EDWARD W. SAID

THE POLITICS
OF DISPOSSESSION

An internationally renowned literary and cultural critic,
Edward W. Said is University Professor at Columbia
University. He is the author of twelve previous books,
including *Culture and Imperialism* and *Orientalism*, which
was nominated for the National Book Critics Circle
Award.

BOOKS BY EDWARD W. SAID

Representations of the Intellectual

The Politics of Dispossession

Culture and Imperialism

Musical Elaborations

Blaming the Victims:
Spurious Scholarship and the Palestinian Question

After the Last Sky

The World, the Text, and the Critic

Covering Islam

Literature and Society

The Question of Palestine

Orientalism

Beginnings: Intention and Method

Joseph Conrad and the Fiction of Autobiography

THE POLITICS
OF DISPOSSESSION

THE **EASTERN MEDITERRANEAN**

CYPRUS

MEDITERRANEAN

Port Said

Alexandria

E G Y P T

Nile R.

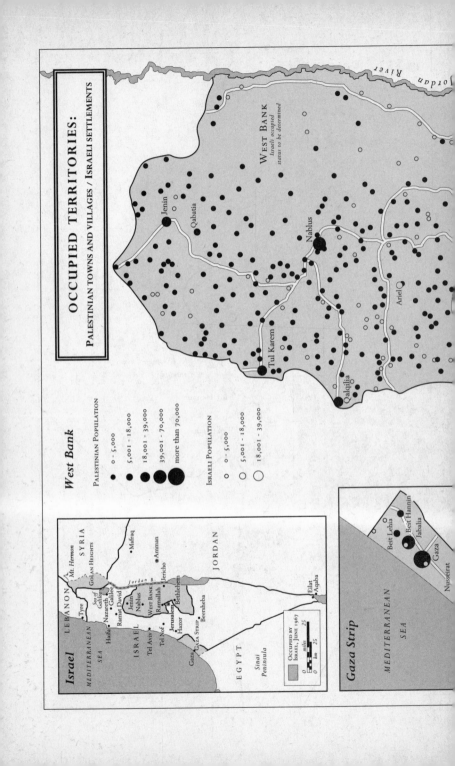

OCCUPIED TERRITORIES:
PALESTINIAN TOWNS AND VILLAGES / ISRAELI SETTLEMENTS

West Bank

PALESTINIAN POPULATION
- 0 – 5,000
- 5,001 – 18,000
- 18,001 – 39,000
- 39,001 – 70,000
- more than 70,000

ISRAELI POPULATION
- 0 – 5,000
- 5,001 – 18,000
- 18,001 – 39,000

WEST BANK
Israeli occupied status to be determined

Jenin
Qabatia
Nablus
Tul Karem
Qalqilia
Ariel

Israel
MEDITERRANEAN SEA
LEBANON
SYRIA
Mt. Hermon
Golan Heights
Tyre
Sea of Galilee
Nazareth
Galilee
Haifa
Ramat David
Jenin
Nablus
West Bank
Ramallah
Tel Aviv
Tel Nof
Jerusalem
Hazor
Bethlehem
Jericho
Amman
Mafraq
JORDAN
Jordan R.
Gaza
GAZA STRIP
Beersheba
EGYPT
Sinai Peninsula
Eilat
Aqaba

OCCUPIED BY
ISRAEL, JUNE 1967
miles 25
0   km   25

Gaza Strip
MEDITERRANEAN SEA
Beit Lehia
Beit Hannin
Jabalia
Gaza
Nusseirat

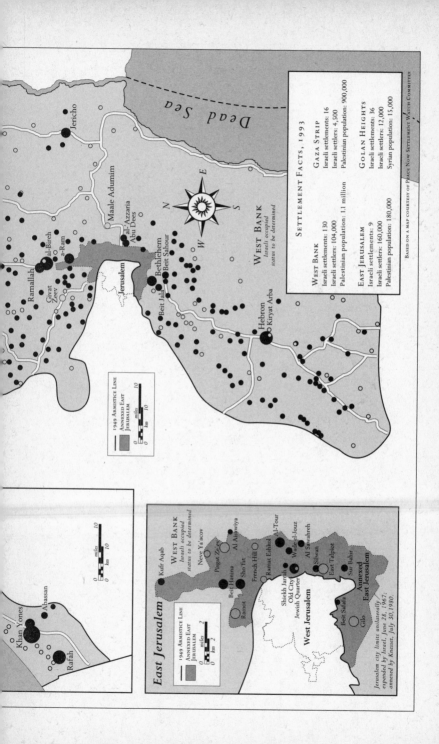

Dead Sea

Jericho

Maale Adumim

al-Azzaria
Abu Dees

Ramallah
al-Bireh
a-Ram
Givat Ze'ev

Bethlehem
Beit Sahour
Jerusalem
Beit Jala

WEST BANK
Israeli occupied
status to be determined

Hebron
Kiryat Arba

N
E
S
W

1949 ARMISTICE LINE
ANNEXED EAST
JERUSALEM
0   km   10
0   miles   10

SETTLEMENT FACTS, 1993

GAZA STRIP
Israeli settlements: 16
Israeli settlers: 4,500
Palestinian population: 900,000

GOLAN HEIGHTS
Israeli settlements: 36
Israeli settlers: 12,000
Syrian population: 15,000

WEST BANK
Israeli settlements: 130
Israeli settlers: 104,000
Palestinian population: 1.1 million

EAST JERUSALEM
Israeli settlements: 9
Israeli settlers: 160,000
Palestinian population: 180,000

Khan Yones
Abassan

Rafah

0   km   10
0   miles   10

East Jerusalem

Kufr Aqab

WEST BANK
Israeli occupied
status to be determined

Neve Ya'acov

Pisgat Ze'ev
Al Aisawiya

Beit Hanna
Sho'fat

Ranot
French Hill
Ramat Eshkol
Al-Tour

Wadi-el-Jouz
Shiekh Jarrah
Al Sawahreh
Old City
Silwan
Jewish Quarter

East Talpiot

Sur Bahir

West Jerusalem

Beit Safafa
Gilo

Annexed
East Jerusalem

1949 ARMISTICE LINE
ANNEXED EAST
JERUSALEM
0   km   2
0   miles   2

Jerusalem city limits unilaterally
expanded by Israel, June 28, 1967;
annexed by Knesset, July 30, 1980.

THE POLITICS
OF DISPOSSESSION

*The Struggle for Palestinian
Self-Determination, 1969–1994*

EDWARD W. SAID

VINTAGE BOOKS

A Division of Random House, Inc.

New York

FIRST VINTAGE BOOKS EDITION, JUNE 1995

Copyright © 1994 by Edward W. Said
Maps copyright © 1994 by Vikki Leib

Permissions acknowledgments appear on page 431.

The Library of Congress has cataloged the Pantheon edition as follows:
Said, Edward W.
The politics of dispossession: the struggle for Palestinian
self-determination, 1969–1994 / by Edward W. Said.
p. cm.
Includes bibliographical references.
ISBN 0-679-43057-1
1. Jewish-Arab relations—1973– 2. Palestinian Arabs—Politics
and government. 3. Arab countries—Politics and government—1945–
I. Title.
DS119.7.S3325 1994
956.9404—dc20 93-38465
Vintage ISBN: 0-679-76145-4

Book design by Maura Fadden Rosenthal

Manufactured in the United States of America
10 9 8 7 6 5 4 3 2

For Bayan and Shafiq al-Hout

Contents

Acknowledgments   xi

Introduction   xiii

ONE: PALESTINE AND PALESTINIANS

1   The Palestinian Experience (1968–1969)   3

2   The Palestinians One Year Since Amman (1971)   24

3   Palestinians (1977)   30

4   The Acre and the Goat (1979)   33

5   Peace and Palestinian Rights (1980)   43

6   Palestinians in the United States (1981)   52

7   The Formation of American Public Opinion on
     the Question of Palestine (1982)   56

8   Palestinians in the Aftermath of Beirut:
     A Preliminary Stocktaking (1982)   69

9   Solidly Behind Arafat (1983)   78

10   Who Would Speak for Palestinians? (1985)   81

11   An Ideology of Difference (1985)   84

12   On Palestinian Identity: A Conversation with
     Salman Rushdie (1986)   107

13   Review of *Wedding in Galilee* and *Friendship's Death*
     (1988)   130

14   How to Answer Palestine's Challenge (1988)   137

15   Palestine Agenda (December 1988)   145

16   Palestinians in the Gulf War's Aftermath (1991)   152

17   The Prospects for Peace in the Middle East
     (1991)   156

18   Return to Palestine–Israel (1992)   175

                    TWO: THE ARAB WORLD

19   U.S. Policy and the Conflict of Powers in the
     Middle East (1973)   203

20   The Arab Right Wing (1979)   224

21   A Changing World Order: The Arab Dimension
     (1980)   231

22   The Death of Sadat (1981)   243

23   Permission to Narrate (1984)   247

24   "Our" Lebanon (1984)   269

25   Sanctum of the Strong (1989)   273

26   Behind Saddam Hussein's Moves (August 1990)   278

27   A Tragic Convergence (January 11, 1991)   283

28   Ignorant Armies Clash by Night
     (February 11, 1991)   287

29   The Arab–American War: The Politics of
     Information (March 1991)   295

30   The Intellectuals and the War (April 1991)   304

Contents

THREE: POLITICS AND INTELLECTUALS

31   Chomsky and the Question of Palestine (1975)   323

32   Reticences of an Orientalist (1986)   337

33   Identity, Negation and Violence (1988)   341

34   The Orientalist Express: Thomas Friedman Wraps Up the Middle East (1989)   360

35   On Nelson Mandela, and Others (1990)   366

36   Embargoed Literature (1990)   372

37   The Splendid Tapestry of Arab Life (1991)   379

38   The Other Arab Muslims (1993)   384

Epilogue   413

Notes   421

Permissions Acknowledgments   431

Index   433

Acknowledgments

The first person to propose that I publish a collection of my political essays was Michael Sprinker, a former student, friend, and colleague at SUNY, Stonybrook. I will always be grateful to him for his support and interest, and especially for his generosity in making the initial selection and preliminary edit of some of my articles. Later, I was fortunate that my dear friends Frances Coady of Vintage (UK) and Shelley Wanger of Pantheon gave me the benefit of their attention and expert help. Once again, Zaineb Istrabadi assisted me ably with the manuscript's preparation; I am most grateful.

This book is dedicated to Bayan Nowaihid al-Hout and Shafiq al-Hout. Bayan is now one of our finest scholars of the history of Palestine, chronicler of the lives of ordinary as well as exceptional Palestinians, teacher and friend. Shafiq is a brilliant orator and wit, writer and political activist. Independent and incorruptible, he deserted neither his post nor his principles. Together, they have lived the politics of Palestinian dispossession with grit and grace.

E.W.S.
New York
November 1993

Introduction

Until the June 1967 war I was completely caught up in the life of a young professor of English and comparative literature at Columbia University. I was born in Jerusalem in late 1935, and I grew up there and in Egypt and Lebanon; most of my family—dispossessed and displaced from Palestine in 1947 and 1948—had ended up mostly in Jordan and Lebanon. Sent to America as a schoolboy in 1951, I had completed my education here by 1963, and began teaching later that year. All through those twelve years, however, I would spend vacations (and once even a full year) in the Middle East, since that is where my family lived and where I continued to feel most at home. All that changed forever in mid-1967.

For the first time since I had left to come to the United States, I was emotionally reclaimed by the Arab world generally and by Palestine in particular. This was a direct result of the war—which I experienced in New York—and of the severely damaged political, cultural, and, of course, military and geographical situation that it created. My generation had been formed by the Arab nationalism represented by the late nineteenth century *Nahda*, the renaissance of Arabic culture that culminated in the great 1917 Arab revolt against the Ottoman Empire. Our sense of our own history was that at the very moment that we were entitled to, and indeed promised, our independence by the British and French, who had urged us to rebel, we were betrayed by them. Between them, the two great colonial powers redesigned the Arab countries into zones of influence which they ruled as mandates or protectorates. In addition, the Balfour Declaration of 1917 promised Palestine to the Zionists as a Jewish national home.

After World War II, when the two European powers were forced to dismantle their empires, a whole series of independent Arab states emerged, most of them led by military men or traditional leaders whose watchword was Palestine. The greatest of these was Egypt's Gamal Abdel Nasser, whose fiery charisma, personal incorruptibility, and almost limitless dedication to pan-Arab unity and anti-imperialist struggle dominated the Middle East during my formative years; even though I was in the United States I felt the great power of his appeal and did not much question his ability to liberate and unify the Arab world. It was also Abdel Nasser's achievement to propel the Arabs into the Third World: During his tenure, Cairo was one of the centers of the Non-Aligned movement, the Afro-Asian movement, and of worldwide anti-imperialist liberation struggle. In a matter of six days, however, everything that Abdel Nasser and his followers had created came apart. To be an Arab meant a sense of defeat, profound shock, and bewildering uncertainty.

Starting that summer, I began to feel that what happened in the Arab world concerned me personally and could no longer be accepted with a passive political disengagement, not least because at the same moment that pan-Arabism lay in ruins, the Palestinian national movement emerged first in Jordan, then in Lebanon, then, more or less, wherever—including North America—Palestinians lived. Friends I had known in America during the 1950s, usually as fellow-students, were suddenly galvanized into new and highly politicized activity. One in particular, Hanna Mikhail, who like me had become an American academic, gave up his teaching position at the University of Washington and flew to Jordan to join the movement (the Resistance as everyone called it then). Within a matter of months, he had become a ranking information officer with whom I had frequent contact until his untimely death in 1976 during the Lebanese Civil War. Another old friend and distant relative was Kamal Nasser, whom I had seen often in Cairo during the early years of the Abdel Nasser era; a political refugee from the Jordanian government, which then controlled the West Bank, he was a native West Banker who after 1967 also joined the movement, where his gifts as poet, orator, and analyst propelled him to its very top. He was its extremely effective chief spokesman when, in April of 1973, he was assassinated by an Israeli hit team in Beirut.

Before the tragedies and losses set in, however, hope was the watchword. Although many of us were shattered by the catastrophe of 1967, we were reinvigorated by the Palestinian national movement whose promise and ideas during its early years after the June War were felt throughout the Arab world. I remained in New York and continued teaching, but beginning in 1968 I started to think, write, and travel as someone who felt himself to be directly involved in the renaissance of Palestinian life and politics. Those of us who were concerned sought each other out across the oceans and despite years of silence. On the cultural and intellectual level, the appearance of an organized Palestinian movement of resistance against the Israeli occupation began as a critique of traditional Arab nationalism whose ruins were strewn about the battlefields of 1967. Not only did Palestinian men and women take up arms on their own behalf for the first time, but they were part of a national experience that claimed primacy in modern Arab discourse by virtue of openness, honesty, realism. We were the first Arabs who at the grass-roots level—and not because a colonel or king commanded us—started a movement to repossess a land and a history that had been wrested from us. Our leaders were popular and accountable to us, not hereditary or imposed on us from above.

Moreover, the Palestinian movement seemed to signal a break with the pomposity, bombast, and mythology of the past. Thus, a new rhetorical style came into being in which things were called by their name—Israel was called Israel and not "the Zionist entity"—for the first time in Arabic publications; and footnotes began to be used systematically in political writing in Palestinian publications. After 1948 most Palestinian refugees had been obliged to take on the identities of the Arab states to which they came as refugees. In Syria, many became Baathists, in Egypt they were Nasserists, and so on. For the first time, after 1967 it became possible not only to become Palestinian again but also to choose Fatah, or the Popular Front, or the Democratic Front as one's movement of choice: each was Palestinian, jealously guarding its own vision of a Palestinian future.

Yet, almost from the beginning, things were not in good order. I was in Amman during the summer of 1969 and then again in 1970. I was a visitor but also an exhilarated participant in the national revival that I saw taking place. One of the very first things I wrote (the first essay in this book) when I got back to the United States was an account of that experience as it suggested to me what, in the context of a general history of dispossession, Palestinians were doing to repossess their history and politics. The bitterness and appalling violence of Black September 1970 followed. But after 1971, when the PLO relocated to Beirut, there were remarkable institutional achievements, the greatest of which was the rise in regional and international visibility of the PLO itself. Then again, as the civil war that began in 1975 attests, this too occurred not in Palestine but in Lebanon.

From the moment I began to write on behalf of Palestinian rights and self-determination, the apprehension that as a people we still had no sovereignty over any part of the land of Palestine has dominated my efforts. Added to that was its consequence that, like most Palestinians today (more than 50 percent of whom live outside Israel and the Occupied Territories), I was pretty far away from the contested land, forced to do my bit at a great distance and, much of the time, for a constituency made up of a minority of compatriots and a far larger number of Americans and Europeans.

From the start, therefore, the platform from which I spoke found an audience in expatriate Palestinians and Arabs, Americans and other Westerners (Jewish and non-Jewish alike) who were likely to be interested in the reconciliation of Palestinians and Israelis. The Israeli occupation was a cruel thing, a further injustice done to a people deprived of all rights, the violence of the relationship between the peoples destined to share the same land—all these were to be resolved at the end of the road. But that was a general goal. My most specific task was, as many of the essays in this book show, to make the case for Palestinian presence, to say that there *was* a Palestinian people and that, like all others, it had a history, a society, and, most important, a right to self-determination. In other words, to try to change the public consciousness in which Palestine had no presence at all. In addition, as these essays also show, I had to make the effort to include considerable discussion of general Arab issues and themes, as well as a constant reassessment of intellectual practices.

Although in 1994 all this may seem fairly obvious, in the America of those days it was extremely difficult to make the effort. Golda Meir had set the general tone in 1969 by denying that we existed at all. The first task was to get a place—literally anywhere—to say that we did exist. It hardly needs pointing out, therefore, that speaking about the Palestinian issue in the United States always has been a very different thing from discussing it in an Arab newspaper published in either Cairo or Beirut; it was even different and required more primitive rituals of assertion than what Hebrew-language papers in Israel were saying. In North America, one was compelled, almost humiliatingly, to keep to a testimonial level: I am Palestinian, we have a collective identity that while Arab is not only generally Arab but specifically *Palestinian,* and an attachment to the actual land of Palestine antedates Zionism and Israel. Therefore, so far as writing was concerned, the major goal was getting ourselves the right, or permission, to tell our story.

In the meantime the turbulent history of the Middle East continued. The October War of 1973 led to Camp David and the Egyptian–Israeli peace agreement, plus the return of Sinai to Egyptian sovereignty. Beginning in 1970, a number of proposals and plans—all of them originating from outside parties—were put forth: the Jarring proposals, the Rogers plan, the Kissinger plan, the Reagan plan, the Fahd plan, the Baker plan, etc. In 1974 at an Arab League meeting in Rabat, the PLO was conceded the status of the Palestinians' "sole legitimate representative"; later that year, Yasir Arafat appeared at the UN, which is where I first met him. Thereafter, the organized Palestinian presence in Lebanon was more and more deeply embroiled (tragically and mistakenly, I believe) in that country's already pronounced unraveling, so that by the late 1970s we had a situation in which the politics of Palestinian liberation were conducted inside Lebanon. One Palestinian leader went so far as to say that the liberation of Palestine will proceed from Jounieh (the capital of Christian Lebanon). By 1982, five years into a period of Likud government in Israel, the growing political threat of the PLO in Lebanon as perceived by Israel had to be attacked, not because of Lebanon or of "terrorism" so much but because internationally the PLO had achieved a modicum of recognition and respect. Hence the Israeli invasion of Lebanon, the siege of Beirut, the PLO's exodus from Lebanon to Tunisia. Not one Arab leader or state did anything to stop the devastation.

With the exception of a relatively brief flourishing of Palestinian national institutions in Lebanon—social welfare agencies, political organizations, cultural and intellectual activities, to say nothing of a minuscule army, and ramshackle civil defense units in the refugee camps—it is difficult to look back at the Beirut years (1971–1982) with much except regret and even anger. First was the almost unbelievable damage to ourselves and others that we caused. There were the massacres and destructions that culminated in the Sabra and Shatila disasters of 1982, which, as a people and a movement in exile, we have survived very badly. Our leaders have had to leave and dismantle the official Palestinian presence, evoking hostility and bitterness among Lebanese friends and enemies alike. Worse, almost 400,000 stateless Palestinians remained behind—unprotected and frequently attacked (as during the camps' war of 1985), forced to endure the hostility brought on by their leaders.

Then in the 1990s the PLO acquired an unmistakable if extremely eccentric prominence. It became a quasi-official Arab state organization, not unlike, indeed far too much resembling, the bureaucracies and dictatorships it was forced to deal with in the region. The problem was that in the Middle East, as well as in the West, there was such a battle to be waged by all Palestinians just to get the *idea* of a national Palestinian authority accepted and recognized, that we did battle on that front and left the fight over the nature of the organization until later. That was a big but perhaps inevitable mistake. The PLO leadership itself became far too concerned with its own survival, not enough with learning from the past, capitalizing and building on strength and potential, remaining focused on principles (like freedom and equality for Palestinians) and real goals, mobilizing its people and their best elements for work in a common cause.

Much of this has had to do with the appallingly difficult circumstances of the Palestinian people in the late twentieth century. It is very, very hard to espouse, for five decades, a continually losing cause. Take our opponents, for instance. Israel and its major backer the United States represent a formidable military and political power, seemingly unchallengeable regionally and, in the main, internationally. Israel is not French Algeria or white South Africa; its Jewish citizens are the remnants of the Nazi Holocaust with a tragic history of genocide and persecution. Moreover, the United States is the only superpower today, and its support for Israel has meant for us an extraordinary multiplication of our woes. With, in addition, a massive lobbying and demographic strength (relative to us) in American civil society, this has made getting out any sort of Palestinian message extremely difficult. Nor have Arab "allies" been allies at all, over the long run. Egypt and Saudi Arabia apply pressure to Palestinians much more than they support our rights; in Lebanon, Syria has often conducted all-out war against us; Iraq, for a time a patron of last resort, since 1990 has been a major liability. Thus, with no superpower patron (the USSR scarcely counted, except for use as a propaganda target serving as a pretext to attack *us!*), no regional ally, and no sovereignty anywhere, just to have a meeting of Palestinians posed a redoubtable logistical problem, and to keep up a national existence, an extremely tough proposition.

So not only was it difficult to absorb and understand what was happening to Palestinians in the Middle East, there was for me the quite distinct challenge of trying to write about it in the West. I had to keep saying that Palestinians were not only the opponents and victims of Zionism, they also represented an alternative: This was what they embodied in fighting for the idea of Palestine, a non-exclusivist, secular, democratic, tolerant, and generally progressive ideology, not about colonizing and dispossessing people but about liberating them. I was always trying to abide by universalist principles and yet be concrete and critical at the same time. I do not think there is a piece collected here that does not attempt to be critical and even aggressive about these principles, particularly when it came to making distinctions and taking stands. In 1983, for example, with large numbers of people deserting the movement in a Palestinian insurrection inside Fatah backed by Syria, I wrote an op-ed piece for the *New York Times* criticizing Syria openly; this was at a time when my family and relatives in Lebanon were directly under Syrian military hegemony. As early as 1979, I explicitly attacked repressive and unpopular regimes in the Arab world; even earlier, I spoke against human rights abuses in Israel *and* the Arab world. I kept my eye on U.S. policy, since as an American citizen resident in the United States—whose own policies were so important in the Middle East—my duty was first of all toward trying to influence opinion and, if possible, policy, on our behalf as a people. There wasn't and has never been a Palestinian lobby in the West, so what one did at the outset was fairly solitary. It became part of my purpose to keep up support for Palestine, to inform, explain, interpret what was otherwise unreported, misrepresented, or falsely portrayed.

None of this was easy and, at first, could be done only intermittently. By about the early 1980s I was able to speak my piece in a number of journals, newspapers, radio and TV outlets, but there were many more that were closed to me. My family and I lived with death threats; my office was vandalized and sacked; I had to endure libelous abuse about my people and cause—not only was I a terrorist but also a professor of terror, an anti-Semite, an accomplice to murder, a liar, a deranged demagogue, etc.

I am still firmly convinced that to defend Palestinian self-determination, and even to pronounce the word *Palestine* has been more difficult than any other political cause today. Despite our relatively modest actualities as a people, because of the understandable vehemence stirred up by a national community that has challenged Israel's behavior—Israel being seen as a state of survivors of the Holocaust—we have been cast as inheritors of the Hitlerian legacy. Israel and its supporters have not hesitated to exploit this.

For those of us who live in the West, the change in public opinion has been very slow in coming, but by the late 1980s it did come, although after the 1982 Israeli invasion, the PLO had become a far-diminished, not to say enfeebled, organization located quite improbably in Tunisia. The *intifadah,* which broke out in Gaza in December 1987, suddenly thrust a population of almost two million unarmed Palestinians before huge television audiences in the West and, with them, an inevitable number of Israeli soldiers who were seen beating and shooting them. No longer confined to the image of a gang of skulking terrorists, the Palestinians began to acquire in 1988 the irrevocable status of a people dispossessed and under a brutal military occupation in international consciousness, a status consolidated by the Palestine National Council meeting held in Algiers later that year.

I participated as an active member of the council. For months preceding it, I had discussed with Palestinians the wisdom of this historical compromise which I felt we had to make definitively then. When it happened—despite the demurrals of many—I was very pleased, since a decade earlier I had known we would have to face this issue. A majority vote carried the motion: Divide historical Palestine into two states, one Israeli and one Palestinian. A month later in Geneva, Arafat made his famous renunciation of terrorism (according to a script written out by the U.S. Department of State), and promptly thereafter a "low-level" dialogue began in Tunis between the American ambassador and three senior PLO officials.

This was the first time that accredited Palestinian representatives had earned some measure of recognition from the major Western power. At the time "the dialogue" assumed fantastic importance for the PLO. The effect of long years of nonrecognition in the West should not be underestimated on a Third World movement whose outlook has been colored by a strange and unseemly dependence on the West for status and a paternalistic approval. Of course, it was galling for Henry Kissinger in 1974, acting at the instigation of the Israeli government, to lay various injunctions against "talking to the PLO." But to think that the key to the Palestinian future was Washington's to formulate was, and remains, a fatal error. It derived principally from two factors, both of them still true of all the current Arab leaders. One, there is an extraordinary ignorance of America: its history, culture, social system, and political attitudes. Lazier and less attuned to the outside world than most leaders, the Arab ruling elites are tied to a romantic vision of America. Two, there is among Arab, and certainly Palestinian, leaders a sense that America cannot be fought or challenged but must be pacified; you may appear to be "radically" nationalist (e.g., Saddam Hussein before he invaded Kuwait, and Hafez al-Assad), but in the end your goal has to be ingratiation.

Anwar Sadat's example was precisely that: Throw yourself on the Americans and they will do the rest for you. At the time of the Camp David agreements (1978), the Palestinian position was, I felt, extraordinarily rigid, and I, along with various people with contacts in the Carter administration, made an effort to make it more flexible. Through my old friend and college classmate Hodding Carter, then Assistant Secretary of State in the Carter administration, I had met and talked with the Secretary of State, Cyrus Vance. This was a year after Sadat's trip to Jerusalem, and a few weeks after my name and that of my old friend and colleague Ibrahim Abu-Lughod had been given by Arafat to Sadat and then to the Americans as possible "low-level" people who might negotiate for the Palestinians. Neither of us was a member of the PLO, but both of us that year had become members of the PNC. Vance was, I thought, very forthcoming and seemed to be frustrated at the hobbles put on his capacity to meet with the PLO by—as he put it—his "predecessor," Kissinger, whose name was never mentioned once. Vance and I were meeting at the UN Plaza Hotel where, as I told the Secretary, a PLO delegation was also staying. I immediately suggested expanding the meeting to include my closest friend in the PLO, Shafiq al-Hout, who while loyal to Arafat was a well-known writer, orator, and wit quite independent of Arafat. Shafiq was always very jealous of his own reputation—he had, after all, been a PLO man before Arafat's advent in 1968–1969—and has always refused all offers to join Fatah, Arafat's own group.

Vance demurred, saying that even though he might have liked to include Shafiq in our discussion it would be indiscreet and wrong. In any case, our conversation progressed sufficiently enough for me to realize that the Carter administration, as represented by Vance, was seriously interested in a resolution to the Palestinian question, which

Vance also told me they realized could not be accomplished without the PLO and Arafat. I laid forth the Palestinian case to Vance as comprehensively and as eloquently as I could, concentrating on my conviction that Arafat was, in fact, a man of peace. Whereupon between us we devised a method by which I would send Arafat a detailed message from Vance via Shafiq, who was leaving for Beirut a few days later, its aim being an open dialogue between the United States and the PLO. The only condition required was a PLO acceptance of Resolution 242. Indeed, Vance added, the Palestinians could accept the Resolution, which contained no mention of the Palestinians at all, with a "reservation" or added clarification, a clause affixed to the declaration that stipulated how the PLO held on to Palestinian rights and self-determination, despite their exclusion from 242.

The message was sent, and a few days later I called Shafiq—who was very close to Arafat—and confirmed that it had been delivered. It was November 1978, and I kept in touch with Vance intermittently but had no response at all from Beirut. Finally, in the spring of 1979—just as the peace agreements were about to be signed—Vance called me and asked me for Arafat's answer. Deeply embarrassed by the whole episode—I wished I had never gotten involved—I explained that I had heard nothing. Vance had Harold Saunders, his assistant for Near Eastern Affairs, redictate the text of what he had agreed the PLO should say in order to get U.S. recognition, and then he urged me to fly to Beirut with the document immediately. This I did and asked Shafiq to arrange a meeting for me with Arafat.

At around midnight that very day, Arafat came to Shafiq's house alone and, after the usual greetings, asked me what was so urgent. I told him that I had received no answer to my message. "I didn't get any message," Arafat said, at which point Shafiq expostulated (with reason) that that wasn't true, since he himself had delivered the message. Denials and affirmations went on for a bit, at which point Arafat asked me to tell him exactly what Vance had said. Then he stood up and said he would give me an answer the next night, again at Shafiq's place. He arrived, a little after midnight, this time with all his major advisers and lieutenants (many of whom were subsequently killed by the Israelis). In effect, he told me, "we" were not interested in the American offer: They were unfair to us and too close to the Israelis, and we don't need the recognition they were offering. Needless to say, I was too embarrassed to say any of this to Vance, even though I had to convey the refusal.

Four years later, the PLO was saved from General Sharon's tanks by the United States' intervention (ironically, Arafat had asked me to help in negotiating with George Shultz), though a short while after the evacuation from Beirut, several thousand Palestinians were massacred in the Sabra and Shatila refugee camps. And a decade later, when Iraq invaded Kuwait, Arafat and his group—consulting no one in particular—decided that Iraq might have had a case after all. After the Gulf War, when the slightest knowledge of American politics and foreign policy would have enjoined a rapid disengagement from Iraq, the PLO found itself imploring the United States for help in the peace process, which—again it was perfectly possible to predict—would be dictated neither by fairness nor magnanimity but by superpower interests and Israel's agenda.

In any event, the great compromise of 1988 did not yield very much for very long: A year and a half later, after a stupidly criminal and useless attempted raid (with only Palestinian casualties) by one of the PLO factions against a Tel Aviv beach, the United States broke off the dialogue in May 1990, with no results for the Palestinians to show for it. Thereafter, Arafat and his inner circle—marooned in Tunisia, forced to bear the humiliation of endless losses, as well as the opprobrium and gradual dislike of its own Palestinian constituencies—became increasingly reclusive. I and many others felt the increasing gap between the rhetoric and the reality. We had already ceased being a people determined on liberation; we had accepted the lesser goal of a small degree of independence. The PLO seemed to be getting more bureaucratic and delivering less and less. After the Gulf War, the money from wealthy Arab governments and states began to shut off, until by the middle of 1993, hundreds of people remained unpaid in PLO offices abroad, more families were left unsupported (the PLO had once established a generous pattern of social and economic welfare for refugees as well as Palestinians in the Occupied Territories), and greater cries of dissatisfaction and despair went up. And still the bluster of yore—"we are at the threshold of a state" Arafat kept on saying defiantly from, of all unlikely places, Tunisia, fifteen hundred miles away from Palestine—poured out.

[I I]

What I have been describing is something of the background of the pieces collected here. My own direct involvement in the tangled history of the Palestinian national movement needs to be summarized. As I said earlier, I first met Arafat when he came to the United Nations in 1974; I translated his speech from Arabic into English and became acquainted with the various officials of the PLO at that time. Two in particular have remained close friends throughout: the famous poet Mahmoud Darwish and Shafiq al-Hout, then representative of the PLO in Lebanon. Both became members of the PLO's Executive Committee in the late 1980s and 1990s. Central to everything about the PLO, including its more and more ineffective opposition (the Popular Front, the Communist Party, and the Democratic Front), was Arafat himself, a mercurial, charming, infinitely complex political animal whose power through the years increased as did his mistakes and the losses endured by his people. Since my mother lived in Lebanon—and after my father's death I was often obliged to make more frequent trips there—my relationship to the Palestinian struggle and to Arafat developed but never my party affiliation. I refused all inducements to join one of the groups or to work in the PLO, largely because I felt it was important to preserve my distance. I was a partisan, yes, but a joiner and member, no. I very often felt the need to engage more fully but was always held back by Arafat's growing dominance and unchecked control over everything of significance within the PLO.

During the 1980s I felt that I became far too publicly identified with him, especially in Europe and the United States, where, for better or for worse, I was called upon regularly by the mainstream media. There was nothing I could do to change my situation. The choice I faced was a stark and extraordinarily unappetizing one: Was I to defend the PLO and Arafat as, in fact, the main instruments of the Palestinian struggle against an overwhelmingly hostile media and public reaction that denied that that struggle was anything more than terrorism and anti-Semitism? Or was I to be someone who joined the general racist chorus in the U.S. of attacks on the Palestinians, Islam, the Arabs, and Arab nationalism in general?

I have always tried to focus on the main aspects of the first alternative, without becoming an uncritical and totally accepting chorus of approval for everything the PLO and Arafat did. What made it more difficult for me is that most of what I said in the West was immediately republished or broadcast in the Arab world. There it was seen in a very different context. For example, in the late seventies I was extremely critical of such phrases as "armed struggle," all the rage in Beirut; and when my book *The Question of Palestine* was published in 1980, I was savagely attacked by both Fatah and the Popular Front for talking about the need for a recognition of Israel and accepting a two-state solution, an idea of which I was one of the pioneers. I was unequivocal in my denunciations of terrorist adventurism and immoral violence, although, of course, I did not spare Israeli violence either. It's an interesting footnote to all this that when *The Question of Palestine* came out in New York, a Beirut research center and publishing house approached me about an Arabic translation. When I agreed, I was stunned to learn a moment later that I would be expected to remove from the English text any criticisms I had made of Syria, Saudi Arabia, and the rest. I refused, and to this day none of my three books on Palestine *(The Question of Palestine, After the Last Sky, Blaming the Victims)* has been translated into Arabic. Mifras, a small Israeli house, published in 1981 an unedited and uncut Hebrew translation of the first of the three.

As the general position of the PLO in the Arab world worsened after 1982, it was obvious that a new strategy was needed. Because my son was gravely ill, I was unable to attend the 1983 PNC meeting that was held in Algiers; nevertheless, I sent a long message to the group saying that we should accept the realities of Israel and its occupation in order to be able, on the one hand, to resist and put limits to their dominance over us and, on the other, so that we might put forward a clear goal (i.e., a Palestinian state) for our own people. Even after its exit from Beirut, the PLO still pretended that its goal was the liberation of Palestine, which to Israel and the United States was made synonymous with the extermination of the state of Israel. Shafiq al-Hout was one of the first to say at that PNC meeting that the liberation of Palestine was neither possible nor really our goal, so why maintain so ludicrous a formula?

I did, however, go to the next PNC meeting in Amman in November of 1984, where, for many of us, support for Arafat against Syrian military and political pressure was a central obligation. There too al-Hout was as fierce in his criticism of PLO hypocrisy and equivocation as he was a year before. Arafat was so desperate for a quorum of independents like Hout and myself that he called Mariam, my wife, and me half a dozen times, begging us to show up in Amman together. Both Shafiq and I were roundly denounced by the Fatah dissidents now housed by the Assad government and threatened with death for our "treasonous" rallying to Arafat.

A year later in Tunis, Arafat told me that he had no intention of ending up as the Mufti did with nothing to show for his decades of effort against the Zionist movement. Already the Reagan administration, which had forged a new strategic alliance with Israel and had increased its levels of aid to new records, totaling close to $5 billion annually (between 1967 and 1990 the grand total was $77 billion), had begun to try to move some sort of peace process, which in every case imposed very harsh terms on the Palestinians. Here is the paradox: Even though, in dealings with the United States, the PLO has been hamstrung by its own ignorance of how the United States works and what its real strategic goals are all about, its own public record vis-à-vis peace has been very consistent since the middle 1970s (although its information policies or its effort to make its policies known in the West have always been sub-par). The problem has been that without any coordinated and planned information policy, the PLO could never get its message out, especially in the United States, whose media has been astonishingly biased in its reporting. As Noam Chomsky has pointed out more clearly than anyone, none of the Palestinian positions taken since the mid-1970s—on a two-state solution, on mutual recognition, on the imperatives for peaceful negotiations—has ever been reported with requisite care or accuracy. On the contrary, one read over and over again how the PLO was dedicated to the destruction of Israel, how its inherently terrorist nature made peace impossible, and how Israel's security was endangered by the mere existence of Palestinians who, unreasonably, demanded self-determination and full human rights.

When Menachem Begin's Likud party came to power in 1977, the official line taken on *all* acts of resistance by Palestinians against Israeli occupation or Israeli attacks in Lebanon was to call them *terrorism,* which from then on became the principal focus of the U.S. media as well. There was never any attempt to compare the scale of Israeli violence with the pitiful level of Palestinian resistance, nor was an effort made to make a connection between the Palestinian struggle against Israel and the undisputed facts of Palestinian dispossession by immigrant settlers. As the Israelis opposed the PLO because the PLO represented Palestinian nationalism, so too did the United States and the media. In print and on television, Palestinians were dehumanized, turned into vast and frenzied collectives bent on killing innocent Jews for the sheer unregenerate desire of it. The United States vetoed no less than twenty-nine UN Security Council Resolutions censuring Israeli practices which contravened—often with quite unashamed explicitness—many of the norms of international behavior. The U.S. media rarely took note, even though the Israeli press, for instance, was extremely forthcoming on these matters. Above all, Israel and the United States took political positions designed in advance to prevent peace: When the Palestine National Council recognized Israel in 1988 (having implicitly done so already in 1974), there was never a demand from the United States that Israel should recognize and deal with the Palestinian nation.

The *intifadah* began in December 1987, in what was surely one of the great anticolonial insurrections of the modern period. The United States urged restraint on all sides. Even so-called peace activists in the United States, like the Reverend Jesse Jackson, who was pilloried by the Israeli lobby for his modest acknowledgment that the Palestinians actually existed (his crime had been to shake Arafat's hand in Beirut), backpedaled when he ran for the presidency in 1988. "Israeli security" was always put ahead of Palestinian human rights. The idea seemed to be that in U.S. and European public opinion you could uphold UN resolutions (on Iraq, for example) and suspend them for the Palestinians. And yet, public opinion finally began to shift; by the third year of the *intifadah,* according to some Gallup polls, 45 percent of the American population was in favor of Palestinian self-determination as opposed to the 24 percent who were not (see *Journal of Palestine Studies,* Winter 1990, pp. 75–86). The image of the Israeli as pioneer and open-faced democrat faded into the Israeli as brutal soldier, killing in full view of European and American viewers. Yet the settlements continued, their number increasing to more than two hundred; more land was confiscated, especially around Jerusalem; more than 80 percent of the Occupied Territories' water was used by the settlers and Israel proper. Meron Benvenisti, former deputy mayor of Jerusalem, director of the West Bank Project, an information and monitoring group, estimated that over 50 percent of the land of the Occupied Territories had been expropriated by the end of the 1980s.

And still the U.S. government, first under Ronald Reagan, then under George Bush, scarcely modified its essentially rejectionist position. All the Middle Eastern Arab countries, including the PLO, were long on record as desiring peace through negotiations; all of them, in conformity with the international community (minus Israel and the United States) had stated that an exchange of land occupied in 1967 would yield full peace. This was formally affirmed as early as the Fahd plan (voted unanimously by the Arab League of August 7, 1981), but, as I said earlier, the PLO had signaled its willingness to make peace in return for Palestinian land seven years before that. The United States has always opposed Palestinian self-determination in no uncertain terms. Its conditions for the various peace plans of the 1980s were: no PLO, no Palestinian state, no pressure on Israel (indeed, always more aid to Israel). The policy of the Reagan administration under George Shultz was, in fact, to give Israel more and more in aid and support on the theory that once it became so incredibly secure, Israel would of its own free will be inclined to make an agreeable peace with the Arabs, including the Palestinians. Nothing of the sort happened. When along with Ibrahim Abu-Lughod I had an official meeting with George Shultz in April 1988, in what was the first meeting between PNC members and the Reagan administration, he talked about nearly everything except the PLO and self-determination.

Yet all through the period from 1969 to 1991, I and many other Palestinians had had private, even secret, meetings and peace discussions with Israelis, American Jews, and others who were concerned with the issue. I found it difficult at first, since the Israelis—even the dissenters among them—were to me representatives of an occupying power inflicting many cruelties and depredations on us. My idea was that by being present I would be able to expose the Palestinian point of view, especially a sense of our history of dispossession, to Israeli and non-Israeli Jews who were disposed toward reconciliation with us but who needed, I felt, a much fuller sense of our actuality, humanity, and history. I participated in many of these encounters from the beginning and addressed many audiences as well on campuses, in synagogues, learned associations, churches, and foreign policy associations. During the 1980s, the PLO began to take an interest in meeting with Israeli Jews, always with an eye to the influential ones—potential members of the Knesset, etc.—never with those courageous individuals like Israel Shahak who were marginal in Israel but were uncompromising defenders of Palestinian rights. By the period of the *intifadah* I had lost interest in the encounter groups principally because they were often manipulated by professional "conflict-resolution" technicians, and also because they were now being used by the PLO not to argue the

Palestinian case but, in my opinion, to try to prove to Israelis how many concessions the PLO was prepared to make.

I also found that most members of the Israeli Left (including Peace Now) were focused on asking for more Palestinian concessions (recognize us, give up on the National Charter, etc.) without offering anything in return. In other words, these private attempts at reconciliation—with some notable exceptions—reflected the exact balance of power between us, a very weak partner and a very strong one, some of whose advocates shamelessly kept asking the victims of military occupation and dispossession for various moral acknowledgments from their victims. Shortly after the *intifadah* began, I stopped attending, and was disturbed to realize that the PLO (quite inexplicably and unjustifiably) thought of these private encounters as a form of negotiation with the Israelis, gradually using more and more visible personages from the PLO (e.g., Nabil Shaath) plus notables from the Occupied Territories (e.g., Faisal Husseini and Hanan Ashrawi) to try to open up areas of agreement and possibly a reconciliation.

There was never any attempt at coordinating such Palestinian efforts internationally. Between late 1982 and the first part of the 1990s Arafat was in Tunis and I visited him there several times. My main effort was to convince him and his colleagues in the "Palestinian Central," as we called it, to coordinate a massive human rights campaign in the United States, and to conduct an orderly, well informed, and coordinated policy of rapprochement with Israeli supporters of Palestinian rights. I often brought European and American colleagues with me to give seminars on the current state of American politics, society, culture—all to no avail. I accepted many invitations to join a Palestinian "think tank" to advise him, but we never had a single meeting. I also discovered that a standing PLO committee set up to deal with the United States never met, and most of its members didn't know any English (although there were plenty of Palestinians who did). All through this period Arafat was neither fighting to expand solidarity for Palestinians in the West nor nurturing the logical Palestinian constituency, which was primarily composed of liberals, dissenters, the women's movement, ethnic and religious groups, and so on. Instead, he and his associates seemed to be looking for patrons in the West who would get them a solution of some sort. This quixotic fantasy originated in and was encouraged by the notion that the United States worked like, say, Syria or Iraq: Get close to someone who is close to the maximum leader and all doors will open, things would get done, prizes were to be had. This idea went along with a total absence of any institutions inside the Arab world that specialized in the study of America or any university departments devoted to American studies. Neither Arafat himself nor his principal lieutenants really knew English or French; none of them had ever lived in the West, and they were therefore incapable of understanding it. Even Israel was known through "contacts" and hearsay rather than through scientific and systematic knowledge.

By the end of the decade of the 1980s, whole congeries of circumstances compounded by bad judgment, the lack of planning, and widespread corruption brought the PLO and Arafat, in particular, to a very low point. True the *intifadah* progressed, but it could not liberate Palestinian territories on its own. The Gulf states on whom the PLO and the Territories depended for financial support had tapered off their grants, thus, in effect, slowly deserting the *intifadah* as well as the PLO. The demise of the Soviet Union and the Socialist bloc removed a putative, if not actual, deterrent to the combined power of Israel and the United States. Syria and Jordan were, each in its own way, at odds with the PLO, the former for strategic, as well as Assad's personal, reasons; the latter because Jordan always saw itself as a competitor with the PLO for the Territories and, of course, for the almost two million Palestinians who had become Jordanians (Jordan was the only Arab country to give Palestinians citizenship and accommodate them decently).

The PLO drifted closer to Iraq, which had given money, institutional support, and accommodation to many Palestinians. Egypt was increasingly a surrogate for the United States, acting to pressure the Palestinians to be more concessive, more pliant, more like Egypt. Finally, Arafat was more and more isolated in Tunis, without a fighting force to back him and, instead, a huge geographical distance between him and the majority of his people. His two most trusted lieutenants, Abu Jihad and Abu Iyad, were assassinated in 1988 and 1990 respectively; he was now surrounded by sycophants, yes-men, and mediocrities.

The Gulf crisis of August 1990 sealed the PLO's unhappy fate. In general, however, it is true that the PLO and Arafat were already closely allied with Saddam Hussein's regime and made no serious effort to dissociate themselves thereafter. The result was that all the Gulf regimes cut off the PLO completely and, worse, made it impossible for the hundreds of thousands of Palestinians there to go on living as before. This was acutely true of Kuwait's case. Kuwait threw out three hundred thousand Palestinians in the spring and summer of 1991; most were innocent of any collaboration with Iraq, all had contributed vitally to Kuwait's prosperity and development. Now not only isolated but also impugned, Arafat and his shrinking band of loyalists readied themselves for the inevitable ax.

This came in the form of an American peace proposal. When, on March 11, 1991, he addressed the Congress as the conquering hero of Desert Storm, President Bush announced the need for a peace process that took account of the new realities. Gone was the Palestinian and international consensus about a UN peace conference; what was now being proposed was, in effect, an American show, with Russia along as a lame-duck cosponsor. Secretary of State James Baker had already canvassed Palestinians in the Territories, and they had deferred to the PLO. The idea for us was to negotiate a statement of guarantees from the United States that would guarantee the Palestinians a bare minimum of assurances that some of their demands would be met.

Self-determination was never accepted by the United States, nor was a Palestinian state. Instead, the PLO was not to attend except as a distant observer; the Palestinians were to be a part of a joint delegation with Jordan; Israel would retain the right of veto over the delegation's members (which could not include any residents of Jerusalem). In addition, what was to be discussed at the conference was to be decided by Israel. The United States went along with all this but also asked the Palestinians to accept.

During August 1991 I went to London several times to meet with leaders from the Territories, plus PLO members from Tunis, in order to draft a satisfactory entrance ticket for us into the conference. I say now, for the record, that I was alarmed at how anxious the PLO seemed to be about accepting American (and, in effect, Shamir's Likud) terms. Every major point had to be sent back to Arafat, who equivocated and came and went and usually opened another channel for himself, leaving us all more or less to mark time. Ibrahim Abu-Lughod and I cautioned against rushing in so precipitously: We reasoned that there could be no peace process without Palestinians, so that, even though we were obviously being made to pay the price of our weakness and lapses in judgment, we could hold out for stronger guarantees. But only if we coordinated honestly among ourselves and only if we stuck to certain principles, like self-determination, equality, and human rights. Instead, there was an extraordinary (and, in my opinion, unseemly) rush to discard principles and strategic goals with equal abandon. And so, in the end, the Madrid conference was set up for early October 1991.

A month and a half earlier, at the very end of August, I convened a meeting of about twenty-five leading Palestinian activists—including several members of the PLO—to try to put a consensus in place among ourselves. In the eventuality of a peace process we would be required to do the talking and, in the usual haphazard way, to provide some planning, so why couldn't we agree that as Palestinians with a knowledge of our own history and our personal record of struggle, we would maintain it at all costs? It was an unsuccessful attempt at the eleventh hour, and a few weeks later, in September 1991, I resigned from the Palestine National Council. Coincidentally, I had been diagnosed with a case of chronic leukemia which forced me to reorder my priorities and rethink what I was doing. In my letter of resignation to the Council's head, I said only that I was leaving for reasons of health. I said not one word more, and because (against hope) I wanted our efforts to succeed I didn't criticize what I felt was a tragically mistaken policy.

For the first time in over two decades I realized that I had no faith in the leadership of the organization I had previously supported. Going to Madrid and throwing ourselves into the arms of the United States and the Israeli government, I strongly felt was a betrayal of our history and of our people. I continued to express support for Palestinian rights and even for Palestinian participation in any negotiations that were ongoing, even those. I was pleased at the new visibility that Madrid gave us, thanks to the efforts of people like Hanan Ashrawi, Haidar Abdel Shafi, and Faisal Husseini, although I was apprehensive that the bilateral talks that began in Washington a month later would open us not only to more pressure but also to the results of our disintegrating national authority, the PLO. And that is exactly what happened: Ten rounds of talks in Washington brought more misery in the Territories, more disillusionment—even fractiousness—among the negotiating Palestinians, and Israel still held the cards. I tried on several occasions—both in the United States and in the Arab world— to press the case for opening up a mass public campaign in the United States to help our position in the talks, but I was unsuccessful. Arafat had, in my opinion, irrationally tied himself to a failing Republican administration, and nothing could change his mind.

One small point needs mention here. In October 1989 in a leading

Arabic magazine I had been publicly critical of the PLO's attitudes toward the United States, attacking its ignorance of the system, its reliance on middlemen and fixers, its unwillingness in a serious way to deal with the media or public information, which were either left to chance or to Arafat. I also accused the PLO of selling "franchises" to individual operators, as if our struggle had become the political equivalent of a large vending machine supervised by the PLO. Arafat and his lieutenants responded in their own defense, and I had a meeting with the Executive Committee in Tunis to explain my views, but all to no avail. Business as usual, no changes at all.

In the meantime, in the summer of 1992, I visited Palestine for the first time in the forty-five years since my family left in 1947 and was able to see for myself what Palestine had now become. I was struck by the fact that people were on the whole both discouraged and immobilized. This was a logical result of the "peace process" taking place in Washington and bringing no results so far as improving the quality of life under occupation was concerned, despite the valiant efforts of the excellent Palestinian delegation (made up of West Bank and Gaza residents). There was almost a magical sense that America would take care of our problems somehow and that Bush—who had temporarily stood up to the Israeli lobby for a time, by opposing (for a time) the $10 billion in loan guarantees requested by Israel—was a real friend of the Arabs. I felt that there was a mass amnesia overcoming us, as if the long and dreadful history of unfulfilled hopes and hypocritical promises that characterized our relationship with the reigning Western power had suddenly been removed from the collective consciousness.

Stronger things were to come when the Labor party won the elections of June 1992: New hope was placed in Yitzhak Rabin as if he wasn't the same man who had tried to crush the *intifadah* and who in 1948 was personally in charge of the dispossession of fifty thousand Palestinians from Ramle and Lydda. By the end of 1992 he had deported four hundred and fifteen alleged Hamas Palestinians as "terrorists" without trial and against all international law. After great unrest in Gaza and the West Bank, Rabin closed the territories off from Israel in late March 1993 (they remain closed); this imposed greater hardship on Palestinian workers who could no longer get to their jobs and to all others who could no longer travel in and out of Jerusalem. But this too was, over time, swallowed by the PLO and the Arabs: We now know that meetings had already begun between Arafat's emissaries and the Mossad to talk about security for Israelis if "autonomy" was to be set up.

[III]

On August 30, 1993, a "historic breakthrough" was announced in the form of a Declaration of Principles negotiated directly between the PLO and Israel. A second set of documents comprising a mutual recognition between Israel and the PLO was also put in place at the same time. With some of the euphoria dissipated after the great celebration surrounding the breakthrough, it now becomes possible to reexamine the Israeli–PLO agreements with the required common sense. What emerges from such scrutiny is a deal that is more flawed and weighted unfavorably for the Palestinian people than many had first supposed. The show biz pomp of the White House ceremony on September 13, the degrading spectacle of Yasir Arafat thanking everyone for the suspension of most of his people's rights, and the solemnity of Bill Clinton's performance—like a twentieth-century Roman emperor shepherding two vassal kings through rituals of reconciliation and obeisance—all these only temporarily obscure the truly astonishing proportions of the quite sudden Palestinian capitulation, which smacks of the PLO leadership's exhaustion and of Israel's shrewdness.

So, first of all, let us call the Declaration of Principles or, as it has become known, "Gaza–Jericho first," by its real name: an instrument of Palestinian surrender, a Palestinian Versailles. What makes it worse is that for at least the past fifteen years the PLO could have negotiated a better arrangement than this modified Allon Plan, one not requiring so many unilateral concessions to Israel. For reasons best known to the leadership, it refused all such previous overtures. Indeed, as the noted Egyptian journalist Mohammed Hassanein Heikal remarked in a lecture given in Cairo on October 6, 1993, the Gaza–Jericho option was offered to Arafat by Sadat in 1977 but promptly turned down. After the Israeli invasion of 1982, and after the Gulf War occurred, because of its disastrous positions then, the PLO lost even more ground. Except for the resolutions of the 1988 PNC, the gains of the *intifadah* were squandered away, and today advocates of the new document say, "We had no alternative." The correct way of phrasing it is, "We had no alternative because we either lost or threw away a lot of others, leaving us only this one."

What is particularly mystifying is how so many Palestinian leaders and their intellectuals persist in speaking about the agreement as a "victory." The fact is, of course, as ex-Secretary of State James Baker said in a TV interview in early September, that Israel has given up nothing, except a bland acceptance of "the PLO as the representative of the Palestinian people." Or as Israeli "dove" Amos Oz reportedly put it during a BBC interview (September 14), "This is the second biggest victory in the history of Zionism."

By contrast, Arafat's recognition of Israel's right to exist carries with it a whole series of renunciations: of the PLO Charter; of violence and terrorism; of all relevant UN resolutions, except 242 and 338, which do not have one word in them about the Palestinians, their rights, or aspirations; by implication, the PLO deferred or set aside numerous other UN resolutions (which, with Israel and the United States, the PLO is now reportedly undertaking to modify or rescind) that have given Palestinians refugee rights since 1948, including either compensation or repatriation. The Palestinians had won numerous international resolutions, including those passed by the EEC, the Non-Aligned movement, the Islamic Conference, the Arab League, as well as the UN, which disallowed or censured Israeli settlements, annexations, crimes against the people under occupation.

It would therefore seem that the PLO has ended the *intifadah,* which embodied not terrorism or violence but the Palestinian *right to resist,* even though Israel remains in occupation of the West Bank and Gaza and has yet to admit that it is, in fact, an occupying power. The primary consideration in the document is Israel's security, with none for the Palestinians from Israel's incursions. In his September 13 Washington press conference, Rabin was straightforward about Israel's continuing control over sovereignty; in addition, he said, Israel would hold the River Jordan, the boundaries with Egypt and Jordan, the sea, the land between Gaza and Jericho, Jerusalem, the settlements, and the roads. Gaza and Jericho are separated by sixty miles of territory to be controlled by Israel; in addition, Jericho is an unspecified territory, which may mean just the city, the district, or the region. In early February 1994, after weeks of sterile negotiations, Jericho was fixed at only 20 square miles. Ehud Barak, the Israeli chief of staff, said on Rosh Hashanah that "we are preparing for the redeployment of the forces in the Jericho area and the Gaza Strip. As to all the rest of the places, our tasks have not changed, and everything continues as usual." For there is nothing in the document to suggest that Israel will give up *its* violence against Palestinians or, as Iraq was required to do after it withdrew from Kuwait, compensate the victims of its policies for forty-five years.

Neither Arafat nor any of his Palestinian partners with the Israelis in Oslo has ever seen an Israeli settlement. There are now more than two hundred of them, principally on the hills, promontories, and strategic points throughout the West Bank and Gaza. Some will probably shrivel and die, but the largest are designed for permanence. An independent system of roads connects them to Israel and creates a disabling discontinuity between the main centers of Palestinian population, which will be divided into ten or eleven cantons. The actual land taken by these settlements, plus the land designated for expropriation, amounts—it is estimated—to over 55 percent of the total land area of the Occupied Territories. Greater Jerusalem alone, annexed by Israel, comprises a huge amount of virtually stolen land, almost 25 percent of the whole. In Gaza, the settlements in the north (three), the middle (two), and the south along the coast from the Egyptian border past Khan Yunis (12) comprise at least 30 percent of the Strip. In addition, Israel has tapped into every aquifer on the West Bank and now uses about 80 percent of the water there for the settlements as well as Israel proper. So the domination (if not outright theft) of land and water resources is either overlooked, in the case of water or postponed in the case of land, by the Oslo Declaration of Principles.

What makes matters worse is that all of the information on settlements, land, and water is held by Israel, most of which it hasn't shared with the Palestinians, any more than it has shared the total amount of inordinately high taxes it has imposed on them for twenty-six years. There have been all sorts of technical committees set up for such questions by the PLO in the territories (in which nonresident Palestinians have participated), but there is little evidence that committee findings (if any) were made use of by the Palestinian side in Oslo or by the negotiating committees that began and still continue meetings with the Israelis on October 13. So the impression of a huge discrepancy between what Israel got and what the Palestinians conceded or overlooked remains unrectified.

What was most troubling in the White House ceremony was that Rabin in effect gave the Palestinian speech, whereas Arafat pronounced words that had all the flair of a rental agreement, words that made no mention of the extent of his people's suffering and loss. The Palestinians saw themselves characterized before the world as its now-repentant assailants—as if the thousands killed by Israel's bombing of refugee camps, hospitals, schools in Lebanon; its expulsion of eight hundred thousand people in 1948 (whose descendants now number about three million, many of them stateless refugees); the conquest of their land and property; its destruction of more than four hundred Palestinian villages; the invasion of Lebanon; to say nothing of the ravages of twenty-six years of brutal military occupation—were reduced to the status of terrorism and violence to be renounced retrospectively or dropped from reference entirely.

In return for exactly what? Israel's recognition of the PLO, undoubtedly a significant step forward. Beyond that, by accepting that land and sovereignty are being postponed till "final status negotiations," the Palestinians have, in effect, discounted their unilateral and internationally acknowledged claim to the West Bank and Gaza: These have now become, in effect, "disputed territories." Thus, with Palestinian assistance, Israel has been awarded at least an equal claim to them. The Israeli calculation is that by accepting the policing of Gaza—which Begin tried to give to Sadat fifteen years ago and which in 1992 Rabin and Peres said they wished would disappear into the sea—the PLO would soon fall afoul of local competitors, of whom Hamas is only one. Moreover, rather than becoming stronger during the interim period, the Palestinians will grow weaker, increasingly more under Israeli control, and thus less able to dispute the Israeli claim when the last set of negotiations begins in two or three years after the signing. But in the absence of any specified mechanism of how to get from an interim status to a later one, the document is purposefully silent. Does this mean ominously that the interim stage may be, in effect, the final one too?

Israeli commentators (e.g., Uzi Benziman, *Ha'aretz*, September 3, 1993) have been speculating that in a matter of six months the PLO and Rabin's government will negotiate a new agreement further postponing elections, thus allowing the PLO to continue to rule. At least twice during the summer of 1993 Yasir Arafat said that his experience of government consisted of the ten years that he "controlled" Lebanon, hardly a comfort to the many Lebanese and Palestinians who recollect that sorry period. Nor is there any concrete way now at hand for real elections to be held should they even be undertaken. The imposition of rule from above, plus the long legacy of the occupation, have not contributed much to democratic grass-roots institutions. There are some unconfirmed reports in the Arabic press (for example, *al-Hayat,* September 27, 1993) that the PLO has already appointed ministers from its own inner circle in Tunis and deputy minsters from among trusted residents of the West Bank and Gaza (Dr. Haidar Abdel Shafi turned down one such offer). There is the question of whether these groups will ever evolve into more truly representative institutions. One cannot be very sanguine given Arafat's absolute refusal to share or delegate power, to say nothing of the financial assets he alone knows about and controls, but I suppose that we should have hope that having resisted Israeli occupation for twenty-six years, Palestinians will prove equally resistant to PLO *diktats.*

In both internal security and development, Israel and the PLO are now aligned with each other. PLO members or consultants have been meeting with Mossad officials since last October (see *Boston Globe,* September 17) to discuss security problems, including Arafat's own security. And this at a time of the worst repression against Palestinians under Israeli military occupation. The intent of this particular Vichy-like collaboration is to silence or deter the Palestinian man or woman who, for instance, will want to demonstrate against the occupation, which will continue given that Israeli troops will redeploy, not totally withdraw. Besides, Israeli settlers will remain and live, as they always have, under a different jurisdiction ruled by the army. The PLO will thus become Israel's enforcer, an unhappy prospect for most Palestinians. Interestingly, even after it won political recognition, the ANC has always refused to supply the South African government with police officials until after power was shared, precisely in order to avoid appearing as the white government's enforcer. It was reported from Amman in late September that one hundred and seventy members of the Palestine Liberation Army, now being trained in Jordan for police work in Gaza, have refused to go along for precisely the same reason. With about twelve thousand Palestinian prisoners in Israeli jails—some of whom Israel has said it might release, while promising to release more (but not all) if the peace negotiations progress satisfactorily— there is an inherent contradiction, not to say incoherence, to the new security arrangements being made.

The one subject on which most Palestinians agree is development, which is being described in the most naive terms imaginable. The realities are considerably more complicated. The world community will be expected to supply the nearly autonomous areas with large-scale financial support; the Palestinian diaspora is expected—indeed preparing—to do the same. Yet all development for Palestine must somehow be funneled through a Palestinian economic agency headed by Arafat and the joint Palestinian–Israeli Economic Cooperation Committee, even though, according to the document, "both sides will cooperate jointly and unilaterally with regional and international parties to support these aims." Israel is the dominant economic and political regional power, of course; in addition, its power is enhanced by its alliance with the United States. Israel's GNP is $60 billion versus a combined GNP of $20 billion for Jordan, Lebanon, and Syria; Israeli per capita income is $12,000 p.a. versus $1,100 for the three Arab countries; 39 percent of Israel's GNP constitutes its foreign debt compared to 125 percent for Jordan, Syria, and Lebanon combined. More than 80 percent of the West Bank and Gaza economy is dependent on Israel, which is likely to control Palestinian exports, manufacturing, labor for the foreseeable future. Aside from the small entrepreneurial and middle class, the vast majority of Palestinians are now impoverished and landless, subject to the vagaries of the Israeli manufacturing and commercial community which employs Palestinians as cheap labor. Almost certainly most Palestinians (the middle class is an exception) will remain as they are economically speaking, although now they are expected to work in private-sector, partly-Palestinian-controlled service industries, including resorts, small assembly plants, farms, and the like.

A recent study by Israeli journalist Asher Davidi (*MERIP* no. 184, September/October 1993) quotes Dov Lautman, president of the Israeli Manufacturers Association: "It's not important whether there will be a Palestinian state, autonomy, or a Palestinian–Jordanian state. The economic borders between Israel and the territories must remain open." With its well-developed institutions, close relations with the United States, the aggressivity and drive of its economy, Israel will in effect incorporate the territories economically, keeping them in a state of permanent dependency. Then Israel will turn to the Arab world, using the political benefits of the Palestinian agreement as a springboard into Arab markets, which it will also exploit and is likely to dominate. This is a chilling prospect.

On September 19, 1993, in an article for *Ha'aretz*, Meron Benvenisti had the following to say about the tenor of the agreements from the Israeli viewpoint:

[. . .] Up to now, Israeli exploitation, discrimination, and domination in the Occupied Territories were justified as necessary for security, nationalistic-political, or even altruistic reasons. Now a new dictionary is being compiled to justify the self-same policies and enrich the same elements [of society], but the arguments will be reversed: it's all for the good of the Palestinians, it's all for the success of peace, it's all so that the Palestinians will finally understand what their fathers refused to understand—that the Zionist enterprise is here to rescue them from the morass of hardship and backwardness—and they must therefore be eternally grateful.

Nevertheless, the PLO, the World Bank, the IMF, the European Community, have put together vast and ambitious development (albeit uncoordinated) plans; funds seem to be available, although as yet no institutions are set up and on the ground in order to be ready to receive them. The general hope seems to be that revenues from taxation, plus outside moneys, will be available first to enable massive infrastructural work (in Gaza especially); this will help Palestinians to go on to establish the rudiments of an independent working economy with perhaps a customs union with Jordan and import possibilities for Palestinians that can get around Israel. Whatever happens, most West Bankers seem certain that their economic situation will improve and that even a kind of economic sovereignty might help to pull them away from Israeli sovereignty and control. Gazans are less optimistic because they are more impoverished and inherently less self-sustaining.

Economic aid for Palestine is being supervised and controlled by the United States, bypassing the UN, some of whose agencies like UNRWA and UNDP are far better placed to administer aid to the Palestinians. Take two recent examples, Nicaragua and Vietnam. Both are former enemies; one, Vietnam, actually defeated the United States but is now economically in need of it. A boycott against Vietnam finally ended in 1994, and the history books are being rewritten to show how the Vietnamese sinned against and "mistreated" the United States for the latter's idealistic gesture of having invaded, bombed, and devastated their country. Nicaragua's Sandinista government was attacked by the U.S.-financed Contra movement; the country's harbors were mined, its people ravaged by famine, boycotts, and every conceivable type of subversion. After the 1991 elections that brought a U.S.-supported candidate, Mrs. Chamorro, to power, the United States promised many millions of dollars in aid, of which only $30 million have actually materialized. In mid-September all aid was cut off. There is now famine and civil war in Nicaragua. No less unfortunate have been the fates of El Salvador and Haiti. To throw oneself, as Arafat has done, on the tender mercies of the United States is almost certainly to ensure the fate the United States has meted out to rebellious or "terrorist" peoples it has had to deal with in the Third World, *after* they have promised not to resist the United States anymore.

Hand in hand with the economic and strategic control of Third World countries that happen to be close to, or possess, necessary resources like oil for the United States, there is also the media system, whose reach and control over thought is truly astounding. For at least twenty years, Yasir Arafat symbolized the most unattractive and morally repellent man on earth. Whenever he appeared in the Western media, or was discussed by it, you could not imagine him without the single thought that he was supposed always to be entertaining: Kill Jews, especially innocent women and children. Within a matter of days, the "independent media" had totally rehabilitated Arafat. He was now an accepted, even partially lovable figure whose courage and realism had bestowed on Israel its rightful due. He had repented, he had become a "friend," and he and his people were now on "our" side. Anyone who opposed or criticized what he had done was either a fundamentalist, like the Likud settlers, or a terrorist, like Hamas. It became nearly impossible to say anything except that the Israeli–Palestinian agreement—mostly unread or unexamined, mostly unclear, minus dozens of crucial details—was the first step toward Palestinian independence.

As in the case of that agreement itself, the problem of the media so far as the really independent critic or analyst is concerned is how to free oneself from the ideological system which both the agreement and CNN now serve. Memory and skepticism (if not outright suspicion) are requisites. Thus, even if it is patently obvious that Palestinian freedom in any real sense has not been, and is clearly designed never to be, achieved beyond the meager limits imposed by Israel and the United States, the famous handshake broadcast all over the world is supposed (a) to symbolize a great moment of success, (b) to blot out past as well as present realities. One of my main reasons for publishing this book is to try to make sure that the past and the present that derives from it are *not* forgotten.

Given a small modicum of honesty, Palestinians should be capable of seeing that the large majority of people the PLO is supposed to represent will not really be served by the agreement, except cosmetically. True, residents of the West Bank and Gaza are rightfully glad to see that some Israeli troops will withdraw to other parts of the West Bank and Gaza and that large amounts of money might start to come in. But it is rank dishonesty not to be alert to what the agreement entails in further occupation, economic control, and profound insecurity. Then there is the mammoth problem of Palestinians who live in Jordan, to say nothing of the thousands of stateless refugees in Lebanon and Syria. Today, *over 50 percent of the Palestinian population does not in fact live on the West Bank or in Gaza*. These people have simply been left out of the Oslo Declaration, deferred until the "final status" negotiations begin several years hence. "Friendly" Arab states have always had one law for Palestinians, one for natives. These practices have already intensified, as witness the appalling scenes of delay and harassment occurring on the Allenby Bridge since the agreement was announced. There is no small irony in the fact that the new Palestinian bureaucracy is reportedly being trained in Egypt, surely the most deadly of all bureaucracies, one with a particularly unsavory record toward Palestinians.

The first thing to be done now is for Palestinians to make clear not only the virtues of being recognized by Israel and accepted at the White House but also what the truly major disabilities are. Pessimism of the intellect first, then optimism of the will. You can't improve a bad situation that is largely due to the technical incompetence of the PLO, which negotiated in complete secrecy and in English, a language that neither Arafat nor his emissary in Oslo know, with no legal adviser (the PLO's two main legal negotiators resigned in protest sometime earlier; Arafat and his three or four subordinates alone faced an entire corps of Israeli Foreign Ministry experts), until on the technical level at least you involve people who can think for themselves and are not mere instruments of a by-now single Palestinian authority. I find it extraordinarily disheartening that so many Arab and Palestinian intellectuals, who a week earlier had been moaning about Arafat's dictatorial ways, his single-handed control over the money, the circle of sycophants and courtiers that have surrounded him in Tunis of late, the absence of accountability and reflection at least since the Gulf War, should suddenly make a 180-degree switch and start applauding his tactical genius and his latest victory. The march toward self-determination can be done only by a people with democratic aspirations and goals, or it is not worth the effort.

After all the celebrating "the [supposed] first step toward a Palestinian state," we should remind ourselves that much more important than having a state is the kind of state it is. The modern history of the postcolonial world is disfigured with one-party tyrannies, rapacious oligarchies, economic ruin, the distortion of society caused by Western "investments," and large-scale pauperization through famine, civil war, outright robbery. Any more than religious fundamentalism, mere nationalism is not and can never be "the answer" to the problems of new secular societies. Potential statehood in Palestine is no exception, especially given so inauspicious a start, in which one can already, alas, see the lineaments of an appetizing marriage between the chaos of civil war in Lebanon and the tyranny of Saddam Hussein's Iraq. Is Arafat going to become Israel's Noriega?

To prevent such an eventuality, a number of quite specific issues need to be addressed. One, of course, is the diaspora Palestinians, who originally brought Arafat and the PLO to power, kept them there, and are now relegated to permanent exile or refugee status. Since, as I said, they comprise at least half of the total Palestinian population, their needs and aspirations are not negligible, especially if, as has already begun to happen, their material as well as political support is being solicited for Gaza and Jericho. A small segment of the exile community is represented by the various political organizations "hosted" by Syria. A significant number of independents (some of whom, like Shafiq al-Hout and Mahmoud Darwish, resigned in protest from the PLO) still have an important role to play, not simply by applauding or condemning from the sidelines but by advocating specific changes in the PLO's structure, trying to change the triumphalist ambience of the moment into something more closely resembling the realities, mobilizing support and building organization from within the various Palestinian communities all over the world for continuing the march toward self-determination. These communities have been singularly disaffected, leaderless, indifferent since the Madrid process began.

One of the first tasks is a Palestinian census, which has to be regarded not just as a bureaucratic exercise but as the enfranchisement of Palestinians wherever they are. It is a perhaps surprising fact that Israel, the United States, and the Arab states—all of them—have always opposed a census: It would give the Palestinians too high a profile in countries where they are supposed to be invisible, and before the Gulf War, it would have revealed to various Gulf governments how dependent they were on an inappropriately large, usually exploited, "guest" community. Above all, opposition to the census stemmed from the realization that were Palestinians to be counted all together, despite dispersion and dispossession, they would by that very exercise come close to constituting a nation and not just a collection of people. Now more than ever, I think, the process of holding a census—and perhaps later even worldwide elections—should be a principal agenda item for Palestinians everywhere. It would constitute an act of historical and political self-realization outside the limitations imposed on them by the absence of sovereignty. And it would give body to the universal need for democratic participation, now ostensibly curtailed by Israel and the PLO in a premature alliance.

Certainly a census would once again raise the question of return for those Palestinians who are not from the West Bank and Gaza. Although this issue has been compressed into the general "refugee" formula deferred until the final status talks sometime in the future, it needs to be brought up now. The Lebanese government, for instance, has been publicly heating up the rhetoric, fed by every faction in the country, against citizenship and naturalization for the 350,000–400,000 Palestinians in Lebanon, most of whom are stateless, poor, permanently stalled. A similar situation obtains in Jordan and Egypt (see *Christian Science Monitor*, September 28, 1993). These people who have paid the heaviest price of all Palestinians can neither be left to rot nor dumped somewhere else against their will.

In the meantime, Israel enjoys the Right of Return for every Jew in the world: Individual Jews can become Israeli citizens and live in Israel anytime at all. This extraordinary inequity, intolerable to all Palestinians for almost half a century, has to be rectified. Certainly it is unthinkable that all the 1948 refugees would either want to or could, in fact, return to so small a place as a Palestinian state, but, on the other hand, it is unacceptable for them all to be told to "resettle" elsewhere, or drop any ideas they might have about repatriation and compensation.

One of the things the PLO and independent Palestinians should therefore do is to open a question not addressed by the Oslo Accords, thereby preempting the final status talks, namely, to ask for reparations to Palestinians who have been the victims of this dreadful conflict. Although it is the Israeli government's wish (expressed quite forcibly by Rabin at his Washington news conference) that the PLO should close, in his words, "its so-called embassies"—a pattern already discernible in the string of many now-bankrupt PLO offices around the world, hundreds of unpaid workers, deep discouragement, and low competence in their performance—these offices should be kept open selectively so that claims such as those of repatriation, compensation, reparations, can be made and pressed.

In sum, we need to move up from the state of supine abjectness with which, in reality, the Oslo Declaration of Principles was negotiated ("we will accept anything so long as you recognize us") into the prosecution of parallel agreements with Israel and the Arabs that concern Palestinian national, as opposed to municipal, aspirations. But this does not exclude resistance against the Israeli occupation, which continues indefinitely. So long as occupation and settlements exist, whether legitimized or not by the PLO, Palestinians and others must speak against them. One of the issues not raised by the Oslo Accords, the exchange of PLO–Israeli letters, the Washington speeches, is whether the violence and terrorism renounced by the PLO includes largely nonviolent resistance, civil disobedience, self-defense, etc. These are the inalienable right of any people denied full sovereignty and independence and must be supported.

Like so many unpopular and undemocratic Arab governments, the PLO has already begun to appropriate authority for itself by calling its opponents terrorists and fundamentalists. This is demagoguery. Hamas and Islamic Jihad are opposed to the Oslo Declaration, but they have said several times that they will not use violence against other Palestinians, although inter-Palestinian violence has already begun and will not easily go away. Besides, the Islamists' combined sway amounts to less than a third of the citizens of the West Bank and Gaza. As for the Damascus-based groups, they strike me as either paralyzed or discredited (for obvious reasons). But this by no means exhausts the Palestinian opposition, which as Mouin Rabbani analyses its various constituencies in an excellent article (*Middle East International,* September 24, 1993) includes well-known secularists, people who are committed to a peaceful solution to the Palestinian–Israeli conflict and are realists and democrats. I include myself in this group, which is, I believe, far bigger than is now supposed.

Central to this opposition's thought is the crying need for internal reform within the PLO, which is now put on notice that reductive claims to "national unity" are no longer an excuse for its by now all-too-habitual incompetence, corruption, autocracy. For the first time in Palestinian history, such opposition cannot, except by some preposterous and disingenuous logic, be equated with treason or betrayal. And, for the first time, opposition means not walking out, killing, or equating disagreement with treason but open discussion, frank language, and, above all, an alternative vision committed to an ongoing democratic political process. Indeed, our claim is that we are opposed to sectarian Palestinianism and blind loyalty to the leadership; we remain committed to the broad democratic and social principles of accountability and performance that triumphalist nationalism has always tried to annul. I think that the emergence of a broad-based opposition to the PLO's history of bungling and incompetence will emerge in the diaspora but will also in time come to include people and parties in the Occupied Territories.

Lastly, there is the confusing matter of relationships between Israelis and Palestinians who believe in self-determination for two peoples, mutually and equally. Celebrations are premature and, for far too many Israeli and non-Israeli Jews, an easy way out of the enormous disparities that remain. Our peoples are already too bound up with each other in conflict and a shared history of persecution for an American-style powwow to heal the wounds and open the way forward. There is still a victim and a victimizer. But there can be solidarity in struggling to end the inequities and, for Israelis, in pressuring their government to end the occupation, expropriation, settlements. The Palestinians, after all, have very little left to give. Now the common battle against poverty, injustice, and militarism must be joined seriously and without the ritual demands for Israeli psychological security, which if they don't have it now, they never will. More than anything else, this is the true test of the symbolic handshake, if it is going to be a first step toward reconciliation and real peace.

No political settlement of a long and bloody conflict can ever fit all the circumstances, of course. To be recognized at last by Israel and the United States may mean personal fulfillment for some, but it doesn't necessarily answer Palestinian needs or solve the leadership crisis. The Palestinian struggle has always been about freedom and democracy; it is secular, and for a long time—indeed, up until the Gulf War—it was fairly democratic. By signing the Oslo Declaration, Arafat rescued himself, throwing himself and his unconsulted people into an alliance with Israel but with possible results in further dislocations, disappointments, and conflict that bode poorly for both Palestinians and Israelis. In recent years, Arafat's PLO (which is our only national institution) refused to mobilize its various dispersed constituencies, to attract its people's best talents. Now it may try to regain the loyalty and compliance it expects before it plunges into a new phase, having seemed to mortgage its future without serious debate, without adequate preparation, without telling its people the full and bitter truth. Can it succeed and still represent the Palestinian nation?

The destiny of the Oslo Declaration of Principles—most of whose details are unclear and yet to be negotiated by two parties very unequal in power—is that for it to be implemented as Israel and the United States intend is for it to be yet another obstacle in the path toward Palestinian freedom and equality. Yet it has been signed and sealed: To oppose it now is like opposing a fact of nature. But the only way for Palestinians to deal with it realistically is to think of *overcoming* its horrendous limitations, going beyond them creatively and courageously. From my point of view, this means overcoming also the weaknesses and flaws of the PLO. True, Arafat may be popular and regarded by some residents of the West Bank and Gaza as a messiah. But he is neither infallible nor sufficient. There is beginning to be talk of alternative structures, a need for a separate human rights campaign, for the kind of professionalism and competence that the PLO has long eschewed. I doubt that all this can occur in collaboration with the PLO, but I would very much like to be proved wrong not only about this but about all my analyses of the Oslo Declaration. We face a tragic dilemma as a people: how to move forward coherently and yet also set limits to the appalling weaknesses of our situation (including the present leadership).

As I said above, there are important Palestinian assets: Hope is one of them. Many of the economies and municipalities of the Gulf were built and run by Palestinians. Everywhere one turns in the Arab world and outside it, Palestinians have proved themselves *individually*, often with extraordinary brilliance. Certainly the most skillful entrepreneurs in the Arab world are Palestinians; the same applies to economists, teachers, doctors, engineers. We must hope then that the combined force of these people can open up opportunities on the West Bank and Gaza undreamed of by the Israelis, who still hold sovereignty, security, and overall power. Unfortunately, however,

> [t]he inherent asymmetry of the Oslo Agreement will be reflected in the fact that every plan for the development of the Middle East, if such there will be, and every bit of openness towards Israel in the wake of this Agreement, will be exploited for the expansion of her international contacts and markets, without her being compelled to take

responsibility for the ruin of the Occupied Territories' economy and their exploitation for fulfillment of her own economic needs. [*The Other Front,* October 20, 1993]

My hope is that this book will be useful, first, in providing a record of twenty-five years of a Palestinian struggle that will continue for some time to come and, second, in reminding readers that the struggle over Palestine contains within it the elements of reconciliation between Jews and Palestinians. Both peoples have to feel that they can and must live together as equals—equals in rights, equals in history and suffering—before a real community between the two peoples will emerge. My ambition is not to stop working or trying to realize that dream but to press the case for reconciliation and equality in such a way as to reengage people again, to raise questions and provide answers, to keep principles and values in a very prominent place before us.

Part One

PALESTINE
AND
PALESTINIANS

CHAPTER 1

The Palestinian Experience

[1968–1969]

Anyone who has tried seriously to examine the contemporary Near East is frequently tempted to conclude that the project is an unmanageable one. Every sort of distraction gets in the way; after a time, a distraction seems as inherent a necessity as an essential. Yet if one believes that the crux of the Near East today is the conflict between Israel and a dispersed, or occupied, population of Palestinian Arabs, then a clearer view of that problem becomes possible. For the major distraction to any scrutiny of the region has been *everyone's* unwillingness to allow for a Palestinian presence. This has been no less true of the Palestinians themselves than it has of the other Arabs, or of Israel. My thesis is that since 1967 the confusions have somewhat diminished because the Palestinians have had to recognize this truth, and have gradually begun to act upon it. This recognition is the source of what I call Palestinianism: a political movement that is being built out of a reassertion of Palestine's multiracial and multireligious history. The aim of Palestinianism is the full integration of the Arab Palestinians with lands and, more importantly, with political processes that for twenty-one years have either systematically excluded them or made them more and more intractable prisoners.

It seems to me a useless dodge to assert—as most anti-Palestinian polemics do—that the Palestinian popular resistance to the exclusions of Zionism is simply a version of Arab anti-Semitism, or still another threat of genocide against the Jews. I have felt that the best way to disprove this view would be to put the Palestinian experience to the reader on both a personal and a public level. Each, I think, is as honest as I could make it, and that has required an approach to Palestinianism by a passage through other Arab countries, notably Lebanon and Egypt. By a happy coincidence both countries have been familiar to the Western reader, accessible to me, and logical geographic and ideological ways of getting to Palestinianism and to its temporary headquarters in Jordan. Another virtue of the approach is that it helps to reduce the difficulty of writing about the Palestinian experience in a language not properly its own. For by moving to the Palestinians through the screens that have surrounded and are now unsettled by them, even as so many continue in exile, an English transcription of the process dramatizes the real difficulties of peripherality, silence, and displacement that the Palestinian has suffered. Palestinianism, then, is an effort at repatriation, but the present stage of the Palestinian experience (as this essay tries to show) is a problematic early transition from *being* in exile to *becoming* a Palestinian once again.

Two of the oldest beach facilities in Beirut are called Saint Simon and Saint Michel; they are also known together in Arabic by a different name, *al-Janah,* that does not approximate a translation of their French titles. To this peculiar cohabitation of French and Arabic, tolerated by everyone without much attention, was recently added a third beach establishment adjacent to the other two: Saint Picot. In June 1969, when I was in Beirut, the new place and its name assumed a powerful symbolic value for me, as did all the *discordia concors* that makes up Beirut. Clearly someone had assumed that "Saint" meant beach, and since Georges Picot was still a name to be reckoned with, what better conjunction than Saint Picot? But then the contradictions and ironies multiply without control. Lebanon was in the midst of its worst internal crisis in many years, a crisis whose dimensions, depending on whom you talked to, seemed at once definitively critical and endlessly analyzable. A caretaker government held office since no cabinet could be formed. One supervening reason for this state of affairs was the lack of a workable definition of Lebanon's sovereignty: An undetermined number of Palestinian *fedayin* were encamped in the south (next to the Israeli border), and although "accepted" as Arab brothers engaged in a legitimate struggle against Israel, the presence of these men had in some very fundamental way unsettled Lebanon's identity, if not its remarkable economy. Yet they remained, the crisis continued, as did Lebanon in suspense for many weeks. Beirut contained this paralyzing collision of views, just as it has contained, indeed exposed and incarnated, almost every contradiction of the Arab Near East. Thus in a small way the endowment of Picot's name (to which the Arabs have no reason to be grateful) with sainthood, and the entitlement of a Lebanese beach to so oddly decorated a European name, was a reflection of the cabinet crisis, of reverberations that came from Syrian, Jordanian, Israeli, Egyptian, American, and Russian unrest, but above all, of Beirut's unique status as a place of natural entry from the West onto the confusing modern topography of the Arab world.

Engaged in the astonishing variety of their history, the Lebanese are used to finding themselves split several ways, most of them contradictory and, as I have been suggesting, utterly Lebanese in the near-freakishness of their resolution. (I use Beirut and Lebanon interchangeably, despite an inevitable slurring of nuances. There are enough nuances to be taken account of, however, without worrying too much about these.) What is Lebanese is the public and direct availability for daily use of these contradictions in so tiny a country. They *are* Lebanon, and have been for at least a century. The order of Lebanon is how miraculously for such a long time it was able to accommodate everything, and how its citizens stood the accommodations that might cripple everyone else. To live in Beirut means, among other things, having the choice of doing, feeling, thinking, speaking, and even being the following, in a huge assortment of possible combinations: Christian (Protestant, Maronite, Greek Orthodox, Melchite, Roman Catholic, etc.), Muslim (Sunnite or Shiite), Druze, Armenian, Jewish, French, American, British, Arab, Kurdish, Phoenician, part of pan-Islamism, part of Arab nationalism, tribal, cosmopolitan, Nasserite, communist, socialist, capitalist, hedonist, puritan, rich, poor, or neither, involved in the Arab struggle against Israel (i.e., for the *fedayin,* for the Israeli airport attack as a sign of involvement), disengaged from the Arab struggle against Israel (i.e., against the *fedayin,* for the airport attack insofar as it demonstrated Lebanon's peaceful position by the absence of any resistance given the raiders), and so on. The poverty of labels like left-wing and right-wing is immediately apparent.

Until the Civil War of 1975 Lebanon stood for accommodation, tolerance, and, especially, representation. It is no accident, for example, that such disparities as the ideas of Arab nationalism, the renaissance of Arabic as a modern language, the foundations of the Egyptian press, the living possibility and continuity of the good life and commercial entrepreneurism (at least for the twentieth-century Arab) originated in Lebanon. Yet the crisis of 1969 developed out of the wealth of what was represented in the country and the lack of suitable Lebanese instruments, for once, to extract the best possible combination for Lebanon's destiny. For if past, present, and future are all readily negotiable with most interests, as I felt they were in Beirut, then crisis ensues. Call it equilibrium, and it still remains critical. As I saw it, Beirut was a victim of its openness and its true cultural virtuosity, as well as of the absence of an articulable foundation upon which to draw.

By comparison Damascus was scarcely visible at all. An accident of personal history made it impossible for me to visit the city: No Americans were permitted there at that time, and since I had American citizenship, despite my birth in Jerusalem into a Jerusalem Arab family, I could not even drive through Syria on my way to Amman. As the plane to Amman flew over Damascus, the city's appearance from the air confirmed my impression of it as the most impenetrable Arab city I had ever known. It seemed gorged on its hermetic involutions. The Syrian regime, which tangled the rhetorical mysteries of Baath politics with the secret intricacies of Alawite religion, had closed the country off and turned away the flavor of its life from the observer.

Everything about Amman, whose central position for the Palestinian had been strengthened since June 1967, testifies to austerity and *Ersatz*. Scarcely a town before 1948, its helter-skelter growth has made it a city by default. Many refugee camps surround it, of course, but unlike Beirut, whatever internationalism Amman possesses remains only in the lingering sense of British discipline one encounters here and there. The streets are hopelessly crowded with pedestrians and cars, although a kind of martial informality pervades all activity. At first I kept asking myself and others which people were Palestinians and which were Jordanians. The number of men in uniforms or green fatigues prompted my questions, but a few hours after arrival I gave up asking. By then it had become evident to me that, in spite of its Hashemite throne, all of Jordan had become a temporary substitute for Arab Palestine. Jordan was the only Arab state to give Palestinians citizenship. Yet, so far as I could tell—and this was certainly true for me—no one really felt at home in Amman, and yet no Palestinian could feel more at home anywhere else now. Aside from a few places on the hills where rather commonly despised parvenus had built ostentatious villas, Amman is a city carrying the single-minded Palestinian energy. No particularly apparent heroism or self-conscious cause mongering are in the air: Both Amman's setting and its means are too daylit in their poverty to permit these futile games. The city has a bustling commercial life, but an impressive dedication to Arab Palestine overrides even that. In Amman one cannot escape the necessity of that cause (and this accounts for the city's austerity): *Everyone,* you feel, has been touched in a concrete way by "the Palestinian question." Cafés, television, movies, social gatherings—all these amenities are permanently subordinated to an overwhelmingly powerful experience.

In Amman today two ways of life enclose all the other ways, which finally connect the main two. These two are being a refugee in a camp and being an active member of one of the resistance groups. It is difficult to remember, as one visits the refugee camps, that such places with their mean rows of neat, ugly tents, are not there to be visited, nor even to impress one in a sentimental way with their poverty and squalor. Each camp provides an absolute minimum of daily existence, where a communal life can be led just because refugees believe that they need continue in this confining fashion *only until* they can return to their place of origin. A Palestinian UNRWA official with whom I chatted said that what never failed to amaze him was how the refugees simply hung on. He had difficulty describing the quality of the refugees' life, and I noticed how anxious he was to avoid the word *passivity.* He went on to say that although each camp contained about 35,000 people, there was no crime to report, no "immorality," no social unrest. I saw that what he was doing—since he himself was also a refugee—was protecting the camp dwellers, or rather protecting their right to be as they were, for the time being: I took this as I think he wanted it taken, that the duration of a refugee's life in the camp was a moral fact with unspoken meaning, attested to by some deep faculty of knowing endurance, and a faith that being a refugee would end at the right time.

Women and children were very much in evidence, but hardly any men or young boys. If they are not engaged as day laborers in the Ghor (the valley between Amman and the river), they belong to one of the guerrilla groups, the boys to the *Ashbal* (cubs), whose regimen includes a standard education and military training. There are almost daily air attacks (about which little is heard in the United States) by the Israelis over the fertile Ghor. The pretext for these raids is military targets, but their achievement is the destruction of crops and of the few inhabited villages left. Yet life there, like that of the camps, goes on because there is some evidence that hope is not entirely baseless. I talked with three Fatah men who had just returned from a raid; five of the original party were killed, but the three who came back had expected a loss of this magnitude. They all had wives and mothers in the camps. Now they also have dead or living comrades and relatives on the West Bank: This investment has made a difference, and no amount of tiresome cant about being refugees who won't settle with, or won't be settled by, the other Arabs, or being "pawns" or "footballs" or "terrorists," can alter it for them.

The other Arab cities are, of course, touched by the experience of the past twenty years, but none today so urgently enlivens that experience as Amman. This has not always been true since 1948, but it is true now, for reasons that have to do with each Arab country. I shall return to those reasons shortly. To the Palestinian Arab the Jordanian border with Israel is *the* border: the closest one spiritually, the one traveled across most painfully, the one that most fully characterizes the displacement and the proximity of its cause. Therefore, as a place Amman has become a terminal with no other *raison d'être* than temporarily to preserve displacement; beyond the city, physically and in consciousness, are a desert and extinction. In Amman the Palestinian either stays on as best he can or he repatriates himself from it as a guerrilla. For a time he seems to have stopped thinking about Kuwait or Beirut or Cairo. He has only himself to consider now, and what he discovers, by whatever techniques he uses, is how he is a Palestinian—or rather how he has already become a Palestinian again and what this must mean for him. For the most recent arrivals in Amman it has been a necessity, and this necessity has galvanized the residents who have been there since 1948. What has emerged, in short, is Palestinianism.

States of the popular soul are, I know, almost impossible to examine scientifically, even discursively. It is no false modesty on my part, for example, to feel that what I am now writing is at too far a remove from the ongoing fortunes of Palestinianism. The realities of the Palestinian experience are both complex and elusive, so much so as to escape the descriptive order of what must appear to be a series of afterthoughts. But this recognition, which I certainly make, is an exact analogy of a significant new aspect of the Palestinian experience. The discontinuity between writing *about,* let us say, and the direct experience of which the writing tries to treat, is like the essential condition for the Palestinian's transformed consciousness. Just as he can see that Amman is not Jerusalem, Beirut not Amman, Cairo not Amman— hitherto interchangeable parts of a collective Arab dream, strung together like identical beads on a string—he can now know that being a Palestinian includes, but does not reconcile, being in Amman *and* being under military occupation in Jerusalem, Gaza, Nablus, or Jericho. Yet what he feels as discontinuity is no longer a void which he had previously tried to forget—by going to Beirut or coming to the United States. That void had been an inert gap that stood for the absence of any real encounter with Israel.

For there has been one major encounter between the Palestinians and Israel since June 1967, an encounter that concentrated and, despite exaggerated accounts of it, thereby symbolized the possibility of popular resistance to a political enemy (despite a whole prior series of sporadic guerrilla operations, which had lacked coherence). That was the battle of Karameh in March 1968. At that moment, when an invading Israeli force was *met* by a local one defending what it could no longer afford to give up, the void changed into a direct experience of true political discontinuity: the actual face-to-face enmity between Zionism and Palestinianism. This conflict thus became a symbolic event, not simply a news release doctored to fit a wildly polemical broadcast.

All occurrences become events after they occur. In part events are mythic, but like all effective myths they record an important aspect of a real experience. An event like the battle of Karameh was a decisive moment which, for the Palestinians, was suited to be a certain demarcation between what came before it and what came after it. At Karameh—unlike the West Bank village of al-Sammu, which Israel had razed unopposed—the opponents were clearly pitted against each other. A regular Israeli force moved against an irregular Palestinian one, and the latter answered with a refusal merely to push off and let Karameh (a village built by refugees: hence its significance) be destroyed; by refusing, it stayed to become a truly popular activation of a conflict that had formerly been left to the Arabs at large. Thus Karameh divides the Palestinian experience into a *before* that had refused an encounter, which meant accepting a retrospective fiat declared against the Palestinian Arab past, and an *after* that finds the Palestinian standing in, becoming, fighting to dramatize the disjunction of his and her history in Palestine before 1948 with his history at the peripheries since 1948. In this sense, then, a void, felt by every Palestinian, has been altered by an event into a discontinuity. And the difference between void and discontinuity is crucial: One is inert absence, the other is disconnection that requires reconnection.

The odds against a reconnection of the displaced Palestinian with his land and with his subjugated compatriot are severe indeed, and the battle has only just begun. Israel's stated policy has been categorically to deny the reality of a Palestinian people, but such a policy is thoroughly consonant with the Zionist vision since Herzl. Nevertheless, morale is probably higher among West Bank Arabs than it is outside, because on the West Bank at least one is an inhabitant (albeit a third-class citizen), whereas outside, the Palestinian is excruciatingly aware of how thin his existence has been during the past twenty-one years. A better way of saying this is that the displaced Palestinian has had his human prerogative—i.e., the right to object to his exile, suffering, loss, death—taken from him in his political struggle. His oppressor has been a political enemy surfeited with this prerogative. But whereas the very most has been made out of Jewish suffering, the very least has been made out of Palestinian–Arab suffering. For example, the diplomatic haggling between Israel and Arab states is always depicted by Israel and its supporters as a quarrel between "Jews" who want peace and a place of their own at last, and "Arabs" who will not let them have either. That Israel has been more than a match for a whole world of Arabs, or that it is presently inflated to three times its original size or, most important, that Palestinian Arabs, who have suffered incalculable miseries for the sake of Western anti-Semitism, really do exist, have existed, and will continue to exist as part of Israel's extravagant cost—about these things very little is heard, apart from the usual unctuous complaints about injustice, the lack of reason, and the necessity of peace.

It is becoming more and more certain to the Palestinian that Israel in its present state of thriving militarism has no immediate need of peace. If it does want peace, that would be because the Israelis wanted some rest from the strain on their economy or on their "image." Most Palestinians fear large-scale sellouts by the Arab states, themselves tired out by the uneven struggle. It is due to this fear that relations between the *fedayin* and the Arab governments are so problematic: each suspects that the other's interest will suffer, as it must, of course. Another danger is that the Palestinian organizations will allow themselves to become more and more enmeshed in local Arab conflicts. Yet from the larger world the Palestinian expects (and is getting) attention, but no more than that. He has no benefits to gain from Western good-thinkers who sympathize so effortlessly with the Vietnamese peasant, the American black, or the Latin American laborer. And this only because he is an "Arab" who is opposed by the "Jew." To live in America, for example, and to know this truth is especially painful. For here the emotional residue of what has been a singularly dirty chapter in world history, from no matter whose side it is studied, has been turned against the Arab. Even the word *Arab* works quite easily as an insult. From the Final Solution, to American unwillingness to permit European Jews entry to the United States, to Lord Moyne's murder, to the sordid role of the British, to the Lavon affair, to Sirhan's assassination of Robert Kennedy (which was stripped of its political significance by the press), to Bernadotte's murder by the Stern Gang, the tracks are messy, yet scarcely recognizable in, for instance, *Commentary*'s clean pages.

Insofar as my personal experience is admissible in evidence, I can try to flesh out a few of these thoughts. In 1948 I was twelve, a student at an English school in Cairo; my immediate family and I had left Jerusalem for the last time in December 1947. Aside from my immediate family, most of my other relatives were in Palestine. During the early months of 1948 all of them became refugees who were to resettle themselves in either Jordan, Egypt, or Lebanon. My closest friend at the time was a Jewish boy who had a Spanish passport. I remember him telling me that autumn how shameful it was that six countries were pitted against one; the appeal, I believed, was to my sporting instinct developed at cricket and soccer games. I said nothing, but I felt bad. On similar occasions many years later I also said nothing (actually I said I was from Lebanon, which was as cowardly as saying nothing, since it meant saying something that was intended to be deliberately not provocative). I was born in Jerusalem; so was my father, his father, and so on; my mother was born in Nazareth. These facts were rarely mentioned. I earned my degrees, I became a professor, I wrote books and articles on European literature. And, as the jolts of Near Eastern politics dictated, I occasionally saw my family on vacations: sometimes in Egypt, in Jordan, finally in Lebanon. In 1967 I was "from" Lebanon.

That did me no good during that awful week in June. I was an Arab, and we—"you" to most of my embarrassed friends—were being whipped. I wrote one or two letters to the *Times,* but these were not published, and with a few other Arabs had sessions of group-think that were really group therapy; then I began compulsively to clip things out of papers and magazines. A year and a half later, out of those smoldering extracts, I wrote an essay called "The Arab Portrayed" (a portion of which reappeared in my book *Orientalism*) in which I lamented and documented the ways in which the Arab, in contrast to the Israeli, had been depicted in America. This vulgar demotion, as I called it, was what made American accounts of the June War so unfair and so disgraceful an example of anti-Arabism. Yet what I was also saying, almost without realizing it, was that a too-integral nationalism, which the Arab himself purported to embody, had failed him as much as it had failed even the Israelis, who in the months after June 1967 were robbed of "Arab" recognition. In the meantime I continued with my own work, and the "Arabs" went on with theirs.

By "Arab work" I mean the way in which, *grosso modo,* the Arab countries set about their national existence as a result of the June War. Much of the very recent work done by the Arabs has been reductive. This is not entirely bad and, to my mind, it has been necessary. Arab independence was, and in some cases still is, a partially Western construction. I am not a political scientist or a social psychologist, but what I am trying to articulate is my sense that Arab independence was not so much earned but granted in forms that suited the former colonizers. One becomes especially conscious of this in, to take a classic case, *The Seven Pillars of Wisdom,* where it is gradually revealed that Lawrence's triumph was in having used the Arabs' vague national aspiration as the stuff out of which *his* chivalric-medieval-romantic dream could be carved. Even if Lawrence and the Arabs both awakened to the dream's betrayal, it has taken the Arabs a longer time to rid themselves of its haunting effects. Therefore, the nationalism of independence, when finally left to itself, was in part borrowed, grandiose, aimless, self-serving, relatively authentic—but fairly inexpensive. The reductive process has been costly, for there has been a realization of these inadequacies, and an attempt to decompose Arab nationalism into discreter units finely sensitive to the true cost of real independence. In most Arab countries today (Egypt, Syria, Iraq, and Lebanon in particular) the reduction has taken the form of left-wing critique among many, but by no means all, thinkers; thus it could be shown that the traditional class structure of those societies has yet to undergo revolutionary change. This may be true, but lurking in everyone's mind is the massive fact of Israel's presence, and the costs of that presence have still to be fully felt universally. Hence the accentuated importance of the Palestinian today, for he is being pragmatically forced to create his identity in accordance with real impingements upon it.

I remarked above that one working psychological change since 1967 was that Amman and Jordan had become more central to the whole Palestinian question than ever before. The reason for this refocusing is not only because the Palestinian has made the change, but also—let it be admitted—because of a general feeling in other Arab countries that Palestine had neither served nor been adequately served by actions taken in the interests of Arab nationalism. I don't want to dwell on this too much because, like my comments on Arab independence, at best I am making general, rather presumptuous speculations about some very complicated movements in the Arab world at large (from which I have conveniently excluded Libya, Sudan, Algeria, Tunis, and Morocco); besides, things have been in too much flux to do more than suggest tentative reasons. First, of course, was the military defeat, as well as the humiliating difference between the exuberance of prediction and the aftermath of rout. For no matter how correct the moral stand, it could not be detached from the methods of its implementation and expression, and those were shown to be disastrously wanting. Second, it became apparent that Arab nationalism was far from unitary; the creed was fed by many subsidiary ideologies, and therefore assumed differing roles. Abdallah Laroui's book *L'Idéologie arabe contemporaine* is an excellent recent account both of what makes up Arab nationalism and of its differences from other Third World movements. I need not go over what he has discussed so well.

On what seemed Arab nationalism's most unanimous argument, opposition to Israel, there could never be real thought since, as Sartre and Cecil Hourani (in an article published in *Encounter* right after the 1967 War) have both observed, one cannot truly oppose what one neither knows nor confronts. The hiatus that prevented Arab unity was Israel, and this the Arabs collectively proclaimed, but a hiatus, like any other rupture, cannot be dealt with by ignoring it. By this I mean that the problem of Israel always remained on *the other side*, literally and figuratively, of what the Arabs collectively did. Israel was always being *left to* the realm of generality (in which, not surprisingly, Arab nationalism also operated), where it was hoped that Zionism could be treated as an interruption to be ignored, or drowned out by a general concert of voices and action. This concert then was the job of Arabism, just as on other levels it was the job of the army, of the ministries of information, of the Arab League, in sum, of the Arab nation. Since Israel was the Other, which of course it still is, it was felt that *other agencies* would take care of it on behalf of *us*. One always felt involved in the sentiments of anti-Zionism, whereas the action always seemed to be taken by proxy, at some distance from the sentiments. That sort of cleavage, then, is what 1967 exposed.

It was as an understandable reaction to the devastations of the June War that in Egypt, to take the principal case in point, open-minded intellectuals recognized the limitations of the pre-War psychology by rediscovering the limits of their own national interests. The Egyptian expedition to Yemen had further irritated their awareness. In refusing to be deluded by proclamations that the June War was only a setback, these intellectuals saw that what one of them called "nationalitarianism" did Egypt itself a disservice. One perhaps minor but fascinating development out of this view was a renewed interest in works like Hussein Fawzi's brilliant *Sindbad Misri (An Egyptian Sindbad)*, which had originally appeared in 1961, subtitled "Voyages Over the Vast Spaces of History." Quite one of the most original works produced in Egypt over the past twenty years, Fawzi's book took for its theme the absolute coherence of *Egypt*'s history, from the pharaohs to the modern period.

Although the book's theme was not a new one, the assured subtlety of his thought enabled Fawzi to construct a series of historical tableaux in which a specifically Egyptian kind of history developed, which, he argued, showed Egypt's people to be "makers of civilization." The implicit point here, made explicitly by other Egyptian intellectuals like Lewis Awad, was that Egypt had its own mission, quite apart from an Arab one, to fulfill, and that that did not *primarily* include violence. Israel's occupation of Sinai has unfortunately vitiated the argument somewhat.

There were comparable redefinitions of the relationship between Arabism and local nationalism taking place, in different forms, of course, and not always as standard left-wing critiques, in the other Arab countries. However, I do not wish to imply that such reassessments had never taken place before; they have been taking place all along—witness the earlier work of Constantine Zurayk, Ra'if Khoury, Ibrahim Amer, and Salama Musa, to mention a few examples at random. It is just that the present redefinitions possess a cumulative thrust that has sharpened and extended the horizon of national self-knowledge. Like the Lebanese cabinet stalemate of 1969, the recent redefinitions and self-criticisms can be understood in psychological terms as what Erik Erikson has called identity crisis, although certainly I am aware that analogies between individual and collective identities are dangerous to make. Another risk is that Erikson's use of his own concept is so ingenious as to make gross adaptations like mine seem clumsy and hopelessly farfetched. Still, there is something to be gained, I believe, from applying the following description by Erikson to the post-1967 period:

> I have called the major crisis of adolescence the identity crisis; it occurs in that period of the life cycle when each youth must forge for himself some central perspective and direction, some working unity, out of the effective remnants of his childhood and the hopes of his anticipated adulthood; he must detect some meaningful resemblance between what he has come to see in himself and what his sharpened awareness tells him others judge and expect him to be. This sounds dangerously like common sense; like all health, however, it is a matter of course only to those who possess it, and appears as a most complex achievement to those who have tasted its absence. Only in ill health does one realize the intricacy of the body; and only in a crisis, individual or historical, does it become obvious what a sensitive combination of interrelated factors the human personality is—a combination of capacities created in the distant past and of opportunities divined in the present; a combination of totally unconscious preconditions developed in individual growth and of social conditions created and re-created in the precarious interplay of generations. In some young people, in some classes, at some periods in history, this crisis will be minimal; in other people, classes, and periods, the crisis will be clearly marked off as a critical period, a kind of "second birth," apt to be aggravated either by widespread neuroticisms or by pervasive ideological unrest.[1]

"Adolescence" must not at all be understood as implying condescension toward a recent history that has so obviously been painful: this is why the present identity crisis is not minimal, but a matter of profound moment. What is crucial to Erikson's definition is awareness of the crisis on the part of those undergoing it—and this, I think, is the new situation among those who together make up the vanguard of the Arab mind today. Whereas Jacques Berque, in some minds the most audacious Western thinker about the Arabs, had deliberately called the first chapter of his book on the Arabs "The Disruption of Traditional Man,"[2] the notion was not commonly recognized to be true, and thereby acted upon, by Arabs themselves.

The identity crisis solicits above all a recognition of disruption. And to have this recognition one needs a very clear idea that something has been left behind in order that a new development based on a stronger identity might become possible. I speculate once again when I suggest that what is now being left behind is the Arab–Islamic idea of reality, staggeringly complex, no doubt, but based, as Berque argues so cogently, on the plenitude of the present. Hitherto the Arab genius had taken the world as fullness and simultaneity; thus, there was no unconscious, no latency that was not immediately accessible to vision, belief, tradition, and, especially, language. Any change in that sort of order can only be a mixed blessing that disturbs confidence, yet in the context of Arab national independence (which roughly coincided with the inception and growth of Zionism), the phase to 1948 was a period of youth and adolescence, of initiation into a new history. After 1967 came the slow realization of what that really meant.

It is useful to compare the course of Arab nationalism with that of Jewish nationalism in order to indicate the traumas involved in the change I have just been discussing. Near the beginning of this century both nationalisms seem to have been phenomena of projection, like all emerging national ideologies. Each had its aims, its plans for realization, and its philosophical and rhetorical styles. The Arab version has been studied and restudied at great length in works like George Antonious's *The Arab Awakening* and Albert Hourani's *Arabic Thought in the Liberal Age*. What 1967 forced upon the Arabs, however, was a gradual attenuation of their projection, and it seemed to them that Zionism—no longer an idea but a state that sprawled over much of their territory—had realized its original projections. Neither side, each occupied with its own problems, was charitably aware of hardships suffered by the other. For the Arab, then, it seemed that quite without him a foreign growth had spread in his midst, forcing him to attenuate his vision from pan-Arabism to collective as well as individual defeat, displacement, loss. To him the Israeli had asked for and received the world's backing in a well-planned project of dissemination and growth. Yet the current emergence of the Palestinian movement is not only, I think, a sign of the diminished vision of Arab nationalism, but also a hopeful sign that the contrast between Arab and Jewish nationalism has been muted. In having to respond to the claims of Palestinians, Zionism must itself undergo the attenuation it had forced on the Arabs at large. If there is to be any future reconciliation between Jewish nationalists and the Palestinians, it must be as a result of this reversal of trends.

It can also be said that during the years up to and including 1967 it never did the Arabs much good to believe that absolute right was on their side. I do not mean by this that Zionism was something to be tolerated passively, but rather that the elevation of a political conflict into a framework of cosmic morality had two noticeably damaging effects. In the first place, it made the Arabs rely on the self-validating moral force of their arguments which, as I said above, isolated the Israelis and insulated the Arabs from the essentially *political* nature of the conflict. Emotion and rhetoric can never be wholly divorced from politics (this is particularly true, as I shall remark a little later, in so fraught a region as Palestine), but it is when they are employed as a substitute for politics that they do most harm. Worst of all, they play directly into the hands of a political argument whose greatest strength is its apparent aloofness from history and politics, and this is the second damaging effect. For Zionism, or Jewish nationalism, has prospered on arguments and actions either *for or against* its exclusivity, whether as positive good or, from the Arab side, as negative evil.

This is not as paradoxical as it may seem. Zionism is historically incommensurate with any sort of liberalism, so long as Zionism is believed by its supporters to be identical with, or at least a logical extension of, Judaism as a religion of secular exclusion and nonassimilation. This is not to say that every Zionist is a Herzl or a Jabotinsky or a Dayan; Buber, Magnes, and, in America, I. F. Stone had argued for some sort of dilution of the extremist view. In the main, however, the moderates have not fared well. The dialectic of polar opposition has been too strong for them. With every apparent consolidation of its national existence Israel seems more and more to represent not only the *place apart* of Judaism but also the concentrated actions of Judaism. And Judaism, in two dimensions, each, commonsensically, incompatible with the other: the universal (timeless) and the secular (temporal). Thus Israel can make claims for its historical presence based on its timeless attachment to a place, and supports its universalism by absolutely rejecting, with tangible military force, any other historical or temporal (in this case Arab Palestinian) counterclaims. I do not think it unfair either to the Israelis or to the Arabs to say that both contributed, each in its own way, to this maelstrom of exclusions. The Arab has acceded to that aspect of Judaism which, as Arthur Koestler put it in *The Trail of the Dinosaur,* "unlike any other [religion] is racially discriminating, nationally segregative, socially tension-creating." In his refusal to deal with Israel at all, the Arab simply enforced the self-segregating tendency in Judaism, for which Israel assumed secular responsibility.

The obvious bearing of the Jewish experience in World War II on present-day Zionism cannot be overestimated. Yet even there, as Hannah Arendt, for one, sensitively exposed the issue in her *Eichmann in Jerusalem,* problems for the non-Israeli Jew, especially for the often conservative American Zionist, persist. It is not my task to consider here the ambiguities of being a Zionist, remaining in America, and thinking of the Arab solely as Israel's opponent, beyond remarking how American Zionism symbolizes the vast range of the Zionist projection and, conversely, the attenuation of Arabism: Both nationalisms have reached their furthest extremities. Yet because of the Palestinian resurgence, the conflict has been compressed into its most economical local form in the present confrontation between the conquering Israeli and the resisting Palestinian. For all its difficulty and violence, this form of conflict strikes me as being more clear, and more hopeful, than the morass of thought which seeks to drag in every conceivable confusion.

Nevertheless, many doubtless imponderable forces also intersect at the essential node of the conflict. These range from overtly bumbling great power competition to, equally irrational and perhaps even more compelling, the subliminal forces of primitive religious emotion, mythic racism, and ideological mythologizing of the worst sort. For it must never be forgotten—and this may be the clue to the entire imbroglio—that Palestine carries the heaviest weight of competing monotheistic totalitarianism of any spot on earth. While it may be dangerously optimistic to pretend that a reconciliation of supernatural arguments can take place in a natural setting, there is some encouragement in remembering that until 1948, Palestine seems simultaneously to have given birth to interconnected ideas of the One *and* the Many, of the individual *and* the community.

Since 1948 the Arab Palestinian has had to endure a political living death. Whatever he or she now experiences in the way of vitality is because, since 1967, there has begun a revitalization of thought just to avoid total extinction, and because the dreams of Arabism have broken on his acutely exposed situation. The two reasons are different sides of the same coin. The main characteristics of the Arab Palestinian's life since 1948 have been peripherality, isolation, and silence—all of those are conditions of displacement and loss. (It cannot fail to escape the Palestinian's notice, by the way, how much their experience begins to resemble that of the Diaspora Jew). Peripherality, like the other two characteristics I've mentioned, is not tolerable past the point where displacement (not being where you ought to be) means not being any place else really, not being able to stand at the center of your destiny, feeling that all your prerogatives have been usurped. If you cede your initiatives to a larger entity, and if you tie your fortunes to others', you are apt to be awakened from this passivity when you discover that your priorities have been disordered. Like all other Mediterraneans, the way Maurice Le Lannou describes them, the Palestinians belong first to their village, land, and tribe, then second, and with many misgivings, to the vaster group. When after 1967 it became apparent that the first fact of the Palestinian's life was Israeli occupation, the second dispersion among the other Arabs, and only third, Arabism, the priorities had righted themselves. Peripherality took on a close literal meaning and was intolerable.

Political silence, in the case of the Palestinians, has meant not knowing to whom or for what to talk, and therefore talking with different voices, none of them their own. The silence was broken under the new, more oppressive occupation of 1967. Here too the priorities emerged more clearly: the Palestinian must first address the Israeli, not as a rebellious prisoner speaking to his guard, or as a challenge to a coercive presence. It is the restiveness of Arabs inside occupied Palestine that, at least as far as the outside world is concerned, has made pre-1967 silence seem inauthentic. A whole range of Palestinian speech has erupted, all originating at the proper source—Arabs under occupation in Palestine—and thereby channeled out to the world. Call them rumors, myths, paraliterature, propaganda, or whatever: They replace the silence with what is now only a substitute political voice (just as Amman is a substitute political center), but which at least derives from an objective, because directly experienced, condition of imposed silence. This essay of mine, I feel, because it is in English, partakes both of the peripherality and of the paradoxical silence that I have been trying to describe.

The Palestinian's isolation has been a disorientation more than anything else. Or so it now appears. Previously a classless "refugee," since 1967 he has become a politicized consciousness with nothing to lose but his refugeedom; that isn't much of a possession, and it is his only political possession at present. The attenuation of the Arab project, or the demystification of the Arab potential, has left the Palestinian with his original starting point, as Gerard Manley Hopkins phrased it, being "a lonely began": the fact that he is a deracinated refugee from Palestine. Karameh presented the refugee with a new alternative, the chance to ground peripherality, isolation, and silence in resisting action. If once it made the Palestinian generally angry and resentful that neither the Arabs, the Israelis, nor the rest of the world fully grasped his predicament, such organizations as the Popular Front for the Liberation of Palestine, al-Fatah, and even the independent Institute of Palestine Studies in Beirut are his way of grasping himself and his predicament alone.

Before discussing the meaning of the Palestinian movement more fully, it may be worthwhile to comment briefly on two sympathetic sources of outside interest in the Palestinian issue. One is the so-called realistic view, which is held by some Zionists and many non-Zionists as well. In this view the word *tragedy* turns up with cloying frequency. Thus, runs the argument, while the Jews have an undeniable right to what they have so laboriously earned, it is a tragedy that a million and a half Arabs, innocent of European anti-Semitism, have had to be one of the costs of the enterprise. Such is the material of tragedy, but life must go on. Reason and negotiation ought now to prevail. The trouble with this argument is that, no less than Four Power settlement, it is an imposition of an occidental aesthetic model on what is in large measure a nonoccidental political situation. Tragedy, as Jaspers put it bluntly in another connection, is not enough. It would be just as silly to try to convince a refugee living in a tent outside Amman that he is the daily victim of a tragedy as it would be to tell an Israeli that he is a tragic hero. Moreover, the tragic vision is a static one, unsuited to the dynamics of political action currently enacted and lived through. If there was a tragedy, it was part of the common Semitic past in its sufferings at the hands of the West: the Jews in World War II, the Arabs in Palestine evicted by the power of Western-backed Zionism. The reality of Palestine remains, however, and that requires action, not tragic suffering.

The second source of sympathy is from the international radical Left. Although wishing to accept that sympathy, the Palestinians—myself included—suggest a number of reservations. One is that the Left argues the case against Israel too much from the outside, whereas what is needed is a corrective from the inside of the situation. It might have been possible to show how Israel was originally a creation of Western colonialism (as Maxime Rodinson has done with such telling effect)[3], yet it does not alter the fact that there is such a thing as Israeli imperialism and that it is now affecting all Palestinians more directly than Western colonialism. The latter, to Israel's immediate credit and to its ultimate disadvantage, has had the function of helping the Israelis remain in the curiously skewed position of assuming territorially sovereign status as well as an historically and politically aloof and repressive position whenever it came to the Arab inhabitants of Palestine. To the Palestinian, what matters now is the troubling immediacy of the Israeli presence, not the contradictions inherent in European and American colonialism.

Another aspect of the Left argument that disquiets me (I can't speak for anyone besides myself) is what bothered me when I quoted Erikson so tentatively, or when I disavowed the tragic view. I simply have no way of knowing how political analyses developed in the West ultimately apply elsewhere. There is, for example, an Israeli Left, just as there is an Arab Left: they are still opposed on more direct nationalist grounds than theoretical ones. I have no answer to this problem, and I raise it only as a symptom of difficulties with any so-called internationalist overview, whether political, psychological, or aesthetic. Finally, no Palestinian can forget three things about the Left. First, that it was Russia and its satellites that went along with the United States in the Partition Plans and in UN creation of Israel in 1948. Second, that there is an alarming symmetry in the manner by which the Left has recently joined or replaced anti-Semitic supporters (who were a source of endless trouble) of the Arabs against Israel. Third, that the new Palestinian ideology owes next to nothing to the Western Left, which, with a few exceptions, bogged down in its dynastic worries and conflicts over racism and/or conflicts and/or its own internationalism, had little to contribute to the Palestinian during the 1967 War.

The present phase of the Palestinian experience is in trying to sharpen the experience by keeping it pertinent to *Palestine,* thereby liberating Palestine, actually and intellectually, from the segregations and the confusions that have captured it for so long. All sorts of difficulties tamper with this effort, Israel most of all. Every Jewish Zionist I have either read, heard, or spoken to, whether he is an Israeli or an American, adheres to a notion whose common denominator is that Israel must remain as it is now in order to safeguard the Jewish *rhythm of life,* a phrase that presumably serves to camouflage the wide social discrepancies between the European, the Oriental, the Orthodox, and the secular Jews in Israel. This, I gather, makes sense to many Jews: I can't tell. For a Palestinian, it is difficult to accept the rhythm-of-life view except as one of two things. Either the phrase stands for a fear that the Holocaust could be repeated, which makes of Israel (after twenty-one years of much-vaunted independence) what the English would call a funk-hole for every still-dispersed Jew. Or the phrase is an argument for preserving Israel from having to face the no less real truth that the Jewish rhythm has supplanted a more inclusive one, the Palestinian, which has and would allow Christian, Muslim, and Jew to live in counterpoint with each other.

Probably the most serious psychological obstacle preventing close and fair political scrutiny of Palestinianism is, as I said above, the heavy emotional pressure of the Holocaust. To this pressure every civilized person must, of course, submit, so long as it does not inhibit anyone's political rights, particularly those of people who are absolutely disso-ciable from what has been an entirely European complicity. It cannot be emphasized enough, I think, that no Arab feels any of the sort of guilt or shame that every Westerner (apparently) feels, or is impelled to show he is feeling, for that horrible chapter in history. For a Palestinian Arab, therefore, it is not taboo: to speak of "Jews" in connection with Israel and its supporters, to make comparisons be-tween the Israeli and the German occupations, to excoriate journalism that reports Jewish suffering but ignores, or discounts, Israel's razing of Arab homes and villages, Israeli napalm bombing, Israeli torture of Palestinian resistance fighters and civilians, Israel's deliberate attempt to obliterate the Palestinian Arab, Israel's use of its understanding of "Arab psychology" to offend the Arab's human status, Israel's callous use of Jewish suffering to blackmail Christians and Muslims by toying with (and then implementing) "plans" for Jerusalem—and so on.

The Palestinian organizations active today have Palestinianism in common. They do not project too far ahead of plans somehow to open Palestine to all Palestinians. Despite Israeli disclaimers, their penetra-tion into occupied territory and the surprisingly tough resistance of the Arab residents in those territories are keeping the possibility of Pales-tine very alive. During a period of a few weeks this past spring al-Fatah claimed 168 raids within Israel; this is a considerable toll on Arabs and Jews, but given the self-defeating Israeli inflexibility, it is not a sense-less toll. If Jews are to stay, the Palestinians argue fairly, then Chris-tians and Muslims must be allowed the same, equal privilege. Interestingly, past tension between Arab Christians and Muslims has been surmounted among the Palestinians. Christians sit on the Fatah Executive Committee, and the leader of the Popular Front is a Christian. While in Amman I spoke with a clergyman who had been active in West Bank resistance—he had been imprisoned by the Israelis, abused, then deported; to him, the Muslims and Christians in the village were exactly alike in their interests and in their enemy. But the plight of Arabs in occupied Palestine is morally awful. To believe in a democratic, progressive, multiconfessional Palestine and yet to be forced to live "cooperatively" under Israeli domination is a condition not borne easily. Only the merchant class, never particularly admirable, has found life not so bad, cooperating with whoever has seemed most profitable to it.

As to methods of achieving self-determination in Palestine, they are shrouded in circumstances as yet not fully known. The essential point is that the goal has to be won from the ground up. It might mean—if Israel were to expand still further—the turning of many more Arabs (Jordanians, Lebanese, Syrians, for example) into "Palestinians." The present regimes everywhere in the Arab world are in a state of tricky balance, but for the moment the Palestinians anxiously avoid involving themselves too deeply in the mire of Arab politics. Most Arab leaders presently can win a measure of popular favor, and much-needed glamour, by openly consulting with Yasir Arafat. For example, al-Fatah still plays its part independently of Nasser, Hussein, or the Syrians. To what extent this can continue and to what extent the Americans and the Russians are (or will be) involved in Palestinian affairs are hard questions to answer. What matters most is that the Palestinian has made of his dismal experience an important political weapon for his purposes, and so long as it remains his own, developed as it is out of attachments to his native land, the cost will not have been too high.

Published in *Reflections on the Middle East Crisis*, edited by Herbert Mason.

CHAPTER 2

The Palestinians One Year Since Amman

[1971]

A year since the predictable battle in Jordan between the Palestinian Resistance Movement and the Hashemite monarchy, the Middle East as a whole jerks about awkwardly, like an ungainly puppet dangling from all-too-obvious strings. Despite innumerable initiatives, agreements, and meetings, King Hussein, the Baathists in Iraq and Syria, President Sadat, the Lebanese and Saudis—essentially the same organs of power *personally* (in some cases) present and responsible for the immense Arab defeat of 1967—are still visible exactly as they were four years ago; so much so, in fact, that King Hussein could continue his royally unhindered decimation of Palestinian *fedayin,* the only estimable force for change in the whole area, from September 1970 to July 1971. For, axiomatically, a symbol of prominent authority is born easily but dies very hard in the Arab world. By the same apparently inflexible law Hussein and the Baathists remain, failures against Israel though they may have been, and the various Palestinian groups and the PLO remain, failures against Hussein. Kaddafi, the new revolutionary, intervened in the Sudanese coup, but naturally did not intervene in the Jordanian–Palestinian events. And the Soviets are present at best; at worst, they are for the Egyptian regime a faded old wife left at home as the husband rushes off after the eternal other woman, in this case the United States.

No conspiratorial view of history is needed to remark how, both since 1967 and since Hussein's war on the Palestinians, American investments in the Middle East have not only remained unharmed but have been enhanced: Several hundred billion dollars' worth of oil are at stake, after all, and with the wealth the usual vague sense of geopolitical interests. Together these have dictated a *logical* (but perhaps not reasonable) U.S. policy in the region. If Vietnam is a continuing American disaster, the Arabs and Israel today are a dazzling American victory: Not a penny has really been lost, and if the United States is still neither loved nor admired, it seems essential to the area, economically, politically, and psychologically. All the technical (but not the moral) lessons of Vietnam—among them, the dangers of actual American military involvement, the true threats of insurgency or of revolutionary movements, the mindless support of internally weak native governments—were skillfully incorporated into American Middle Eastern policy. Since 1967 setback after setback has been circumvented, or to use a phrase from the 1967 Presidential Commission on the Middle East, "revolution has been nipped in the bud."

Hitherto little-known studies done in universities or by the RAND Corporation, the Hudson Institute, or agencies of the Department of Defense enabled the United States to outmaneuver the Palestinian guerrillas by using, and financing, all governments in the area who stood to lose most if the Palestinians were to have fulfilled their revolutionary role. In the end this strategy proved cheap and stunningly effective. The fruits of such "war games" as Project Sierra, or the Rand study by W. M. Jones, *Predicting Insurgent and Governmental Decisions: The Power Bloc Model* (December 1970), enabled the U.S. government to *contain* the Palestinians by using primarily the Arabs' governments *against* them since, as Jones comments, in a "perverse sense, the *fedayin* and Israel are allies" when it comes to competition for the control of Arab resources (p. 51). Above all, U.S. antirevolutionary policy performed the essential task of making it impossible for Palestinians (or Arabs) and Israelis ever seriously to confront each other, militarily or otherwise, or to permit Arabs and Israelis to institute change that benefited them. Instead, a series of fratricidal outbursts between Arabs, with Israel standing as untouched as possible, erupted, if not by design, then at least by the creation of favorable conditions. (An interesting detail is that as many Israelis were killed on the Suez front as there were Palestinian-caused Israeli casualties; neither figure, however, compares with the number of Arabs killed by Arabs.) Every wave of repression has been accompanied by further

U.S. grants in aid, sometimes called the Rogers plan: the puppet master jerks the string gently, and the puppet dances, a little incoherently, it is true, but to an intelligible beat.

Within the Arab countries, and indeed within Israel, noticeable rifts separate governed from governing. Perhaps the most bizarre sight of all is the way governments seem allied together against the large mass of their people, in a fashion that respects neither ideology, political structure, nor race; these latter causes are nevertheless the theme of persistent and usually bloodcurdling rallying cries. Who believes them these days, I wonder. Israeli tankers may carry Saudi oil; Jordan, the United States, and Israel have had a jointly agreed-upon policy against the Palestinians, and, after repeated debacles, the PLO, the Jordanians, the Egyptians, and Saudis negotiate yet another agreement to create "good" Palestinian guerrillas and to allow Jordanian Bedouins to continue being "noble" defenders of the fatherland. The expense in human life, in blood and treasure, has been truly appalling, but the end is not near. The recent summary crushing of labor disputes in Israel, in Egypt (at Helouan), and the bloody reprisals against working-class leaders in Sudan argue a long-term policy of government by unpopular force and protected privilege, of which the Egyptian–Syrian–Libyan entente on the one hand, and the U.S.–Israeli quasi-alliance on the other are major examples. With rights for intervention in attempts against one government guaranteed to other governments of the federation, change has been permanently banished by constitutional, even international decree. Collectively, then, Arabs and Israelis enjoy even less autonomy than ever before.

In July and August 1970 the organized Palestinians outside Israel and those inside the occupied West Bank seemed the brightest popular hope in the Middle East. A year later nothing to me so humbly and yet significantly demonstrates the Palestinian fall from favor, their almost total paralysis, as the sight of some young men in a car trying unsuccessfully in Beirut to *give* away a copy of the *Fatah* newspaper. The Palestinian middle classes prosper; the camp dwellers and the wretched are as lost as ever. Nevertheless, Arab insurrection persists in Gaza, seemingly unconnected with Palestinian misfortunes elsewhere, perhaps because directly connected with a clumsily brutal Israeli occupation policy there. Gaza is the only place now where Palestinians and Israelis, those chief original parties to the great dispute, are in warring confrontation. Everywhere else Israel has, for the

Palestinian, become either a very distant thing, or (as is the case for the Israeli Arabs) a passively tolerated authority.

The reasons for this state of affairs can be analyzed in two interconnected ways, one having to do with the Palestinian movement itself, the other with the international, that is, the inter-Arab and Israeli arena. Common to both sets of reasons is the special fact that ever since 1917 the fate and the political struggle of Arab Palestinians for their national rights has been conducted geographically *outside* Palestine. Palestinians therefore have always had an extra-national or extra-geographical dimension to their existence. By September 1970 this extra dimension had taken the form of a para-governmental, in some ways bureaucratic, presence in Jordan, against which it was politically inevitable for the king to react.

Some Palestinians today still maintain that the September War could have been avoided, but such arguments are scarcely convincing given the challenging direction already taken, not a little blindly, by the movement. For the indications are that Hussein had been preparing for war against the Palestinians since 1969. Tragically enough, however, only the Palestinians themselves seem to have been unaware of how truly revolutionary their role was. One slight measure of this insouciance was the premature, somewhat ill-conceived visibility of their apparatus, their offices, their tireless public self-advertisements, their social services, their political philandering. By contrast preparations for a complex political and military *strategic* battle against a host of enemies were woefully inadequate. Rather understandably for a constantly hounded and betrayed people, Palestinians were seduced by the ease with which they momentarily filled the lusterless vacancy of post-1967 Arab regimes, but as *Palestinians* (not as *Arabs*) they remained curiously indecisive about their goal. Were they irredentists, or were they social revolutionaries? Was a return to the Palestine of 1948 their aim, or was the building of a true socialist democracy, for Arab and Jew alike, their objective? These were the human dilemmas facing a much-abused, dispossessed people, but they can also be traps into which an oppressed people can be forced, by themselves almost as much as by others.

Politically, the hard truth is that the vacillation destroyed them—in their present form at least. The "cause" remains, and the Palestinian people are still grievously sinned against, but it must be for a new generation of leaders to define the cause more adequately and operationally, totally, systematically, coherently, and to organize politically for it, to assess forces accurately, to ascertain foe and ally precisely. One of the most depressing things today is the inverse connection between ideological anti-Zionism and practical means for implementing the ideology; as the ideological sentiment intensifies, the means for its implementation seem less adequate. The reverse is also true, for as the guerrilla program in practice focuses more on Arab affairs, anti-Zionism recedes in importance.

Modern Arab politics generally have so far been like a brew dissolving and blurring every substantial issue: Palestine, at least as defined by the generation of militant Palestinians between 1967 and 1971, has been the latest victim. This truth, alas, still needs recognition if a genuine resurgence is to take place. Although awaiting precise articulation, the even more difficult view that Israeli domination has much to do with Arab cultural and political vulnerability is, I think, a correct one, and is capable ultimately of mobilizing Palestinians and Arabs together toward a democratic state in which Jews will play an equal political role.

Internationally the Palestinian Resistance met enemies of a truly formidable resourcefulness, the chief of which was the economic *status quo*. A U.S. Defense Department study estimated that militarily a Palestinian guerrilla could inflict an Israeli casualty twenty-two times more cheaply than an Egyptian soldier could. Such potential force had to be blunted and divested lest it upset a hugely profitable (for the West) economic paradise. And so—as I mentioned above—the American scientific management of insurgency was put at the service of Israel, Jordan, and less directly the other Arab regimes. All together they were too much for the Palestinians, whose action, paradoxically, continues to be the crux on which the whole region's stability depends. In this context the extra-dimensionality of Palestinians, whether as captives in Israel and Jordan or as the cultural and scientific elite of the Arab world, is a decided weapon if it can be held in their own hands. That the Palestinians themselves have underestimated this tremendous asset of theirs indicates the current quality of their despondency. For as a people whose national existence is a virtual nexus of oppressions—imperialist and racial, native and foreign—they represent the ills of the Middle East most acutely, and are therefore most immediately at the origin and at the source of alleviation of these ills.

Not surprisingly, the aftermath of Palestinian travails during the past year has been a busy universal effort to wrest Palestinian destiny from Palestinian hands. Now that Palestinians have been defused, there are more pro-Palestinians (mainly liberal Zionists) around than can be imagined. With their organizations dissipated and blocked, Palestinians no longer speak directly for themselves, whether at the UN, in Arab councils, or in innumerable peace and reconciliation groups. Yet again, in other words, *agencies* rather than authentic Palestinian voices clamor for attention, and for the vast money available for settling Palestinians (and their Pandora's box of troubles) once and for all. Here, though, one must remain optimistic, since there is indeed a Palestinian Arab people—and a unique history such as theirs finally does speak affirmatively for itself. No makeshift organization can totally represent it, nor mechanical settlement efface it. If the phase of their history that began in Amman's Black September 1970 and was concluded in Jarash in July 1971 can be said to have led them further into the unhospitable desert, then at least the outlines of things, away from the hazy fantasies of pseudo-havens like Amman, Cairo, Damascus, or Beirut, will face them directly. Perhaps the first thing a Palestinian now sees is himself alone. That is a hard sight to endure, especially for Arabs, so much the hybrid, enmeshed creatures of both East and West; however, in this case, I think, solitude will be an achievement. But only if it is not squandered another time: 1936, 1948, 1967, and 1970–71 have been enough.

Published in *Le Monde Diplomatique,* October 1971.

CHAPTER 3

Palestinians

[1977]

I had been away from Lebanon (and family) for two years when I returned there this past summer. Almost as much as by the terrible scars of war in downtown Beirut one is struck by relatively insignificant changes. Nearly everyone seems to be wearing either an oversized cross or a replica of the Koran around the neck—ostentatiously announcing not a religious conviction but a political assertion.

There are Syrian Army strong points, but just away from them, into an either "Christian" or "Muslim" quarter, you can see an occasional armed man, a reminder that factions are ready to mobilize and fight immediately.

The worst thing is the large number of newly dispossessed poor. Whole sections of the city were razed by the Christian warriors. The luckless inhabitants fled and occupied houses in other districts. Groups of high-rise apartments have become ghettos; the hulks of damaged buildings are overcrowded tenements; the Gold Coast beach area is now a slum. Only the politicians are unchanged.

I come from a Christian Palestinian family, which has a sizable Lebanese Christian branch. My natal connections in Lebanon are principally with Lebanese Christians to some of whom I turn for explanations. Yet everything I hear of Muslim savagery, Palestinian treachery, communist conspiracy is unacceptably xenophobic. None of that is capable of producing the awful results on all sides—60,000 dead, thousands more injured, and billions in property damage. And more to come.

Many relatives and old friends are unapproachable now. Some families are divided as the country is divided, even though both sides are alike in their fear, their needless isolation, their endless anecdotes about "them." At least South Lebanon, which I visited, is an open battlefield. There Israel fights Palestinians with an aim to extending Israeli hegemony over Lebanon through a discredited right wing.

Lebanon is but the latest and the most dramatically articulated instance of what has taken place in the once romantic Near Orient since World War II. Crisscrossed with incredibly complex and amoral weapons deals, the whole region is miserable, the people poor, frightened, and abused despite pockets of enormous wealth.

What happened in former Palestine has not been a good model for the region, especially not for Lebanon. True to its roots in the culture of European imperialism, Zionism divided reality into a superior "us" and an inferior, degenerate "them." Today, if you are an Arab in Israel, you are a third-class person; you cannot ever be equal, so far as landowning and immigration rights, free movement, and state institutions are concerned.

On the Israeli-occupied West Bank, daily civilian protests are dealt with summarily. Now there is no secret about state-sanctioned torture, illegal detention without trial, occasional murder. Above all, it is religion or race understood in the least universal sense that defines political attitudes. The Western liberal mind refuses to accept any of this, doubtless because "they," the Arabs, are mere Orientals.

Into this unattractive mess, President Carter's rhetorical spotlight on human rights has yet to penetrate. There has been no widespread call for attention to human rights in the Middle East—except by Palestinians. Yet now, clumsy, cautious to a fault, an October 1 pronouncement on Palestinian human rights has appeared, formulated by the two superpowers. Surely on some level this is an instance of the two nursing and jerking about their clients and their interests. Yet just as surely this is the first public acknowledgment that the Middle East generally, Israel and Lebanon particularly, are not simple problems of "instability" and "security," but coarse parallel instances of bloody injustice, terrible sufferings, violations of basic human rights.

Geneva clearly can have another dimension than that of a big international conference. It must be the first occasion when the whole principle of modern Middle Eastern politics is honestly challenged. There must be recognition of the fact that *citizens with rights* (and not movable anonymous populations) are the moral norm. Hence, the importance of Palestine Liberation Organization representation at Geneva. The minority ideologies dominating Middle East political life have to be shed at Geneva and replaced by a more generous conception of human variety.

We need to distinguish between surface explanations of Middle Eastern problems like Lebanon, Israel, and the Palestinians, and the underlying realities. Two generations of men and women have been reared only on ideas like security, protection against extermination, minority sovereignty, an unappeasable need for weapons and their symbolism. Yet unless the pitiless logic of these concerns yields to some understanding of their human origins, the future will be still more murderous. On the other hand, a reconvened Geneva conference is an opportunity *now* that cannot be missed for Palestinians and Israelis above all.

Published in *The New York Times,* October 6, 1977.

CHAPTER 4

The Acre and the Goat

[1979]

There are two striking differences between the Zionist movement and the Palestinian national movement, and these have remained constant for about a century. One is that in terms of getting things done (mainly acquiring territory) Zionism was essentially a Benthamite policy of detail, whereas the Palestinian tendency— scarcely a policy—was to rely on unassailable general principles, which never prevented the ground from being literally cut out from underneath them. The result of this, in starkly contrasting realities, is that Zionists have a state. Palestinians don't. Of course Zionism proved the militarily stronger of the two antagonists, and it had broad principles upon which to rely, but the focus of mobilization was definable in relatively small terms, "another goat and another acre," as Weizmann said, according to Michael Bar-Zohar in *Ben-Gurion: A Biography*.[4]

I remember being stirred as a boy by accounts of how, when the time came and the Mandate ended, the Zionists would be "driven away" by our valiant Hebronites (the proverbial Palestinian strongmen), who needed only sticks to shoo them all back to where they came from. But what I also remember were the endless discussions, testimonial declarations, complaints about the justice of our cause, and the visual evidence, which is still very clear in my memory, of row upon row of Jewish farmers, schoolchildren, pedestrians even, going on about their business with their backs turned, so to speak, to the urgent aimless life among the Arab Palestinians, whose much larger numbers and land holdings proved later to be of little moment. No detail, no itemized organization, no carefully demarcated separation in Arab existence between it and Jewish life of the sort that made a percentage of one's cinema ticket price go to the Jewish Agency.

The second difference follows interestingly from the first. Because the Diaspora by definition was not in Palestine, a great deal of what was done in the Promised Land on Zionism's behalf was also presented—perhaps *projected* is the better word here—as if on to a kind of world-theater–stage. The acre and the goat, the hospital and the school, the settlements themselves: all these seemed to be taking place as part of a drama which the world was witnessing, the reconstruction or (as Weizmann called it) the reconstitution of Palestine. For the Diaspora this drama had very different meanings at different times. It was always meant to be a didactic alternative picture to the way Jews were habitually viewed, even by one another, in the West. Later the reconstruction with its redemptive message was changed to meet the situation created after the Holocaust: Palestine as refuge, as affirmative action for those dispossessed Jews not massacred by Nazi Germany. Still later there came the Zionists as early (Puritan) pioneer, then as Spartan, then as existential hero.

Some of the self-conscious drama was caught last year by the Israeli novelist Amos Oz, who is quoted in *Time* as saying:

> For as long as I live, I shall be thrilled by all those who came to the Promised Land to turn it either into a pastoral paradise or egalitarian Tolstoyan communes, or into a well-educated, middle-class Central European enclave, a replica of Austria and Bavaria.[5]

Not only was Zionism to restore Israel then; it was also to show the world that Jews could be Bavarian, Tolstoyans, or Marxist—in Asia in the midst of land that had been "neglected" for centuries. One is reminded of the surrealistically white-suited accountant in Conrad's *Heart of Darkness,* who sits amid the "great demoralization of the land" in darkest Africa, going through a Londoner's routine.

But there *were* other people already in Palestine, and the slow accumulation of land by a policy of detail as well as the painstaking drama of the state taking shape before the world's eyes came together more or less to blot out the natives entirely. Why these natives in all their untidy backwardness could not impress the Zionists, much less the rest of the world, with their presence is something I cannot really understand, although one can see parallels between Zionists and American Puritans, say, or between Zionists and nineteenth-century European theorists of "empty" territory in Asia and Africa. What is still more perplexing is how the same blindness is repeated painstakingly by modern Zionist historians who retell the story not so much with the luxury of hindsight but with the same narrowness of vision that spurred on the early Zionists. Martin Gilbert's *Exile and Return: The Emergence of Jewish Statehood* narrates the events as if Palestine were teased out of a few offices in Whitehall, as if "the Arabs"—the phrase has a certain symptomatic anonymity to it—were miscellaneous weeds to whom no great statesman paid much attention as he cultivated grander gardens than *that* miserable patch. For an antidote one must go straight to A. I. Tibawi's *Anglo-Arab Relations and the Question of Palestine,* an impressively detailed work that chronicles British duplicity from the standpoint of Palestinians who finally lost the land—more justified zeal than Gilbert's. Neither book (and certainly Tibawi's is the more original and important) furnishes one with a history of Palestine as the place where Arab life, Zionist settlement, imperialist machinations were happening together. This also happens to be true of A. W. Kayyali's otherwise useful *Palestine: A Modern History.*

Surely Zionism's genuine successes on behalf of Jews are reflected inversely in the absence of a major history of Arab Palestine and its people. It is as if the Zionist web of detail and its drama choked off the Palestinians, screening them not only from the world but from themselves as well. And indeed, as the noted Palestinian thinker Ibrahim Abu-Lughod has written, Palestinians for a decade after 1948 adopted "a politics of accommodation" to the Arab and Israeli realities all around them: They became Egyptian Palestinians, or Israeli Palestinians of the sort whose life Sabri Jiryis has chronicled in *The Arabs in Israel* (1976). During the Nasser period, Palestinians were caught up in a general wave of anti-imperialist, Arab nationalist sentiment, hence in those years what Abu-Lughod calls "a politics of rejection." Then, after 1967, Palestinian nationalism asserted itself in the breach made by the Arabs' defeat, and this has been called "the politics of revolution and hope." But in all these phrases, with the exception of a handful of literary works, the concrete human detail of Palestinian existence was regularly subordinated to big general ideas. For their pains in having devised a theory of armed struggle against Israel, the Palestinian became associated in the world's eyes with "terrorism."

These are perhaps pessimistic and critical things to have to say, and yet by no means do they tell the whole story. The general Palestinian idea of opposition to Israeli exclusionary practices has become a potent symbol of what it means to be an adversary to the seedy *status quo* everywhere in the Middle East. Palestinians are touted now by Iranians as they had been previously by Egyptian students and intellectuals, Syrian workers, Third World liberation groups. The emergence of the PLO—always hovering between some revolutionary ideas and the more practical aims of a national independence movement—has brought forth a wide array of Palestinian institutions (schools, factories, hospitals, research and publication networks) that are sensitive to the scatterings of Palestinian life today. The central fact remains, of course: This is a people without a land of its own. But for the first time in their history, one can see Palestinians in a sense *producing themselves,* and this self-production has had a noticeable effect on how, for the first time in *its* history, Zionism's policy of detail and its dramatic self-projection are faltering.

Take some recent instances as a start. Whereas the early Zionists simply ignored the Palestinians and everyone like them, the tone (and the substance) of how the Palestinians, as well as Third World natives, are now considered has become strident, openly vicious. General Dayan put it this way in January: If Palestinians inside Israel are going to support the PLO, then we shall evict them as we evicted the others. General Eytan (Israeli Chief of Staff), in an interview with *Yedioth Aharonot,* January 19: "Before the State of Israel existed we came here [to] conquer this country, and it was for this purpose that the state was established." Asked about Arabs in the Galilee, he replies: "In my opinion, the Arabs today are engaged in a process of conquest of the land, conquest of work, illegal immigration, terror there." This is presumably the overture to some new wave of Israeli repression in the Galilee, which is where the largest number of Arab Israelis is found. A cartoon on January 12 in *Maariv:* a huge black genie with a leering face that is meant to resemble Khomeini, who seems to have emanated from an oil drum. This overtly (and paradoxically) anti-Semitic creature is identified as "Islam—the reaction." Standing off to the side are a decent-looking, worried gent who represents the West and a little boy wearing a yarmulke. The latter says to his older friend: "When do you mean to move?"

It is not as if Menachem Begin hadn't moved, verbally at least. From the moment that Khomeini returned to Iran, Begin was warning the world of this return to the Middle Ages and to religious fanaticism, without so much as a pause in his remarks when he went on to justify holding "Judea" and "Samaria" on the basis of Old Testament promises. Begin's appeal was to age-old Western fears of the Orient, although characteristically he was unable to see the beam in his own eye as he spoke. This is not to say, however, that the Israeli press hasn't been recording in detail the pronouncements and threats I have mentioned above, but what is interesting is how the old Zionist world-drama can no longer hide its less savory accomplishments.

The most offensive recent example of all is Chaim Herzog's *Who Stands Accused? Israel Answers Its Critics.* Herzog's scowl adorns the cover, as if to alert the world to his prophetic wrath, and without a trace of irony he accepts himself as Israel's very incarnation. And what an incarnation! Most of the book is full of anxious self-praise accompanied by all-out attacks on the Palestinians, wherever and in whatever form they happen to be. Nowhere does this ex-intelligence officer let on that it was he who helped the Iranian monarchy set up the SAVAK in the early sixties, so that democracy could flourish in torture rooms, in complicity with the Light of the Aryans, in a rhetoric that mangled people and reality. (Herzog's interesting past is sketched in Richard Deacon's *The Israeli Secret Service.*) Herzog has the gall to defend Israeli settlements on the West Bank by accusing the world of anti-Semitism. If the Arab population of Israel has grown from 150,000 in 1949 to 550,000 today, that is not considered a "demographic change," he says sarcastically, "but if a total of approximately 6,000 Jews settle in Judea, Samaria, Sinai, Gaza and Golan, in an area populated by 1.5 million Arabs, this is termed a 'demographic change.' " Leaving aside the fact that the 150,000 Arabs who "remained" in Israel after 1949 were a small fraction of the 800,000 who were driven out, allowing for the generosity of Israel *letting* those 150,000 grow to 550,000, overlooking the fact that most of the Israeli population today was imported into Palestine in the form of colonial settlers on someone else's land, and accepting the 60,000 Jews who have settled on seized lands in Arab Jerusalem as constituting no demographic change at all, General Herzog's way with the truth is still incredible. He simply does not mention that the Israeli army has demolished 17,000 houses on the West Bank alone, or that the settlers (and the occupation itself) are considered illegal by the entire world; he wants us all to celebrate Israel's achievements in his person, in his words, and in his presence before the world.

Part of Herzog's angry zeal is surely due to his nagging realization that Palestinians (and for that matter Arabs in general) will not so easily be made to lie still today under the Zionist tarpaulin. There are infinitesimal signs of this in the slips he makes while describing Arab matters in a prose that is meant to convey expertise and professional competence. The same symptomatic failures crop up in Aviezer Golan's *Operation Susannah*. Arab names like "Khaled" and "Sahyuni" become "Haled" and "Sayoni"; a statement by Arafat is first dated 1975, then changed to 1976. "Khawaga" becomes "Hawaga," "Emad el-Din" is changed to "Ahmad al Din," the PLO is said to have "introduced" terrorism—but the list is too long and dispiriting to rehearse any further here.

The larger failures are very apparent in Golan's woefully padded and sentimentalized spy tearjerker about the *Lavon* affair which began in 1954: Israeli attempts at manipulation and hegemony fail not so much because there is more and more credible Palestinian resistance, but because there are inherent short circuits to any policy of detail based mainly upon denial and coercion. Clearly we are meant to feel a kind of spectatorial admiration for the misled young Egyptian Jews who during the early 1950s threw bombs in American-owned Cairo cinemas and libraries (no admonition here from the author about "terrorism" and vandalism) as part of an Israeli-intelligence plot to make the United States angry with Egypt: This is all part of the Zionist way of engaging the world theatrically in exploits that are not all positive. But in Golan's unskillful hands, the shabby morality shows through. After all, it was the same Israeli intelligence services that sent bomb-throwing conspirators Ninio, Dassa, Levy, and Natanson to Egyptian jails for having failed in their mission to stir the United States against Abdel Nasser's Egypt, that *also* brought forth General Herzog, the failure to predict an Arab attack in 1973, etc. These are not all failures in competence as much as they are failures in principle. No matter how carefully you plan in detail, you cannot indefinitely go on acquiring lands, populations, support, as if all reality and all people were simply reducible to the dictates of your will or your justification.

The franker and less mendaciously apologetic Zionists seem always to have known this, but their ways of expressing it are encoded very differently, depending on age, position, political preference. The thin hagiographic mists surrounding Bar-Zohar's portrait of Ben-Gurion are soon dispelled by the critical reader. For one, the word *conquest* turns up with unhappy frequency whenever the man's ideas for Palestine are mentioned; the curious feature of these, however, is that the conquest in question is always Jewish, whereas the Arab things being conquered are never mentioned. An adulation for Lenin gives way early on in Ben-Gurion's life to a rapproachement with Jabotinsky and longings to join the Commonwealth; he also falls away from the workers' movement (incidentally, what *was* Labour Zionism?). Not a victim of persecution himself, Ben-Gurion appears to have found the Zionist cause an instrument for his will, and later in life he even advised De Gaulle on the wisdom of setting up another Israel in North Africa. The colonial venture had become a habit of thought.

Like Begin today, Ben-Gurion saw what he did in two perspectives, one based on the Bible (his war aims in 1948 were, in his own bloodcurdling terms, that "a Christian state should be established [in Lebanon], with its southern border on the Litani river. We will make an alliance with it. When we smash the Arab legion's strength and bomb Amman, we will eliminate Transjordan, too, and then Syria will fall. If Egypt still dares to fight on, we shall bomb Port Said, Alexandria, and Cairo. . . . And in this fashion, we will end the war and settle our forefathers' account with Egypt, Assyria, and Aram"). The other is based on white supremacy ("Israel is the bastion of the West in the Middle East"). Already in Ben-Gurion's politics one watches the emergence of future difficulties in what I have been calling Zionism's theater, whose less attractive features are not usually referred to in Israel's liberal addresses to the West. Thus it is Ben-Gurion's deliberate plan *not* to mention the state's specific boundaries in the 1948 Declaration of Independence; just as it is strikingly odd that a liberal democracy is *not* the state of all of its citizens, but "of the whole Jewish people." Bar-Zohar records these little matters without commentary.

Roughness, directness, determination (translate these as force, force, and more force) are Ben-Gurion's main characteristics in this portrait. They are occasionally tempered by softening references to his passion for books—the Greek classics, Tolstoy, and so forth. Set beside Nahum Goldmann's second book of miscellaneous but engaging memoirs, Ben-Gurion's cultural aspirations seem a little makeshift. Goldmann makes no bones either about his dislike of Ben-Gurion or about the old soldier's clumsy efforts at culture. The bond that mattered for Goldmann was always the one with Chaim Weizmann, whose line the redoubtable head of the World Zionist Organization felt himself to be continuing. Although the rift between Weizmann and Ben-Gurion was important, it amounted only to a question of style and taste: Weizmann and Goldmann after him were subtler, Ben-Gurion coarser. All of them, however, felt that Palestine ought to be taken

from the Arabs, Weizmann and Goldmann opting for later reconcilia-
tions with them, Ben-Gurion for clobbering them whenever possible.
With someone like Begin around, Goldmann's value today is obviously
crucial. An urbane, clever, and serious man, he has the vision (if not
the power) of a statesman to see that Israel's present course is almost
certainly disastrous. Yet what is troubling about Goldmann's thought
in *The Jewish Paradox* is his altogether easy slide into notions of irony
and paradoxicality whenever he must seriously face up to disturbing
features of Zionism. Can one simply say that Zionism and the Jews are
paradoxes when, for example, their claims to universality and a tran-
scendental ethical sense get literally translated into some of the most
chauvinistic and exclusionary (the word *discriminatory* comes very easily
to mind here) social policy toward non-Jews under their rule? One
wants things called by their name, not disguised as tidy rhetorical
sweets.

There are signs of hope elsewhere within the Zionist movement. I
have been suggesting that by and large the policy of detail has until
recently obliterated the realities this policy has been designed to hide;
and I have also suggested that Zionism conceived of its activity dramatically, with an anxious, liberal world in the West as its audience, the
very same audience that Sadat's strutting autobiography is now entertaining. To a great extent, as I and others like me would like to believe,
the allure of such a strategy has weakened not only because it is so
epistemologically wrongheaded, but because it has had to deal with a
rising oppositional tide as represented by the Palestinians. But there is
another reason for what is undoubtedly Zionism's new crisis: Israel has
in fact produced a society—and not a caricature of one, as many Arabs
prefer to imagine; it has also produced people who, despite their
political loyalties, are in the course of things going to have to confront
themselves, their history, and their political ethos. When this happens
(and of course I am speaking about this as taking place at the center
of Zionism, not in the profoundly moral and iconoclastic individual
visions of Jews like Magnes, Shahak, Chomsky), then we can expect
the veils very slowly to be rent.

That in the cases at hand it should occur in the work of two young
Israeli social scientists, neither of whom on the face of it is a radical,
is something remarkable. Saul Mishal's argument is simple. The Pales-
tinians, he says, have a "primordial attachment" to their land. During
Jordan's hegemony over the West Bank between 1949 and 1967, the
Hashemite monarchy manipulated those Palestinians under its tutelage,

but was never able to subdue their nationalist aspirations. Those always were—and have clearly still remained—Palestinian, independent, genuine. Notwithstanding Mishal's muddy later pages on "the return of Islam" (a concept he borrows from one of the least serious of modern Orientalists) as a device for discrediting, or at least devaluing, Palestinian secular nationalism, Mishal's argument on the whole is an upright one. In the Israeli context of today, it is an argument about honesty, and also about some attempt to recognize the Palestinian reality for what it is. If the political implications are not exactly spelled out, we should still be pleased that this book has emerged from Israel.

Were it not that it is saturated, indeed dripping, with jargon of an almost unbearable ugliness, we should be still more grateful for Sammy Smooha's *Israel: Pluralism and Conflict.* I cannot and certainly will not try to reproduce the academic "model" that Smooha employs throughout his book: at bottom it serves only to give an elephantine shape to its author's modest, slightly conservative temperament— namely, his preference for accommodation over revolution in a society as riven with contradictions and conflict as Israel's.

He may be right in his preference, as even Palestinians have seriously concluded and said in public. Israel has perpetrated an injustice, it still oppresses Palestinians and Oriental Jews, it cannot deliver on its early promises. Smooha goes as far as saying that in time the Palestinian Arabs inside Israel will become the country's most pressing problem. But he backs away from anything more drastic than an assertion of Israel's "pluralistic" society ("pluralism" is where his description of the country's contradictions, inequalities of power, absence of homogeneity always ends up), and the need for a coming "to grips with its structural pluralism, intergroup inequality and conflict and to do justice to its disadvantaged groups." This assertion is forcefully supported by a rigorous and disenchanted analysis of Israeli society, an analysis which needs to be supplemented by Elia T. Zureik's severely excellent *The Palestinians in Israel: A Study in Internal Colonialism* for its basic pessimism to stand out.

But what does it mean, *to come to grips?* For Smooha it certainly does not mean revolution, and if it means gradual change, then he isn't true to the spirit of his analysis which, plus Likud hegemony, events in Iran and in other parts of the region, tells me at least that gradualism is a Panglossian hope. My sense of things is that Zionism's choices all along the way have overdetermined its current political possibilities, and among those possibilities a renunciation of accumulation by detail and

of self-dramatization as the liberal West's hope *simply do not figure.*
After all, people like General Arik Sharon are not responsible for
settlement in the Occupied Territories by chance (see the long interview with him in *Maariv* on January 26, 1979, for a chilling statement
of Israeli intentions). Conversely—as Rosemary Sayigh argues convincingly in her impressive book *The Palestinians: From Peasants to
Revolutionaries*—Israeli society has claims made on it not only by
Palestinians inside the country but also by those armed, politicized
farmer refugees who live in the *ghurba,* exile. Add to this economic
pressures, increasing social turbulence, and one gets a most unrosy
picture of the prospects for "coming to grips" by academic recognition or tragic *anagnorisis.*

Perhaps we ought to remember that neither an artificial tranquillity
induced by Camp David TV appearances nor Sadatian hyperbole about
"psychological factors" can transform the real conflict between Zionism and the Palestinians into a simple misunderstanding. And this
alleged misunderstanding cannot, we must hasten to add, be dissolved
by "problem solving," or by getting people together in seminars
where the "barriers" between them will disappear. A national movement whose provenance and ideas were European took a land away
from a non-European people settled there for centuries: That is a
displacement, a conflict, a fact of history which both Israelis and
Palestinians *live,* and it is not something that rhetoric or drama can long
either conceal or prettify. For anyone who undertakes to write about
these matters, that is what must be dealt with candidly, and *in detail,*
though whether it can most usefully be done—as it is now—before an
audience of outsiders and in seminar rooms, or only on various battlefields, is something for Palestinians and Israelis to decide among themselves. As for the future, one can assert with reasonable confidence that
the conflict will continue and, if the amount of oblivious self-deception
and empty posturing decreases on both sides, will be settled (if it *can*
be settled) appropriately. Where and how this will take place are the
questions that Palestinians and Zionists together must now, after the
soporifics of Camp David, try to take up.

Published in *The New Statesman,* May 11, 1979.

CHAPTER 5

Peace and Palestinian Rights

[1980]

The Palestinian autonomy talks between Israel, Egypt, and the United States were to have produced a result by May 26, 1980. In April, President Carter brought Anwar Sadat and Menachem Begin to Washington in order to impress on them and their constituencies that progress had to be made by the agreed-upon deadline. One surmised that if nothing as spectacular as the Camp David agreement was being proposed at this time, it was still worthwhile politically for the President to appear in public with the two men, keep the talks going, preserve the appearance of serious deliberations in course. A climactic summit could always be arranged later on, as now it appears a summit will occur after the elections in November. Israeli spokesmen in the meantime have been unyielding on important points: no Palestinian self-determination, no Israeli withdrawal, no change in an increasingly aggressive settlements policy, no Palestinian control over anything as important as water resources or security, or foreign policy, or immigration, or East Jerusalem. To this series of provocations, Egypt has responded by breaking off the talks for a time, and agreeing to resume them in a transparent effort to help with the President's reelection. Undeterred by world opinion and international law, Israel for its part formally annexed East Jerusalem on July 22, and a few days later announced four new illegal settlements. Repression on the West Bank and Gaza continued, as did the bombardment of South Lebanon. In the cycle of violent fanaticism and the predictable resistance to it in Hebron in early May, as well as the subsequent maiming of two

Palestinian mayors by Israeli extremists, and the deportations of three other leading Palestinians, the sheer mass of questions separating, and ironically uniting, Israelis and Palestinians is starkly conveyed.

Yet, one asks, how is it that Palestinian autonomy talks include no Palestinians? Is it not manifestly odd, and does it not require some explanation, that the party whose ''autonomy'' is being discussed is not present? Why, since a supposedly comprehensive peace is being sought, should a major protagonist in the conflict—the exiled Palestinian community of nearly three million people who do not now happen to reside on the West Bank and Gaza—be so deliberately left out? And why does anyone expect Palestinians to be encouraged by a ''peace process'' that not only excludes them but seems actively designed to give them less under ''autonomy'' than they now have under an illegal occupation?

No answers to these questions can possibly be obtained today in the terms afforded one by American public discourse on the Middle East. In this, a presidential election year, more even than in preceding years, what the various candidates have said about the Middle East has been especially depressing. Every one of them salutes Israel and Israeli accomplishments with reckless abandon: Israel is not only ''our staunch ally''; it is also a ''bastion of democracy,'' and a state beleaguered by terrorism, Communism, and anti-Americanism. Unilateral Israeli moves such as the annexation of East Jerusalem, the setting up of more and more settlements, the routine collective punishments of entire communities on the West Bank and Gaza, the merciless bombing of civilians in and the gradual depopulation of South Lebanon, are either ignored or warmly supported by candidates eager to show what each has ''done for Israel.'' Not only does this indecent scramble for Jewish votes indefinitely postpone any serious coming-to-grips with what goes on in the Middle East—it actively eliminates history and reality from American thinking about a region of the world that has become uniquely important to American interests.

The immediate prognosis for any sort of fair settlement on the ground is not good. In August there was a well-publicized move in the Knesset to begin the formal annexation of the Golan Heights, much as Jerusalem had been annexed. On May 23, 1980, Ha'aretz, a leading Israeli daily, quoted Knesset member Aharon Yariv as saying that ''there are opinions to exploit a situation of war in order to expel 700,000 or 800,000 Arabs [from the Occupied Territories]. Such opinions are common. Persons are speaking about this and means for this have been prepared." Given what appears to be a period of political emptiness in the United States, Israeli military men obviously plan to take advantage of the lull in order to create new *faits accomplis*. The attack on Palestinian positions in South Lebanon on August 19 and 20 was part of this policy, as is the ominous possibility of similar attacks coordinated with southward forays on the Palestinians made by the Maronite Phalangist militias. (Parenthetically, it is worth mentioning that Israeli designs on Lebanon go back for many years, as the recently published Moshe Sharett *Diaries*[6] attest with extraordinary vividness: As early as 1954 and 1955, according to Sharett, people like Moshe Dayan were speaking of cajoling a Maronite in the South—"he need only be a Major"—into proclaiming himself the savior of Christians; then he would be persuaded to secede from the country and openly become an Israeli agent. All this has come true, of course, in the case of Major Saad Haddad.[7]) Syria's situation, internally and regionally, is highly volatile, and the risks of all-out war—perceived as in Israel's interest at this point—are therefore considerable.

Yet the United States today (1980) persists in taking Israel's side in questions of war and peace, and persists also in speaking portentously of a peace process. On the other hand, the entire international community has achieved consensus on the ingredients for a Middle East peace, in which neither Israel nor the United States has shown any real interest. Yet Israel still gets a huge slice of the U.S. foreign aid budget (43 percent in the coming year), at the same time that its economy and its relations with its neighbors and much of the world are at an all-time low. The Arab and Islamic worlds recognize the PLO, of course, and have recently expressed strong impatience with an unconvincing American policy of expecting unlimited oil supplies, political support, and willing alignment from these states, while giving them very little in return. In this connection Prince Fahd's recent declaration on Jerusalem and the necessity of a *jihad* are to be taken with a little seriousness, I believe. All in all, then, the official U.S. position, aided and abetted by an uncritical media and an uninformed public, is in strong discord both with Palestinian hopes and with manifest international backing for these hopes (as reflected, for instance, in the July 29, 1980, UN General Assembly Special Session, on the Question of Palestine, and the subsequent resolution produced during the Session affirming Palestinians' rights).

A CONCRETE HISTORY OF LOSS

Yet Diaspora Jews and Israelis at present would concede, I think, that the Palestinians have suffered unjustly at the hands of Zionism. There is agreement therefore that the Palestinian claim should at last be addressed with some seriousness, although very few Jews or Israelis (members of the Peace Now movement included) have found it possible to speak consistently and equitably of *Palestinian* rights. Thus it is no less true that most Jews still are fearful of what such a subject might portend; the risk for the Jewish people of a competing Palestinian nationalism, whose history is in its own way as severe in its traumas and sufferings as that of Jews, cannot therefore be lightly put aside or even approached. Conversely, however, Palestinians endure an existence of dispersion and exile. Many of them live under astringent Israeli control, inside Israel as well as in the Occupied Territories. Many, too, bear the living scars of frequent bombardments, mass expulsions, systematic humiliation. Every Palestinian represents a concrete history of loss—of a society, a country, a national identity. For many, armed struggle has seemed the only logical course to guard against the threat of complete extermination.

The Palestinians and the Israelis are therefore two asymmetrical communities of fear, one now dominating, and yet fearful of, the other. Add to this the effects of internal political struggles, plus superpower and regional disputes, and the situation appears hopelessly intractable.

The whole structure, method, and aim of the autonomy talks unfortunately symbolize, without in any way ameliorating, this abysmal state of affairs. Little in the present negotiations tries to break the deadlock or dissolve the fear or end the domination. The Palestinians cannot even be present as equals in the autonomy talks, except in terms that limit them still further, which, of course, they have rejected, for it is proposed that they be stripped of their history as the longtime majority resident in Palestine, stripped also of a large fraction of their number, and of almost all of their real political existence and of an astounding international legitimacy, to say nothing of 80 percent of their land. The Israelis retain all their advantages—military occupation and unilateral rule over the Palestinians chief among them—thus confirming and intensifying their fear of the future. For shortsighted reasons of his own, President Sadat has gone along with this, even as internal opposition to his regime grows more significant every month and as even *he* has begun to chafe at relentless Israeli intransigence. Worst of all, the United States has placed its redoubtable power around the whole business, sealing off the grim drama of prolonged stalemate and impasse with what has come officially (and, alas, self-delusively) to be known as "the spirit of Camp David." Even when U.S. policy is openly proclaimed to be against Israeli occupation practices, President Carter has been unable to sustain his policy for any length of time or to any effective end: In March a positive U.S. vote in the UN Security Council was disavowed apologetically a day later (at a time when the U.S. government was unwilling to concede even a hint of an acknowledgment of past interference in the internal affairs of Iran), while the UN resolution on May 8 calling on Israel to take back the three Palestinian leaders (Bassam el-Shaka'a, Mohammed Milhem, Shaikh Abdel Hamid el Sayeh) just deported drew forth a craven U.S. abstention.

It has now been sixty years since Britain's Lord Balfour spoke imperiously of not being willing "even to go through the form of consulting the wishes of the present inhabitants of Palestine." Four million Palestinians have little to be grateful for if today Egypt, Israel, and the United States go through the form not of actually *consulting* the present Arab inhabitants of Palestine (forgetting about the three million refugees who have already been denied residence there by Israel), but *perhaps of getting ready to consult them* on such momentous matters as sanitation.

Where, then, are Palestinian rights? Why, each Palestinian asks himself or herself, is it so hard for the United States, whose administration has declared itself in support of human rights in principle and in practice, to grant even the theoretical possibility that Palestinians are entitled to the same basic human rights to which people are entitled everywhere else (in theory at least) on earth? What is so monstrous, so unthinkable, so prohibitive in the fact that Palestinians, having been turned out of their homes and their lands, having for thirty years endured an existence of suffering and exile, having also resisted this fate and having affirmed their national identity in so brave and unmistakable a way, now claim for themselves the independent sovereign national existence which every known moral precept gives them the right to? What is so difficult to accept in the idea that Palestinians should, like all other people, be free of the travail of deportations, curfews, exile, bombardment, and general misery? To these questions virtually no one in the modern industrial West has begun to supply answers.

Yet, as I said above, the nub of the conflict is the impasse between two intertwined communities of fear. During the past few months, however, despite the worsening West Bank and Gaza situation, there have been a minuscule number of encouraging signs of change in Israel, in Europe, in the American Jewish community, among Palestinians. There is for the first time an active, visible peace community in Israel, with important ties to sectors of the American Jewish world. Austria, Spain, Great Britain, France, Greece, among other European countries, have begun in earnest to reckon with the PLO. The Third World, as well as the nonaligned and Islamic countries, support clearly stated Palestinian ideas about self-determination. A considerable number of statements by responsible Palestinians have indicated willingness to end armed struggle with Israel in return for an independent sovereign Palestinian state. As recently as May 8 PLO chairman Yasir Arafat told Anthony Lewis of *The New York Times* that he wanted a final negotiated settlement.

INEQUITY VERSUS RECONCILIATION: TWO STYLES

I would submit therefore that the important question is whether the best hope for the future lies with the rigidity, discrepancies, and inequities represented by the autonomy talks, or with an alternative, largely United Nations framework for reconciliation and peace that is now beginning to emerge with hopeful resolve among Palestinians, Israelis, as well as people in the United States, Europe, and the nonaligned world who can look past the *status quo* toward a reasonable, peaceful settlement. These two alternatives represent two outlooks, two styles. On the one hand is the polarizing, confrontational style, in which you stop the historical process of people's development at a stage that is most near at hand. You give in to fears of the past. You say, in effect, there is an Israeli state, a powerful army, an intransigent government and, in the United States, an electorate that can always be roused to unquestioning support of Israel. Then you ask, why should one tamper with that? You ignore the world's opinion, except for what official Israel and South Africa have to say. You shut yourself away from other voices, voices of hope, reconciliation, and understanding. You say anachronistically that the Palestinians are not fit to represent themselves and therefore must be represented by powers that know better. You do nothing to convince the media or the various political candidates that there are any other ways to proceed. You simply deny Palestinian rights even while affirming that all people have rights.

This style, I have said, has lowered the standard of public discussion. It has hindered the United States from perceiving that such a vision of reality is neither true to its people's interests nor to the way the world is going. It is the style that in effect produced the Iranian revolution; it is probably what may produce similar revolutions in Egypt, Turkey, and Pakistan, among other places. Above all, I believe, it is a style that betrays certain fundamental traits in American culture and in the history of the American people. For after all, there is in the United States a great native tradition of fairness, compassion, openness to change. Why must this be sacrificed to the policy of governments that close themselves to the real experiences of people, that resort to fossilized naysaying when they meet resistance, that seem to believe that peace is arranged by proxies and patrons, and enforced unilaterally by Phantom jets, new military bases, and rapid deployment forces?

On the other hand, there is a style more in keeping with a world sick of war and of superpower posturing, invasions, and geopolitical strategies. This style is focused upon principles and ends, rather than on gimmicks and quick-fix formulas. It asks communities to define their aims with an eye toward final, negotiated settlements, and it asks further that such settlements be based on justice, self-respect, and human rights for all, not just for members of certain ethnic groups, religions, nationalities. With reference to Israel and the Palestinians, the *priority* in this mode of trying to settle the conflict would have to be getting Israel for the first time in its history to recognize Palestinian national rights unequivocally. Israelis and Palestinians are two communities that will neither go away nor leave each other alone. What better way of beginning to come to terms with each other than to open one community to the other's history, actuality, and aspirations?

But for such mutual recognitions there can be no limiting preconditions. No one can demand of the other anything in advance *except* the serious wish (a) to end hostility; and (b) to make certain that no human rights are infringed or abrogated. This procedure seems to me to be unquestionably the alternative for today and tomorrow.

Where, then, does one go from here, now that the autonomy talks seem to have embarked on a phase of almost pure ritual? In the first place, anyone seriously concerned with the Middle East is under immediate obligation to seek to change the present context: Confrontation, hostility, "us" versus "them"—forms of seeing the conflict between the Palestinians and Israel that are encouraged by Americans with far less excuse than the parties themselves have—must be converted to exchange, dialogue, reconciliation. The European Community and the United Nations have already played a considerable role in providing a forum that is less debased and less subject to ignorance or bigotry than the domestic American scene, although there are plenty of opportunities in this country also for stimulating new discussion. Like-minded people should courageously seek one another out.

Secondly, we need to hammer it home that the present collision course, in the Middle East and elsewhere in the world, serves the interest of only a tiny minority of the world's people. A new world is struggling to be born; now that the old bankrupt games are being revived after Afghanistan and Iran, the imperative for some more generous political outlook on life to emerge is very great.

Thirdly, we should always be conscious of the fact that nothing exists in a vacuum: Every action by every group or individual is part of a whole history. The sooner we try consciously to be aware of our own and others' history, the sooner we appreciate the urgent need for a common framework of political intercourse; then we will not so much need war or hostility or blustering. The U.S. government, often singularly afraid of these realities, should be on notice that potentially effective things like peace talks had better be lined up with human concerns for real peace, not left in the form of fantastic charades. For if one does not require it of the U.S. government to face the reality of both the Palestinian and the Jewish peoples, and if this government is permitted to continue making patronizing and irrelevant pronouncements on behalf of people who have not even been consulted, one might as well say that war for several more generations is what the peace talks are really about.

Is there no hope for compassion or for simple common sense? Is there no way of making U.S. policy depend on the fact that there is a Palestinian people which, like all other people, is entitled to its own representatives, to a state of its own, to a life free from endless war and exile? For as the scenario of increasing polarization and hardening hostility gradually takes unshakable hold of the Middle East, visions of peace and understanding human community will seem more and more remote. And thereafter, no one will benefit—not even those stubborn enough to claim victory after the Holocaust.

Published in *Trialogue*, no. 24, summer/fall 1980.

CHAPTER 6

Palestinians in the United States

[1981]

The largest concentrations of Palestinians in America are to be found in Detroit, Chicago, and Los Angeles. A web of affiliations extending from those cities across the Midwest and into the East (to Washington, the metropolitan Boston and New York area) binds the almost 200,000 or so Palestinians in the United States to one another. A number of characteristics in this recently visible ethnic group are uniquely Palestinian. Perhaps because officially and traditionally public sentiment here is overwhelmingly pro-Zionist, and also because Jewish groups are well organized and extraordinarily verbal about matters pertaining to Israel, the American Palestinian community bristles with organizations, many of them militant, all of them articulate, most of them self-consciously making use of the word *Palestine* as a central part of their activity (an act of defiance both here and in the Occupied Territories). These organizations mostly contain Palestinian–American life, so far as the outside world is concerned, and they give that life internal coherence as well. Their reference point, though, is not so much the situation in the United States, but Palestine, and this kind of geographical bias is, of course, the very essence of the politics of exile.

The smallest number of these organizations is cultural. Next in size come the regional associations—e.g., the Ramallah clubs, since in some instances whole villages and clans have been transplanted to this country. Then, crisscrossing all the others, are the political groups (Palestine Red Crescent, Palestine Congress of North America, etc.), all of them linked not simply to the PLO, but in some cases to specific groups within it. One must candidly say, however, that even though all these organizations are more active and effective than are most other Arab–American organizations, they are beset with problems, which again are peculiarly Palestinian.

One is isolation. If you feel yourself to be in a hostile place, you are likely to band together with compatriots who will readily join you in shutting off the environment and its pressures, real ones in this case. Another difficulty is nostalgia, which tends to prettify not only the past but the present and future as well. Third is a brooding sense of universal suspicion, a feeling that everyone—including the occasional Palestinian—has really sold out, betrayed the cause and certainly the revolution, made an easy peace with America and Israel. Lastly there is a persistent habit of seeing the world more or less exclusively in terms of Palestine. Not surprisingly, the old elephant story which has the Frenchman discussing the elephant's love life, and the Pole discussing the elephant and the Polish question, now circulates among Palestinians, with the Palestinian interminably connecting the elephant to the loss of Palestine.

All of these problems nevertheless are dialectically linked to the American Palestinian community's strengths, its sociology, its relatively important place in contemporary America. Compared to other ethnic groups here, Arabs (mainly Syrians and Lebanese) have always been politically conservative, interested in seeing themselves in a sort of harmless folkloric light (of the kind used, say, by Danny Thomas in his career), tirelessly assimilating and accommodating. I think it is fair to say that the 1967 War and the emergence of the Palestinian Resistance Movement eclipsed that traditional role for Arabs in America. Within a year after the June War, the first Middle East teach-ins took place on American university campuses, and for the first time Palestinian rights and activists played a leading role. For once, the "Arab" position—not usually credible, often shabbily rhetorical in the extreme—was sharply differentiated into such specific, highly effective components as Palestinian claims against Zionism, liberation, freedom from oppression. This, then, was the positive consequence of Palestinian isolation, although it should be noted that during the height of domestic opposition to the Vietnam War almost all other American antiwar associations and individuals stayed away from Palestine— Father Daniel Berrigan, Noam Chomsky, I. F. Stone, Eqbal Ahmad, and a number of black radicals being among the notable exceptions.

Palestinian memory, or nostalgia in its weak version, has kept alive what numerous American administrations and one generation after another of the Zionist movement have tried to efface: the existence of a Palestinian Arab nation, generating in turn a healthy self-consciousness. Socially this has taken the form in America of an exceptionally well-educated community, dominated by a sizable professional class, small and middle-level business people, and a large number of students. Palestinians here were the first Arab–Americans to investigate their own history seriously, to see that history in terms similar to those of other oppressed peoples, to go a little beyond the clichés of the hour. They went on to project their sense of themselves as potentially liberated people at the same time that Zionists seemed to be looking anxiously at the future only as a security problem, or backward to the Old Testament to justify more colonization of the West Bank and Gaza.

In time, however, this Palestinian self-consciousness brought on a cycle of American responses, some unpleasantly reactive, some unintentionally favorable. Beginning in 1972 with Operation Boulder, the government has placed the Palestinian community on its priority surveillance list; one noteworthy fact today is that only Palestinians can be (and in two cases actually are) threatened with deportation, without arousing press attention, much less liberal hue and cry. Zionist organizations, directly orchestrated by the Israeli government and in some cases enjoying the unrestricted support of prominent members of Congress, much of the media, and many intellectuals, wage unremitting war against the Palestinians as terrorists pure and simple. Yet this, I think, testifies to how much the language and the position of Palestinian rights have achieved in American public discourse. Slowly, too, some of the society's progressive elements have been addressing themselves to the whole question, and, in the case of many Jewish progressives who have broken with the strict Zionist consensus, this has caused deep consternation in the organized Jewish community. Everyone for the most part still treads very carefully where Palestine is concerned, the suspicion of one's closest friends being the first consequence of getting involved.

From the start the Reagan era augured badly, though. For the first time since Harold Saunders of the State Department made his statement about Palestine to Congress in 1975, the "Question of Palestine" is no longer considered to be a central issue in U.S. Middle East policy. Individuals and groups here struggle on, but there is some risk that the American Palestinians might be so concerned with their internal, not to say idiosyncratic, problems as to become just another ethnic community like the Ukrainians or the Serbs. Oil and terrorism (translated into arms for Saudi Arabia and Israel, a Rapid Deployment Force for the Gulf, a relentless opposition to Arab nationalism) signal continued U.S. hostility to Palestinian national aspirations. For Palestinians resident in America the atmosphere has turned sharply darker. Domestic surveillance and harassment are on the increase, the politics of intervention and resurgent Americanism casts them by inference in the role of the enemy, and Arab divisiveness, exported to America, has split Palestinians, Egyptians, Lebanese, Iraqis, and others from one another. But the fighting Palestinian spirit of survival remains, and doubtless it will be strengthened by the current adversity.

Published in *The Guardian*, March 23, 1981.

CHAPTER 7

The Formation of American Public Opinion on the Question of Palestine

[1982]

In Western Europe, generally speaking, public attitudes toward the Palestinians, which on the whole only grudgingly and very recently have begun to show some improvement, are considerably in advance of the United States. In America the situation has genuinely improved over the past five or six years, although judging from recent pronouncements about the Middle East by various presidential candidates, the low level of talk and of quick public acceptability of such talk are depressingly evident.

I would like therefore to analyze the background of these American attitudes insofar as they reflect and embody a rarely questioned consensus and an unconscious ideology, both of which derive from certain specific features of American society and history. That will take up the first part of this essay. In the second part I shall give concrete examples of how the consensus and the ideology work with reference to the Palestine question.

AMERICAN CONSENSUS AND IDEOLOGY

Because the United States is a complex society made up of many, often incompatible subcultures, the need to impart a more or less standardized common culture through the media is felt with particular strength. This is not a feature associated only with the mass media in our era, but one that holds a special pedigree going back to the founding of the American republic. Beginning with the Puritan "errand into the wilderness," there has existed in the United States an institutionalized ideological rhetoric expressing a particular American consciousness, identity, and destiny whose function has always been to incorporate as much of American (and the world's) diversity as possible, and to re-form it in a uniquely American way. (This rhetoric and its institutional presence in American life have been convincingly analyzed by numerous scholars, including Perry Miller and, most recently, Sacvan Bercovitch.) One result is the illusion, if not always the actuality, of consensus, and it is as part of this essentially nationalist consensus that the media, acting on behalf of the society they serve, believe themselves to be functioning.

The simplest and, I think, most accurate way of characterizing this consensus is to say that it sets limits and maintains pressures. It does not mechanically dictate content, nor does it mechanically reflect the interest of a certain class or economic group. We must think of it as drawing invisible lines beyond which a reporter or commentator does not feel it possible to go. Thus the notion that American military power might be used for malevolent purposes is relatively unthinkable within the consensus, just as the idea that America is a force for good in the world is routine and normal. Similarly, I think, Americans tend to identify with foreign societies or cultures projecting a pioneering spirit (e.g., Israel), with those who are wresting the land from ill-use or from savages. On the other hand, Americans often mistrust or do not have much interest in traditional cultures, even those in the throes of revolutionary renewal. Americans expect that Communist propaganda is guided by similar cultural and political constraints, but in America's case the media's setting of limits and maintaining of pressures is done with little apparent admission or awareness. And this, too, is an aspect of setting limits. Let me give two simple examples. First, Palestinians are systematically considered to be terrorists: For a long time, nothing else about them was as consistently referred to, not even their bare human existence. Second, when the U.S. hostages were seized and held in Tehran, the consensus immediately came into play, decreeing more or less that only what took place concerning the hostages was important about Iran. The rest of the country, its political processes, its daily life, its personalities, its geography and history, were eminently ignorable. Iran and the Iranian people were defined in terms of whether they were for or against America. But these matters are best understood in practice, and we shall see what this entails when we come to specific cases.

After World War II the United States took over the role formerly played by imperial France and Britain. A set of policies was devised for dealing with the world that suited the peculiarities and the problems of each region affecting (and affected by) U.S. interests. Europe was designed for postwar recovery, for which the Marshall Plan, among other similar U.S. policies, was suited. The Soviet Union, of course, emerged as the United States' most formidable competitor, and, as no one needs to be told, the Cold War produced policies, studies—even a mentality—which dominated the relationship between one super-power and the other. That left what has come to be called the Third World, an area of competition not only between the United States and the USSR but also between the United States and various native powers only recently independent of European colonizers.

Almost without exception, the Third World seemed to U.S. policy-makers to be "underdeveloped," in the grip of unnecessarily archaic and static "traditional" modes of life, dangerously prone to Communist subversion and internal stagnation. This is the framework into which the Palestinians have fitted. For the Third World, "modernization" became the order of the day as far as the United States was concerned. And, according to James Peck, "modernization theory was the ideological answer to a world of increasing revolutionary upheaval and continued reaction among traditional political elites."[8] Huge sums were poured into Africa and Asia with the aim of stopping communism, promoting U.S. trade, and, above all, developing a cadre of native allies whose *raison d'être* seemed to be the transformation of a backward country into a mini-America. In time the initial investment required additional sums and increased military support to keep it going. And this in turn produced the interventions all over Asia and Latin America that regularly pitted the United States against almost every brand of native nationalism.

The history of U.S. efforts on behalf of modernization and development in the Third World can never be completely understood unless it is also noted how the policy itself produced a style of thought, and a habit of seeing the Third World, which *increased* the political, emotional, and strategic investment in the very idea of modernization. Vietnam is a perfect instance. Once it was decided that the country was to be saved from communism—and, indeed, from itself—a whole science of modernization for Vietnam (whose last and most costly phase was known as "Vietnamization") came into being. It was not only government specialists who were involved, but university experts as well. In time, the survival of pro-American and anti-Communist regimes in Saigon dominated everything, even when it became clear that, on the one hand, a huge majority of the population viewed those regimes as alien and oppressive, and, on the other, that the cost of fighting unsuccessful wars on behalf of these regimes had devastated the whole region and cost Lyndon Johnson the Presidency. Still, a great amount of writing on the virtues of modernizing traditional societies acquired an almost unquestioned social and certainly cultural authority in the United States, while in many parts of the Third World "modernization" was connected in the popular mind with foolish U.S. spending, unnecessary gadgetry and armaments, corrupt rulers, and brutal U.S. intervention in the affairs of small, weak countries.

Among the many illusions that persisted in modernization theory was one with special pertinence to the Islamic world, namely, that before the advent of the United States, Islam had existed in a kind of timeless childhood, shielded from true development by an archaic set of superstitions, prevented by its strange priests and scribes from moving out of the Middle Ages and into the modern world. The Islamic world seemed indifferent to the blandishments of "Western" ideas altogether. What was especially troubling about its attitude was a fierce unwillingness to accept any style of politics (or, for that matter, of rationality) that was not deliberately its own. Above all, the attachment to Islam seemed especially defiant.

Ironically, few Western commentators on "Islamic" atavism and medieval modes of logic noted that a few miles to the west of Iran, in Begin's Israel, there was a regime fully willing to mandate its actions by religious authority and by a very backward-looking theological doctrine. Whereas Western journalists and intellectuals became expert at derisively quoting various Islamic edicts in Iran (which seemed quite reactionary), no one bothered to point out, for example, that the modern Israeli edition of the Babylonian Talmud (edited by Rabbi Adin

Steinzaltz), which is taught in many Israeli and some American schools, has in its Tractate Berachot such passages as the following: "A Jew who sees tombs of Gentiles should say: 'Your mother shall be sore confounded, she that bore you shall be ashamed, behold the end of the Gentiles shall be a wilderness, a dry land and a desert,' Jeremiah 50: 12."

Religious intensity was thus ascribed solely to Islam. A retreat into religion became the way most Islamic states could be explained—from Saudi Arabia, which, with a peculiarly Islamic logic, refused to ratify the Camp David accords, to Pakistan, Afghanistan, and Algeria. In this way, then, we can see how the Islamic world was differentiated in the Western mind generally, in the United States in particular, from regions to which Cold War analysis could be applied. There seemed to be no way, for example, in which one could speak of Saudi Arabia and Kuwait as parts of "the free world"; even Iran during the shah's regime, despite its overwhelming anti-Soviet commitment, never really belonged to "our side" the way France and Britain do. Nevertheless, U.S. policymakers persisted in speaking of the "loss" of China, Vietnam, and Angola. In this context it has been the singularly unhappy lot of the Persian Gulf's Islamic states to have been considered by American crisis managers as places ready for U.S. military occupation. Thus George Ball, in The New York Times Magazine of June 28, 1970, warned that the "tragedy of Vietnam" might lead to "pacifism and isolation" at home, whereas U.S. interests in the Middle East were so great that the President ought to "educate" Americans about the possibility of military intervention there.

One more thing needs mention here: the role of Israel in mediating Western and particularly American views of the Islamic world since World War II. In the first place, as I have already said, very little about Israel's avowedly religious character is ever mentioned in the press. Only recently have there been overt references to Israeli religious fanaticism in the Western press, and all of these have been to the zealots of Gush Emunim, whose principal activity has been the violent setting up of illegal settlements in the West Bank. Yet most Western accounts of Gush Emunim simply leave out the inconvenient fact that it was the "secular" Labour government that first instituted illegal settlements in occupied Arab territory, not just the religious fanatics now stirring things up. This kind of one-sided reporting is, I think, an effect of how Israel—the Middle East's "only democracy" and "our staunch ally"—has been used as a foil for Islam. All the social and ideological peculiarities that over the years have allied Israel and South Africa tend to get no attention whatever. Instead, Israel has appeared as a bastion of Western civilization hewed (with much approbation and self-congratulation) out of the Islamic darkness.

Secondly, Israel's security has become automatically interchangeable with fending off Islam, perpetuating Western hegemony, and demonstrating the virtues of modernization. At this point, of course, Orientalism and modernization theory dovetail nicely. If Orientalist scholarship traditionally taught that Muslims were no more than fatalistic children tyrannized by their mindset, their *'ulama,* and their wild-eyed political leaders into resisting the West and progress, was it not the case that every political scientist, anthropologist, and sociologist worthy of trust could show that, given a reasonable chance, something resembling the American way of life might be introduced into the Islamic world via consumer goods, anti-Communist propaganda, and "good" leaders? The one main difficulty with the Islamic world, however, was that, unlike India and China, it had never really been pacified or defeated. For reasons which seemed always to defy the understanding of scholars, Islam continued to sway over its adherents, who, it came regularly to be argued, were unwilling to accept reality or at least that part of reality in which the Western superiority was demonstrable.

Efforts at modernization persisted throughout the two decades following World War II. Iran became in effect the modernization success story and its ruler the modernized leader par excellence. As for the rest of the Islamic world—Arab nationalism, Egypt's Gamal Abdel Nasser, Indonesia's Sukarno, and the Palestinian national movement, Iranian opposition groups, thousands of Islamic teachers, brotherhoods, orders—all of this was either opposed or not covered by Western scholars with a heavy investment in modernization theory and in American strategic and economic interests in the Islamic world.

During the explosive decade of the 1970s, Islam seemed to give more and more proof of its fundamental intransigence. There was, for example, the Iranian revolution: Neither pro-Communist nor pro-modernization, the people who overthrew the shah were simply not explainable according to the canons of behavior presupposed by modernization theory. They did not seem to be grateful for the quotidian benefits of modernization (cars, an enormous military and security apparatus, a stable regime). In these ways, therefore, three sets of illusions economically buttress and reproduce each other in the interests of shoring up the Western self-image: the view of Islam, the ideology of modernization, and the affirmations of Zionism.

In addition, to make "our" attitudes to Islam very clear, a whole information and policy-making apparatus in the United States depends on these illusions and diffuses them widely. Large segments of the intelligentsia, allied to the community of geopolitical strategists, deliver themselves of expansive ideas about Islam, oil, the future of Western civilization, and the fight for democracy against both turmoil and terrorism. For reasons that I have discussed elsewhere, the Islamic specialists supply more material, despite the fact that only a fraction of what goes on in academic Islamic studies is directly infected with the cultural and political visions to be found in geopolitics and Cold War ideology. Adding to this are the mass media, which take from the other two units of the apparatus what is most easily compressed into images: hence the caricatures, the frightening mobs, the concentration on "Islamic" punishment, and so on. All of this is presided over by the great power establishments—the oil companies, the mammoth corporations and multinationals, the defense and intelligence communities, the executive branch of the government. When President Carter spent his first New Year's Day in office with the shah in 1978, and said that Iran was "an island of stability," he was speaking with the mobilized force of this formidable apparatus, representing U.S. interests and covering Islam at the same time.

AMERICAN PUBLIC POLICY AND
THE QUESTION OF PALESTINE

On September 9, 1979, ABC broadcast a conversation between Barbara Walters and Yasir Arafat. The program was part of the network's "Issues and Answers" series, taped on September 8 in Havana during the last hours of the conference of nonaligned countries. Much of what was said about the conference in the U.S. press focused on tensions between President Tito and Fidel Castro, yet ABC's choice of Arafat for what was to be the only major television coverage of the conference indicated accurately enough that, even in Havana, the PLO and the Palestine question stood at the center of the issues being discussed.

Walters' prominence as a journalist star gave the interview more gravity, as did the Middle East expertise she had gathered from having interviewed Anwar Sadat, Menachem Begin, and Arafat himself on previous occasions. I do think it is wrong to assume that viewers were supposed to understand that Walters' "doing" Arafat meant that in some vague, undefined way history was being dramatized before their eyes. In this case the historical event was Arafat's trial for harboring intentions to destroy Israel and kill all the Jews.

Every so often in the interview Walters would ask routine political questions: What did Arafat think of the resolutions (still to be voted on) condemning Israel and supporting the PLO? What sort of aid was Cuba giving the PLO? Was it correct that Arafat had intervened to forestall a UN Security Council vote on Palestinian rights so that Andy Young would not be embarrassed at having to cast a U.S. veto? But the interview's main business consisted in a more and more impassioned Walters asking Arafat questions, not of policy, but of destiny. Isn't it true, she asked three times, that the PLO's charter advocates the destruction of Israel? Each time she asked the question, and each time she rephrased it, her insistence declaimed moral partisanship. She was not "just" a reporter doing her job; she was Right asking (perhaps potential) Evil to cease and desist from genocide. She was, in fact, raising the specter of the Holocaust before her audience's eyes, and quite decently exposing Arafat's latent Nazism to the world. He, on the other hand, hesitated—his poor English forcing him time and again to counter the question with the wrong question. Have you actually read the charter? And what disreputable translation did you use, he asked, as if the charter guided his every move and as if only a linguistic philosopher could really decode the charter's deep mysteries. How could Walters, scrupulously doing her job, know (and how much less likely was it that her viewers could know) that most of the frequent *Palestinian* criticisms of Arafat were that he did not truly observe one or another clause in the charter? But that could not possibly emerge in such an interview anyway. What was astonishing was how quickly and easily a journalist could escalate the rhetoric from politics to the grandiose level of history and destiny, and, perhaps more maddening, how little of the same kind of rhetoric is ever directed against Israeli or Zionist leaders being interviewed.

Consider that as recently as 1969 Golda Meir said that Palestinians do not exist; since then every Israeli prime minister has referred to the more than four million Palestinians in terms that have been intended

dramatically to express doubt about their genuine existence. General
Rabin referred to them as "so-called Palestinians," and Menachem
Begin called them "the Arabs of Eretz Israel." Israel has no constitution, but in none of its Basic Laws is there a provision made for (much
less a reference to) the 650,000 Palestinians who are in fact Israeli
citizens. Moreover, in having literally destroyed about four hundred of
the original five hundred Palestinian villages, Israel not only eradicated
a society but dispossessed its people and occupied the remainder of its
territory. And Israel continues to bomb, strafe, and punish the civilian
refugee population without respite. Begin's party, the Likud, states
quite explicitly in its constitution that Israel intends to hold on to the
West Bank, and even to occupy the East Bank (that is, the sovereign
state of Jordan). Yet there has never been an occasion when a reporter
in the United States has publicly asked an Israeli politician questions
about these matters. The great questions about existence, about genocide, about recognition are regularly asked of the Palestinians, who
have been turned into metaphysical abstractions all signaling the destruction of the Middle East's most powerful state, and the end of the
Jewish people, and protracted terror and violence.

In this state of affairs, which is primarily a public information and
policy question of very great moment indeed, print and broadcast
journalism are seriously implicated. Barbara Walters is no especially
culpable figure in this respect: she is, I believe, a well-intentioned
reporter who has followed unquestioningly the trend, the rhetorical
space opened at least a generation before her. The result is that few
people have been prepared to open the Palestinian file as something
representing a direct challenge to certain concrete Israeli policies and
to concrete aspects of Zionist history. On the one hand, therefore,
most things about Israel appeared sacrosanct, since as an idea the
country was a once-empty land now filled with those Jews not destroyed by Nazism. On the other hand, since the Palestinians did not
really "exist," and since their narrative continuity as a people could
not easily be ascertained (there are practically no works in English
about them; they belong to the exotic Islamic Orient, not the West;
they were an essentially backward peasant people whose world silence
could be interpreted as indifference), they came to represent nothing
more than an obstacle to Israeli existence. In time, when it became
clear after 1967 that Israel was going to have to deal with its "non-
Jewish" subjects, Palestinians were an immediate flaw in Israel's actuality: How could Israel be said militarily to occupy territory not its

own? How could mere Arabs unanimously resist Israeli "preventive detention?" How could an organization such as the PLO make claims on Israel's hitherto unqualified legitimacy and assert the presence of another people on the same Palestinian soil? All these questions were unilaterally equated with "terrorism" and a threat "to eliminate Israel," and for politeness' sake not asked.

What happened, and why did it happen? The answer has in the end very little to do with a Zionist lobby, although such a lobby obviously played a role of some sort. Let us start charitably with the understandable explanations first. Zionism can easily be said to have achieved remarkable things for Jews. However much the record may have caused disagreements within the Jewish community, I think it is true that in the liberal Western world's eyes the struggle for Palestine was seen to be an affirmative thing. Certainly after World War II the struggle seemed irresistibly important, and Israel was established—part of the same effort that included the Marshall Plan, as one historian (Fritz Stein) has recently said. No attention to speak of was given to what Israel cost the native Palestinian, whose actual numerical majority was, as late as the spring of 1948, three times greater than that of the growing number of incoming Jews. Except for the odd UN report, neither the academic experts on the Middle East nor the press devoted much space to the Palestinian side of the story, which was mainly a story of loss, exile, and dispersal. History seems always to be written from the victors' standpoint, and the Israelis were the winners. In addition, it was Israelis and pro-Zionist Americans who provided the local consumer of news with what was happening: After all, how many Palestinians spoke or wrote English, and what did it mean to the average American to be a Palestinian and to suffer for it? Even today, when the Arab world is full of civilian casualties, how many Arab funerals are shown on American television? Whereas hundreds of thousands of Palestinians actually lost their country and became for the most part stateless exiles, no one could sympathetically name a single Palestinian or identify with a Palestinian story the way readers of *Exodus,* admirers of Moshe Dayan, and students of Martin Buber could.

Into this vast gap about the Palestinians flowed a limited number of clichés, endlessly deployed, repeated, and rephrased almost unthinkingly. In the background lurked a strong Western prejudice against Arabs and Muslims—violent and uncultured terrorists—while in the foreground one could go on about Israeli modernity and democracy, about the *kibbutzim* (all of which programmatically exclude non-Jews), about the marvelous army, and so forth. For journalists and politicians it was *de rigueur* to be "for Israel," as if that automatically meant being for civilization, against the Holocaust, and with the American way of life. By 1967, when Israel came into possession of approximately a million more Palestinians, to be "for Israel" meant being for life, for values, for civilization itself. The Palestinians were just there in order for Israel's "benign occupation" to be carried out. To be critical of Israel was to fall into the pattern set forth by Nazism. In the process, of course, the history of Zionism, which to some extent created today's militant Palestinian resistance, disappeared: Israel stood alone in the eastern Mediterranean, a virtuous plot of land without time, without any history but that of anti-Semitism, without people except surviving Jews and terroristic "Arabs."

As one watched Barbara Walters, one could begin to understand why neither she nor her colleagues ever asked Begin, for example, where the Palestinians came from anyway, and why Palestinians should feel animosity toward Israel, or why most Africans and Asians identify with them and not with Israel. She did not know—and, what was more important, there was no rhetoric for her to use easily even if she did know. To a very great extent the recent U.S. interest in the PLO is a function both of a renascent Palestinian political struggle and of a backward, novelty-seeking press, as well as of the phenomenon referred to as "the return of Islam." The shortcomings of that interest are equally a function of all three factors. In any case, were Arafat to have spoken naturally about his own life or the lives of his friends and relatives, then the concrete punishments of Zionism for the Palestinian might have emerged. And were Walters to have asked him a personal question—"Why do you and your young men and women willingly endure Israeli bombardment in your camps and still wage the struggle for Palestinian self-determination?"—the interview might have been informative. But the journalist could not escape the false positions into which one habitually falls in talking about the Palestinians and the Middle East. From one perspective, too much rhetoric and metaphysics; from another, not enough human detail.

The results of this skewed situation have recently been unimaginable for any other foreign policy question. Consider some recent grotesqueries in which the U.S. media and the politicians have followed along for the most part uncritically.

1. The Camp David events of September 1978. Following much talk about the Palestinian problem, a simple question arises: Why were

no Palestinians present or consulted? Even if Carter, Sadat, and Begin were treated by Cronkite, Walters, and Brinkley with the respect normally given to prophets, would it not have been possible for someone to venture out loud that it was a bit peculiar to speak *about* and *for* Palestinians, but not by any means to speak *to* them? And still we are informed every few days that Jimmy Carter, perhaps only to ensure his reelection, will, in his best Presidential manner, bring Sadat and Begin to the White House to get the autonomy talks off dead-center. Yet, *The New York Times* tells us, there is no chance that Sadat and Begin will agree on the really crucial question governing the colonial settlements: the question—however metaphysical it might seem to ordinary mortals—of Israeli security. No one asks (perhaps because it is too naive a question): Why bother with an autonomy agreement, since none of the major questions except sanitation can be talked about, and since it will not be accepted by anyone—least of all the Israelis, who hold all the power, or the Palestinians, to whose benefit it is supposed to be occurring?

2. The March 1980 UN vote censuring Israel after which, having first supported it, the United States disavowed its own position. We now know that Ambassador McHenry flew to Washington with the text of the resolution in his pocket the night before the vote. What exactly caused the failure to communicate? Did the text drop out of his pocket between the airport and the White House? Or was it that the President, the ambassador, the secretary of state, and the national security adviser, neither singly nor together, understood the language of the resolution? Or was it that somebody else—perhaps Robert Strauss—instructed the President that the vote would have to be disavowed if the campaign were to continue successfully?

One cannot know, of course, but these are not the really consequential questions. What counts, in my opinion, is that every candidate, including the President himself, has attacked a policy declared to be our policy in the name of that policy. Lewis Carroll could not have dreamed up a nicer conundrum, nor a cleverer logical and political absurdity. And still the U.S. constituency has not been heard from, just as the press—which has been on the wrong side of every argument or prediction in the Middle East—follows along sheepishly, reporting the idiocies with no indication that it is aware that they are in fact idiocies, not to be tolerated by any rational human being.

3. The question of human rights. On this point words fail me, or, if they do not, they ought to be extremely strong words indeed. Let

me venture a few. It is a scandal that Palestinian rights are assumed to
be negligible and that such an assumption has become the common
currency of everyday politics and discourse in the United States. When
the press and the government can whip up sentiment in America in
favor of treating the ex-shah as a charity case, hardly anyone except a
courageous Australian journalist, Claudia Wright, has the courage to
tell the story of Ziad Abu Ein, a Palestinian who is being extradited by
the United States at Israel's simple request, in flagrant violation of
every decent human sentiment and every known legal precept. Palestinian rights have been trampled on; they have been ripped up, torn
to shreds in legal fact and in the bodies of our people. And yet no one
says anything. Instead we have Senator Kennedy's fatuous words about
Israel's security, as if the mere mention of the word *Israel* were enough
to assure him of a place in posterity. One could go on and on.

But in the end the Palestinian problem is *the* Middle East problem.
It is about the denial of human rights for "natives." It is about
unremitting war waged by Israel against the non-European Arab inhabitants of Palestine, a war that continues today in war-destroyed southern Lebanon and in the Occupied Territories. It is about unrestrained
militarism, destruction, and overspending. Palestine is the human truth
hidden beneath propagandistic thought-stopping headlines, like "RE-
SURGENT ISLAM," "MIDDLE EAST CRISES," and "ISRAELI DEMOC-
RACY." The Palestinians are everywhere in the region: The Gulf is
dependent on them, every Islamic movement supports them, every
liberation movement sees their struggle as the vanguard struggle.
Above all, the independence and democracy of the Palestinian political
struggle represents a genuine alternative to superpower maneuvers in
outmoded, unacceptable spheres of influence. After all, the Palestinian
idea in its essence opposes religious and ethnic exclusivism, which have
dispossessed all four million "non-Jews" (as Israel designates them
officially), and proposes instead equality for Jews and Arabs alike. This
is not an idea to be backed away from, especially at a time when
Americans have been fed a diet of ideological hatred for nonwhites
and for "Islam," and when no criticism of Israel is the easiest line to
take in a country that is less critical of Israeli policies than Israelis
themselves.

Published in *Palestinian Rights: Affirmation and Denial*,
edited by Ibrahim Abu-Lughod.

CHAPTER 8

Palestinians in the Aftermath of Beirut: A Preliminary Stocktaking

[1982]

[I]

There is slight consolation for Palestinians in the realization that Israel did not achieve all its war aims in Lebanon. The accelerating propaganda efforts at convincing the world—the United States especially—that Israel delivered Lebanon to the "free" world appear more preposterous every day, but totally in keeping with the ingrained Israeli habit of supplanting reality with fantasy. True, the immense physical and human damage done to Lebanon has receded in memory somewhat, and true also there is a meliorist and euphemistic aura surrounding Lebanon's new president, who aspires to be more a national leader and more a symbol of unity than either the tradition of his predecessors or of his party might allow. But in the main Israel has not been able to turn its military successes into anything resembling a clear-cut political victory. The universal opprobrium heaped upon Begin and Sharon for the siege of Beirut and the Sabra-Shatila massacres, the intensified international awareness of the Palestinian issue, the minimal but definite steps forward taken by President Reagan and the Arab heads of state—all these are indications that Likud's plan for a Palestinian final solution failed to sweep the board clean to Israel's advantage. As the war bill of $2.5 billion is presented by Israel to the United States, it is likely that more rather than fewer regrets about the whole episode will be expressed; talk of the war's "opportunities for creative diplomacy" have long since given way both to disapproval of Israel's peremptory annexationist militarism and to a temporary widening of the chasm between U.S. and Israeli interests. This chasm corresponds to the difference between a major imperial and a minor subimperial power. Nevertheless, all this will not necessarily be to the Palestinians' advantage. The all-but-formal annexation of the West Bank and Gaza proceeds unchecked; the dispersal of more Palestinians to more places continues; the isolation of individual Palestinians, and of Palestinians collectively, increases the difficulty of their anomalous status; statehood seems further away.

In 1948 Israel was created as the culmination of a long process initiated in Europe, as an integral aspect of the great age of expanding colonialism. European Jews, having suffered centuries of Christian anti-Semitism that were to climax in the horrendous Nazi slaughters of World War II, sought to create a Western colony in the East. Their efforts succeeded, although in the process hardly anyone in the West who supported Zionism as a postwar reconstructive phenomenon noticed that Israel's birth erupted out of the ruins of Palestinian society. An Ottoman colony for many years, Palestine was nevertheless the communal home of the Palestinian Arabs. After decades of Jewish immigration into Palestine, the Jews there in 1948 numbered only a third of the total population; these Jews also owned no more than 6 percent of the total land surface of Palestine. Yet this relatively new community of Jews defeated the unorganized, basically unarmed Palestinians, and along with them a miscellaneous force of other Arab armies, ill-equipped, poorly trained, unmotivated. Well over 800,000 Palestinians were evicted from their homes by the Zionist forces. In 1967 the rest of Palestine—occupied by the Hashemite Kingdom of Jordan in 1948—was taken over by Israel. Today the four million Palestinians exist in three dispossessed, dispersed, subjugated groups: There are 650,000 Israeli Arabs, colonized internally; there are the 1.3 million Palestinians of the West Bank and Gaza, under Israeli military occupation; and there are the Palestinians in total exile from Palestine. Of the latter, the largest group is in Jordan; next in size is the community of 500,000 Palestinians who have been in Lebanon since 1948 (with the exception of a handful who went there in 1971). It is sometimes forgotten that Israel's war against the Palestinians in Lebanon is but a continuation—as brutal, as inhumane, and as contemptible—of its war against those innocent Palestinian civilians who were driven from their homeland in 1948.

At the very least, then, the Lebanese conflagration provides Palestinians with some urgent opportunities for reflecting on the future, and of course on those aspects of the past that directly affect the future. Lebanon was a disaster: There is no way of avoiding the facts, each of which, separately or as part of a whole, confirms a picture whose tragedy and loss exceed the events of 1948.

From one point of view, Palestinian involvement in the Lebanese Civil War and subsequently in free-for-all Lebanese politics was an unhealthy thing. Because Lebanon's style of politics is essentially combative but indecisive (no winner and no loser, runs the motto), Palestinians were involved in the frequently draining activity of holding on to unimprovable positions. Palestinian politics became a function of Lebanese politics; Palestinian sections of Beirut were mirror images of strictly Lebanese sections; Palestinian leaders adopted the style of traditional Lebanese leaders. In the meantime, essential goods and services were provided by the PLO to the largely indigent civilian and urban population whose representative it was: This was true in Beirut, of course, but also in Sidon, Tyre, and Tripoli. The camps were protected as political domains ruled over by Palestinians, and on every level an impressive array of health care, educational, social, occupational self-help, and economic organizations provided Palestinians and Lebanese with the communal and political identity denied them everywhere else. It is forgotten today that Amal, the southern Lebanese Shiite militia, began with Palestinian help.

Above all, the Lebanese period in the history of the Palestinian national movement—a period of eccentricity, unresolvable paradox, extraordinary international gains—was the first truly independent period of Palestinian national history. That it should have taken place outside of Palestine, even though a formidable nationalist consciousness arose in the Occupied Territories, is one index of how utterly difficult the Palestinian struggle is today. It is also an index of how seriously Israel took the emergence not only of a national movement but of a national history: Israel completed the destruction of a country, killed thousands of innocent civilians with outlawed weapons, earned itself the lasting disapproval of many Jews, in order to strip Palestinians of their national identity and of their newly formed national (as opposed to merely colonial) history. The climax to this campaign occur-

red when, in West Beirut, Israeli soldiers carted off Palestinian archives, destroyed the private libraries and homes of prominent Lebanese nationalists and Palestinian personalities, and literally heaped
excrement over valuable rugs and cultural artifacts almost at the same
moment when, in Sabra and Shatila, a gang of Lebanese Maronite
psychopaths—armed, trained, and supported by Israel—was slaugh-
tering Palestinian civilians under the light of flares provided by Israeli
soldiers. This was all a concerted, deliberate attempt to roll back the
history of the past several years: Palestinians, in Begin's rhetoric, were
to be treated as terrorists and two-legged beasts, and neither as human
beings nor as potential citizens. This made it easier to bomb them and
to pretend that Israel was doing the work on behalf of humanity.

[I I]

A curious symbiosis developed between Palestinians and Israel
that was nurtured in Lebanon. Certainly the Israeli side of this
relationship was more destructive and immoral: The ruins of
Lebanon are ample proof. But there is a peculiar Palestinian syndrome
that should not go unnoticed here although it can be discerned in
perspective only if the relevant data are taken into account. On the one
hand, the Palestinians in exile are a nation and a people without
territory; oppressed on all sides, this nation nevertheless evolved from
the status of miscellaneous refugees into a considerable proto-state
formation. On the other hand, none of this would have been possible
without the political education undertaken by the PLO on behalf of a
program foreseeing some sort of communal, multi-ethnic existence
between Jews, Muslims, and Christians in former Palestine. People are
not easily mobilized out of their present misery without such a goal
before them. To its credit, therefore, the Palestinian national movement argued the case for more than one equal national community in
Palestine; to its discredit, the State of Israel and its Western supporters—with the exception of a few dissidents—argued no such thing.
Palestinians were to be "inhabitants of Judea and Samaria," or they
were terrorists; in either case they could not be considered true
interlocutors of Israel. Throughout its history, Zionism in the main has
tended to this sort of narrowing vision, and certainly it can be said that
since 1967, since the Begin government came to power, since Camp
David, since the almost complete colonization or annexation of Occu-

pied Territories, the Palestinians have almost disappeared from the official Israeli *Weltanschauung* except as docile (or rabid) natives. That the invasion of Lebanon could be covered by so inappropriate a phrase as "Peace in Galilee" reveals how far the moral and political impoverishment of Israel had advanced with regard to the Palestinians.

All the propaganda emanating from Israel and its supporters—not least the United States—about the Palestinians hardened, narrowed, made more uninviting the field for the Palestinians. Change the charter, we have been told; renounce violence; recognize Israel; agree to Camp David; allow your representatives to be chosen by others. Few people discriminated between the violence of the oppressor and the violence of the oppressed. Still fewer reflected on the issue of proportionality: By what right did Israel claim for itself the privilege of killing dozens of Palestinians for every Israeli? To this series of injuries Israel has commonly been asked to offer nothing by way of argument or political sense, nothing except more repression, more outrage, more dehumanizing actions and rhetoric.

For every Palestinian advance internationally, however, there was a small retreat internally—and now we come to the Palestinian side of the symbiosis. On the political level, in Lebanon, the unmovable Israeli wall of denials and attacks, coupled with a U.S. policy as rhetorically empty as it was mendacious, caused Palestinians to dig in, gradually to relax strenuous political mobilization in favor of consolidating entrenched positions inside Lebanon, gradually to think less about liberation and independence and more about defending the crucial political and territorial gains made in Lebanon. After all, there has been no liberation movement in this or any other century that, like the Palestinian movement, has been so beset with such immense difficulties: No movement has had to deal with colonizers so morally creditable as the Jews. No movement has had to deal simultaneously with expulsion, dispossession, colonization, and a terrifying kind of international illegitimacy. No movement has had to fight from a hundred different locations (excluding a national base) against a military-political alliance (Israel and the United States) that would outclass any but one or two modern nation-states in strength, resources, and institutional power. No movement has been so unfortunate in its allies and its surrounding context.

Given these factors, then, Lebanon for the Palestinians became an increasingly more eccentric, more ironic place over time. Achievements like the territorial autonomy, the social and political administration of the refugee camps in Beirut, Tripoli, Sidon, and Tyre, as well as the border areas of the South, were too quickly converted into quasi-permanent enterprises; the connection between those achievements and freeing the Occupied Territories from Israeli military occupation was not reflected upon enough, was not therefore a central project. International accomplishments—at the United Nations, in Europe, and elsewhere—were thought of as inhabiting a different world. They are part of another department which had little to do with day-to-day life in Beirut. Slogans like "armed struggle" that date from the late 1960s, from a very different moral environment and a purely insurrectionary phase lingered on unattended by reflection or political work. It was as if every Israeli advance on the ground was responded to by a Palestinian advance on a different territory, one of our own choosing. For this we were all responsible, those in Beirut and those residing elsewhere.

[I I I]

Nevertheless, there was a healthy evolution of institutions and maturity in Lebanon, although faced with Sharon's tanks and his U.S.-made air force, Palestinians on the ground were not protected enough. Undoubtedly the Palestinian defense of Beirut was heroic, almost miraculous, given the paucity of advanced weapons, air-defense systems, strategic advantages. No one in the world could have fought better in the Palestinians' place, just as it is also true that for the first time Arab resistance provoked thousands of Israelis to a radical reconsideration of what their nation was all about. But the question is, and remains to haunt us all: Was the end in Lebanon avoidable? Was the substitutive nature of Lebanon a necessary phase or a disaster in the long run around which we should have maneuvered? Were the fruitless but encumbering ties with various Arab states inevitable, or were they pursued as an end in and of themselves? Was there enough understanding of the larger, the enormously complex global dynamic that involves the question of Palestine today? Were Palestinian politics and ideological struggle concentrated, directed, disciplined enough? Above all, has the new Arab environment of corruption, petrodollars, and mediocrity presided over by the United States, seriously, if not definitively, affected the Palestinian national struggle?

It is far too early to answer these questions with anything more than impressions and emotions. Imperatives for the future nevertheless impose themselves immediately. For the first time in the history of the struggle between Zionism and the Palestinians, two things have emerged, and together these alter the face of things irrecusably; together they must determine the future course of Palestinian history, or there can be no Palestinian history to speak of. One new thing is that a constituency of disaffected Jews, Zionist supporters, Israeli nationalists, as well as fully aware Palestinians has emerged. The second is that an unusual ideological-cultural-political space has opened up, making it possible for the first time to discuss and act on the question of Palestine in its own terms, not simply as a function of superpower rivalry or of the so-called Arab-Israeli conflict.

The defense and the fall of Beirut swept away a great deal, including a lingering faith in the United States, which did not even abide by its commitment to guarantee the safety of Palestinians left behind after the PLO evacuation. But, as I have been saying, the aftermath has created new political formations in a new political territory. The limits to which Israel can go in its ethnocide against the Palestinians for the moment are defined internationally and regionally; the PLO remained intact as the actual political expression of Palestinian nationalism, Sharon's murderous actions and the Village League quisling notwithstanding. Yet on all sides the problems continue to accumulate. Dispersal and dispossession are accentuated in the post-Beirut period. Arab pressures on the PLO increase, as do the temptations simply to start replaying the old Arab game of summit conferences with its attendant collective ineptitude and functional disunity. The immediate possibility of a credible military option, to say nothing of a credible Arab deterrent, is not very high. Yet everywhere that Palestinians are to be found—Lebanon and the Occupied Territories especially—the political pressure to achieve a solution to the question of Palestine is exerted in ways designed to reduce Palestinians to uncountable statistics, the better to absorb them mutely and anonymously to someone else's scheme. Thus Reagan wishes them associated with Jordan, Israel sees them as uncomplaining resident natives, the Arabs want them as the spearhead for the wars they either cannot or will not fight.

It is of the essence, therefore, that much of the residual force that went into the defense of Beirut should now go into formulating a clear Palestinian political program. Historically, our formulations of where we are going also included such detritus as laments about an unacceptable past, attacks on our enemies, ideological pronouncements aimed at a complex web of interlocking, sometimes contradictory, Arab (and even Palestinian) constituencies. There can be no return to this impure style. Our constituency, given the Arab nonresponse to what happened in Lebanon, is neither the old one nor a collection of salvaged remnants. There is first a Palestinian constituency that emerged from outside the barren avenues of official routines, positions, and structures. This constituency can be nurtured only by someone of Yasir Arafat's partially enhanced stature, sensitive to its makeup, to the innovative claims it makes, to the novel maneuvers it can allow. The other important, indeed crucial constituency, is that of Israeli and non-Israeli Jews who find Israel's present course unacceptable and disastrous.

Moreover, the loss of Beirut as a substitute for Palestine and the gain of many new places of exile accentuates the focus on the Occupied Territories, those last bits of Palestine still inhabited by Palestinians. The urgent issue now becomes the problem of keeping Palestinians there—despite, and because of, Israeli desires to expel them all—and expanding the juridical, political, and cultural framework in which they live. Here, too, the old formulae don't apply anymore, as the disasters that overtook Camp David amply prove. The conflict in Palestine is not simply a territorial one: This fact cannot be strategized, Sadatized, or Kissingerized. There is a radical conflict between a view stating that Jews have more rights than non-Jews, and a view—as yet to be formulated with the cogency and power it deserves—stating that all present communities and individuals have civil rights in Palestine, equal in principle. Every departure from this second view has brought sustained disaster to opponent and proponent alike. The need for a new politics on the Occupied Territories is the need for a new effective theory for combating tyrannical exceptionalism, by which one community's claim is given divine status, the other's reduced to an occasional appearance from time to time.

None of what is being said here can minimize the unimaginable complexity of the tasks ahead. No Palestinian is ever afraid to admit that the struggle we face may be far bigger than we are. Certainly any political theater that incorporates the swirl of Arab nationalism, Zionism, the history of anti-Semitism, anti-colonialism, Islamic, Jewish, and Christian apocalyptic millenarianism, decolonization, imperialism, the threat of nuclear annihilation, to say nothing of every variety of human degradation and exaltation, is an epochal stage indeed. To be a Palestinian is then to stand at the nexus of these forces, either to be swept away by them or in some way to comprehend and employ their force constructively. If an Israeli military solution, no less than a cosmetic American or Arab solution, will not serve, this is the exact moment for Palestinians collectively, using all the means at their disposal, to state what will serve. Rarely in human history has the articulation of a program acquired so much revolutionary and far-reaching significance. But rarely too has so much of a people's political identity depended on the collective act of counting, rendering, and projecting themselves—beyond the armies, the states, the lamentable stabilities of the present.

Published in *Arab Studies Quarterly,* vol. 4, no. 4, fall 1982.

CHAPTER 9

Solidly Behind Arafat

[1983]

What does Syria hope to accomplish by backing the mutiny within the Palestine Liberation Organization? Nothing less than the final rout of Yasir Arafat—at a cost of many innocent lives. President Hafez al-Assad wishes to replace King Hussein of Jordan as the negotiator for Palestine, and thereby to extend his influence well beyond Lebanon. Yet Palestinian rights cannot be recovered by Syrian guns or maneuvers.

In early September Mr. Arafat returned to the northern Lebanese city of Tripoli—a tragic but inevitable decision. Tripoli meant that he preferred to be with the refugee-camp dwellers who were his first and most loyal constituency. It also meant that he would inevitably confront Syria and the PLO mutineers it controlled.

For most Palestinians today, Mr. Arafat's era in the PLO has been the decisive political and psychological fact of their national identity. Between 1948 and 1968, when Mr. Arafat emerged as a major leader, Palestinians were a forgotten people—refugees, displaced persons, a nation dispossessed and unrecognized. Mr. Arafat and his al-Fatah loyalists set out to shape them as a national community: He built institutions, dispensed arms, and instilled a sense of hope and pride.

Beyond that, Mr. Arafat did two supremely important things. First, he made the PLO a genuinely representative body. Even his enemies knew that Mr. Arafat and the Palestinian will—though not always clearly and consistently articulated—were in a sense interchangeable. By 1974, when he appeared at the United Nations, he had put the

Palestinian people and their cause before the world. To speak about the Middle East now, everyone had to reckon with the Palestinians.

Second, he was the first popular Palestinian leader to formulate the notion that Palestinian Arabs and Israeli Jews would—indeed must— seek a future together on an equal footing in a shared territory. To this day, no Israeli leader has responded to the moral challenge and humane audacity of this vision.

True, Mr. Arafat's leadership was endlessly problematic. His vacillations, his questionable involvements with extreme groups and nations, his legendary toleration of corrupt and incompetent subordinates, his frequent inability to seize political opportunities (some would say his incapacity for real leadership)—all these earned him a just share of criticism, most notably after the Jordanian debacle in 1970 and the Lebanese disaster of 1982. But he was always open and personally incorruptible. His commitment to his people and cause had no limits. He seemed both fearless and gentle to those who encountered him—though far too few Americans and Israelis saw him as anything but a terrorist thug.

Nor is there a credible alternative to Mr. Arafat. Certainly the mutineers have no popular backing of any consequence, and many have deserted to rejoin Mr. Arafat. He cannot be dislodged democratically and had to be challenged by force. The Syrians claim that they are rescuing the Palestinian cause: Syria, which requested a ceasefire in Lebanon after merely five days of fighting the Israelis, dares to challenge the man who held off Israel for nearly three months.

The Syrian government has made Arab nationalism its general creed and Palestine its particular cause. In fact, its true interest in Palestine is Syrian domination. Unpopular and repressive, the Syrian government has made a vocation of impeding and manipulating others. It thrives in an environment—both Arab and Israeli—largely devoid of ideas and values beyond those of tribe. The other Arab regimes offer advice at least, money at most—and all sit by idly while innocents are massacred. Israel goes on annexing, occupying, oppressing. The superpowers offer little except arms and, in the case of the United States, a confused hodgepodge of schemes, support, and money, too much, too late, and to the wrong people.

The months to come will bring the ruthless deployment of American, Israeli, and Syrian military power. Palestinian nationalism will not be canceled, though it will undoubtedly be set back. On the West Bank and Gaza, in the camps of Lebanon and Syria, in the Persian Gulf, in

Europe and North America, Palestinians are solidly behind Mr. Arafat. This following represents much more than a commitment to a man: It is a commitment to a view of the future based on pluralism, justice, and political resolution of the claims of both Jews and Arabs in Palestine.

If this kind of future is put off indefinitely, there will be upheaval, violence, and misery for a long time to come. Certainly, the PLO insurgents, Syria, Israel, and the superpowers have little else to offer.

Published in *The New York Times,* November 15, 1983.

CHAPTER 10

Who Would Speak for Palestinians?

[1985]

Who would represent the Palestinians in talks with Jordan and Israel over the future of the West Bank and Gaza? Many Palestinians are wondering just that—wondering which of us would be acceptable to the United States and on what grounds. We have always known that we were a special people; only recently have we understood just how special.

According to the proposal for negotiations put forward in February by Yasir Arafat and King Hussein of Jordan, Palestinians and Jordanians would form a joint delegation to the talks. The United States has, however, added several conditions.

First of all, it has made clear that none of the Palestinian representatives can be members of the Palestine Liberation Organization or affiliated with it. Never mind that for some fifteen years virtually all Palestinians have said they consider the PLO their sole legitimate representative—our only national authority. Never mind that it is recognized as such by more than one hundred countries. But what is the point of holding talks about the Palestinian question that are designed from the outset to bypass the one organization that even its enemies agree is the only body capable of delivering an agreement?

No one has suggested that the Israeli, Jordanian, or American negotiators who would participate in such talks shouldn't have any affiliation with their governments. Only Palestinians are required to

detach themselves in this way—and be represented by people designated by non-Palestinians. It is as if the American delegation at the
arms control talks in Geneva decided to negotiate with only anti-Soviet
Armenians.

Washington has several explanations for its position. The PLO is a
terrorist organization, whose sole business, it is said, is not to help
Palestinians gain their national rights but only to destroy Israel. The
PLO is also non-Western: It has relations with the Soviet Union; it is
Islamic, disliked by Henry A. Kissinger, and most of its members do
not speak English. These are grave charges, especially when the PLO
is compared with Israel, whose military forces just happen to be in
occupation of all of what was once Palestine, the Syrian Golan Heights,
and, for the time being, South Lebanon.

Although Israel's army is responsible for the destruction of Palestinian society, the expulsion of hundreds of thousands of Palestinians,
and the deaths of many thousands more, all resistance to it is considered terrorism—because Israel and the United States say so. And of
course, no one should have anything to do with terrorists—not even
former terrorists.

Second, we are told that any Palestinian negotiators would have to
endorse United Nations Security Council Resolution 242. It doesn't
seem to matter that the resolution makes no mention of Palestinians,
except as nameless "refugees," or that it has no real application to us;
its central point is, after all, that territory acquired by force must be
returned, and Palestinians haven't acquired any territory—by force or
otherwise.

We have also been requested to renounce the Palestinian National
Charter and recognize Israel's "right to exist"—a metaphysical phrase
never used before in international, domestic, or religious law. None
of us are stupid enough to pretend that Israel does not exist. What we
dispute is that its existence should depend on the negation of our
national existence. I and many other Palestinians are ready to accept
Jewish self-determination in Israel so long as there is a reciprocal
recognition by Israel of Palestinian self-determination on our territories.

We have, in effect, been told that if we concede our national
claims to any part of Palestine, if we accept Jordanian tutelage, if we
recognize Israel, if we forget our history and our identity, if we say
and do all that is required of us, in the interest of peace, we might
qualify for a stool near the bargaining table. We might also get a

brief meeting with Secretary of State George P. Shultz or some other American notable. But a state, or national status, or even a hint of self-determination? No chance.

To achieve peace, Israelis and Palestinians must speak with each other's credible and legitimate representatives—and they must get on with it immediately. The rest is wasted time.

Published in *The New York Times,* May 24, 1985.

CHAPTER 11

An Ideology of Difference

[1985]

[1]

The Israeli invasion of Lebanon in 1982 seems for the first time to have broken the immunity from sustained criticism hitherto enjoyed by Israel and its American supporters. For a variety of reasons, Israel's status in European and American public life and discourse has always been special, just as the position of Jews in the West has always been special, sometimes for its tragedy and horrendous suffering, at other times for its uniquely impressive intellectual and moral triumphs. On behalf of Israel, anomalous norms, exceptional arguments, eccentric claims were (and still are) made, all of them carrying the force that Israel does not entirely belong to the world of normal politics. Nevertheless Israel, and with it Zionism, had gained that unusual status *politically,* not miraculously, by attaching itself to a variety of currents in the West whose power and attractiveness operated in such a way as to distance Israel from anything as concrete, for example, as a policy of rigid separation between Jew and non-Jew, or a military rule over hundreds of thousands of Arabs that was (and is) as repressive as anything to be encountered in Latin America or Eastern Europe. Any number of credible accounts exist, from daily fare in the Israeli press to studies by Amnesty, by various UN bodies, Western journalists, church groups, and, not least, dissenting supporters of Israel. In other words, even though Israel was a Jewish state established by force on territory that was already inhabited by a native population of largely Muslim Arabs, in a part of the world that was overwhelmingly Muslim and Arab, it appeared to most of Israel's supporters in the West (from which Zionism increasingly drew its greatest help) that the Palestinian Arabs who paid the price for Israel's creation were neither relevant nor necessarily even real. In 1982, the distance between Arab and Jew was for the first time perceived more or less universally as not so great; indeed, any consideration of Israel, and any perception of Israel at all, would henceforth have to include some consideration of the Palestinian Arabs, their travail, their claims, their humanity.

Changes of this sort seem to occur dramatically, although it is more accurate to comprehend them as complex, cumulative, often contradictory processes occurring over a long period of time. Above all else, however, no such process can be viewed neutrally, since, for better or for worse, many interests are at work in it, and therefore many interests are also at work whenever it is interpreted or reported. Moreover, while it is worthwhile and even possible to reduce and curtail the gross pressure of those interests for the purpose of analysis or reflection, it is useless to deny that any such analysis is inevitably *situated in,* or inevitably affiliated to, a particular historical moment and a specific political situation.

I repeat these truisms because, as I noted above, discussions of Israel and of Zionism have regularly been conducted as if the actualities of interpretation either could be suspended or did not obtain. Why and how this has been so is one of the themes of this essay, but—given the odium commonly attached to the 1975 UN Resolution on Zionism as a form of racism—we must first plant ourselves squarely on some historical as well as existential realities. I shall begin with a few basic points.

1.   Even though most of what is said either "for" or "against" Israel is debatable, there is common consent on one major point: Israel was established in 1948 as a Jewish state. In this context, "Jewish" must be construed as different from Christian and Muslim on the one hand, and on the other, different from French, Arab, Chinese, or British. How it was established, what existed in Palestine before its establishment, what justified its establishment, what forces brought it about—all these are matters of immense controversy or, more often, apologetic. No one, as far as I know, disputes the Jewishness *in intent* of Israel, for in this lies its uniqueness and, to the contemporary

Palestinians, *their* uniqueness with regard to the Jewish state. A Jewish
state is on national, religious, cultural, juridical, and political grounds
different from any other state.

2.   In its own public, juridical, and international practice, Israel is
the state of the Jewish people, and not a sovereign, independent state
of its citizens, who happen to be non-Jewish as well as Jewish. This was
a matter discussed and then resolved in the earliest period of Israel's
existence, during which time it was decided in the People's Council
debates that as a state Israel would and could not be independent of
all the Jewish people, Israeli and non-Israeli.[9] The result has been that the
non-Jewish Israeli has fundamentally fewer rights than Jewish Israeli
members of "the Jewish people": The inequity between Jew and
non-Jew in Israel is therefore radically antidemocratic, as Rabbi Kahane has had the boldness to proclaim. Moreover, Israel has no constitution, and no internationally declared boundaries, even though its
Basic Laws press the claim for Jewishness on the Land of Israel with
unmistakable clarity. One example will stand for many: The Law of
Return and, with it, the Nationality Law, together stipulate that any
(but only a) Jew anywhere is entitled to immigrate to Israel, and to
acquire Israeli citizenship or nationality. No Palestinian Israeli—who
in this formula is reduced to the status of "non-Jew"—has any such
right, even though he or she may have had generations of family
resident in Palestine.

3.   Yet there are—also according both to Israeli and Arab rhetoric
and practice—"non-Jews" in Israel. About their status, their history,
their national as well as political identity, their intentions, their present
situation, much controversy has raged. Nevertheless, two things can be
agreed upon: First, that these people are, in fact, "non-Jews" and
therefore separated and in numerous ways different from Jews in the
Jewish state; second, that to a vast preponderance of the world's
population (including also themselves), they are referred to as Palestinians, that is, present or former native Arab inhabitants of what is
now referred to as "historical (because it does not exist today, but
once did exist) Palestine."

Beyond these three observations very little can normally be said
without contest, challenge, and debate. Later I shall refer to two very
recent books symptomatic, at this late date, of the desire to maintain
that Palestinians do not exist, and if they do, that they are a murderous
race of mindless fanatics. On the crucial issue of "difference," which

is central to many recent theoretical and interpretive discussions, one can, however, declare oneself *for* difference (as opposed to sameness or homogenization) without at the same time being for the rigidly enforced and policed separation of populations into different groups. As a touchstone for examining the political issues raised by "difference" we can use a combination of two commonly held positions. One is the uncontroversial view based on experience and common sense that all social situations, and hence all populations, states, groupings, are *in fact* mixed. Therefore, there cannot be any such things as a pure race, pure nation, or a pure collectivity, regardless of patriotic, ideological, or religious argument. A corollary to this view is that all efforts (particularly the efforts of governments or states) at making pure one or several of these human agglomerations are tantamount to organized discrimination or persecution: The examples of Nazi Germany and South Africa argue the force of such a judgment with considerable authority in today's world. Second, we have the UN Declaration of the Elimination of All Forms of Racial Discrimination (December 20, 1963), which proscribes all forms of segregation, separation, discrimination on the basis of race, color, religion, national origin. The Declaration's premise, of course, is that all modern states are made up of mixed populations. Both Israel and the United States, among most UN member states, subscribed to this premise and voted to confirm the Declaration.

Insofar as there is a Palestinian argument, it runs as follows: Not only is it manifestly the case that different national, ethnic, and religious groups exist, but no one has an inherent right to use "difference" as an instrument to relegate the rights of others to an inferior or lesser status. Not incidentally, Palestinians employ this argument not only against Israel but against the Arab states which, almost without exception, have over time created a separate set of laws for resident and transient Palestinians. On the other hand, the Jewish case for possessing Palestine—a case expressed politically by Zionism—has derived from and rested on what is supposed to be an inherent right, first articulated in the modern period during the nineteenth century, as a special relationship between Jews and "The Land of Israel," and later—once the land was gained—institutionalized on all levels of life in the Israeli state.

As applied to "The Jewish People" on "The Land of Israel," difference takes various forms. Theologically, of course, "difference" here means "the chosen people" who have a different relationship to

God from that enjoyed by any other group. But that sort of "difference" is, I confess, impossible for me to understand. On a purely secular plane, however, difference means the unique bond to the land of Palestine/Israel distinguishing Jews from all other peoples. Tradition, custom, ethos, the experience of suffering and exile—these carry "difference" through time and historico-social identity. Inside Israel, the "difference" that counts is that between Jew and non-Jew. So far as land in Israel is concerned, for instance, much of it (nearly 90 percent) is held in trust for the Jewish people, whereas non-Jews cannot juridically derive equal benefits from it simply because they are not Jews. Indeed, even if we exclude Arab land acquired by Israel in 1967 and after, land either annexed (Jerusalem, portions of the Golan Heights) or occupied and settled (the West Bank, Gaza, South Lebanon), hundreds of thousands of acres of Palestinian Arab land were expropriated by the State of Israel since 1948 on behalf of the Jewish people. Note that when the 1948 War broke out, the total amount of land owned by Jews in Palestine amounted to only 6 percent of the country. The means employed to "transfer" the land from Arab to Jewish ownership were "legal," but their consequence to the Palestinian Arab was dispossession *tout court*. Thus the Law of Return is exactly commensurate with these means, and no less absolute in differentiating between all Jews anywhere, and the non-Jewish Palestinians, who are not entitled to rights of return and Israeli citizenship.

Difference consequently then extends to non-Jews as well. For if a Jewish state is created by and for the Jewish people, then it must be the case that non-Jews are posited as radically *other*, fundamentally and constitutively different. There is by now a small but excellent literature on the condition of non-Jews (Palestinian Arabs) in Israel, of which the principal works are Sabri Jiryis, *The Arabs in Israel;* Davis, Mack and Yurval-Davis, *Israel and the Palestinians;* Elia Zureik, *The Palestinians in Israel: A Study in Internal Colonialism;* Ian Lustick, *Arabs in the Jewish State.* Nothing in this literature indicates anything but a radically subordinate and consequently disadvantaged position for the Arab citizens of Israel, a position hardly in consonance with the sustained praise in the United States for Israeli democracy. As for the condition of the West Bank, Gaza, South Lebanon, and Golan Arabs that, as I said earlier, is the subject of a regularly documented journalistic as well as specialist literature, all of it reiterating evidence of the gross difference in treatment between the captive Arab population and the Jewish settlers who, in the words of every major figure in the

Israeli government and establishment, have the right to settle anywhere in the land of "Eretz-Yisrael," which according to numerous authorities includes South Lebanon, the East Bank of the Jordan, the Golan Heights, as well as all of historical Palestine.

None of this literature, however, has had much purchase upon intellectuals in the West, for whom issues of tyranny, social justice, and the violation of human rights are supposedly central. What is to be observed in the case of Israel is how the practice of separation between Jew and non-Jew has been translated ideologically into a separation of that practice from all other similar practices, so that—as a case in point—comparisons between the Palestinians and American Indians, or South African blacks, are routinely *not* made, even though similarities between them all are striking. Moreover, we will find that during the years around and after 1948 Zionism was especially supported by liberals and socialists, precisely those political communities who in similar circumstances would be the first to champion the cause of downtrodden populations, mistreated minorities, discriminated-against ethnic groups, victims of policies of separation. Whereas during the sixties few such intellectuals had any difficulty in criticizing U.S. napalm bombing of Vietnam, hardly any of them said anything about continued Israeli use of napalm (and later of cluster bombs) against Arab civilian populations. Subsequent invitations to connect Palestinian militancy, say, with Afghan resistance to Soviet occupation, or with Polish workers' action against the Jaruzelski regime, were either ignored or vehemently rejected. E. M. Forster's injunction, "only connect," was regularly circumvented: Israel and what Israel did were special, were not connected to similar practices elsewhere, were therefore regularly overlooked.

As I said at the outset, Israel's status has somewhat changed now, and one of the consequences of the change is that we can begin to see retrospectively how connected the practice of separation between Jew and non-Jew has been with a complex ideological formation that was built upon an epistemology of forcible separation between things *for the sake of separation itself.* The reason for the change is that Palestinian nationalism has appeared and has made possible a critique whose premise is the need for forging connections and, more important, the existential need to find modes of knowledge, coexistence, and justice that are not based on coercive separation and unequal privilege. Let us then say that we can reinterpret ideologies of difference only because we do so from an awareness of the supervening actuality of "mixing," or crossing-over, of stepping beyond boundaries, which are more creative human activities than staying inside rigidly policed borders. And that awareness is the achieved product of a political process responding to the travail and expense of separation imposed upon— and to some extent creating—a national community, the Palestinian Arabs. Perhaps more important, we develop in the process a heightened critical consciousness not only of what difference can do, but of where its politics can lead.

[I I]

To be a non-Jew in Palestine/Israel is first of all to be marked negatively. This is no less paradoxical a thing than one of the Laws promulgated in Israel for gaining Palestinian land, the one designating so-called present-absentees (nifkadim nochachim), non-Jews defined on the one hand as absentees by virtue of abandoning their place of residence during the 1948 War, and, on the other, present by virtue of current residence in Israel as Israeli citizens.[10] If in a Jewish state normality is defined by Jewishness, abnormality is the normal condition of the non-Jew. The logic extends itself to history and society more generally considered. Thus the routine and by now orthodox view of the Palestinians is that they are not a people, but rather only individuals who are Arab, as if the threshold for a positive national identity had not yet been crossed. Most Israelis and Zionists to this day do not deviate much from this position, a relevant sign of whose strength is that active, positive support for Palestinian rights is upheld only by a tiny segment of the Jewish population. Thus, to consider one small index, Elia Zureik points out that the principal research paradigm in mainstream Israeli social science holds the Arab in a "psycho-cultural" vise. Such supposedly real and stable objects as the Arab mind, temperament, and cultural weakness predominate, while little attention is devoted to foreign domination or, for that matter, to developments within Arab history. Talal Asad further notes that Israeli ethnographic research on Palestinian Arabs, presented as indisputable fact, employs abstract categories like "ethnicity" or the "hamula" (village "clan") in ideological terms, for the "resolution of a Zionist problem," which of course was the existential presence in Palestine of a long-standing and settled population. Like all such populations, this one developed and changed historically, so that social structures like the *hamula* played greater or lesser roles at different times; it changed along with the rest of the population, its centrality diminished over time. Yet for Zionist anthropology, the *hamula* is fixed as an invariant structure, Asad says, for epistemological as well as political reasons: "it constituted a mode of control and an imputed identity for the only political existence allowed to Arab villagers in Israel."[11] Hence, the Palestinian Arabs could be regarded as at best a collection of village clans, not a people, certainly not an evolving nation.

Ideology and practice thus support each other. Of the earliest Zionist thinkers it is correct to say that the presence of resident Arabs played very little part in their views of the future Jewish homeland. The structures of Zionist settlements in Palestine itself reflected this skewed awareness, in that they were designed to emphasize Jewishness by including only Jews within their confines; conversely, non-Jews were programmatically excluded as outsiders. To this day, for instance, the *kibbutz* has never admitted Arabs except, in the years since 1967, as manual daily wage laborers. With the establishment of the Jewish state, then, the non-Jew was marked again, this time by inferiority and secondariness. As an example of what I mean, consider an article published in *Ha'aretz* on December 30, 1983. Written by Ran Kislev, it concerns the remaining Arab residents of Jaffa, an Arab city adjoining Tel Aviv, captured in 1948. The Israeli official in charge of the Arab population in what is now called "Tel Aviv-Jaffa" can only *estimate* the number of Arabs in his charge, and indeed confesses that he has very little information about the group that he oversees. This paucity of statistics must be seen against the background of data in Israel about Jews, information that is as refined and plentiful as any on earth. Kislev then concludes:

> But the main reason for the lack of information is not that the inhabitants don't want to give it. So far, there has not been one Israeli authorized institution—the state, or an academic or municipal body—that bothered to make any serious survey of the Arab population of Jaffa. Obviously no one bothered to examine the socio-economical conditions of this population. This situation continued while surveys and plans have been made concerning the urban future of Jaffa, and considerable sums of money have been given to prepare

these plans. All this is done as if the Arabs are not there, as if this obstacle, which no one knows what to do with, has disappeared because no one wants it. As if Arab Jaffa does not exist.

The point is that Kislev's account is itself part of the ideology of difference it attempts to impugn. His speculation is that Israeli Arabs are the victims of a neglect that is neither organized nor deliberate; no one bothers, no one cares, no one knows whether or not to do something, he says. Whereas:

the problems between Arabs and Jews [in Israel only] appear to lie in differences in attitudes, values, and understanding. The logical out- come of many of these studies [and of remarks such as Kislev's made by Israelis about "their" Arabs] when considered in isolation is that injustice appears to be rooted in the irrationality of individual men and not in the collective and institutional aspects of Israeli society which are rationally directed.[12]

A far stronger sign of what has issued from "the collective and institutional aspects of Israeli society" is the following item, which I reproduce in full:

As part of my job, I organized some seminars about current issues for youngsters about to be conscripted. I met with ten such groups of fifty boys each, who can be described as a representative random sample of Israel's Jewish population. The boys came from all sections of society and from all groups of ethnic origin existing within that age group. Since this happened after Finkelstein from Upper Nazareth had been interviewed on television on November 1, I chose as one of my topics the attitudes towards the Arabs of Israel. [Finkelstein's cam- paign to expel the Arabs from Upper Nazareth has stirred up a stormy debate inside Israel.] Almost all the participants in the debate said they fully identified with Finkelstein's racist attitude towards the Arabs. When I argued that the Arabs in question were citizens accorded equal rights by our laws, the typical response was that they should be deprived of Israeli citizenship.

In every discussion group there were several boys who argued that the Arabs of Israel should be physically eliminated including the old, women, and children. When I drew comparisons between Sabra and Chatila and the Nazi extermination campaign, they voiced their approval and declared in all honesty that they were willing to do the exterminating with their own hands, without guilt feelings or hang-ups. Not a single boy voiced his horror or even reservations about these remarks, but some did say that there was no need for physical extermination. It was enough to expel the Arabs across the border.

Many argued for South African style apartheid. The idea that the Arabs of Israel regarded this country as their homeland was received with amazement and contempt. Any moral arguments presented were rejected with sneers. In any one group there were never more than two or three boys with humanitarian and antiracist opinions, and I felt that they feared to express these publicly. Those few who dared to present unpopular views were indeed immediately silenced by a chorus of shouts.[13]

No ideological or social system, however, is completely effective, and we should not make the mistake of ascribing to Israel and Zionism what it is about both of them that we criticize. No more than the "non-Jew" or "the Palestinian" are they stable and essentialized objects. For within Zionism and Israel, almost as much as within the Palestinian community, it has been true—in Raymond Williams' formulation—that

> however dominant a social system may be, the very meaning of its domination involves a limitation or selection of the activities it covers so that by definition it cannot exhaust all social experience, which therefore always contains space for alternative acts and alternative intentions, which may not yet be articulated as a social institution or even project.[14]

Hence the emergence not only of a Palestinian nationalism responsive to Israeli practice, but also of many currents within Israel and Zionism challenging the systematic view (and treatment) of non-Jews. Such phenomena as draft resistance, the appearance of a civil rights movement, of organized dissent, of various acts and movements of protest, of public debate and revision—all testify to the truth of Williams' observation.

Yet these "alternative" acts and intentions, both Palestinian and Israeli, have themselves bred counteralternative practices, especially on the ideological level, and these, alas, have been extremely, if not totally, effective. Certainly the rise of Begin's Likud, its Lebanese campaigns of 1978 and 1982, the emergence of Gush Emunim, Jewish terrorism, and Meir Kahane, testify to the counterweight to which I refer. We must therefore view "difference" as challenged by many kinds of counterdifference: Internally and existentially a real and internationally acknowledged Palestinian people has appeared on the scene, rifts have appeared within the ranks of Israel's supporters and citizens, Israel now sits on vast new amounts of Arab land whose occupation and potential annexation it must justify to an increasingly critical world public. Most of all, however, major discrepancies between the discourse of Israeli democracy and knowledge of what Israeli state practice has done to non-Jews are beginning to appear, particularly in places where support for Israel is historically crucial. Whereas in the past it almost went without saying that the cause of Israel was a liberal and even progressive one, new encroachments on its ideological privileges within Western discourse are constantly being felt. The period since the 1967 War is consequently of vital importance once this perspective is kept in mind.

Since 1967 "difference," therefore, has had to be reasserted by Israel's supporters in ideologically antinomian terms. *Where* this assertion takes place has been a matter of strategic moment, but let us confine ourselves to the generally Western, more particularly American liberal constituency, especially given the fact, which totally contradicts almost all the normal complaints about Israel's vulnerability, that after Israel's enormously conclusive military victory in 1967, there can be no serious doubt that the dangers to Israel's existence are illusory. Its military is commonly held to be weaker only than those of the two superpowers; it is the world's sixth largest exporter of arms; it has at will penetrated the borders of Egypt, Lebanon, Jordan, Syria, Iraq, Saudi Arabia and taken territory from four of these states; it rules millions of Arabs in occupied lands; it intervenes with impunity in the daily life of each of these Arabs; it has killed, tortured, displaced, and deported hundreds of thousands of Arabs at a factor of forty Arabs killed for each Jew killed—all these acts are accomplished with little abatement in the praise for Israeli democracy and decency by its Western supporters. Not that these supporters have been ignorant of what Israeli policy means for non-Jews. They *have known,* but have allowed this information either to be ignored or casually to coexist with their continually positive views of Israeli society. Noam Chomsky calls this situation the Orwellian syndrome. At the same time, however, some of the leading pro-Israeli left liberal intellectuals have modified their views and theories of other matters to keep pace with the increasing drift toward extremism in Israel, as reflected in Israeli state practice. For instance, when it comes to equality, justice, or war, left liberals have altered their old views rightward as a way of not allowing these views and theories to furnish even implicit criticism of what Israel does. This is a phenomenon worth examining closely.

Consider Hannah Arendt. For many years she was closely associated with the efforts of Judah Magnes and Martin Buber on behalf of binationalism in Palestine. Although she worked for the emigration of Jews to Palestine before the war, she was always critical of mainstream Zionism, as her collection of essays, *The Jew as Pariah,* and her remarks in *The Origins of Totalitarianism* and *Eichmann in Jerusalem* testify. Yet in 1967 she supported the Jewish Defense League with money, and did so again in 1973. This information—presented without any awareness of the contradictions at work here by Elisabeth Young-Bruehl in her biography of Arendt—is remarkable for someone otherwise so compassionate and reflective on the subject of what Zionism did to Palestinians. How did the supporter of Magnes and Meir Kahane mediate the discrepancy? Significant also is Young-Bruehl's implicit (and perhaps unconscious) attempt at explaining the difficulty when she prefaces her remarks on Arendt's excited concern for Israel in 1973 with the sentence "Egypt and Syria invaded Israeli territory on Yom Kippur."[15] It should be noted that what Egypt and Syria literally invaded were, respectively, the Sinai peninsula and the Golan Heights, Egyptian and Syrian territory occupied by Israel in 1967. Thus do wishes override truth!

During the antiwar uprisings of the sixties, Israel was characterized as "not Vietnam," in the words of two prominent American liberals (Michael Walzer and Martin Peretz), as if to say that Israeli acts of conquest belong to a different genre of conquest from those of French and American interventions in Indochina. This acceptable conquest emanates from what Barbara Tuchman called the country's "terrible swift sword."[16] Not all wars are just, Walzer later went on to argue in his book *Just and Unjust Wars,* and in the main, canons of justice established for all other states were suspendable in Israel's case. Similarly for the civil libertarian Alan Dershowitz, preventive detention is elsewhere unjustifiable. But in Israel, where the "terrorist" threat is a real, present danger, the state can abrogate the norms of democratic process (although only Arabs are concerned) without ceasing to be a democracy. Such forms of legitimation for Israel's actions went on during the years after 1967 as responses to the by-now inescapable problem of Palestinian and other Arab populations visibly affected by the warlike actions of Israeli soldiers, by curfews and the blowing-up of houses, by the rampages of militant Zionist settlers. The legitimation was needed even more because Israel had by now become almost wholly dependent upon the United States for military and economic support. With continually increasing levels of aid, Israel received more U.S. dollar aid than any other country, about $1,000 per Israeli man, woman, and child every year. This includes assistance to the Israeli defense industry, outright grants, proceeds from the sale of tax-free bonds, forgiven loans, all at a rate of about $7.4 million per day ($25 billion between 1948 and 1982, and in fiscal 1984—85 more than $2.6 billion in direct military and economic assistance). These figures give some meat to the fantasy of idealism and fascination sketched by Peter Grose in *Israel in the Mind of America,* whose ideological premises almost obliterate the material foundations of the U.S.–Israeli partnership. .

Thus, Israel is a unique country, in that what it did and how it lived bore no obvious relationship to its productivity or resources. With a rate of inflation of over 300 percent in 1984, military expenditures at more than 40 percent of the GNP, dependence on underpaid Arab labor, occupation and settlement policies far in excess of production or revenue, Israel, says Gideon Spiro in a trenchant passage spoken before the MacBride Commission in 1982, does not:

> pay the price of anything that we are doing, not in the occupied territories, because Israel is in this a unique miracle. There is no country in the world which has over 100 percent inflation, which is occupying the West Bank, occupying another people, and building all those settlements with billions of dollars, and spending 30 percent of the GNP on defence—and still we can live here. I mean, somebody is paying for everything, so if everybody can live well and go abroad and buy cars, why not be for the occupation? So they are all luxury wars and people are very proud of the way we are fighting, the quick victories, the self-image of the brave Israeli—very flattering![17]

Even so, there are limits to what luxury can do. The main one for Israel during the period 1967 to 1982 was the active determination of the Palestinian people to resist the inferior, quasi-invisible, nonnational fate decreed for them by mainstream Zionist ideology and by Israeli state practice. No one needs reminders of the dramatic appearance of

Palestinian *fedayin* first in Egypt, then Jordan and Lebanon, who challenged the bankruptcy of the "Arab" armies, as well, of course, as the tyranny of Israeli occupation. The Israeli counter-response (leaving aside the Arab response, which belongs to a discussion of the ideology of "sameness") was to view Palestinian nationalist activity in essentially *reductive* terms, given that with few exceptions most Zionist ideologists had never considered the existence of Palestinian Arabs on land designated as Eretz Israel as anything more than a collection of miscellaneous people possessing no intrinsic historical or political nationalist dynamic of their own: even a quick glance at Shlomo Avineri's *The Making of Modern Zionism*—despite its Hegelian mode and show of sophistication—verifies precisely this fact. A common ideological program connects the large number of expert Israeli and Israeli-supported studies in the late sixties and seventies (all of them studying "the Palestinian problem"), with the resurgence of Zionist Revisionism in 1977 and the doctrine that Palestinians were essentially terrorists. Here, too, the convergence between left liberal and right-wing positions is notable, just as today American liberals and right-wing evangelical Christians (Jerry Falwell, Jimmy Swaggart, et al.) compete in intensity of support for Israel.

For affirmative proof of what I have just said, we can look first at official Israeli positions, which have dictated policy and which command the use of Israeli military power. True, the Israeli government concluded a peace agreement with Egypt, but it is important to remember that Zionism never had a territorial dispute with Egypt, nor, for that matter, an ideological one of a fundamental kind. Yet during the same time that Israeli policymakers and social scientists (e.g., Yeheshofat Harkabi, Shimon Shamir, Shlomo Avineri—to mention only the ones best known and quoted in the West) were discussing the unprecedentedly impinging Palestinian problem from the "socialist" labor party perspective, one Israeli government after another—Labour and Likud—refused to compromise on the issue after 1967. Jerusalem was annexed, as were sections of the Golan Heights. Gaza was brutally pacified (by Ariel Sharon mainly) by the early 1970s, and vast amounts of land were expropriated and settled in what came to be called Judea and Samaria (the change of name legitimated after 1977 simply announces what had clearly been done in fact). A whole series of severe measures—curfews, detention, long prison sentences, torture, school and university closures, houses blown up, censorship, denial of rights to build, to water access, to improvement, plus numerous deaths by shooting, dynamite, and booby traps—in the Occupied Territories made it plain that Israeli declarations of the need for direct negotiations with "the Arabs" bore little relationship to what Israelis themselves referred to as "creating facts" designed expressly to make negotiations impossible, or at least very unattractive for any Arab interlocutor who, unlike Egypt's Sadat, would press the Palestinian claim.

In the light of these developments, the role of the Zionist doves, as they came to be called, was highly ambiguous. Plausible, humane, liberal, these people, I think, were successful in getting a Western audience for their views, even though those views stopped very far short of saying anything that might restrict the ideology of difference constantly operating in Israel's favor on the ground. Others, e.g., Matti Peled, Uri Avineri, Lova Eliav, Simha Flapan, remained Zionists, but took the far more explicit and courageous position advocating Palestinian rights and national coexistence. In the course of time, both in Israel and abroad, the New Left critique of Imperialism and the Establishment would have come to focus upon Israel and its policies as a state, like others in Asia, Africa, or Latin America, which ruled an oppressed native population. What happened instead was that that sector of the liberal (or democratic) socialist Left to which I have referred stood still and prevented a true critique of Israel from taking place, a critique, that is, which would touch the ideological premises upon which Zionism acted toward the Palestinians. For a while, then, Zionist doves like Amos Oz—in Shlomo Avineri's formulation— spoke of the conflicts in Palestine as the struggle of two competing national movements, of right versus right. Reconstructing this argument, we note that its logic was based upon an admission of the Palestinians' belated appearance as a national movement, but not as a people already in Palestine before the advent of Zionist colonization. This acknowledgment of a present fact but not of its historical background required only a small adjustment in Zionist views of the ideological importance of the difference between Jew and non-Jew. Ever the ideological tactician, Avineri spoke of Israeli administration of the West Bank and Gaza as "brilliantly" improvisatory (as if there had been no precedent in Israeli history of Jews ruling over non-Jews), and in keeping with this extraordinary fiction, proposed the establishment of a two-state settlement, not as a solution to the fundamental problem of difference but as a clever, pragmatic, and tactical answer to the problem for Israel of hundreds of thousands of non-Jewish Palestinians.

Thus, you adjust to the existence of non-Jews by making no essential change in your ideological belief that Jews should rule over, be different and separate from, non-Jews.

The dovish argument therefore did not take into sufficient account the real forces (or the real interests) either of the Israeli government or of the Palestinian grievance, the two radically incommensurate with each other, and yet systemically related. The first stemmed from the historical bases of Zionist thought, concerned with Jewish settlers on a land believed to be inhabited either by no one or by an inferior people without nationhood or national aspirations: The Palestinian grievance stemmed from the revenge of an abused people who, in the words of the Palestinian National Covenants of 1964 and 1968, persisted retroactively (and ineffectively) in considering the Zionist invasion to be null and void. But as the Israeli government's line hardened, and as Menachem Begin's policies began to take effect, instead of understanding these ominous realities deriving from the original ideological separation of Zionism from the Palestinian realities on the ground, the doves and their liberal constituency gradually accommodated themselves to what Begin did. No one did this more completely than Avineri, a socialist who during the Israeli siege of Beirut was used by the army to indoctrinate the troops on the advisability of taking West Beirut by force![18]

But to return to "pure" ideology. In the first place, the conflict between Palestinian non-Jew and Israeli Jew was never discussed in the theoretical or philosophic terms that might have elucidated its core as an ideology imposed upon a "different" (i.e., non-Jewish) population. The Palestinians were routinely discussed in pragmatic and essentialist terms, pragmatic when their claims were felt at all (ergo, let us solve the Palestinian problem), essentialist when their claims were felt as too great (ergo, Palestinians are nothing but terrorists). The pragmatic bias always challenged the liberal intellectual to come up with "solutions," as if solutions could come about because intellectuals proposed them to waiting politicians. The essentialists would regularly revert to describing Palestinians as "the inhabitants of Judea and Samaria." Usually both exercises concluded with Zionists berating Palestinians for not being forthcoming enough, for not recognizing Israel, for not renouncing violence, for not being like Peace Now, as if all of these things were equal in magnitude to the destruction of Palestinian society and the continued ethnocide waged by the Israeli government, in possession of all the land and all the weapons, against the Palestinian people.

Along with this performance went another, which was to be *for* Palestinian rights in general but *against* them and their representatives in particular. This move has been preferred by socialists like Irving Howe and Michael Walzer, who speak openly against Begin (as they should)—but also speak cold-bloodedly of *destroying* the only authentic representatives of Palestinian nationalism, and with undisguised revulsion at the "unspeakable" Arafat. There is no other way to understand such thinkers, who claim to be positive about the need for a Palestinian solution, but adamantly oppose the Palestinians' right to represent themselves and their own program.

This line was entirely understandable, since after the 1982 War there has been a tremendous Zionist effort—to which I shall return in a moment—to bludgeon the media and the public back into line. Everything shown on TV screens in the West has now been called into question, as if the traumatic siege of Beirut and the enormous human cost of the war to Palestinians and Lebanese never really occurred. What took place, runs the Zionist argument proliferating more or less everywhere, was the implementation of an anti-Semitic media bias, deliberately misrepresenting a clean, relatively painless surgical Israeli entry into Lebanon to purify South Lebanon of a few terrorists. The result of putting this preposterous message across has been that anyone writing about Lebanon and Israel either has had to reinvent the wheel, so to speak, or to compile so overwhelmingly complete a set of facts as to preclude any discussion of the radical problem of the ideology of separation itself. In other words, you must either try to tell the story of the Palestinians from scratch, or—no less onerous—you have to put forth the most detailed facts possible, facts restricted to what is taking place.[19]

[III]

That such distinctions, separations, disconnections are still made boggles the mind. To the Palestinians, Israel is a Jewish state programmatically associated with the systematic denial of Palestinian national, human, and political rights. On almost every conceivable level of history, contemporary actuality, ideological argument, this has always been the case. Its denial is therefore a dramatic symptom of an ideology of difference blind to the origin which has brought about the present horrors. As I write these lines, we must remember, for instance, that Israeli administrators have just shut down a West Bank university for four months on the grounds of its endangering Israeli security in having sponsored a festival of Palestinian culture. Thousands of students are deprived either of entrance or of graduation. And all this occurs simultaneously with the total disruption of life in South Lebanon and the devastation of its economy due to Israeli occupation. In addition we need to think of the perpetually occurring detail of Israeli encroachment on Palestinian life—the dozens of illegal settlements, the humiliating searches and detentions, the torture and imprisonment of "suspects," the prevention of development and building, the control of water supplies to every Palestinian community.

As I said, none of this is secret, although it is routinely circumvented by Israel's European and American supporters. Faced with the evidence, the supporters of conscience resort to anguished dirges on the death of the Zionist dream, as if that dream weren't always a bad one for the Palestinians who watched their land being taken away from them, and they and their families displaced. And as if laments for the loss of early Zionist idealism were not also effective in shutting out the painful truth that, no less than the present leaders of Israel, the early Zionist settlers either overlooked the Arabs completely or actively sought their removal. But at least these conscience-stricken critics of present Israeli policy see what is taking place now with some degree of regret, even if they use that regret to exonerate—and hence differentiate from all other white settlers in Africa and Asia—the early Zionist dreamers who, it is claimed, were not really interested in doing what other colonizing Europeans did to *their* natives.

As for Israel's more muscular supporters, their current behavior is characterized by a different, far more brutal and less nostalgic atavism. Since the Israeli invasion, the largest, wealthiest, and most organized Jewish community in the world, the American, has moved on several fronts. Its publicists and agents have attacked anyone criticizing Israel as anti-Semitic, pro-terrorist, and a Soviet stooge. Once laid down, this framework is used in the various books and hit lists published by AIPAC as a device for discouraging any criticism of Israel and as a means of actively punishing the critics. The goal is to assure continued and unqualified congressional, financial, and military support for Israel so that even vaguely "anti-Israel" sounds will not come out of official Washington: a formidable task. The most visible aspect of this campaign, however, has occurred on the ideological level, in the discourse of culture and of history. I referred earlier to two books published in

1984, both of them with enormous public attention (and, in the case of Uris's *The Hajj,* enormous sales), both of them with—for the Palestinian people—clear political messages. One is Joan Peters' *From Time Immemorial,* whose subject is nothing less than the Palestinians' nonexistence, a theme unimaginable during the period 1974 to 1982, although as anyone familiar with Israeli social science literature will confirm, well known during the fifties. Using various sources and documents, Peters undertakes to prove that the people who call themselves Palestinians today are in fact a myth: Most of them are 1948 refugees, yes, but almost all really came from neighboring Arab countries, attracted to Palestine during the years immediately before 1948 by the success and prosperity of Jewish settlements. For them to claim repatriation in Palestine now is, she says, inappropriate. Her other major point is that since most of the Israeli Jews from Arab countries were expelled by Arab regimes, there was an exchange of populations—Arab refugees for Jewish refugees—to which Israel has accommodated by resettling the Jews as Israeli citizens, but of which the Arabs have remained oblivious, allowing the Palestinians to remain as a political nuisance to themselves and to the world in general.

Peters' book has been launched with accolades and testimonials of every variety; the jacket is blazoned with approving quotations from political figures of nearly every stripe, authors and intellectuals like Barbara Tuchman and Saul Bellow, august personalities and all-purpose sages. The book has been presented on various radio programs and talk shows, and of course it has been reviewed in prominent journals and newspapers. This is not the place to refute its specious arguments or its almost incredibly coarse attempts at proof. Nor should we spend much time demonstrating how an only slightly altered version of its thesis can, with a good deal more justice, be applied to European Jewish settlers in Palestine who after an "absence" of 2,000 years came to claim Palestine from its native residents. At least Peters' Palestinian frauds want repatriation after two or three years' residence in Palestine: The Polish, Russian, and American *olehs* came to Palestine only with a millennial absence and promises from God and Lord Balfour. Nor is it worth going into the racist impulses dictating her book's main line, which is that of denying people-hood to a non-European, non-Jewish people simply on the basis of supervening (but doctored and totally misleading) statistics and facts, irrespective of historical experience, demonstrated communality, or actual political will. What is noteworthy about the book, on the contrary, is what it does not say, what is implicit in its appearance, what constitutes it as an event.

In the first place, it represents a natural analogue to the concerted, sustained Israeli attack upon Palestinian nationalism, the invasion of Lebanon, and the unstated desires of the Jewish state (and of the Zionist dream) that the Palestinians do not exist, or, if they do, they are to be wished away, expelled, or slaughtered. To deprive the Palestinians of their legitimacy *as Palestinians* is nothing less than declaring them Orwellian nonpersons, as the Ministry of Truth does to those it eliminates in *1984,* finding evidence that disputes the existential reality, and then using it retroactively to wish away a person's historical presence. If you thought you were a Palestinian, you were wrong. You really came from someplace else, and therefore *are* someone else.

In the second place, Peters' book exactly reproduces the schizophrenic ideological formation within Israel and doctrinal Zionism that decrees the Palestinians to be present-absentees. The difference is that this is now done for a general American audience, and not simply in the pages of a specialized journal or for a local Israeli audience. The book depends upon the general audience's knowledge of "the Palestinians," who have become a staple of contemporary Western journalism, to say nothing of numerous UN resolutions, countless studies, and innumerable declarations almost everywhere in the world. Before 1982 such an exercise as Peters' would have seemed improbable, even preposterous. Now, however, it is both reactive and overstated, as if Generals Sharon and Eytan were given license in print to finish the job they couldn't complete in Lebanon. It displays the confidence and defensiveness of a political line unconcerned with credibility or persuasion. Willfulness and assertion have become paramount, much as the Reaganism to which the book is closely tied asserts that the world must either behave as America says it should behave or it risks being nuked. Ideology has entirely overridden truth. If Zionist propaganda in the West had once denied the Palestinians' presence by not talking about them, now it talks about them obsessively by saying that they really do not exist. You are not who you say you are because I can prove you were never really you.

Yet Joan Peters' *From Time Immemorial* is mild and even benign when compared with Uris's *The Hajj.* I must confess at the outset that I could not finish its 600 pages, so filled with sheer disgusting hatred are they. This book is a best-seller that makes the worst Nazi anti-Semitism seem restrained. It is intended as a "fiction," offering to place before a wide audience the reality of Arab Palestinian life, Islamic religion, contemporary Middle Eastern history and politics. Its premises are simple: The Arab is a lecherous, deceitful, murderous, irrational, larcenous, and utterly reprehensible subhuman, whereas the Jew (Uris is at least totally uncompromising in his portrayals) is noble, intelligent, understanding, courageous, and, above all, deserving of Palestine. Of this diseased work it can be said without fear of serious contradiction that in its hatred, fear, and demented inability to deal with reality, it could only be the production of an American supporter of Israel writing about the Muslim Arabs generally, the Palestinians in particular, at this moment. It expresses the horror and loathing of someone so gorged on strength and contempt for what he has been attempting to destroy that he can suspend even the elementary protocols writing about another group of people. And lest we think of Uris as a vulgar aberration, we should remember that he has been published by Doubleday, that he has been on the best-seller list for many weeks, and that his book is advertised publicly as a work of penetrating, compassionate, and courageous humanism. Only the Zionism of Begin, Sharon, and Gush Emunim could have brought forth Uris.

But Uris's brand of gutter racism has its "high-class" equivalent: that of *The New Republic,* whose suave deceits and rabid pronouncements still earn it the respect of liberals and right-thinking intellectuals who write for and read it. Consider the following, by the magazine's editor, Martin Peretz. It is a description of a play put on at the American Repertory Theater in Cambridge,

> in which a visiting German businessman, an American Jewess come as an immigrant, and an Arab Palestinian find themselves taking refuge in a bomb shelter in Jerusalem under Arab siege. If there is something a bit startling about the merging empathy between the play's German and its Jew, even less have the universalist prejudices of our culture prepared us for its Arab—a crazed Arab, to be sure, but crazed in the distinctive ways of his culture. He is intoxicated by language, cannot discern between fantasy and reality, abhors compromise, always blames others for his predicament, and in the end lances the painful boil of his frustrations in a pointless, though momentarily gratifying, act of bloodlust. This is a political play and what makes it compelling is its pessimism, which is to say its truthfulness. We have seen this play's Arab in Tripoli and in Damascus, and in recent weeks hijacking a bus to Gaza and shooting up a street of innocents in Jerusalem. On

the Rep. stage he is a fictional character, of course, but in the real
world it is not he but his "moderate" brother who is a figment of the
imagination.[20]

Such remarks, which impugn an entire race, *cannot today be printed
in the West about any other people:* They are, however, legitimized by
liberals not because of any long-standing "blood feud" between Arabs
and Jews, but entirely because the ideology of difference fueling
Zionism has evolved to the point where any Arab, any non-Jew, any
Palestinian can be tolerated only in the terms employed by Uris and
Peretz. Note how "the Arab" is decontextualized entirely, then made
to play the role of crazed terrorist run amok—all without reference
to the history of occupied Gaza, for example, brutally pacified and
ruled without quarter or mercy, or any reference to the remarks of
General Eytan, who unlike a camp-dwelling refugee can and does
deliver on promises to turn West Bank Palestinians into "drugged
roaches in a bottle." To say of such writers as Uris and Peretz that
what they write about Arabs is traceable to what Nazis said about Jews,
or what South African whites have said about blacks, is not to exaggerate. Finally, we may note with regret, if not alarm, how this ideology
of difference has become almost a touchstone of apostasy for former
Left-liberals who have abandoned an earlier politics for a safer one.
The Conor Cruise O'Brien who once censured Camus for not even
mentioning the name of the Arab killed by Meursault, has now become a Zionist publicist who regularly says absolutely nothing about
Palestinian dispossession in his attacks on "terrorism"; similarly,
O'Brien—once an anti-imperialist specialist on Africa—now gives
Naipaulian lectures to Third World leaders on how imperialism is not
to blame for their difficulties, but that they themselves are.

Difference, in short, can become an ideological infection and a
generalized *trahison des clercs.* I note its ravagements not to turn the
clock back to an earlier, presumably less unpleasant period, nor to
score points, but as a method for understanding the unprecedented
miseries of a part of the world beset with massive socioeconomic
problems as well as numerous inhibiting ideologies and doctrines, most
of them glossed over by fraud, deceit, and utter contempt for the
truth. Rarely has the Middle East seemed as factionalized and as riven
as today—Zionism, Shiite zealotry, Maronite exclusivism, plus every
kind of reactive nationalism, underwrite a political setting as stagnant
as it is deadly. Anyone proposing political community as an alternative

owes it to his or her audience to understand the dangers of what we have now; otherwise it is all too easy to fall into another version of the Zionist dream. I do not think as Palestinians that there is even a remote possibility that we can return to a pristine, undivided past. For us, the only hope is a community with Zionist and non-Zionist Jews on the land of historical Palestine. We have yet to find the way to achieve this goal, especially since conflict and hostility are imposed on us by our far more powerful opponents. But if we can at least succeed in getting people to testify to what conscience and common sense tell them, we shall have done something to mitigate the effects of an ideology of difference hitherto unrestrained by reason or humanity.

The only way to do this, I believe, is to grasp and understand the problem of difference, as exemplified in the relationship between Israel and the Palestinians, and to do so as radically, as fully, and as variously as possible. We must reckon with the history and actual facts of Israel as a state and a society with a continuity and integrity of its own. To do so, I hasten to add, is not simply to enumerate what Israel did to the Palestinians; it is certainly more than that. Even if it is impossible for Palestinians to assent to the many paeans of praise for "the miracle of Israel," it is quite possible for us to appreciate the impressive social, political, and cultural gains of the Jewish state for Jews themselves.

One must distinguish, then, between two existing, powerful, and deeply felt views about the current state of Israel. On the one hand is the unqualified assent to its present structure and practices; on the other is the rejection of this situation felt by most Palestinians. If we reify the ideology of difference that dominates views on either side, we either prolong what has been for nearly two decades effective stagnation, or we authorize the inevitable annihilation of one or the other antagonist. But if we strive toward a more creative sense of "difference," one that acknowledges the historical, cultural, and material distinctions between Jews and Palestinian Arabs, while refusing to privilege the experience or the contemporary situation of either, we shall, it is to be hoped, produce a whole new dynamic in this relationship. The choices are evident enough. The difficult task is to realize them in the world, a task that must begin with a new logic in which "difference" does not entail "domination."

Published in *Critical Inquiry*, September 1985.

CHAPTER 12

On Palestinian Identity: A Conversation with Salman Rushdie

[1986]

SALMAN RUSHDIE: The purpose of this evening is to talk about Edward's new book, *After the Last Sky*.[21] First I would like briefly to introduce Edward—although, judging by the number of people who have come and are unable to get in, that may hardly be necessary. For those of us who see the struggle between Eastern and Western descriptions of the world as both an internal and an external struggle, Edward Said has for many years been an especially important voice. Professor of English and Comparative Literature at Columbia and author of literary criticism on, among others, Joseph Conrad, Edward has always had the distinguishing feature that he reads the world as closely as he reads books. We need only think of that major trilogy which precedes *After the Last Sky*. In the first volume, *Orientalism*, he analyzed "the affiliation of knowledge with power," discussing how the scholars of the period of Empire helped to create an image of the East which provided the justification for the supremacist ideology of imperialism. This was followed by *The Question of Palestine*, which described the struggle between a world primarily shaped by Western ideas—that of Zionism and later of Israel—and the largely "Oriental" realities of Arab Palestine. Then came *Covering Islam*, subtitled "How the Media and the Experts Determine How We See the Rest of the World," in which the West's invention of the East is, so to speak, brought up-to-date through a discussion of responses to the Islamic revival.

After the Last Sky is a collaborative venture with Jean Mohr—a photographer who may be known to you from John Berger's study of immigrant labor in Europe, *A Seventh Man*. Its title is taken from a poem, "The Earth Is Closing on Us," by the national poet of Palestine, Mahmoud Darwish, and I would like to start by reading this.

The Earth is closing on us
pushing us through the last passage
and we tear off our limbs to pass through.
The Earth is squeezing us.
I wish we were its wheat
so we could die and live again.
I wish the Earth was our mother
so she'd be kind to us.
I wish we were pictures on the rocks
for our dreams to carry as mirrors.
We saw the faces of those to be killed
by the last of us in the last defence of the soul.
We cried over their children's feast.
We saw the faces of those who will throw
our children out of the window of this last space.
Our star will hang up mirrors.
Where should we go after the last frontiers?
Where should the birds fly after the last sky?
Where should the plants sleep after the last breath of air?
We will write our names with scarlet steam.
We will cut off the hand of the song to be finished by our flesh.
We will die here, here in the last passage.
Here and here our blood will plant its olive tree.[22]

After the last sky there is no sky. After the last border there is no land. The first part of Edward's book is called "States." It is a passionate and very moving meditation on displacement, on landlessness, on exile and identity. He asks, for example, in what sense Palestinians can be said to exist. He says:

Do we exist? What proof do we have? The further we get from the Palestine of our past, the more precarious our status, the more disrupted our being, the more intermittent our presence. When did we become a people? When did we stop being one? Or are we in the process of becoming one? What do those big questions have to do with our intimate relationships with each other and with others? We frequently end our letters with the motto "Palestinian love" or "Palestinian kisses." Are there really such things as Palestinian intimacy and embraces, or are they simply intimacy and embraces—experiences common to everyone, neither politically significant nor particular to a nation or a people?

Edward comes, as he puts it, from "a minority inside a minority"—a position with which I feel some sympathy, having also come from a minority group within a minority group. It is a kind of Chinese box that he describes: "My family and I were members of a tiny Protestant group within a much larger Greek Orthodox Christian minority, within the larger Sunni Islam majority." He then goes on to discuss the condition of Palestinians through the mediation of a number of recent literary works. One of these, incorrectly called an Arab Tristram Shandy in the blurb, is a wonderful comic novel about the secret life of somebody called Said, *The Ill-Fated Pessoptimist*.[23] A pessoptimist, as you can see, is a person with a problem about how he sees the world. Said claims all manner of things, including, in chapter one, to have met creatures from outer space:

In the so-called age of ignorance before Islam, our ancestors used to form their gods from dates and eat them when in need. Who is more ignorant then, dear sir, I or those who ate their gods? You might say it is better for people to eat their gods than for the gods to eat them. I would respond, yes, but their gods were made of dates.

A crucial idea in *After the Last Sky* concerns the meaning of the Palestinian experience for the form of works of art made by Palestinians. In Edward's view, the broken or discontinuous nature of Palestinian experience entails that classic rules about form or structure cannot be true to that experience; rather, it is necessary to work through a kind of chaos or unstable form that will accurately express its essential instability. Edward then proceeds to introduce the theme—which is developed later in the book—that the history of Palestine has turned the insider (the Palestinian Arab) into the outsider. This point is illustrated by a photograph of Nazareth taken from a position in what is called Upper Nazareth—an area which did not exist in the time of Arab Palestine. Thus Arab Palestine is seen from the point of view of a new, invented Palestine, and the inside experience of the old Palestine has become the external experience in the photograph. And yet the Palestinians have remained.

> It would be easier
> to catch fried fish in the milky way
> to plough the sea
> or to teach the alligator speech
> than to make us leave.[24]

In Part Two, "Interiors," which greatly develops the theme of the insider and the outsider, Edward refers to a change in the status of the Palestinians who are inside Palestine. Until recently, among the Palestinian community in general, there was a slight discounting of those who remained inside, as if they were somehow contaminated by the proximity of the Jews. Now, however, the situation has been inverted: Those who go on living there, maintaining a Palestinian culture and obliging the world to recognize their existence, have acquired a greater status in the eyes of other Palestinians.

This experience of being inside Palestinianness is presented as a series of codes which, though incomprehensible to outsiders, are instantly communicated by Palestinians when they meet one another. The only way in which to show your insiderness is precisely through the expression of those codes. There is a very funny incident in which Edward receives a letter, via a complete stranger, from a man who has built his *Palestinian* identity as a karate expert. "What was the message to me?" Edward asks.

> First of all he was inside, and using the good offices of a sympathetic outsider to contact me, an insider who was now outside Jerusalem, the place of our common origin. That he wrote my name in English was as much a sign that he too could deal with the world I lived in as it was that he followed what I did. The time had come to demonstrate that the Edward Saids had better remember that we were being watched by karate experts. Karate does not stand for self-development but only for the repeated act of being a Palestinian karate expert. A Palestinian—it is as if the activity of repeating prevents us and others from skipping us or overlooking us entirely.

He then gives a number of other examples of repeating the behavior in order to make it Palestinian behavior, and thus existing through that repetition. There also seems to be a compulsion to excess, illustrated in various ways, both tragic and comic, within the book. One of the problems of being Palestinian is that the idea of interior is regularly invaded by other people's descriptions, by other people's attempts to control what it is to occupy that space—whether it be Jordanian Arabs who say there is no difference between a Jordanian and a Palestinian, or Israelis who claim that the land is not Palestine but Israel.

The third part, "Emergence," and the fourth part, "Past and Future," turn from such passionate and emotive—or certainly moving—writing to a discussion of what it actually is or might be to be a Palestinian. There is also an account of the power to which Palestinians are subject, of the way in which even their names have been altered through the superimposition of Hebrew transliteration. As a mark of resistance, Palestinians are now seeking to reassert their identity by going back to the old Arabic forms: Abu Ammar, for example, instead of Yasir Arafat. On various occasions the very meaning of names has been changed. Thus the largest refugee camp in Lebanon, Ein el Hilwé, becomes Ein el-Khilwé in the Hebrew transliteration: a name which means "sweet spring" has been turned into something like "spring in the empty place." Edward sees in this an allusion to mass graves and the regularly razed and not always rebuilt camps. "I also register the thought," he writes, "that Israel has indeed emptied the camps with its Palestinian wellspring."

The text goes on to talk about Zionism, which he addressed in his earlier book, *The Question of Palestine.* I hope that we will return to this later, but we should note the difficulty in making any kind of critique of Zionism without being instantly charged with anti-Semitism. Clearly it is important to understand Zionism as a historical process, as existing in a context and having certain historical functions. A further idea in these later sections of the book is that, in the West, everyone has come to think of exile as a primarily literary and bourgeois state. Exiles appear to have chosen a middle-class situation in which great thoughts can be thought. In the case of the Palestinians, however, exile is a mass phenomenon: It is the mass that is exiled and not just the bourgeoisie.

Finally Edward poses a series of questions which come down to the original one of Palestinian existence: "What happens to landless people? However you exist in the world, what do you preserve of yourselves? What do you abandon?" I find one passage particularly valuable, as it connects with many things I have been thinking about. "Our truest reality," he writes, "is expressed in the way we cross over from one place to another. We are migrants and perhaps hybrids, in but not of any situation in which we find ourselves. This is the deepest continuity of our lives as a nation in exile and constantly on the move." He also criticizes the great concentration of the Palestinian cause on its military expression, referring to the dangers of cultural loss or absence.

I would like to begin by asking a question. Some of you may know that Edward recently received threats to his safety from the Jewish Defense League in America, and I think it is important for us to appreciate that to be a Palestinian in New York—in many ways *the* Palestinian—is not the easiest of fates. I shall tell two stories, one tragic and one comic, and then ask Edward to talk about how it feels to be a Palestinian in New York.

The comic one is of my sister, who was repeatedly asked in California where she came from. When she said, "Pakistan," most people seemed to have no idea what this meant. One American said: "Oh, yes, Pakestine!" and immediately started talking about his Jewish friends. It is impossible to overestimate the consequences of American ignorance on world affairs. The less comic story is that in January, when I was at the PEN Congress in New York, the American writer Cynthia Ozick took it upon herself to circulate a petition which described Chancellor Kreisky of Austria as an anti-Semite. Why was he an anti-Semite—this man who is himself a Jew and has given refuge to tens, perhaps hundreds, or thousands of Jews leaving the Soviet Union? Because he had had a conversation with Yasir Arafat. The alarming thing is that this petition, on the face of it quite absurd, should have been taken so seriously by participants at the Congress. There was even a moment when I felt nervously that since no one else seemed to be speaking about Palestine, I might have to myself. But the defense came from Pierre Trudeau, of all people, who spoke very movingly about the Palestinian cause. These are some of the extraordinary things that happen in New York. Edward, you are the man on the spot. Is it getting worse or better? How does it feel?

EDWARD SAID: Well, I think it is getting worse. First of all, most people in New York who feel strongly about Palestine and Palestinians have had no direct experience of either at all. They think of them essentially in terms of what they have seen on television: bomb scares, murders, and what the secretary of state and others call terrorism. This produces a kind of groundless passion, so that when I am introduced to someone who may have heard of me, they react in a very strange way that suggests "maybe you're not as bad as you seem." The fact that I speak English, and do it reasonably well, adds to the complications, and most people eventually concentrate on my work as an English professor for the rest of the conversation. But you do feel a new kind of violence around you, which is a result of 1982. An important break with the past occurred then, both for people who have supported Israel in the United States, and for people like us, for whom the destruction of Beirut, our Beirut, was the end of an era. Most of the time you can feel that you are leading a normal life, but every so often you are brought up against a threat or an allusion to something which is deeply unpleasant. You always feel outside in some way.

SR: Has there been any change in your ability to publish or talk about the Palestinian issue?

ES: To some extent. This is one issue on which, as you know, there is a left-right break in America, and there are still a few groups, a few people—like Chomsky, Gore Vidal, or Alexander Cockburn—who are willing to raise it publicly. But most people tend to think that it is better left to the crazies. There are fewer hospitable places, and you end up publishing for a smaller audience. Ironically, you also become tokenized, so that whenever there is a hijacking or some such incident, I get phone calls from the media asking me to come along and comment. It's a very strange feeling to be seen as a kind of representative of terrorism.

SR: Yes. There seems to be a quite extraordinary assumption that you should know so much.

ES: You're treated like a diplomat of terrorism, with a place at the table. I remember one occasion, though, when I was invited to a television debate with the Israeli ambassador—I think it was about the *Achille Lauro* incident. Not only would he not sit in the same room with me; he wanted to be in a different building, so as not to be contaminated by my presence. The interviewer said to the national audience: "You know, Professor Said and Ambassador Netanyahu refuse to speak to each other, the Israeli ambassador won't speak to him and he won't . . ." But then I interrupted and said: "No, no, I am perfectly willing to speak to him, but he won't . . ." The moderator replied: "Well, I stand corrected. Mr. Ambassador, why won't you speak to Professor Said?" "Because he wants to kill me." The moderator, without batting an eyelid, urged: "Oh, really, tell us about it." And the ambassador went on about how Palestinians want to kill the Israelis, and so on. It was really a totally absurd situation.

Perhaps I should mention that I had taken along my young son to the TV studio—a very alert boy, quite different from his sister, who is only twelve and finds it very difficult to handle her background or that of her parents. My son has a great interest in the whole issue: He went with me in 1984, for example, when I attended the meeting of the Palestinian National Council in Jordan. In fact, he is two people: At times he's simply Wadie Said, speaking with a normal American accent; at others he's a Palestinian speaking English, with a rather heavy Arabic accent, calling me *Doktor* and generally treating me with ironic veneration.

SR: I'd now like to ask you the opposite question. How is it to be a New York Palestinian in Palestine?

ES: Sometimes I have the strange feeling that I'm the only Palestinian in New York—partly because there aren't many Palestinians in the city, and partly because even they probably think of me as a kind of freak. There is something peculiar about meeting me there, and it's odd that I persist in this crazy New York existence in which nobody feels at home, except probably myself. You should remember that I haven't been to Palestine since the mid-sixties, and since 1982 I haven't been to many parts of the Arab world. Many of us in this strange situation are beginning to form a different kind of community, which is based not on everyday experience but on long-distance telephone calls and other activities that occur infrequently. It is a marginal existence, with no center to it.

SR: You say you don't like calling it a Palestinian diaspora. Why is that?

ES: I suppose there is a sense in which, as one man wrote in a note to me from Jerusalem, we are "the Jews of the Arab world." But I think our experience is really quite different and beyond such attempts to draw parallels. Perhaps its dimension is much more modest. In any case the idea that there is a kind of redemptive homeland doesn't answer to my view of things.

SR: So let me put to you your own question. Do you exist? And if so, what proof do you have? In what sense is there a Palestinian nation?

ES: First of all, in the sense that a lot of people have memories or show great interest in looking into the past for a sign of coherent community. Many, too—especially younger-generation scholars—are trying to discover things about the Palestinian political and cultural experience that mark it off from the rest of the Arab world. Secondly, there is the tradition of setting up replicas of Palestinian organizations in places as far afield as Australia or South America. It is quite remarkable that people will come to live in say, Youngstown, Ohio—a town I don't know, but you can imagine what it's like—and remain on top of the latest events in Beirut or the current disagreements between the Popular Front and al-Fatah, and yet not even know the name of the mayor of Youngstown or how he is elected. Maybe they will just assume that he is put there by somebody rather than being elected. Finally, you can see from Jean Mohr's pictures that the Palestinians are a people who move a lot, who are always carrying bags from one place to another. This gives us a further sense of identity as a people. And we say it loudly enough, repetitiously enough, and stridently enough, strong in the knowledge that they haven't been able to get rid of us. It is a great feeling—call it positive or pessoptimistic—to wake up in the morning and say: "Well, they didn't bump me off."

SR: To illustrate this point, that things could be worse, you tell the story of a mother whose son died very soon after his wedding. While the bride is still mourning, she says: "Thank God it has happened in this way and not in another way!" The bride then gets very angry and says: "How dare you say that! What could possibly be a worse way?" But the mother-in-law replies: "Well, you know, if he grew old and you left him for another man and then he died, that would be worse. So it's better that he dies now."

ES: Exactly. You are always inventing worse scenarios.

SR: It's very difficult to work out whether this is optimism or pessimism. That's why it is called pessoptimism. Would you like to say something now about the codes by which Palestinians exist and recognize each other—and about the idea of repetition and excess as a way of existing?

ES: Let me tell you another story that will show you what I mean. A close friend of mine once came to my house and stayed overnight. In the morning we had breakfast, which included yogurt cheese with a special herb, *za'tar*. This combination probably exists all over the Arab world, and certainly in Palestine, Syria, and Lebanon. But my friend said: "There, you see. It's a sign of a Palestinian home that it has *za'tar* in it." Being a poet, he then expatiated at great and tedious length on Palestinian cuisine, which is generally very much like Lebanese and Syrian cuisine, and by the end of the morning we were both convinced that we had a totally distinct national cuisine.

SR: So because a Palestinian chooses to do something it becomes the Palestinian thing to do?

ES: That's absolutely right. But even among Palestinians there are certain code words that define which camp or group the speaker comes from— whether from the Popular Front, which believes in the complete liberation of Palestine, or from the Fatah, which believes in a negotiated settlement. They will choose a different set of words when they talk about national liberation. Then there are the regional accents. It is very strange indeed to meet a Palestinian kid in Lebanon who was born in some refugee camp and has never been to Palestine but who carries the inflections of Haifa, or Jaffa, in his Lebanese Arabic.

SR: Let us turn to the idea of excess. You talk about how you find yourself obliged to carry too much luggage wherever you go. But more seriously, I remember that dialogue between a captured Palestinian guerrilla and an Israeli broadcaster in which the guerrilla appears to be implicating himself in the most heinous crimes but is in fact sending up the entire event by a colossal excess of apologies. The broadcaster is too tuned into his own set of attitudes to realize what is going on.

ES: Yes. It was in 1982 in southern Lebanon, when Israeli radio would often put captured guerrillas on the air as a form of psychological warfare. But in the case you are talking about, no one was deceived. In fact, the Palestinians in Beirut made a cassette recording of the whole show and played it back in the evening as a way of entertaining people. Let me translate à sample:

Israeli broadcaster: Your name?

Captured Palestinian: Ahmed Abdul Hamid Abu Site.

Israeli: What is your movement name?

Palestinian: My movement name is Abu Leil [which in English means Father of Night, with a rather threatening, horrible sound to it].

Israeli: Tell me, Mr. Abu Leil, to which terrorist organization do you belong?

Palestinian: I belong to the Popular Front for the Liberation . . . I mean terrorization of Palestine.

Israeli: And when did you get involved in the terrorist organization?

Palestinian: When I first became aware of terrorism.

Israeli: What was your mission in South Lebanon?

Palestinian: My mission was terrorism. In other words, we would enter villages and just terrorize the occupants. And whenever there were women and children in particular, we would terrorize everything, and all we did was terrorism.

Israeli: And did you practice terrorism out of belief in a cause or just for money?

Palestinian: No, just for money. What kind of cause is this anyway? Is there still a cause? We sold out a long time ago.

Israeli: Tell me—where do the terrorist organizations get their money?

Palestinian: From anyone who has spare money for terrorism.

Israeli: What is your opinion of the terrorist Arafat?

Palestinian: I swear that he is the greatest terrorist of all. He is the one who sold us and the cause out. His whole life is terrorism. [Of course, to a Palestinian this could mean that he is the most committed of all, but it sounds as if he is just a total sellout.]

Israeli: What is your opinion of the way in which the Israeli defense forces have conducted themselves?

Palestinian: On my honor, we thank the Israeli defense forces for their good treatment of each terrorist.

Israeli: Do you have any advice for other terrorists, who are still terrorizing and attacking the IDF?

Palestinian: My advice to them is to surrender their arms to the IDF. What they will find there is the best possible treatment.

Israeli: Lastly, Mr. Terrorist, would you like to send a message to your family?

Palestinian: I would like to assure my family and friends that I am in good health. I would also like to thank the enemy broadcasting facility for letting me speak out like this.

Israeli: You mean the Voice of Israel?

Palestinian: Yes, yes, sir. Thank you, sir. Yes, of course, sir.

SR: And this went out over the air?

ES: Absolutely. It was put out on a daily basis, and recorded in Beirut and played back to the guerrillas. It's a very funny and wonderful story.

SR: You also talk about a photo-article in a fashion magazine, under the headline "Terrorist Couture," which claims that the Palestinians are not really Palestinians because they have simply hijacked Arab dress and renamed it Palestinian.

ES: We do it all the time!

SR: The article also claims that this supposedly distinctive dress is not that of the people but of the upper middle class. Referring to the American author of the article, Sharon Churcher, you write: "In the larger scheme of things . . . she is somebody doing a hack job on a hack fashion magazine." And yet you say you feel the need to go right back to the beginning, to explain the whole history of Palestine in order to unmake Sharon Churcher's lie and show that this is in fact genuinely popular Palestinian dress. Doesn't this need to go back again and again over the same story become tiring?

ES: It does, but you do it anyway. It is like trying to find the magical moment when everything starts, as in *Midnight's Children*. You know midnight, and so you go back. But it is very hard to do that because you have to work out everything and get past a lot of questions in the daily press about why Palestinians don't just stay where they are and stop causing trouble. That immediately launches you into a tremendous harangue, as you explain to people: "My mother was born in Nazareth, my father was born in Jerusalem. . . ." The interesting thing is that there seems to be nothing in the world which sustains the story; unless you go on telling it, it will just drop and disappear.

SR: The need to be perpetually told.

ES: Exactly. The other narratives have a kind of permanence or institutional existence and you just have to try to work away at them.

SR: This is one of the things you criticize from within Palestinianness: the lack of any serious effort to institutionalize the story, to give it an objective existence.

ES: That's right. It is interesting that right up to 1948, most of the writing by Palestinians expressed a fear that they were about to lose their country. Their descriptions of cities and other places in Palestine appeared as a kind of pleading before a tribunal. After the dispersion of the Palestinians, however, there was a curious period of silence until a new Palestinian literature began to develop in the fifties and, above all, the sixties. Given the size of this achievement, it is strange that no narrative of Palestinian history has ever been institutionalized in a definitive masterwork. There never seems to be enough time, and one always has the impression that one's enemy—in this case the Israelis—is trying to take the archive away. The gravest image for me in 1982 was of the Israelis shipping out the archives of the Palestine Research Centre in Beirut to Tel Aviv.

SR: In the context of literature rather than history, you argue that the inadequacy of the narrative is due to the discontinuity of Palestinian existence. Is this connected with the problem of writing a history?

ES: Yes. There are many different kinds of Palestinian experience, which cannot all be assembled into one. One would therefore have to write parallel histories of the communities in Lebanon, the Occupied Territories, and so on. That is the central problem. It is almost impossible to imagine a single narrative: It would have to be the kind of crazy history that comes out in *Midnight's Children*, with all those little strands coming and going in and out.

SR: Yes, it's full of lies! You have talked of your namesake novel, *The Pessoptimist*, as a first manifestation of the attempt to write in a form which appears to be formlessness, and which in fact mirrors the instability of the situation. Could you say some more about this?

ES: It's a rather eccentric view, perhaps. I myself am not a scholar of Palestinian and certainly not Arabic literature in general. But I am fascinated by the impression made on everyone by, for instance, Kanafani's novel *Men in the Sun,* whose texture exemplifies the uncertainty whether one is talking about the past or the present. One story of his, called, I think, "The Return to Haifa," follows a family who left in 1948 and resettled in Ramallah. Much later they return to visit their house in Haifa, and to meet again the son they had left behind in a panic and who was adopted by an Israeli family. Throughout the novel there is a powerful sense of endless temporal motion, in which past, present, and future intertwine without any fixed center.

SR: Perhaps we could now turn to the lengthy discussion in *After the Last Sky* about the unheard voices of Palestinian women. You write:

> And yet, I recognize in all this a fundamental problem—the crucial absence of women. With few exceptions, women seem to have played little more than the role of hyphen, connective, transition, mere incident. Unless we are able to perceive at the interior of our life the statements women make—concrete, watchful, compassionate, immensely poignant, strangely invulnerable—we will never fully understand our experience of dispossession.

The main illustration you then give is a film, *The Fertile Memory*, by the young Palestinian director Michel Khleifi, which deals with the experience of two Palestinian women.

ES: Yes. This film made a very strong impression on me. One of the most striking scenes revolves around the older woman, who is actually Khleifi's aunt. She has a piece of property in Nazareth which a Jewish family has been living on for many years, but one day her daughter and son-in-law come with the news that this family now wants to buy up the title-deeds. She makes it clear that she is not interested. "But what do you mean?" they insist. "They are living on it; it's their land. They just want to make things easier for you by giving you money in return for the deeds." "No, I won't do that," she replies. It is a totally irrational position, and Khleifi registers the expression of stubbornness, almost transcendent foolishness, on her face. "I don't have the land now," she explains. "But who knows what will happen? We were here first. Then the Jews came and others will come after them. I own the land and I'll die, but it will stay there despite the comings and goings of people." She is then taken to see her land for the first time—it had been left to her by her husband, who went to Lebanon in 1948 and died there. Khleifi records her extraordinary experience of walking on the land that she owns but does not own, treading gently and turning around and around. Then suddenly her expression changes as she realizes the absurdity of it all and walks away. This scene typified for me the persistent presence of the woman in Palestinian life—and, at the same time, the lack of acknowledgment which that presence has elicited. There is a strong misogynist streak in Arab society: a kind of fear and dislike existing alongside respect and admiration. I remember another occasion when I was with a friend looking at a picture of a rather large and formidable yet happy Palestinian woman, her arms folded across her chest. This friend summed up the whole ambivalence with his remark, "There is the Palestinian woman, in all her strength . . . and her ugliness." The picture of this woman, by Jean Mohr, seems to say something that we have not really been able to touch upon. That experience is one that I, as a man, in this Palestinian sort of mess, am beginning to try to articulate.

SR: In *After the Last Sky* you say that, having lived inside Western culture for a long time, you understand as well as any non-Jew can hope to do what is the power of Zionism for the Jewish people. You also describe it as a program of slow and steady acquisition that has been more efficient and competent than anything the Palestinians have been able to put up against it. The problem is that any attempt to provide a critique of Zionism is faced, particularly nowadays, with the charge that it is anti-Semitism in disguise. The retort that you are not anti-Semitic but anti-Zionist is always, or often, greeted with: "Oh, yes, we know that code." What you have done in this book and in *The Question of Palestine* is to offer a very useful, emotionally neutral critique of Zionism as an historical phenomenon. Perhaps you could say a few words about this.

ES: In my opinion, the question of Zionism is the touchstone of contemporary political judgment. A lot of people who are happy to attack apartheid or U.S. intervention in Central America are not prepared to talk about Zionism and what it has done to the Palestinians. To be the victim of a victim does present quite unusual difficulties. For if you are trying to deal with the classic victim of all time—the Jew and his or her movement—then to portray yourself as the victim of the Jew is a comedy worthy of one of your own novels. But now there is a new dimension, as we can see from the spate of books and articles in which any kind of criticism of Israel is treated as an umbrella for anti-Semitism. Particularly in the United States, if you say anything at all, as an Arab from a Muslim culture, you are seen to be joining classical European or Western anti-Semitism. It has become absolutely necessary, therefore, to concentrate on the particular history and context of Zionism in discussing what it represents for the Palestinians.

SR: The problem, then, is to make people see Zionism as being like anything else in history, as arising from sources and going somewhere. Do you think that Zionism has changed its nature in recent years, apart from the fact that it has become subject to criticism?

ES: One of my main concerns is the extent to which people are not frozen in attitudes of difference and mutual hostility. I have met many Jews over the last ten years who are very interested in some kind of exchange, and events since the sixties have created a significant community of Jews who are not comfortable with the absolutes of Zionism. The whole notion of crossing over, of moving from one identity to another, is extremely important to me, being as I am—as we all are—a sort of hybrid.

SR: I would like to ask you a couple of more personal questions before we open out the discussion. You say that to be a Palestinian is basically to come from a Muslim culture, and yet you are not a Muslim. Do you find that a problem? Have there been any historical frictions in this respect?

ES: All I can say is that I have had no experience of such frictions. My own sense is that our situation as Palestinians is very different from Lebanon, where conflicts between Sunnis, Shiites, Maronites, Orthodox, and so forth have been sharply felt historically. One of the virtues of being a Palestinian is that it teaches you to feel your particularity in a new way, not only as a problem but as a kind of gift. Whether in the Arab world or elsewhere, twentieth-century mass society has destroyed identity in so powerful a way that it is worth a great deal to keep this specificity alive.

SR: You write: "The vast majority of our people are now thoroughly sick of the misfortunes that have befallen us, partly through our own fault, partly because of who the dispossessors are, and partly because our cause has a singular ineffectuality to it, capable neither of sufficiently mobilizing our friends nor of overcoming our enemies. On the other hand, I have never met a Palestinian who is tired enough of being a Palestinian to give up entirely."

ES: That's rather well put!

SR: This brings me to my final point that, unlike your previous three books, which centered on the dispute between Eastern and Western cultures, *After the Last Sky* focuses much more on an inner dispute or dialectic at the heart of Palestinianness. After a period of extroversion, you suggest, many Palestinians are themselves experiencing a certain turning inward. Why is this so? What has been your own experience?

ES: Well, obviously much of it has to do with disillusion. Most people in my own generation—and I can't really speak for others—grew up in an atmosphere of despondency. But then in the late sixties and early seventies, a tremendous enthusiasm and romantic glamour attached to the rise of a new movement out of the ashes. In a material sense it accomplished very little: No land was liberated during that period. Moreover, the excitement of the Palestinian Resistance, as it was called in those days, was a rather heavy atmosphere, forming part of Arab nationalism and even—in an ironic and extraordinary way—part of the Arab oil boom. Now all that is beginning to crumble before our eyes, giving way to a sense of disillusionment and questioning about whether it was ever worthwhile and where we are to go from here. It was as an expression of this mood that I wrote *After the Last Sky*. The photographs were important in order to show that we are not talking just of our own personal, hermetic disillusionment. For the Palestinians have become a kind of commodity or public possession, useful, for example, to explain the phenomenon of terrorism. I found myself writing from the point of view of someone who had at last managed to connect the part that was a professor of English and the part that lived, in a small way, the life of Palestine. Luckily Jean Mohr had built up quite a large archive of pictures since he worked for the Red Cross in 1949. We came together under strange circumstances: He was putting up some pictures and I was working as a consultant for the United Nations. Since they would not let us write captions for the pictures at the UN, we said: "Let's have a book and do it in our own way." It represented a very personal commitment on both our parts.

SR: The picture on the cover is really quite extraordinary—a man with a kind of starburst on the right lens of his glasses. As you say, he has been blinded by a bullet in one eye but has learned to live with it. He is still wearing the spectacles . . . and still smiling.

ES: Jean told me that he took the photo as the man was en route to visit his son, who had been sentenced to life imprisonment.

SR: I would now like to throw open the discussion to the audience. Who wants to ask the first question?

FIRST VOICE: If and when you are invited to speak to Jewish audiences, what do you tell them about the future of Jews in Palestine?

ES: My goodness—what a powerful question that is! It is very difficult for me to talk about the future of another people, which feels itself, for the most part, to be so different from the Arab Palestinians. But the Palestinian experience, for all its ineffectualness and even shabbiness in places, is a struggle to achieve a mode of coexistence. Over the last generation a strong bond has been formed between the Israeli and the Palestinian on the basis of fear. Let me tell you a story to illustrate this. About three months ago I was at a conference of the International Society for Political Psychology. I don't know exactly what I was doing there, but we seemed to be experimenting with how Israelis and Palestinians might speak to each other. During the second half of a discussion between six Palestinians and six Israelis, the theme was: "What Are the Psychological Obstacles to Peace?" I was fascinated by the fact that the Israelis—in marked contrast to the Palestinians, myself included—had so far appeared very relaxed and academically dispassionate. It was as if their possession of the land allowed them to be in charge of everything, and thus to assume a detached air. Finally, however, when the moderator asked what they saw as the obstacles to peace, one of them nearly floored me with his answer: "We are afraid of the Palestinians." I couldn't understand it. Here was a serious scholar, closely linked to the Israeli government and army, who was saying: "We are more afraid of the PLO than we are of all the Arab armies." This fixation on the Palestinians and the PLO in particular—a disadvantaged minority in our own country—only made sense in terms of a peculiar bond that we are just now beginning to grasp. But when he said, "We are more afraid of the PLO than we are of all the Arab armies," he was making a statement, I think, about how he saw the future.

SECOND VOICE: I would like to follow on by asking you about the nature of Zionist discourse, which seems to have become completely institutional-ized in such a way as to shut out the Palestinian discourse whenever it is raised. Since the fear of another Holocaust continually supports this blockage, how can we ever begin to institutionalize the Palestinian dis-course? And if you don't change things in discourse, you can't change them in reality.

ES: This is a very interesting and complicated question, but I will make just two points. Today I think that a lot of people—despite the wild imagin-ings of Meir Kahane—realize that there cannot really be an Israeli military option against the Palestinians. Even the most cataclysmic war, of the kind that was perhaps intended in 1982, is not going to achieve the obliteration of the Palestinian people. On the Palestinian side, whatever the occasional rhetoric and outbursts of emotion, there is a parallel awareness that the Jews cannot be simply sent back to Europe or wherever. Thus, one of the peculiarities of the present situation is the great emphasis on discourse or on the realm of the cultural and ideological, and the possibility that some change may be accomplished. On the other hand, we have to recognize that military power and the actual holding of land are real forces in the world in which we live. The problem is how to use the emotional or imaginative dimension to affect those realities. Cinema, various irregular or unconventional means of association and political organization will certainly have to be mobilized, because otherwise I see nothing but a rather bleak prospect down the road. If the stalemate is not to continue, we have to think in terms of a new beginning of some kind.

THIRD VOICE: The problem I find is that when someone says something about the Palestinian issue, you soon realize that they know absolutely nothing and that you have to tell them all the stories we've heard before. That can be very frustrating, as you never know where to start. Have you developed a system whereby you can answer the question in a simple way?

ES: Unfortunately, there is no system. I once had a relative who had a card printed with two messages: on one side, "Your story is very moving. Thank you very much, but I can't contribute"; on the other side, "Here's the story, and if you want to know everything . . ." But in reality every challenge with which you are presented requires a different retelling of the story. The most frustrating experience is the kind of exchange I had with Cynthia Ozick seven or eight years ago. In a special issue of *The New Leader* devoted to Jimmy Carter and the Jews, she had argued essentially that Carter's interest in the Palestinians demonstrated that he was anti-Semitic. In the course of the articles she wrote something like: "Edward Said, for example, who professes to teach English at Columbia University and is a member of such-and-such, is regularly paid to go to Beirut to plot the murder of innocent Israeli children." I don't usually respond to such nonsense, but someone brought it to my attention and I sat down and wrote what I thought was rather a clever reply. I concentrated on my particular story: that my family lived in Beirut, that my way is never paid, that I go there to visit my family, and so on. A series of narrative denials, if you like. Whereupon she wrote a letter saying: "Ah, so he pays his own way to go to Beirut . . . !" You see the scale of the problem.

FOURTH VOICE: In your thinking about the heart of the Palestinian issue, do you see a contest between two stories, one of which is vocal, in place, and has a reality to its expression; and one of which is denied, or fragmented, or difficult to locate? Are we talking about two conflicting histories, with Realpolitik and displacements of power as the only resolution? Or is there also a moral dimension, a question of justice that is relevant to the matter? And if so, where can it be articulated? How can it be brought to bear on events?

ES: I am strongly convinced that there is indeed justice and injustice. Most professed or committed Zionists find it very difficult to respond at such a level and generally say nothing about it. As to where the justice resides, I don't think it can be a matter only of asking: "Would you like it done to you?" The other way of formulating it would be to say: "If you don't see the justice and the injustice, then you are on one side or the other." One of the great problems with the Palestinian experience is precisely that its justice and its truth have not been recognized as such. At that conference I was talking about earlier, one of the Palestinians suddenly said to the Israelis: "Look, what you don't seem to understand is that although I'm from Haifa and my family left there in 1948, I don't really want my house back. I can tell you that. But what I do want from you is a sign that you did wrong to me." There was a lot of fudging, but in a curious way we all felt the need for an acknowledgment, even perhaps for an act of atonement. Unlike other peoples who suffered from a colonial experience, the Palestinians do not primarily feel that they have been exploited but that they have been excluded, denied the right to have a history of their own. When you continually hear people say: "Well, who are you anyway?" you have to keep asserting the fact that you do have a history, however uninteresting it may appear in the very sophisticated world. Take that astounding book by Joan Peters that came out a couple of years ago. Its basic argument was: "They weren't there to begin with; they only came because there was settlement in Palestine in 1946 and 1948. When they had to leave they weren't refugees; they were all going back to where they came from." It is not only the historical truth that has been constantly denied but the very experience of the hurt, the very fact of injustice.

To answer your question, I don't think it is just a matter of two stories contesting with each other. The whole essence is that despite all the sufferings of the Jews in Europe, there was a willful transporting of that history to Palestine, a conscious dispossession, dislocation, and displacement of another people. You might say that this was inevitable, that there was no other solution, but even then quite a lot of people in the Jewish community saw it as an injustice. The classical and, in my view, liberal perception of a clash between two rights does not do much to address the situation. For there is a truly profound, irreducible injustice for which the injured side needs to get institutional recognition. Perhaps I could mention in this context the book by Edward Thompson, father of E. P. Thompson, *The Other Side of the Medal,* which was published in 1926. Talking about India, the book describes the different versions of history that developed in India and Britain: the Mutiny of 1857, for example, was an act of just rebellion for one side and an outbreak of appalling savagery for the other. Toward the end of this little book, Thompson writes almost in passing: "What is needed now for the English is an act of atonement for what it is that we have done." This struck me as a deep idea, which applies in other contexts where the side with the power has denied certain things to the side without any, or with relatively less, power.

FIFTH VOICE: Granted that there is this feeling of injustice, would you say that it is now more or less widely recognized among Jews than in the past? Perhaps things are different in America or the West, but in Israel itself the tendency seems to be in the opposite direction. Fewer and fewer people are willing to give due recognition to the sense of grievance.

ES: You may well be right, although I can only judge from what I read and hear about the situation inside Israel. On the other hand, a number of people have emerged in the last few years who strike me as quite remarkable in their forthrightness, and whether this is a sign of a diminishing or a declining trend, it ought to give some basis for encouragement. Probably the crux of the matter is the unprecedented munificence that the United States bestows on Israel—the moral equivalent of a blank check to do what it likes. When another country is given U.S. aid, it is always for a particular purpose—say, the purchase of wheat—and the proper receipts have to be provided. But in the case of Israel it is simply categorized as "budgetary support" to the economy in general. Thomas Dine, head of the American-Israel Public Affairs Committee, recently gave a speech at its annual convention in which he more or less said that his was the most powerful lobby in the United States today. At the drop of a hat, it can get the entire Congress to vote yet more aid for Israel. He even boasted: "It is the only country in the world in which aid is not tied to specific items." This settles as a cloud on the whole Palestinian issue. But you would be surprised at some of the recent signs of change, expressed in opinion polls and other ways. When people are appealed to in a simple and direct manner, they are often able to see beneath the surface. I am not a political scientist, nor do I have visions of any neat solution, but it is necessary to register the changes as they take place on the long road that undoubtedly lies ahead of us.

SIXTH VOICE: In the United States it seems that the invasion of Lebanon in 1982 gave the press a greater freedom than it had had before to write about the activities of the Israeli government. But in the last four years that door has been closed again. How do you explain that?

ES: I see it as a kind of compensation for the very ugly things that were momentarily revealed on the screen about Israel and the invasion of Lebanon. Already in the academic year 1982–83 there was a kind of traveling show, put on by one of the large Jewish organizations, that went from campus to campus screening a film called *NBC Versus the Jews*—an attempt to prove, on the basis of video footage from the summer of 1982, how NBC slanted the news to show the Jews in their worst light. This opening salvo was followed by the trundling out of all the references to the Judeo-Christian tradition, increasingly counterposed to Islamic fundamentalism, terrorism, and so on. My impression is that they were running scared and had to slam the door behind them. Zuckerman, owner of the once-liberal *Atlantic Monthly* and *U.S. News & World Report,* laid down the line in typical, if unusually open, fashion when he said: "I will not have a word of criticism of Israel in any of my publications." Yet no repression of that sort can exhaust all the possibilities. It is now much easier for many of us to go around speaking—we may be threatened with loss of limbs or even of our lives, but there is now an interested audience.

SEVENTH VOICE: What lessons have been learned from the experience of the years 1976 to 1982, when the Palestinians virtually ran West Beirut and southern Lebanon, only to be driven out in the way that they were? What is the next phase after the failure of this episode of Palestinian nationalism that was born after the disaster of '67 and ended with the disaster of '82?

ES: I don't really know the answer to your question. A process of fragmentation is certainly taking place, as I can see in the United States, where organizations and associations of Palestinians are beginning to fall apart. In many ways this is reflected in the person of Arafat himself, a tragic and fascinating figure, paradoxical and extraordinarily complex. The Western media present him as a straightforward mass murderer, the sort of person to whom you would say: "How does it feel after killing five thousand innocent people before breakfast this morning?" But he is a very rich figure, and his ability to survive somehow expresses a quality that is central to the Palestinian experience. He just keeps going on and on— repetition again!—with a remarkable persistence in the political objective. It is true that he had a little thing going with Jordan, but that never worked and never deflected him from his consistent goal that Palestinians should be represented everywhere and should be allowed to represent themselves. For many Palestinian intellectuals and the younger generation, what happens to Arafat is a very important index of what is going to happen to the rest of us.

Published in *The New Left Review*, November/December 1986; the discussion took place at the Institute of Contemporary Arts, London, in September 1986.

CHAPTER 13

Review of *Wedding in Galilee* and *Friendship's Death*

[1988]

Palestine on Film is the title of a pamphlet by the British filmmaker Taylor Downing that I recall reading a few years ago. Taylor surveyed the archival material available on this quite extraordinary spot of land and concluded by remarking how dominated it all was by either the imperial or the Zionist viewpoint. Part of the reason was, I suspect, that Downing—who went on to make a three-part documentary on the Zionist–Palestinian conflict for Thames Television that was sympathetic to the Palestinian position—had access only to Western sources and therefore could not have looked at newsreels or documentary films about Palestine (not of very high quality anyway and with no influence to speak of) produced in the Arab world. There is no doubt at all, however, that recent television and feature film work in England and America is almost ludicrously slanted against the Palestinians. And, alas, there is virtually nothing comparable now being produced in the Arab world to compete with it, with the result that Western audiences are getting a steady, and quite invidious, diet of pro-Israeli films.

Beginning with *Exodus* (which Otto Preminger's grateful Israeli friends said as recently as last year did more for the Jewish state in its early years than almost any other outside support) and continuing throughout the sixties and seventies, Israel in films has become unquestioningly identified with heroism, pioneering enterprise, and anti-

communist anti-terrorism. Rarely has the situation seemed more unforgiving, so far as contemporary representations of Palestinians are
concerned. Hollywood and various international consortia together
churn out fast-paced, objectionably violent adventure films at a furious
pace. *Delta Force* and *Black Sunday* show the Palestinians as murderous
terrorists whose only victims are innocent civilians. Sylvestor Stallone
is making another Rambo film in Israel, and CBS in this country has
just prepared a film about a Palestinian terrorist's trial, in which the
chief technical adviser is Alan Dershowitz, an unabashedly enthusiastic
Zionist who also is known to be an intrepid courtroom defender of
unpopular, seemingly hopeless, cases. As for the television news, it
routinely lingers over Israeli grief during funerals after a violent action,
and just as routinely ignores any such sequence on the Palestinian side,
as if to confirm the supposition that Palestinians do not suffer, do not
value life as "we" do.

Eight or nine years ago in Beirut, an energetic young Palestinian
woman, Abir Dajani, introduced me to a group of people who were
scouting for Costa-Gavras. Having done a number of political feature
films on difficult subjects, Costa-Gavras was now said to be exploring
the Palestinian issue. One of the people I met was his renowned
screenwriter, Franco Salinas, who had worked with Pontecorvo on *The
Battle of Algiers,* and therefore had impeccable credentials. I then sat
down with the group, plus Abir, to discuss story possibilities, an
encounter that was like sitting in a leaking canoe. Yes, we want a
Palestinian story, but it can't address the issues frontally. No, we don't
want to appear cowardly; yes, we must engage the West on this highly
emotional issue, but we cannot be sure either of funding or of audiences. Hints were uttered about Jewish pressure. I recall Salinas, I
think, fixated on the idea of using the letters "home" of a Palestinian
worker in Germany. Which "home," I said, Palestine or refugee
camps in Lebanon or Jordan? *"C'est très difficile"* was the only answer
I got.

The sidling and the backing and filling got us nowhere, so I left in
exasperation. Abir Dajani persisted, however, and Costa-Gavras finally
did make his film, which appeared in 1984 with Jill Clayburgh (who
hasn't worked much since) and Gabriel Byrne. *Hanna K* was its name,
the story of an Israeli lawyer (Clayburgh) who defends and has an affair
with a Palestinian activist, maybe a terrorist—the film was deliberately
unclear on that point—despite the pressure of her Israeli detective
boyfriend (played unconvincingly by Gabriel Byrne). Costa-Gavras

engineered some powerful cross-examination scenes during the Palestinian's trial, there were a number of dramatic interchanges elsewhere in the film, and there was an especially remarkable opening sequence in which the Israelis cold-bloodedly blew up a Palestinian house. Yet, as a whole, the film was unfocused and distracted in its attempts to hook the Palestinian story onto Clayburgh's love life, while at the same time containing any serious damage to Israel and its supporters. Although *Hanna K* was woefully unsuccessful and was hardly booked anywhere (not at all in London, I think), I defended it anyway, as at least going a step beyond the caricatural nonsense proffered by every other Western film in which Palestinians appeared.

Films produced in the Arab world, especially in Egypt, which has always been the heart of Arab film culture, have not generally been part of the international network. The only Arab director to have made a name for himself abroad is Youssef Chahine, and aside from the occasionally interesting Syrian, Iraqi, or Tunisian feature, films by and for Arabs are of strictly regional import; Egyptian comedies and melodramas in particular continue to delight huge Arab audiences that have still not made the switch to *Dallas* and *Dynasty*.

Thus, I routinely (even hopelessly) scan film festival programs to see if an Arab film, or a European film on a decently sympathetic Arab subject, has made it through. This year's London Festival presented two, Michel Khleifi's *Wedding in Galilee* and Peter Wollen's *Friendship's Death*. (Neither, I believe, would ever have been part of the New York Film Festival.) It is, I think, some sort of testimony to the stubborn durability of the Palestinian narrative that fascinating aspects of it have emerged in these two radically different and eccentric works. Khleifi is from Nazareth (which is a city in Israel proper, not the Occupied Territories), but he has lived and worked in Belgium for a decade; his film is listed as a Franco-Belgian-Palestinian coproduction, although it was filmed in Israel/Palestine. His earlier film, *The Fertile Memory* (about which I wrote in *After the Last Sky*), was a lyrical documentary about two Palestinian women. *Wedding in Galilee* is a much more ambitious drama that takes place during a very long day in the life of a Palestinian village.

Khleifi's cuts between the dozens of scenes that make up his film are abrupt and, I feel, awkward. A lot is going on, the cast is a sizable one, the conflict and ideas operate on several levels. But *Wedding in Galilee* is nevertheless a profoundly affecting representation of the Palestinian quandary today, seen not exclusively as the result of Israeli occupation but also as the extension of problems endemic to Arab society in the late twentieth century. An elderly man (Ali el Akili), whose village has been punished by curfew, secures permission to hold a big wedding for his son on condition that the Israeli military governor (Makram Khoury) and his staff attend and stay through the ceremonies along with the other guests. This is not to everyone's liking in the village, but the wedding proceeds anyway. Khleifi interweaves a number of strands, all of them connected to the main event and illustrative in various and quite inventive ways of the central impasse in Palestinian society, the failure of continuity and settled existence for Palestinians that has resulted from Israel's presence. The son, Adel (Nezih Akleh), cannot consummate his marriage because the patriarch's imposing authority blocks him; his sister, Sumaya, played by the devastatingly attractive Tunisian Sonia Amar, wants out of the village but can visualize herself doing so only as a man; a group of young men plots but fails to kill the Israeli soldiers; assorted relatives voice and demonstrate attitudes of loud defiance or undignified collaboration; a pair of elderly relatives wander in and out like Chekhovian retainers who cast a deepening shadow over the festivities; Tali (Tali Dorat), an Israeli woman in uniform, passes out but is revived by Arab women in a seduction scene that is dangerously close to a Pierre Loti fantasy.

Khleifi's method is to keep the surface pretty much to the mundane matters at hand, a tactic that would have the effect for most Palestinians and Arabs of a quaint folkloric scene. But then he brings you up short with a gesture or a sequence that harshly rends the veil of forgiving sentimentalism. Most of the actors are in fact amateurs, but they perform the required volte-face with total conviction. Thus, for example, the old man is seen talking tenderly to his sleeping son, trying somehow to communicate a dream to him; then the boy awakens, and the old man's tone changes abruptly to sharp reproof. During the feast, the Israeli commander and his crew together savor the food (which one of them remarks is much better than kibbutz meals), until the seasoned officer says without embarrassment that it is not as good as the food in Lebanon; someday, he adds with confidence, you will have a meal in Aleppo.

Rituals often go awry, as when the thoroughbred mare used to transport the groom breaks out of its stall and runs off into a nearby field that happens to have been mined by the Israelis. A disquieting sequence ensues. The Israeli soldiers hold a map with the mines' location and, firing their rifles, try to scare the animal into moving safely between the mines and then to freedom; the old man, petrified that his lovely mare will either be blown up or driven stir-crazy, takes over, and coaxes her out, but he is forced to do so of course under the Israelis' thumb, between their mines and their maps. One is left with a remarkably reflective portrait of Palestinian life trapped inside various boxes, all of them reconfirming the present impasse. The film's affectionate frankness, without any macho posturing, is indebted both to Italian *verismo* and to the visionary clarity of many Third World films of the past two decades.

Wollen's work is much more self-consciously avant-garde, but like Khleifi's, his view of things is stunningly coherent and original. He is a well known film theorist and director, whose *Signs and Meanings in the Cinema* and the more recent *Readings and Writings* have given him his reputation as an intransigently original and politically engaged figure. *Friendship's Death* was originally a short story first published in *Bananas,* later collected in *Readings and Writings,* and is based on Wollen's sojourn in Amman during the early days of September 1970, i.e., Black September. In the story, Friendship is a creature from outer space whose voyage to MIT (where he has been sent to visit Noam Chomsky to study linguistics *and* peace) has been deflected, and he has ended up in Amman. The narrator is a left-wing sympathizer with the Palestinians, who is introduced to Friendship—a foreigner who strayed into the battle zone—by one of the combatants. Narrator and humanoid become friends, both of them trapped in Amman as the contest between Jordanian regulars and Palestinian guerrillas rages furiously around them.

This is already enough to establish the peculiarity of Wollen's science fiction perspective—but it gets stranger. Friendship is fascinated with machines (clocks, vacuum cleaners, and typewriters in particular), and of course he is interested in language. Nevertheless, two things become clear together: that Friendship's ability to comprehend earthly ideas is curiously limited (he can't understand the narrator's explanation of the Oedipus complex, for example), and that because he is a victim of sorts, he sides with the Palestinians. In doing so, "he would be a representative, not so much of machines today, as of the potential oppressed class of intelligent machines and servomechanisms of tomorrow." Joining one of the militias, Friendship is separated from the narrator, who leaves Amman just before the final defeat. Friendship, he assumes, has been captured and killed; his sadness at the Palestinian debacle shades imperceptibly into his melancholy incomprehension of Friendship's visit. He is pushed into memorializing the episode (he feels, he says, "rather like the Evangelists must have felt before starting to write, many years after the death of their protagonist") and reproduces Friendship's translation of *L'Après-midi d'un faune,* a virtuoso misreading of Mallarmé that features such ingenious renderings as, "I vault to persecute these white water-lilies," for *"Ces nymphes, je les veux perpétuer."*

In the film, Friendship is a woman (Tilda Swinton) whose gender and placid beauty are perfectly suited to the curiosity, concern, oppression, and wisdom Wollen wants to convey in his portrait of the victimized but saintly robot. The narrator is a tough Hemingway–like character called Sullivan (Bill Patterson), whose probing confidence provides a satisfying foil for the outsider and for the historical moment. Wollen's filmic style is understatement, although his realization of the story greatly amplifies and elaborates the narrative. Odd bits of comedy and apocalypse jostle each other. Thus, Friendship is interested in shaving and in human hair, being hairless herself; she dreams of succulence or of impossible objects; Sullivan is fascinated by maps; Friendship comes from the period after nuclear winter; rows of tombstones in Jordan point the way to the events of Beirut.

When Friendship and Sullivan part for the last time, he gives her a razor in exchange for one of her memory-chips. Back home in England, Sullivan's young daughter figures out a way to decode the chip by playing it on a VCR. What ensues is Wollen's visual transposition of the Mallarmé translation left behind by the robot. The terminal sequence is an extraordinary montage of biomathematical symbols, geometric patterns, nuclear explosions, and incomprehensible sequences. But the final effect of this articulate and calm film, so unusual and intelligent, is a deep and strangely moving melancholy, almost religious in its intensity and poignance.

What makes *Friendship's Death* and *Wedding in Galilee* so extraordinary is their postmodern unexpectedness, their eccentricity, and almost tangential connection to the Palestine story. Neither goes over the well-known territory, although in both films the human tragedy of Palestine has been transmuted into a quasimystical celebration of sacrifice and elegiac immobilization. It is as if both of these remarkable works of cinematic mastery, by turn witty and unutterably sad, might have established a new nondiscursive medium for the Palestine story, which has now gone beyond the brassy triumphalism of its military phase and has settled into the travail of a difficult but far from ordinary everyday life. Clearly, however, significant treatments of the Palestinian drama can come, as it were, only from nonestablishment and counterinstitutional viewpoints, although there will be a long wait before more films of this caliber will come along. Wollen's achievement is particularly distinguished, not only because of the nobility and purity of his daring but because he is, after all, an outsider. To have done the right thing and to have done it so authentically, this says a great deal about Wollen—and about Palestine.

Published in *The Nation*, May 28, 1988.

CHAPTER 14

How to Answer Palestine's Challenge

[1988]

For the past nine months, the Palestinians who have lived under Israeli military occupation for twenty years on the West Bank and Gaza Strip have mounted what is by all accounts one of the most extraordinary anticolonial and unarmed mass insurrections in the whole sordid history of the modern period. What has made this uprising, or *intifadah* as it is called in Arabic, so unusual is that the antagonists—Palestinians and Israelis—are no ordinary people, and what they dispute is perhaps the most unusual piece of territory in history: Palestine, a land drenched in historical, religious, political, and cultural significance. What we have been witnessing for the past several months is an eruption of history, an uprising of unarmed civilians whose political, cultural, civil, and human rights have been violated repeatedly for at least forty years.

One important result of the *intifadah* is that it has brought together the three major sectors of the Palestinian people, who, taken together, constitute a nation in exile. First is the group of about 700,000 Palestinians who are Israeli citizens and who have gone on strike in solidarity with their West Bank and Gaza compatriots; second are the inhabitants of the West Bank and Gaza, 1.5 million strong; third is the exile population of about 2.2 or so million, dispersed throughout the Arab world, Africa, Latin America, Europe, and North America (almost 200,000 here). I belong to the exile community, which has played a major role in political, social, and economic support of the *intifadah*. As a member of the Palestine National Council, the parliament in exile of which the PLO is a constituent member, I have written and spoken on behalf of our struggle. That we are in fact one people, and at last recognized as such, was symbolized in the meeting held between Secretary Shultz, my PNC colleague, Professor Ibrahim Abu-Lughod of Northwestern University, and myself on March 26, 1988.

The challenge of Palestine to people in the United States, which virtually underwrites the occupation of the West Bank and Gaza and in effect pays for the bullets that kill Palestinians, is an especially serious one. Since 1948, the United States has poured dozens of billions of dollars into Israel. Israel absorbs the largest portion of the foreign aid budget, and no other state gets aid without strings attached. No other country gets $1,000 per capita for every man, woman, and child in subsidies; no other military power gets an average $10,000 per soldier subsidy from the United States.

Today, because of the massive uprising on the West Bank and Gaza, the world is being asked to confront reality as if for the first time. A new truth has emerged, a truth Palestinians have been proclaiming during this entire century, that far from being a national liberation movement of Jews who came, in the commonly cited phrase, "to a land without people, as a people without land," the Zionists in fact came to Palestine, found another people already there, and then for several decades have dispossessed, alienated, and brutalized that people, the Palestinians, with the moral approval and support of the West generally and the United States in particular.

An Israeli prime minister—Golda Meir—could say in 1969, "Who are the Palestinians? There are no Palestinians." We have now had a slew of Israeli officials calling Palestinians "two-legged vermin," or according to General Eytan in 1983, "drugged roaches in a bottle," enjoining Israeli armed troops and illegal settlers to break their bones and use systematic beating, might, and crushing (this is Rabin). Most recently, we have had the grotesque Mr. Shamir telling the Palestinians that they had better behave or be "crushed like grasshoppers." I suppose we ought to feel grateful that the descriptions of Palestinians by responsible Israeli officials show a small vertical rise, as we move up the scale from nonexistence, to vermin, to roaches, to grasshoppers. Perhaps we can someday look forward to achieving the status of cattle or of monkeys.

Americans should be asking how it is that an entire people, living under inhuman conditions, should take on the most formidable fighting machine outside of Europe and the United States armed with only stones and their minds. The *intifadah* did not just begin on a certain day—in this case December 9, 1987. It should not be forgotten that over the previous twelve months, 3,500 acts of resistance to the occupation were recorded. The *intifadah* has been long in the making, deep in its intensity, force, drama.

The Palestinian Arabs were promised independence by Britain after World War I as a *quid pro quo* for joining the war against the Ottomans on the Allied side. In 1917, however, Palestine was also promised to the Zionists by the British, even though the population of Palestine was at that time about 90 percent Arab. After decades of Jewish immigration to Palestine, aided and abetted by the British, Palestine in 1948 was still only 30 percent Jewish and about 70 percent Arab. Zionist settlers still owned only about 6 percent of the land surface of Palestine, the Arabs owning all the rest. Yes, the Arabs contested the Partition project of 1947 for perfectly sound reasons then: that it would allot 55 percent of Palestine (and the best part of the country, at that) to a Jewish state comprising less than a third of the total Arab and Jewish population.

When war broke out in 1948, the British suddenly exited the country, leaving behind a Jewish army ten times larger and a hundred times better equipped than the one the native Palestinians could muster. As for the Arab armies, they were there to get the part of Palestine not conquered by the Zionists; Egypt took Gaza, Jordan the West Bank. In the spring of 1948, a series of deliberate massacres and a campaign of terror by the Israeli military provoked residents of the major Arab rural and urban centers into panic and flight, pushing out about 800,000 Palestinian Arabs. In the course of the 1948 war, almost four hundred Arab Palestinian villages were destroyed—as Moshe Dayan admitted publicly on several occasions. Thousands of people were killed and/or dispossessed.

When Ben-Gurion declared the independence of Israel in May 1948, he omitted to mention the actual borders of the state. To this day Israel is the only state in the world with no officially declared borders, just as it is the only state in the world posited not as the state of its citizens but as the state of the whole Jewish people. Just imagine what would happen if America would be declared the state only of WASPS. Israel, moreover, has racially discriminatory immigrations laws that allow any Jew anywhere to become a citizen—the Law of Return—whereas people like myself, any of the five million Palestinians who were born in Palestine, enjoy no comparable right of return. When Palestinians today are asked to recognize the state of Israel, most of us are hard put to know which Israel we are to recognize, within which borders intending which territories, claiming which prerogatives.

Nor is this all. Recent Israeli scholarship has brought new historic facts to light and dispelled a series of carefully maintained myths, among them the myth of Palestinian exodus ("They left because Arab leaders told them to"), or the myth that Israel truly accepted the idea of a partitioned Palestine (Ben-Gurion always made it clear that partition was a step toward acquiring *all* the territory). Immediately after the state of Israel was declared in 1948, every major Arab state—Syria, Jordan, Egypt—petitioned Israel for peace. Yet Ben-Gurion systematically refused their offers, preferring to maintain Israel in a state of war. These hitherto unacknowledged facts have been documented in Simha Flapan's *The Birth of Israel* and Tom Segev's *1949*.

Since 1948, Israel's policy has been to eliminate all traces of Palestinian national life, to treat the Palestinians not as a people but as a bunch of inconsequential nomads who could be driven out, killed, or ignored, regarding them as subhuman coolies whose life, property, and national rights could be trampled underfoot. By 1950, vast amounts of Arab land in Palestine, now Israel, were expropriated arbitrarily or consigned to a Jewish authority which safeguards the land in perpetuity for "the Jewish people." The Arabs were reduced to a sullen minority ruled, until 1966, by the same military laws applied by the British against both Jews and Arabs in colonial Palestine; moreover, the institutions and programs of the state discriminated rigidly against Arabs, or non-Jews as they were juridically known.

In 1967, Israel acquired the West Bank, Gaza, the Golan Heights, and the entire Sinai peninsula. It returned Sinai to Egypt in 1982, in a treaty—the Camp David Accord—that explicitly reduced Palestinian rights to nearly nothing, even as more illegal settlements were being built on the West Bank and Gaza. Today, after twenty-one years of occupation, more than 50 percent of Palestinian land in the Occupied Territories has been expropriated; 120 settlements and 65,000 settlers sit provocatively on land taken from Arabs, settlers who can more or less do what they want, since they are permitted to bear arms and enjoy Israeli military protection.

In the face of this escalating repression, Palestinians—the victims— have preposterously been identified with terror and violence, as if by blaming the victims Israel can obtain the peace and security it has claimed to be wanting these past forty years. The fact is that Israel has no peace and security, and has killed incomparably more Palestinians than the number of Israelis killed by Palestinian action. The great, perhaps the greatest, irony is that it is precisely the central party, the Palestinians, the PLO—vilified, caricatured, and attacked without limit—who have proposed the only decently humane and politically acceptable peace plan to surface in the region.

I shall let the facts speak for themselves. Since 1974, the Palestine National Council has articulated under the leadership of Chairman Arafat—whose name is scarcely pronounceable in polite company these days—a program for Israel and a new Palestinian state to divide historical Palestine between them. In April 1987, at a meeting in Algiers, the PNC (including *all* the main factions of the PLO) voted in favor of the political settlement in the context of an international conference, as a result of which peace would be obtained in exchange for land. And for at least four years Yasir Arafat has been declaring his willingness as the representative of the Palestinian people to negotiate on the basis of UN resolutions 242 and 338, plus all relevant UN resolutions that deal directly with the Palestine conflict.

It is perhaps worth recalling that 242 and 338 were UN resolutions passed after the 1967 and 1973 wars, respectively. Resolution 242 in particular made no mention of Palestinians, but of anonymous "refu- gees." The main lines of the resolution underline the inadmissibility of the acquisition of territory by war (Israel should withdraw), arguing that all states are entitled to live within secure and recognized bounda- ries. The irony is that Israel has in fact controverted most of the provisions of 242 and 338, even as (more ironically) both Israel and the United States continue to insist that the PLO should accept 242. The understandable unwillingness of Palestinians to do so without qualification rests on a major principle: that in speaking of us only as refugees, 242 deliberately ignores the *national* rights of the Palestinian people. Thus insistence on 242 is tantamount to asking Palestinians to renounce their national aspirations, especially self-determination: This, and not peace, is the reason it is hectoringly waved at us. Still, we have accepted 242, so long as it is not isolated from but taken in conjunction with the other UN resolutions that recognize Palestinian rights.

No declarations by Palestinians seem to be sufficient for Israel and the United States. We have accepted Israel's existence, we have said we are willing to live in peace and coexistence, we have spoken positively about mutual recognition and mutual self-determination, we have said we would negotiate a final settlement of the conflict directly with Israel, we would accept UN auspices, internationalization, demilitarization. And what does Israel say? No, no, and still again, no. This is as true of Labour as it is of Likud. Israel will not withdraw its military occupation, will not recognize Palestinian rights, will not deal with Palestinian representatives, will not—even in principle—accept the idea of a Palestinian state, won't come to a conference, will only negotiate the control, which must be perpetual, of every bit of Palestine. No one seems to have asked Israel what it wants to negotiate (since it has explicitly rejected 242) if it says all of its positions are nonnegotiable. The Labour party chief, Peres, is credited with a somewhat more advanced position than the truculent Shamir, and yet let us look closely at what Peres does say: No PLO, no Palestinian state, no return of the territories except here and there, and no sovereignty for the Palestinians, no representatives of the Palestinians except those acceptable to Israel. Why are Palestinians asked always to let someone else negotiate for them, Jordan, the Arabs in general, docile Palestinians, who in any case don't exist now, as the uprising has shown? Has anyone heard any Palestinian or Arab in the past decade say that we should negotiate only with Peace Now? Has anyone asked Israel to negotiate peace using as its delegates the Rumanian boxing team or the Belgian foreign minister?

There are hopeful signs, however, the greatest of which is the Palestinian people's continued resistance. Certainly the uprising has continued even though (predictably enough) the American media have lost interest in it. Local organizations have increased in scope and power, the infrastructure of independence from Israel's authority is now well under way, and the will of the resistance is irreversible: The Israeli army has been unable to destroy the leadership; the pamphlets and imaginative actions (strikes, the creation of liberated zones, discovery of alternative means of support, etc.) keep coming, as do, alas, the string of Palestinian deaths and sacrifices. Their message is that we will not go away, we will not submit to tyranny, we will resist, but we will do so in terms of a vision of the future—the Palestinian idea—based not on exclusivism and rejection, but upon coexistence, mutuality, sharing, and vision. I think Palestinians now universally realize, along with most Arabs, that Israel and Israelis are part of the Middle East, and they cannot be expected to leave. We will live with them. Therefore we must seek means to do so. Our duty is to work with those Israeli and other Jews who have begun, because of the uprising, to understand the main premises of the Palestinian case and to criticize the rejectionist Israeli position. There has emerged an Israeli opposition, whose focus today is not the vague one of peace or political solutions but, in the Israeli and American context, the end of the occupation. That is now the nub of the question: ending the occupation, since national self-determination, from either the Israeli or the Palestinian point of view, is incompatible with the domination of one people by another, in which one people enjoys all the rights, the other none.

Palestinians present themselves as interlocutors with the Israelis for peace. We are not an inconsiderable people, and our achievements in education, business, science, and engineering testify to intelligence, will, and foresight. We say to the Israelis and their U.S. friends, live with us, but not on top of us. Your logic, by which you forecast an endless siege, is doomed, the way all colonial adventures have been doomed. We know that Israelis possess a heritage of suffering, and that the Holocaust looms large over their present thought. But we Palestinians cannot be expected merely to submit to military rule and the denial of our human and political rights, particularly since our attachment to Palestine is as significant, as deep and as lasting as theirs. Therefore we must together formulate the modes of coexistence, of mutuality and sharing, those modes that can take us beyond fear and suffering into the future, and an extraordinarily interesting and impressive future at that.

As the uprising continues, with the inevitable brief spells of waning that are the result of Israeli repression and Palestinian fatigue, the need for political action increases. An Arab summit (held in Algiers in early June) has voted both political and economic support. A PNC meeting will surely be convened before the end of 1988. As U.S. opinion gradually shifts, the elections and a new presidency will bring new urgency to the question of Palestine, hitherto shielded from reality by a congressional blank check for everything Israel does. As the *intifadah* demonstrates, however, only forceful and creatively original action can make a difference. Here the challenge clearly before us all is to break the barriers of ideological fiction and uncritical ethnic solidarity, to move toward beyond the present impasse, and to guarantee decent self-determination for Israelis and Palestinians in historic Palestine.

Published in *Mother Jones*, September 1988.

CHAPTER 15

Palestine Agenda

[DECEMBER 1988]

The nineteenth session of the Palestine National Council, formally entitled the *"Intifadah* Meeting,'' was momentous and in many great and small ways unprecedented. Held in Algiers, there were fewer hangers-on, groupies, and "observers" than ever before. Security was tighter and more unpleasant than during the 1987 PNC session, also held in Algiers; Algeria had just had its own brutally suppressed *intifadah,* so the presence of several hundred Palestinians and at least 1,200 members of the press was not especially welcomed by the Ben Jadid government, which paradoxically needed the event to restore some of its tarnished revolutionary luster. This was also to be the shortest PNC meeting ever held. Barely three and a half days long, it accomplished more by way of debate, discussion, resolutions, and announcement than any other Palestinian meeting in the post-1948 period. Above all, this PNC secured for Yasir Arafat the certainty of his place in Palestinian and world history for, as one member put it, "We're not only living through a Palestinian revolution; it's also Abu Ammar's revolution.''

None of the approximately 380 members came to Algiers with any illusion that Palestinians could once again get away simply with creative ambiguity or with solid affirmations of the need to struggle. The *intifadah*'s momentum and its ability to have created a clear civil alternative to the Israeli occupation regime now necessitated a definitive statement by the PNC of support for the *intifadah* as an end-to-occupation and relatively nonviolent movement. This required an unambiguous claim for Palestinian sovereignty on whatever Palestinian territories were to be vacated by the occupation. Together with this, there also had to be an equally unambiguous statement on peaceful resolution of the conflict between Palestinian Arabs and Israeli Jews based on UN Resolutions 181 (partition), 242, and 338. In short, the PNC was asking of itself nothing less than emphatic transformation: from liberation movement to independence movement. Jordan's recent withdrawal of claims for the West Bank made the need for transformation urgent and compelling.

If you live in the United States, participating in Palestinian discussions, debates, and soul-searching reappraisals is particularly poignant. Palestinians meet rarely enough, given the widespread dispersion among our five million people, and the fact that we have no center, no territorial sovereignty of our own makes our distance from most other Palestinians in the midst of a U.S. society whose government's hostility to us is limitless, a continuously frustrating experience. Tunis serves the role of occasional headquarters, but since Abu Jihad's assassination Arafat's presence has necessarily been fitful and erratic. Yet most of us in the PNC made at least one trip there; many documents and drafts went through fax, express mail, or over the phone. And the date of the PNC kept getting postponed, but was definitively set by late October, not without trepidation, since Algeria's internal volatility remained high.

PNC members were to be quartered in bungalows adjacent to the enormous meeting hall set in a conference-cum-vacation center built by Ben Bella in 1965, approximately thirty miles west of Algiers. Four of us traveled together overnight to Paris from New York, transferred from De Gaulle to Orly airport, and arrived in Algiers at 2 P.M. on November 11. Ibrahim Abu-Lughod and I were driven off to one bungalow, only to find it already occupied; a second choice turned up the same fact, so we settled for a downtown hotel, which came to mean no hot food and hardly any sleep for three and a half days, as we commuted back and forth at the craziest hours. Despite jet lag, we went back to the conference center late that Friday night to call on Arafat, who seemed involved in three concurrently running meetings. He was confident but looked tired. Everyone knew that this was his step first to articulate, then to persuade everyone to take, then finally to choreograph politically. He handed me the Arabic draft of the declaration of statehood and asked me to render it into English. It had been drafted by committee, then rewritten by Mahmoud Darwish, then, alas, covered with often ludicrously clumsy insertions, and inexplicable deletions. Later Darwish told me that the phrase "collective memory" had been struck by the Old Man because, we both opined, he took it for a poetic phrase. "Tell him it has a serious and even scientific meaning," Darwish implored me; "maybe he'll listen to you." He didn't, and I didn't listen to Arafat when he wanted other phrases inserted, often lifted out of inappropriate contexts.

Nobody was to see these texts until much later, and indeed perhaps the oddest part of this PNC—with its obsessive postmodern rhetorical anxieties—was how the two main documents (declaration of statehood, and political resolutions) were discussed in public debates for hours on end without a piece of paper before us. After the opening ceremonies on Saturday the PNC divided itself into two committees, the political and the *intifadah*. Arafat had the texts memorized, and Nabil Shaath, brilliantly adroit chairman of the Political Committee, had them before him. All significant discussion about what we were doing took place in the riveting atmosphere of that committee, with speaker after speaker sounding off on what after all was the most significant political moment in Palestinian life since 1948. Words, commas, semicolons, and paragraphs were the common talk of each recess, as if we were attending a convention of grammarians.

The heart of the discussions occurred in the speeches given late Sunday and midafternoon on Monday by George Habash and Abu Iyad (Salah Khalaf) respectively, the first an opponent of the by-now well-known substance of the political program; the second, Arafat's key supporter and one of the main leaders of al-Fatah. Habash's express reservations concerned the clear acceptance of 242 and 338, resolutions not only unfriendly to us because they treat us only as "refugees," but also because they contained an implicit prenegotiating recognition of Israel. This, Habash said, was going too far too soon; there had been agreement that such tough issues as recognition, 242, borders, etc., would be handled at the international conference. Why, Habash asked, was it so necessary to go forward on everything *before* the conference? He spoke passionately and clearly, saying without hesitation that he and the Popular Front wished to remain within the PLO, no matter the outcome or the disagreements. To which, in a meandering and yet always fascinating speech, Abu Iyad responded by saying that decisions had to be made now, not only in the face of the discouraging realities of the Israeli elections, but because our people needed an immediate, concrete statement of our goals. What clinched it for me as I listened to Abu Iyad was the logic of his thesis that decisive clarity was needed from us principally for ourselves and our friends, not because our enemies kept hectoring us to make more concessions.

Arafat remained throughout the debate, occasionally intervening, and yet maintaining his office, so to speak, from his seat in the house; an endless stream of secretaries, delegates, messengers, experts came to him, and yet he seemed attuned to every phrase uttered in the hall. He had told me early on that he had planned the declaration proclamation to occur shortly after midnight November 15, after a whole night's debate November 14. By about 9:30 P.M. on Monday, November 14, the political program had been passed by a large majority in the political committee, and immediately afterward the whole PNC was reconvened in plenary session. Habash and supporters fought each sentence almost word by word on the crucial 242/338 paragraph, which was voted on in different forms half a dozen times. The somewhat garbled paragraph that resulted shows the effect of these battles in its ungainly phraseology, although the actual substance remains unmistakable. At one point Arafat stood up and recited the entire program from memory, indicating, as the Chair hadn't done, where the clause, sentence, and paragraph breaks occurred, so that there could be no mistake about meaning, emphasis, conclusion. For the first time in PNC history voting by acclamation wasn't going to be enough; Habash insisted on precise tallies, which emerged to his disadvantage, 253 for, 46 against, 10 abstaining. There was a sad nostalgia to what he represented, since in effect by voting against him we were taking leave of the past as embodied in his defiant gestures. The declaration ceremonies that closed the meetings were jubilant, and yet somehow melancholy.

About this break with the past there could be no doubt whatever. To declare statehood on the basis of Resolution 181 was first of all to say unequivocally that an Arab Palestinian and an Israeli state should coexist together on a partitioned Palestine. Self-determination would therefore be for two peoples, not just for one. Most of us there had grown up with the reality (lived and remembered) of Palestine as an Arab country, refusing to concede anything more than the exigency of a Jewish state, won at our expense in the loss of our land, our society, and literally uncountable thousands of lives. A million and a half of our compatriots were under brutal military occupation (as we met, the entire 650,000 people of Gaza were under total curfew), fighting tanks and fully armed soldiers with rocks and an unbending will. For the first time also, the declarations were implicitly recognizing a state that offered us nothing whatever, except the by-now empty formulas of Camp David, or the openly genocidal threats of population transfer and extreme brutality.

The declaration of statehood spelled out principles of equality, mutuality, and social justice far in advance of anything in the region. Call them idealistic if you will, but better that than the remorseless sectarianism and xenophobia with which Palestinians have had to contend for these five decades. Then, too, the *principle* of partition was asserted, not the territories specified in the 1947 UN resolution. All of us felt that since Israel had *never* declared its boundaries, we could not declare ours now; better to negotiate the question of boundaries with Israel and confederation with Jordan directly with both than to spell them out fruitlessly in advance. There was no doubt, however, that we were in fact discussing the territories occupied in 1967.

Secondly, there was absolute clarity in speaking of a peaceful settlement to the conflict. "Armed struggle" does not appear in the resolutions, the key sections of the much longer political statement in which they appear as binding conclusions. Central to the resolutions is a long and awkward sentence on the international peace conference based on "Resolutions 242 and 338." Everything that surrounds acceptance of the resolutions is a statement of the obvious, not a reservation about acceptance. For example, representation by the PLO on an equal footing with other parties, the aegis of the Security Council, the *implementation* of 242 and 338, the centrality of the Palestinian–Israeli conflict, the inalienable rights of the Palestinian people—all these are mentioned as the *context,* the history, the Palestinian interpretation of what we were accepting. This was especially necessary since 242 and 338 say literally nothing about Palestinian political acualities, which in 1967 seemed scarcely evident, except as the detritus of the Arab-Israeli June War.

Thirdly, the rejection of terrorism in all its forms (also asseverated in the declaration) makes an emphatic distinction between resistance to occupation (to which Palestinians are entitled according to the UN Charter and international law) and violence whose aim is to terrorize civilians. Note that no all-purpose definition of terrorism exists today, one that has validity and clarity of application internationally. Yet the PNC took a step that is unusual in its attempt to make distinctions between legitimate resistance and a proscribed indiscriminate violence of states or of individuals and groups. Also note that Israel has always arrogated to itself the right to attack civilians in the name of its security. These facts highlight the courage of what is ventured in the Palestinian statement.

Finally and most important, all the resolutions, however they are read, clearly intend willingness to *negotiate* directly. There are no disclaimers about the "Zionist entity," or about the legitimacy of Israeli representatives. All of the relevant passages about peace, partition, statehood in the 1964 Covenant are flatly contradicted by the 1988 PNC resolutions, which give their statement added, not lesser force. All the refusals, attacks, and insults heaped on the Council's results, both by Israel and the usual array of U.S. "experts," signifies consternation, a sign that the more Palestinians take responsible and realistic positions, the less acceptable they become, not just because Palestinians want peace, but because Israelis don't know what to do when peace is offered to them. There is a dispiriting continuity here between the early days of Israel's existence when Ben-Gurion refused peace with the Arabs, and the all-out rejection trundled out today by Likud and Labour alike.

The point is not that the Council documents are perfect and complete, but that they must be interpreted as everyone there intended— as a beginning that signals a distinct break with the past, as a willingness to make sacrifices in the interests of peace, as a definitive statement of the Palestinian acceptance of the international consensus. A few days before the Algiers meeting Sharon appeared on Italian television vociferating loudly about the need to kill Arafat. That no comparable sentiment was expressed at any time in Algiers is a fact that furnishes its own eloquent comment on the real difference now between Israeli leaders and Palestinian leaders. These are dangerous times for Palestinians; the occupation will get worse, and assassinations and all-out political war will intensify. For once, however, the record is unmistakable as to who is for peace, who for more senseless bloodshed and suffering. But our campaign for peace must be joined, since sitting on the sidelines is no longer any excuse.

What I cannot either understand or condone is why the U.S. media—quite unlike the rest of the world—have internalized the rejectionist norms promulgated by the Israeli and U.S. establishments. Far from reading the texts as they were meant to be read, commentators persist in suggesting that no matter what was said in the texts it could not by definition be enough. As to why Israel itself is not asked whether it is willing to coexist with a Palestinian state, or negotiate or accept 242, or renounce violence, or recognize the PLO, or accept demilitarization, or allay Palestinian fears, or stop killing civilians, or end the occupation, or answer any questions at all, perhaps the media will break their silence, as Palestinians already have.

Published in *The Nation,* December 12, 1988.

CHAPTER 16

Palestinians in the Gulf War's Aftermath

[1991]

As Iraq endures tragic paroxysms of disintegration and suffering, a solution to the question of Palestine seems more or less to be on, with an amazingly durable cast of the usual suspects trying to appear different and more effective than before. Let them try by all means, but let them approach matters honestly. For it is also true that large numbers of Palestinians—essentially unarmed and un-protected—are more dramatically vulnerable today. Consider that West Bank and Gaza Palestinians are presided over by a far-right, essentially fundamentalist Israeli cabinet, two of whose members have been implicated in the 1982 Sabra and Shatila massacres; in Lebanon, where about 300,000 Palestinians reside, the cabinet also contains two members implicated in the same camp killings. Pogroms against Pales-tinians have begun in Kuwait, where an indefinite martial law is likely to entail mass deportations, internment camps, and an even less envi-able status for an unjustly scapegoated people with basically nowhere else to go.

And still the search for "acceptable" Palestinian representatives continues strenuously, a grotesque and time-wasting effort if there ever was one. Everyone knows exactly who representative Palestinians are. A few days ago the Saudi and Kuwaiti foreign ministers went to Damascus to meet the Palestinian dissidents maintained as wards by Syria as a goad to Yasir Arafat, who is seriously crippled by his foolish positions on Iraq; between them these Syrian Palestinians represent no significant number of Palestinians at all, so the Gulf effort is quite simply to try to bleed, confuse, and divide this long-suffering and dispossessed nation even further. In addition, the Gulf potentates who speak in terms of reasonable moderation to their American patrons, finance Hamas, the West Bank–Gaza Islamic activists who, to evident Israeli satisfaction, proclaim the destruction of Israel as their goal (Iraq used to give Hamas money, too). With a few exceptions, the Israeli peace movement has waltzed sanctimoniously off the scene, its excuse being Palestinian support for Iraq, as if the Palestinian situation under Israeli military occupation had been just wonderful before the Gulf War.

The Palestinian tragedy therefore continues, with murderous villainy and preening hypocrisy exacting a dreadful price from students who have no schools or universities, men and women who have little food, no jobs, no political rights, no certainty at all of life, residence, or even subsistence nourishment a week hence. What could be more disheartening than for the superpower that has completely destroyed Iraq as a functioning country, all the while claiming a UN mandate for its actions, now to send Secretary of State James Baker around the Middle East to "consult" with its various clients on what to do about Palestinians—even as Security Council Resolution 681, which was passed unanimously on December 20, 1990, goes unheeded, unimplemented, unrecalled? According to that resolution (blocked for a month by the United States), the UN was supposed actively to protect Palestinians from brazen violations of the Geneva conventions by Israel. Nothing has changed, except that Israel continues the violations and has been given an additional $750 million to settle many Russian Jews on Palestinian land. Such dishonesty and immorality are breathtaking.

What Palestinians have suffered at the hands of Israel, the United States, and the Arab states well antedates what PLO leaders are now being preached at for having said (which was often both wrong and embarrassingly silly) during the Gulf crisis. Arab support for Palestinian self-determination was (as the history of the Gulf attests) *always* the result of popular pressure on the rulers, and not of their goodness of heart. The Egyptian president now promotes what he does mainly because he wants some Arab legitimacy to dress up his domestically unpopular American-Saudi stand against Iraq. To look past the cant and hypocrisy that clot the scene is to realize that the main hope for any serious Palestinian resolution cannot be in a *pax Americana* brokered by dithering enemies of the Palestinian people, but by a renewed all-Palestinian effort to take the case directly in hand.

On the minus side, the odds against success are obviously staggering, with widespread dispersion and economic hardship now greatly increased. On the plus side, a perfectly plain linkage (there all along, of course) exists between the illegal occupations of Kuwait and Palestine; in addition there is the tremendous resilience and unconquerable will of the people themselves; and lastly there is a solid world consensus on behalf of Palestinian rights. What to do? Herewith the proposals of a nonexpert but independent and committed Palestinian partisan:

1.   A return to the ways and means of the past is unconscionable. Palestinians must be the first to describe things as they are, avoiding euphemism and servility, requiring accountability and seriousness of purpose from leaders and each other alike. The situation is not only bleak, it is terrible. There is hope, but only Palestinians can articulate their vision creatively, and only they can say whether it is satisfactorily being realized.

2.   A provisional government or government in exile has to be formed by and for the Palestinian people, under UN auspices. An agreement with Israel, and with Jordan, for a form of independence acceptable to the residents of the West Bank and Gaza must be directly negotiated, and must be validated right away by the PLO. The basis should be UN Resolutions 242, 338, and 181 (partition), according to the terms of the PNC resolutions of November 1988. These prescient and peacefully accommodating terms have never been repudiated or modified, as few commentators seem to recall.

3.   The situation of Palestinian exile populations has to be normalized, by giving people options for compensation, citizenship, or if at all possible, repatriation. Here the terms of the Geneva conventions and Resolution 681, plus all other human rights protocols, must apply. There is no reason for further Palestinian statelessness, and none for punitive and invidious laws against residence; there can be no excuse for discrimination, abuse, insecurity. As an early step, a census of Palestinians should be taken. Only an active Palestinian government and the UN (preferably with direct U.S. support) can take charge of such things.

4.   Ideally we would also need a worldwide moratorium on efforts to find "a solution to the Palestinian problem" that does literally

everything except address Palestinian grievances themselves. Looking for (a) "alternative" representatives, (b) ways of endlessly trying to allay Israeli insecurity as Israeli troops sit on top of Palestinians, (c) circumlocutions to avoid discussing the most flagrant abuses of reason or morality: All these ought to be abandoned on grounds of rudimentary decency. Almost five million Palestinians constitute a nation. Like the members of other nations, they expect not to be killed and punished *because* they do not now have a state to defend, repatriate, or enfranchise them. The calculated, leisurely sadism of the current high-level tours and parlays is an affront to humanity and, I think, forecloses the compassion and insight that ought to prevail.

Published in *International Herald Tribune*, March 18, 1991.

CHAPTER 17

The Prospects for Peace in the Middle East

[1991]

E ver since he addressed the Congress on March 6, President Bush has seemed set on convening a Middle East peace conference. There is now a tentative, if not completely clear willingness on the part of the concerned Arab and Israeli governments to participate in the conference, which is scheduled to begin sometime later this month. During its meeting in Algiers at the end of September, the Palestine National Council voted decisively in favor of entering the peace process. Despite the fact that the Palestinian people is the principal aggrieved party to the conflict between the Arabs and Israel, and although this nation of people now suffers under the twin burden of exiled dispossession and military occupation, it alone has been prevented from supplying the conference with its own freely chosen representatives. Still, all the parties—including the Palestinians who will participate in a non-PLO grouping within the Jordanian delegation—will be present under the aegis of the United States and the Soviet Union for two days of a politically insignificant ceremonial inauguration, to be followed by two weeks of bilateral discussions. My subject here is not so much the conference itself, but to what crisis the conference is meant to be a solution, what sort of human problem and political conflict it seeks to address, and what we can and cannot expect.

When it comes to the subject of Israel and the Palestinians, public discourse in the United States lags considerably behind that in Israel itself or in Europe where it is possible to speak, write and represent critical views of Israel and to talk about the Palestinian people with affection and support. This is very difficult to do here for reasons that are familiar to everyone.

Neither the Palestinians nor the Israelis have a military option against each other. Both peoples must learn to live in peace, and in mutual acknowledgment of each other's history and actuality. Yet today only one people, Israeli Jews, has sovereignty, has achieved self-determination, even as the other people, the Palestinian Arabs, live in a state of subordination and oppression. That the Palestinians struggle against and resist this state of affairs is a function of how injustice and sufferings do not defeat a people, nor compel it into submission, but rather drive that people to resist more, and to struggle further for political justice and rights. It is because the Palestinians' side of the conflict is most urgently in need of attention and help that I want to accentuate their tragedy and travail, and I want to do so in such a way as befits Palestinian history, the continued resistance of the people of Palestine, and their political perspectives.

Let us look first then at what has generally engaged and affected Americans most recently, the war with Iraq. Arabs and Americans are parties to the opposing sides of what appears to be one of the longest, the deepest, and most complex conflicts of the modern world—that between the Arab-Islamic world on the one hand, and on the other, the Western, and more particularly the North Atlantic world. Neither side, it seems to me, did itself much credit.

The behavior of the Iraqi regime has been disgraceful: repressive at home, mischievously adventurous and violent abroad. Most recently in its illegal occupation and annexation of Kuwait, it brought destruction upon its people, first through American bombing and mass devastation, then through a merciless persecution of its own population, especially the Kurds, persecuted, betrayed, and in danger yet again of being abandoned. Certainly Iraq's government did important things domestically to build a secular society, to take major steps in development, education, health, agriculture, oil, and housing. But along with almost all the other Arab governments it did very little for human rights. Democracy does not really exist as a result, and the shocking rampage against the sovereign state of Kuwait indulged in by the Iraqi army cannot at all be characterized as having anything to do with the best things about Arabism, Arab civilization, or the Arab people. Neither has the restored government of Kuwait done itself credit, as the abuse of innocent expatriates continues, the mindless corruption and despotism remain unruffled and the likelihood of further stagnation, inaction, and political hopelessness increase each day.

As for the United States this was another imperial intervention, inspired by oil, not principles, mainly to consolidate a faltering empire, distract from the troubles at home, acquire a military aura at the expense of a tailor-made villain whom, interestingly enough, the United States in a certain sense supported and apparently still wants to live with as a useful foreign devil. It is perfectly obvious, however, that along the way, getting Iraq out of Kuwait has accomplished next to nothing; and once again the United States and its allies show themselves to be largely devoid of ideas, values, and any appreciable sort of moral or statesmanlike courage, except bellicose declarations and saber rattling.

This war must really be seen as an episode in a much longer and deeper contest. After its European wars, for instance, the United States quickly came to terms with Europe; the same was true of its conflict with Japan and Indochina which even after both were devastated seems to have settled into a sustained mode of doing business with the United States. Only with the Arab–Islamic world does one feel that after this particularly violent chapter the problems remain pretty much unsolved, pretty much simmering beneath the surface. There are wounds, betrayals, misunderstandings, and antipathies that seem to be reproduced generation after generation, each of them quite different but each of them sharing with all the others the sense that an overall contest between the West and Islam is still in place and still unresolved. To this level of tension President Bush has never addressed himself—and more's the pity.

Because of history and tradition, many people in the West and in the Islamic world like to think that they are part of a contest that has world-historical significance. In speaking about the West we are not really speaking about anything so concrete and so fully inclusive as to be monolithic. There are many Wests: there is a Catholic West and a Protestant West, there is a Judeo-Christian West and a secular liberal West, there is the West as represented by Europe and that West represented by the United States, there is the West that colonized Ireland, Africa, Asia, Australia, and Latin America, and the West that fought for abolition, for decolonization, for justice and freedom. Much the same points can be made about the Arabs and Islam: there is the Arab world of Abbasid and Andalusian culture and that of militant fundamentalism, the Arab world of the *intifadah* and the Arab world of the Gulf *Amirs*, of writers like Abdel Rahman el Munif, Kanafani, Jabra and of the official regime-sponsored journalism of nearly every leading Arabic daily.

The officially designated Arab world and the officially designated West are in conflict because in a strange way their official establishments require each other as enemies. Certainly it was true of George Bush and Saddam Hussein that each saw in the other an embodiment, in one case of Western imperialism, in the other of a foreign devil, each of whom had to be defeated not just militarily, but morally and culturally as well. This was why in the Arab world people supported Saddam, and certainly not because he was a real champion of Palestinian or human rights, and why also in the United States so many people supported Bush as the personification of Western civilization reversing aggression. For those Arabs who were also of the West it was a peculiar misfortune to fall into both of these rhetorical and almost exclusively negative traps, yet there was little space or opportunity afforded anyone to dispute either the notion that Saddam was equivalent to the Arabs and Islam, or the equally false notion that George Bush represented America and the West.

There is much more, however, to be gained by critically discussing and disengaging from the large collective passions. As we look around in the aftermath of Desert Storm, no one can be convinced that today the collective Arabs any more than the collective Americans who speak the language of justice and rights are doing anything different from what they did *before* Desert Storm; and that what they do now has anything very much to do with improving the concrete human rights of Palestinians, say, or women, or disadvantaged minorities in the Arab world, or enabling free expression, or freedom of the press, opinion, assembly, and the rest.

Every Arab state today proclaims the self-determination of the Palestinian people as one of its chief aims in life. All of the Arab states visited several times by Secretary Baker refused to take any steps toward a bilateral peace with Israel because, the leaders of these states said, there had to be movement on the Palestinian question first. Now steps toward a peace conference have been taken because the United States, as the major power, has taken them. In the meantime the *intifadah* is well into its fourth year. Now what is interesting about the *intifadah is* that it is the very thing that collective official Arab rhetoric has been speaking about for so long. The *intifadah is* Palestinian self-determination, and is not a figure of speech. As part of the *intifadah,* Palestinian men and women have taken their difficult lives under Israeli military occupation into their own hands; they have tried to construct a system of self-help and relative independence from the occupation, and they have thus roused themselves and the other Arabs into creating a model for communal life that is not based upon the exclusive authority of one party, one sultan, one repressive state apparatus.

To this the Arab states well before the Gulf crisis have responded really very little. If you compare everything published, all the words spoken in the Arab world, in support of Palestine since the *intifadah* began, you will see that none of it amounts to the financial and political support the *intifadah* really needed.

Roughly the same argument can be made about the United States' official rhetoric of support for freedom and the rights of people everywhere. While the President sent off over 650,000 troops to resist aggression, his government continued to block votes in the United Nations that supported agreed-upon rights for the Palestinian people. Over the years there have been sixty-four UN resolutions on the books, an additional twenty-nine of them vetoed unilaterally by the United States, some of them even supported by it, enjoining Israel to stop its dreadful abuse of the Palestinian people, and its annexation and settlement of Arab territory. None of them was ever as enthusiastically supported by the United States as was the liberation of Kuwait.

In the late twentieth century it is the case, I believe, that the language and the rhetoric of large-scale national and cultural identity is now seriously in disrepair. If we look at the contest between the West and the Islamic world, it is too vast and too unreal in many ways either to be won or lost conclusively. Even more important, there are too many exploiters of the situation who have wrapped themselves in the virtuous rhetoric either of the West or of the Arabs to do much more than keep themselves going.

That is why it is important now, with the Arab world sunk in a dispiriting torpor, with the absence of collective vision and leadership mostly the case in the West and in the Arab world, to stand back and look at the situation before us, on the eve of a likely peace conference, with a broader awareness of history, cultural possibility, and human responsibility, with a heightened sense of moral purpose, than the usual clichés about the Arab world, Islam, and the West afford us.

In the relationship between Europe and the Islamic–Arab world there is a very different history of problems, profits and encounters than that between the United States and that world. Europe first encounters Islam as an Arab religion, when it emerges from the Arabian peninsula in the seventh century and swiftly sweeps across Western Asia, North Africa, and southern Europe. Throughout the Middle Ages and the Renaissance, the Arabs and Western Europe were linked in all sorts of way, ways military as the history of the Crusades attests, ways cultural as the transmittal of knowledge from the Arabic scientific and philosophic tradition to European culture shows, ways theological as the whole history of Christian polemics and religious disputation against Islam beginning with John of Damascus testifies so eloquently and, alas, in so hostile a manner.

Norman Daniel, Hisham Djait, Maxime Rodinson, and Albert Hourani have correctly stressed the presence in this extended encounter of a great many contradictions. True the anti-Muslim polemics of Pascal and later of Renan characterize much that has remained as a prevailing attitude to Islam within European culture, but what has also remained is what Rodinson has called a fascination with Islam. The first non-Arabic version of the Koran was produced in the eleventh-century Abbey of Cluny by Peter the Venerable, a labor of interest and attention emulated by many later scholars, poets, travelers, and religious figures. Goethe, Hugo, Burton, Massignon: the list of great and gifted Europeans with a deep and abiding interest in the Arabs and Islam is a long and honorable one.

Yet since the late eighteenth century the relationship between the Arab world and Europe has been shaped by a largely political contest that has taken many forms. Beginning with Napoleon and continuing with the British expeditionary force to the Eastern Mediterranean, the French occupation of Algeria in 1830, the British occupation of Egypt in 1882, European powers have viewed the Arab world as a place to exercise their colonial energies. And this in turn has provoked a series of resistances to European colonialism that climax not only in various insurrections and nationalist agitations between World War I and World War II but also in such variously misconceived attempts as the partition of the Fertile Crescent, the promise of Palestine by the British government to the Zionist executive as a national home for the Jews, and—after 1870—the annexation of Algeria as a department of France. After a particularly bloody war, however, Algeria did achieve independence from France in 1962, and many of the countries of the Eastern Mediterranean also gained independence and liberation from either Britain or France, except Palestine.

Along with the struggle for political domination has gone a long-standing cultural and technological contest between Europe and the Arab–Islamic world. This too has been well studied and documented by a whole range of scholars and intellectuals. All of them agree in the main on three points. First is that European advances in industrialization, technology, and economic power rendered the Arab world especially vulnerable to domination. In this the Arabs were hardly more unfortunate than, say, the Indians, the Irish, or the Africans, as the global reach of European navies, missionaries, merchants, and scientists impressed on the entire globe the fact of what the historian Michael Adas has called "machines as the measure of man." In short non-European man and woman were found wanting, inferior, less developed, a fate which condemned many of them not only to subservience but also to slavery, poverty, and ignorance.

Second, the unbound Prometheus referred to by David Landes, which was Europe, instigated in the Arab world and across a wide front a great wave of nationalist sentiment. This ran the gamut from religious fundamentalism (still present in different forms today), to modernization of the sort that stimulated mass education, translation, local industrialization, and reformism, to a very various assortment of local as well as pan-Arab nationalisms. Much of this too has been well studied both by Arab and European scholars, although the tendency has been to see things according to a simple model of the West acting, the Arabs reacting. For surely there were aspects of Arab cultural activity, for instance, that answered to an internal logic within Arab society that was neither available nor permeable to Western influence. But there is little doubt that much of the animosity felt by Arabs toward the West today bears within it the history of defensive responses to encroachments from Britain, France, Italy, and so forth, all of them, in my opinion, shaped by such less than noble attitudes as the search for cheap resources, for ready markets, for strategic dominance, and the like. Rarely was the encounter an equal one, and even more rarely did it result, from the Arab standpoint, in a humane exchange.

Third and most interesting, there developed a certain intimacy between Europe and the Arabs that in another context Germaine Tillion has referred to as complementary antagonism, a sort of hostility that also included a knowing affection, long years of mutually engrossing experience, and grudging acknowledgment of each other's actuality. This never precluded the most savage repression visited by one on the other, nor, in the case of European colonial attitudes toward the

Arabs, did it prevent attitudes of the most rabid racialism, many of which still persist today. But—and this is the point—it was about knowledge and experience of a kind that has literally *never* existed between the Arab world and the United States, which in effect has succeeded Europe as the great outside power exercising hegemony over the Arab world, from the Atlantic to the Gulf.

In 1936 the leading Egyptian intellectual, scholar, and public figure Taha Hussein published a tract entitled *The Future of Culture in Egypt,* in which as a man deeply involved in university education as professor (later to become Rector of Cairo University) and as senior administrator (he was to become Minister of Culture), he outlined the topic from a perspective that was taken by many to be an official one. He spoke at length about Egypt's Islamic and Arab legacies and mission, but when he came to the country's future cultural orientation, he spoke exclusively about Europe. For Taha Hussein Egypt's role as the principal Arab country meant its recognition of its debt to the Greeks, the European Enlightenment, and above all to European industrial and scientific modernity. For indeed Hussein accurately articulated the Eurocentrism of an Egyptian elite that ever since Mohammed Ali's reign had locked itself into the European orbit, consciously and happily, despite the travail of colonial rule and imperial exploitation. Hussein makes no mention at all of Egypt's cultural links with Africa and Asia, both of which in the revolutionary era that succeeded his, Abdel Nasser's, were to be of central importance. [Interestingly enough, in the recent scholarship of Martin Bernal and Basil Davidson these links are also of the first magnitude.[24]] For Taha Hussein the mainly Arab–Islamic character of Egyptian culture would be oriented toward Europe, and not the United States.

Now most Americans have little idea of the world beyond the United States' borders, and most seem convinced that the United States is the world's policeman, entitled to intervene at will more or less everywhere and, having intervened and (as was the case with Panama, Vietnam, and Grenada) savaged whatever the place, thereafter to leave that place behind, forgotten, consigned to oblivion. I felt this in particular about the tremendous media campaign against Iraq. No matter what one feels about Saddam Hussein, and his government, it is also true that the United States did nothing serious to avoid war or to help Iraq in its search for freedom and democracy. One had the impression that Iraq was a tremendous desert with a mad Hitler-like figure sitting on top, and that it was not only all right but an excellent thing for the United States to pour a huge amount of firepower onto the place and virtually destroy it as a functioning country.

In fine, Iraq was reduced to a noncivilization, a noncountry, and its people were simply ignored, although it was, of course, they, far more than Saddam and his supporters, who bore (and continue to bear) the terrible brunt of the United States' attack. Now during the whole of the war, as well as the period before and after it, no one who had access to mainstream public discourse (in the media or the government) suggested that in spite of the current U.S. war with Saddam, Iraq was, after all, the inheritor of a great culture, its people were remarkably gifted and had done perhaps more than any other Arab people in the twentieth century to further artistic, literary, and architectural production in the Middle East. This, I think, might have been a small deterrent to the fury of the military attack on Iraq—but that deterrent was not there in the United States precisely because relationships between the Arabs and the United States are so humanly, culturally, historically attenuated, so abstract, so dehumanized, and in so many significant ways nonexistent. In the United States the Arab world has no cultural status at all; the few images of the Arabs that circulate are essentially negative and frightening, images such as those of terrorism, fundamentalism, and so on.

So far then I have been arguing that far from there being a monolithic West and an equally undifferentiated Arab world, there are important distinctions to be made, of which one of the most important so far as the West is concerned is the one today between the United States and Europe. When we turn to the question of Palestine—surely the longest-lasting matter at issue between the modern Arab world as a whole and the West—it first engaged modern Europe in conflict with the Arabs, before it engaged the United States in a continuation of the same conflict, not just with one Arab people, the people of Palestine, but with the whole Arab world. The present struggle between the Palestinian people and the state of Israel very much belongs to the historical relationship created over time between the Arabs and the West, and that so far as any Palestinian is concerned, the destruction of our society in 1948, the expulsion and dispossession of our people since then, as well as the military occupation of the West Bank and Gaza since 1967 is seen as extending and deepening the ravages in our midst of what began originally when Napoleon invaded Egypt in 1798, Western European colonialism.

In its earliest stages Zionism was of European provenance: its

institutions referred to and identified themselves as colonizing under-
takings in the manner of European colonization of Africa and Asia; its
whole rhetoric and ideological language borrowed heavily not only
from Jewish theology but also from the rhetoric and language of the
British in Africa and India, or the French in Algeria. (Later interpretations of Zionism as a "liberation movement" are retrospections of
fantasy, not of history or truth.) Central to the enterprise was the
qualitative distinction between incoming Jews from Europe, and those
natives who were variously depicted as absent altogether or, in the
words of Ben-Gurion, like red Indians, that is, a negligible quantity
entirely.

As I suggested, the complexity and richness of Palestine, however,
have involved Europe well before the onset of modern Zionism in the
late nineteenth century. One could say of this small, largely unprepossessing bit of land between the Jordan River and the Mediterranean
that more than any other on earth it is literally drenched in religious
and cultural significance, not only for Judaism and Christianity but also
for Islam, in whose tradition it has always had a unique sanctity. Until
the Renaissance, Jerusalem—the city of my birth—was placed at the
center of the earth in most European maps of the world. Crusades
were fought over Palestine, and although the actual physical territory
was unknown to most of the people who referred to it, it was the
center of imagination, of culture, of world history for generations of
Europeans, from Shakespeare and Dante to the humblest village dwellers in France and Ireland. Without actually ever being seen, Palestine
informed the iconography of Western art; it underlay Rome and the
Roman Church and, ironically, it also undergirded the entirety of the
Protestant Reformation. It is perhaps a comic, perhaps even a pathetic
fact that when Western European and American missionaries came to
Palestine in the nineteenth century they ended up by converting no
Jews and no Muslims; they succeeded only in making converts of the
local Eastern Christian sects who, for reasons having to do with a free
education and other emoluments of this world, joined the Anglican
community (like my paternal grandfather in Jerusalem) or the Baptist
Church (like my maternal grandfather in Nazareth). The point is that
Europe in particular and the West in general had designs on Palestine
that go back to the beginning of the Christian era, designs that entailed
the overriding of native communities in Palestine, designs that entailed
a huge amount of conflict with the native cultures of the place.

Yet when it came to the politics of an actual Palestine and the wishes of its actual inhabitants, one always senses that in the Western consciousness an agenda of far greater consequence is at stake than that imagined by some essentially insignificant Palestinian individuals. Consider the following sentences from a memorandum written by Arthur Balfour in 1919:

> The contradiction between the letter of the Covenant [the Anglo-French Declaration of 1918 promising the Arabs of former Ottoman colonies that as a reward for supporting the Allies they would have their independence] is even more flagrant in the case of the independent nation of Palestine than in that of the independent nation of Syria. For in Palestine we do not propose even to go through the form of consulting the wishes of the present inhabitants of the country, though the American Commission has been going through the forms of asking what they are. The four great powers are committed to Zionism, and Zionism, be it right or wrong, good or bad, is rooted in age-long tradition, in present needs, in future hopes, of far profounder import than the desires and prejudices of the 700,000 Arabs who now inhabit that ancient land. In my opinion that is right.[25]

Not merely the expression of an opinion, this remark and many others like it made possible the availability of Palestine for literally millions of Jewish immigrants, in the past as well as in the present, and they in turn took over the land, dispossessed and exiled the natives, and today sit in military occupation over approximately two million Palestinians on the West Bank and Gaza. In 1948 my entire family was turned into a scattering of refugees, none of whose older members ever recovered from the trauma. Since the occupation began in 1967, the Palestinian people have had no political rights at all; since the *intifadah* began in late 1987 until the end of June 1991, 983 have been killed by the Israeli military (this is three times the number of blacks killed by South African troops under *apartheid* for the same length of time); more than 120,000 wounded and beaten, and 15,000 political prisoners in continuous incarceration, most of them without benefit of trial, defense, reprieve, or even a charge; more than 112,000 trees have been uprooted, and 1,882 houses have been punitively demolished; at least 50 percent of Palestinian land has been confiscated, and more than 220 Israeli settlements established, all by force of Israeli arms, all by official Israeli policy. Over time, books have been routinely banned, for example, Plato's *Republic* and Shakespeare's *Hamlet*, as is the word *Palestine* and the colors of the Palestinian flag. Many schools and the leading universities were, and often are still closed, so determined has Israel been to criminalize Palestinian education. Two hundred or so Palestinian leaders have been deported, and literally thousands of days of total twenty-four-hour curfew have confined almost two million unarmed and essentially defenseless civilians to their houses. All of these measures by the Israeli authorities have been condemned as violations of the Geneva and Hague conventions by Amnesty International, the Human Rights Watch, even the U.S. Department of State—to no avail.

Despite Israel's unqualified hostility to the Palestinian people, and as one Israeli government after another has moved further to the right, become more and more intransigent and rejectionist, Palestinians have become more moderate, more reasonable. The Palestinian political program as set forth in 1988 by the Palestine National Council (PNC) has been unambiguously clear: Although official Israel has refused to accept any of the provisions of the Palestinian political program, that program remains as is, despite the Gulf War. Passed in late 1988, the Palestinian program calls for two states on a partitioned Palestine; it recognizes Israel; it accepts the validity of UN Resolutions 242 and 338, and it envisions an end to the armed conflict between Israelis and the Palestinian people through political negotiation. Israel's response has been unambiguously clear and unambiguously negative: no withdrawal, no Palestinian state, no end to settlement, no end to confiscation, no dealings with the PLO.

Now of course the political positions of the Israeli government are well known and have played far too great a role in determining the U.S. position in the upcoming peace conference. What Israel does to Palestinians it does against a background, not only of the long-standing Western tutelage over Palestine and the Arabs that I discussed earlier, but also against a background of an equally long-standing and equally unflattering anti-Semitism that in this century produced the Holocaust of the European Jews. We cannot fail to connect the horrific history of anti-Semitic massacres to the establishment of Israel; nor can we fail to understand the depths, the extent and the overpowering legacy of suffering and despair that informed the postwar Zionist movement. But it is no less appropriate for Europeans and Americans today, who support Israel because of the wrongs committed against the Jews, to realize that support for Israel has included, and still includes, support for the exile and dispossession of the Palestinian people.

Palestinians today and since 1948 are the victims of the victims, and are kept in this position to a great extent by Europe and the United States, both of whom look away and excuse Israeli behavior because Israel is seen as a state of survivors. Moreover, as a state whose economic and political well-being depends to an enormous degree on generally Western and specifically American support—almost 25 percent of Israel's GNP today takes the form of American aid, which since 1967 has totaled the staggering figure of 77 billion dollars—we are entitled to draw the conclusion that Israel's occupation policies on the West Bank and Gaza are in fact subsidized by the West.

Nor must we overlook the sad fate of Israel's Palestinian citizens, 780,000 of them who today constitute 18 percent of Israel's population. They are underrepresented in the Knesset—that is, at about 1 percent of the entire membership. Their juridical status in the State of Israel—which unlike every other state in the world today is not the state of its citizens but the state of the entire Jewish people—their status is confined to that of "non-Jews"; they receive less than 1 percent of the education budget, and their life expectancy and rate of infant mortality are dramatically worse than those of Jewish citizens of Israel. But it is when it comes to landholding that the worst discrimination is enacted against them. Since 90 percent of the land of the state of Israel is held in trust for the Jewish people, non-Jews are allowed neither to buy nor to lease land, privileges reserved totally for Jewish citizens.

As recently as September 16, 1991, residents of the town of Ramyah—close to the development town of Carmiel—have had their land expropriated for use by incoming Russian Jewish immigrants. Thus it is clear that far from being a threat only to the well-being and landholding of Palestinians in the Occupied Territories (where Israel has expropriated 90,000 acres, more than 50 percent of the land), the massive wave of Russian and Ethiopian immigrants to Israel, whatever the obvious humanitarian reasons for their arrival, are also a threat; their arrival means that Palestinians will be dramatically, catastrophically less well off as a consequence. To make matters worse, the ordinary democratic freedoms of expression and opinion allowed Jewish citizens of Israel are curtailed for non-Jews. Thus a well-known Palestinian–Israeli writer, a distinguished poet who is also a non-Jewish citizen of the state of Israel, has been on trial and convicted of terrorism because a book of his poetry has been found "dangerous" to the state. Were it not for groups such as PEN, abuses against

Palestinian writers and artists would go unreported and unprotested by Western liberals, who on the other hand, and quite justifiably, supported Salman Rushdie's right to publish freely.

But it would be too simplistic to say that the West, especially Europe, no longer owed the Jewish people restitution for what is a terrible history of anti-Semitism. In the United States, for example, a long history of enslavement and racial discrimination against the black people has subsequently produced what I think is a fair practice of affirmative action—that is, minorities are actively helped to achieve what historically they have been deprived of. And whereas it is scant reparation for what white American society did to the African-American people, it is something. So, one could argue, this is what Israel represents, reparation for what the West did to the Jews, up to and including the dreadful exterminatory massacre of European Jews. There has therefore been little time for and scant inclination to listen to the pathetic bleats emitted by Palestinians. But in reality the situation has been changing, as more and more Palestinians have forced themselves upon the Western consciousness, as more and more of them actively resist the colonial measures administered against them in their ancestral land by Israeli soldiers and colonial officials.

At a time when most of the tyrannies of Eastern Europe, Latin America, the Soviet Union, have collapsed, three places remain— Ireland, South Africa, and Palestine/Israel—where hostility between communities has prevailed for decades. In each of them, a minority is surrounded by an unreconciled majority; it has appeared important therefore for the embattled minority to maintain a state of siege—that is, for a minority, like the Israelis or the white South Africans, to maintain a state of siege against the majority, the Muslim and Arab majority in one instance, the black majority in the other. The problem with this model, as any visitor to Ireland or South Africa or Palestine can readily see, is that it is flawed in at least two ways: first, it suggests that the minority just because it is a minority is to be forgiven, despite any or all of its provocations and sins against the majority; second, the model ignores the fact that important change can take place and has taken place in at least two places, South Africa and Ireland. Far from the situation being frozen into an unending siege, an immensely significant transformation has occurred to require a change in perspective. A scant eighteen months ago the ANC was considered a terrorist organization, banned from the country, most of its leaders either in exile or in jail; today you can visit ANC headquarters, as I did recently when I went to Johannesburg, in the downtown Shell House, and its leaders, Nelson Mandela, Oliver Tambo, Walter Sisulu, and Joe Slovo, are major political figures in the country. There are negotiations, and of course, there are still huge problems: The point, however, is that the situation is now transformed so that both the majority and the minority are involved in discussions about the future of the country, about power sharing and about enfranchisement.

The Irish situation is also vastly different today than it was a decade ago. There is an Irish state, there is an Anglo–Irish Agreement, and even though there is partition and British forces are still in Northern Ireland, discussions are under way about the future of Northern Ireland. People speak about unification, and they also speak about the past, and about the British occupation, with frankness and passion, but change is occurring, not soon enough, not quickly enough, but unmistakably. In both Ireland and South Africa, of course, violence is still a major ingredient of the current political situation.

For at least ten years it has been internationally impossible to say a good word about South Africa, because South Africa has been irrecusably attached in the public mind of the West with apartheid. Not only was South Africa banned from international artistic and sports events, but a widely sustained policy of economic sanctions and a cultural boycott have remained in effect for a considerable period of time. In the United States a successful campaign against investment in South Africa was waged on the campus, with results in divestment policies and a raised political consciousness that have been dramatic. To a large degree change has come about due to the ANC's international success in connecting South Africa's identity as a nation directly to its deplorable racial policy.

No such connection has been made with regard to Israel and its treatment of the Palestinians, half of whose number now resides outside of Palestine as refugees, stateless persons, and persecuted exiles. Today people can oppose apartheid in South Africa and say not one word about Israel's practice of apartheid on the West Bank and Gaza. Writers and intellectuals can quite easily refuse—as many do— to visit South Africa in observance of the cultural boycott, whereas they can go and give lectures in Israel, completely ignoring what Israel has done to Gaza, which is a great deal worse than Soweto. If today a film or theatrical producer wishes to put on a Palestinian play or film the dangers of commercial suicide are too great; think of what happened to Vanessa Redgrave. Books and articles are prevented from being published and they are opposed so forcefully when they are published, not because they don't tell the truth, but because *they do*. A new tactic has been to impugn the person and completely ignore what he or she says if that happens to be accurate and sheds an unflattering light on Israel.

In both the American and the Israeli cases I have discussed there have, of course, been instances of courage, of speaking out, of intellectual responsibility, but these cases have been overridden by the fear and self-censorship of the majority concerned. People follow dogmas quietly on their own since these have been internalized as constituting unquestioned norms for what should or should not be said. Yet I want to underline my conviction that only a revitalized conception of the intellectual vocation itself can remedy the situation.

Almost seventy years ago Julien Benda accused intellectuals of failing in their mission when they compromised with the truth and succumbed instead to what he called the organization of collective passions. We live in a more difficult world today. Intellectuals have become vastly specialized in their field of expertise; they do not cross over from one to another, nor do they challenge the prevailing consensus, which in the West is like a lucrative Kuhnian research paradigm that guarantees consultancies, jobs, promotion, and the like.

To return to the Palestinian–Israeli case and the challenge it offers to the intellectual conscience: I do not want to be interpreted as saying that Palestinians are innocent, or that as a people they have been passively tolerant of their fate. Such words as *innocent* have no place in discussions of this sort. We are discussing attributions of responsibility based on an intellectually discriminating and accurate representation of the collective historical reality. It is therefore important to insist that Israelis are not white Afrikaners; nor are they like French settlers in Algeria. They have a history of suffering and of persecution that has made the state of Israel a compellingly attractive resolution for that history.

For Palestinians there is now a major threat to their culture and national existence, a threat which is neither theoretical nor just a vague possibility. The question to be asked is how long can the history of anti-Semitism and the Holocaust in particular be used as a fence to exempt Israel from arguments and sanctions against it for its behavior toward the Palestinians, arguments and sanctions that were used against other repressive governments such as that of South Africa. How long are we going to deny that the cries of the people of Gaza—a recent visitor told me that she could not open her window for three days, so great was the stench—are directly connected to the policies of the Israeli government and not to the cries of the victims of Nazism?

At the very threshold of a Middle East peace conference we should understand concretely that what is truly at stake in it, is neither a ten-billion-dollar loan guarantee to Israel, nor a patched-together arrangement between unpopular Arab rulers and Israel. The real issue is Palestine. The Palestinian people have accepted an extraordinary set of compromises, required of no other participant. As a result, only *we* will not be represented by our political representatives, the PLO; no one from East Jerusalem will be allowed to attend; no one from *outside* the West Bank and Gaza will be allowed to participate even though the Palestinians are one people, half of whose number live in forced exile outside Palestine. So not only will Palestinian participants be a subordinate part of the Jordanian delegation, they will have to face an Israel armed with what might be unconditional U.S. support and a series of inflexible positions that commit it to no withdrawal, no end to settlements, no negotiation on Jerusalem, no compromise on Palestinian *self-determination*. As Michael Lerner put it in his lead editorial for the September/October 1991 *Tikkun*:

> The conference is set up in such a way as to make substantive progress extremely unlikely. Israel will get its way on matters of procedure. After a largely ceremonial opening session, separate negotiations between Israel and the surrounding states will take place. But Shamir has reassured his constituency over and over again that there will be no compromise on the Golan Heights—and no compromise that would grant sovereignty or national self-determination to the Palestinian people . . . [They would get "limited autonomy" which] would allow Palestinians control over municipal functions such as fire and police services, garbage collection and street repair. Shamir's plan would not allow Palestinians' control over land and water resources, would not protect them from the increasing expropriations of land on behalf of Israeli settlers. . . .

In spite of all this, Palestinians have accepted what even Abba Eban has said is something unprecedented in the history of conflict—that one side, Israel, can pick the team both for itself and for the other side as well as the agenda. The United States has in effect gone along with this, although President Bush's position on the loan guarantees is the first instance of his administration's even suggesting that not everything about the Middle East should be dictated by Israel and the Israeli lobby.

We have no choice but to support the President's position, of course, but we must also speak out and say that the realities on the ground are too horrific and violent for the Palestinian people as to permit only a cosmetic peace to occur. One cannot in good conscience condone the endless enslavement of a people and the exile of many of its number and also expect silence and compliance. But that, I am sorry to say, is what the peace conference might portend if Israel and its supporters work their way further on the United States, which has already incorporated too many Israeli designs into the structure of the agenda of the conference. These designs—I must say categorically— are scandalously unjust, unworthy of the Jewish people in whose name Mr. Shamir (and later Mr. Rabin) and his colleagues purport to speak. To the current Israeli government Palestinians are at most aliens on Jewish land; according to Mr. Shamir and his colleagues, they cannot have a status that in any way diminishes exclusive Jewish control over the entire land of historic Palestine. Even to Israel's staunchest supporters such a vision of the future must clearly appear to be a formula for virtually unending conflict. No one can suppose that having resisted decades of unjust Israeli rule, the Palestinian people is about to give up and play dead. We have no strategic ally, the Arab environment is deeply hostile, Israel has an almost complete monopoly on the means of violence and coercion. But we do have hope; we are a resourceful and unendingly courageous people who will never submit to brute force; and above all we have a more just and, I think, a truer picture than our enemies of a future built on reconciliation and peace.

What we worry about is indifference and silence, especially in the United States, where it has too long been the case that because people are afraid of the Israeli lobby they simply turn away from the truth and continue to pour in the economic support, $4 billion plus per year. This must no longer be the case. The issues are clear, the dangers too obvious to be gainsaid. Peace is for everyone, not just for one people which happens to be in the ascendant. As Americans we have an urgent role to play as witnesses and referees to what might be the last chance in a generation for an opening toward peace in the Holy Land. Yet no one must shy away from the responsibility to speak out, to call injustice injustice, and to appeal not to present fears of the past but to future actualities and to the abiding truth about justice and peace.

Published as *Peace in the Middle East* in the Open Magazine Pamphlet Series, November 1991.

CHAPTER 18

Return to Palestine–Israel

[1992]

[I]

On Friday June 12, 1992, at about 7:45 P.M., our Air France flight touched down at Tel Aviv's Ben-Gurion Airport. My children, Wadie, twenty, and Najla, eighteen, had never before been to any part of the Holy Land; my Lebanese-born wife, Mariam, had visited Arab East Jerusalem a couple of times in the early sixties, when the city had been a part of Jordan. I was born in Talbiya, West Jerusalem, in November 1935, but since the end of 1947 just before Talbiya fell to Jewish forces in the early winter of 1948, I had not returned for a variety of political and personal reasons. True, I once spent a few days on the West Bank and East Jerusalem twenty-six years ago, but the Palestine I left as a twelve-year-old and the Israel we had just set down in were different places.

Arab Palestine was destroyed in 1948, its people, all but 120,000 of them, driven out in a terrifying mass exodus; a new Jewish state, Israel, came into existence. The virtual transformation of the Middle East through political upheaval, war, technological and social development and major shifts in population had also occurred. Then in June 1967 Israel occupied the 22 percent of Palestine that comprises the West Bank and Gaza, which had been under Jordanian and Egyptian control respectively since 1948. I had remained close to the Arab world, where even the idea of Israel was anathema, throughout this period, even though I came to the United States as a schoolboy in 1951 and stayed on as professor and writer. Most of my extended family, all of which had left Palestine as refugees in early 1948, had gone to and remained in Beirut, Amman, and Cairo. I had made many regular visits there since 1967. In addition, I had become very involved politically in the struggle for Palestinian rights. Forty-five years of my life had elapsed, and at last I was returning.

"Just a minute, please," said the young immigration officer, taking my American passport with her to a nearby office, leaving the three others on her desk. We were all extremely nervous as we waited. Would they send us back, would they grill us—me especially—and go through our bags, or (this was my private nightmare) would they march me off to prison? Between 1977 and 1991 I had been a member of the Palestine National Council proscribed as an enemy organization by Israel, and I had played a visible role in Palestinian advocacy in Europe, the United States, and the Middle East. I knew Yasir Arafat, was (crudely) referred to as "his man," and was even, as the scurrilous propagandists of the pro-Israeli lobby in the United States occasionally ventured, described as an accomplice of terrorists. We had planned to make the trip four years ago, but an announcement from Mr. Shamir's office indicated that we would not be allowed entry. This time we came without first asking, except to alert Mohammed Miari, a friend who was an Israeli Knesset member.

The immigration officer came back ten minutes later and, pushing the four passports through the little window, said somewhat indifferently, "OK. You can go now." No questions at all. Then we proceeded to the next stop and another young woman who guarded a security barrier. Exactly the same thing happened, except that this time we were also greeted by Miari's familiar face. His parliamentary immunity allowed him access to the arrivals hall. What immediately struck me about Mohammed, and indeed about all the Palestinian Israelis we met, was how easily, unaffectedly, casually they spoke with Israeli Jews, civilians and uniformed personnel alike. I had assumed that there would be a manifest uneasiness or even fear, as between members of subaltern and dominant groups, but it was always matter-of-fact, casual, and often cocky. I remarked on this to friends, who invariably responded that it was "our" country too, and we (unlike them) spoke Arabic *and* Hebrew, so why be uneasy? The national snubbing of Palestinians by Israel is evident in road signs, all of which are in Hebrew, of course, some with English translations, only a few in Arabic.

A few moments later we were out, minus my suitcases, which were apparently "lost" (not to worry, said the El Al lost-and-found person, with a couple of winks and a smile. "They'll turn up in forty-eight hours," which they did, a little untidy inside.) That ended the ordeal. Mine was the generation raised in an Arab world according the Jewish state no recognition at all. This odd proposition made possible a policy of nonknowledge, a void that erected a wall around itself, allowing both Israeli and Arab leaders to get away with literally everything in the name of security. Until 1967 the Arab world, including the millions of floundering Palestinians in exile, nearly forgot about their compatriots who remained after 1948. Until 1967 it was even impossible to use the word "Israel" in Arabic writing. Until our visit two months ago states like Jordan, whose leaders have met regularly in acknowledged "secrecy" with Israeli leaders, would not allow citizens of any nationality to enter the country with passports stamped by Israeli border officials. All this was supposed to cost Israel in legitimacy and resolve, so that if we didn't acknowledge its presence it would go away. Of course it didn't, although many of us (those whose passports and safe jobs made it feasible) needed a long time to make the return trip, cross the barrier, and confront the difficult reality.

Miari, plus his wife and daughter and Rashid Khalidi, an American-Palestinian friend spending the summer in Jerusalem, drove us up to that extraordinary city in the quickly darkening twilight. When we arrived, a brilliant star-dotted sky swept by cold winds overhung the city's heights, and as we crossed the handsome stone threshold of the American Colony Hotel, I was already conscious of trying to stem the torrent of memories, expectations, and disoriented impressions that assaulted me. Tentatively at first, boldly later, I found myself repeating inwardly that I did have a right to be here, that I was a native, and that nearly everything in my early life could be traced to the city of my birth. I was baptized in St. George's Anglican Cathedral (built in 1899), a couple of hundred yards from our hotel; along with most of the male members of my family, I had attended the Cathedral school, St. George's; my family had owned property in Jerusalem barely a mile from where I now stood, was connected to a whole network of other families, was in fact as Palestinian as you could be. What is it that remained now, I kept asking myself, what could be reconstituted through memory and then experienced in a ten-day visit, despite the politics of extreme antagonism that I had lived for forty-five years?

With the Miaris and Rashid we had a pleasant supper in the hotel garden that first night, and began to plan for the next few days. I thought of the visit as having two parts, one personal—to see for myself and show Mariam and the children the Palestine I grew up in but which had become Israel—the other contemporary and political: to discover what and where the Palestinians were on the West Bank and Gaza, where as a people we claimed sovereignty and the right to establish a state. In both places, Israel intervened. My Palestine had become a Jewish state, in which the Palestinians who stayed behind now numbered almost 850,000 people, 18.5 percent of the predominantly Jewish population. The West Bank and Gaza were Occupied Territories, militarily under the control of Israeli soldiers, settlers, and colonial officials. About two million Palestinians lived there.

The distances I remembered never corresponded to the distances we actually traveled. Jericho and Jerusalem, for example, were much closer than I had supposed. My saintly grandmother used to spend her winters in Jericho, which seemed like another country when she prepared her bags meticulously and laboriously several days before she went: it turned out to be less than thirty minutes away, a dusty and unprepossessing place that we first passed on our way to Tiberias and the north. Acre was much farther away than I remembered, and Haifa, where an uncle of mine used to live on Mount Carmel, overlooking the city, was almost a different country. Early memories of regions like the Galilee were overlain with more recent visual impressions— photographs, film scenes, tourist commercials for Israel, and pictures conjured up by reams of prose. This visit was to clear away years of neglect and weedlike growth, to see for the first time in four and a half decades what exactly it was about.

Jerusalem was the hub of it all. The Holy Sepulcher, that center of centers, was exactly as I recalled it, an alien, run-down, unattractive place full of frumpy middle-aged tourists milling about in the decrepit and ill-lit area where Copts, Greeks, Armenians, and other Christian sects nurtured their unattractive ecclesiastical gardens in sometimes open combat with each other. I remember being carried around in it on my father's shoulders, wondering who those bearded foreigners were, and could *this* be the actual site of Christ's last hours? Both Najla and Wadie seemed perplexed and upset by its incongruities: Najla was particularly disturbed by the third-rate commercialization—''Like a market,'' she said—and Wadie by the rambunctious, seemingly hostile priests.

The four of us wormed our way into an ongoing Greek Orthodox service, where much incomprehensible muttering, chanting, and jostling did little, alas, to compose our irritated souls. All of the tour groups were led by Israeli guides now; this was equally true at the splendid Dome of the Rock, one of Islam's holiest shrines. A friend later told me that no Palestinian guides now worked, since the Israeli occupation forces held the sites and trained the guides; after all, it was through Israel that most groups today entered the West Bank and East Jerusalem.

To me this was a privately disquieting sign: My paternal grandfather had for a time worked as a tour guide, and my father as a boy sold crowns of thorns to tourists near the Sepulcher. That particular association was now ended. Yet a few yards away, underneath a declivity in the city wall, we stumbled on Zalatimo, the renowned pastry shop whose specialty *mtabaqa* was a great family favorite. A wizened old baker was in there stoking the oven, but his ancient form suggested something only barely surviving. As we headed away from the Old City toward West Jerusalem by taxi that afternoon, I sensed for the first time that odd combination of exhilaration and mournfulness I felt as we visited familiar sites in (which was it mainly?) Israel or a recollected Palestine.

There were four prosperous and new Arab quarters largely built during the Mandate period (1918–1948): Upper and Lower Baqaa, Talbiya, and Qatamon. I recall that during my last weeks in the fall of 1947 I had to traverse three of the security zones instituted by the British to get to St. George's School from Talbiya; by December 1947 my parents, sisters, and I had left for Egypt. My aunt Nabiha and four of her five children stayed on but experienced grave difficulties. The area they lived in was made up of unprepared and unarmed Palestinian families; by February Talbiya had been taken over by the Hagganah. Now as we drove around, looking for my family's house, I saw no Arabs, although the handsome old stone houses still bear their Arab identity.

I remembered the house itself quite clearly: two stories, a terraced entrance, a balcony at the front, a palm tree and a large conifer as you climbed toward the front door, a spacious (and at the time) empty square, designated as a park, that lay before the room in which I was born, facing toward the King David and the YMCA. I do not recall street names from that time (there are none, it turns out) although Cousin Yousef (now in Canada) drew me a map from memory that he

sent along with a copy of the title deed. Years before, I had heard that
Martin Buber lived in the house for a time after 1948, but had died
elsewhere. No one seemed to know what became of the house after
the middle 1960s.

Our guide for the trip was George Khodr, an elderly gentleman
who had been a friend of my father's and an accountant for the family
business, the Palestine Educational Company. I vividly recalled the
main premises (comprising a wonderful bookshop at which Abba Eban
had been a regular customer): These were built against the stretch of
city wall running between the Jaffa and New gates. All gone now, as
we drove past the wall, and up the Mamila Road, then a bustling
commercial center, now a gigantic construction site where a Moshe
Safdie settlement was being built. Khodr's family had also lived in
Talbiya in a house he took us to so as to orient himself. Despite the
Mediterranean foliage one might have been in an elegant Zurich sub-
urb, so patently did Talbiya bespeak its new European personality. As
we walked around, he called off the names of the villas and their
original Palestinian owners—Kitaneh, Sununu, Tannous, David,
Haramy, Salameh—a sad roll call of the vanished past, for Mariam a
reminder of the Palestinian refugees with the very same names who
fetched up in Beirut during the fifties and sixties.

It took almost two hours to find the house, and it is a tribute to my
cousin's memory that only by sticking very literally to his map did we
finally locate it. Earlier I was detained for half an hour by the oddly
familiar contours of Mr. Shamir's unmistakably Arab villa, but abandoned that line of inquiry for the greater certainty of a home on Nahum
Sokolow Street, 150 yards away. For there the house was, I suddenly
knew, with its still impressive bulk commanding the sandy little
square, now an elegant, even manicured park. My daughter later told
me that, using her camera with manic excitement, I reeled off twenty-
six photos of the place which, irony of ironies, bore the name plate
"International Christian Embassy" at the gate. To have found my
family's house now occupied not by an Israeli Jewish family, but by a
right-wing Christian fundamentalist and militantly pro-Zionist group
(run by a South African Boer, no less, and with a record of unsavory
involvements with the Contras to boot), this was an abrupt blow for
a child of Palestinian Christian parents. Anger and melancholy took me
over, so that when an American woman came out of the house holding
an armful of laundry and asked if she could help, all I could blurt out
was an instinctive, "no, thanks."

More than anything else, it was the house I did not, could not, enter that symbolized the eerie finality of a history that looked at me from behind the shaded windows, across an immense gulf I found myself unable to cross. Palestine as I knew it was over, reminding me of my last view of my father a few days before he died in Beirut as I was about to return to my work in New York; he lay in bed, already slipping in and out of a cancer-caused coma, and then after I hugged him good-bye he turned his face to the wall and seemed quickly to fall asleep. That was January 1971. Exactly four days after we saw the house in Jerusalem in June 1992, I took my family to St. George's to visit the old "Bishop's School," as it is known in Arabic. There I showed my son Wadie his grandfather Wadie's name on the cricket and football First Eleven boards for 1906 till about 1911. In the assembly room where morning prayers used to be held, a seventy-year-old caretaker asked us shyly whether we'd like to see old school pictures. He brought up four—a class picture from 1942, the staff in 1927, etc.—from the cellar (they're about to be thrown out, he said), one of which riveted my attention. A work of great formal beauty, it was signed "Kh. Raad," the name of Palestine's most famous photographer, Khalil Raad, a nervous but gifted man whom I remember would fussily arrange and rearrange us for group pictures during weddings and confirmations. There seated on the floor next to a young man carrying a football with "1906" written across it, was in fact my father as a boy of twelve or thirteen.

The coincidence was too much for me at that point, suddenly vitalizing my family's history with this astonishing serene likeness of my young father as I really never knew him, and, as I thought back to the silent Talbiya house, with its lamentably foreclosed destiny now in "Christian" hands, that world seemed condemned to intermittent scraps and shards of memory and melancholy. I think I knew at that instant why I should have left politics and resigned from the PNC, as I did, in late 1991, and why I felt I had to return to Palestine just then. Wasn't it that the shocking medical diagnosis I received in September of a chronically insidious blood disease convinced me for the first time of a mortality I had ignored, and which I now needed to experience with *my* own family, at the source, so to speak, in Palestine? And then the reminder of other earlier histories starting and ending in Jerusalem seemed for me a fitting accompaniment to the ebbing of my life on the one hand, and, on the other, a concrete reminder that just as *they* had started and ended, I did and would too, but so too would my children, who could now see for the first time the linked narrative of our family's generations, where that story belonged but from which it had been banished.

I didn't then know why it was that the rest of our trip in Israel/Palestine was focused on associations with my mother's family, originally from Safad, then Nazareth. Retrospectively, I guess that I felt it as some sort of balance—in its less middle-class tone, its more eccentric and inspired waywardness—for the dour finality of what in effect was my father's Anglican, formal, mortuary Jerusalem. (Until her dying day my father's sister, Nabiha, referred to her closest friend as "Mrs. Marmura," who in turn always referred to "Mrs. Said," and this after more than fifty years of friendship.) As we drove north toward Safad and then Nazareth, we passed Beisan, which I remember as a sleepy, mostly Arab village, but which has become an unattractive, exclusively Jewish town—Beit Shean—with rows of nondescript tenements paralleling both sides of the highway. The striking disparity between the gentle and rather dry rolling hills, with their moderate-size evergreens, gray rocks, and brown sands, and the unyielding uniform buildings put up by the Israelis everywhere suggests not so much incompatibility as a kind of unfriendliness, as if the land as they took it had to be disciplined, compelled into submission.

Then, as we drove along toward Tiberias, I noticed something I had seen all along the coast, up from Jerusalem, to the ports of Haifa and then Acre: how practically every open space, whether football field, orchard, or park, seemed surrounded by barbed wire. This fixation on enclosure blended in tidily with the numerous prisons I saw (like Telamund) along the Haifa road, with its largely Palestinian prisoners, and its unending rows—two, three, four deep—of wire. I noted another contrast, particularly in resorts like Tiberias: the sudden, overblown assertiveness of luxury hotels, high-rise condos, and the like, blaring out a message of Expensive Holidays. We stopped for coffee at the Miami Beach-style Moriah Plaza, where a young Palestinian with whom we had an appointment impressed me by his ease in a totally Jewish enclave. This was our first entry into a place like that, so instinctively I think did we tend to emphasize our American provenance, speaking English protectively, and so forth. Not Mohammed (who didn't know English anyway): he insisted on speaking Arabic to us rather loudly, and then with equal aplomb, talking away in Hebrew to the pretty young Israeli waitresses.

After Tiberias we stopped at Tabgha, a tiny village near Capernaum at the north end of Lake Galilee, which I hadn't seen since 1945, a beach of singular calm and modest beauty that I also associate with roast corn, sold at the water's edge by itinerant peddlers. There is now an ostentatious German chapel that spoils the view, and as we left quickly I marked in my mind something I had not known, that Tabgha was where the miracle of the loaves and fishes took place. We used to go down to Tabgha from Safad, which is where my maternal uncle Munir lived, and where as a unique treat we would spend time in the summer. A renowned doctor, he and his wife were refugees in Jordan. They have been dead for fifteen years.

Clinging to the side of a steep mountain, Safad today has been entirely purged of its Arab inhabitants. A combination religious and artistic colony, it so sprawls in different clusters and directions as to have never afforded me a sense of where Uncle Munir's house (last visited in 1945) actually was. We met an old Arab-looking man trudging up the road, but he (a) didn't know where the "center of town" (my extremely vague landmark) was, and (b) averred as how he was from Morocco, and despite his ostensibly fluent Hebrew preferred to speak Arabic. Then as we rounded a curve I saw the long stair passage whose sinuous curves would bring us up and down as children from the house to Jamile's (I never knew her last name) little set of rooms, where she entertained us with gaudy postcards and a minuscule magic lantern. It was an extraordinary feeling to lunge up those stairs, now lined with shops selling Judaic religious objects, and suddenly see my uncle's house at the top, with its oddly high balcony, decorative Ottoman arches, and steep stairs flanking its side wall. But how changed was old Safad! Across the street were a group of Lubavitcher Hassids doing exactly what they do in New York—giving away their literature, looking for converts, standing apart from all. No vehicular traffic is permitted on the newly cobbled streets, crowded with tourists, soldiers, shoppers ambling through cafés, electronic shops, and the like.

The same gloomy feeling soon came over me here as it did in Talbiya, of a history finished, packed up, taking place elsewhere. The house was identified by a plaque as being the Municipal Building, but to look through one of its less soiled windows was to ascertain immediately that not only was it unused, but that its interior, chairs and tables scattered desultorily about, seemed frozen in time like Miss Havisham's Satis House.

Nazareth jolted me startlingly back to life. Of all the Palestinian sites I visited, it is among the richest in significance and the dimmest in memory. My maternal grandfather, Shukry Musa-Bishouty, died (in the late twenties) and is buried there, after having founded and built the Baptist church and brought up a gifted, perhaps even remarkable brood of children: my mother, Hilda, and four boys—a doctor, a lawyer, a physicist, and a banker—all charming, all fluent, all musical, in sum, very different (despite or perhaps because of their father's unrelenting Baptist fundamentalism) from the gray Victorian Anglicanism, in some ways like that of Theobald Pontifex's family in *The Way of All Flesh,* that I associate with my father's Jerusalem family. What also courses through the Musa-Bishouty family is a Lebanese current that connects us to the Levantine archness and hedonistic dash of that quixotic land, with its perplexing combination of wit and bloody-mindedness.

Nazareth today is really two towns: one, the bustling Arab *madina* where the Musas once flourished, and two, upper and Jewish or new Nazareth, set ostentatiously on hills that command the Arab, or lower, city. For Mariam and myself, Arab Nazareth was the only place we visited where we could quickly feel at home, so similar was it to a small-scale Amman or Beirut, the only pre-1948 Palestinian site not totally violated and interrupted by subsequent history. We were welcomed and then guided around by close family friends, the Abbouds, whose sumptuous table gathered in other friends (such as the celebrated writer Emile Habiby), and this respite allowed us a leisurely exploration of Nazareth's geography before we set out to see it. Then, as we entered the main square, I almost instinctively made out St. Mary's Well very close to where my mother was born and where she grew up. The topography has remained unchanged. My uncle Emile, who now lives in Athens and left Nazareth fifty years ago, had given me enough information to locate the house from landmarks like the Well and the Moscow Seminary (as it is still called), a large square building now functioning as local police headquarters. Unlike West Jerusalem, Nazareth was in effect the same place it was in 1948.

How peculiar then that, although the Musa house and the Baptist church have either been totally transformed (the former) or completely rebuilt (the latter), I felt more life in Nazareth, and considerably less sorrow than in Jerusalem. The new Baptist church, incidentally, has an unbecoming honeycomblike facade and, as a friendly American voice told me over the phone, my grandfather's tomb had been moved from the old church to a nearby cemetery. "We did it very well," he assured me, with Israeli health inspectors to ratify the proceedings, and then added, as if apologetically, "All we found inside were some bones and a Bible!" I prevented myself from asking what else he had expected.

A week later in Amman an American journalist questioned me about the visit and, somewhat reluctantly, I obliged with a summary description. After a few minutes from me, he deflated my recital: "Not to belittle your experience, Professor, but if I visited the New Jersey town I grew up in the changes would be similar." Perhaps . . . but I really doubt it, since a new country of (mostly) Europeans hadn't displaced New Jersey out of existence forty-five years ago; besides, he didn't seem to have returned to register the change. I had, and I was shaken.

[I I]

Midway through my stay in Jerusalem, a journalist from a leading Israeli daily, *Hadashot,* rang me at the American Colony Hotel and asked for an interview. I said that I was in the country on a personal visit and that the only interview I would give was to *Ha'aretz* which was conducted by Joseph Algazy. That had been arranged for me by an old and admired Israeli friend, Professor Israel Shahak, a great intellectual and uncompromising fighter for Palestinian rights. Five minutes later the same man called again, "Could we at least take a picture of you?" he asked. I again refused, and was therefore both irritated and unpleasantly surprised when a couple of days later *Hadashot* ran a story about me complete with an old file photograph proclaiming me to be in Israel on Arafat's instructions. These were nothing less than to persuade Palestinian Israelis to vote Labour (which in fact was to win) during the upcoming elections. To me, this offensive journalistic license illustrated the vast distance that separated Palestinian realities from Israeli fantasies about them. On a deeper level it demonstrated again that there was no private realm so far as individual actions were concerned, so politicized and entangled have we become with the Israelis.

But even this reality is difficult to handle, given that we are so much weaker, with dramatically fewer assets than the Israelis. Not having communicated with the PLO at all, I had no political agenda except to see for myself and then try to grasp the Palestinian situation inside

Israel and the Occupied Territories. This was difficult but important to do, especially since I was a creature of exile, a fate I shared with more than 50 percent of my compatriots, most of whom lived in Jordan, Syria, Lebanon, and, before the Gulf War, in the Gulf states. For us, the experience of living under Israeli rule was something we heard and read about but did not know directly. The majority of expatriate Palestinians have different problems: they suffer the tribulations of statelessness and, except for those in Jordan, which is the only Arab country to have granted them citizenship and relative security, they also suffer chronic uncertainty, and even persecution, about their fate.

In Israel, on the other hand, Palestinians are clearly marked inside the state as second-class citizens: Their average per capita income (in 1986–87) is about 282 shekels per month, versus more than 542 shekels for Israeli Jews. One needs only to glance at the figures supplied by Israel's Central Bureau of Statistics to see how Jews and "non-Jews" (the designation for Arabs in Israel who constitute 18.5 percent of the population) are separated into two classes, one of which is *always* considerably lower in status. This is true for health, education, unemployment, quality of life, right across the board.

Yet what impressed me on this visit is that inside Israel Palestinians do in fact survive as a community. Everywhere they live that is next to or in the midst of Jews, one has the impression of crowding and confinement. As we drove through Haifa, once a pretty Mediterranean city, now a cluttered hodgepodge of tenements, we were struck by the way Wadi al-Nissnass—an Arab quarter—was hemmed in on all sides as if like a cowering ghetto. It was an incidental irony that on the two occasions that we asked Haifa passersby for directions (in Hebrew), we were met with uncomprehending stares; later we discovered that we were talking with Russian Jews, one of whom I think I later recognized on a beachfront in Tel Aviv playing a forlorn Bach violin sonata with an alms cup next to him. Even though Palestinians are less favored than Jews in Israel, they are rarely separated from their compatriots because they don't know the language or are from someplace else.

Although we were there on the eve of the elections, I didn't have the impression that as a people the Palestinian citizens of Israel show little interest in organized politics. That my erstwhile airport host, poor Mohammed Miari, ended up by losing his seat was most likely a function of how the tiny number of Arab Knesset candidates couldn't work together. No, the Palestinian community inside Israel survives first of all by a fantastic, even maddening, and almost inadvertent stubbornness, and second, by here and there undertaking imaginative and courageous schemes for self-development and improvement.

One instance of the latter is to be found in Acre, a very sad place today. We walked through the medieval Arab port at the water's edge and were depressed by the sense of life being slowly and systematically choked off, buildings left unrepaired and empty, desolate people walking about in poor and yet curiously defiant circumstances. The great mosque has a leaking roof, yet no repairs are forthcoming because there is no public (i.e., Israeli) money for it, nor for any of the other buildings, for whose reinstatement I was told the government would not give permits.

In stark contrast there is the shining example of the Acre Pedagogical Center, headed by Mariam Marei, a woman I had met in Europe and the United States. An attractive and strong personality Ms. Marei has set up a small teacher training unit whose purpose is to train young people in the art of teaching Palestinian children unconventionally. Rather than rote methods or attempts to ape techniques from more fortunate, generally European or American, contexts, she helps teachers to draw on materials from their own environments—wood, say, or colored cotton fabrics—to animate, enliven, move the children's minds, which would otherwise be occupied with the poverty and relative hopelessness of their situation. Her methods are improvisatory, refreshingly unbureaucratic: puppet shows, cardboard models, folk poetry, incredibly colorful displays, invigorating talk. Her center is located in a nice old Arab house, and exudes a sense of discovery and optimism, totally undeterred by the lack of funds and the obstacles put in the way. The point she made to me was that by training teachers, who in turn taught young kids, "we" would have a better alternative than those offered by Israel.

This is another point to be mentioned. Everywhere I went I didn't feel like an outsider—which in many ways I was—but rather like a partner, one of the "we," in the problems and hopes encountered by people in daily life. I'd be sitting at breakfast at the hotel, and a young man or woman would come up to me with great politeness, and ask for a minute of my time. "There's this notion I have," one of them would say to me, "for a research project of some sort or other," and then would ask me for my ideas on the matter; no one I met asked me for direct help such as money or contacts. It was regularly ideas,

sources, or books. This, of course, was a relatively small sector of the
Palestinian population, but I noticed it equally among Palestinians on
the West Bank and also inside Israel.

And yet every time I went around the West Bank and especially
Gaza I was impressed with the sheer intrusiveness of the Israeli military. Nowhere have I ever seen such a profusion of green fatigues and
uniforms as there, not even in the Syria or Egypt of two decades ago.
It was nowhere worse and, in my opinion, more deliberately offensive
than in Hebron, where I was obliged to walk through small groups of
soldiers lounging around at the entrance to and inside the mosque. The
reason given for such coarse reminders of the appalling religious
muscle-flexing of Judaism in an Islamic holy place is that the mosque
is also the site of the Patriarchs' tombs: hence the soldiers, and the
recently opened Jewish Library just off the mosque's main hall. The
other particularly unpleasing military presence I noted is only slightly
less unattractive. As you enter the Jerusalem city walls at the Damascus
Gate and turn left, you immediately come upon a group of soldiers
sitting at the entrance of an imposing house at the top of which there
is an incongruously large menorah. This is where Ariel Sharon has
planted his banner, enlisting a small battalion of soldiers to make his
ideological proclivities stick.

Rashid Khalidi's cousin Haifa invited us to lunch in the Old City on
our first day. She lives there with her elderly parents and uncle, in a
house her family has owned for generations. Its main problem is that
one of its sides gives out on the Wailing Wall and is therefore a
prospective site for the settlers to pick, as they try to change Arab East
Jerusalem into a new Jewish city. Routinely she has found some of
these zealots peering over into her house, taunting her, threatening to
take the house from her, provoking her with catcalls and jeers from
adjoining houses. Wherever I went in the Old City, which has been
Arab for hundreds of years, I saw these settlers walking through
crowds of Palestinians, completely oblivious of them, usually armed
with handguns or Uzis (sometimes both), always—it seemed to me—
flaunting their power to be there, in the heart of the Arab *casbah*. After
lunch that day I was introduced to an elderly widow whose house had
been summarily expropriated by a group of settlers. Because the house
is all the wealth she has, she has been forced to move into a tiny
basement room of it, whose dark, airless interior is damp and unimaginably crowded, although it has miraculously accommodated six or
seven people. One of her daughters was laboriously blowing a hair

dryer onto some wet clothes. "They won't let us hang our washing outside," she said, pointing to her former home above. "When we try to, they pour garbage and dirty water on it."

The man who took me to the poor widow's house was in late middle age, a Mr. Sandouqa. He has the quiet, if sad, authority first of a longtime teacher, second, and more important, of the head of a local defense committee against settler incursions in Jerusalem. He showed me a modest house around which settlers had taken rooms and various bits of the courtyard, thus making entrance to the Arab house impossible except by walking through their ranks. The committee's first priority is to organize links between Palestinian inhabitants of the Old City, quarter by quarter, house by house. Then, Sandouqa told me, we pinpoint the houses that are immediately threatened, either because the settlers are trying to force people out coercively, or because they try to do it using phony (or, alas, authentic) real estate Arab middlemen, collaborators, who are in it for the money. He told us of another widow—they are a prime settler target—who had taken her case against squatters to court, had won the case, but was now trying rather fruitlessly to get the court order implemented. In the meantime she had been helped financially by her neighborhood committee branch and is also helped to pursue further legal procedures with lawyers provided by the committee. Another family I was introduced to had come home one evening to find a lone settler wandering about inside their house. When asked what he thought he was doing, he responded that he was there to look over "my house."

These episodes are at the core of the Palestinian predicament today, which is essentially territorial and geographical. Little about the peace talks has had much effect on the slow and relentless advance of the Israelis into more and more Palestinian space. Aside from the constant military presence everywhere on the West Bank and in Gaza, there is the equally constant settler presence on most of the hills. These take the form of the dreaded settlements; the most dramatic thing about them that I could immediately see—and an important clue to the year-long wrangle between the Bush administration and the Palestinians on the one hand, and both the Shamir and Rabin governments on the other—is that all of them are made up of two parts. First is the group of prefab houses that are finished and lived in. Usually behind them, standing in row after row in weedlike profusion, is the second part, houses (sometimes only the barest approximation to a structure, sometimes only a set of caravans) that are unfinished, empty and awaiting money for completion. No Israeli government, and certainly not Rabin's, has undertaken to abandon or let them remain incomplete. Their number is undetermined, but they are there to "thicken" the settlements, provide cheap subsidized housing in Arab territory so as to maintain pressure for irreversible Israeli sovereignty. So when George Bush gave Israel the ten-billion-dollar loan guarantees these unfinished houses were accepted as already "existing," with a further loss in Palestinian territory. The West Bank and Gaza together comprise only 22 percent of the whole of former Palestine, and of that 22 percent it is estimated that nearly 50 percent is expropriated and settled by Israelis.

The government has also devised a network of roads to the settlements that are laid out deliberately to avoid glimpses of Arab towns and villages; thus new Israeli pioneers can duplicate the feat of their immigrant predecessors who came to Palestine and did not seem to see and consequently ignored the native inhabitants. As we drove south of Jerusalem toward Bethlehem, Beit Sahour, and Hebron, I could see a new parallel road about two miles to the west. Aside from its wasteful allocation of scarce money, the road's purpose is also to connect settlements to each other and, in a sense, to disconnect or encircle the Arab populations. Driving in Ramallah later that week, I noticed a bold yellow line that first appeared on the main road in town and then swerved away out of town on a side road. I was told its purpose was to direct settlers out of the town who had come in to an Arab town either because they were lost or because no separate road existed yet.

Making matters much worse for Palestinians in the Occupied Territories is that the only functioning, that is, legal, authority in their lives is the Israeli military and civil administration. Speaking to Raja Shehadeh, one of the most gifted and subtle lawyers on the West Bank, I got the impression of a Kafkaesque struggle to make sense, keep abreast of and somehow get responses from a constantly changing, essentially obscure fabric of laws that govern every aspect of Palestinian life. All Palestinians are assessed extremely high and even punitive taxes, yet no one knows how that money is spent since there is no published Israeli budget for the West Bank and Gaza. No Palestinians are elected to office, none allowed to vote (as Israeli Palestinians can) for Israelis either. Anyone can be picked up, jailed, and tried, or not—just because an Israeli official or military person says so. There are now about a thousand laws passed by the Israelis, all of them regulating Palestinians in such a way as to prevent development, building, water, travel, electricity, education, journalism, political organization. "Occupier's Law," Shehadeh called it, and, he has argued, it is this body of laws that has gradually taken over Palestinian life in a legalistic, extremely methodical manner since 1967, and which must be just as methodically and deliberately taken back, dismantled by Palestinians acting through the peace process.

This is by no means to suggest that Palestinians are otherwise powerless or supine. As was the case with Palestinians in Israel, I noticed much the same resilience and enterprise in the Territories. When the schools and universities were closed for long periods during the *intifadah,* classes were held in alternative sites that I was shown (the schools were all open when I was there). Yet the most interesting thing I noticed about the structure of political authority on the West Bank and Gaza (especially the former) was the new legitimacy, visibility, and patronage of the peace delegation. Of course I visited Faisal Husseini shortly after we arrived in Jerusalem; he has visited me in New York several times, so I was reciprocating on one level. On another I was paying my respects to the acknowledged but unofficial head of the Delegation (as it is now called—*al-wafd,* in Arabic, with its unmistakable echo in memories of the great Egyptian nationalist party, also called al-Wafd, established in 1919 and headed by Saad Zaghloul who negotiated for independence for Egypt from the British). Husseini is an unaffected, unintellectual man whom it is impossible not to like. He is a born leader because, as another West Bank intellectual and prominent political figure, Mahdi Abdel Hadi, told me over dinner, he has the famous Husseini name (and an idealized father, Abdel Kader Husseini), he has institutions, the blessing of the PLO—still by far the most important source of Palestinian authority in the Territories—an unimpeachable record, and is accessible to and known by all.

Without him the Delegation, as well as Palestinian participation in the peace process, would have been impossible; yet without Yasir Arafat, Husseini probably wouldn't enjoy all the authority on the West Bank he now has. Going to see him in his modest Jerusalem home reminded me of seeing Arafat in Beirut, or Tunis. There is the same endless coming and going of different petitioners, supplicants, colleagues, family members, retainers, visiting dignitaries, all of it punctuated by phone calls and cups of coffee. Husseini is, like Arafat, very modest in manner, so that you are never given the impression of speaking up, so to speak, to an authority figure; on the contrary Husseini shares ideas, he has a neat sense of humor, and has never in my presence lapsed into bombast. The night I saw him he showed me a piece of paper announcing an agreement between him, as representative of the "National Movement," also known as the Delegation, the PLO, Fateh, whatever, on the one hand, and Hamas, the Islamic movement in the Territories, on the other. All sweetness and light, the document presented a reasoned argument for peaceful cooperation and political savvy in dealing with the Occupation and the peace process. Then, Husseini said, "Look at this other paper," which was dated a week later than the other. It was a circular purporting to issue from Hamas, denouncing Husseini and the Delegation as collaborators, traitors, sellouts. Internecine Palestinian conflict is a major threat to the future of the West Bank and Gaza.

I had spoken about Hamas rather anxiously with Husseini and others, including Arafat, in the past. "They have no more than fifteen percent," was the standard answer I used to get. Now Husseini admitted to somewhere around 30 percent. My son, Wadie, who has been taking university courses in classical Arabic, was struck by and drew my attention to the war of one-line, and often one-word slogans, on walls all over East Jerusalem, Hebron, Nablus, and elsewhere; some said simply "Fateh," others, written with numbing frequency next to or around or on top of "Fateh," said "al-Islam huwal hal" (Islam is the only solution) or more tersely, al-Islam. Occasionally one could see visible signs of some attempt to erase both sets (the Israeli occupation forbids wall slogans and graffiti), but the battle for hearts and minds is a very fierce one. I asked everyone I met, including Husseini, what "the only solution" really was, and got no very satisfactory answer except that it meant militant struggle of some sort. Abdel Hadi also suggested that, while strong indeed, Hamas has no visible or acknowledged leadership, although another friend also suggested that the Israelis and possibly the Saudis were behind Hamas.

This hasn't at all deterred Husseini and the Wafd. The main group is made up of university professors like Hanan Ashrawi, lawyers like Shehadeh, and various other personalities from the Territories, all of whom have become relatively well known through meetings and rallies, as well as the press, of course, and a gradually expanding (often shady) arc of influence-peddling, jockeying for position, and outright patronage. Husseini has hit on an ingenious device for giving the core group additional visibility. This was shown to me by Nazmi al-Jo'beh, an affable and trilingually articulate Islamic archaeologist, who took us on a tour of his native Hebron, and who is also a member of the

Delegation. He had a little laminated card in his wallet, which he exhibited with some amusement, as well as, I thought, some pride. It read "Member, Palestinian Delegation," in Arabic and Hebrew, and was signed by Faisal Husseini. As Jo'beh explained it to me, the card had no legal status whatever; it was a device for identifying members of the Delegation so that in dealings with the Israelis they would be treated respectfully. Unsaid was the fact that the card identified a member of the new Palestinian Interim Self-Governing Authority—PISGA—which is what is being negotiated (without any advances at all) with the Israelis in Washington, in effect, a Palestinian government. Attached to the Delegation are many subsidiary committees, advisers, research institutes, and the like, all of them helping to document, articulate, and present the Palestinian position on everything at the peace talks. All this is closely coordinated with the PLO, with the usual rumors of incompetence and corruption hanging over the whole thing.

It was while traveling around the West Bank and Gaza that I began to notice the minute difference in idiom between Palestinians there and those of us in exile. No one there, for example, refers to the Israelis except as "the Authorities." This has a distancing effect, but it is also precise enough to distinguish between ordinary or sympathetic Israelis, and those directly implicated in what is in effect colonial rule. No one I spoke to ever used the name of the month; dates are given entirely in numbers. Thus you say, "I came back from Amman on four, eight" (August 4), or, "They imprisoned Ali on ten, twelve," and so on. There is a whole political shorthand for identifying parties, trends, histories. For someone who grew up in the Arab world you have to keep translating quite consciously, since even when the words are the same they quite mean quite different things. Whenever I heard the phrase "the Front" inside Israel it required an effort to remember that the reference was not to the Popular Front (George Habash's party) but to the Israeli Communist Party, Rakah, in a later metamorphosis of which Palestinians, and not Israeli Jews, predominated. I would say that nearly every young (or youngish, up to the mid-forties) Palestinian man that I met made a passing, extremely unforthcoming, but unmistakable reference to time spent in Israeli jails. No one volunteered information to me about which jail or where it was, but I caught a glimpse of the protracted struggle with the Israelis inside the jails (for better conditions, for books, the right to hold study groups, etc.) that was maintained even after people left. An estimated 200,000 (15,000 of them are still incarcerated) men have passed through the jails, so no family has been spared.

It was when, on about the fourth day of our visit to the Holy Land, we went down to the Gaza Strip that my recent memories of a trip to South Africa kicked in with considerable force. In 1991 I had been invited to give the T. B. Davie Academic Freedom Lecture at the University of Cape Town; this required clearance from the cultural boycott committee, which I got, as well as additional sponsorship from the ANC and two other universities. One of the first things I did in Johannesburg was to visit Soweto, as well as other such townships in the vicinity and in Cape Town. Nothing I saw in South Africa can compare with Gaza in misery, in sheer programmed oppression, in confinement and racial discrimination. Yet like the West Bank Dhei-shah Camp south of Jerusalem, Gaza as a whole impressed me with a similar sense of transported and then confined delinquency that you get from the marginalized South African townships. Both Mariam and I quickly noticed in Gaza the proliferation of military observation posts, the incongruously high street lights (so that they can't be hit by stones), the acres of barbed wire, and the large number of patrolling "white" soldiers that you see in South Africa. Curiously, though, Israel has been spared universal criticism—because somehow viewed as unconnected to its practices in Gaza—as South Africa hasn't.

The day we drove down from Jerusalem began ominously with an unusual hail and thunderstorm. By the time we got to Gaza two hours later vast pools of mud and stagnant water made passage extremely messy, especially in the Jabalya Camp, which has the highest popula-tion density in the world, and houses over 65,000 refugees, displaced from as far north as Acre. You enter the Gaza Strip through what in fact is a large gate, which is locked at night, and gives the place the appearance of an enormous concentration camp. Numerous Israeli soldiers man barriers that stop each car, empty out passengers, check the magnetized pass cards, and in every way make transit both unpleas-ant and regrettable. As Jerusalem cars cannot enter without a permit, we were met at the gate by a close Gazan friend, Raji Sourani, a young lawyer who has won a number of human rights awards in the United States and Europe for his heroic efforts on behalf of Palestinian prison-ers, although he always tells people with a wry smile that he's never won a case. Most of what he does therefore is to visit his clients, making them feel that someone is looking out for them, keeping contact between them and their usually forlorn and often quite helpless family: This gives him additional prestige but has not at all protected him from Israeli attention (four jail sentences varying from a few months to a couple of years).

Jabalya Camp is the most appalling place I have ever seen. The numerous children that crowd its unpaved, potholed, and chaotic little streets have a sparkle in their eyes that is totally at odds with the expression of sadness and unending suffering frozen on adult faces. There is no sewage system, the stench tears at your gut, and everywhere you look you see masses of people falling all over each other, poorly dressed, glumly making their way from one seemingly hopeless task to the other. The statistics are nightmarish: the worst infant mortality rates, the worst unemployment, the lowest per capita income, the most days of curfew, the least medical services, and on and on. Raji had gathered about twenty men, leaders in fields like health, education, employment, and the like, for me to talk to in Jabalya. The house we met in was spotlessly clean on the inside, but surrounded with tiny little houses made of wood, mud, and tin, jammed together like so many empty boxes heaped up on each other. No zoning, no landscaping or beautification here. Any changes in the physical layout of the place, any attempt to drain the putrid stagnating water, for instance, or to improve a house, is forbidden, or requires a permit that is next to impossible to get.

I didn't hear a single hopeful thing in the two hours I spent with the men. One of them spoke of being in jail for seventeen years, his children sick, his parents and wife going from illness to destitution, to occasional improvement, all without a trace of self-pity. There was a lot of anger. The phrase I kept hearing, which will haunt me forever was *mawt bati'*, slow death. There seemed to be considerable animus against West Bankers, who were variously characterized by Gazans as spoiled, or privileged, or insensitive. "We are forgotten," they all said, and because of the unimaginably difficult job of dramatically (or even slightly) improving the general lot of Gazans, I was repeatedly enjoined *at least* not to forget.

Even as I write about it now I cringe at the memory of the place, despite (or perhaps because of) the unfailing generosity and gentleness of the people we met. Raji arranged for us to see Dr. Haidar Abdel Shafi, an eminent doctor and official head of the Palestinian Delegation, in his home a few miles from Jabalya. The Strip itself is made up of several towns (Rafah, Khan Younis, Gaza City), of refugee camps and, most offensive, of a number of posh-looking Israeli settlements, whose spacious lawns and swimming pools are so removed in appearance from the enforced squalor all around us as to make Marie Antoinette in comparison seem like an anxious radical. Abdel Shafi immediately communicated a sense of calm decency that has elevated him to universal admiration in Gaza and throughout the Palestinian world in part because, unlike Husseini and Arafat, he is not principally a political man, but someone whose life and relatively few words suggest an abiding sense of Palestinian nationalist struggle in Palestine. Speaking to him and his wife, I suddenly felt the whole fragmented picture of Palestinian society making some collective sense because in people like the Shafis and Raji and so many others that I met during that fateful trip to Gaza, the idea of an actual society that bound us all together somehow *did* survive the ravages of our history, its tragic mistakes, misfortunes, and the destructive course of Israel's policies.

An affecting reinforcement to what I had experienced earlier in Gaza took place as we came to leave, and more pieces fell into place. Raji wanted me to meet the mother of one of his clients, again a widow, whose imprisoned son was slated for deportation; there were some legal points to be discussed, and as the daily curfew time was approaching the visit had to be a brief one. This was in Rafah, a few yards away from the Egyptian border; here the two parts of the town are grotesquely separated by a barbed-wire fence into Egypt and Israel. The house was nondescript, but the woman herself, Um Mohammed, was surprisingly self-possessed and politicized. We had been told that her oldest son, a PLO cadre, had been killed in Lebanon; we met his young daughter whose name was "Beirut." In a matter of minutes I discovered that Um Mohammed's brother was Yusif Najjar, one of the three PLO leaders assassinated in Beirut by the Israelis in 1973. Kamal Nasser, one of the three, was a close friend and poet with whom I had had dinner the night before he was killed.

So there on a dusty side street in Khan Younis, as Raji Sourani explained to the family how their son was to be deported (a sentence rescinded by the new Rabin government), several additional strands of the Palestinian experience came together and were illuminated for me as rarely before: the gifted young lawyer, a native of Gaza, the refugee woman a camp dweller whose three sons were either killed in battle, in jail and sentenced to deportation, or recently released, and whose brother, an early guerrilla leader, had also been killed, while in Arab exile, myself the American Palestinian, still tied to this strange and tormented land after forty-five years of expatriation, and finally, my wife and children seeing Palestine and meeting Palestinians together for the first time.

My children, too, tied their own strands. My daughter's way of being connected was her delight in the children, who surrounded her wherever we went and whose sprightly vitality affected her more than their difficulties; Wadie, on the other hand, has been studying Arabic and Palestinian history passionately, so for him the visit was a goad to renewed effort, fortified commitment.

The very last thing I did before leaving the Occupied Territories for Jordan was to spend half a day at Birzeit University, near Ramallah. I can barely recall the Birzeit I knew as a child, which was then only a secondary school. It was founded in the 1920s, but its new campus today stands on land given it by the Nasir family, connected to mine through marriage and a long history of associations. Earlier in the week, I had been scheduled to go there for a seminar and lecture, both of which had to be canceled because Hamas had called a strike. (Parenthetically I must say that these periodic shutdowns of the West Bank strike me as colossally stupid and wasteful. No one is hurt by them except Palestinians, with shops and schools closed, and an immense amount of time lost in stupid posturing.) Rescheduled for our last day, our visit was shortened to a lunch given for us by Acting President Gaby Baramki and a public lecture-discussion. Not only was I eager to engage with an audience of Palestinian students and professors for the first time in my life, but I was particularly moved that the event was to take place in Kamil Nasir Hall, named for my dear friend, the Birzeit native son who had given his life for Palestine in 1973. This strange combination of new experiences with symbolic associations and selective memory was more and more the hallmark of the whole trip, threatening to overburden what I did.

Birzeit had only recently been permitted to reopen after a four-year shutdown. I am particularly bitter about this facet of the Israeli occupation, which seems to have targeted Palestinian education as a particularly vulnerable enemy. The criminalization of teaching and learning has been made worse by the incredible silence of Western academics and intellectuals who regularly waltz in and out of Israeli universities without protest and without making any significant noise about the outrage. Miraculously, however, Birzeit battles on. We visited a rich exhibition of architectural models and drawings set up by the students, as well as various labs where inventive work on Palestinian agriculture and nutrition is being carried out. A heavily politicized faculty and student body exist at Birzeit; many of the former are involved either in the ongoing peace process or in opposition to it, so the public encounter—preceded by a lively meal—was bound to be rousing. I was a little hesitant to go in for oratory in classical Arabic style (which is always expected of me) because living for years in an environment where my public speaking is based on an essentially conversational model, I find it difficult to transmute myself into a (for me) stiff public rhetorician. I ended up using a slightly refined variant on the spoken language, without the requisite eloquence but also without obfuscation.

A very large crowd filled the hall. I suspected that many had heard of me, some had read me, but most were there to find out what I thought about the current peace process. I was warmly introduced by philosophy professor George Giacaman and then gave (by request) a short précis in English of my forthcoming book on culture and imperialism.[26] Thereafter discussion switched back to Arabic, and was moderated by Giacaman and Professor Ali Jerbawi. The first questions sought clarifications of what I had just said, most of them having to do with the role of the United States as a sort of new imperial power which, I kept reiterating, is scarcely understood in the Arab world, despite the tons of verbiage spewed out about it. Then came the first challenge, a simple question that asked me to spell out my "real" position on the Gulf War. Throwing all caution to the winds, I denounced Saddam Hussein as a dictator and a fool, his occupation of Kuwait as an unacceptable aggression, but was unsparing in my criticism of the American-led war, as well as the Arab members of the coalition. In no time we were heavily into Salman Rushdie, whom I defended categorically, and political Islam, which I also criticized somewhat impetuously. I made, I think, one rather far-out analogy between the Israeli penchant for barbed-wire fences and the now current separation of "us" (Palestinians, Arabs, Muslims) from the West, saying that all cultures were in fact hybrid, and any attempt to push a homogenizing line was not only false but demagogic.

As we left Birzeit, Albert Aghazarian, the genial man who runs Birzeit's public programs, introduced me to two young men who were the campus leaders of the Islamic movement. Expecting the worst (the public reception earlier had been warm enough, but I suspected that politeness, not passion, had ruled the day), I bravely confronted the two. I was thunderstruck when they told me that although "there were points of disagreement," they appreciated my honesty (that's colloquial Arabic for you, I said to myself), and would I please come back.

The next day we crossed into Jordan at the Allenby Bridge, greeted by a sign announcing "You are in Jordan. Smile." This brought unexpected relief, especially that the omnipresent barbed wire had disappeared once we got over the river. We hadn't been questioned by the Israeli border people at all, even though we were kept waiting for ninety minutes for the bus, and an incongruously large group of soldiers milled about us, one of them ogling my pretty daughter with charmless intensity.

The first thought that came to me after we left both Israel and Palestine was how small a role pleasure now seems to play in those two places. In Gaza, for example, swimming seems to be forbidden not by the Israelis, but by the Gazans. A harsh driven quality rules life, by necessity for Palestinians, by some other logic, which I can barely understand, for Israelis. After so many years of thinking about it, I now feel that the two peoples are locked together without much real contact or sympathy, but locked together they are, and very slowly perhaps they will improve the relationship. Perhaps I would find it very hard to live there: exile seems to me a more liberated state but, I have to admit, I am privileged and can afford to feel the pleasures, rather than the burdens, of exile. Yet I also feel that as a family the four of us need the connection, need the assurances that Palestine and Palestinians have really survived, and this we now have. I think I needed the chance metaphorically to bury the dead, and what with the large number of funerary associations for me, Palestine/Israel was indeed a mournful place. But I can feel and sometimes actually see a different future as I couldn't before.

Published in *The Observer*, October 25–November 1, 8, 1992.

Part Two

THE ARAB WORLD

CHAPTER 19

U.S. Policy and the Conflict of Powers in the Middle East

[1973]

We are delighted with the fact the cease-fire lasted this long and the area is relatively stable. . . . Contrary to the views I hear expressed occasionally, we still have good communications with the Arab countries and we still have hopes that negotiations can start sometime.

Secretary of State Rogers, March 14, 1972

In our new approach to security assistance we have adjusted, and in some areas eliminated, practices which did not reflect the realities which are inherent in the Nixon doctrine and our national security strategy of realistic deterrence. We have sharpened our managerial procedures to assure better allocation of our scarce resources, and have included specific guidelines for the integration of security assistance into overall force planning under the total force concept. And most importantly . . . we are moving forward with our allies on programs which do improve their self-sufficiency and increase their contributions to our mutual security.

Secretary of Defense Laird, March 15, 1972

[I]

Asimple working definition for what is involved when foreign powers come into conflict in the Middle East is that one power seeks a presence (whatever the form) of some sort, and this presence is actively struggled for with other powers who have the same general ambitions. There can never, of course, be an absolute victory of one power over all the others, since the historical pattern tells us that powers begin by hoping for the total dislodgment of other powers, but end by settling for a type of coordinated presence with these powers, within which one finds it possible quite ably to maneuver. The mode of conflict is rather more complicated and various than the underlying fact of conflict. The reason for this is—and here modern experience in the Middle East is a very advanced school for the historian—the extraordinary lengths to which the powers have gone in defining their "interests" in the Middle East. Thus, for every interest there is a mode of conflict and a type of goal more or less special to it. A general rule, however, is that no matter what the "interest," a power will seek its enhancement or growth or realization as forcefully and as inexpensively as possible. Where direct intervention or great risk and expense appear as alternatives, they have not always been categorically avoided (e.g., the Anglo–French–Israeli invasion of 1956), although I think that the Middle East of the 1970s presents unique opportunities for a "logical" and, for the United States, a relatively lucrative policy of conflict management that make violence between the powers almost totally unattractive. I believe this to be a sophisticated short-range policy, given U.S. objectives, but it is misguided in the long run.

Part of the enormous confusion that exists in the Middle East today about the conflict of powers there is that the Western powers have been a major factor in political life from the very beginning of the twentieth-century struggles for national independence. It has therefore become difficult to examine the policy of powers whose involvement in the modern history of a dozen states seems to have *enabled* that history to come about even as it has later become an encroachment upon it. Hence my simple definition of conflict perfectly suits the way Britain and France, for instance, assisted Arab and Jewish nationalisms in their seemingly successful struggles within the Ottoman framework. It is the intertwining of foreign interests with local ones, however, that has made contemporary Middle Eastern history a battleground for competing perceptions of how, what, and which regional autonomy is to be achieved. What gives these perceptions an almost frightening vitality is the sheer number of levels at which the foreign powers and the Middle East interpenetrate, levels which are economic, political, cultural, and psychological. So that if the historian wishes to avoid using general labels to describe the interpenetration, he or she is virtually trapped into saying that matters are too complex for judgment, that every issue has to be judged separately, etc. In trying to discourage this kind of surrender to what seems to be an irrationally large aggregate of details, I hope also to be advancing a view that is accurate and particular even as it volunteers judgment.

In the final analysis what is important in all such investigations as this one is what is too often obscured or forgotten: that there is a legitimate "interest" in the Middle East to be held for its resources and potential development *by its people*. Any policy that suppresses this interest can do so only in the short run since there is a limit to how long the Middle East will submit inertly to being so handled. At least three decades of seemingly endless agitation, turmoil, self-deception, and wasted effort have—not without the paternal encouragement of the powers—turned both the Arab and Jewish peoples into a mosaic of warring factions. The result has been to divert a sense of self-interest into subsidiary, less crucial interests. While outside powers strengthen central state governments in the Middle East, the great mass of people seems to me more abused.

A major reason for this state of affairs, which is a symptom of the Middle East's unique history, is that the contemporary Middle East is the result of "combined and uneven development." Trotsky's phrase is doubtless apt for most of the Third World, but in no place more than the Middle East is the difference between levels of development that coexist simultaneously in time so dramatic. The three major religions which originate in the area have welcomed foreign cultures linked dynastically to them, but separated from them in terms of economic development and historical awareness; at the same time they have also reacted conservatively in trying somehow to preserve the identity of their national roots. On the Western side, this clash between traditional cultural affinities and sensitivity to the external world is also reproduced schizophrenically in the Western radical who is silent (or worse) about Israeli actions in the Middle East, even as he or she has had a lot to say about Vietnam or Cuba. An accurate political awareness therefore suffers from exposure to regressive emotional sympathies. Yet this has benefited neither the Western radical nor the Middle Easterner. The fact is that Middle Eastern realities are rationally intelligible, if not simple, and amenable to analysis; aside from U.S. policymakers, not enough people have grasped this fact.

[II]

It is instructive to see, from the outset, how the Western European and Atlantic powers dealt with the Arabs (or the Jews) in a set of three interrelated moves; these involve a number of attitudes still present and employed today. First of all, there is the step of dealing with smaller groups (oligarchies, hereditary elites, minority factions) in terms more appropriate to a much greater mass of people. Thus the Sharifian dynasty is encouraged to aspire toward, and ironically to settle for, "Arab" goals; similarly, a Zionist faction is identified as a spokesman of the Jewish people. With this maximalist tendency nurtured among minorities comes a second step: through the dialectic of partnership in an allied cause, whether it is anti-Ottoman or anti-communist, a set of national goals and priorities is formulated and, in some cases, granted. In fact, however, these goals turn out really to be the legitimation by the powers of their presence and the presence of their minority native partners. As Aaron S. Klieman has recently shown, the Cairo Conference of 1921 is a watershed for this type of arrangement, in which a conflict between rationales for imperial stability and the logic of appeasing nationalist aspirations multiplies, rather than dampens, confusion and expense.[1] Not the least important is a third move, which is for one power (or sometimes a group of powers) to promote policies designed neatly to do a double but contradictory job. On the one hand, competing powers are dislodged, forestalled, removed; on the other hand, the locals are convinced of having achieved a step toward independence.

As most commentators agree, only since World War II have the United States and the Soviet Union entered the conflict of powers in the Middle East. Britain and France by then had begun an attenuation of their presence, which was slowly to be reasserted, though to a lesser degree than before the war, after 1967. The decade of the fifties saw an exchange of interventions, musical invasions we might call them, the upshot of which was to bring U.S. and Soviet rivalry to the fore.[2] Today there is generally thought to be an absolute symmetry in the

Middle East between, on one side, the U.S.–Soviet conflict, and on the other, the Arab–Israeli conflict. How this peculiar view has come to be held, particularly when it has a basis neither in history nor current actuality, must be counted as one of the dubious achievements of "public diplomacy." For I submit that one of the most ominous developments in the Middle East since the era of avowedly secret agreements by the powers on the disposition of spheres of influence has been the rise of a public policy consisting of the traditional *Realpolitik* but incorporating the terminology of a liberal mutual interest, respect, and assistance platform against *extremism* and *disorder;* even as the far less evident underside of that platform is a thoroughly ruthless instrument for quashing or containing the slightest social restiveness or protest. I shall be concentrating upon U.S. policy behaving this way, simply because that policy has hitherto proved most effective. *I am not at all arguing,* however, that other powers are either blameless or uninvolved in the same kind of techniques. I shall also be arguing that the *technical* lessons of direct intervention (as in Vietnam) have not been lost on this policy; thus it is possible to say that in the Middle East, United States strategies have made their greatest inroads by conceiving of the U.S. role primarily in behavioral science terms, with an eye toward social and economic, as opposed to overt military, control. The military imperatives remain, of course, but they have, I think, been made far less obtrusive.

The effectiveness of such a policy is most easily seen in the successful internationalization and defusing of the Palestine question, at bottom a direct conflict between two peoples as well as the accepted genesis for all Middle Eastern unrest. The rise of an armed and organized Palestinian movement since 1967 should be interpreted, I believe, as a popular determination to nationalize (much as Abdel Nasser had done with the Suez Canal in July 1956) the right to one's political fate. To a very great degree, however, the defeat of Palestinian nationalism in its present form has been the product of a policy of viewing Palestinian–Israeli conflicts as secondary to *international* instability. When, in a study commissioned by the Office of the Assistant Secretary of Defense, International Security Affairs, the RAND Corporation surveyed Palestinian nationalism, it characterized the whole movement as a two-time "trigger" to armed conflict in the Middle East.[3] The movement's defeat by 1971, according to the analyst, William Quandt, had proved that any extraterritorial, or paramilitary, or conspiratorial force could not "be reflected in any future political arrangements.''[4] The future is thus determined by the nations that presently neutralize social conflict, having put a so-called order between nations above everything.

Such conclusions as this are symptomatic and consistent, even though they neither make nor substantially alter policy. Obviously they protect the *status quo*. But they make the smallest possible allowance for the basic values to which the Palestinians dedicated themselves, and this is a disservice a research study ought not to perform. Such conclusions cannot therefore adequately deal with the human forces that might again stimulate Palestinian insurgency, especially since those forces by no means regard the *status quo* as unchangeable. Besides, analyses such as Quandt's only reinforce norms—military stability, political unity, etc.—that derive from a view of things held to be without serious challenge; everything discussable is, given a sufficient number of facts, predictable, since the model of political action invoked is essentially a simple linear process from "ideology" to "adaptation to reality."[5] A political force is seen as a potential power bloc: if it is prevented from engaging directly in "political arrangements," then it will inhabit a "political limbo."[6] The complexity of human activity is denatured and falsified into what one critic has called "the rat view of human nature."[7]

For what purpose? Chiefly to assure the sponsor of such research, and possibly even the researcher, that human activity might be susceptible to what behaviorist psychology calls negative reinforcement. This is a corollary of the view that human nature is simpler than it really is. Moreover, while research of this sort is driven by a desire greatly to increase the sophistication of United States foreign policy, such sophistication as I have been able to discern is found initially in the large amounts and the great variety of information being gathered rather than in the quality of the approach. In the case of the Middle East these quantities of information are directly commensurate with the growth of U.S. interests felt to be in need of protection there. Certainly these interests are conceived in a more complex, although menacingly holistic, way, but the principle that they must be preserved has not changed much from the "new research" methods I described above. To this end, therefore, all information about the Middle East is highly political in nature. Research on popular attitudes toward a given regime helps, for example, to assess whether or not there would be a strong response to the regime's dislodgment; a survey of political thought can assert or deny the true influence of radical ideas upon the political culture. The apparent randomness of such analyses conceals an integral goal binding them together. Borrowing from President Johnson, Barnet has called this goal keeping America the number one nation.[8] Of course, this is a general goal capable of being reached in many different ways.

It is worth considering in more detail now what the U.S. sees as its interests in the Middle East, how they are defined, and what attitudes their formulations strengthen. The Nixon administration has made it clear since 1969 that the Middle East is its number-one trouble spot, the most dangerous place on earth. Aside from the contradiction and entanglement given rise to by the Arab-Israeli conflict, inter-Arab rivalries and the struggle between the powers, the Middle East seems inherently to present itself as *disorderly,* so complex are even the native currents that make for instability there. Thus, whether it is the Senate Foreign Relations Committee, or a U.S. Army area handbook, the accepted view has come to find disorder and instability in need of pacification and stabilization.[9] But since the United States has interests "that command concern," a policy must steer a course between maintaining "traditional friendships" and maintaining a net dollar inflow of some $1.7 billion per year from the Middle East.[10] In addition there are politico-strategic interests such as containing the Soviet Union, cultural interests, and so on. More recently, Arab petroleum has become essential for U.S. home consumption, at least from the mid-1970s on, even as OPEC militancy tightens its demands for increased revenue and ownership.[11] With a U.S. investment in it through the decade of at least $100 billion (relatively cheap oil, military assistance, institutional aid) and the likelihood of a cash surplus for the oil-producing states of about $50 billion, the Middle East and its disorders therefore present some difficulties for policymakers.

After Vietnam there is an evident consensus that, according to a 1970 paper by Campbell, "a foreign physical presence could be a political liability in countries characterized by nationalist sensitivity." He goes on to say that the Pentagon acquiesced in this judgment, the key to which "could be found in the effects of technological change on military geography."[12] Thus, since there was a general regional coalition aligned with the United States—Spain and Turkey are mentioned by Campbell, but Eqbal Ahmad has persuasively shown the paramount importance to this strategy here of Iran, Greece, Ethiopia, and Israel[13]—a more delicate policy, less obtrusively dependent on conventional military means, is possible. For the unstable environment is now accepted as a starting point of policy; this is a roundabout way of saying that the causes of instability will perforce remain deliberately untouched, through benign neglect, in the safeguard of U.S. interests. Hence:

> . . . American policy will have to prove itself amid interlocking struggles for political power involving both the big and small powers against a background of crisis which is more or less continuous but stops short of war. American policy and strategy will therefore be primarily political, with the double aim of preventing war and preventing any major shift in the world balance, whether that balance is viewed in political or military terms. Fundamental to those purposes are a necessary minimum of control over the level of conflict between the Arabs and Israel; maintenance of present commitments to NATO countries and of relations of confidence and solidarity with them including some tolerable regulation of the present awkward situation of Greece and of the Greece–Turkey–Cyprus imbroglio; support for the economic and social progress of *all* Mediterranean countries; maintenance of open channels of communication to all of them, hostile as well as friendly; and, in all probability, a measure of cooperation with the Soviet Union. This last point could be the key to success or failure in all the others, but such cooperation requires two willing partners.
>
> The instruments for such a grand strategy are primarily political, economic, diplomatic.[14]

This "mixed situation" requires subtle crisis management of a particular kind, as we shall see.

The central principle for policy-making is that there must be as protected and sustained a flow of income as possible, viewed as both economic and strategic, from the Middle East to the United States. This consideration overrides all others; it is the one value whose importance is accorded *a priori* objectivity and not unnaturally a kind of freedom from examination. Therefore, since crisis in the Middle East still enables this flow, there is no reason to change the crisis in its present form. Furthermore, some objectivity and permanence are given the crisis because of its association with the continued production of income. A small example will suffice here. Since December 1969, the United States has not strenuously maintained that the return of Israeli–occupied territory to Egypt be one condition for a settlement.

It had done so before, notably in UN Resolution 242 of November 1967, and in the Four Powers negotiations. The change signified the degree to which U.S. policy had adapted to the crisis, and a return to earlier principles would now mean an expensive alteration in the "balance" U.S. policy had taken for granted,[15] (all this despite the presence in the State Department of legendary Arabists!).

Conversely, though, the reasons for such a view of things cannot be ascribed to a Zionist conspiracy, or even to Jewish pressures on U.S. policy.[16] Those pressures play a role but only to the extent that they coincide with the overall U.S. interests. I realize that I am suggesting a great degree of selectivity and discrimination in U.S. foreign policy, to which Vietnam gives the lie. But one must not forget that there is a much older, and discriminating, relationship between the United States and the Middle East that guarantees at least a greater amount of interaction and knowledge than has existed between the United States and Southeast Asia. There are institutes, university regional studies curricula, cultural dynamics of very long standing and enormous funds available for all sorts of projects—some of them bordering on whimsy—from foundations. (The Lilly Foundation, for instance, awarded $25,000 in 1970 for something called "private diplomacy" in the Middle East.) All this, then, makes it practical for even so lumbering and cumbersome a complex as the foreign policy body of the United States to put into effect a viable program for the Middle East.

We can distinguish two main approaches which a prodigiously generous supply of intelligence keeps viable. Both approaches are multi-dimensional and work together, but they are most profitably understood as an updated version of the conflict-of-powers moves I enumerated earlier. I shall call these approaches coordination and isolation. Both of them depend heavily upon identifying and predicting levels of tension, although clearly a level of tension—for example, between Jordan and the Palestinians—is not unacceptable simply because it is violent. Perhaps because of Vietnam, a rule is that U.S. military intervention is a last resort, never an immediate response. Above all, an optimum result is to employ regional and adjacent (NATO for instance) forces in the crisis: This, of course, is the famous linkage principle. The overall effect can then be viewed as the result of "an engineering approach."[17]

1. COORDINATION

A. *Analysis*

The analysis of antagonistic forces has now discarded the old communist–versus–free world polarity as a conceptual tool. Regional homogeneity is not assumed except, as I said above, insofar as it contributes integrally to the flow of economic and strategic income from a region. For the purposes of identifying components of the crisis, diversity is the norm. Here we can begin to see the fruits of what Glen H. Fisher has called the behavioral science approach in foreign affairs.[18] Sociological, anthropological, and psychological methods expose a region in all its ethnic and subcultural diversity, pointing to the interests, dynamics, and sensitivities of each unit. Since the Middle East is manifestly a mosaic society, it is not only important to tell the groups apart, but also to record each group's self-perceptions. To this end we have studies of the Palestinians such as Quandt's and studies of how Palestinians are seen by Israelis, and by themselves.[19] If, as is often the case, regional institutions can do research of this sort—so much the better.[20] There is nothing secret or esoteric about this research (which is often produced in the routine of business, cultural, and educational relations between the United States and the Middle East), primarily because no discrete part of it has real value without the rest. Presumably only the sponsor—the Department of Defense, RAND, Hudson, Ford Foundation, etc.—has all the results immediately available. Yet we might digress a moment to remark (with Senator Fulbright, Admiral Rickover, and others) that the *total* amount of research is so vast as to defy the digestive capabilities of even the largest organization. Fulbright put his finger on it by saying that even though the aggregate was irrational, the sheer power demonstrated in sponsoring the research was a way of containing it.[21]

Ethno-sociological analyses feed next into higher levels of interpretive analysis: The economic and the military-strategic. RAND, for example, has since 1954 conducted Project Sierra "to examine possible limited war situations in Southeast Asia, the Far East, and the Middle East, with particular reference to Air Force effectiveness."[22] In later years the Institute for Defense Analysis conducted a "study of the problem of literacy training for conscripts in underdeveloped countries . . . [which was] applied to the ground forces of a country in the Middle

East." And with this went another IDA study done for the Joint Chiefs of Staff, on "the multiplicity of military and political problems facing the United States in the Mediterranean, Middle East, Persian Gulf, and Arabian Sea begun in July 1968."[23] There are literally dozens more such projects—Rainbow scenarios, strategic forecasts, etc.—undertaken by universities and by large corporations like Douglas Aircraft, Westinghouse, and General Electric. To these must be added research done on economic, sociological, agricultural, and demographic features of the Middle East, features whose influence on the U.S. position is felt to be decisive. A comprehensive analysis of this sort underlies a RAND series on the Middle East, underwritten by the Ford Foundation and Resources for the Future.[24] The annual expenditures, roughly guessed at, are in the many millions of dollars.

It is difficult to assume that many of these projects are disinterested scholarship. It is equally difficult to understand how critics of U.S. policy in Vietnam cannot see, and will not be critical of, the U.S. attitude common both to Vietnam and to the Middle East. The major difference between the two areas is that Vietnam is manifestly a battleground, but the Middle East seems not to be. Yet U.S. policy in the Middle East—as the general nature of the analyses suggests—conforms closely to conflict game plans discussed, say, by Thomas Schelling in *The Strategy of Conflict.* Furthermore, Vietnam has been judged a series of costly mistakes (as the Pentagon Papers amply demonstrate) which it has become the duty of a major power to avoid. An impressive demonstration of the link between Vietnam and the Middle East is a series of studies done at MIT on the control of small wars. Having amassed a large amount of data, the authors proceed to construct a model of small wars. The model's function is to predict and select stages in the war for the United States to use in planning pressure upon the combatants ("nipping them in the bud"). No distinction is made between one war and another; all are considered equally small and "dangerous," and therefore in need of pacification.[25] Obviously, every bit of information about a region is useful intelligence, from meteorological characteristics to social stratification, in the pursuit of a pax Americana,[26] presumably a plan with optimum cost effectiveness.

B. Decision Making to Enforce Coordination

Some good hints on the relations between vast pools of accumulated research findings and implemented policy can be garnered by the

recent history of U.S. relations with the Middle East. The countries of
the area have never really been treated as a group, much less as the
vaunted Arab–Israeli dichotomy, simply because only the most careless
observer will fail to miss the divisions that animate the place. U.S.
policy therefore proceeds along many axes, each with its own options
for intervention, active support (economic, social, military), tacit
support, containment or isolation. In the eastern Mediterranean there
are eight Arab countries, aside from the Gulf states. Between these
states there are numerous ties, some antagonistic, some not. In addition there are dozens of minorities extending in some cases (Druze,
Christian sects, Kurds, Shiites, etc.) across frontiers. To these have to
be added elites and interest groups both inside and outside the governments. By the time one adds Israel to this pattern, as well as the active
interests of other states (France, Britain, USSR, Japan, India, Iran),
policy options cease to be of the either-or type, and instead become
and-and propositions. By contrast the policy of the Arab states and
Israel seems increasingly limited to one-dimensional assent or abstention. Since policy options are frequently a direct product of information, the following evidence of limited Arab initiatives (despite the
enormous sums expended on military hardware by the Arab League)
is significant: There is not a single institution in the Arab world
devoted exclusively to the study of the United States, a country whose
involvement in the Arab world far outstrips that of *any other power*.
Compared to the institutions and programs in the United States whose
exclusive job is to monitor the Middle East, this is lamentable. The
point, however, is that because they have never fully explored their
options, the Arabs have had to deal with the powers and Israel *as if*
there were a true collective Arab coordination. In reality this inauthentic collectivity makes the Arab vulnerable to the divisive policies of the
powers.

With regard to Israel, for a great many obvious reasons, the United
States there has thoroughly insinuated its market and strategic interests. The defense of Israel, which according to Fulbright means a
literally unprecedented supply of military assistance, has become a
plank in the platform of every major political candidate in the United
States. The key to this policy is that the Israeli air force—the object
of evident Pentagon-approving interest[27]—is seen as a unique cost-
effective deterrent to Soviet moves in the Mediterranean.[28] After all,
why do it expensively by direct intervention if it can be done far less
expensively by an ally already there? Israel, furthermore, is the only

power between France and the Indian subcontinent to have a nuclear option, and this, as Fuad Jabber shows, could scarcely have been achieved without aid solicited from the United States and the West generally.[29] One clue to the extent to which Israel and the United States have interlocking military-industrial establishments is that after Canada and the United Kingdom, Israel is the recipient of the largest amounts for DOD research.[30] Since 1968 it is estimated that Israel has received at least $1.5 billion in military goods from the United States; thus, "by these calculations the United States has sent a greater value of weapons to Israel than to any of the three forward defense countries that formerly accounted for 90 percent of U.S. military transfers in the region (Turkey, Greece, Iran)."[31]

The growing complexity of arms dealing by the powers is a subject too often reduced to the false U.S.–USSR/Israel–Arab states symmetry I mentioned above. In the years since 1967, the United States has supplied arms to Iran, Jordan, Lebanon, Saudi Arabia, and Kuwait, aside from those to Israel. While there is no gainsaying the supply of Soviet arms to some Arab countries, I think it can be confidently said that the U.S.-supplied arms are delivered with two principal objectives in mind, both of them more flexibly adaptable to U.S. interests than the monolithic (and only modestly successful) Soviet policy of arming a very few Arab states for defense against Israeli attacks. The two U.S. objectives in arms supply are: (1) preserving an *internal* balance within the Middle East and assuring oil supplies; and (2) outflanking the Soviets to the east and south. I have already discussed the reasons for such a policy; what requires comment now is the policy's implementation, particularly (2). One consistent tactic is to confuse ties among the Arabs, thus making states with sharply different constitutions, populations, economies, and avowed foreign policies (Israel, right-wing Arab states) unwittingly similar in the positions they adopt. Any force challenging these regimes, either externally or internally, is labeled radical, and an unspoken alliance develops, for economies and class balances are deeply threatened by change.

The case of Jordan since 1967 is classical in the intricacies of its front-line position, not only facing Israel, but also its neighbors, the Palestinians, the more distant Arab states and the United States. An indication of the pressures upon it in September 1970, and the high importance attached to them by Washington, is the fact that during that single month the National Security apparatus of the U.S. government met twenty-one times; for a period of *ten* months, between

March and December 1971, the same group met only twenty-five times to deal with the East Pakistan crisis.[32] Moreover there are grounds for believing (as substantiated years later by the work of Seymour Hersh) that in September 1970 the United States, Israel, and Jordan had a concerted plan of action, which would have entailed appropriate military responses, had the Palestinians and the Syrians gained the upper hand. During those days in September, it must have seemed that the Middle East was poised on the brink of a popular social revolution. The Palestinian insurgency was at its apex, and it is, I suppose, to the credit of the United States, Jordan, and Israel that all three governments took the *fedayeen* for a genuine revolutionary force.[33] Even the slight chance of a revolutionary victory in Jordan suggested a wave of dissidence right through the area; together with Nasser's acceptance of the cease-fire in July, a stroke that was intended to parallel in diplomatic terms the Palestinian challenge, these movements threaten the calm by replacing a seemingly ingrained Arab habit of sheer stubbornness with a suddenly fresh initiative.

Had Jordan fallen, Syria, Iraq, and Egypt would have presented Israel and the United States with a battery of new difficulties: an offer of peace in the West, plus escalating demands from the East, unrest on the West Bank, and renewed Soviet support for a resurgent Arab position. The wider repercussions included threats to the oil, as well as to all of the Gulf monarchies. The U.S. response to the Jordanian crisis was impressive, for it set in train a remarkable series of events that almost literally destroyed every progressive movement in the Arab world, and of course strengthened the U.S.–Israel position accordingly. The Sixth Fleet and U.S. troops in Europe were placed on much-publicized alerts. Any rents in the Jordanian monarchy's power were repaired immediately:

> Jordan's economy had lost about $25 million through the 45 days of fighting and economic disruption (*Le Commerce du Levant,* Beirut, 1/71). The United States immediately offered $5 million in economic aid and replenished lost military supplies. Then Spain gave Jordan 240 tons of rice and 30 tons of sugar, and Iran, which had always refused to buy Jordanian phosphates, changed its mind (*ibid.,* 2/71). Tapline in principle agreed to raise its payments to Jordan for oil transit rights, to the tune of perhaps $4 million per year (*ibid.,* 3/71). Then Taiwan offered to furnish agricultural products in great quantity, if Jordan would only pay for shipping (*ibid.,* 6/71). And finally, the World

Bank's soft-loan branch, the International Development Association, offered $6 million for highways in Jordan."[34]

Economic aid was only part of the picture. The army was later provided with "nearly ninety M60 tanks, about two hundred M113 armored personnel carriers, about forty thousand M16 automatic rifles, together with considerable radar and other modern equipment." As a result—and this is the pattern elsewhere in the Arab states—there was a shift in Jordanian military priorities. In order these became "major forces in the north, facing Syria and Iraq; internal security; Israeli borders a distant third priority."[35] Since September 1970, the harsh turning inward of the Jordanian regime upon demands for social justice has been followed by similar developments in Sudan, Egypt, Iraq, and Syria. This cannot at all be discordant with the general lines of U.S. policy.

With the defeat of the Palestinian resistance as a political presence in Jordan, it remained for Israel to secure its hold upon the West Bank and Gaza, which together comprise the choicest of the territories occupied in 1967, the most heavily populated and the most complex to administer. In its 1970 report on the *Development and Economic Situation in Judea, Samaria, the Gaza Strip, and North Sinai,* the Israeli Ministry of Defence states that "the areas are a supplementary market for Israeli goods and services on the one hand, and a source of factors of production, especially unskilled labour, for the Israeli economy on the other." Israel's political and economic absorption of this new colony very closely corresponds to this assertion. Agricultural, industrial, employment, and import-export plans for the West Bank have kept the territories in a viselike hold; industrial development is carefully inhibited, Arab labor is significantly less well paid than Jewish labor, type and quantity of produce is tailored for the Israeli market, labor is kept to a semiskilled and unskilled level, and generally the West Bank is looked to as an economic conduit between Israel and the Arab world.[36]

Since, as Michael Bruno has remarked, "the most natural markets for Israel would be Arab countries, but these are closed to Israeli trade," and since Israel's traditional exports (i.e., citrus fruits, polished diamonds, textiles, plywood, cement, tires) are inadequate, there will have to be a shift to "growth" industries: "electronic equipment, scientific instruments, fine chemicals, and the like—for which transportation costs are of less importance, skill and know-how could be developed, and potential markets exist.''[37] Israel's economic links are strongest with the West generally, in particular with the United States and the European Economic Community. The continued Israeli occupation of Arab territories (there are now more than fifty settlements there, with many more to come, and great amounts of Arab land have already been expropriated in Hebron, Jerusalem, Nablus, etc.) suggests therefore a more lasting *dependent* involvement between Israel with its satellites and the Western economies. With Israel supplying management and know-how, and the Arabs inexpensive labor, the Middle East can serve the United States as an intermediate link to Africa and perhaps later to the subcontinent. (Israel has already begun to export U.S. electronic and military products—manufactured in Israel on a concession basis—to African countries.)[38] On the whole the picture has strong analogies with plans for the incorporation of Vietnam into the U.S. economic orbit once ''stabilization'' has occurred.[39]

At present Israel and Egypt allocate more than 25 percent of their budgets for defense purposes, which not only benefit the defense establishments (no different there) but also outside suppliers like the United States and the USSR. Much of the focus of attention in the press has been on Arab–Soviet economic dependence, while United States–Arab economic relations have gone largely unnoticed. The facts are, however, that Arab–USSR relations remain relatively pale, and less substantial in the years between 1967 and 1970 than (a) the *increase* in U.S. exports to the Arab countries, (b) the *decrease* in Arab exports to the United States, and (c) the *quarter* of the total U.S. trade surplus between 1967 and 1970 that came from the Arab states.[40] A further insight into the worth of the Arab–United States trade exchange is gained when one remarks how perfectly it fits the sociology of relations between advanced and less developed economies. As usual the whole-scale purchase and transfer of technology from one cultural level to another impoverishes the poorer partner even as it feeds his illusions of progress. For not only are the services of acquired technology badly distributed to the population, but technology itself is raised worshipfully to a dangerous eminence that overshadows far more urgent social and political considerations.

Far from holding its own precariously in the Middle East, therefore, the United States is synonymous politically, psychologically, and economically with power capable literally of absorbing every inherent difficulty presented to it in the Middle East. Social unrest, the enormous gap separating elites from the population at large, minority aspirations and majority afflictions, military ambition and the stark reality of poverty—all these are flattened into statistics and made to work in the interests of perpetuating U.S. dominance. Whatever follies presently exist in each area of the Middle East are protracted, since U.S. policy is calculated institutionally to nurture "balance" rather than change. To its Western allies the United States has so far been inclined to be generous—as in the parceling out of oil subconcessions, military sales, etc.—but only under a coordinated umbrella whose reaches extend nearly everywhere.[41]

2. ISOLATION

The logical concomitant of a fully articulated policy of coordinated presence for the United States and its allies is that forces hostile to this presence be isolated from each other and away from any means of interfering with that presence. What the United States and countries or groups allied with it cannot absorb are intractable revolutionaries both of the left and, interestingly, of the right. That is, any group that sees itself as not driven by motives immediately translatable into technological advance or new capital. Pressure upon the radical Palestinians, for example, since their heyday in 1968 and 1969, has always first taken the form of incentives to settle down and share, for a change, in the profitable movement in goods and services. Most recently the carrot took the shape of a Palestinian state, which has tragi-comically been put forward from three separate national quarters, not a single one of which has any moral or historical right to dispose of Palestine by secret agreement or by proxy blueprint.[42] Failing compliance with such pacification schemes, the Palestinian organizations—whose financial and intellectual strength came importantly from a significant slice of the technocratic elites in the Gulf, a fact not unnoticed in the United States—were all but destroyed. What was noticeable, however, was the convergence of unanimity by an astonishing majority of Middle Eastern regimes during 1970 and 1971 on the wisdom of so isolating and destroying opposition.

The isolation of opposition, then, has been proved possible on a local, controlled scale opposed to the earlier type of an expanding conflagration. I think that this is a development of capital importance in the Middle East, and this change from the past is unfailingly linked to the U.S. policy

> of achieving a stable and progressive order in the area. The risk of war cannot be exorcised until the environment is transformed by funda-mental changes in the relations of states and peoples of the region. Such transformations are occurring in Europe, under the powerful influence of the ideas and arrangements of the European Community. Similar efforts have been launched in other areas of the world—in Central America and in Southeast Asia, for example.[43]

That an environment's transformation to suit these prescriptions may not be to the Middle East's advantage, or that a just war or a change in the structure of government may not be unprofitable for the area's people—these eventualities are wholly ignored. If, as Rostow says, "peace is not the natural state of affairs in the Near East,"[44] there is no reason why controlled war against either a very much expanded and genuine peace or a conflict (both of which would substantially diminish the U.S. presence) cannot be made the fate of the area. Controlled conflict, after all, can take relatively peaceful economic and political forms.

CONCLUSION: THE PERSPECTIVE
FROM FEBRUARY 1973

In seeking to broaden or to narrow at will the opportunities for change in the Middle East, the United States since 1967 has been extraor-dinarily alert to the consequences of its policy in the region as well as sensitive to the interplay of political forces within each country. Every attempt has been made, by research and analysis, to understand the potential in present social instability that could develop into political movements capable of challenging the U.S. presence. There is little doubt that such a systematic program has evolved partly as a result of already existing U.S. resources for the penetration and manipulation of markets and societies. Therefore, to argue that the U.S. presence in the Middle East is dictated simply by executive fiat is incorrect, since its investments, institutions, and historical personality in the area are regional instances of its global attitudes and political structures. It remains for the present generation of radical historians and political scientists in the United States to attempt an understanding and a transformation of these attitudes, as well as of the processes of the Middle East. For the peoples of the region, and especially those like the Palestinians, for whom state authority has meant state usurpation of the popular right to self-determination, one very pressing task, I believe, is essentially the acquisition and diffusion of information without which their politics will be childishly ineffectual. Until precise determinations are made about the United States, its policy, its meaning, its allies, its foreign and native instrumentalities in the area, there is not much use merely in hoping for a people's war or a revolution. So artfully has illusion obscured the complex but intelligible realities of economic and political life in the Middle East, so powerful have been the authentic sentiments for deep social change, that glib analogies with Vietnam, Cuba, Algeria, and China have predominated without doing very much good. There is now the most urgent political need for seeing precisely which forces have been manipulated, which isolated, which detoured; that these forces are to be found everywhere, among both Arabs and Israelis, has been a truth far too often overlooked in the rush toward poorly clarified objectives.

As this essay goes to press, President Nixon has been reelected, the Vietnam War seems ended, U.S. policy is increasingly geared toward what some analysts have called a "pentanodal" world (the United States, USSR, EEC, Japan, and China), and U.S. dependency upon imported oil is more publicly marked than before. There seems little reason to doubt that the United States will try, in the words of James M. Gavin, Chairman of Arthur D. Little, Inc., "to achieve national goals without the necessity of employing tactical forces. *The measure of success of a strategy is the degree to which battle becomes unnecessary.*"[45] Yet even if the battle becomes unnecessary, a battleground still exists, and according to the *Guardian Weekly* (February 3, 1973):

the battleground is the Middle East. The EEC's French-inspired efforts to create a free trade area stretching right around the Mediterranean are regarded with the deepest hostility and distrust in Washington, the more so since the Americans have come to realize that they, like the Europeans, are dependent on Middle East oil reserves—nearly three-quarters of the known world reserve.

With the USSR out of Egypt, the terms of confrontation between the United States and other powers in the Middle East have shifted: The battle, such as it is, is economic, and foreign policy is based yet more solidly upon economics. For the parties to the conflict in the Middle East—the Arab states, the Palestinians in and out of occupation, Israel, and Iran—what they now do will depend on the political price they are willing to pay in order to secure a larger share of the coming oil and money boom. Territorial problems (e.g., Israeli-occupied Sinai, the West Bank, Jerusalem), though still "hot," seem distinctly secondary to the overall economic stakes now at issue. The present Jordanian and Egyptian diplomatic campaign and the promised Israeli one obviously have peace with increased economic benefits and some territorial flexibility in mind. I can now only sketch this new commercialization of international relations in the Middle East.

Jordan has already stated its willingness to make peace without waiting for Egypt.[46] Saudi Arabia and Iran in December 1972 declared a policy of mutual military and security cooperation in the Gulf, the better to protect their oil interests from "disruptive tendencies"[47] and the better to straddle both their economic demands and their obvious need of the United States: On the one hand, the shah's demands for a greater share of oil revenue increase in militancy; on the other, Shaikh Yamani volunteers Saudi oil revenue for reinvestment in the United States. The Iranians, according to M. A. Adelman in *The Wall Street Journal* (quoted in the *International Herald Tribune* of February 12, 1973) "in one important respect—the Trans-Israel Pipeline—actually cooperated with Israel more than the United States." Nevertheless, Israel, Iran, Saudi Arabia, and Jordan are heavily dependent upon U.S. military assistance. In addition, *The Economist* suggested on December 9, 1972, that even though the Middle East oil producers:

> may also make good their expressed wish to invest in the downstream operations of the oil industry, taking an interest in tankers, refineries, and even service stations . . . there is great doubt whether they have the technical and managerial resources to do this on their own. Their likeliest partners in such ventures would be the oil companies, so how much control would the oil companies lose?

"It's helpful to get all points of view," said President Nixon to King Hussein in February 1973; Mrs. Meir's visit to the United States in March presumably added to the banquet of viewpoints. Rowland Evans and Robert Novak reported on February 2, 1973, that there is considerable Arab pressure to involve Dr. Kissinger in Middle East peace efforts, another instance, I think, of Arab nostalgia for the Eisenhower–Dulles period. Though preoccupied with Vietnam, Kissinger has not been idle on other fronts.

The Associated Press said on January 30, 1973, that, under his direction, a national security study of the energy crisis is under way, soon to be "floated around" the Pentagon, State Department, and CIA. A principal point to be analyzed by the study is the "growing contradiction between U.S. aid to Israel and increased need by the United States for Arab oil." Despite a continuing barrage of Israeli "peace" plans, each one stressing opposition to peace imposed from the outside, there is no good reason why a U.S.-imposed peace for the Middle East cannot be worked out in stages lasting up to ten years, especially if the plan were to be initiated at present when the main parties to the conflict are disoriented internally. The only national group at present that is capable of seeing what irreparable harm to a great mass of the people such a commercial settlement will do is regrettably silent. I am speaking of the Palestinians in exile. I remain convinced, as I hinted in my comments above, that only a politically extraterritorial group can formulate concrete alternatives for genuine national freedom in a Middle East whose central state governments are so deeply embroiled in—and I think corrupted by—great power strategy. So far, however, the Palestinians have responded only negatively: no peace, no deals, no talk. There must nevertheless be many thousands of people in the Middle East and elsewhere for whom these negatives cannot be sufficient. If national liberation remains a goal, there can be no more urgent task than articulating it now, when—as *The Washington Post* phrased it on February 10 while recommending U.S. "peace" activity for the Arabs and Israel—the Middle East is *still* "next on the agenda."

Published in *Journal of Palestine Studies,* vol. 2, no. 3, spring 1973.

CHAPTER 20

The Arab Right Wing

[1979]

The time has come to acknowledge the fact more or less officially that there is such a thing as an Arab Right Wing, for it is this Arab Right Wing, despite our best efforts to ignore it, that now sits in a central place in the Arab world.

In discussing the Arab Right, the first thing I am inclined to say is that it is neither reductively fascist nor does it have a coherent ideology. Fascism historically has always had a mass base, and this the Arab Right does not have; The Right elsewhere usually has a dogmatic set of beliefs—like Zionism, for example—and this, of course, the Arab Right doesn't have at all. What does it have then? First, it has power and a large measure of control over dwindling, and very poorly distributed, economic resources which it conceives of less as power than as cash to be exchanged for consumer goods. Yet if the Right doesn't have a coherent ideology—there are exceptions, such as the Christian Right Wing in Lebanon—it does have a state of mind, and, alas, a very large appetite. The problem is how analytically to deal with the Arab Right as a whole, given, of course, not only its ideological reticence, but also the fact that there is a large variety of Arab Right-Wing theory and practice.

We must remember at the outset that in most Arab countries during the 1970s there has been a vivid contradiction between internal and external policy, not only in rhetoric but also in actual practice. There is no Arab state today that does not publicly associate itself with such progressive positions as international anti-Zionism, anti-apartheid, anti-imperialism, and yet the fact remains that—as the cases of Lebanon, Syria, and Jordan go very far to show—internal tolerance for the local equivalent of international progressivism is very low indeed. In practice this means that an Arab ambassador can lead the anti-Zionist struggle at the United Nations even as at home his government's position on the PLO in Lebanon is radically different—and this is putting the contradiction very politely. Similarly, the Arab position on Israel at UNESCO, which was purportedly and correctly a cultural and political objection to Israel's occupation practices, is hardly matched by the broad range of censorship, political repression, and intellectual thought control practiced virtually everywhere in the Arab world. If the attack on Zionism is a correct one, there is no reason at all to say that those who attack Zionism are innocent of every other variety of political evil.

One thing we can easily say about the Right Wing, or rather the Right Wing thinking which dominates Arab capitals and governments and institutions, is that it is fundamentally schizophrenic. It is quite able to carry out brutality at home and alleged sweetness and light abroad, with no necessarily felt sense of hypocrisy or contradiction. Why is it possible for the language and rhetoric of radical nationalism to cover the antidemocratic practice of political, social, and economic repression at home? Put differently, the question is how it was that the great wave of Arab nationalism that carried us all forward since the earliest days of Arab independence after World War II, and in particular since the initial victories of the 1973 War, has now been subverted, inverted, perverted into nothing so much as what I term schizophrenic Right Wing brutality, a brutality without ideological coherence or mass political grounding, even though in some instances it employs the machinery and language of progressive Arab thought?

The Right Wing, for better or worse, operates under the legitimacy—or the cover—of central state authority. It has inherited the barely surviving carcass of Nasserism and the other nationalist charismatic ideologies of the fifties and sixties. As such it is representative of the state and ideological structure we have endowed ourselves with as Arabs since World War II. It is also representative of the legitimacy given to the national state authority by the Arab Left—and here we begin to see the origins of the contradiction I first spoke of, that the Arab states take progressive international positions, and regressive political and economic positions at home. Insofar as the Arab National Movement was a progressive movement, and insofar as since World

War II the Arab National Movement impelled the Arab states into an anti-imperialist and anticolonialist struggle in Palestine and elsewhere, then the regime was felt automatically to be the bearer of progressive struggle, regardless of what it did at home. The act of endowment, the act of making legitimate the central state authority, no matter what its actions—this is the source of that easily practiced schizophrenia, by which in Lebanon, to take one example, Syria feels itself to be acting not against, but *on behalf of* the Palestinian and Lebanese national movements. Once you grant the State the legitimacy of its international good positions, then you turn it automatically into an unchecked central authority at home.

The reality of what I am trying to describe, the current of Right Wing thinking and practice that now rules the Arab world, can be illustrated by an experience that for me at least perfectly symbolizes the kind of thing we should be more concerned with than we are. During the summer of 1975, I spent a week in Egypt where I had heard that it would be instructive to see a performance of the hit play in Cairo, *Yahya al-Wafd*. It was reported that the play had been closed down a couple of times for political reasons, but it was running strong when I was in Cairo. So on a steamy July night I found myself in the Miami Theater in midtown Cairo watching a performance of one of the most grotesque and vulgar plays that I, or anyone else, has ever seen. The story—which ran on for about five interminable hours—is about a village couple who are fed up with the foreign delegations—mostly from Eastern Socialist countries—foisted on their village by the Arab Socialist Union and who decide to emigrate to the United States. By the end of the play they have returned to Egypt, full of American gadgets, stories of American wonders, but nevertheless happy to be back in Egypt, free of foreigners, especially Eastern European foreigners.

The play was probably supposed to be a broad attack on any kind of foreign influence in Egypt, since both the Russians and the Americans came in for their share of digs, the Russians more savagely since they are represented as clumsy, barbaric idiots who take over the little peasant village. More broadly still, the play was designed as a not very subtle attack on Nasser's Egypt, for its having opened the country to "Soviet imperialism." The point I want to make about this enormously successful play is that the attack on "imperialism" is made from the Right, using the sentiments and even the personality of the Left. One of the most depressing and yet interesting things about the play was that the peasant woman who, with her husband, is the play's main character was played by Tahia Carioca, the famous Egyptian dancer. Only now Tahia had physically tripled in size since her best days as a dancer. She portrayed the peasant woman with a vulgarity and a reactionary nationalism that took my breath away, even though it was also funny in a base sort of way. It was not only that Tahia had been an extraordinarily graceful dancer and now looked like a pickle barrel, scarcely able to move except with a thousand wheezes and squeaks, but that Tahia Carioca had once been a member of the Egyptian Communist Party, had been imprisoned for subversive activities, and for a long time was in public disgrace as a Leftist agitator. Here she was vulgarly representing a return to the pre-Nasser past, and more or less extolling the virtues of the Sadat policy of *al-Infitah* (or "free" market profiteering). To make matters worse, but to illustrate my point even better, she was in real life married to the play's author, a man at least twenty years her junior, who also played the part of her husband in the play.

I don't want my remarks about *Yahya al-Wafd* to be interpreted as an attack on Tahia Carioca, or even the play. What I am trying to do is dramatize the essentially Right Wing state of mind that rules over the Arab world, and to portray it as a living thing; it involves schizophrenia, anomalies, cruelty, contradictions, grotesquerie, success and all, all together. Wherever you look in the Arab world, you will see that combination of *arrivisme* with commercial rapacity and national irresponsibility that characterizes the new classes that are the main supports of the Right Wing. These classes are totally dependent on the Western market economy; they are principally sellers of services and comparatively cheap labor; they pride themselves on their enlightened liberality and technical know-how; they are totally cut off, ideologically and economically and socially, from the rapidly increasing masses whose accelerating poverty probably outstrips the increase in the birthrate; moreover, these new classes are mainstays and even mirror images of the regimes and armies they support. Like these regimes they are managerial oligarchies with no roots either in the native tradition or in the West they so desperately emulate. And it is these classes, this small minority, which have taken upon themselves the task of carrying our foreign policy and guiding the destiny of the Arab people as a whole. If Tahia Carioca represents the aesthetically and politically displeasing transformation of the revolutionary nationalism of the fifties and sixties into a small-minded, vulgar chauvinism, then what has taken place in Lebanon represents the same transformation in a

tragic and bloody form. The Lebanese Right Wing in its sectarian
and isolationist theory and practice could not have thrived as well as
it did without both the active and passive support of most of the
Arab regimes. What they saw in the plight of the Lebanese Right
Wing was the plight of their own threatened bastion of privilege and
minority rule.

Take as a start the question of vast Arab oil wealth. I'm not enough
of an economist to be able to give you all the relevant facts and figures,
but it is certainly true that much of this wealth has found its way back
into the West. Even after the trumpets of the boycott and the price
rises of 1973 and 1974, we are more, not less, in thrall to New York,
Bonn, and London. In early 1976 it was reported that $17 billion of
Arab money was on short-term cash deposits in the West; now the
figure is closer to $50 or $60 billion. If you were to visit London, you
would see, too, that Marks & Spencer and Harrods have benefited from
Arab oil wealth in a grand, not to say disgusting way. I've been told
that real estate investments in London, in New York City, and elsewhere in the West are excellent, that the purchase of 15 percent of
Mercedes-Benz is a wise long-term investment, but is there any doubt
that the investment of Arab oil wealth for the most part is as visionless
and incoherent as the Right Wing I have been describing. Where are
the investments in universities and libraries, in hospitals, in projects
that will improve the moral, physical, and intellectual lot of our
teeming underprivileged masses? Isn't it clear that the huge expenditures on arms and weapons systems are fundamentally reactionary,
since who but a self-serving military establishment and companies like
Lockheed and Grumman have benefited? Certainly the arms are used
less to fight Zionism and imperialism than to fight the people; isn't this
what Syria's role in Lebanon proves, where several thousand Syrian
troops have expended their valor and ammunition on their Palestinian
and Lebanese sisters and brothers?

The Arab world has been given up to economic adventures: the
building of luxury hotels, the importing of senseless quantities of
consumer goods—cars, tape recorders, hair sprays, and the like. The
Arabian Gulf is crawling with speculators and international sharks of
every sort, as high-rise apartment buildings for real estate speculation,
and numerous airports go up like so many mushrooms. The appalling
greed for enormous new stocks of military goods in the Gulf hinders
development of the Arab world as a whole.

Where is the vision, where are the values guiding the investment of this great national treasure of ours, which will not last forever? How many castles in England, how many Cadillacs, how many Lockheed jets need to be bought before we can turn to other things? For this Right Wing I've been describing is not finally interested in its own preservation so much as it is interested in having a good time; no ruling class in history is as unintelligent as this one. If it does not have faith in its people, it has no faith in any other values either. The universities languish. The student population increases—which is good—yet the curriculum is as antiquated as anything can be. We must face the fact that there are no achievements to speak of in modern Arab science or most intellectual effort, at least none that have come out of our universities. Don't you wish you could wake up one day and read that plans were afoot to build a great Arab library instead of a new hotel? There isn't a single decent library in the entire Arab world. To do research on our own past, our culture, our literature, we still have to come to the West, to study at the feet of Orientalists, many of whom have openly declared themselves enemies to Islam and the Arabs. The effort to build a great Arab research center has never succeeded. Similarly, there has been no effort to pour money into Western universities to promote the study of Arab and Islamic civilization, to promote that study in *our* interests. The field of Arab/Islamic study, to which our best students are sent, is in the West still dominated by a handful of old-boy networks. Why have we never tried to build an institute for the promotion of a non-Orientalist, non-antiquated study of our own traditions past and present?

On all sides it is evident that as Arabs we are the world's intellectual and moral *lumpenproletariat*. True, we have vast hordes of clever computer specialists and experts in various industrial techniques, but even in this we are either consumers or we simply serve the Western market economy, which needs valueless and politically neutral technocrats to run its international conglomerates. Everywhere you turn you are met with the truth that the Arab world is undergoing a premature technocratization. We need to remember that without social values, without innovative science, our expertise is useless and perhaps even harmful to us. The Right Wing has produced a technical class like itself, good only for knowing how to press the button, uninterested in what the process is all about and what the process will ultimately result in. A direct result of this blindness can be seen in Lebanon, where the technocratization of military power hasn't, it seems, caused the Syrian officer to wonder whether his missile is hitting a brother Arab or an enemy. To me the greatest indication of our moral and intellectual *lumpenproletarianization* is our failure as Arabs to mobilize around the root political issue of the area, the problem of Zionism. Lebanon is another confirmation of this tragic failure.

I could go on and on—but my point is clear. We are living through a period in the Arab world of unparalleled economic prosperity on the one hand, and of unparalleled political and social and intellectual poverty on the other hand. In what Arab capital is it possible to write and publish what one wishes, to say the truth, to stem the tide of repressive central state authority, intolerant of everything except its own fantasies and appetites? Most of our best writers and intellects have either been co-opted or jailed into silence. It is not only in Israel—I must remind you—that human rights are trampled on. Where is our Israel Shahak, our Felicia Langer? We may not be Zionist racists, but we can scarcely call ourselves revolutionary democracies. Everywhere the individual is brutalized by the secret police, by huge unthinking bureaucracies, by a heedless Central State authority. Everywhere the democratic opposition is not tolerated, its leaders silenced, its voices muffled.

We must acknowledge that this Right Wing wave is interested in nothing really except blundering on from second to second. It is uninterested in the past or present, and looks at the future blankly and unknowingly. In the meantime the Arab world collapses inward on itself. The course of social and economic justice in the Arab world generally is crushed. For in the Arab world, from the Gulf to the Atlantic, the reality is for the most part very ugly. Our role here and elsewhere as serious intellectuals is not to acquiesce in this decadence, nor to cooperate with its processes. Our obligation is to the truth, and also to our people as a whole. We must be able to discriminate between national priorities and ruling-class priorities. We must see the issues concretely, not in terms of the happy and airy abstractions that tend to dominate our discussions. What distinguishes the truly struggling intellectual is, first, his or her effort to grasp things as they are in the proper methodological and political perspective, and, second, the conception of his or her work as activity, not as passive contemplation. Our task as Arab-Americans, it seems to me, is clear—and most urgent.

Published in *Information Paper No. 21*, September 1978, by the AAUG.

CHAPTER 21

A Changing World Order: The Arab Dimension

[1980]

[I]

During 1979 a newly sharpened and intensified set of polarities has endangered world peace and the harmonious development of peoples. Of these polarities, the renewal of the Cold War—marked both by the decision last December to introduce U.S. Cruise and Pershing missiles into Western Europe and the Soviet Union's invasion of Afghanistan—has been among the most ominous, and certainly the widest in its repercussions. It has set in motion what the British historian E. P. Thompson has called the logic of exterminism, not a salutary one by any means. The effect of the new Cold War, which is likely to be further exacerbated after the Reagan victory, has been to deepen other tensions only indirectly related to the superpower confrontation. Thus the great North–South disparity, recently addressed in the Commission, and the subsequent report bearing Willy Brandt's name, has increased: The poor are poorer, the rich richer. This pattern seems destined to continue for the foreseeable future. Exploitative relationships between dependent and metropolitan societies are more the norm now than the exception. And nearly everywhere the cultural relationships between societies have taken starkly primitive, oppositional forms, even as "the new information order," recently the topic of debate at UNESCO, has shown how it is that the extraordinary Western media and information monopoly continue to saturate every corner of the globe, with nothing but the most ineffective, generally retrograde response from the post-colonial Third World. In the face of Western control of the media, Third World countries have only been able to counter with ideas about centralized control imposed by their own governments: Thus one problem is simply compounded, and even aggravated, by another.

All of this has had an especially bad effect on the Arab world. For the past ten years regions of the Arab world have been spoken about openly as targets of direct military intervention. The Carter doctrine has transformed the Mediterranean and the Indian Ocean into American seas; this has become a matter of unchallenged public U.S. policy. Camp David has split Egypt from the Arab world, just as the Lebanese civil war, the rift between the Syrian and Iraqi wings of the Baath party, the rapidly shifting alignments between various Gulf and other Arab states have placed heavy pressures on the idea, to say nothing of the actualities, of Arab unity. In the overall turbulence of our region, certain other ideas—most of them unfortunate departures from the great emancipating currents of Arab unity and anti-imperialist liberation struggle—have gained widespread currency. One is local nationalism, whose aim (as we see it in Lebanon, Israel, Egypt, and elsewhere) is the reestablishment of millets, cantons of sectarian or confessional groupings, in the region. These millets would be hostile to each other although tied by a client–patron relationship to outside powers. In such ways, a nineteenth-century sort of imperialism has returned to our region.

Another idea is the return to primitive and reductionist brands of religion; this is the case nearly everywhere in the Christian and Judaic world, and it is also the case in the Islamic world. The reasons are different, for after all the Gush Emunim wants to steal Arab land in order to fulfill supposedly religious imperatives, whereas the various Muslim opposition groups in the Arab world, like the Iranian revolutionaries, seek to liberate their people from oppression by means of religion. Yet religion is, I think, a diversion from the mainly secular goals that impel all people everywhere—the desire for economic and social justice, the desire to enjoy human rights, the desire for freedom and knowledge, and so forth.

Finally, the Arab world has been completely overtaken in recent years by the ideology of the national security state. To this has been sacrificed the idea of democratic rights, freedom of expression, investigation, and political activity, all of which have always been found in the Arab tradition and certainly in the best modern expressions of Arab unity. But the alleged imperatives of national security have superseded everything, with the net result that citizens are alienated from their governments and governments from the people, the quality of life has diminished, and the absence of democratic participation has narrowed the popular base of most governments in the Arab world to a very great degree.

As a long-standing corrective (and certainly not the only one) to all these ideas, there is the Palestinian struggle, which continues now as before in the face of almost unimaginable difficulties. It would be wrong to consider the struggle for Palestine only as a local struggle for land; it is that, of course, but equally, it is a far-reaching struggle for democratic rights and principles now denied or hidden far beneath what Israel Shahak calls an ideological system of democratically supported racism. Yet even though the Arab world is unanimous in its support of Palestine, there is an obvious discrepancy between expressed and actual support.

One cannot speak therefore of an Arab world mobilized or even motivated enough to respond to what is taking place over Palestine, much less in the world order as I have sketched it briefly. On the contrary, what one sees is a series of unfortunate signs that whatever mobilization there is is focused on mistaken and in some instances destructive goals. Arab money, with its vast potential for regenerating modern Arab life and culture, is for the most part scattered everywhere in the West, associated not with intelligent power, but with conspicuous, even laughable consumption. Stripped, in a way, of its national origins, deprived of institutions (except those in the West that use it for their own ends), undirected and unmotivated except by short-range profit, Arab money in the changing world order is homeless. Worst of all, the national class associated in the Arab world with that money seems to have little sense of building or revitalizing a civilization. Perhaps because the money is essentially derived by them from commission and relatively unearned royalties, these new Arab entrepreneurs are also homeless, concerned only with earning more, storing away more, avoiding even the common civil responsibilities of taxes and doing good works, both of which have always characterized the Arab and Islamic traditions. Lastly, the internecine quarrels—the latest of which is between the most successful anti-imperialist revolution in the Middle East, Iran, and a great center of Arab nationalism,

Iraq—bleed away common energies and divert attention from worth-while goals.

Because of these things, a climate of opinion has developed in the West perfectly prepared to take advantage of them. Take the case of J. B. Kelly, a New Zealander who was once employed as an "adviser" to Shaikh Zayid of the United Arab Emirates. Kelly has recently emerged as the latest "expert" on the Arabs and their oil: His book, *Arabia, the Gulf and the West* (1980), has been saluted publicly by nearly every major Western journal and newspaper. What is extraordinary about the book is not simply its inaccuracy and its irresponsible way with history, but the astonishingly frank atavism of the line he proposes for the West to take toward the Arabs. None of the reviews mentions this fact, just as scarcely an Arab voice has been raised either in criticism against it or in a clear announcement of the fact that of no other national group in the entire world could such a book have been written, and approved so widely in the West. Take as a small example Kelly's final paragraph, which for its sheer desire of imperial conquest and its barely concealed racial hatred deserves quotation:

> How much time may be left to Western Europe in which to preserve or recover its strategic inheritance east of Suez it is impossible to foretell. While the pax Britannica endured, that is to say, from the fourth or fifth decade of the nineteenth century to the middle years of this century, tranquillity reigned in the Eastern Seas and around the shores of the Western Indian Ocean. An ephemeral calm still lingers there, the vestigial order of the old imperial order. If the history of the past four or five hundred years indicates anything, however, it is that this fragile peace cannot last much longer. Most of Asia is fast lapsing into barbarism—into the condition, in short, they [*sic*] were in when Vasco da Gama first doubled the Cape to lay the foundations of Portuguese dominion in the East. . . . Oman is still the key to command of the Gulf and its seaward approaches, just as Aden remains the key to the passage of the Red Sea. The Western powers have already thrown away one of these keys; the other, however, is still within their reach. Whether, like the captains-general of Portugal long ago, they have the boldness to grasp it has yet to be seen.[48]

Although Kelly's suggestion that fifteenth- and sixteenth-century Portuguese colonialism is the most appropriate guide for contemporary Western politicians may strike some readers as a little quaint, it is his simplifying falsifications of history that are most representative of the current mood. Colonialism brought tranquillity, he says, as if the subjugation of millions of people amounted to no more than an idyll; their abused feelings, their distorted history, their unhappy destiny do not matter, so long as "we" can continue to get what is useful to us—valuable resources, geographically and politically strategic regions, a vast pool of cheap native labor. After centuries of colonial dominion, the independence of countries in Africa and Asia are dismissed as "lapsing into barbarism." The only course left open, after what he characterizes as the craven demise of the old imperial order, is a new invasion. And underlying this invitation to the West to take what is rightfully its own, is a profound contempt for the native Arab–Islamic culture.

The point about Kelly is not what he writes (since this kind of mentality is that of the nineteenth-century imperial raj, which has been with us for a long time), but: (1) that his voice should be as eagerly listened to as it is now; (2) that what he says is said only about the Arabs in the changing world order; and (3) that the Arabs as a group apparently have no response to give him, and therefore no real defense against the message of conquest he proposes.

For let us face it, there is no collectively reinforced Arab position toward the U.S. doctrine of intervention in the Gulf or toward the Rapid Deployment Force, which is very likely to turn the Arab world into a disaster area. There is not yet a collectively reinforced Arab position toward Israel either, and there is not yet a collectively reinforced position toward the new economic, social, and information order. Therefore, when we speak of the Arab dimension in the changing world order, we must speak of an unarticulated, unannounced dimension, one that is as yet unconscious, unfocused, and unformulated. This is the moment and the predicament we find ourselves addressing.

[I I]

One of our most common activities has been to bewail the distorted image of the Arabs that exists in the West. This complaint has the virtue of acknowledging the fact that Arabs as a people have become so specialized and so isolated as to have become only robed, sandaled, hook-nosed, lecherous, and over-moneyed fools in Western media and in public discourse. But what has not been sufficiently acknowledged is that even though our isolation is the result of some of the political trends that I mentioned earlier, the representation of the Arab itself is a cultural phenomenon. It derives from the cultural confrontation between the Arab–Islamic world and the West, and it is on this that I now want to reflect. My purpose will be to show that even if politically and militarily the Arab world does not now occupy a strong position in the changing world order, there are enough Arab economic and cultural resources to be mobilized to enhance the overall Arab dimension. By this I do not at all mean that what we must do is "improve" the image of the Arab, which is at best a superficial and cosmetic undertaking. Rather, there is a great need to enter the information and knowledge world system at an appropriate and productive conjuncture, and there to use our considerable resources to wage the battle that we must win if we are not, in a matter of decades, to disappear as a cultural force in the world. The burden is not only that we must do something, but also that what we can do is entirely within the range of possibility today, whereas direct political and military action are not. What I propose, in other words, is an analysis deriving from political, military, and economic actualities, but not confined to them, because it has been our disabling confinement to those realms that has brought us to the present, extremely limiting pass in the changing world order.

I shall discuss two things only: the use of Arab money, and the struggle over information. Both are related to each other. I will discuss them by way of a well-known incident.

On May 12, 1980, PBS ran the film *Death of a Princess,* which had been made by Anthony Thomas, a British filmmaker. A month earlier the film had created a diplomatic incident between the United Kingdom and Saudi Arabia, resulting in the withdrawal of the Saudi ambassador from London, the boycott of England as a Saudi vacation spot, and the threat of further sanctions. Why? Because, according to the Saudis, the film insulted Islam and gave a wrong picture of Arab society in general, and Saudi justice in particular. Based on the well-known execution of a young princess and her commoner lover, the film was done in the docudrama form of a search for the truth: A British reporter tries to find out exactly what happened to the couple, and in so doing he travels to Beirut, where he talks to Lebanese and Palestinians, then to Saudi Arabia, where he is, of course, given an official runaround. In the process he learns only that the princess's story was interpreted by the people with whom he spoke as a symbol of their political and moral dilemmas. The film's conclusion is open-ended; all the explanations have some truth to them, although no one of them is adequate to cover what seemed to have happened.

In the United States the Saudi government made known its opposition to the film's showing; two unpopular results were that Warren Christopher of the State Department brought the Saudis' displeasure publicly to PBS's attention, and Exxon took out advertisements in leading newspapers asking PBS to "review" its decision. In several cities the film's showing was canceled. As a concession to the film's controversial nature, PBS ran a sixty-minute panel discussion immediately following the broadcast. Six individuals plus a moderator talked about the film; the participants were the Arab League representative; a Harvard law professor; a Boston-area Muslim clergyman; a young American described as an "Arabist"; a young woman with business and journalistic experience in the Middle East; and finally, a British journalist who was honest in his dislike of the Saudi scene. Together these six individuals delivered a reasonably incoherent hour of talk. Those who knew something about the region were bound by their positions to stick to a conventional "Muslim" and Arab line. Those who knew only a little showed it, of course, and the rest were fairly irrelevant.

Pressures against the film's showing correctly raised the issue of First Amendment rights. I believe it should have been shown. The important, but unstated, things about the film (which from the standpoint of cinematic art was, in my opinion, quite banal) were: (a) that it was *not* made by an Arab or a Muslim; (b) that it was likely to be the only, or if not the only, then certainly the most impressive film about Arabs the average viewer was likely to see; and (c) that discussions of the film, both on the panel show and elsewhere, very rarely touched on the questions of context, power, and representation. Thomas's undertaking obviously had the ready-made glamour that a film about Yemen, for example, would not have: sex and "Islamic" punishment (particularly of the sort confirming "our" worst suspicions of Arab barbarity). These two dressed up as an earnest docudrama could command a very wide audience. As *The Economist* said on April 19: "Islamic law to most Westerners means Islamic punishment: a simplified myth that this film will have fostered." The audience became still wider once it was known that the Saudi government had been pulling strings (involving Exxon, to boot). And all of this emphasized that *Death of a Princess* was clearly not an Arab or Muslim film, but a film about which Muslims had only very limited, relatively unpopular, and ineffective things to say.

The filmmakers and PBS had to be conscious—as indeed any Arab or Third World individual would be conscious—that no matter what the film contained, the making of the film, the very act of representing scenes in images, was a prerogative coming from cultural power, in this case the West's. It was simply irrelevant that the Saudis had more money: The actual production and distribution of news and images were more powerful than money because they, more than mere capital, were the system that counted in the present world order. As against this system, official Saudi objections about the film being an insult to Islam were in their turn an attempt to mobilize another, far weaker system of representation (the regime's self-image as a defender of Islam) in order to neutralize the so-called Western one.

There was a further victory for the system in PBS's discussion. On the one hand, the network could accurately claim to have responded to Saudi unhappiness by *sensitively* airing a discussion of issues; on the other hand, PBS controlled the discussion by making certain that a "balance" of views, disparate and not very well articulated by relatively unknown "representative" individuals, would blunt any intense or protracted analysis. The appearance of a discussion alone served as a substitute for careful analysis. It was part of the event's success that no one commented on how both the film's *Rashomon*-style structure and the "balanced" panel left judgment on the film's actual subject—a contemporary Muslim society—misleadingly open-ended. We never know (nor perhaps do we really care) what the princess actually did, just as we had the panel saying, "the film was bad" as well as "it was honest and good." But underlying both film and discussion is the hidden fact that such a film could be made and shown with far more consequence than a Saudi film that was considered to be damaging to Christianity, the United States, or President Carter.

Besides seeking actively to prevent the film from being shown, the Saudi regime was put in the position of denying something (the incident itself) it really could not deny, and at the same time being unable to offer anything as a competing version of Islam. For one could either say, yes, that is the way Islam is, or Islam is not really like that, it is this way, provided, of course, there were some way of saying such a thing effectively, as well as someplace in which to stand and say it. For the official Saudi spokesperson there was no way and no place, except in the culturally discredited mode of wanting to prevent the film from being shown at all. Saudi officials made some halfhearted efforts to suggest "good" aspects of Islam, but these did not resonate in the debate. In addition there seemed to be no American constituency strong enough on *cultural* grounds to point out that the film was too inconsequential either as art or as politics to communicate anything of great moment. Unfortunately, there was nothing worse, both in the United States and in England, than for opponents of the film to appear to be puppets of Saudi financial interests (as suggested with unconcealed contempt by J. B. Kelly in *The New Republic,* May 17, 1980). In fine, the film's opponents commanded no apparatus to challenge the film critically. How trite the controversy was is quickly evident when discussions of it are compared with the debate over Marcel Ophuls' *The Memory of Justice,* or over *Holocaust,* or when various Leni Riefenstahl films were revived.

The *Death of a Princess* showing enables one to note more things than that. Both the American media and the surrounding intellectual and cultural milieu, well before *Princess* was ever heard of, have been literally teeming with overt anti-Islamic and anti-Arab slurs. On at least two occasions in the past, a Saudi Arabian king was directly insulted by New York City's mayor, who refused to greet him or show him even the commonest form of courtesy. Assiduous research has shown that there is hardly a prime-time TV show, for example, without several episodes in it of patently racist and insulting caricatures of Arabs, all of whom tend to be represented in unqualified categorical and generic terms: One Arab is therefore seen to be typical of all Arabs and of Islam in general. High school textbooks, novels, films, advertisements—how many of them are really informative about, much less complimentary to, Islam?

After the *Princess* controversy died down, the Saudis unfortunately forgot to take offense when in its June 1980 issue the *American Spectator* published an article by Eric Hoffer called "Muhammad's Sloth," subtitled "Muhammad, messenger of plod." Nor did the Saudis include in their list of misperceptions of Islam some reminder that the only three countries in the world whose territory was under occupation by a U.S. ally were Arab–Islamic states. Only when the royal family's reputation was directly tarnished did the Saudi regime threaten punishment. How was it, then, that the Arabs and Islam were hurt only in the one instance, not in the others? Why until the present have the Saudis done relatively little to help in promoting an understanding of the Arabs?

The full context of the *Death of a Princess* episode is still more complex, however. As noted earlier, U.S. military intervention in the Gulf has been a common topic of discussion for at least five years. But only since late 1978, when the Saudis did not join the Camp David peace process, have articles highlighting the regime's numerous faults and weaknesses cropped up regularly. It was acknowledged in late July 1980 that the CIA was behind some of these stories: See "The Washington Leak that Went Wrong: A CIA Gaffe that Shocked Saudi Arabia," by David Leigh (*The Washington Post,* July 30, 1980). For sixteen of the seventeen years of its existence, the *New York Review of Books* virtually ignored the Gulf, then during the year immediately following Camp David, it published several articles on the region, all of them stressing the fragility of the present Saudi ruling arrangement. At the same time, the daily press discovered Islam's ascendancy and the medieval attributes of its punishments, jurisprudence, and conception of women; no one remarked at the same time that Israeli rabbis, for example, expressed remarkably similar views on women, non-Jews, personal hygiene, and punishment, or that various Lebanese Christian clerics were just as bloodthirsty and medieval in their views. The selectivity of focus on Saudi Arabia's Islamic regime seemed orchestrated around its vulnerability and its peculiarity, all of which made it no less vulnerable and peculiar. But the intention seemed to be that because it had defied the United States, Saudi Arabia should not endure the benefit of "honest" reporting, as well as submit to demands for ending cover-ups of Saudi censorship (whereas no one complained about the fact that every news item coming out of Israel had to pass the military censor). There was widespread outrage routinely (and justly) expressed at the absence of freedom of the press in Saudi Arabia. How many no less apt feelings of outrage were expressed about Israeli rules against Arab newspapers on the West Bank? Saudi Arabia all of a sudden became a unique case to be upbraided by liberals and Zionists in one chorus, praised and nearly coddled by conservative financiers and senior Establishment figures in another. This further demoted Saudi Arabia and the Arab cause, made it more unacceptable and intellectually preposterous.

Two things will be apparent: First, Arab money as it is presently deployed is useless except for the short-term realization of purely commercial profits or small-scale cosmetic projects; second, there is no such thing as Arab information on the Arab world; there is only an Arab reaction to the unrestrained production of information (or disinformation or misinformation—the differences are important) about the Arab world. In both instances we see that Arab power is constrained, limited in the extreme, specialized, and isolated. Consider, as another example, the fact that Arabs cannot even give money to universities for Arab studies without a public outcry, whereas when the Japanese or German government donates money to places like Columbia or Harvard for Japanese or German studies, the chorus of approval is positively overwhelming.

[III]

In conclusion, the rule I propose for our attention is: either one intervenes alertly and responsibly in the current world order or one is intervened against brutally and irresponsibly. What I have been describing is a systematic intervention against the Arabs on the cultural and informational level. There is nothing natural or given about this, just as there is nothing natural or given about Arab inaction and passivity hitherto. Improving your image is not something you set out to do: It is something that accrues to you after you have done something about yourself, which improves you in fact, and your image as a consequence.

The Arabs therefore must be prepared to intervene *productively*—that is the key word—not cosmetically, in the changing world order, and to affiliate with the productive cultural and informational processes of the world system. We must not accept the allegation that Arabs are only Arabs as they are defined at present by everyone else except Arabs. Above all, we must show ourselves capable of being an organic part of the world, not a scapegoat for all its ills.

These are practical matters, not simply philosophical ones. Why do we need always to think in terms that limit us? Why cannot Arab money outside the Arab world support, let us say, liberation movements *and* a great library, or a civil rights group *and* a research institute in the United States, and why must it forever be limited either to coopting people like Billy Carter, or to finding academic experts willing to accept our money in order to write nice things about us (while secretly despising us for not being able to do even that for ourselves)? So far as the image of the Arab is concerned, it seems to me far more productive and interesting to deal with that question through discussions of the media in general, or analyses of disseminative systems. In other words, if we remain within the ethnic and narrowly political orbit to which we are presently confined, we will always be on the receiving end of things, never at their source. During the past year, on at least three occasions, international Arab money lost the chance to make itself productive and set itself up at the level of production internationally: first, when Random House was for sale; second, when *Harper's* was for sale; third, when the London *Times* was for sale. There is a kind of self-constraining timidity in the uses of international Arab capital which keeps it enclosed within the unproductive system of commissions, unearned royalties, relatively safe or quick off-the-top profits.

One could go on giving example after example; all of them can be reduced to a matter of will, and to will that needs collective focusing. The question is on what? I would submit that it must be focused on the idea of *production,* not reception or re-production or consumption. Those of us who live outside the Arab world and are therefore relatively free of all the distracting pressures of daily life there are in a unique position by the example of our work to provide that sort of focus. The various overseas Arab organizations that have developed in recent years were in part responses to the disastrous political situation the Arabs are in at home, but they are also, to their immense credit, responses to the cultural war against the Arabs, conducted within the changing world order. They—and each of us individually—have now reached a point of maturity. They can go in either of two ways. Either they become in essence ethnic clubs, groups, and organizations which, in the West at least, represent assimilated immigrants who wish to retain a bit of the old country in their lives. Or—and this is more what I think befits those of us Arabs who belong to one of the great world civilizations (and not simply to a charming ethnic group)—they can participate directly in the struggle for a new world order on the side plainly of freedom, knowledge, human rights—that is, on the side of everything that enhances life and humanly productive values. Beyond our imperative to survive as a distinct culture, we need to strive for a transformation of the conditions that hold all oppressed cultures in thrall.

Published in *Arab Studies Quarterly,* vol. 3, no. 2, spring 1981.

CHAPTER 22

The Death of Sadat

[1981]

As consciously as anyone since Charles de Gaulle, Anwar Sadat successfully set about acquiring a symbolic personality on a world scale. His death was ironically more of an American than an Arab event, so strongly did his presence impress itself on the Western media, on the Establishment, on the government, and, it would seem, on vast numbers of ordinary citizens.

He was the one Arab Muslim "we" could accept. In his person, he made possible everything we had traditionally supposed to have been impossible. At the very center of the Third World, he "threw out" the Soviet Union, he made peace with and benignly accepted Israel, he welcomed the United States—its style, its fantastic obsessions, blindness, and power, its statesmen and tourists—with an endless patience; he turned Egypt into an obligatory part of the "reasonable," moderate world.

Saudi Arabia may have offered the United States more tangible things, but it has remained a strangely remote, persistently unattractive quantity in the official and the public consciousness. Sadat overshadowed the Saudis completely. He was not just a substitute. He actually replaced the whole Arab world, the Middle East, Islam. The "loss" of each presumed island of stability added to his worth, increased his size, obliterated more history and, alas, more reality. He almost managed to shoulder Israel off center stage altogether.

Yet in the Arab world Sadat never succeeded in carrying the burdens more or less automatically placed on his shoulders in 1970.

For five years he bore them routinely, then he went looking for (and found) an identity elsewhere. Even the mystique of Mit Abul Kom, his native village, was designed for outside consumption. The myth of origins has never been a part of contemporary Arab lore and, for that matter, neither has the motif of autobiographical self-fashioning. For Arabs, Sadat was principally Gamal Abdel Nasser's successor and Arab Egypt's leader. Neither of these two facts has any place in current U.S. media or foreign-policy attention, given that Arab leadership and nationalism have always been the elusive prizes sought and never won by U.S. policymakers. Nasser embodied resistance, will, and unbowed failure. He was the way Arabs saw themselves in their weakness and in their potential for nobility. Oil and petrodollars never figured in Nasser's theater. His defeat did not cancel the validity of the impulses that moved him. On June 9, 1967, after he resigned in responsibility for a catastrophically bad military performance, millions of people poured into Cairo streets to reclaim him as their leader. When he died three years later Cairo was convulsed with a spontaneous outpouring of emotion, the likes of which it will not soon see again.

Nasser was what Sadat was not. To Arabs, Sadat was easily captured by the United States and Israel. He promised Arabs things he could not ever deliver, and this, of course, the Israelis knew, and he knew too but scarcely dared admit. To promise things at Camp David is not the same as keeping those promises at home. Sadat worked *outside* Arab history, society, and actuality, outside their rhetorical extravagances, their infatuation with form, their dizzyingly collective incoherence. In his last years he abused the Arabs mercilessly. He seems to have lost touch with his people (as witness their silence now), with most of his advisers, with most things except an abstract peace process. The list of his recently jailed opponents is far from adequately covered with a phrase like "Muslim fundamentalism," although his was not an exceptionally repressive regime.

As an emblem of his policies, Camp David signified disaster for the Arab world. After Camp David, Israel annexed Jerusalem, colonized the West Bank and Gaza relentlessly, devastated South Lebanon, attacked Iraq, rained blow after blow on Palestinian refugees. With the Arab world in a state of turmoil, Sadat just went on being the great statesman—at a distance, in a kind of U.S. daydream of what great native "rulers" ought to be.

In one sense, then, he was too big and could not carry the weight of what was expected of him. In another, he was small and irrelevant, however much people in the Arab world may have secretly admired his theatrical resourcefulness. His moment was a very short one: when he stood before Israel, placed the full Arab case before its government, and waited for the answering gesture that never came. The Arab world, for its part, could not keep pace with his movements. Even his natural constituency, Egypt's Egyptians, were, in the end, too Arab in their consciousness, too accustomed to the Arab world's historical love and cultural respect for them, to stay close to him.

Sadat's assassination ends the covenant ruling the Middle East since the 1950s. No longer will heads of state and prominent leaders be immune from bodily attack. Vice President Hosni Mubarak, who was Sadat's Saudi liaison, will try to hold on till the rest of Sinai is supposed to be returned in April 1982. Then, just as Sadat veered off his predecessor's path, he will almost certainly look for a time with more favor on his Arab context, and Egypt's Arab role.

Saudi Arabia, not the Camp David accords, will define the regional consensus, including Egypt. But until then, Israel, with the ferocious Menachem Begin and Defense Minister Ariel Sharon in charge, will seize opportunities in Lebanon against Syria and the Palestine Liberation Organization it had only begun to exploit behind the amiable screen that was Sadat. Turbulence will continue elsewhere. And U.S. policy, mindlessly supportive of Israeli military adventures and enamored of a regional alliance that exists only in the geopolitical mind, will be lost until the next Sadat comes along. The United States has built its largest embassy in Egypt, but its importance will inevitably be diminished—inevitably, as U.S. policy has always picked *against* the regional or nationalist currents everywhere in the Third World.

As for reason and peace, they will be in short supply. The superpowers define their peace and their "moderation" in ways that scant human life, as well as livable concepts of justice. Sadat's grandiose structure was a function of American credibility. It did not repatriate a single Palestinian nor lessen Egypt's amazingly high military expenditures and its abysmal poverty. One should mourn his passing as a man, and profoundly regret the violence of his assassination. But until there is some realization outside the Palestinian refugee camps that peace in the Middle East cannot be thought of without Palestinian self-determination, there will be more illusions, more waste, more senseless violence. If, as the cliché has it, Sadat was the victim of peace, then a much better and different peace is needed now.

Published in the *Los Angeles Times*, October 11, 1981.

CHAPTER 23

Permission to Narrate

[1984]

As a direct consequence of Israel's 1982 invasion of Lebanon, an international commission of six jurists headed by Sean Mac-Bride undertook a mission to investigate reported Israeli violations of international law during the invasion. The commission's conclusions were published in *Israel in Lebanon* by a British publisher[49]; it is reasonably clear that no publisher could or ever will be found for the book in the United States. Anyone inclined to doubt the Israeli claim that "purity of arms" dictated the military campaign will find support for that doubt in the report, even to the extent of finding Israel also guilty of attempted "ethnocide" and "genocide" of the Palestinian people (two members of the commission demurred at that particular conclusion, but accepted all the others). The findings are horrifying—and almost as much because they are forgotten or routinely denied in press reports as because they occurred. The commission says that Israel was indeed guilty of acts of aggression contrary to international law; it made use of forbidden weapons and methods; it deliberately, indiscriminately, and recklessly bombed civilian targets— "for example, schools, hospitals, and other nonmilitary targets"; it systematically bombed towns, cities, villages, and refugee camps; it deported, dispersed, and ill-treated civilian populations; it had no really valid reasons "under international law for its invasion of Lebanon, for the manner in which it conducted hostilities, or for its actions as an occupying force"; it was directly responsible for the Sabra and Shatila massacres.

As a record of the invasion, the MacBride Commission report is therefore a document of importance. But it has had no appreciable effect on the one outside force—America—whose indulgent support for Israel has made possible continued turbulence in Lebanon. The political question of moment is why, rather than fundamentally altering the Western view of Israel, the events of the summer of 1982 have been accommodated in all but a few places in the public realm to the view that prevailed before those events: that since Israel is in effect a civilized, democratic country constitutively incapable of barbaric practices against Palestinians and other non-Jews, its invasion of Lebanon was *ipso facto* justified.

Naturally, I refer here to official or policy-effective views and not the inchoate, unfocused feelings of the citizenry, which, to judge from several polls, is unhappy about Israeli actions. U.S. aid levels to Israel since the siege of Beirut have gone up to a point where Israel received roughly half of the entire American foreign aid budget, most of it in outright gifts and in subsidies to Israeli industries directly competitive with American counterparts. Presidential candidates, with the exception of George McGovern and Jesse Jackson, outbid each other in paeans of praise for Israel. The administration has refurbished the strategic "understanding" it made with Israel during Alexander Haig's time as Secretary of State, as if the invasion had never happened, the theory being that, given unlimited aid, Israel will be assured of its security and prove a little more flexible. This has not happened. And, of course, Israel now sits on even greater amounts of Arab land, with occupation policies that are more brutally and blatantly repressive than those of most other twentieth-century occupation regimes.

Gideon Spiro, an Israeli, testified to the MacBride Commission:

> We don't pay the price of anything that we are doing, not in the occupied territories, because Israel is in this a unique miracle. There is no country in the world which has over 100 percent inflation, which is occupying the West Bank, occupying another people, and building all those settlements with billions of dollars, and spending 30 percent of the GNP on defense—and still we can live here, I mean, somebody is paying for everything, so if everybody can live well and go abroad and buy cars, why not be for the occupation? So they are all luxury wars and people are very proud of the way we are fighting, the quick victories, the self-image of the brave Israeli—very flattering![50]

Yes, Israelis have fought well, and for the most part the Arabs haven't, but how is it that, as has been the case for much of this century, the premises on which Western support for Israel is based are still maintained, even though the reality, the facts, cannot possibly bear these premises out?

Look at the summer of 1982 more closely. A handful of poorly armed Palestinians and Lebanese held off a very large Israeli army, air force, and navy from June 5 till the middle of August. This was a major political achievement for the Palestinians. Something else was at stake in the invasion, however, to judge by its results a year and a half later—results which include Arab inaction, Syrian complicity in the unsuccessful PLO mutiny, and a virulent American hostility to Palestinian nationalism. That something was, I think, the inadmissible existence of the Palestinian people whose history, actuality, and aspirations, as possessed of a coherent narrative direction pointed toward self-determination, were the object of this violence. Israel's war was designed to reduce Palestinian existence as much as possible. Most Israeli leaders and newspapers admitted the war's *political* motive. In Rafael Eytan's words, to destroy Palestinian nationalism and institutions in Lebanon would make it easier to destroy them on the West Bank and in Gaza: Palestinians were to be turned into "drugged roaches in a bottle." Meanwhile the clichés advocating Israel's right to do what it wants grind on: Palestinians are rejectionists and terrorists, Israel wants peace and security, the Arabs won't accept Israel and want to destroy it, Israel is a democracy, Zionism is (or can be made consonant with) humanism, socialism, liberalism, Western civilization, the Palestinian Arabs ran away in 1948 because the other Arabs told them to, the PLO destroyed Lebanon, Israel's campaign was a model of decorum greeted warmly by "the Lebanese" and was only about the protection of the Galilee villagers.

Despite the MacBride Commission's view that "the facts speak for themselves" in the case of Zionism's war against the Palestinians, the facts have never done so, especially in America, where Israeli propaganda seems to lead a life of its own. Whereas, in 1975, Michael Adams and Christopher Mayhew were able to write about a coherent but unstated policy of unofficial British press censorship, according to which unpleasant truths about Zionism were systematically suppressed,[51] the situation is not nearly as obvious so far as the British media today are concerned. It still obtains in America, however, for reasons to do with a seemingly absolute refusal on the part of policy-makers, the media, the liberal intelligentsia to make connections, draw conclusions, state the simple facts, most of which contradict the premises of declared U.S. policy. Paradoxically, never has so much been written and shown of the Palestinians, who were scarcely mentioned fifteen years ago. They are there all right, but the narrative of their present actuality—which stems directly from the story of their existence in and displacement from Palestine, later Israel—that narrative is not.

A disciplinary communications apparatus exists in the West both for overlooking most of the basic things that might present Israel in a bad light, and for punishing those who try to tell the truth. How many people know the kind of thing suggested by the following incident—namely, the maintenance in Israel of a rigid distinction between privileged Jew and underprivileged Palestinian? The example is recent, and its very triviality indicates the by-now unconscious adherence to racial classification which pervades official Israeli policy and discourse. I have this instance from Professor Israel Shahak, chairman of the Israeli League of Human Rights, who transcribed it from the Israeli journal *Kol Ha'ir*. The journal reports, with some effect of irony:

> The society of sheep raisers in Israel (an entirely Jewish body from which Arabs are totally excluded) has agreed with the Ministry of Agriculture that a special sheepfold will be built in order to check the various immunizations on sheep. Which sheep? Jewish sheep in Israel, writes Baruch Bar Shelev, secretary of the sheep raisers' society, in a circular letter to all sheep raisers. In the letter they are asked to pay, toward the cost of the sheepfold, twenty shekels for Jewish sheep. This demand was also received by Semadar Kramer of the secretariat of "Neve Shalom" near Latron.
>
> Semadar Kramer sent the society of sheep raisers only half of the sum requested for building the Jewish sheepfold because "Never Shalom" is a Jewish–Arab village, and therefore its sheep are also Jewish–Arab. They also claim that they have no certain knowledge about mixed marriages among the sheep, and that lately some difficulties about the conversion to Judaism were encountered in their sheepfold.

This, one might think, is either insanity or some comic fantasy produced in the imagination of a Swift or Kafka. Jewish sheep? The conversion of Arab sheep to Judaism? Surely these things cannot be real. Such distinctions, however, are part of the system of possessive exclusivism which has been imposed upon reality by central forces in Israeli society. The system is rarely discussed at all in the West, certainly not with anything resembling the intensity with which Palestinian terrorism is discussed. When an attempt is made to speak critically of Israel, the result is frightening—if the attempt succeeds in getting any diffusion at all. One small index is the fact that the Anti-Defamation League in America and the American–Israel Public Affairs Committee have each published books identifying Israel's "enemies" and employing tactics for police or vigilante action. In addition, there is the deep media compliance I have referred to—so that effective, and especially narrative, rendering of the Palestine–Israel contest are either attacked with near-unanimous force or ignored. The fortunes of Le Carré's novel *The Little Drummer Girl* and Costa-Gavras's film *Hanna K* illustrate these alternatives.

Having made a strong impression regionally and internationally during the years 1970 to 1982, the Palestinian narrative, as we shall see in a moment, is now barely in evidence. This is not an aesthetic judgment. Like Zionism itself, post-1948 Palestinian nationalism has had to achieve formal and ideological prominence well before any actual land has been gained. Strange nationalisms these, conducted for years in exile and alienation, for years protective, stubborn, passionately believed in. The major difference is that Zionism was a hothouse flower grown from European nationalism, anti-Semitism, and colonialism, while Palestinian nationalism, derived from the great wave of Arab and Islamic anticolonial sentiment, has since 1967, though tinged with retrogressive religious sentiment, been located within the mainstream of secular post-imperialist thought. Even more important, Zionism is essentially a dispossessing movement so far as non-Jews are concerned. Palestinianism since 1967 has generally been inclusive, trying (satisfactorily or not) to deal with the problem created by the presence of more than one national community in historical Palestine. And for the years between 1974 and 1982, there was a genuine international consensus underwriting the Palestinian communal narrative and restoring it as an historical story to its place of origin and future resolution in Palestine. I speak here of the idea that Israel should return the Occupied Territories and that a Palestinian state be created alongside Israel. That this went against the grain of Zionism, despite its many internal differences, was obvious: nevertheless, there were many people in the world both willing and able to contest Golda Meir's 1969 fiat that the Palestinians did not exist historically, had no communal identity, and no national rights. But when the whole force of the Palestinian national movement proposed a political resolution in Palestine based on the narrative shape of alienation, return, and partition, in order to make room for two peoples, one Jewish and the other Arab, neither Israel nor the West accepted it. Hence the bitter Arab and Palestinian infighting, which has been caused by Arafat's—i.e., the mainstream PLO's—failure to get any real response to the notion of partition from those Western nations most associated with the fate of Palestine. Bruno Kreisky puts the case forcefully in "L'Échec d'Arafat, c'est notre faute" (*Les Nouvelles*, December 1983). The symbolism of Palestinians fighting each other in the forlorn outskirts of Tripoli in North Lebanon is too stark to be misinterpreted. The course taking Palestinians, in Rosemary Sayigh's phrase, from peasants to refugees to the revolutionaries of a nation in exile has for the time being come to an abrupt stop, curling about itself violently. What was once a radical alternative to Zionism's master code of Jewish exclusivism seems reduced to mere points on the map miles away from Palestine. Lebanon, the Soviet buildup, Syria, Druze and Shia militancy, the new American–Israeli quasi-treaty—these dominate the landscape, absorb political energies.

Two anecdotes give a sense of the political and ideological problem I am trying to describe. Between August 29 and September 7, the United Nations held an international conference, mandated by the General Assembly, on the question of Palestine. The conference was to be held in Paris, but, worried by the threat of demonstrations and incidents from French Zionist organizations, the Mitterrand government requested that it be held elsewhere: France's *quid pro quo* to the UN, which was actually entitled to hold the conference in Paris at UNESCO's extraterritorial headquarters, was to be full participation by France. The conference was duly moved to Geneva, and France, just as duly, reneged on its promise and participated only as an "observer." One hundred thirty-seven nations showed up, a fact repeatedly changed to seventy-five nations by the U.S. press. The central document of the conference was to be a "Profile of the Palestinian People"—the title and the study's focus were specified by the General Assembly. With a small group of other "experts," I was engaged to produce the Profile. It went to the Secretary General's office for three months, and was returned for discussion to the Prepar-

atory Committee of twenty-odd nations. There it sat until the beginning of June, at which point I was told that the Profile could not, and
would never, be approved for use at the conference. The reasons given
were, as usual, diplomatic and diverse. But, as an apologetic ambassador from a friendly Arab country made clear to me, by positing the
existence—and historical narrative—of a Palestinian people, the Profile had "created" a dual-nationality problem for the Arab countries
in which Palestinians had been dispersed since 1948. The same strictures and fears applied to the proposal I made to conduct the first-ever
census of refugee and expatriate Palestinians, most of whom live in the
Arab world. There is an Arab context and an Israeli context, I was told:
to speak of Palestinians outside the Occupied Territories was to challenge the collective Arab narrative and, in the words of a young Arab
Third Secretary, to view history in too "liberal and Western" a way.
Thus no Palestinian narrative, no Profile, no census: Palestine yes,
Palestinians no.

The second anecdote is taken from the other side of the aisle,
where, as we have seen, things are no less peculiar. The Israeli commentator Yoav Karni wrote in 1983:

> Last week I was invited to the Israeli Army Radio program *Correct Till
> Now* to speak about the historical backgrounds of Armenian terrorism.
> Against their usual custom, the editors insisted on taping the talk
> beforehand. Afterwards, I understood why. I was asked if the Ar-
> menian holocaust really occurred. I answered: "There is no doubt that
> genocide occurred. For thousands of years people lived on its land,
> and suddenly it was no more. This is genocide," or words to that
> effect. The Israeli Army Radio refused to broadcast the talk. They
> were ready to do it only on condition that I should change the text,
> and say, "There was a massacre, which perhaps approaches geno-
> cide."[52]

He concludes that "perhaps it was the great mistake of the last
Jewish generation which caused it. It should have been forbidden to
Jews to treat the concept of 'genocide' as applying to them alone. It
should be told in every Israeli school that many other peoples were,
and still are, expelled and massacred."

Conversely, Israelis are told by Chaim Herzog that when Israel
fosters good relations with Right Wing regimes which practice racial
discrimination and kill their own people, the only criterion ought to

be: "Is it good for the Jews?" A related sentiment was expressed by a Jewish-Israeli resident of Upper Nazareth about his Israeli-Arab neighbors: "Love is more dangerous than hate. It's dangerous to our existence."

The Palestinian narrative has never been officially admitted to Israeli history, except as that of "non-Jews," whose inert presence in Palestine was a nuisance to be ignored or expelled. With the exception of a small and marginal group of Israelis, most of Israel has as a result not found it difficult to get over the story of the Lebanese war and its subsequent horrors. Take Abba Eban—liberal, humane, judicious. In his introduction to the Israeli Kahan Commission report, published as a book in the West, he praises the "meticulous" analysis that, in a sense, exonerates Israel: yet in so doing he nowhere mentions such things as the explicitly fascist nature of Israel's chief allies, the Lebanese Phalanges, or the fact—which doesn't speak for itself—that the Palestinians in Lebanon were not *ipso facto* "terrorists," as the report has it, but were there because they had been driven out of Palestine in implementation of an admitted policy of expulsion.

Thus, as much as Begin and Sharon, Eban refuses to consider the PLO as more than a gang of terrorists. Indeed, he makes it seem that the PLO and the Phalangists, both of whom are "the chief agents of the tragedy," are equally culpable for killing the Palestinians at Sabra and Shatila. As to whether "terrorism" is adequately defined simply by ascribing it to Palestinians because of Israeli deaths (the figures are interesting—between 1967 and 1982, 290 Israelis were killed in Palestinian attacks, whereas Lebanese police, UN, and Red Cross figures put Israeli-caused Arab casualties at 20,000 deaths for July and August 1982 alone), or whether any act of Palestinian resistance is terrorism, Eban does not say. Yet the *other* Israeli report on Sabra and Shatila is perfectly clear on Israeli responsibility for, and even complicity with, what took place: I refer here to the Israeli journalist Amnon Kapeliouk's powerfully concise book, *Sabra et Chatila: Enquête sur un massacre,* which has still found no established British or American publisher.

Facts do not at all speak for themselves, but require a socially acceptable narrative to absorb, sustain, and circulate them. Such a narrative has to have a beginning and an end: in the Palestinian case, homeland for the resolution of its exiles since 1948. But, as Hayden White has noted in a seminal article, "narrative in general, from the folk tale to the novel, from annals to the fully realized 'history,' has to do with the topics of law, legality, legitimacy, or, more generally, *authority.*"[53] Now there are numerous UN resolutions certifying the Palestinians as a people, their struggle as a legitimate one, their right to have an independent state as "inalienable." Such resolutions, however, do not have the authority of which White speaks. None has drawn any acknowledgment from Israel or the United States, which have restricted themselves to such nonnarrative and indefinite formulae as—in the language of lackadaisical U.S. pronouncements— "resolution of the Palestinian problem in all its aspects."[54]

No television watcher could have had any doubts that the Israelis were savage and ruthless during the siege of Beirut. Yet a campaign has been waged in the media attacking the media for a pro-PLO slant. It got started, well before the Israeli invasion, in pro-Zionist publications like *The New Republic,* and it continues long after in *Encounter, Commentary,* and *Policy Studies,* as well as on college campuses where lectures entitled "NBC in Lebanon: A Study in Misrepresentation" are regularly given. The basic line is that the media have taken liberties with language, that analogies between Warsaw and Beirut are wrong, that any images showing Israeli troops engaged in bombing plainly civilian targets are anti-Semitic, that the millions of feet of newsreel are less trustworthy than the impressions of a supporter of Israel who spent a day in Lebanon touring the place as a guest of the Israeli army. Underlying all attacks on the media is the allegation that the PLO has intimidated or seduced journalists into partisan, anti-Semitic, and anti-Western attacks on Israel, a charge grandiloquently pronounced by Norman Podhoretz in his imitation of Zola, "J'Accuse."[55]

The repetition and accumulation of these claims amount to a virtual orthodoxy, setting limits, defining areas, asserting pressures, and the Chancellor incident of July 1982 stands as something of a monument to the process. John Chancellor is a leading American television commentator who arrived in Beirut during the siege and witnessed the destruction brought about by the indiscriminate bombing that was taking place all around him. The report he produced in full view of a vast national audience included references to "savage Israel," "an imperialist state that we never knew existed before." Yet a week later he reappeared in Jerusalem more or less retracting his remarks from Beirut: what he had seen there, he now said, was a "mistake," Israel did not intend the city's siege but had "bumbled into it." Commenting on this volte-face, Richard Poirier wrote in *Raritan Review* that "the feelings aroused in Chancellor (and in millions of viewers presumably)

by the television footage simply had no place to go outside the program.'' Far from just changing his mind from one week to the next,
Chancellor:

> unwittingly exposed the degree to which the structure of the evening
> news depends on ideas of reality determined by the political and social
> discourse already empowered outside the newsroom. Feelings about
> the victims of the siege could not, for example, be attached to an idea
> for the creation of a Palestinian homeland, since, despite the commit-
> ments, muffled as they are, of the Camp David accords, no such idea
> has as yet managed to find an enabling vocabulary within what is
> considered ''reasonable'' political discourse in this country.[56]

What needs to be added to Poirier's astute comments is that the
''idea'' of a Palestinian homeland would have to be enabled by the
prior acceptance of a narrative entailing a homeland. And this has been
resisted as strenuously on the imaginative and ideological level as it has
been politically.

While it is true that the ideological dimension is always important
in political contests, the oddity here is that the physical distance from
the territory aspired to, and the heavily saturated significance of that
territory, make crucial the need for antecedent ideological projection
in narrative form in the West. For Palestine is a privileged site of origin
and return for both Judaism and Christianity—all the more so given
the fact that Palestine for one and a half millennia had been in non-
Jewish and non-Christian hands. It figures prominently in such momentous events as the Crusades, the nineteenth-century imperial
conflicts, in Zionism, and in a whole congerie of major cultural texts
from Augustine's autobiography, to Dante's vision, to Shakespeare's
dramatic geography, and Blake's apocalypse. In more material and
mundane terms, Palestine has also been important to the Arab and
Muslim experience: a comparative study of that experience with the
Judaic and Christian would be of extraordinary interest. The point I am
trying to make is that insofar as the West has complementarily endowed Zionism with a role to play in Palestine along with its own, it
has stood against the perhaps humble narrative of native Palestinians
once resident there and now reconstituting themselves in exile in the
Occupied Territories.

With this background in mind, the current disapproval of terrorism
can more easily be understood. As first articulated during the late

months of the Carter administration on, and amplified in such books as *The Terror Network* and *The Spike,* as unrestrainedly used by Israel—and now by American—officials to describe "enemies," terrorism is the biggest and yet for that reason the most precise of concepts. This is not at all to say that terrorism does not exist, but rather to suggest that its existence has occasioned a whole new signifying system as well. Terrorism signifies first, in relation to "us," the alien and gratuitously hostile force. It is destructive, systematic, and controlled. It is a web, a network, a conspiracy run from Moscow, via Bulgaria, Beirut, Libya, Tehran, and Cuba. It is capable of anything. One fervent anti-Communist Israeli has written a book revealing the Sabra and Shatila massacres to be a plot engineered by Moscow and the PLO to kill Palestinians (using Germans) in order to frame democratic Israel. Most of all, terrorism has come to signify "our" view of everything in the world that seems inimical to our interests, army, policy, or values.

As such, it can be used retrospectively (as in the cases of Iran and Lebanon) or prospectively (Grenada, Honduras, Nicaragua) to justify everything "we" do and to delegitimize as well as dehumanize everything "they" do. The very indiscriminateness of terrorism, actual and described, its tautological and circular character, is antinarrative. Sequence, the logic of cause and effect as between oppressors and victims, opposing pressures—all these vanish inside an enveloping cloud called "terrorism." Israeli commentators have remarked that the systematic use by Begin, Sharon, Eytan, and Arens of the rubric "terrorist" to describe Palestinians made it possible for them to use phrases like "terrorists' nest," "cancerous growth" and "two-legged beasts" in order to bomb refugee camps. An Israeli paratrooper said that "every Palestinian is automatically a suspected terrorist and by our definition of the term it is actually true." One should add that Likud's antiterrorist language and methods represent only an increase in intensity over previous Israeli policies, which were no less callous about Palestinians as real people with a real history.

No wonder, then, that "facts" and the truth of a consecutive historical experience stand very little chance of wide acceptance or distribution in this wilderness of mirrors. To know, for example, that Shamir's Stern Gang treated with the Nazis,[57] or that everything the Israelis now do to Palestinians constitutes brutality and oppression easily rivaling the deeds of the Polish or South African regimes, is also sadly to know that antiapartheid activists regularly avoid discussion of

Israel when they criticize one of its chief allies, South Africa, or that American journalists do not report the details of daily life on the West Bank with the tenacity they bring to reports about daily life behind the Iron Curtain, or that leaders of the antinuclear movement have nothing to say about the Israeli nuclear threat. Worse yet, there is every chance that ignorance about Israel's attitude toward Palestinians will keep pace with sustained encomiums on Israel's pioneering spirit, democracy, and humanism. On the uprooting of Palestinian orchards in Gaza in 1972 to make way for settlements, Chomsky notes here: this is "what is called in technical terms 'making the desert bloom.' "[58]

There have been refugees before. There have been new states built on the ruins of old. The unique things about this situation is Palestine's unusual centrality, which privileges a Western master narrative, high-lighting Jewish alienation and redemption—with all of it taking place as a modern spectacle before the world's eyes. So that when Palestini-ans are told to stop complaining and to settle elsewhere like other refugees before them, they are entitled to respond that no other refugees have been required systematically to watch an unending ceremony of public approbation for the political movement, army, or country that made them refugees and occupied their territory. Occu-pying armies, as Chomsky observes, do not as a rule "bask in the admiration of American intellectuals for their unique and remarkable commitment to 'purity of arms.' "[59] To top it all, Palestinians are expected to participate in the dismantling of their own history at the same time.

As long as discussions of Palestine and Israel are conducted on this level, the superior force of the ideological consensus I have been describing will prevail. Palestinians will initially have to play the major role in changing the consensus and, alas, characteristically, they have not been very successful. I recall during the siege of Beirut obsessively telling friends and family there, over the phone, that they ought to record, write down their experiences; it seemed crucial as a starting point to furnish the world some narrative evidence, over and above atomized and reified TV clips, of what it was like to be at the receiving end of Israeli "antiterrorism," also known as "peace for Galilee." Naturally, they were all far too busy surviving to take seriously the unclear theoretical imperatives being urged on them intermittently by a distant son, brother, or friend. As a result, most of the easily available written material produced since the fall of Beirut has in fact not been Palestinian and, just as significant, it has been of a fairly narrow range

of types:[60] a small archive to be discussed in terms of absences and
gaps—in terms either prenarrative or, in a sense, antinarrative. The
archive speaks of the depressed condition of the Palestinian narrative
at present.

This does not, however, make any of the works in question less
valiant, less indicative of a new moral isolation enveloping Israel—for
all the absence of a Palestinian narrative. Each functions on some
inevitably primitive level as valuable testimonial, as raw information
for a setting, Europe and America, where definitions of the Middle East
serve to screen the reality of Israeli actions. Jonathan Randal—a senior
American foreign correspondent, veteran of Vietnam, Cuba, and Algeria—like John Bulloch of the *Daily Telegraph,* like Kapeliouk, like Salim
Nassib and Caroline Tisdall, like Tony Clifton, is a journalist writing
what is in effect surplus reportage, as if the constraints of newspaper
columns could not contain what was seen. This is an interesting
phenomenon, perhaps a new journalistic mode. Each of these writers,
except Chomsky, tells a story sympathetic to the Palestinians, if not
always in political agreement with them; there is also a solidarity with
those Lebanese who have suffered for decades the unmitigated stupidity of their leaders and foreign friends. All of these writers chronicle
the relentless brutality of the siege, the outrage felt at the unctuous
language of military communiqués glossing over massacres and heroism. Although their works overlap in many ways, each contributes a
piece to the larger picture attempted in his redoubtably encyclopedic
way by Chomsky.

As straight narrative of the battle culminating in Beirut between
Israel and the PLO, Bulloch's book is difficult to better, though it is
dotted with careless errors (Said Aql for Basil Aql). Its economy of line
and unsparingly harsh perspective allow a clear but circumscribed
picture to emerge of what forces were engaged together; his conclusion is that Israel lost the war. But even though he makes an effort at
describing the momentum of Palestinian nationalism, its lopsided
anomalous achievements in Lebanon, its inevitably messy involvement
in Lebanese and Syrian politics, its better than expected efforts to cope
with circumstances too complex for anyone to overcome, he writes as
an outsider, and there is little in his narrative to prepare one for the
continuing drama of the PLO, or for the bloody Israeli occupation of
South Lebanon, or for the unfolding national catastrophe that has been
Lebanon since August 1982.

Bulloch is of the school which thinks of Lebanon's history as the

time-honored story of *zaims* (or semifeudal patrons), factions, and
loyalties. He follows Lebanon's leading historian, Kamal Salibi, in
this,[61] although unlike Elie Salem (Lebanon's current foreign minster),
Bulloch hasn't concluded that Lebanon's sudden modern prosperity
was ever, or could ever be, maintained without disastrous upheaval—
Salem's prediction, as recently as twelve years ago.[62] It would be hard
to be more unfortunately wrong. Not that anyone was more correct
in predicting the two-decade cataclysm, first of wealth, then of civil
war, which is tearing Lebanon apart.

David Gilmour's first chapter exposes the jungle that was "the old
Lebanon" with merciless precision, and his last chapter presciently lays
for the scenario now being enacted. His account of the overwhelming
mess unleashed by piratical commerce, governmental incompetence,
regional and ideological confusions, tremendous demographic change,
and utter cynicism is unique. It gives one a compelling rationale for the
emergence of the PLO inside (rather than its "invasion" of) Lebanon,
where among a largely destitute and confined refugee population no
one could survive at all without some form of political organization for
protection. One senses in Gilmour's book, however, some frustration
at the recalcitrant, nonnarrative character of Lebanon's problems. No
other modern society has torn itself apart with that crazy mixture of
brutality and style. Few countries have concentrated within their
borders so impossibly heterogeneous a collection of interests, most of
them having coarse domination, profit, and manipulation as their goal.
Some adumbration of this is conveyed in the American title of Randal's
book—*Going All the Way*—and much of its substance similarly delivers
the irrationality of Lebanon: the relentless Lebanese willingness to see
yet another car bomb (surely, at this "post-political" stage, an art
form), the stupid, opportunistic ideological fantasies constructed by
different factions. There are cultural and intellectual roots to the things
that move Maronites, Sunni, and Shia Muslim, Greek Orthodox Christians and Druze in Lebanon, and these Randal does not explore. A pity,
since, as he notes, for a corps of Western journalists afflicted with too
rapid and frequent a turnover in complicated places like Lebanon,
there is by now a specialist literature that ought not to be ignored: the
pioneering studies of Lebanon and Syria by Albert Hourani and Dominique Chevalier have been elaborated in the work of younger colleagues and students. Instead Randal relies on his instinct for relevant
observation. His sketches of the checkmating, of the multiple "nega-
tions," between communities on which modern Lebanon has rested

are good, as is his portrait of U.S. ignorance, bumbling, and mistimed and misplaced pressures.

There has never been an American policy on Lebanon, as anyone today can quite easily ascertain. Randal, however, takes the further step of characterizing American weakness in the face of Israeli strength as actively promoting Lebanon's destruction. At most, "Lebanon, for the United States, ended up a disposable place of unknown loyalties and complicated working, not to be entirely trusted." This by no means explains the presence of 2,000 Marines and a Navy flotilla, but it goes a long way toward telling us that no coherent mission for them will ever be found, and, unfortunately for those Lebanese who have put their trust in U.S. military policy, that the Marines are almost certain to be pulled out ungracefully fairly soon. Randal's best moments come when he narrates Bashir Gemayel's rise to power—a chilling tale that lays to rest any illusions about the Maronite–Phalange claim to be defending the values of "Western civilization." It is difficult to understand the romance that lingers about Bashir's short life, in which he was just as capable of killing as of marshaling the members of his own community. Randal also helps one to grasp the basic premises of Israeli policy on Lebanon, and Israel's only recently challenged alliance with the fascist Phalanges. (Interestingly, it was an interagency conflict that brought these matters into the open—between the Mossad, who promoted the Phalanges, and Israeli military intelligence, who felt that Mossad had lost "objectivity" by overidentifying with their Lebanese clients.)

Randal's book goes back to the period just after World War I to show how Zionists envisaged incorporating South Lebanon into the future Jewish state, but the bulk of his evidence dates from the fifties and after, when it became a matter of official Israeli policy—fascinatingly documented in Moshe Sharett's *Diaries*—to intervene directly in Lebanese affairs, sponsor militia, bribe officials, collaborate with Maronites to help maintain an imbalance between dramatic rises in the Muslim population and the increasingly unyielding Christian control which was handed to the Maronite oligarchs by French colonialism in 1943.

Two other journalists' books deserve mention. One is Tony Clifton's *God Cried*, which, with Catherine Leroy's graphic and painful photographs, narrates the agonies of conscience, sympathy, and rage felt by an Australian correspondent reporting the Palestinian and Lebanese experience that culminated in the siege. Clifton pours it out—all the anger at Israel's detailed, almost fastidious effort to humiliate and pain the very refugees it had expelled in 1948, and has been stamping on ever since. As with Randal's work, we are obliged in the end to rely on one man's sensitive and informed testimony. There is some slight resemblance between Clifton and Jacobo Timerman, whose rambling but affecting account of an Israeli's awakening of conscience has been criticized by some for unfairness to Israel, by others for reducing the whole war to a problem for one Jewish witness.[63] In both instances, nonetheless, there is an urgency in the author's conviction that what he writes is unfairly matched against a public narrative skewed very much in Israel's favor.

It may have been with some of these problems of subjectivity in mind that Salim Nassib and Caroline Tisdall shaped their book the way they did. *Beirut: Frontline Story* has the effect of a montage sequence: interviews with a wide spectrum of political figures interspersed with vignettes of daily life, of which the best is a lively "cross section of the war—five stories of a Beirut apartment block" whose occupants are Greek Orthodox, Maronites, Sunni Muslims, Druzes, and Shia Muslims. This is the Israeli invasion seen in vivid microcosm, daily life surgically rendered, but, as in a Zola novel, there is an active sympathy at work. Nassib's pieces were his dispatches for *Libération,* and they conclude with Arafat aboard the Greek freighter *Atlantis* on his way from Beirut to Athens, speaking about the war. Caroline Tisdall's pages of eyewitness description relive the Sabra and Shatila massacres, and end with this telling Palestinian comment:

> Before the war they said we were terrorists and that we were training terrorists in our camps. Everyone who knows us knows we were fighters you could trust, and that we were trying to build a progressive mentality. Why didn't they write that every day? It's related to philosophy: when you are building something and the enemy comes and destroys this thing again and again, it means you are on the right road, however long it may be.

This comment (and especially the image of repeated destruction followed by repeated efforts to rebuild) should be kept in mind as one proceeds through Chomsky's panorama of stupidity, immorality, and corruption, *The Fateful Triangle,* which, for its documentation, may be the most ambitious book ever attempted on the conflict between

Zionism and the Palestinians viewed as centrally involving the United States. But this, too, is not the narrative that is missing.

For Chomsky's book is decidedly not written from the point of view of a Palestinian trying, as it were, to give national shape to a life now dissolving into many unrelated particles. *The Fateful Triangle* is instead a dogged exposé of human corruption, greed, and intellectual dishonesty. It is also a great and important book, which must be read by anyone concerned with public affairs. The facts for Chomsky are there to be recognized, although no one else has ever recognized them so systematically. His mainly Israeli and U.S. sources are staggeringly complete, and he is capable of registering contradictions, distinctions, and lapses which occur between them. But, as we shall see, his work is not only deeply and unacceptably pessimistic; it is also a work not critical and reflective enough about its own premises, and this is partly because he does not, in a narrative way, look back to the beginning of the conflict between Zionism and the Palestinians.

These criticisms cannot be made at all lightly, or without acknowledging the unparalleled energy and honesty of his achievement. There is something deeply moving about a mind of such noble ideals repeatedly stirred on behalf of human suffering and injustice. One thinks here of Voltaire, of Benda, or Russell, although more than any of them Chomsky commands what he calls "reality"—facts—over a breathtaking range. He has two aims. One is an account of the origins of Israel's attack upon the Palestinians during its invasion of Lebanon in 1982; out of that account comes a survey of diplomatic, intellectual, economic, and political history that connects these disparate realms with each other. His major claim is that Israel and the United States—especially the latter, seen by Chomsky as the archvillain of the piece—are rejectionists opposed to peace, whereas the Arabs, including the PLO, have for years been trying to accommodate themselves to the reality of Israel.

The other aim of Chomsky's book is to compare the history—so profoundly inhuman, cynical, and deliberately cruel to the Palestinian people—with its systematically rewritten record as kept by those whom Chomsky calls "the supporters of Israel." As with another book of his, it is Chomsky's contention that the liberal intelligentsia (Irving Howe, Arthur Goldberg, Alan Dershowitz, Michael Walzer, Amos Oz, Jane Fonda, Tom Hayden, Shlomo Avineri, Martin Peretz) and even segments of the organized Left are more culpable, more given to lying, than conservatives are. The Western media come off badly in comparison with their Israeli counterparts, although Chomsky notes, shrewdly, that media accuracy is rarely a matter of goodwill or of unhypocritical journalists: it is just that "the totalitarian mentality" ruling the West since Vietnam can't always keep up with the swarming life of fact in the Western democracies.

So the book can be read as a protracted war between fact and a series of myths—Israeli democracy, Israeli purity of arms, the benign occupation, no racism against Arabs in Israel, Palestinian terrorism, peace for Galilee. Although Chomsky's model for these myths is Orwellian newspeak and doublethink (aspects, he says, of a revision of history in the post-Vietnam era), the process of dismantling to which he submits the myths is actually a form of deconstruction, since all of the material he uses against texts like *The New Republic, The New York Times,* the *Jerusalem Post* is itself textual. Nearly everywhere he looks he finds either suppression or outright apologies for gangsterism (as when *The New Republic* on July 27, 1977, prints "the first explicit defense of torture to have appeared in the West apart from the ravings of the ultra-right in France during the Algerian war"), all done in the interest of sustaining Israeli and U.S. hegemony. Having rehearsed the "official" narrative, he then blows it away with vast amounts of counterevidence, leading us to the conclusion that the Middle East, along with the rest of the world, is on the road to Armageddon.

I can give only a hint of his tremendously effective methods and recourse—his thousands of footnotes, his frequently angry irony, his compassion for the weak, the forgotten and calumniated. Thus as he tells us of older Israeli soldiers testifying that even in European service during World War II they saw nothing to compare to the destruction of Ein-el-Hilweh Camp, or that "long and repeated interrogations were accompanied by constant beating, or attacks by dogs on leashes," or that Israeli border guards force people to crawl, bark, laud Begin, or that during collective punishment in the West Bank village of Halhul "people were ordered to urinate on one another, sing 'Hativka' . . . lick the ground," or that the director-general of the Israel Broadcasting Authority in 1974 wrote an article expressing his preference for South African over black Africa, complete "with citations of research proving the genetic inferiority of blacks"—as he gives these and literally thousands more such horrifying details, he notes the silence of *The New Republic,* the praise for Israeli purity of arms, the defense of Israel's occupation (collective detention, torture, and murder) policy, the high praise for Israel's moral values, the testimony of cultural authorities such as Saul Bellow, who sees in Israel a land "where almost everyone is reasonable and tolerant, and rancor against the Arabs is rare." Worse yet, there are the many cases where apologists for Zionism and socialism like Irving Howe ignore the killing of Jews by the Irgun, speak about the evils of Begin (although much of Chomsky's evidence is that Labour was at least as bad as Likud), and then go on to pronounce on the "habitual violence" of Arab politics. Chomsky gives much attention to the organized racial persecution of Arabs and of "Oriental" Jews, usually abetted by learned or religious authorities, or by figures like Elie Wiesel who use the Holocaust to legitimate excesses; he also notes that none of Israel's liberal supporters has anything to say about this.

Chomsky is not especially gentle to the PLO, whose "self-destructiveness" and "suicidal character" he likes no more than he approves of its program of armed struggle and erratic violence. The Arab regimes, he says, are not "decent," and, he might have added, not popular either. But this—and not incidentally—is one of the gaps in this almost preposterously complete book. I am referring to its relative inattention to the Arab world. He is certainly right to say that there exists a standard Western practice, racist in origin, of dismissing Arab sources as unreliable, and he suggests that the unavailability of written Arab work in the West is in part due to the same "democratic" censorship that promotes the image of Israel. Yes, but the dynamic of "a fateful triangle" would make more sense if, included in it, there could be some account of political, social, and economic trends in the Arab world—or if it were changed to the figure of a square or circle. Among such trends one would have to place the economic dependence of the Arab states on the United States (amounting, in some instances, to objective collaboration with Israel); the almost total absence of democratic freedoms in the Arab world; the peculiar relationships that obtain between Palestinians, or for that matter the PLO, and various Arab countries; Western cultural penetration of the Arab world and the Islamic reactions this has bred; the role of the Arab Left and the Soviet Union. Despite their stated willingness to have peace, the Arab regimes have not been able to make peace, or to mobilize their societies for war; such facts—which are not entirely a consequence of Israeli–American rejection—Chomsky does not fully consider.

There is also some confusion in the book, some inconsistency at the level of principle. The normative picture proposed by Chomsky—with which I am in agreement—is that Palestine should be partitioned into two states, and that the PLO, plus most of the Arab states, have had this end in mind at least since the early seventies. I think he is absolutely right to say that because, in the words of Israeli commentators like Yehoshua Porath and Danny Rubenstein, Israel feared moderate and responsible Palestinians more than terrorists, it was Israel, aided by the United States, which prevented any realization of this reasonable if imperfect plan. But it isn't clear to me how you can recognize that Zionism has always excluded and discriminated against Arabs—which you oppose—and yet maintain that Jews do have a communal right to settlement from abroad in Palestine. My point is that here you must more explicitly define what those rights are, and in what way your definition of those rights is not like that of those Zionists who simply disregarded the fact of Arab inhabitants already in Palestine. How can you formulate the right to move people into Palestine despite the wishes of all the already present native Palestinians, without at the same time implying and repeating the tragic cycle of violence and counterviolence between Palestinians and Jews? How do you avoid what has happened if you do not more precisely reconcile *allowable* claims?

In leaving this problem unresolved, Chomsky is led to one of the chief difficulties of his book—namely, his pessimistic view that "it is too late" for any reasonable or acceptable settlement. The facts, of course, are with him: The rate of Jewish colonization on the West Bank has passed any easily retrievable mark, and as Meron Benvenisti and other anti-Likud Israelis have said, the fight for Palestinian self-determination in the Occupied Territories is now over—good and lost. Pessimism of the intellect *and* pessimism of the will . . . But most Palestinians would say in response: If those are the facts, then so much the worse for the facts. The supervening reality is that the struggle between Zionism, in its present form, and the Palestinians is very far from over; Palestinian nationalism has had, and will continue to have, an integral reality of its own, which, in the view of many Palestinians who actually live the struggle, is not about to go away, or submit to the ravages of Zionism and its backers. And curiously this is what Chomsky does not or perhaps cannot see, although he is right to forecast a worsening of the situation, increasing levels of violence, more polarization, militarization, irrationality. In having accepted the Zionist first principle of a right to settle Jews in Palestine against the wishes of the native inhabitants, Chomsky almost unconsciously takes the next step of assuming that the Palestinian struggle is over, that the Palestinians have given up—maybe because their historical existence hasn't totally convinced him of its permanence. Perhaps giving up is the rational thing to do, yet—and here Chomsky's own fighting energies contradict him—injustice is injustice, and no one should acquiesce in it. Chomsky himself, with this massive volume, is a case in point.

That raises another problem. His isolation from the actual arena of contest, his distance from power as a fiercely uncompromising intellectual, his ability to tell the dispassionate truth (while no longer able to write in previously hospitable places like the *New York Review of Books*) have made it possible for him to avoid the ideological traps and the dishonesty he perceives in Israeli and U.S. apologists. There is, of course, no state-worship in Chomsky, nor is there any glossing over uncomfortable truths or indecent practices that exist within one's own camp. But are isolation, the concern for justice, the passion to record injustice, sufficient to ensure one's own freedom from ideology? When Chomsky claims to be dealing with facts, he does deal with more facts than his opponents. But where are facts if not embedded in history, and then reconstituted and recovered by human agents stirred by some perceived or desired or hoped-for historical narrative whose future aim is to restore justice to the dispossessed? In other words, the reporters of fact, like Chomsky, as well as the concealers of fact, like the "supporters of Israel," are acting within history, according to codifiable norms of representation, in a context of competing ideological and intellectual values. When he states the facts as widely, as clearly, as completely as any person alive, Chomsky is not merely performing a mechanical reporting chore, from some Archimedean point outside propaganda and cliché: he is doing something extremely sophisticated, underpinned by standards of argument, coherence, and proof that are not derived from the merely "factual." But the irony is that Chomsky does not reflect theoretically on what he does; he just does it. So, on the one hand, he leaves us to suppose that telling the truth is a simple matter while, on the other hand, he compiles masses of evidence showing that no one can really deal with the facts. How can we then suppose that one man can tell the truth? Does he believe that in writing this book he will lead others to tell the truth also? What makes it possible for us as human beings to face the facts, to manufacture new ones, or to ignore some and focus on others?

Answers to these questions must reside in a theory of perception, a theory of intellectual activity, and in an epistemological account of ideological structures as they pertain to specific problems as well as to concrete historical and geographical circumstances. None of these things is within the capacity of a solitary individual to produce, and none is possible without some sense of communal or collective commitment to assign them a more than personal validity. It is this commitment that national narratives authorize and represent, although Chomsky's understandable reluctance to hew to any national or state line prevents him from admitting it. But in a situation like that of the Palestinians and Israelis, hardly anyone can be expected to drop the quest for national identity and go straight to a history-transcending universal rationalism. Each of the two communities, misled though both may be, is interested in its origins, its history of suffering, its need to survive. To recognize these imperatives, as components of national identity, and to try to reconcile them rather than dismiss them as so much nonfactual ideology, strikes me as the task at hand.

Published in the *London Review of Books,* February 16–29, 1984.

CHAPTER 24

"Our" Lebanon

[1984]

The resignation of Lebanese Prime Minister Shafik al-Wazzan and his cabinet last week and the outbreak of total civil war are the logical consequences of a willful and disingenuous U.S. foreign policy. The administration's attempts to hold Syria culpable and Reagan's sudden decision to "redeploy" the Marines ought not to distract us from the facts. We are witnessing a repetition of the policies the Carter administration followed in Iran prior to the revolution; the situation also bears a striking resemblance to U.S. efforts in El Salvador. Now we see another cycle of violence and counterviolence from which, but for U.S. policy, the country might have been spared this time.

It requires no expertise to understand the U.S. role. After the Israeli invasion, whose appallingly destructive results Washington hailed as a "diplomatic opportunity," Reagan gave unqualified encouragement to the Christian Phalangist Party: Israel's ally in the invasion, perpetrator of the massacres in the Sabra and Shatila refugee camps and, above all, professedly fascist group dedicated to Maronite Christian rule in a country whose demographic balance has shifted dramatically in favor of the Muslims. True, there was almost unanimous support among the Lebanese for Amin Gemayel's presidency, but most of that was conditioned on his promise to reform the 1943 National Covenant, a power-sharing scheme left over from French colonialism which benefits the Maronite oligarchy.

So the United States threw its support, and the Marines, behind the President and mythologized his youth and promise. We forgot that the civil war had been going on for almost eight years, claiming 100,000 lives, and was being fought because of the anomalies in the National Covenant. We forgot that Israel had demolished and occupied southern Lebanon and that Lebanon—despite its veneer of Franco-American manners—is an Arab country adjoining and dominated by Syria. We also forgot that the Third World regimes we favor in our mania for anti-communist stability tend to get more intransigent and more insensitive to their internal circumstances the longer they hold power. In time such regimes are perceived as American lackeys and are therefore isolated. Not incidentally, we also bought the myth that the PLO had destabilized Lebanon, not noticing that instability increased dramatically after it left and that the 450,000 Palestinian refugees who remained in Lebanon became the objects of persecution by the Phalanges-dominated army and security services.

The United States backed Gemayel when he brought in a weak unrepresentative government of technocrats. The Reagan administration gave him money and weapons to strengthen the army, without regard for its composition or leadership. In its haste for Lebanon to reach a withdrawal agreement with Israel in May 1983, Washington forgot about the civil war and the need to revise the 1943 pact, and it overlooked the fact that, weak as it was, the government refused to ratify the agreement. When Begin resigned in August, a casualty of his disastrous Lebanon policy, Reagan paid little heed. When fighting broke out in September between the Lebanese army and the Druze, whose traditional territories in the Shuf had been handed over to the Phalange by the Israelis, the United States sided with a government headed by a Phalangist leader. Naturally, the White House blamed his troubles on the machinations of Syria and the Soviet Union, on Shiite fanatics and on Arab radicals.

By late September the administration had persuaded Gemayel to hold national reconciliation talks in Geneva, but they were too little, too late. America's blank check had allowed the Lebanese government to accomplish its purposes, unnoticed by the U.S. media, which were content to follow dutifully the State Department's changing assessment of the situation, or to rely on Orientalist clichés about "volatile" Arabs and "unstable" national mentalities.

Among other things, the Gemayel government deployed the Lebanese army in strength in Muslim areas while maintaining only a token presence in Phalanges strongholds. The officer corps was staffed with ex-Phalangists, and in keeping with an announcement by Pierre Gemayel, the president's father, the "victorious" Phalangist Party secured its hold on "the institutional bases of power: the presidency, the army, the judiciary." And so it happened. Although the party controls only nine seats in Parliament, the government's economic, social, military, and judicial policies and appointments have favored the minute part of Lebanon it represents, and those policies were unconditionally supported by the United States. Foreign policy was made by "Americanist" Lebanese advisers and ratified by the party's political bureau. Graft and profits from the arms trade, the customs administration, and new construction benefited Gemayel's cronies. As for the public sector, which was withering from lack of attention by the central government, such programs as did exist were skewed outrageously to favor the minority. For example, £120 million was allocated for a sewer project in the Northern Metn (the Maronite heartland, with a population of 150,000), while a similar project for the Muslim southern suburbs of Beirut (population 700,000) received £30 million. Much of this was reported in the European press but not in the United States.

The Phalangists made a strenuous attempt to break the labor unions. Water shortages and electric power failures were frequent; telephone and health services deteriorated. The economy of southern Lebanon was severed from the rest of the country by Israeli occupation. There was pressure on the universities to promote Phalangist sympathizers at the expense of non-Phalangists, Palestinians, and foreigners. The security services selectively harassed citizens along confessional and political lines. Throughout 1983, opposition to the central government solidified. In July non-Phalangist Maronites united in a common front with the Druze, the Shiites, and a large portion of the Sunni establishment. Still, the United States pressed Gemayel to enter into the unrealistic withdrawal agreement with Israel, as if the latter's demands were the only important ones in Lebanon. Afterward, of course, the security of American Marines became Washington's primary concern.

By late 1983, when it had become impossible to ignore Lebanon's disintegration, the Marine barracks in Beirut had been destroyed in a shockingly destructive manner, the White House and many foreign policy experts began to speak of partitioning the country into Syrian and Israeli zones, as if external forces rather than internal struggles were ripping the country apart. By then the United States had become a belligerent in the conflict, its fleet offshore flattening villages to protect the Marines, and maiming Lebanese in the process.

Religious passions have acquired a dialectic of their own and have intensified frighteningly. But we should understand that Christian and Jewish currents are at work in the region as well as Muslim ones, and they are creating new realities which Reagan's self-righteous pronouncements can do little to change, except for the worse. The United States has played a lamentable role in Lebanon, doling out arms, supporting the wrong parties, demonizing groups it doesn't like and ensuring the ascendancy of greater violence and political conflict. Despite his early promise, Gemayel is on his way to becoming America's Lebanese shah, another ally pressed into misguided policies.

America presides over the cataclysms of a distant society, and just as the situation becomes unbearable, Reagan prepares to leave. No country deserves such a fate. Even if the Lebanese are largely responsible for the disasters they have suffered, the United States and its allies have contributed more than their share of the damage.

Published in *The Nation,* February 1, 1984.

CHAPTER 25

Sanctum of the Strong

[1989]

Secretary of State Baker's May 22 speech to AIPAC appeared to be and was greeted by some of his audience and some Arabs as a new departure for U.S. Middle East policy. He was explicit about ending the occupation of the West Bank and Gaza; he told Israelis and Palestinians to give up ideas about Greater Israel and the whole of Palestine, respectively; he reiterated the principles of exchanging territory for peace, of confidence-building measures, of an emerging new political reality for Palestinians. Yet what he said was not really new and, in fact, given his invocation that Arabs and Jews should use the global desire for democracy as a new pattern for thinking about the Middle East, was outright rejectionist. He opposed the creation of a "new" Palestinian state and did not refer to the significant changes in the Palestinian political position since the *intifadah* (the PNC resolutions, the recognition of Israel, UN Security Resolutions 242 and 338, the two-state solution, the proposal for a comprehensive settlement through an international conference). He repeated formulae about the Israeli–United States connection and United States and Israeli love for "democracy" that took the discourse back several decades.

Most significantly, however, Baker stressed the importance of the Israeli proposal for elections without addressing the central problems with the proposal to which he referred only in passing. Thus what was novel about the speech turned out either to be a matter of "tone" (he didn't prostrate himself before the Israeli lobby, and appeared to be speaking more plainly than other U.S. politicians have in the recent past) or a matter of recently sharpened U.S. and Israeli thinking—i.e., the idea of holding elections on the West Bank and Gaza as a way of bypassing the PLO, of splitting the Palestinian community in half, of entirely defusing the movement toward self-determination. The rest was a restatement of U.S. policy since 1967, repeated countless times even as Israel has been acting unilaterally since 1967 to try to change the *status quo* unalterably. Without holding Israel to a strict timetable, without specifying more concretely what conditions had to obtain for elections to be useful and free, without allowing that Palestinians would be justifiably apprehensive about holding elections for "self-government" under a more and more brutal Israeli military occupation, Baker's speech, I think, can be interpreted as extending the already extensive level of complicity between the United States and Israel a good deal further, thereby causing more, rather than less, Palestinian suffering.

Consider that since his return from the United States in April Prime Minister Shamir has seemed to view his visit as licensing an escalation of measures against the *intifadah*. What he and Defense Minister Rabin have said repeatedly is that having proposed the relatively unspecified formula of "elections," the Palestinians have been given an alternative to the *intifadah:* Unless they unconditionally comply, Israeli attacks on Palestinian national life in all its aspects will increase. Clearly the Israeli tactic is legitimized by the U.S. acceptance of Israel's election proposal. Whatever might give substance to the proposal—e.g., the participation of East Jerusalem residents, freedom of speech and organization, release of political prisoners, participation of international observers, is relegated to the status of "details," which might be discussed later. When Palestinians are occasionally allowed to respond, as Bassam Abu Sharif did in *The Washington Post* (May 31, 1989), by saying that as a population enduring the travails of military occupation, we need concrete and detailed safeguards against arrest, deportation, curfew, and we also need protection to safeguard the *results* of our vote (in 1976 after municipal elections on the West Bank three elected mayors were maimed by "unknown" (probably) Israeli assailants, some deported, imprisoned, removed from office by the occupation authorities); there is refusal to discuss as well as more repression. The Nahhalin massacre took place right after Shamir returned. All of Gaza has been under curfew since that time. Israel has kept all Palestinian schools and universities closed, denying education to an entire generation of young people. The number of dead in April was thirty-four, almost twice as many as the previous month. Mosques have either been attacked (Hebron) or closed to worshippers during Ramadan (al-Haram al-Sharif in Jerusalem).

As for discussion, Shamir revealed what kind of bamboozling of Palestinian nationalism he had in mind in an interview he gave to the *Jerusalem Post* on May 9, ignored by the U.S. media and, of course, the U.S. government. Introduced with a vignette from Arab history about how "they" might try to cheat us the way "Mohammed (the Prophet)" did when he hoodwinked his opponents in Mecca, Shamir makes it clear that he has no interest in "details" (such as giving the vote to residents of East Jerusalem), but he's opposed to that and all other such ideas "absolutely." What if, after elections, the Palestinian representatives declare themselves a government? No, answers Shamir, "there has to be prior agreement to the process as a whole." "Q: But agreement by whom? A: By the body with whom we will negotiate. Q: So the agreement won't come before the elections? A: It must come before the elections. Q: But before the elections no one has been elected. So who will agree? A: So how will you vote? Elections will be held only after agreement with a body which is going with us to the negotiations. . . . Q: But who is this body? A: It will have to be a Palestinian body [but never the PLO]. Perhaps if Egypt and Jordan will want to join, we will welcome them." As for goals, Shamir allows that Palestinians will have "wide-ranging rights . . . to manage the [*sic*] affairs, except for matters of security, which will be under our full and absolute responsibility, and foreign affairs."

No wonder, then, that to Palestinians the coincidence between U.S. approval of the Israeli election proposal (uncluttered with any details about observers or free speech) and Shamir's phrase "interim arrangements" appears ominous. "We must," he says to the *Post* "resolutely stand by our [peace plan and] . . . prove to the people of the *intifadah* that it [the *intifadah*] is not an alternative, that we can suppress it, that we can break it. . . ." Indeed, he implies that he prefers Palestinian rejection because, he adds, the Arabs have good reason not to accept Israel's existence.

By leaving the next, and crucial, period of time under Shamir's direction and allowing it to bear the innocuous title of "interim arrangements" (Baker's phrase in his speech was "transitional arrangements"), the United States is giving Israel the opportunity it needs to try to go for an all-out final onslaught against the *intifadah*. Without

stricter injunctions, recommendations, and explicit sanctions from the
United States, Israel can try to do what it wants, undeterred by the
latest Amnesty condemnation about political prisoners, or even the
State Department's recent human rights report. Although U.S. public
opinion polls are running at rates of 60 and 70 percent for a Palestinian
state, and even though Western Europe has accepted the new pro-
peace Palestinian position by welcoming Arafat in places like Paris and
Vienna, the United States has shilly-shallied without scruple or misgiv-
ing. It has opposed the recent UN Security Council resolution condemning Israeli practices; it has had no congressional hearings on the
intifadah; aid levels are unchecked; according to Thomas Friedman of
the *Times* it has opted to use the PLO–U.S. dialogue as a "carrot" for
inducing the PLO to go along with its (and Israel's) ideas. Above all,
the United States has not required of Israel any clarification on 242, or
on the Palestinian proposals crystallized at the Algiers PNC, openly
welcomed by many Israeli and American Jews.

Thus, Baker's speech in context gives Israel yet another chance to
do what it and the United States clearly want: to postpone Palestinian
claims for as long as possible, with the idea that under more pressure
they might dissolve entirely, or become once again subservient to
Jordan. What Baker proposed as a way of acknowledging these claims
without taking them too seriously was to "create an environment"
conducive to reducing tension. It is a notion that turns up first in
Building for Peace, a report issued in 1988, published by the Washington
Institute for Near East Policy, a pro-Israeli think tank. Among the
authors of the report were Walter Mondale and Lawrence Eagleburger, plus Charles Krauthammer, Steven Spiegel, Daniel Pipes—
and Dennis Ross, now Baker's Middle East policy man.

The report makes Baker's ideas in his speech much clearer. It is an
unremittingly pro-Israeli recommendation, in which *everything* in U.S.
Middle East policy is made secondary to a strong relationship with
Israel. Thus, one item on the list is "a Palestinian willingness to reduce
the level of violence and disorder coupled with an Israeli readiness to
ease the restrictions imposed in response to the *intifadah*": not the
occupation itself, but "just" the unpleasantness of having to respond
to Palestinian "violence and disorder." Palestinians, according to the
report, must accommodate to "Israel and its security concerns," and
can only hope for assuming "authority over certain aspects of self-
government." Ultimately, in pursuit of that modest goal Israel "might
be convinced to permit free elections to produce a representative

Palestinian leadership,'' of the sort Shamir describes in his *Jerusalem Post* interview.

In the short run, therefore, time is against the Palestinians. Because of their greater power, Israel and the United States have established a new agenda, i.e., elections. But the realities are such that even with so obviously unattractive a scheme as this the PLO has not performed as sensibly and as wisely as it can, leaving things to drift without planning, or long-term strategy, or day-to-day assessment. We are now at a critical moment which requires a major offensive whose aim is to put forward a modified election plan. Unless the tremendous suffering and heroism of the *intifadah* are connected in detail with the emerging discussion of elections, unless, that is, Palestinians work seriously to alter the framework and the substance of the proposal— interpreting, criticizing, changing, bargaining, etc.—in the context of our realities on the ground, exchanging ideas and proposals imaginatively, with a view to gaining our self-determination and independence, free of occupation and domination, we will have sacrificed a great deal in vain. Politics is not a matter of flashy declarations, flying visits, or heartfelt dialogues, nor is it a statement here and there with no focused attention on the complexities of the U.S. and Israeli political arenas. It requires detailed knowledge to be synchronized with vision, responsibility with serious, tireless commitment. The road from Algiers to a Palestinian state has only just begun to shimmer before us, but if we don't get our act together now, we'll be back out in the cold once again.

Published in *The Nation,* July 10, 1989.

CHAPTER 26

Behind Saddam Hussein's Moves

[AUGUST 1990]

S addam Hussein is an appalling dictator whose rule in Iraq has turned the place into a graveyard for democracy. Everyone knows that, especially Arabs. But in the American campaign to demonize, isolate, and destroy him for his shocking invasion of Kuwait, he has been inaccurately separated from the environment and politics that have produced him. These latter, it must be said, have been shaped to a considerable degree by U.S. Middle East policies, which have now come to a temporary end after nearly five decades of relative success from the American standpoint. Yet despite the rousing self-righteousness of U.S. military and diplomatic moves against Iraq, it is important to realize that the Middle East is not just an oil-producing desert, but an overwhelm- ingly Arab and Muslim region, filled with its own histories, societies, and political dynamics. This, I think, urgently requires consideration now, not only because Arabs will bear the brunt of suffering and destruction, but because the current crisis is otherwise incomprehensible. The events now unfolding are not simply a matter of good versus evil.

The disappearance of a society due to invasion and annexation is grave and tragic. The scale of human sorrow that will attend Kuwait's demise is horrific: Lives will be permanently disrupted or lost, families separated, work and livelihoods ended. It is disturbing that in all the pious Western denunciations of Iraq's aggression little concern has been shown for the unfortunate residents of Kuwait itself. Yet all had not been well in the Gulf before. The regimes were viewed by most Arabs as flawed, complicit in oil production geared not to Arab requirements but to American needs, powerless to object when American support for Israel was infinitely permissive and hypocritical. In return for the unimpeded flow of oil, Gulf leaders got promises (and in the Saudi instance the presence) of American military support. The Gulf rulers—the Kuwaitis were typical—spent some money on regional development and gave considerable help to the Palestinian movement, but the bulk of their vast wealth has been deposited in the West. A mounting Arab resentment perceived that the main natural resource of the Arab world was held in thrall to Western consumers, for whom cheap oil necessary to maintain their "life-style" overrode any awareness, consideration, or regard for the culture and aspirations of the region. In addition, Gulf leaders were forced to endure public rituals of abasement and humiliation by Israel's supporters when petitioning Washington for the privilege of buying U.S. weapons at extortionate prices; that these weapons have been insufficient to protect the Arab world from Israeli incursions added salt to the wound.

Saddam is a deeply unattractive, indeed revoltingly tough and callous leader, who has suppressed personal freedoms, subjected his considerably gifted and hardworking people to unimaginable rigors, harassed and invaded his neighbors at already considerable cost. His invasion of Kuwait is aggression pure and simple. But he is neither mad nor, I would suggest, an unlikely figure to emerge out of the desolation that has characterized recent Arab history. He is admired today by many Arabs who also deplore his methods, but who say that the world we live in is essentially dominated by powers that invade, grab land, attempt to change governments with scant regard for the principles and moral imperatives they proclaim exclusively against Arabs, nonwhites, wogs, and the like. Turkey seized part of Cyprus a few years ago; the Russians invaded Afghanistan; the United States has bombed and invaded Grenada, Libya, and, only a matter of months ago, Panama, because it suited its interests, as defined by the President; above all, every Arab is agonizingly aware that because of an American green light, the Israeli army in 1982 invaded Lebanon, killed 20,000 people, attempted to destroy the PLO, set up a basically puppet government, not to mention earlier violations of Syrian, Jordanian, and Saudi airspace, and bombings of Iraq and Tunis.

The United States did not apply sanctions against Israel, and it continues to subsidize the Israeli occupation of the West Bank, Gaza, the Golan Heights, and a part of South Lebanon. At the UN the United States has consistently blocked any censure of Israel; together the two countries have defied the entire world, with the United States permitting only resolutions to pass that "regretted" the "violence on both sides," a phrase both cynical and insulting. In the light of the sanctions against Iraq, into which the UN has been peremptorily bullied by the United States, the habitual American leniency toward Israel confirms the long-held Arab and Third World claim that an indecent double standard is at work.

Saddam thus sees himself as acting not only to secure Iraqi interests—Kuwait has long been regarded as part of Iraqi territory and for the past several months has increased oil production at considerable cost to Iraq—but also Arab interests. To this latter mission he brings significant credibility. He fought, and was supported, in his Arab war against "Persia." He has expressed contempt for the Arab "moderates" (the word has a pejorative resonance in the Arab world today) who became American clients and who, like Mubarak of Egypt and al-Saud of Arabia, have slid from the center of Arab politics to the margins. He opposed both Camp David (which split the Arab world) and a debased Arab nationalism, which had turned its hopes for unity and splendor into factionalism, civil wars, the sway of weak and unpopular rulers, the ideological dominance of petty local nationalisms. All this was believed to be abetted by the United States, the great enemy of Arab nationalism, and Israel's unfailing prop.

We should not therefore underestimate Saddam's appeal to Arabs who feel that nothing less than the future of Arab civilization is at stake. Historically opposed by the West, which has generally regarded Arabs with contempt and through a racist optic that considers them mainly as greasy oil suppliers, terrorists, or camel jockeys, a resurgent Arab nationalism has taken heart from the resistance embodied in the Palestinian *intifadah,* the various Islamic groupings, and the Iraqi president.

What America and its allies have continually offered (besides unrestricted support for Israel) is an endless postponement of Palestinian self-determination—Palestine remains the Arab world's most potent dispute with the West—and a denigration of Arab sovereignty over Arab destiny. In aiding Abul Abbas against Yasir Arafat's flagging PLO policy of moderation and compromise, Saddam was beginning to collect as many of his major nationalist cards for the big confrontation which, one feels certain, he knew he would have to face. As he saw it, the failure of a halfhearted and insultingly one-sided U.S. policy unsuccessfully to persuade Israel even to talk to Palestinians, as droves of Soviet Jews headed for Israel/Palestine, as Arab oil seemed perpetually hostage to local oligarchies in cahoots with Western oil companies and governments, and as his own society suffered the traumatic after-effects of a war he believed he had fought on behalf of all the Arabs—all this seemed to propel him, so to speak, to the head of a fragmented, demoralized, and cowering Arab world, apparently in need of his brashness, courage, and overweening will.

The consequences will be tragic and dreadful to contemplate. What we shall probably watch is not a skirmish or two but a full-scale engagement between a long-suppressed, long-deferred, and often penalized nationalist program in whose moral conviction and promises Saddam has wrapped himself, and, on the other side, an American-led campaign designed principally to punish Saddam and, as present signs bear out, to mutilate the wings of Arab nationalism yet again.

Nor is this all. The Palestinian drive toward self-determination is being dealt a grievous, perhaps even catastrophic blow: It now seems to be both the Israeli and the Arab impulse to drive things back to the way they were in 1948, with the Arab states and Israel dealing with each other over Palestinian heads. Governments in Egypt, Saudi Arabia, and perhaps Jordan (to say nothing of those in the smaller Gulf states) are likely to recover badly, if at all, from the U.S. rush to military reaction. Immense economic and ecological changes unforeseen in their scope will, I think, radically alter the face of the whole Middle East. And I greatly fear that what will once again get pushed under—Arab nationalist hopes and cultural assertions—will be rechanneled into xenophobia, religious revivalism, the politics of hostility and revenge.

We are now watching the terminal throes of the period that began after World War II with the establishment of Israel and the coming to power of various Arab nationalist and independent governments. No Arab can excuse today's ghastly spectacle of corrupt and unjust regimes, massive social and economic inequities, horrendously backward educational and cultural establishments, overblown security apparatuses, and abrogated democratic freedoms. These are all there for everyone to see and feel ashamed about. But, I submit, has the Western and especially the American failure not to draw out the Arabs in a real dialogue, to take their hopes and fears seriously, to address their grievances responsibly—has this not also contributed to much of what is unattractive in the Arab world, deflected and distorted its development into the politics of revenge, resentment, and angry hostility? Rather than leaving the U.S. response to Iraq in its present bare-knuckled form, must we not also expect George Bush to address the Arab world as he would any other great people or culture, offering understanding and community instead of the stony preachiness, the unbending and inhumane formulas the United States has presented to Arabs for a generation? The United States would reap even greater disasters were it now simply to return to the old *modus vivendi* and fail concretely to link the unacceptability of Iraq's occupation with Israel's.

Published in *The Christian Science Monitor*, August 13, 1990.

CHAPTER 27

A Tragic Convergence

[JANUARY 11, 1991]

For many Americans and Arabs—as well as Americans of Arab origin—the slide into an appalling and horrendously costly war provokes feelings of a barely statable apprehension. The main reason for silence up to this point is that either to be for or against Iraq, or for or against the United States and its allies, exhausts the positions offered by current discussion, whereas the tragic quality of what is unfolding in the Gulf has gotten little attention. Many Arabs, for example, are against the Iraqi aggression, are also for a total withdrawal of Iraqi troops, and yet are not at all in favor of a U.S. attack against Iraq. I include myself in this group, as I also include myself among those Americans who feel that our military presence in the Gulf is far larger, more expensive, and potentially disastrous than is merited by the case the United States has been making for its intervention during the past few months. On the other hand, a principled stand against aggression *can* be made in and with the United Nations, and the sooner we start working to deescalate the confrontation the more persuasive such a case will be. The difficulty, however, is that the fundamental reason for so massive a buildup of U.S. and Iraqi forces in the Gulf has not been sufficiently understood.

Each of the provocations listed by the Bush administration and its supporters as justifying its actions—deterring Iraq, reversing the occupation, not giving in to aggression, assuring oil supplies, etc.—could have been dealt with by something less than a war of a million combatants. Yet the underlying reason for the continuing American buildup and the increasing likelihood of war is that the United States seems unable to tolerate the idea that its power should not be projected anywhere it pleases, for its own ends, wrapped in its own "higher" morality and principles. This is an imperialist ideology. For in the new world now dominated by only one superpower, policymakers feel an urgent need to make sure that whenever American interests are challenged, the challenger should be confronted and, if necessary, routed.

Who has given us the right to project our power all over the world, at the same time proclaiming our higher purpose and superior wisdom? The United States is in fact repeating the practices employed by the British and the French in the nineteenth century. The big differences are, first, that today we are capable of much greater destruction than they were, and, second, that we are unable to state openly and candidly our engagement in the business of empire, and damn the results.

The counter to this anachronistic and dishonest line is not simply a matter of bringing the troops home, or of waiting for sanctions to take hold, or of deciding whether air or land forces are best. Rather, it consists in starting immediately to dismantle the imperialist mission that the United States has set itself from its beginning as a nation two centuries ago. The first step is to remove the taboo that forbids Americans to regard their country's actions as imperialist. Then what we must learn to do is to live like other people in a world grown much smaller and much more interdependent than ever before. Since ours is a precariously balanced world, with ecological, economic, and social pressures that are barely containable, it is sheer folly to suggest that we are naturally entitled to cheap oil or to a better way of life than anyone else. Or that we can survey the world and decide whom "we" regard as punishable or not. That we also have the military power to enforce these often petulant, not to say narcissistic, desires makes things a great deal worse. The Gulf is not merely an empty desert with a large pool of "our" oil underneath and a whole bunch of shaikhs, terrorists, or Hitlers on top, but a place with living peoples, traditions, and societies whose aspirations and values have to be viewed as having merit independent of our needs and attitudes.

The history of U.S. interventions over the years has not been salutary, to say the least. Panama, for example, has not recovered, nor has Indochina. The idea that faraway places are either required to accept the dictates of American will or risk destruction is virtually unexamined, and, alas, much too influential an idea in U.S. history.

We are insulated by our wealth and our immense power; those who have felt the devastations imposed by our wrath have been forgotten, consigned to oblivion or perdition.

It is terrifying to watch Iraq now being readied for mass destruction. First its leader (who like so many of our friends is a tyrant) is made the personification of evil, and our new allies the embodiment of virtue; then Iraq's people and society are reduced to "military assets" and a demonized "Islamic *jihad*"; then finally, after some arbitrary deadline has expired, both leader and people are declared a virtual nonentity, cities are to be smashed from great distances and heights, agriculture and economy are to be torched, infrastructure reduced to rubble, military capability nullified. In all this frightening rhetoric, the sustained ignorance of Arab and Islamic culture is turned into a useful mode of warfare: The enemy has been so dehumanized for so long that we never hesitate to deliver the final blow.

For his part, however, and despite his tedious protests, Saddam Hussein is scarcely a representative of the Arabs. True, a lot of people have clambered aboard his vessel, but I know no one who is fooled by what his captaincy is all about. But the time for such posturing as his, and for the self-pity many of us employed (perhaps unwittingly) in justifiably rejecting the American military expedition, has passed. The traditional discourse of Arab nationalism, to say nothing of the quite decrepit state system, is inexact, unresponsive, anomalous, even comic. It is as if Saddam had collected all the tattered remnants—anger at colonialism, despair at being unable to deal with the challenge of Israel, noble rhetoric about Arab honor—and forced them into a row of banners that people will salute because there is little else to like or respect.

A central casualty has been language. Today's Arab media, for instance, are a disgrace. It is difficult now to speak the plain truth in the Arab world. The Egyptian and Saudi press almost without exception seem committed to the destruction of Iraq; their pages permit few demurrals and little trace of reservation, doubt, hesitation. Conversely, various pro-Iraqi newspapers and journals are equally polarized against their enemies. Nowhere is it really possible to articulate a third position. Intellectuals, writers, artists have an unenviable predicament before them. They can either opt for silence, which is prudent, of course, or they can be mobilized for battle, which can be profitable. One misses the presence of reliable statistics, concrete and undoctored case histories, the raw and documented actualities of life in the Arab world today with its terrible inequities, its self-inflicted wounds, its mediocrity in science and many cultural fields. Allegory, complicated symbolism, and arcane innuendo have to work overtime where plain talking and common sense would have been both simple and desirable.

So overbearing have Arab rulers and states become that the most grotesque situations are tolerated with scarcely a smile. Most national newspapers today solemnly report the comings and goings of the ruler as if they were central events for all mankind. No Arab president or king is accountable to his people in any serious way; this is as true of Saddam as it is of the others. The bureaucracies and the secret police rule more or less without challenge, although they are universally hated and feared. Only some of these debilities can be blamed mainly on imperialism or Zionism, for, after all, it was the Arab states that deserted the Palestinian *intifadah,* not vice versa. No Arab country today can adequately defend itself or its borders, yet national security arguments are used to justify gigantically large outlays of money for imported weapons, standing armies, praetorian guards. Above all, the movement toward war today has overridden any rational consideration of what as Arabs we want our future to be. Where is the real discussion of "Arab" wealth, poverty, society? All of us feel connected to an Arab nation, yet we allow massive amounts of polemic to cover hypostasized Arabs, while not enough detailed attention and care are given to individual, actual Arab lives and bodies.

The tragedy of this moment, therefore, is the convergence between an imperialist American will to war against an upstart Third World state, and an almost equally remorseless Arab propensity to violence and exterminism that began with Iraq's aggression against Kuwait and continues in the Iraqi–Kuwaiti–Saudi–Egyptian drive to war. A further irony is that this convergence is beginning to look like a conflict between Islam and the West, those always convenient rubrics. A sobering look at the *concretely* terrible consequences of the war that seems ever more likely might chart a different course—less imperious and dreary—for Americans and Arabs alike. There can be no real winner in this war, despite braggadocio and threats. It must not begin at all.

Published in *The New York Times,* January 11, 1991.

CHAPTER 28

Ignorant Armies Clash by Night

[FEBRUARY 11, 1991]

From the moment that George Bush invented Desert Shield, Desert Storm was all too logical. Saddam Hussein, a dictator of the kind the United States has typically found and supported, was almost invited into Kuwait, then almost immediately demonized and transformed into a worldwide metaphysical threat. Iraq's military capabilities were fantastically exaggerated, the country verbally obliterated except for its now isolated leader, UN sanctions and Arab (as well as other) diplomatic efforts at a solution were given a ludicrously short run, and then America began the war.

Since 1973 the United States has wanted a physical presence in the Gulf: to control oil supply, to project power, and above all, recently, to refurbish, refinance, reinvigorate its military, still supposedly suffering the Vietnam syndrome. With his crude brutality no match for U.S. and Israeli propaganda, Saddam became the perfect target, and the best excuse to move in. The United States will not soon leave the Middle East.

The electronic war to destroy Iraq as a lesson in retributive power is now in full swing, the press managing patriotism, entertainment, and disinformation without respite. As a topic, civilian "collateral damage" has been avoided and unasked about; no one discusses how Baghdad, the old Abbasid capital, might survive the appalling rigors of technological warfare, or how the bombing of its water, fuel, or electrical supplies, which sustain four million people, is necessary to this "surgical" war (a larger replay of Israel's destruction of Beirut).

Few commentators have questioned the disproportion of 50,000 plus air sorties against a country roughly the size of California, or explained why many days into the war Iraq's air force, artillery, Scuds, and major armored force still stand, or even how radio and television still work. That no one asks about the effect and placement of B-52 carpet bombing—a mass murder technique—is doubtless a psy-war achievement, but it is not a credit to the independent press.

It is curious, but profoundly symptomatic of the present conflict, that the one word that should be tediously pronounced and re-pronounced and yet left unanalyzed was *linkage,* an ugly solecism that could only have been invented in late-twentieth-century America. Linkage meant not that there was, but that there was no connection. Things which belonged together by common association, sense, geography, history, were sundered, left apart for convenience's sake, and for the benefit of imperious U.S. policymakers, military strategists, and area experts. Everyone his own carver, said Jonathan Swift. That the Middle East was linked by all sorts of ties, *that* was irrelevant. That Arabs might see a connection between Saddam in Kuwait and Israel in Lebanon, that too was futile. That U.S. policy itself *was* the linkage, the same policy that tolerated Israeli and Turkish aggression but started a war against Iraqi invasion—this was a forbidden topic to broach.

Never in my experience have nouns designating the Arab world or its components been so bandied about: Saddam Hussein, Kuwait, Islam, fundamentalism. Never have they had so strangely abstract and diminished a meaning, and rarely does any regard or care seem to accompany them, even though the United States is not at war with *all* the Arabs but might very well be, except for its pathetic clients such as Mubarak of Egypt and the various Gulf rulers.

In all the mainstream debate here since August 2, much the smallest component in the discussion has been Arab. During the Congressional hearings that went on for two weeks in December, no significant Arab–American voice was heard. In Congress and in the press, "link-ages" of all kinds went unexamined. Little was done to report oil company profits, or the fact that the surge in gasoline prices had nothing to do with supply, which remained plentiful. The Iraqi case against Kuwait, or even the nature of Kuwait itself, liberal in some ways, illiberal in others, received next to no hearing; the point would not have been to exculpate Saddam but to understand the complicity and hypocrisy of the Gulf states, the United States, and Europe, during the Iran–Iraq war. Efforts were made to grapple with Arab popular rallying to Saddam, despite the horrid qualities of his rule, but these efforts were not integrated into or allowed equal time with the distortions in American Middle East policy. The central media failing was an unquestioning acceptance of American power: its right to ignore dozens of UN resolutions on Palestine (or even not to pay its UN dues), to attack Panama, Grenada, Libya, and also to proclaim the absolute morality of its Gulf position.

From prewar television reports of the crisis I cannot recall a single guest or program that raised the issue of what right "we" had to get Iraq out of Kuwait, nor any exploration of the enormous human, social, and economic costs *to the Arabs* of an American strike. Yet on January 7, I heard a well-known "Middle East expert" say on TV that "war is the easy part; what to do afterward?" as if "we" might, in an afterthought, get around to picking up the pieces and rearranging the area. At the furthest extreme have been the unmistakably racist prescriptions of William Safire and A. M. Rosenthal of *The New York Times,* as well as Fouad Ajami of CBS, who have routinely urged the most unrestrained military attacks against Iraq. The underlying fantasy strongly resembles the Israeli paradigm for dealing with the Arabs: bomb them, humiliate them, lie about them.

From the beginning, when Arabs have appeared on television, they have been the merest tokens: an Arab journalist or two eager to show Arab failings and weaknesses (which were real and had to be pointed out); the Saudi or Kuwaiti ambassador, more enthusiastic about war than most Americans; the Iraqi ambassador, who defended the Husseinian view of the world with cautious amiability; the tiny group of Arab–Americans like myself whose position was neither with Iraq nor with the United States–Saudi coalition. Once, in the fifteen seconds I was given, when I began to elucidate an argument about the relationship between Iraqi aggression and American imperialism, I was cut off abruptly: "Yes, yes, we know all that."

Seen from the Arab point of view, the picture of America is just as constricted. There is still hardly any literature in Arabic that portrays Americans; the most interesting exception is Abdel Rahman Munif's massive trilogy *Cities of Salt,* but his books are banned in several countries, and his native Saudi Arabia has stripped him of his citizenship. To my knowledge there is still no institute or major academic department in the Arab world whose main purpose is the study of America, although the United States is by far the largest outside force in the Arab world. It is still difficult to explain even to well-educated and experienced fellow Arabs that U.S. foreign policy is not in fact run by the CIA, or a conspiracy, or a shadowy network of key "contacts." Many Arabs I know believe the United States plans virtually every event of significance in the Middle East, including, in one mind-boggling suggestion made to me last year, the *intifadah!*

This mix of long familiarity, hostility, and ignorance pertains to both sides of a complex, variously uneven, and quite old cultural encounter now engaging in very unmetaphorical warfare. From early on there has been an overriding sense of inevitability, as if George Bush's apparent need to get down there and, in his own sporty argot, "kick ass," *had* to run up against Saddam Hussein's monstrous aggressiveness, now vindicating the Arab need to confront, talk back to, stand unblinkingly before the United States. The public rhetoric, in other words, is simply undeterred, uncomplicated by any considerations of detail, realism, or cause and effect.

Perhaps the central unanalyzed link between the United States and the Arabs in this conflict is nationalism. The world can no longer afford so heady a mixture of patriotism, relative solipsism, social authority, unchecked aggressiveness, and defensiveness toward others. Today the United States, triumphalist internationally, seems in a febrile way anxious to prove that it is Number One, perhaps to offset the recession; the endemic problems posed by the cities, poverty, health, education, production; and the Euro–Japanese challenge. On the other side, the Middle East is saturated with a sense that Arab nationalism is all-important, but also that it is an aggrieved and unfulfilled nationalism, beset with conspiracies, enemies both internal and external, obstacles to overcome for which no price was too high. This was especially true of the cultural framework in which I grew up. It is still true today with the important difference that this nationalism has resolved itself into smaller and smaller units. In the colonial period as I was growing up, you could travel overland from Lebanon and Syria through Palestine to Egypt and points west. That is now impossible. Each country places formidable obstacles at its borders. For Palestinians, crossing is a horrible experience, since countries that make the loudest noises in support of Palestine treat Palestinians the worst.

Here, too, linkage comes last in the Arab setting. I do not want to suggest that the past was better; it wasn't. But it was more healthily interlinked, so to speak. People actually lived with each other, rather than denying each other from across fortified frontiers. In many schools you would encounter Arabs from everywhere, Muslims and Christians, plus Armenians, Jews, Greeks, Italians, Indians, and Iranians, all mixed up, all under one or another colonial regime, interacting as if it were natural to do so. Today the state nationalisms have a tendency to fragment and fracture. Lebanon and Israel are perfect examples of what has happened. Apartheid of one form or another is present nearly everywhere as a group feeling if not as a practice, and it is subsidized by the state with its bureaucracies and secret police organizations. Rulers are clans, families, and closed circles of aging oligarchs, almost mythologically immune to change.

Moreover, the attempt to homogenize and isolate populations has required colossal sacrifices. In most parts of the Arab world civil society has been swallowed up by political society. One of the great achievements of the early postwar Arab nationalist governments was mass literacy: In countries such as Egypt the results were dramatic. Yet the combination of accelerated literacy and tub-thumping ideology, which was undoubtedly necessary at some point, has proved far too long-standing. My impression is that there is more effort spent in bolstering the idea that to be Syrian, Iraqi, Egyptian, Saudi, etc., is a quite sufficiently important end, rather than in thinking critically, perhaps even audaciously about the national program itself. Identity, always identity, over and above knowing about others.

Because of this lopsided state of affairs, militarism assumed too privileged a place in the Arab world's moral economy, just as today proclamations about "Islam" have taken over from military slogans. Much of both these regressive tendencies goes back to the sense of being unjustly treated, for which Palestine was not only a metaphor but a reality. But was the only answer military force—huge armies, brassy slogans, bloody promises, and, alas, a long series of concrete instances, starting with wars and working down to such things as physical punishment and menacing gestures? Is the only answer today a slogan such as "Islam is the only solution"? I speak superficially and even irresponsibly here, since I cannot have all the facts. But I do not know a single Arab who would disagree with these impressions in private, or who would not readily agree that the monopoly on coercion given the state has almost completely eliminated democracy in the Arab world, introduced immense hostility between rulers and ruled, fanned the flames of religious intolerance, placed a much higher value on conformity, opportunism, flattery, and getting along than on risking new ideas, criticism, or dissent.

Taken far enough, this produces an exterminism common to the

Arabs and the United States, the notion that if something displeases you it is possible simply to blot it out. I do not doubt that this notion is behind Iraq's aggression against Kuwait. What sort of muddled and anachronistic idea of Bismarckian "integration" is this that wipes out an entire country and smashes its society with "Arab unity" as its goal? The most disheartening thing is that so many people, many of them victims of exactly the same brutal logic, appear to have identified with Iraq and not with Kuwait. Even if one grants that Kuwaitis were unpopular (does one have to be popular not to be exterminated?) and even if Iraq claims to champion Palestine in standing up to Israel and the United States, surely the very idea that nations should be obliterated along the way is a murderous proposition, and not fit for a great civilization like ours.

Then there is oil. While it brought development and prosperity to some, wherever it was associated with an atmosphere of violence, ideological refinement, and political defensiveness, it created more rifts than it healed. It may be easy for someone like myself to say these things from a distance, but for anyone who cares about the Arab world, who thinks of it as possessing a plausible sort of internal cohesion, the general air of mediocrity and corruption that hangs over a part of the globe that is limitlessly wealthy, superbly endowed culturally and historically, and loaded with gifted individuals is a great puzzle, and of course a disappointment. We all *do* ask ourselves why we haven't done more of what other peoples have done—liberate ourselves, modernize, make a distinctive, positive mark on the world. Where is excellence? How is it rewarded? There are really first-rate novelists, poets, essayists, historians, yet all of them are not only unacknowledged legislators, they have been hounded into alienated opposition. For an author today to write is perforce to be careful, not to anger Syria, or the Islamic authorities, or a Gulf potentate or two.

What seems intellectually required now is the development of a combination discourse, one side of which is concretely critical and addresses the real power situation inside the Arab world, and another side that is mainly about affection, sympathy, association (rather than antagonism, resentment, harsh religious fundamentalism, vindictiveness). Many of the Arab thinkers of what Albert Hourani calls the liberal age, late-eighteenth to the early-twentieth centuries, were reformers, eager to catch up with developments in the West. We've had too much since then of thinkers who want to start from scratch and zealously, not to say furiously, take things back to some pure, sacred origin. This has given all sorts of pathologies time and space enough to take hold in the middle distance, now, with their structures left unscrutinized, while intellectuals can go off looking for what *would* have been better, what *would* have been just, and so on. We need to know what it is about the present that we should hold on to, and how. What is just, why is it just, why should we hold on to it? We need odes not to blood or mythology or uprooted, mourned, or dead plants but to living creatures and actual situations. As the novelist Elias Khoury says, we need a language that allows one to write neither of a discredited past nor of an immensely distant future.

The supreme irony is that we Arabs are *of* this world, hooked into dependency and consumerism, cultural vassalage and technological secondariness, without much active volition on our part. The point has come when we cannot simply accuse the West of Orientalism and racism—I realize that I may be vulnerable on this point—and go on doing little about providing an alternative. If our work isn't enough in the Western media, for example, or isn't known well by Western writers and scholars, a good part of the blame lies with us. Mohammed Hassanein Heikal, the distinguished Egyptian journalist, has proposed a broadly focused pan-Arab cooperation authority for such things as development, coordinated industry, agriculture, and the like. But we should also devote energy to an intellectual coordination effort that opens lines of communication among Arabs internally and externally with the rest of the world. The idea of equal dialogue and rightful responsibility needs to be pressed. The provincial and self-pitying posture that argues that a largely fictional and monolithic West disdains us ought to be replaced with the discovery that there are many Wests, some antagonistic, some not, with which to do business, and the choice of whom to talk to and how depends greatly on us. The converse is equally true, that there are many Arabs for Westerners and others to talk to. Only in this way, I think, will imperial America not be our only interlocutor.

If as Arabs we say correctly that we are different from the West, as well as different from its image of the Arabs, we have to be persuasive on this point. This takes a lot of work, and cannot be accomplished by a resort to clichés, stereotypes, or myths. George Bush's idea that the new world order has to flow from an American baton is as unacceptable as the idea that Arabs can muster a big army led by a big tough hero and at last win a few wars. That is dangerous nonsense. Americans, Arabs, Europeans, Africans—everyone—need to reorient education so that central to common awareness is not a paranoid sense of who is top or best, but a map of this now tiny planet, its resources and environment nearly worn out, its inhabitants' demands for better lives nearly out of control. The competitive, coercive guidelines that have prevailed are simply no good anymore. To argue and persuade rather than to boast, preach, and destroy—*that* is the change to be made.

The war will be catastrophic and will only distort the Arab world further. And there will be enough residual problems to start up another confrontation in the Middle East in a matter of seconds. We should be looking for political mechanisms with Europeans and the nonaligned that would get a cease-fire and send everybody—including Palestinians—home. It is good to be reminded of that phrase by Aimé Césaire which C.L.R. James, that great champion of liberation, liked to quote: "No race possesses the monopoly of beauty, of intelligence, of force, and there is a place for all at the rendez-vous of victory." This may be utopian idealism, but as a way to think about an alternative to conflicts that go from cultural hostility to full-scale war it is both more inventive and practical than shooting off missiles.

Published in *The Nation*, February 11, 1991.

CHAPTER 29

The Arab–American War: The Politics of Information

[MARCH 1991]

The United States is at an extraordinarily bloody moment in its history as the last superpower. Perhaps because I come from the Arab world, I have thought often during the past few months and more anxiously during the past few days that such a war as we Americans are now engaged in, with such aims, rhetoric, and all-encompassing violence and destruction, could now have been waged only against an Arab–Islamic–Third World country. It does no one in it any credit, and it will not produce any of the great results, however ostensibly victorious either side may prove to be, and whatever the results may prove to be for the other. It will not solve the problems of the Middle East or those of America, now in a deep recession, plagued by poverty, joblessness, and an urban, education, and health crisis of gigantic proportions.

A war like this could only have occurred in a part of the world beset with huge inequities of endowment and rule, bearing within itself the history of postponed and endlessly betrayed promises for justice and fairness at the hands of the West, and now exploding in an agony of hatred, anti-Americanism, and tremendous, largely unforeseen upheaval. I do not excuse and have not excused the aggression of Iraq against Kuwait. I have condemned it from the beginning, just as I have long condemned the abuses of Saddam Hussein's government, and those of the other governments of the region, whether Arab or Israeli.

Democracy in any real sense of the word is nowhere to be found in the Middle East; there are either privileged oligarchies or privileged ethnic groups. The large mass of people is crushed beneath dictatorship or unyielding, unresponsive, unpopular government. But I dispute the notion that the United States is a virtuous innocent in this awful conflict, as I dispute that this is not a war between George Bush and Saddam Hussein—it most certainly is—and that the United States is acting solely and principally in the interests of the United Nations. The United Nations resolutions have already been exceeded, and the bombing campaign against Iraq's population is now murderous. Yet at bottom this is a personalized struggle between, on the one hand, a Third World dictator of the kind that the United States has long dealt with, whose rule it has encouraged, whose favors it has long enjoyed, and, on the other, the president of a country which has taken on the mantle of empire inherited from Britain and France and is determined to remain in the Middle East for reasons of oil and of geostrategic and political advantage.

There continues to be a great deal of talk about *linkage,* a word I continue to find ugly and a concept I find slippery. "Analogy," "relationship," "association" are three possible alternatives, which suggest to me that the United States has no record of consistent opposition to aggression—the instances of Namibia, South Africa, Cyprus, Panama, Nicaragua, and the Israeli-occupied territories come quickly to mind— and that Iraq and Kuwait do not exist only in some unhistorical region of the mind or a map in Dick Cheney's office. For two generations the United States has sided in the Middle East mostly with tyranny and injustice. I defy anyone to tell me of one struggle for democracy, or women's rights, or secularism, and the rights of minorities that the United States has supported. Instead we have propped up compliant and unpopular clients, and turned our backs on the efforts of small peoples to liberate themselves from military occupation, while subsidizing their enemies. We have prompted unlimited militarism and engaged in vast arms sales everywhere in the region, mostly to governments which have now been driven to even more desperate actions as a result of the United States' obsession with and exaggeration of the power of Saddam Hussein. To conceive of a postwar Arab world dominated by the rulers of Egypt, Saudi Arabia, and Syria, all of them working in a new pax Americana, is neither intellectually nor morally credible.

Two things have occurred, quickly and completely, over the past few months. One is that, in the information blitz which has been going on since the summer of 1990, the media and its personnel have, with few exceptions, internalized norms, which prevent dispassionate analysis and induce self-censorship, as well as a very shallow sort of news presentation. The other is that we have not yet developed a discourse that does anything more than identify with power, despite the dangers of that power in a world which has shrunk so small and has become so impressively interconnected. The United States cannot belligerently declare its right, as 6 percent of the world's population, to consume 30 percent of the world's energy, nor for that matter can it unilaterally declare a new world order because it exercises the military power to destroy a few complaining countries along the way. There was no evidence that Iraqi expansion would continue after Kuwait. Indeed, there is now ample evidence that an arrangement between Iraq, Saudi Arabia, Jordan, and Egypt had been worked out in early August: This would have involved Iraqi withdrawal and an adjudication of the dispute with Kuwait. Like every other regional compromise, this was rejected out of hand by the United States. There was considerable evidence that, if further provoked by an exterminist gesture on the part of the United States, Iraq might settle for universal destruction rather than back down. Even the anti-Saddam Iraqi opposition outside Iraq has now closed ranks and sided against the United States.

There are many Arabs who agree, as do I, that Iraq's invasion and occupation must be reversed, but few would agree with the strategy of immediately sending troops because George Bush and Margaret Thatcher assumed that wogs could be told to behave by the white man; there is a pattern of such contemptuous attitudes toward the Arab world, from the days of the British expeditionary force sent to Egypt in 1882 to put down the Orabi rebellion, to the 1956 attack on Egypt undertaken by Anthony Eden in collusion with Israel and France— Eden's attitude, delivered in the accents of petty and vengeful stubbornness, strangely prefigures Bush's personalized hatred of Saddam Hussein. The question that none of the media has asked is: What right does the United States have to send a massive military force around the world in order to attack Iraq in this tough, relentless, preachy way? This is very different from opposing aggression, which many Arabs would have been anxious to do. What the American move has done is effectively to turn a regional issue into an imperial one, especially since the United States has shown no concern over other aggressions— its own or those, like Israel's, which it supported and paid for. Bush has treated Saddam as his personal Moby Dick, to be punished and destroyed—the war plan was designed for that—as if bombing and frightening natives would be sure to lead to a crumbling of their will.

I have written elsewhere in this book of the dreadful situation inside the Arab world: In countries that are now allied with the United States and in those that are not, there is a lot to be disturbed about, all of it attributable, not to the Arab character or to Islam, but to specific political and social distortions, all of them remediable by strenuous secular policies of reform. What concerns me here is the United States.

For decades in America there has been a cultural war against the Arabs and Islam; the most appalling racist caricatures of Arabs and Muslims have conveyed that they are all either terrorists or shaikhs, and that the region is a large arid slum, fit only for profit or war. The very notion that there might be a history, a culture, a society—indeed many societies—to be thought of as interlocutor or as partner has never held the stage for more than a moment or two. A flow of trivial books by journalists has flooded the market, and has gained currency for a handful of dehumanizing stereotypes. Nearly every recent movie about American commandos pits a hulking Rambo or a whizlike Delta Force against Arab/Muslim terrorist–desperadoes. Now it is as if an almost metaphysical need to defeat Iraq has come into being, not because Iraq's offense, though great, is cataclysmic, but because a small non-white country has rankled a suddenly energized supernation imbued with a fervor that can only be satisfied with subservience from shaikhs, dictators, and camel jockeys. The truly acceptable Arabs are those like Sadat who can be made to seem almost completely purified of their national selfhood—folksy talk show guests.

Arabs may only be an attenuated example of those others who in the past have incurred the wrath of a stern white man, a kind of Puritan superego whose errand into the wilderness knows few boundaries and who will go to very great lengths to make his points. One of the ingredients conspicuously missing from today's discussions about the Gulf is the word ''imperialism.'' But it is difficult not to catch in the moralistic accents of American leaders, and in their obedient media echoes, repetitions of the grandiose self-endowment of previous imperialisms (muffled though they may be by the pious formula that Saddam's wrong against Kuwait is to be righted by the United States). And as the Iraqi infraction seems to grow before our eyes, Saddam has become Hitler, the butcher of Baghdad, the madman who is to be brought low.

"All roads lead to the bazaar," "Arabs understand only force," "Brutality and violence are part of Arab civilization," "Islam is an intolerant, segregationist, medieval, fanatical, cruel religion." No other major cultural group could be spoken of in this way, yet the context, framework, setting of any discussion has been limited, indeed frozen, by these ideas. There has seemed to be a kind of pleasure in the prospect of the Arabs as represented by Saddam at last getting their comeuppance. Scores would be settled with Palestinians, Arab nationalism, Islamic civilization. Most of these old enemies of the "West," it should be noted, had the further cheek to be anti-Israeli.

The worst offenders in all this have been the academic experts on the Arab mind, the usual suspects who can always be rounded up and counted on for egregious displays of phony expertise. The public mood has been such as to decontextualize and isolate Iraq, to exaggerate its power fantastically, to subsume its entire population in the two routinely mispronounced words "Saddam Hussein"—as if all "we" were doing was fighting the one dreadful specter of evil. This enables us to bomb Iraq without a twinge of compunction, and to do it, indeed, with a horrific sense of righteous exhilaration. This is something the media has encouraged, even promoted, as if Iraq could most appropriately be seen through the sights of an F-15 or a smart missile. Note also that after the sudden disappearance of April Glaspie and John Kelly, the present war-making administration has been run without a single professional who has any real knowledge or experience of the Arab Middle East, its languages or its peoples. Such as it was, Iraq's case against Kuwait—a case to some degree encouraged and bolstered by the United States, as the transcript of April Glaspie's conversations with Saddam in late July testifies—was given no hearing, thereby ensuring the need for war. It is my supposition that Iraq is being destroyed today, not because of its aggression against Kuwait, which could have been reversed patiently, regionally, economically, and politically, but because the United States wants a physical presence in the Gulf, wants to have direct leverage on oil to affect Europe and Japan, because it wishes to set the world agenda, because Iraq was perceived as a threat to Israel.

I know that loyalty and patriotism come into all of this, but these should be based on a critical sense of what the facts are, what our interests are, and what as residents of this shrinking and depleted planet we owe our neighbors and the rest of mankind. Uncritical solidarity with the policy of the moment, especially when it is so unimaginably costly, cannot be allowed to rule. America's survival is not at stake in the Persian Gulf and never has been. Why have we no criticism of such ridiculous statements as "We have to stop him now, otherwise it will be harder later?" Why have we not heard anyone say that the UN resolutions were bullied out of the Security Council, and that these resolutions say nothing whatever about destroying a country in order to liberate Kuwait and restore to its throne a dynasty which, along with the other Gulf monarchies, has put two and a half trillion dollars on deposit outside the Arab world? These are monarchies which respect neither human rights nor the priorities of their own people.

Desert Storm is ultimately a war against the Iraqi people, an effort to break and kill them as part of an effort to break and kill Saddam. Yet this is largely kept from the American television audience, as a way of maintaining the image of the war as a painless Nintendo exercise, and the image of the American as a virtuous, clean warrior. On January 27, in the lead *New York Times* article by R. W. Apple, Bush was described as "a strict Marquess of Queensbury rules man" as if what the United States was doing was not, in effect, carpet bombing the cities and towns of Iraq, violating the Geneva and Hague conventions by destroying water and fuel supplies for civilians, and doing only very unascertainable damage to the armed forces in the process. It might make a difference even to Americans who are not interested in history to know that the last time Baghdad was destroyed was in 1258 by the Mongols, to know what precedents there are for what we are doing.

What else in the many pictures we are getting is deliberately manipulative? I would say that the lingering over the scenes of Israeli cities where a few missiles have hit is part of the same distortion. Not that such scenes shouldn't be shown, or that I condone Scud attacks against civilians: They should be shown and I am against these attacks. But why is it granted that only Israeli and Western affliction should be to this extent available—if not to maintain the fiction that Arabs are not equal with "our" side, that their lives and sorrows are not worth listening to?

The claim that Iraq gassed its own citizens has often been repeated. At best, and according to U.S. official sources, this has sometimes seemed uncertain, depending not on truth or principle, but on the policy of the moment. There is at least one War College report, done while Iraq was a U.S. ally, which claims that the gassings of the Kurds in Halabja was done by Iran. Few people mention such reports in the media today, although references to them turn up occasionally in the alternative press. Now, the "gassings of his own citizens" has become a fact about Saddam, elevated into one of the proofs that the United States should destroy him, as if by doing so it wouldn't also destroy Iraq, kill thousands of people, sacrifice thousands of American lives (mostly the poor and disadvantaged), and create a whole host of new problems.

The whole premise of the way the war was prepared and is being fought is colonial: The assumption is that a small Third World country doesn't have the right to resist America, which is white and superior. I submit that such notions are amoral, anachronistic, and supremely mischievous, since they not only make wars possible, but also prevent diplomacy and politics from playing the role they should. When the historical record is fully revealed, we shall know what we already partly know now: that the United States steadily resisted and subverted every attempt at mediation, compromise, or adjudication, and pressed for war almost from the very beginning. Thus one can have only the slightest hope that Bush will react positively to an Iraqi–Soviet proposal for withdrawal.

It would therefore seem that the point of this war is to *prevent* lesser nations and subject peoples from enjoying the same privileges that "we" do. Had the United States from the beginning earned moral authority by getting behind Arab and UN action, following up on the numerous proposals for solving the crisis, expanding the rule of UN resolutions to include the whole region and not just one demonized and demeaned country, there would have been no war, and we would be able to speak about dialogue and reconciliation. How absurd and morally repugnant George Bush's phrase that to resolve the Palestinian question now would be "to reward aggression," as if a peace conference on an issue that antedates not only Saddam but George Bush himself could be spoken of in so coarse and schoolmasterish a way.

There has been scarcely any serious thought about the aftermath of war: the tremendous economic, ecological, and human waste, estimated for the Arabs to have cost over $620 billion; the strengthening of powerful religious sentiment and the defeat of secularism, dialogue, and moderation; the destruction of Iraq, its possible dismemberment, the long and awful period of depredations for its citizens; the rise of extremism, of calls for vengeance and more killing and destruction; the instability of many governments, especially unpopular U.S. allies like Egypt, Syria, and Saudi Arabia; the endless prolongation of an American presence, with occupation, killing, and collaboration as our legacy;

the growth of intransigence in Israel, which will use its U.S. lobby to extract more concessions; the destruction of the environment; of the economy. The list is very long.

An article in last winter's issue of the journal *Foreign Affairs* is entitled "The Summer of Arab Discontent" and contains the following passage:

> No sooner had the Arab/Muslim world said farewell to the wrath and passion of the Ayatollah Khomeini's crusade than another contender rose in Baghdad. The new claimant was made of material different from the turbaned saviour from Qum: Saddam Hussein was not a writer of treatises on Islamic government nor a product of high learning in religious seminaries. Not for him were the drawn-out ideological struggles for the hearts and minds of the faithful. He came from a brittle land, a frontier country between Persia and Arabia, with little claim to culture and books and grand ideas. The new contender was a despot, a ruthless and skilled warden who had tamed his domain and turned it into a large prison.

The merest schoolchild knows that Baghdad was not only the seat of Abbasid civilization, the highest flowering of Arab culture between the ninth and twelfth centuries which produced works of literature still read today as Shakespeare, Dante, and Dickens are still read, but as a city is also one of the great monuments of Islamic art. In addition, Baghdad is the city in which, along with Cairo and Damascus, the nineteenth- and twentieth-century revival of art and literature took place. Baghdad produced at least five of the greatest twentieth-century Arab poets, and without any question all of the top artists and sculptors. To say of Iraq that it has no relation to books and ideas is to be amnesiac about Sumer, and Babylon, and Nineveh, and Hammurabi, and Assyria, and all the great monuments of ancient Mesopotamian (and world) civilization, whose cradle Iraq is. To say that Iraq is a "brittle" land with the suggestion of aridity and emptiness is also to show ignorance which an elementary school child would be embarrassed to reveal. What happened to the Tigris and the Euphrates? What happened to the fact that of all the countries in the Middle East Iraq is by far the most fertile?

The author sings the praises of contemporary Saudi Arabia, more brittle and out of touch with books, ideas, and culture than Iraq ever was. The point is not to belittle Saudi Arabia, which is an important country and has much to contribute. I do, however, want to say that such writing as this, appearing as the United States was poised on the edge of war in the pages of the country's most influential foreign affairs quarterly, is neither informative, nor illuminating, nor valuable. Even more important, it is symptomatic of the intellectual will to please power, to tell it what it wants to hear, to say to it that it can go ahead and kill and bomb and destroy, since what is being attacked is really negligible, brittle, with no relationship to books, ideas, cultures, and no relation either, it gently suggests, to real people. There is only the Iraqi dictator and, like a monstrous disease, he must be extirpated.

With such information, then, what forgiveness, what humanity, what chance for humane argument? Very little, alas. Yet there are signs that all over the country, beneath the misleading euphoria, and the manufactured consent put together by the media, people are dissatisfied, consciences disturbed, spirits anguished. Our duty as intellectuals is to the truth, as Benda said, and not to the encouragement of collective passions in the interests of mass slaughter. When one hears philosophers like Michael Walzer or columnists like Anthony Lewis proclaim this as a "just war," albeit an unwise one, one realizes once more that words are the first casualty in any conflict.

Published in the *London Review of Books,* March 7, 1991.

CHAPTER 30

The Intellectuals and the War

[APRIL 1991]

HARLOW: In recent articles you describe linkage as an ugly concept. Nonetheless, some kind of larger analysis that would challenge the efforts of the United States to divide up the Arab world is necessary. How would you describe that kind of larger analysis?

SAID: I prefer the words "making connections," which to me means seeing things in their context, seeing them as they develop together and as they have to be looked at together. There is a very pernicious dialectic between nationalisms—American and postwar Arab nationalism, between American imperialism and a certain kind of local tyranny. Since I was speaking in an American context, there is a very dramatic American responsibility for a lot that has taken place in the Middle East since World War II, which must be at least admitted by some analysts and intellectuals in the United States. I am not a believer in totalizing views of anything. I don't think you can take every injustice, every abuse of power, every suffering, and just lump it all together and say it has to be dealt with all at once. There are questions of sequence, there are questions of inflection and questions of emphasis.

HARLOW: Maybe we could take this question of specificity in two different directions: the representation of the crisis and the war in the United States and in Europe, on the one hand, and then how different areas of the Arab world responded to the crisis so differently.

SAID: Representation of the conflict in the West, by the first week of the crisis in August, had succeeded, first, in demonizing Saddam; two, in personalizing the crisis and eliminating Iraq as a nation, an economy, a people, a culture, a history; and third, completely occluding the role of the United States and its allies in the formation of the crisis.

HARLOW: But even within the West there were divergent opinions, particularly among intellectual figures.

SAID: I'm talking about policy and mainstream media. The media mobilized for the war in perfect synchrony with the administration.

Regarding the alternative media and in the statements of intellectuals, there has always been a reluctance of intellectuals—not the policy people in Washington, but the people who come to the Socialist Scholars Conference, who attend the Marxist Literary Group, generally speaking, left or independent or liberal intellectuals in this country—there's been a general reluctance to deal with the Middle East, for all kinds of reasons. One of the reasons is not only the nature of this particular regional conflict, I mean its setting and the people involved, but also there's been a fundamental shift, perhaps due to the onset of so-called postmodernism. The United States, as the last empire, has, in the case of intellectuals, internalized imperial rule. That sets intellectuals above such issues, perhaps because of a general sense of helplessness and impotence and fragmentation due to specialization.

The intellectual community doesn't operate according to principles, and doesn't consider itself bound by responsibilities toward the common weal. Or doesn't feel itself responsible for the behavior of the United States internationally. In the Middle East the United States has routinely obstructed the struggle for human rights, not just the Palestinian struggle. The United States has sided with every entrenched and rooted power against the struggle for women's rights, the struggle for minority rights, the struggle for ethnic or religious rights or rights to free assembly, free speech. All of these things are matters of U.S. policy. To this history, which has very little to do with the Palestinians, the large body of American intellectuals is basically provincial, drawn only by virtue of expertise. If they're Latin American specialists, they don't talk about anything other than Latin America.

Then there is the sense of responsibility to the public sphere, affiliation with the cause. I remember once a friend of mine, a literary Marxist in this country, said, "Well, you're lucky, Edward, you were born Palestinian, but this other person, who's an American, doesn't have a cause to which he was born." As if there were some tremendous privilege to being subjected to the travails of the Palestinians. If you are an American, you're sort of above all causes. It's as if unless you're born to the thing or you've been given a degree in expertise on the subject, it doesn't matter.

Secondly, the experts among them, among the senior rank, were dying to be called to Washington. They were not saying things that would disturb the policy train. Third, the rest of us—yourself, myself, many others—were fragmented, didn't have access to the media, and they had to rely on samizdat publications.

I want to contrast that with the remarkable interview in January with Jacques Berque, in which he was able to distinguish between Saddam and Iraq and the Arabs and imperialism, between the state of human rights in the Arab world and in, let's say, Europe historically, and butchery and violence which are not the monopoly of Iraq by any means. And got it published in a prominent journal, *L'Autre Journal* (February 1991). Nothing like that happened in this country, where the scholars of his stature and prestige, man or woman, affiliated themselves with the administration.

HARLOW: Despite the Jacques Berque interview, French intellectual circles, just as in the United States and the United Kingdom, saw a considerable failure to respond coherently and with any principle. So how has this crisis challenged the intellectual class to begin to examine its own history?

SAID: Not at all. They were glad it was as short as it was. The problem is a history of disengagement from international questions and, above all, disengagement from the Middle East, the Arabs generally. I don't see any signs of change. If anything, it's confirmed that the whole thing is just a nasty can of worms. The small number of us who continue to try to engage them in general questions of responsibility was too few. Why? Because in the meantime this country has produced an entire literature of instant expertise and knowledge, now on the best-seller list of *The New York Times* and other leading newspapers, all of which put forward a view of the Middle East and of this conflict in particular which entirely supports the administration's position.

HARLOW: Maybe we could talk a little bit about that cult of expertise and the main institutional and individual practitioners of intellectual policing today with regard to the Middle East.

SAID: In contrast to Vietnam, when a powerful and vocal group emerged in the universities that became an alternative power center that challenged the administration. This had a noticeable effect upon the media. They were generally working in the social sciences. Here we ought to say parenthetically that everything I'm talking about more or less excludes the humanities. The various literary people, the theorists, and so on, who have absolutely no presence in any of this, they're the most pathetic group of the lot.

The difference from the Vietnam situation in the 1960s is that Vietnam developed and evolved over a longer period of time. Secondly, in the Middle East, in 1991, the presence of Israel is a complicating factor. With very few exceptions, the leading scholars in the field of the Middle East gravitated either toward Washington or to the media and were made use of there. In other words, their sights were not focused on the region, they were focused on ways to the region as provided by CBS, NBC, *The New York Times,* and whatnot, or the policy-making institutions in Washington. You didn't, therefore, see the emergence of a strong and well-profiled opposition sympathetic to the Arabs as a people and a culture, to Iraq as a nation, one that opposed the Iraqi invasion and annexation of Kuwait but also opposed the American military presence.

Instead the media hooked on to the war policy, in its wake bringing up not only a lot of retired military men—men, always men, and what I call the scholar-combatants—Fouad Ajami, Daniel Pipes, Bernard Lewis, and so on—and with them a handful of journalists like Tom Friedman and Jim Hoagland, who were really indistinguishable from policymakers.

HARLOW: These scholar-combatants also seem to be contributing to a kind of curriculum building—for example, the reading lists that Fouad Ajami presented in *The New York Times Book Review.*

SAID: There was a reading list published by National Public Radio, which didn't have a single work on it either by or about an Arab. *The New York Times,* a couple of weeks before Ajami, published an entire page in which there wasn't a single book listed on Iraq after about the seventh century B.C.! Iraq was left, to a modern reader, pretty much at Sumer! And there were five Israeli novels, there were three or four histories of the Jews, there was Conor Cruise O'Brien, but nothing on the modern history or culture of Iraq. What you have is a canon, which now includes Samir al-Khalil's book, *Republic of Fear,* Ajami's *Arab Predicament,* the instant books by journalists and, of course, Thomas Friedman's *From Beirut to Jerusalem,* David Fromkin's *Peace to End All Peace in the Middle East,* which is considered to be a very important book, and occasionally, Albert Hourani's book. Now, if you exclude Hourani's *History of the Arab People,* which although it's now on the best-seller list, is not a book that's going to be read and digested easily, if you exclude that, and perhaps Fromkin, these are books that are generally unsympathetic to the Arabs and advance the thesis that the feuds and the violence of the Middle East are due to, relatively speaking, prehistoric causes. They're sort of inscribed in the very genes of these people. And that such things as a rational argument presented by some or all the Arab people of the twentieth century about their own sense of history, their sense of identity, their achievements—all of these are really fraudulent, and essentially self-deluding, and, in the words of Ajami, the problems of the Arab world are the result of "self-inflicted wounds." This literature pretty much exonerates the United States and its policymakers, and of course Israel, from any role in this appalling mess that we're living through today.

HARLOW: What are the strategies available to us now to counter that oppressive canon-building?

SAID: Let me just say one more thing that hooks into a very interesting argument advanced by Regis Debray in his book *Teachers, Writers and Celebrities*. These people are all, without exception, people without any significant scholarly attainment or expertise. Friedman is a journalist. Ajami is a second-rate scholar who has written one collection of essays that appeared about twenty years ago, and a very bad history of Musa Sadr. These are all people who belong to the genre of celebrities, they have no particular anchor in the process of intellectual work or in institutions of intellectual production. They are therefore paradoxically much more difficult to dislodge, precisely because they have no particular institution to which they belong. They are creatures of the moment and of the media.

HARLOW: That's why their media and government credentialing process is so serious.

SAID: Exactly.

HARLOW: What kind of scholarly combatants can be developed to contest this? And what kind of effect has the Gulf crisis had on Arab political culture?

SAID: I haven't lived in the Arab world for a long time, and for various reasons, mostly political, find it very difficult to visit there now. But my impressions are quite strong and are roughly as follows. Number one, I don't know of any part of the Arab world, or any part of Europe or the United States, where there is an Arab presence, journalistically speaking, that can be described as doing anything tangible. All of what is now published in the daily newspapers—more or less, one can always find exceptions—in the Arab world is politically motivated, in the narrow and most vulgar sense. To write, you have to be affiliated with a particular line or regime or ruler. If you're independent, unorthodox, creative in some way, it's either extremely difficult or impossible to make a break, or to have an effect.

HARLOW: Do you think this crisis could have destabilized those structures to allow for reconfiguration of intellectual projects?

SAID: That's the optimistic side of it. The more realistic and, in my opinion, accurate assessment is that the credibility of the right has been undermined. Almost everything that is written today directly reflects a political influence in the narrow, most literal sense. Nothing that anyone can write is going to be above question. There's not going to be something you're not going to be skeptical about. The essential authorial credibility on which analysis and writing depends is undermined. Opportunities will open up, new alignments will take place, but the first question asked is not whether what he or she's saying is true or not, but who is this person really speaking for. As they say in Arabic, *min warrah,* "Who's behind it?"

Second, there is now because of the Gulf War and the horrific aftermath, a general collapse of cultural institutions in the Arab world. The pattern of funding, of staffing—all of these things have been changed in ways that we're just only now beginning to assess. Where Palestinians used to be sought after to attend various kinds of conferences, to be in various institutes, that's all stopping now. There's a seismic shift in the intellectual and cultural topography of the Arab world, which is very hard to assess but can't be good.

HARLOW: It's shifting against the emergence of a humane and democratic civil society?

SAID: Absolutely. An Arab world divided between victor and vanquished. Palestinians are now identified as the losers, because they "sided with the wrong person." And the Egyptians now are desperate to cast themselves as winners because they sided with the United States. This has an effect on the micro level, at institutes, at cultural and political endeavors.

Suspicion across borders has increased. Egyptians versus Sudanese, Sudanese versus Saudis. The Saudi deportation of 800,000 Yemeni workers in late 1990 and early 1991 is not about a fifth column or destabilization; it's an act of petty vengeance against an entire people.

And there's also something which is quite new in the Arab world, and that is the idea that if you stand inside one of these borders, people are homogenized in some way. The myth of the homogeneous Arab state, that Syrians are homogeneous Syrians. The "Who is a Jew" debate is something that is quite foreign to our culture and history, because the essence of the region and one of the reasons why we call it the Middle East, is precisely that it's a mongrel region, it's made up of a tremendous diversity, what in Latin America is called the *mestizo* factor. There's no purity at all. It's a consecrated hybridity. And that's why people began to object to the various comical nationalisms that appeared in one or another of these countries. But now it's a situation in which, for example, the king of Jordan can say, "I am a Sharif." In other words, there's now a contest to ground one's identity in some distant, pure, and primitive first state, whether it's Islam or a tribe or a border. That's something very new; it's not a world I grew up in.

HARLOW: What has been the effect of all this on the Palestinian national movement? The Palestinian question has represented something more than integrated nationalism. What's happening to Palestinian nationalism?

SAID: A certain part of it has maintained itself as really quite different from the other kinds, where people are attracted to the cause precisely because it is in a certain sense transnational, it's about principles. It's a struggle about justice. And because it's the only nationalism in the region that talks about its opponents in a humane and comprehensive way. And many of the Palestinians' friends in the West and the Third World generally have remained attached to it precisely for this reason.

Having said all of that, yes, we too have been afflicted by this. We don't live in a vacuum. In 1985, the one time I went to Kuwait, as a guest of Kuwait University, Palestinians and Kuwaitis worked there together as professors, and because I was an outside visitor, both of them sought my ear to accuse the other of malfeasance, usually on national grounds. You can sympathize with the Palestinian who is a minority in a country like Kuwait, but it breeds that whole atmosphere of people being identified ethnically and through the prism of a very narrow and narrowing nationalism, it breeds even in the victim a general lack of generosity. That's what's happened certainly with Israel and the Palestinians, and I think some of that is coming out in our behavior. That people were *happy*—of course, I'm privileged, I live in New York, I don't have this problem— but I was very disappointed when Palestinians on the West Bank and Gaza identified with Iraq bashing the Kuwaitis. Even if the Kuwaitis are not popular and are not liked and they're arrogant—even if you accept all that, it's still strange why a victim would identify with the oppressor.

That's one of the roles intellectuals could play, and leaders could play, and one of the things that we missed in our part of the world, where people said, look, this is a matter of principle. Invasion is invasion. You say in Israel the Arabs have deserted the *intifadah;* that's a fact. It's a very unhealthy mix. That's part of the fraying of inter-Arab connections, of inter-Arab cooperation, solidarity, and thought.

HARLOW: Do you see, within the Palestinian *intifadah* right now, given the devastating effect that this relocation of concerns has had, any possibilities for rehabilitation?

SAID: I'm actually relatively optimistic about that. The difficulties are tremendous and the sufferings horrific, but there has been a cataclysmic shake-up. That, if it doesn't kill you, can induce a reorientation and a clarification of priorities. It's also the case that the alliance of the Palestinian national movement with Gulf money has been not such a wonderful thing. The building of institutions, hospitals on the West Bank, libraries, kindergartens, that sort of thing, with help from the Palestinian community in the Gulf, but also from the Gulf states themselves, made a difference; it was important. But the political price has been high. It's turned our attention away from the actual building process which is so necessary to us. It's also taught an entire generation of Palestinians to depend on shortcuts induced by money—that you could buy certain things. You could buy people by bringing them on planes, buying plane tickets. The removal of all that means that the Palestinians are thrust back on their own, and there has to be a shift back to the resources and the energies of the people themselves, and not these outside interests which I think have been distracting.

The third thing is that in the last couple of weeks, as a result of the Baker trips, all the Arab rulers, when asked by Baker whether they would move forward on normalizing their relations with Israel, to a man said no. We cannot do anything unless there is movement on the Palestinian question. So, in an ironic sort of way, the Palestinian question has been moved back up to the top of the agenda—for whatever reasons—and gives us a reason to put our house in order and to organize politically the campaign for peace in which we are going to be central.

HARLOW: But why are the Arab rulers saying that, despite all the pressure from the United States?

SAID: It's a way of restoring, they think, their own legitimacy and popularity. Palestine remains the only inter-Arab cause. It's the one nationalism
that hasn't been realized. Kuwait's rulers began their involvement in
Palestine in the 1930s because their people urged them to, not because
they wanted to. It's also to restore their aura, which has been sullied by
their association with this appalling war. Palestine remains a popular cause
on the street.

HARLOW: Does this also suggest a message to the Palestinian movement?
One could say that this crisis demonstrated the failure of the Palestinian
movement to provide a leadership for the Arab world and of democratic
forces within the Arab world, leaving a vacuum into which Saddam
Hussein was able to move.

SAID: Yes, Palestinians will tell you that Arafat's positions during the war
followed from the fact that Palestinians in the West Bank and Gaza took
those positions. I disagree. One of the things that leaders do is lead. Many
of us failed in this role. It would be unfair to ascribe it entirely to the
Palestinian leadership. It's a general failure over the last two years, the
abandonment by the Arab regimes of the *intifadah.*

I've often felt the PLO has been remiss in not releasing publicly the
minutes of the meetings between the United States and the PLO in Tunis,
so that people could see what little we had gotten as a result of our
historical compromise. That kind of enterprise—above all, making political gains out of the lessons of the *intifadah,* which are a blueprint for
democracy and solidarity between people, not on a hierarchical but a
communal basis, in the Arab world. That is the role of the Palestinians
today. We are the only national movement still in existence today in the
Arab world that functions according to democratic, largely noncoercive
and inventive modes of association and coordination, which remain for
the most part secular.

It would be foolish not to recognize that the odds against us are
horrifically great. But you can't give up. One of the lessons that we've
learned in the last twenty years as Palestinians, and I think many Israelis
have learned, is that we have no military option against each other. That
leads to emphasizing *persuasion* as a modality of political action. We cannot
credibly and politically, with any serious or desirable result, fight each
other militarily. They could slaughter us, but they're not going to get rid
of every Palestinian, and they won't snuff out the flame of Palestinian
nationalism. Conversely, we have no military option against the Israelis.

What we do have is a vision, a way of including them in the Middle East based on respect of nationalities for each other, the right to live within secure and safe borders, and to coexist in a profitable way with other peoples, with differences.

That is our main weapon. I do not think that most of us have realized it. We still either believe in outdated and now useless slogans of an Arab nationalist movement based upon military means, upon the one-party state, and above all the cult of the great leader, or we believe in Soviet military hardware governed by great dreams of victory. Those are not necessary to the Palestinian struggle and have never been a central part of it. To the extent that we are still a part of the Arab world, that we speak Arabic, that we read the same literature, that we employ the same discourses, it's very important for our discourse to emerge as distinctive from that of the other ones, and lead the others rather than drown—as we did.

HARLOW: The Arab regimes, for all that they have been bullied into cooperating with the United States in the war, are nonetheless saying that the Palestinian question needs to be addressed. The Palestinian national movement, with its representability and its democracy offers a blueprint for the Arab world. In the Arab countries democratic movements are more or less moribund at the moment. How can those movements be reactivated? What kind of coalition building does it make sense to talk about?

SAID: There are generally two time frames we have to work on. One is the immediate one: that of consecutive, chronological, everyday succession. That agenda is dominated now by the regimes. As the events in Iraq demonstrate, even the worst of them are not easily dislodged, and if they're dislodged it's simply by alternative versions of themselves. In that time scheme, the game of the regime is now dominated by the United States and its allies. There are some fairly opportunistic things to be done, given the presence of the Palestinian issue high on the agenda. You have to play that game.

Then there's the other agenda, a "slow politics" that takes place over a long period of time, which can allow for the coalition building. There one has to begin with the premise that most of the national and nonstatist groups and associations in the Arab world today, except perhaps for Saudi Arabia and the other Gulf states including Kuwait, which are actively opposed to Palestine, are all disaffected from the issue. The really popular position in the Arab world, if you were to study it carefully, is a rejection of what Saddam stands for, and the disastrous results which he brought to his own country and people, as well as a rejection of the American military solution.

The coalition would have to be between people in different parts of the Arab world who are actively involved in local struggles for democracy, economic justice, women's rights, human rights groups, university groups—for example, the Jordanian student university movement of the middle 1980s. There are gatherings now of intellectuals in some of the transnational Arab institutes, like the Institute of Arab Unity, the Arab Human Rights Organization, various lawyers' groups and so on, university and intellectual groups who collaborate on small projects, some of the journals like *Mawaqif* and *Fusul*. These things are going back and forth, and there are discussions between secular and Islamic forces in the Arab world for the first time in a serious way.

That's where the coalitions have to occur, between those kinds of largely informal but disaffected groups, both religious and secular. The whole question of education in the Arab world has never been posed adequately. We live in one world, after all; it can't be entirely Arab and Islamic and removed from it, and it can't simply be a copy of the dominant Western paradigm.

One has to make that distinction between two agendas and two types of coalitions; one based on the regimes that are taking place, of necessity, which one has to exploit and use, and the other one, a longer one, which exists across state barriers and national boundaries.

What we really need is a critical language, which should be able to do two things. One is to assess and critique power in the Arab world. This is where a Gramscian vision is so important: to be able to give accurate assessments not according to grandiose schemes imported from Hegel and Stalin and so on—the miseries of the Arab left, many of them are ascribable to this importation of methodological instruments of perspective brought from abroad having no relation to our life, or Orientalist models. Rather, we must indigenously and imaginatively develop models of the sort, for example, that Laroui in North Africa was able to do, or Anwar Abdel-Malek, or Jabiri. You find it among brilliant individuals, but a critique of power assessment has to be given a greater currency in discussion by other like-minded intellectuals.

Second, we need a language of appreciation, care, and attention based not on dogmatic orthodoxy or reverence for religious, Quranic, and authoritative ideas, but rather one that develops out of this critique of power. Being able to say what we are for in *our* world and in *our* lives, as opposed to using the fundamentalist model of saying that we're for the way it was done in the past. I'm talking about a developed sense of what it is that we care about.

Out of this combined critique of power and discourse of care and attention can come accountability. This can lead to participation, which is something in Arab intellectual life that has struck me as very problematic. There is the sense in the Arab world of a tremendous provincialism and isolation. We're not—whether in the case of our literature or intellectual work, historical and other—we're not part of the ongoing debate in the world. There is a world debate—about world literature, about issues affecting humankind generally, issues of the environment, of media, of intellectual excellence—and the Arab contribution to that is tiny. Our inability to enter and take part in that is largely due to ourselves. We are almost like Macondo in *A Hundred Years of Solitude*. We are the focus of a lot of world attention, but we're always outside it, we're not participants in the determination of our own future, intellectually. There's no reason for that.

HARLOW: There probably are reasons; you yourself have analyzed them.

SAID: Well, yes. There are reasons, but there's no reason to acquiesce in it; that's what I meant.

HARLOW: And there's no reason for intellectuals here to be complicit in the exclusionary practices. There do seem to be possibilities for connections here around these issues. This brings us back to the role of the intellectual—Arab and non-Arab—here in the United States.

SAID: Yesterday I heard a panel discussion on the lessons of the Gulf War. One participant was Samir al-Khalil. What struck me as extraordinarily sad, not to say desolate, was his appeal to the United States, which had just devastated his country militarily, to enter further into Iraq and unseat Saddam Hussein. Here is this Arab intellectual, suddenly galvanized into public appearances on American media, and all he does is talk about the evils of Saddam Hussein. Not a word about the American war that devastated his country, nothing about the situation in the Arab world. For him the only issue is the one that he as an Iraqi, genuinely in pain, feels. And that seems to me to be part of the misery of this whole story. He is intelligent, fluent, but unable to attach himself to anything but an issue of the moment, with no consecutive history behind him, with no realism in his perspective. He's suddenly discovered he's got to do something, and what does he do? He appeals to the United States, which has just destroyed his country, to come and rescue him!

It's astonishing. One of the roles Arab intellectuals sometimes play in the West is that of a sort of guinea pig witness. Since you're from Iraq, you tell us about Iraq. When we're not interested in Iraq, we don't want to hear from you. The native informant. The Uncle Ahmad. That's simply an unacceptable role. We have to be everywhere. We have not only to deal with general problems in the Arab world, but we have to be able to say things about this country, where we are.

What is the constituency he represents? He assumes that he is speaking for Iraq, and the Iraqi people who are all opposed to Saddam—I'm sure that's true. But here what Gramsci talks about, organic relationships, become very important. You can't do these one-man things, where you appeal to the American State Department to try to send in an army to do what you please. The world isn't bound by getting on or not getting on the Op-Ed pages of *The New York Times*. His perspective is a bit like Gulliver's: either people are too big for you or they're too small. The corrective is to be organically connected with a movement, with a people, where you're responsible to and responsible *for* certain things. You can't just sort of burst in and do this kind of Tolstoyan grandiloquence which is going to rescue your people. The horror of it is that he appeals to the very same people who are responsible for a large part of the present tragedy of his country. They collaborated with Saddam, and now they've destroyed the country; they're propping him up after destroying the infrastructure. After such knowledge what possible thing can emerge?

HARLOW: What are the political, intellectual, and cultural imperatives for combating this agenda? In 1967 Chomsky wrote the essay "Responsibility of Intellectuals." What would be the main components of such an essay today?

SAID: One would have to pretty much scuttle all the jaw-shattering jargonistic postmodernisms that now dot the landscape. They are worse than useless. They are neither capable of understanding and analyzing the power structure of this country nor are they capable of understanding the particular aesthetic merit of an individual work of art. Whether you call it deconstruction or postmodernism or poststructuralism or post-anything, they all represent a sort of spectacle of giving back tickets at the entrance and saying, we're really out of it. We want to check into our private resort and be left alone.

Reengagement with intellectual processes has very little to do with being politically correct, or citing fashionable names, or striking acceptable poses, but rather having to do with a return in a way to a kind of old-fashioned historical, literary, and above all, intellectual scholarship based upon the premise that human beings, men and women, make their own history. And just as things are made, they can be unmade and re-remade. That sense of intellectual and political and citizenry empowerment is what I think the intellectual class needs.

There's only one way to anchor oneself, and that is by affiliation with a cause, with a political movement. There has to be some identification, not with the powers that be, with the Secretary of State or the great leading philosopher of the time or the sage; there has to be an affiliation with matters involving justice, principle, truth, conviction. Those don't occur in a laboratory or a library. For the American intellectual, that simply means, at bottom, in a globalized environment, that there is today one superpower, and the relationship between the United States and the rest of the world, based upon profit and power, has to be altered from an imperial one to one of coexistence among human communities that can make and remake their own histories together. This seems to me to be the number-one priority—there's nothing else.

An American has a particular role. If you're an anthropologist in America, it's not the same thing as being an anthropologist in India or France; it's a qualitatively different thing.

HARLOW: We're both professors in English departments, despite the fact that the humanities have been quite irresponsible, unanswerable . . .

SAID: Not the humanities. The professors of humanities.

HARLOW: Well, OK, the professors. But there is this question . . .

SAID: I take the general view that, for all its inequity, for all its glaring faults and follies, the university in this society remains a relatively utopian place, a place of great privilege. There needs to be some sense of the university as a place in which these issues are not, because it is that kind of place, trivialized. Universities cannot afford to become just a platform for a certain kind of narcissistic specialization and jargon. What you need is a regard for the product of the human mind. And that's why I've been very dispirited, I must tell you, but some aspects of the "great Western canon" debate, which really suggest that the oppressed of the world, in wishing to be heard, in wishing their work to be recognized, really wish to do dirt on everything else. That's not the spirit of resistance. We come back to Aimé Césaire's line, "There is room for all at the rendezvous of victory." It's not that some have to be pushed off and demeaned and denigrated. The question is not whether we should read more black literature or less literature by white men. The issue is excellence—we need everything, as much as possible, for understanding the human adventure in its fullest, without resorting to enormous abstractions and generalizations, without replacing Euro-centrism with other varieties of ethnocentrism or, say, Islamo-centrism or Afro-centrism or gyno-centrism. Is it a game of substitution? That's where intellectuals have to clarify themselves.

HARLOW: I agree, but at least within certain university contexts there have been lately two major issues: the Gulf War and multiculturalism. I have not seen any linkage between the two.

SAID: The epistemology and the ethic of specialization has been accepted by all. If you're a literature professor, that's what you talk about. And if you're an education specialist, that's what you talk about. The whole idea of being in the university means not only respect for what others do, but respect for what you do. And the sense that they all are part of a community. The main point is that we ascribe a utopian function to the intellectual. Even inside the university, the prevalence of norms based upon domination and coercion is so strong because the idea of authority is so strong—whether it's authority derived from the nation-state, from religion, from the ethnos, from tradition—is so powerful that it's gone relatively unchallenged, even in the very disciplines and studies that we are engaged in. Part of intellectual work is understanding how authority is formed. Like everything else, authority is not God-given. It's secular. And if you can understand that, then your work is conducted in such a way as to be able to provide alternatives to the authoritative and coercive norms that dominate so much of our intellectual life, our national and political life, and our international life above all.

HARLOW: What can alternative publications do to interrupt that particular way of presenting authority?

SAID: One is to remind readers that there are always other ways of looking at the issue—whatever it happens to be—than those that are officially credentialed. Second, one of the things that one needs to do in intellectual enterprises is to—Whitehead says somewhere—always try to write about an author keeping in mind what he or she might say of what you're writing. To adapt from that: some sense in which your constituency might be getting signals about what you're doing. The agenda isn't set only by you; it's set by others. You can't represent the others, but you can take them into account by soliciting their attention. Let such a publication be a place in which in its pages that which is occluded or suppressed or has disappeared from the consciousness of the West, of the intellectual, can be allowed to appear. Third, some awareness of the methodological issues involved, and the gathering of information, the production of scholarship, the relationship between scholarship and knowledge. The great virtue of these journals is that they are not guided by professional norms. Nobody is going to get tenure out of writing for these journals. And nobody is trying to advance in a career by what he or she does there. So that means therefore that one can stand back and look at these things and take questions having to do with how do people know things. In other words, a certain emphasis on novelty is important and somewhat lacking. You don't want to feel too virtuous in what you are doing: that I'm the only person doing this, therefore, I must continue doing it. Wit is not such a bad thing.

Published in *Middle East Report*, July/August 1991.

Part Three

POLITICS AND INTELLECTUALS

CHAPTER 31

Chomsky and the Question
of Palestine

[1975]

Chomsky's work in linguistics and politics is much better known among Jews and Jewish communities than it is among Arabs and Arab communities. This is not entirely because Chomsky himself is a Jew who has written on subjects like Israel and Middle East politics that affect Jews very closely. Rather, I think, it is because Chomsky deals in terms as well as subjects in which Jews have been and continue to be prominent: His principal intellectual and professional contributions are to linguistics, a science whose existence is virtually dependent upon the university, which is where, more demonstrably and effectively than elsewhere in the United States, the Jewish presence is at once irresistibly attractive on some moral and most intellectual grounds and deeply troubled on some political ones. Moreover, Chomsky has not only appropriated for himself the turf of political philosophy and hard contemporary analysis; he has done it with great moral authority, a style recognized by many Jews to be central to an important Judaic tradition in the West (which it is), and—here Chomsky begins to be problematic for Jews—with an insistence that no subject, not even Israel, can be exempt from rational analysis. I suspect that to many Jews Chomsky has pushed his Jewishness too far and too wastefully. As a brilliant Jewish colleague of mine put it to me recently, Chomsky hates Israel with such vehemence and in such tones of harsh judgment that only a Jew could have done his hating so effectively. By contrast, those Arabs who know Chomsky or his work are likely to have a far less prickly sense of him. Not only has there been very little Arab knowledge of his professional accomplishments; there is a rather limited Arab familiarity with the terms, as well as the settings, of his political work. To us, generally, he is either known as a big name of some sort or as someone to whom we can point with fairly uncomplicated (and yet quite mistaken) confidence that he is "with" us and against "them."

To a great extent, both these cant Jewish and Arab attitudes to Chomsky are inadequate, but for very different reasons. It is not only that his political positions are intended as refutations of purely national and even ethnic positions. More interestingly, Chomsky can, and indeed should, be read as an intellectual who is completely suspicious of cant or herd or "accepted" notions of *for* or *against,* especially as they creep insidiously into and then take over all forms of political, moral, and professional discourse. Go back to his work during the Vietnam War, and you will find that in arguments about political attitudes or about philosophical accounts of linguistic action, Chomsky has opposed concepts that mask themselves as rigorous, infallible, expert, objective, value-free, professional (in the sense of being understandable only by professionals in a field) and so on.[1] He has been especially concerned with intellectuals as a class, those who, whether in or outside the university, inside or outside "back rooms" where so-called policy is studied and enacted, have created a cult of fraudulent technology that overrides not just morality and human decency but reason itself. The title of a recent collection of his essays—*For Reasons of State*—fairly delivers his notion of how *a state* (of anything: a political state, a state of mind, a state of an art or science) too easily becomes orthodoxy. And orthodoxy quickly arms itself with such self-confirmations as "responsible," "realistic," and "pragmatic," which lay upon the intellectual the burden to "stop questioning our values and threatening our privilege."[2] "Our" in this sentence is the possessive of the apologist, who will pay any moral or intellectual price in order not to trouble himself with the radical issues. Thus, a purely Arab position, no less than a purely Jewish one, has its own self-serving, nationalistic reasons of state, which, when it comes to the Middle East question, bring out Chomsky's antagonism.

In recent years, and most insistently in this latest book, Chomsky's polemic is directed explicitly against liberalism. It is this specific polemic that more than anything else makes *Peace in the Middle East?*[3]

(the question mark is eloquently ironic) an *American* book. Not that Chomsky is sparing either of the standard Israeli and Arab positions. He is critical of both but is, I think, more truly concerned with debate in the United States about the Middle East generally, and American Jewish pieties toward Israel in particular. He writes as an American Jew with a history of engagement in left-wing Zionism; in addition, he has also taken and argued for generally left-wing positions in American and international politics, principally, of course, against the Vietnam War. What he opposes in American debate on the Middle East is the left-liberal attitude that uses righteous support of Israel as a sort of magic slate rewrite of American failure in Vietnam. This he calls the rebuilding of Camelot. He argues that the conforming left-liberal during the sixties was ambiguous about Vietnam. To be for Vietnam was to be tied to Nixon and later to Watergate; to be against it was to be in some ways "in opposition to state power, often in direct resistance." Therefore the left-liberal orthodoxy was to lie low, then after the "peace" was signed to emerge more anxious than ever in taking revenge on both right and left, in trying to retake power, and once again in occupying a position of moral authority in the United States. "It was much more convenient to denounce one's enemies as totalitarians, radical-chic suburbanites, anti-Semites, or backers of Arab genocide."⁴ The more serious opponents of the Vietnam War, from Chomsky himself to the Berrigan brothers to I. F. Stone, continued to oppose the same sorts of positions represented by the war itself; if, for instance, this meant opposing either Israel or Israeli policies, they were as likely now to speak their minds as they had been then. Chomsky gives numerous examples to show that the left-liberal today is the same fainéant he was over Vietnam during the sixties.

This is an unexceptionable thesis. But it does not fully prepare one for the near-hysterical anger that Chomsky's book on the Middle East has aroused. It appeared in early September 1974, virtually unannounced; for the latest book by a very prominent intellectual on *the* foreign policy issue of the day, this was a peculiar beginning, at least for Chomsky's publisher if not for the media and booksellers. Later, when it was skimpily reviewed, an appalling uniformity was evident in the commentary. Even for one who has been hardened to the surprising ingenuity of unfairness in this most "fair" of all societies—where for decades a total, systematic exclusion of the Palestinians has been practiced in fact and in discourse, and where any individual *mention* of Palestine can be construed as a victory against the system—that was remarkable. Of the four major reviews I saw, the mildest, surprisingly, was in *Commentary;* the bitterest were by Michael Walzer and Theodore Draper in *The New York Times* and *The New Republic,* respectively.[5] Chomsky replied to those reviews for the inordinate misquotation, misreading, and misinterpretation indulged in by authors whose work on other subjects would not have been so transparently flawed. To Arab eyes, it would appear that Draper and Walzer were infuriated by the effrontery of a Jew criticizing Israel, using as evidence not only Israeli sources but precisely the sort of argument liberal American Jews have employed against white South Africans, Thieu's South Vietnamese, and southern American rednecks. The mere mention of Palestinian resistance, or Palestinian rights, stirred up in Walzer and Draper that special combination of enthusiastic anger fed by blind ethnocentric ignorance present in American Jewish discourse about Israel. In both their cases, there was a wish barely concealing itself that Chomsky and his book *not be.* It was as if Chomsky raised a specter far better left forgotten.

What is this specter? I think it has to do with Chomsky's vision of the past and the future, the Jewish past and future. Here was a famous Jew who was quite prepared not only to deal with Israel as if it were a state like all others, but also with the whole Jewish question outside the totally invulnerable category of threatened genocide. In other words, Chomsky makes statements that do not rely for their moral or rational force upon the Holocaust. When he says that "the Nazi massacre, though unforgettable in its horror, no longer determines the choice of action. Rather, it is the living death of the refugee camps and the steady dirt towards further misery yet to come that set the term for policy,"[6] he is saying that the problems of the contemporary Middle East are not all reducible to memories of Jewish suffering in World War II. He is also saying that, just as there is nothing sacrosanct about a Jewish state *per se,* there was an estimable current in pre-1948 Jewish and *Zionist* history resolutely against the establishment of a Jewish state (Ben-Gurion was himself of this current). In the context of American discussion of the Middle East conflict, these are scarcely allowable thoughts, especially since Chomsky's political sympathies are anarcho-socialist. Above all, one senses that Chomsky, perhaps without intending it, lifted a corner of the wall-to-wall carpet on which liberal Americans have pranced for three decades. Not only has he released Arab Palestinians from the sacrifice imposed on them by Israel, but he asserts that the only solution is to take their grievances seriously. As a moral absolute above criticism, Israel is thereby nullified.

To those who cannot sympathize with such a view, enter now the demons of atheism, revolutionism, socialism, radicalism, popular "unrest," anarchism, syndicalism, and on and on. Worse, enter the demon of a genuinely well informed man, a man well informed about *all* the injustices, the anti-democratic practices, the state-run systems of oppression and repression in the Middle East. Still worse, enter the dispeller of hopes in Rogers, Kissinger, Sadat, Rabin, the Knesset, and the PLO. Worse yet, enter the chronicler of American imperialism and Arab–Israeli sub-imperialism in the Middle East. Worst of all, enter the pitiless adversary of special pleading on the basis of abstract "right" or concrete "realism." But what, then, is this as a political stand?

Whereas Chomsky's position is not a rigidly systematic one, it is nonetheless unified. True, his book is a loose collection of essays, and it does not include a precise blueprint for the binational socialism it wishes for Palestine; but then why should it include such an absurd thing? Chomsky's task is to keep hope for a binational solution alive "until such time as popular movements within Israeli and Palestinian society, supported by an international socialist movement that does not now exist, will undertake to make such a hope a reality."[7] For him, certain truths cannot be avoided: that there are two communities in the former Palestine; that the Arabs have been done a monstrous injustice but that the Jews have a symmetrical case to be made for their presence; that the imperialist powers, with the United States chief among them, have played havoc with the area; that states operate according to a certain political and economic logic, and this is equally valid in the case of Israel as it is of the United States; and, finally, that there is no group at present in whom one can have long-term confidence. But everywhere Chomsky takes some account of the situation in the United States, where political debate is petrified by "bomb-them-into-the-stone-age" attitudes to the Arabs, attitudes dressed up in liberal admiration for Israeli democracy.

Chomsky is at his most ideologically firm when he seeks to prove that once fundamental libertarian tenets are betrayed to state interests there can be no democracy, no true solution to nationalist conflict, and no political struggle in the real sense except as resistance to the state and to imperialism, its international ally. There are brief excursus into

Palestinian history (admirably commented on by Irene Gendzier in her foreword to the volume) and fairly detailed analyses of the immediately pre- and post-October War period: Chomsky finds no reason for believing that that war changed anything so far as basic U.S. strategy in the area is concerned. He is perhaps right in thinking that U.S. policy will tend to revert to earlier options (pressure on Israel, as during the Dulles period), and, I think, certainly right in believing that Israeli positions on occupation and withdrawal will remain essentially unchanged, even harder in some cases, as time goes on. He connects Israeli intransigence both with the fallacy of equating Israeli security with Israel's capability of guaranteeing that security, and also with the fanatical, near hysterical lobbying of American Zionists, who "bear a measure of responsibility for the events of October 1973, a very close call for the State of Israel. Furthermore, the lesson has not been learned."[8] Like I. F. Stone recently,[9] Chomsky repeatedly urges attention to the Palestinians, not only on moral but also on political grounds: Palestine, after all, is the center of his view, the point of reference. His reservations about the PLO, however, strike me as on the whole too unexamined; this is a predictable fault since he seems far more familiar with history, social reality, and political philosophy in the United States and in Israel, where, as if to prove his own point, very little is either said or known (sympathetically or otherwise) about the Palestinians. I shall return to this fault a little later.

It is possible to be legitimately uncomfortable with the tone of Chomsky's analyses. The impression he gives is that politics work according to identifiable principles, and these are rarely violated once they have been spelled out. Thus, Vietnam, Korea, and the Japanese empire in World War II are situations for him that seem to act as touchstones for U.S. policy in the contemporary Middle East. This is a correct assumption as far as it goes. Nevertheless, what if, unlike Vietnam, Korea, and Japan, the United States has interests in the Middle East that articulate themselves in different and problematic ways? I am speaking not of a difference in kind only but also a difference in degree and in kind. The peculiar strength in the United States of the Zionist lobby, the strength also of the military-industrial lobby, of the conservative Arab lobby, of the oil lobby—all these are more specialized, less representative of the broad mass support than pro- or anti-war forces during the Vietnamese, Korean, and Japanese wars. Such specialized lobbies are more inclined to hysteria and over-reaction, as well as underreaction on foreign policy questions. In addition, and most important, the Zionist lobby (perhaps because of an odd combination in classical American liberalism of pro-Semitism and anti-Semitism, a subject that is worth examining) has attracted the really volatile and unpredictable elements in the other lobbies to its side, which it has been portraying as the most rational and moral of all sides.

Only in this way can one explain the mounting campaign since Chomsky's book appeared to promote the idea of a U.S. invasion of the Arab oil-producing countries, and even—in no less a place than *Foreign Affairs*[10]—the idea of a salutary U.S. military intervention in Israel. Robert Tucker's article in the January 1975 issue of *Commentary* has been exceeded by a pseudonymous piece, full of revoltingly "expert" military details, in the March 1975 issue of *Harper's*[11]: both have elicited numerous columns, letters, editorials, mostly enthusiastic in that they have actually discussed these ideas as ideas. There have been extraordinary moral acrobatics proving that the main thing to be remembered is that the present Middle East should not be misinterpreted by liberals as another possible Vietnam.[12] But aside from Stone's piece in the *New York Review of Books,* there has been no response made against the idea of a military intervention to seize Arab oil, and certainly not from any of those lobbies traditionally associated with the Arabs in this country.

There are a number of reasons for this. One is that traditional Arab lobbies are now confused and torn between support for Arab–American business interests and Arab–Israeli–American military options (which include antagonism toward Arab–Israeli–American radicalism). Second is that there is no developed intellectual position in the United States or in the world at large which supports the Arabs as a people: I believe that the whole history of academic Western and U.S. "Orientalism," which has for so long masked itself as friendly to Islam and the Arabs, is basically to blame. As a result, Orientalist pro-Arabs (in the oil industry, in the government, in the academy, in the churches) are racists, whose interest in the Arabs is supported by a fraudulent Islamology underlying which is condescension to an unself-conscious, primitive, pastoral, and backward people. But, then again, there is no Arab countertradition of anti-Orientalism, and for this, of course, the Arabs themselves are to blame. Third, and this is extremely important, there is no real U.S. policy in the Middle East mainly because the United States is institutionally incapable of dealing with the root problem in the area, the question of Palestine and the Arab Palestinians. One must distinguish here between an Israeli refusal to deal with the Palestinian issue at all and the U.S. incapacity for dealing with nonstate groups (very much in evidence throughout the Pentagon Papers).

To say that there is no real U.S. policy in the Middle East is to say a number of things, among them that far from there being a conspiracy to eliminate the PLO, there is likely to be a much stronger impulse to recognize the PLO in order to *place* and coopt it once and for all on the final maps of the area. Such a quasipolicy can be justified on the basis of "pragmatism" (spelled out by the still-dominating conceptions of Charles D. Creamens and John Badeau[13]) and according to "eclectic" interests. Clearly, the United States today is much closer than it was before Rabat to recognizing the presence, if not the national existence, of Palestinians; pragmatic eclecticism dictates the necessity of coming to terms in some way with this presence, so long, of course, as it does not seriously threaten other presences and other interests. Therefore, the U.S. tendency will be to consider the Palestinian issue as *part* of an interstate problem, rather than one having independent status. Thus, the United States conceives the Palestinians—more accurately the PLO—primarily as a problem marginal to and divisible into an aspect of Egypt, Israel, Jordan, Syria, etc. Since the main interpretation placed on the 1973 war is that it was an irredentist war, and since the main trajectory of all peace negotiations will focus upon territorial issues, then clearly the question of Palestine will be dealt with pragmatically in the context of other territorial issues.

What policymakers in the United States will look for, then, is not the realization either of their blueprint or of Israel's, Egypt's, or Syria's. Rather, they will unimaginatively organize their efforts around a certain set of reified givens: a controlled level of conflict, manageable Soviet, Arab, and Israeli pressure on each other and on the United States, fundamental stability of economic and social structures in the area. Anything that does not touch off and skew this almost irrational mix of elements is called "peace"; anything that does is "war." The great dilemma faced by the Palestinians, less so by the other Arabs, is that, on the one hand, the PLO must keep itself "present" if it is not to disappear as a political entity, yet, on the other, by doing so it acquiesces conceptually to the U.S. view of things. For the worst thing about U.S. policy is not, as Chomsky implies, the logic of its moves but the confidence it has in being able to manage what is, after all, an impossible, irreconcilable amalgam of variables. As much as a decade ago, Creamens saw this danger quite cannily, but he resolved it by advocating a cosmetic improvement of U.S. "style"; this, he said, "is not so much a matter of discovering how to preserve what we have . . . as of understanding how to participate creatively in the processes of change, while maintaining as the overriding objective of U.S. policy the expansion of the area of freedom in the world."[14] Charitably considered, Kissinger's shuttle politics *is* the creative participation Creamens spoke of; less charitably, but more accurately, it is imperial maneuvering and tinkering, trying, for example, to pry Egypt away from the rest of the Arabs and sink it as a once-radical–national force with bits of "regained" land tied around its neck.

Chomsky is very sensitive to these possibilities, and he is properly antagonistic to them—always, as I have been saying, in a tone that insists on the situation's internal logic working itself out inevitably. I myself believe that, even though Chomsky's analyses of U.S. policy and Israel are powerful, they do not take in all, or even a major part, of what the present (as well as past) Near East situation contains. For it is more complex, hence less easy to predict, than Chomsky implies. Let us see if we can add to what he has portrayed.

Although in his analysis to reactions of the Daniel Berrigan speech during the October War,[15] Chomsky refers to positive social developments in the Arab world, his references there and elsewhere to what is taking place in the Arab world are either very allusive or of the opinion generally that Arab societies "are subject to the will of external powers and dominated by reactionary forces within."[16] That there is what seems to be a turn to the right in the Arab world is not totally inaccurate. But does this adequately characterize the Arab world as the rather large aggregate of forces, developments, and conflicts that it is? I think not. Chomsky's very detailed familiarity with Israel and the United States highlights, I think, the lack of attention he pays to the Arab world as a relatively autonomous force to be reckoned with in Middle East and international politics. There can be no doubt that with the growth of multi-nationals, the absorption of Arab oil money into Western economies, the patent dependence of the Arabs and the Israelis on foreign military aid, the Middle East is grossly affected by Great Power strategy. But this is not to say that *everything* that goes on in the Arab world is subject to, and finally understandable as "the will of external powers." Neither is it true that such phenomena as Arab nationalism or movements of Arab national liberation or independence are best understood as subordinate, belated reactions to "external powers" (i.e., the West and Western culture). There is an integral Arab experience of politics, there are integral Arab social and political and cultural developments, that proceed according to problematics that are specific to given Arab societies; these cannot, I believe, be reduced to attenuated and derivative functions of external powers. Or if they are, they have to be documented in more than the allusively assertive terms Chomsky employs. One need, for instance, only read Mahmoud Hussein's *La Lutte des classes en Egypte*[17] to get a sense of popular struggle conducted on a more complex and nuanced level than we might otherwise imagine. And such popular movements have a not inconsiderable role to play in Middle Eastern politics, independent of "external powers."

We can give a further example, a very pertinent one for the chapter of Chomsky's book entitled "Nationalism and Conflict in Palestine." His account of the binationalist idea and experience, as well as Gendzier's reflections on the same material, curiously has little to say about Arab–Palestinian activity and thought on behalf of the same idea during the Mandate. Aside from Fawzi al-Husseini, who is referred to along with Sami Taha as an Arab martyr to the cause of Arab–Jewish cooperation,[18] Chomsky's rapid survey of political developments among Arab Palestinians gives no real sense, for example, of the continuing presence, struggle, and political culture embodied in the Palestine Communist Party. A recent study by Musa Khalil gives a most impressive account of that party's history, from about 1924 to 1948.[19] Although originally a predominantly Jewish organization, by the late twenties the PCP had an Arab majority, and it was an offshoot of the PCP, the "Usbat al-Muthaqqafin al-'Arab" [League of Educated Arabs]—originally a student group dedicated to eradicating illiteracy, helping the peasant masses, activating political life in the Arab village, in the middle thirties an openly anti-fascist and anti-imperialist party—which first formulated the political slogan of a democratic, secular Palestine now adopted by the PLO. In other words, there has been in Palestine an *unbroken* Arab political structure and culture advocating a version of the binationalist ideal for which Chomsky argues. Yet not only does he seem unaware of it, he does not, cannot, connect this Arab Palestinian activity with the present PLO and PLO-inspired political activity. The continuity is there, and it counts for a great deal in Palestinian experience, which by now ought perhaps to have been accustomed to being treated in secondary terms.

There is also a generalized Arab Palestinian political consciousness as described (in a rudimentary way) by Adnan Abu-Ghazaleh in his *Arab Cultural Nationalism in Palestine,* [20] and embodied in such militants as Izzedin al-Qassam. The point to be made is that the whole question of Palestine from the Arab point of view need not be, though it frequently is, understood exclusively as a reaction to Zionism; by the same token, Arab nationalism need not be understood exclusively as a belated reaction to and unwitting repetition of Western culture. Such views of Arab politics prevailed much too confidently. We need to remember, as Ibrahim Abu-Lughod put it in a trenchant essay, that:

> the new [Arab] leaders, intellectuals or policymakers, have learned many lessons from the travail of their predecessors. They have also been aided by the structural and institutional transformations accomplished in the intervening period and by the fact that they are to a great extent more at liberty to fashion the future of their countries. They are also much more confident and perhaps slightly aggressive. No longer do they have to function hoping to obtain a favourable verdict from the invisible jury of the West. Their dialogue is not with the West, it is with their fellow citizens. [21]

For too long the province of Orientalists and so-called Arabists in Israel and the West, the problems of Arab society and culture have an independent life of their own, and, more important, a sufficient morality of their own, at least with regard to Palestine. One's fundamental disagreement with Chomsky thus extends beyond his neglect of the independent life within Arab society to his unwillingness in conceding that Arab Palestinians *as a people* had an unprecedented unilateral wrong done them by State-Zionism. Whatever the "right" we may concede to the persecuted European Jews, we must not forget as Palestinians that "except for the extermination of the Tasmanians modern history recognizes no cases in which the virtually complete supplanting of the indigenous population of a country by an alien stock has been achieved in as little as two generations." [22] Thus, what separates Chomsky from Israel Shahak, both of whom condemn terrorism and some PLO policies, is that the latter makes it absolutely clear that there is a moral distinction to be emphasized between Palestinian violence and Israeli state terrorism. [23]

But having said that, as Arabs we must concede that it would be very difficult for us as a group to match the individual courage and vision of men like Chomsky and Shahak. Their involvement in the questions they treat is primarily moral and intellectual; neither earns anything more than vituperation and solitude for what they say. They are men whose humanity is armed with learning, with an indefatigable energy for seeking out uncomfortable truths and little-known (because deliberately buried) facts. *Peace in the Middle East?* is an encyclopedia of such information, all of it testimony to Chomsky's prodigious efforts, independent, unassisted, extraordinarily informed. If we remember—and this is crucial—that what he writes about mainly in this book are Israel and the United States, even allowing that he neglects unduly the Arab side of things, we must note that he deals with societies and cultures that are his own and deals with them critically, harshly, truthfully.

We cannot as Arabs say the same for ourselves. No matter how many extenuating circumstances we plead (colonialism, imperialism, and the cultural backwardness attendant upon both), we cannot justify the near total absence of such self-criticism among us. Of course, there are exceptions to what I have been saying, but these prove the orthodoxy of Arab self-vision. What underlines this orthodoxy is not the too-ready excuse that all communal self-visions are orthodox but rather the claim that we are a beleaguered Third World community, victimized by the West, beset by endemic problems of underdevelopment and poverty. In other words, our claim to be a society in the throes of revolution ironically reveals the inadequacy of our efforts to live up to that revolution. Except among a handful of writers, philosophers, left-wing activists, the cause to which as a people we have sacrificed our blood and treasure has not earned a comparable revolutionary vision. In the world we represent ourselves *justifyingly*; we have not developed, as I said above, a coherent intellectual position because that position would require real criticism, real innovation, real effort of the sort we have neither yet created nor expended. Arab money, vast and recently acquired, finds its way unremittingly into Fifth Avenue real estate, British and Swiss banks, conspicuous consumption of appalling vulgarity and short life. So far as I know no comparable Arab plans for building a great library, or endowing scientific or cultural research on an inter-Arab basis or consolidating institutional development, or willing the wholesale eradication of poverty, social and civic injustice, disease and illiteracy, have been announced. We are threatened with the very extinction as a people that all our struggles and money have been employed to avert.

The great challenge of Chomsky's book for an Arab reader is not simply the discovery of a friend among the admirable Jewish intellectual community. Rather, Chomsky's challenge is to force us, as a people and as individual intellectuals, to answer the threat of our continued domination by others in terms that we must articulate and then stand by. His problematic rests upon a desire to understand freedom and knowledge within human and social restraints, or, rather, freedom and knowledge as facts not of uninformed (or pseudo-informed) domination but as facts of fraternal cooperation. Not enough is said by Chomsky's critics of his sense of limits, which is to me salutarily developed and rationally defended in all of his political and linguistic writing. Ideologically, this means that no answers are to be found either in unrestrained assertion of absolutes or in wanton ignorance of particular and *other* human experience. Freedom and knowledge in Middle East politics ought to draw forth partisanship, of course, but more than that they require sustained effort of a sort that does not flinch from examining history, short-term realities, long-term prospects. Chomsky himself is a special case—I paraphrase crudely from the opening of Theodore Draper's hectoring account of *Peace in the Middle East?*—with whom we must reckon; it seems to me that the framework he proposes for discussion (if not all the conclusions to which this leads him) is eminently suited to engage our intellectual and moral energies.

Probably the greatest obstacle Chomsky presents to immediate engagement is his capacity for seeing the state not as a necessity but as a hindrance to social and political justice. It is this opinion, I think, that puts him in opposition to ideas circulating now about a Palestinian state; this and, of course, the source of these ideas, which he correctly ascribes for the most part to ruling elites and their interests (and not the Palestinian people necessarily) in the Middle East and the United States. He is more explicit about this antagonism of his than he is about another one, which does not really get articulated in his book, although much of what he says implicitly suggests it. That is the antagonism toward war in the Middle East. If the best solution to the question of Palestine is a set of decentralized communal structures, loosely federated into a larger but not repressive main one, it would seem to follow that war between nation-states in the present Middle East enhances imperialism rather than the popular lot and the optimal solution Chomsky espouses.

What of the Palestinians? Is their present course wholly without merit in Chomsky's eyes? Here he is suitably qualified both in his approbation and disapprobation. I myself regret the distance (and even disparagement) with which he treats the PLO (but not all of its components) as much as I regret the absence among Palestinian activists of awareness for Chomsky's ideas. But, at least, there is a good deal in common between both corners, a community with much to suggest to the future. The main question, however, persists: What violence, what arms, what force are we to advocate, employ, or discover if the best goals for the area are to be realized? That we feel the urgency of the question after reading Chomsky, the more works like this are of the utmost moment. And the more are our best faculties, as Arabs and Jews for whom the question of Palestine is no mere game of nations, exercised and committed.

Published in the *Journal of Palestine Studies* 4, no. 3 (Spring 1975).

CHAPTER 32

Reticences of an Orientalist

[1986]

Bernard Lewis is a British Orientalist now living in the United States where he has become a prolific neoconservative Cold War polemicist whose hostile attention is focused on the Arabs and Islam. He has now patched together a disorganized and tendentious book out of articles that have appeared elsewhere (in *Commentary* among other places).[24] The first half of *Semites and Anti-Semites* is a potted history of anti-Semitism that advances very little beyond what can be found in the work of Leon Poliakov. That is frequently Lewis's way, since it enables him to set the stage with a great show of scholarship before he gets to his main ideological business. In this instance it is to advance the view that the Arabs and Muslims have now become anti-Semites in the European sense of that term, a charge from which he somewhat exempts them before the nineteenth century.

The extraordinary thing about this effort is how little evidence Lewis's allegations actually dredge up. Readers of his contribution to a recent symposium on "terrorism" will recall his habit of saying both that Islam cannot be said to produce terrorism, and yet that it does, all the while letting popular media clichés about the association between "Islam" and terrorism do the work of incriminating an entire culture and religion for him. A similar procedure is followed in *Semites and Anti-Semites,* with equally problematic (to say the least) results. Thus in one place he will speak of a "sudden outburst of anti-Semitic literature," a phrase suggesting mountains of books and tracts, but which on closer inspection yields only two titles, one published in Beirut in 1869 and another in Cairo in 1893. The cause of this "outburst," we are told, was the Dreyfus case, which since it didn't occur until 1894, one supposes it to have infected the Arab world retroactively. A random quotation from an Egyptian newspaper, a reference to the presence of the *Protocols of the Elders of Zion* in Arabic, an account of the contents of a magazine in 1964—these supposedly establish the existence of anti-Semitism in the Arab world, although no distinctions are made between instances, trends, beliefs, and policies; usually, however, Lewis is omniscient in ascribing anti-Semitism to the people and culture themselves. This is the Orientalist practice of knowing only by reading in snippets, of generalizing imperiously without sympathetic or living knowledge of the condemned society and its culture.

In other places Lewis refers to Arab tirades that link Menachem Begin to Jenghiz Khan and Hitler (the latter purportedly "a much admired hero"), but he will not give more than an item of evidence "proving" that Hitler was admired by some people, and he obscures the fact that it was a few anti-British Arab leaders who negotiated with the Nazis in their war against British colonialism. He also forgets to mention that the present Prime Minister of Israel, Mr. Shamir, and his party also negotiated with the Nazis. Moreover, Lewis prudently overlooks the fact that Labour and Revisionist Israeli governments made common cause during the 1970s and 1980s with the Lebanese Phalanges, an openly fascist, anti-Semitic Christian party. Lewis seems to rely completely for his information about Arab anti-Semitism on a handful of Zionist propagandists, though he is scandalously misinformed about recent Israeli historical research (by Tom Segev and Benni Morris, among others) that incriminates the Israelis for the systematic military expulsion and dispossession of the Palestinians in 1948–49.

That there is anti-Semitism in the Arab world and elsewhere is a fact: a sorry, appallingly ugly, and inexcusable fact, but a fact just the same, although Lewis is too shoddy a historian ever to do more than allude and insinuate, letting his audience deduce the worst about Islam and the Arabs. All facts, however, are located in contexts, and it is the two contexts of Lewis's facts that are carefully left out. One context is America after the 1982 Israeli invasion of Lebanon, when it was felt by the Zionist lobby that the spectacle of ruthless Israeli power on the TV screen would have to be effaced from memory by the strategy of incriminating the media as anti-Semitic for showing those scenes at all. Since then the reconstitution of a primitive ideology eliminating both the siege of Beirut and the Palestinians from history (as in Joan Peters' book, *From Time Immemorial,* which thanks Lewis for his help) has gone forward. This ideology has put up a figurative fence around Israel, decreeing that any criticism of the state is tantamount to old-style Nazi anti-Semitism. Lewis has played that reprehensible trick for all it is worth, with results in this book for the uninformed or the unaware (George Kennan, for one) that are intended to be alarming. That, for example, Israel speaks of itself as the state of the entire Jewish people, its Palestinian citizens merely as "non-Jews," is not considered to enter into either the semantics or the epistemology of Lewis's disgracefully incomplete argument. That these facts might also be more pertinent to an Arab Palestinian population either exiled or colonized by Israel than "anything which might arouse sympathy for the Jews"—a sorely wanting quality among Palestinians and their supporters, according to Lewis—does not occur to him, as he ambles on with his nasty little newspaper references, shorn of any substance, any social reference, any sense of history or institutions.

This is natural enough in the work of a journalist who has made a recent name for himself as a political enemy of the Arabs and Islam. It is worse in the work of an historian who simply suppresses the second context of his work—that is, the full contemporary history of the Middle East. Who could deny that there is atavism in the Islamic revival, or that the Arab regimes are a corrupt, incompetent lot, able neither to wage war courageously and unhypocritically, nor to conclude a peace with Israel decently? But do these facts allow us simply never to mention the fantastic outpouring of official religious and political literature in Israel whose proclaimed attitude toward the *goyim* is startlingly racist, horrifically exclusivist? What about the library of Israeli works on the Arab mentality, on the laziness of the Arab character, the degradation of Islam, etc.? Why do Israeli consulates around the world hand out John Laffin's disgustingly racist *The Arab Mind*? What about the tradition of anti-gentile polemic in historical Judaism? Does not this warrant so much as a disapproving sneer, and is it not part of the anti-Semitism that Lewis pretends to deplore? What are we to make of rabbinic pronouncements to the Israeli army, legislating that whereas it is humane to help a wounded Jew on the Sabbath, it is correct to let a wounded gentile die? As for Gush Emunim, Rabbi Kahane, the Jewish underground and company, all of whom have in one way or another been abetted not only by Zionist supporters in the West, but by Israeli governments as well—Lewis is too delicate to do more than allude quickly to them. One could go on about Lewis's tactful omissions, from the wholesale dispossession of the "non-Jews," to the minute details of apartheid on the West Bank, to the rampant fanaticism of supporters of Yuval Neeman, Sharon, Eytan, etc., all of it coming from the essentially racialist difference between Jew and non-Jew. Somehow Lewis exempts all of this from consideration, preferring instead to let himself linger over the one sin he considers worthy of mention—the anti-Semitism of newspaper quotations and few books.

There are interesting issues here, which Lewis's book is too intellectually feeble, too drenched in pious cant, to debate. For example, is anti-Semitism best understood apart from, say, the oppression and slavery of blacks, the genocidal massacres of Armenians by the Turks, the extermination of the Native American peoples by numerous European populations? Is anti-Semitism, as Lewis implies, a metaphysical thing, or is it one among many historical trends? How has the Palestinian case altered the status of the Jews, from that of victims to that of oppressor? What about the Western philo-Semitism that supports Israel so munificently? And is there some important way in which the terrible sufferings of the Jews can no longer serve to exempt them from opprobrium when in the name of the Jewish people Israeli armies or jet bombers ravage refugee camps, raze Palestinian villages, impose wholesale collective punishments on Arab towns, bomb Arab cities, massacre civilians, even as Israel's propagandists in the West proclaim the state's "purity of arms," the sanctity of its moral politics, its right to preemptive strikes that produce dozens of Arab deaths for every Jewish death? You would never know from Lewis's prose that the Jewish state and not "international anti-Semitism" militarily dominates the Middle East, and that it is Palestinians, and not Jews, who today are marked with special identity cards, license plates, and "pales of settlement."

These are matters worthy of attention, difficult though that may be in so inflamed a situation as that obtaining between Israel and the Arab world. But no, none of it is tackled by Bernard Lewis, whose posture of historical gravity is restricted to the canonical topics of anti-Jewish extremism and the proclivity of Islam to infection by the worst Western imports. What *Semites and Anti-Semites* adds up to is not so much history as sleazy propaganda in the age of Reagan and Begin.

Published in *The Guardian,* November 21, 1986.

CHAPTER 33

Identity, Negation and Violence

[1988]

[I]

As something to be talked and written about, as a phenomenon with nearly hysterical descriptions and pronouncements routinely added to its name as a mobilizing theme for politicians, armies, navies, and air forces, "terrorism" has now temporarily lost a good deal of its power. Only a few months ago, thousands of Americans canceled trips to Europe because they feared the terrorist threat; in April 1986 the United States raided Libya during the prime time evening TV news in order, it was said, to deal with the terrorist threat posed by Libya (on a pretext—the bombing of a West Berlin disco—which has since proved *not* to have been Libya's doing). All during the period from 1983 through 1985 and 1986, "terrorism" claimed public attention on a scale hitherto unknown. Numerous governments at the behest of the United States and the dutiful, unreflecting amplification of its media, made pronouncements about, and any number of moves against, terrorism, so much so that during this period the secretary of state elevated terrorism to the status of "number one" foreign policy problem for the United States and, he went on to suggest imprudently, for the world.

As a result, even though attention to terrorism has quite noticeably diminished now, the word still comes easily, trippingly to the tongue. Now it would be disingenuous at this point for me *not* to connect terrorism as a word and concept with perhaps one reason for my examining the subject in these reflections. The reason, of course, is that terrorism in the United States mainly, but also generally speaking in the West, is by now permanently, almost subliminally, associated in the first instance with Islam, a notion no less overused and vague than terrorism itself. In the minds of the unprepared or the unalert, Islam calls up images of bearded clerics and mad suicidal bombers, of unrelenting Iranian mullahs, fanatical fundamentalists, and kidnappers, remorseless turbaned crowds who chant hatred of the United States, "the great Satan," and all its ways. And behind the wave of "Islamic" images battering the United States' unprotected shores stand the string of Palestinian terrorists—hijackers and masked killers of airport crowds, athletes, schoolchildren, handicapped and elderly innocents—who in the unexamined popular mythology of our day are presumed to have begun the whole shameful and frightful thing. Since I am known as having associations both ethnic and national with Palestine and with Islam, I am therefore presentable before audiences as someone who, when it comes to terrorism, really knows (in the insidious sense of the word) what he's talking about.

I will not waste the reader's time by saying any more about this deplorable concatenation of assumptions than quickly to allude to that combination of discomfort and resentment which has remained with me ever since I began to take on the subject. Nevertheless, it has seemed to be also true that despite the tremendous damage caused by "terrorism" itself and representations or reactions to it, there are some reflections that can be made about both, reflections made possible by the abatement in organized public hysteria I spoke of a moment ago. Precisely that abatement will, I think, enable us to reconnect representations of "terrorism" to contexts, structures, histories, and narratives from which during the word's period of greatest prominence its representations appeared to be severed.

For the one thing about "terrorism" as a phenomenon of the public sphere of communication and representation in the West that seems most striking is its isolation from any explanation or mitigating circumstances, and its isolation as well from representations of most other dysfunctions, symptoms, and maladies of the contemporary world. Indeed, in many discussions of terrorism, there is often a ritual of dismissing as irrelevant, softheaded, or in other ways suspicious, anything that might explain the actions of terrorism: "Let's not hear anything about root causes," runs the righteous litany, "or deprivation, or poverty and political frustration, since all terrorists can be explained away if one has a mind to do it. What *we* should be after is an understanding of terrorism that helps us defeat it, not an explanation that might make us feel sorry for the terrorist.'' Thus terrorism was stripped of any right to be considered as other historical and social phenomena are considered, as something created by human beings in the world of human history. Instead, the isolation of terrorism from history and from other things in Vico's world of the nations has had the effect of magnifying its ravages, even as terrorism itself was shrunk from the public world into a small private world reserved tautologically for the terrorists who commit terrorism, and for the experts who study them.

No less strange was the common agreement among experts on terrorism in their literature and rhetoric, that no real definition of terrorism was actually possible. It is true, of course, that writers like Claire Sterling and Benjamin Netanyahu felt no compunction about defining terrorism as whatever seemed inimical to the West, Israel, the Judeo-Christian tradition and goodness, but it would be wrong and misleading to accuse all writers on terrorism of such robust self-confidence. Many are like Walter Laqueur, who is among the most respectable academic specialists on the subject and began his work on it well before the recent vogue. Laqueur frankly admits that ''no definition of terrorism can possibly cover all the varieties of terrorism that have appeared throughout history: Peasant wars and labor disputes and brigandage have been accompanied by systematic terror, and the same is true with regard to general wars, wars of national liberation and resistance movements against foreign occupiers.''[25] Later he tries somehow to rescue his topic from this welter of ubiquity, valiantly suggesting that even though terrorism resists definition it can be discussed in the context of movements that have used ''systematic terrorism as their main weapon.''[26] But when he asserts that that practice begins in the second half of the nineteenth century,[27] we will, I think, have lost faith not only in his philosophical acuity for trying to describe something that he says cannot adequately be described, but also in his historical sense for studiously ignoring the much-proclaimed revolutionary Terror of France a full seventy-five years earlier.

It is less on Laqueur's own failings than on terrorism as an apparently isolated but identifiable disturbance that I wish to concentrate. In fact the appearance of isolation given to terrorism has almost always been misleading. For terrorism has regularly appeared in contemporary conjunction with, among other stigmatized groups, Islam, Palestinians, Iran, and Shiism, that is, objects, concepts, peoples, and cultures poorly and antithetically known, and therefore more liable to technical, metaphysical, and ultimately ideological constructions. There is first the powerful aura of the exotic, and even the literary, that surrounds terrorism. Its literary roots are Eastern, and if one thinks of Dostoyevski's *Possessed* or Joseph Conrad's *The Secret Agent,* the Assassins and Thuggees, there is in addition the *louche,* the gratuitous, the senselessly cruel that adheres to it. Moreover, the terror of terrorism appears indiscriminate and generalized; no one is safe from it, none insulated, none immune. Facts and figures are not easy to get hold of, although the hint of vast numbers of casualties is always there, from the random explosive let off in a marketplace to the much-vaunted nuclear device that just might kill uncounted thousands. Rarely does one hear the tonic reminders of the disparity in violence between individual terrorists and conventional armies, given by Gillo Pontecorvo to Larbi Ben M'Hidi in *The Battle of Algiers,* "Give us your bombs and you can have our women's baskets."

These techniques of decontextualization and dehistoricization are not new and have occurred elsewhere in colonial or postcolonial situations. Irish resistance to British rule, for instance, was routinely classed as terrorist by British writers, who then built on the classification a theory of retributive response that quite ignored historical specificity, proportion, or concrete analysis. Thus Robert Louis Stevenson in 1888 writes in "Confessions of a Unionist" that so unsuccessful had British policy been in Ireland ("Through sentimentality, through the craven vagaries of a popular assembly, we have suffered the law to tumble in the muck") that "Irish lawlessness" had triumphed, along with the "Irish appeal to violence." In consequence, he advocates no change in British colonial abuses "until the whole machinery of terrorism is destroyed," and this by a wholesale brutality meted out by "vigilance committee." Any other policy would be succumbing to "maudlin sentimentality." Curiously enough, Stevenson's editor in 1888, Jeremy Treglown, does not flinch from Stevenson's "call for an end to terrorism in Ireland," only from his inability to say "how the extirpation of violence is to be brought about in practice." Thus does the inebriatively self-justifying revulsion provoked by the word leap across the years with little regard for context or power. Similar rhetorical flights were routinely in evidence when Cypriot or Mau Mau "terrorists" were discussed during the postwar years.

But the issue that chiefly concerns me here is terrorism as it engages public awareness of the Middle East and of the Arab-Islamic world in particular. The uniqueness of this region and its people to discussions of terrorism is, I believe, quite special. To my knowledge, of no other country, no religion, culture, or ethnic group except Islam and its societies has it been said that terrorism is, after a fashion, endemic. This is argued by several of the Orientalists who contribute to perhaps the most visible and influential of the popular antiterrorist manuals, the collection edited by Benjamin Netanyahu, *Terrorism: How the West Can Win*. By the nature of the argument, evidence is problematic, but it is bandied about anyway, with curious results. All sorts of strange objects appear—for example, the Islamic mind, ancient feuds, remarkable but unnameable proclivities to wanton violence—all of them attesting to essential traits that supposedly have been there eternally and are susceptible neither to historical change nor to any sort of amelioration.

Since "terrorism" is undefinable and entirely negative, these arguments for the connection between it, Islam, and/or Palestinians have rarely been opposed. The point is that there is hardly any way, there are few enunciative opportunities, to oppose such arguments about terrorism without also seeming to be *for it*. Unanimity is intimidating, particularly on this scale, but during a full-scale terrorist alert—for example, during the 1986 bombing of Libya or the 1985 TWA hijacking—you could not deny the Islamic ingredient, you could not present supervening arguments, you could not prevent the guilty associations from spreading, without also appearing in some way to explain, hence condone, the outrage. The framework was entirely hostile to anyone who did not accept the perfect equivalence between the State which seemed to be attacked, and injured innocence; indeed, very little inhibits the framework from expanding to include, on the part of the United States, the Western heritage, morality, and outraged virtue.

Perhaps the most sensible intervention in the verbal dust storm induced by terrorism has been Eqbal Ahmad's, which appeared in the May–June 1986 issue of MERIP Reports. Ahmad's premise is that terrorism—"acts of intimidating and injuring unarmed, presumably innocent civilians," acts for which there are five sources, "state, religion, protest/revolution, crime, and pathology," of which "only the first three have political motivation"—does exist and is a source of genuine concern, but needs analysis and discrimination if we wish to do "justice to its victims, or to understanding" on both sides of "the ideological boundary." Ahmad offers a set of half a dozen guidelines for analysis. These are: Terrorism is connected to "the need to be heard,'' since it ''is a violent way of expressing long-felt, collective grievances. When legal and political means fail over a long period, a minority of the aggrieved community elicits the sympathy of the majority with violent acts.'' Moreover, Ahmad continues, ''Anger and helplessness produce compulsions towards retributive violence,'' a factor that explains not only the violence of the helpless, but also of the powerful: ''I have pounded a few walls myself when I am alone,'' said President Reagan in 1985. Then we should acknowledge the sad truth that ''the experience of violence at the hands of a stronger party has historically turned victims into terrorists.'' Similarly, ''when identifiable targets become available, violence is externalised,'' that is, people pass from the stage of pounding walls to shooting what stands before them.

Ahmad's last two points are the most complex, and have to do with a subtle interplay between the technology of weapons and of the media on the one hand, and political ideology on the other. Examples of massive and senseless violence enable the spread of terrorism. Thus the Indochinese war, history's most visible superpower intervention, conducted at a high level of organization, effectiveness, and cruelty, showed the way governments can plan violence against civilian populations; the emulations of this violence by poorly organized and goalless small groups are also attempts to imitate the legitimization asserted by states who use violence to gain dubious and unclear ends. Finally Ahmad suggests that the more detailed, territorially grounded, and concrete the ideological goal as set forth by insurgent and revolutionary groups (e.g., the Vietnamese, Algerian, Cuban, Angolan, and Nicaraguan uprisings), the less likely the possibility of spectacular and intimidating violence.

> Revolutionary violence tends to be sociologically and psychologically selective. It strikes at widely perceived symbols of oppression—landlords, rapacious officials, repressive armies. It aims at widening the revolutionaries' popular support by freeing their potential constituencies from the constraints of oppressive power.

To dispersed or homeless peoples the appeal of terror is the ease and instantaneity of transportation, whose symbols are the airplane and airport, of coercion, whose instrument is the small lethal hand weapon, and of communication, whose mode is the electronic media, which offer an immediate means of directing a message. Thus have the invisible and terror-filled wars waged by states been challenged by the frightening visibility of unpredictable acts of violence by small bands of adventurers.

What further distinguishes Ahmad's contribution to the enormous literature, the widely diffused imagery, the much marketed expertise on terrorism is something left implicit in his remarks, the role of the interested observer. He writes from the perspective of a militant whose support of anti-imperialist struggles has not, however, stilled his *critical* sense. Without exception much of the current discussion and representation of terrorism simply *assumes* the disinterestedness, detachment, and objectivity of the author. Yet it is a truism of contemporary interpretive theory that no such position can or ever did exist. Thus, to take as an example a social discourse premised on the construction of an observer who articulates the discourse, *anthropology* presumes to offer scientific material about "Others" afforded to ethnographic experts, whose power to observe, live among, participate in the lives of foreign societies is premised on *their* capacity to travel abroad, do anthropology, etc. Similarly, with few exceptions the discourse of terrorism is constituted by an author whose main client is the government of a powerful state officially opposed to terrorism but anxious to shield itself from arguments about and perceptions of its own (quite routinely barbaric and violent) behavior. Why this is so should be obvious, since the disproportion between state violence and (so to speak) private violence is, and always has been, vast.

Nowhere is this paradigmatic rhetorical combination of client appeal and blockage more clear than in the work of political scientists in Israel and the United States, states whose recent foreign policy has been staked on the fight against terrorism, a political decision arrived at consciously and therefore ideologically as a method for dealing with resistance to United States–Israeli power; in addition this decision made it possible for the government-sponsored outpouring against terrorism either to screen or to legitimize the governmental violence of both countries.

Consider Israel, which in many ways has pioneered the notion that democracies, because they are democracies, are especially liable to gratuitious terrorism. According to the respected Israeli journalist Amnon Kapeliouk, writing in *Le Monde Diplomatique* in February 1986, Israeli policymakers began in the mid-1970s the discipline of describing everything done by Palestinians to combat Israeli military occupation as terrorism; the decision coincided with the growing international prestige and legitimacy of the Palestinian national movement. In this decision, of course, Israel was following the path taken by other regimes of colonial occupation (the French in Algeria, the Americans in Vietnam, the South African government in its description of the ANC and its resistance). By the summer of 1982, this campaign of indiscriminate disinformation led to some of the tactics of Operation Peace for Galilee, where what was a massive war against a sovereign country and a national liberation movement could be described as a campaign against terrorism. The distinction of the Israeli informational manipulation of the word *terrorism* was that it was done more or less in conjunction with the most powerful media apparatus available, since no other sub-imperial power in history could avail itself of so formidable an imperial system as the American. The result has been that more or less anything that disturbed the peace and was ostensibly done by someone of whom Western civilization is thought to disapprove was called a terrorist outrage.

Until the television screen was suddenly filled with images of Israel's siege and devastation of Beirut and South Lebanon during the summer of 1982, "terrorism" was supposed by most journalists and audiences to be an almost Platonic essence inherent in all Palestinians and Muslims, without historical, social, or political circumstances or conditions to provoke it. Even more important, however, the discourse of "terrorism," counterterrorism, terrorist expertise obliterated all the historical processes that might conceivably have produced so many terrorists and so many acts of terror. In the case of Israel, the Palestinian argument had posited for itself the existence of a society and of a people, of a nation, in short, whose continuity had been shattered in 1948, and whose subsequent travail was, in the main instance, the result of a continuous war against the Palestinian people by Israel which to the Palestinians proclaimed itself to be conducting a war that made no distinctions between civilians or armed combatants, between refugee camps, hospitals, schools, orphanages, and what the Israeli military command regularly referred to as terrorist nests. Readers will appreciate that I speak here as an engaged Palestinian and not as a political scientist, and they will, I trust, grant me the right to say that despite the wall-to-wall coverage of the Palestinian struggle as an extended terrorist assault upon Israel, the record is a dreadful one, in the loss of thousands of Palestinian lives, of homes destroyed, of literally uncountable human catastrophes suffered by this nation of "Palestinian terrorists." I do not need to say here how the recent mass insurrections and sacrifices of unarmed Palestinians in Gaza and the West Bank testify dramatically to an entire history of iron-fisted, antiterrorist Israeli policy of repression, on the one hand, and to the vacant political message, equally antiterrorist, delivered to them by the Israeli government which has acknowledged only a conflict between terrorism and democracy, on the other.

Gradually the *intifadah,* or uprising, in the Occupied Territories has increased in intensity, has further laughed away the notion that Palestinian resistance equals terrorism, has irreversibly transformed the shadowy status of Palestinian nationalism into proto-statehood, and Israeli policy into a dying colonialism. But what to Palestinians has been revealed by the *intifadah* is the true political mass basis for all national liberation movements, in which neither the uninstructed gun alone nor the random (if understandable) outrage, has anything like the moral and mobilizable force of coordinated, intelligent, courageous human action. When one of the uprising's leaders in Gaza was asked by a journalist how unarmed children, men, and women defied Israeli troops so routinely, the answer testified elegantly to how a popular movement had in fact banished terror. "Fear," he said, "has been forbidden." And that was that.

But I also want to say that in the specific case of "talking terrorism" in the Middle East, crucial distinctions have characteristically been elided. There *has been* terrorism, there has been cruel, insensate, shameful violence, yes, but who today can stand before us and say that violence is all, or even mainly, on the side of the labeled "terrorists," and virtue on the side of civilized states who in many ways do tend in fact to represent decency, democracy, and a modicum of "the good"? I must therefore confess that I find the entire arsenal of words and phrases that derive from the concept of terrorism both inadequate and shameful. There are few ways of talking about terrorism now that are not corrupted by the propaganda war even of the past decade, ways that have become, in my opinion, disqualified as instruments for conducting rational, secular inquiry into the causes of human violence. Is there some other way of apprehending what might additionally be involved when we now unthinkingly use the word *terrorism*? Is there a style of thought and language that pretends neither to get past the word's embroiled semantic history, nor to restore it, cleansed and sparkling new, for further polemical use?

[I I]

Throwing up unfamiliar, or at least newer settings in which to set the unpleasant tingling induced by the word *terrorism* is a worthwhile alternative to simply attacking habitual uses of the word. The very totalism, the radical and impermeable oppositions that set off the word from its use by the enemies of terrorism, furnish a beginning. We normally encounter the word not when used by terrorists to describe what they do, but rather to identify and fix a particularly pernicious assault upon humanity, like Conrad's throwing "a bomb into pure mathematics" in *The Secret Agent*. But things are rarely left to indirection and suggestion. Contemporary "terrorism" is thereafter identified with terrorists, who, as I have been saying, are most often "our" enemies, and are Muslim, Palestinian, etc. Similarly, "we" are the West, moral, collectively incapable of such inhuman behavior, etc.

Even when the analyst of terrorism tries to take a "middle path," the compacting of identities proceeds apace. I have in mind the rather ambitious book by Beau Grosscup entitled *The Explosion of Terrorism*, in which the author tries quite intelligently to separate out the ideological hype and flat-out exaggeration that mars most of the writing on the subject. His approach is what he calls a middle way between polemic and apologetic, and is historical and situational, but he too is obliged to incorporate cultures, peoples, traditions, and regions of the world, with more or less complete congruence, to the practice, if not the essence, of terrorism. To some degree this is an exigency of writing and exposition—how, for instance, can you talk about people who describe themselves as Iranian fighters without somehow associating Iran as a whole with their style of fighting?—but to some degree also the difficulty stems from the modern habit of connecting people with their identities as members of a national group.

So deeply ingrained is the tendency to funnel society into the mold prepared for it by the nation-state that we cannot conceive of societies except as thoroughly congruent with the state, as if the teleology of all social entities were the state. To some extent, of course, this is an understandable tendency for thought in an age so dominated by nationalism, the nation-state, and various statist ideologies. Any reader of the vast literature on modern nationalism, especially some of its better works like Hugh Seton-Watson's *Nations and States* or Benedict Anderson's *Imagined Communities,* will testify to the compelling logic of statism, and to the manifest difficulty of escaping its premises, or of thinking outside its limits. This is one among many reasons for admiring the efforts made by Pierre Clastres in *Society Against the State* to criticize the biases that have infiltrated most of our thinking about society, but he is a singular exception to the rule pervading most political discourse.

Terrorism, in short, must be directly connected to the very processes of identity in modern society, from nationalism, to statism, to cultural and ethnic affirmation, to the whole array of political, rhetorical, educational, and governmental devices that go into consolidating one or another identity. Either one belongs to one group or to another, one is either in or out, one acts principally in support of a triumphalist identity or to protect an endangered one. Very often "terrorists" end up by reproducing the very structures that have "alienated" them (e.g., Sendero Luminoso or the Abu Nidal group). The interplay of identity and alienation is therefore total, and it can be observed in a brilliant epitomization in one of the daring mytho-poetical archeologies offered by Vico in an early section of *The New Science*. Vico speaks here of the origins of authority in "the world of the nations," and is trying to explain the prevalence everywhere of matrimony and religion as the two fundamental components of the modern state. The passage deserves quotation in full because Vico quite amazingly and presciently stakes social order and identity upon the confinement of disorderly energies by the fearful terror of Jove's power:

> Authority was at first divine; the authority by which divinity appropriated itself the few giants [these are Vico's first human beings] we have spoken of, by properly casting them into the depths and recesses of the caves under the mountains. This is the iron ring by which the giants, dispersed upon the mountains, were kept chained to the earth by fear of the sky and of Jove, wherever they happened to be when the sky first thundered. Such were Tityus and Prometheus, chained to a high rock with their hearts being devoured by an eagle; that is by the religion of Jove's auspices. Their being rendered immobile by fear was expressed by the Latins in the heroic phrase *terrore defixi,* and the artists depict them chained hand and foot with such links upon the mountains. Of these links was formed the great chain of which . . . Jove, to prove that he is king of men and gods, asserts that if all the gods and men were to take hold of one end, he alone would be able to drag them all. . . . Hence it was that the giants gave up the

bestial custom of wandering through the great forest of the earth and habituated themselves to the quite contrary custom of remaining settled and hidden for a long period in their caves.[28]

Vico is trying first to describe the birth of divine authority, then in the section about the giants' settling down, of human authority. According to the Sophists, he says, this is the way the world is "girdled and bound." Tityus and Prometheus seem to be models for heroic individuals who have gone too far in living beyond the strictures laid down by Jove; therefore they must be visibly punished and permanently fixed in place, their hearts eaten out. Most other human beings, however, are prepared to accept the places offered them as domestic beings—hence matrimony and religion—by Jove. These early peoples come to inhabit caves, and later houses, but the important thing is that they cease wandering around. Jove's terror is used to tame human terror, to fix it in social and subsequently in national pigeonholes, although Vico does not minimize either the heroic or the transgressive terror of Jove, whose imposing gifts for authority and punishment in Vico's view directly antedate the modern state's monopoly on coercion.

Thus terror emanates from any attempt to live beyond the social confinements of identity itself, and terror is also the means used to quell the primal disorderliness of the unconfined human being. This latter idea is carried over after Vico by social theorists whose vision of the modern social or state order is like his, that authority is based principally upon the organization of coercive power, and neither upon national consent nor upon a benignly ordained and preexistent harmony. Thus, for example, Georges Sorel's notion of the general strike as a violent disruption of an unreasonable social nexus stems from such a supposition. Frantz Fanon's whole theory of colonial counterviolence (which contains in it some of the transgressive heroism that Vico assigns to the vanquished titans) answers to the rationalized violence of the colonial order, with its separation of the colonial from the native city, its attempts to include the native as a subordinate example of universalized "Graeco-Roman" values, its swiftly retributive inclination when it is challenged or otherwise inhibited by its subaltern victims. Finally, there is Michel Foucault's description of the order, discipline, discourse of society, gathering into itself the numerous specialized technologies for controlling, surveying, and manipulating knowledge and its producers, subject only occasionally to the heterogeneous, quixotic, venturesome counterviolence of the outcast, the visionary, the prophet.

In the contemporary contest between stable identity as it is rendered by such affirmative agencies as nationality, education, tradition, language, and religion, on the one hand, and all sorts of marginal, alienated, or, in Immanuel Wallerstein's phrase, antisystemic forces on the other, there remains an incipient and unresolved tension. One side gathers more dominance and centrality, the other is pushed further from the center, toward either violence or new forms of "authenticity" like fundamentalist religion. In any event, the tension produces a frightening consolidation of patriotism, assertions of cultural superiority, mechanisms of control, whose power and ineluctability reinforce what I have been describing as the logic of identity. What I have been articulating is somewhat abstract, almost metaphysical; let me then be more immediately concrete.

I want to look at two instances in which the power of what Adorno, in an English phrase coined for him by Martin Jay, has called "identitarian thought" is deepened. These are, first, media practice, and, second, recent debates on education. Of the way in which immediate experience is emasculated by "the consciousness industry," Adorno says:

> The total obliteration of the war by information, propaganda, commentaries, with cameramen in the first tanks and war reporters dying heroic deaths, the mishmash of an enlightened manipulation of public opinion and oblivious activity: all this is another expression for the withering of experience, the vacuum between men and their fate, in which their real fate lies. It is as if the reified, hardened plastercast of events takes the place of events themselves. Men are reduced to walk-on parts in a monster documentary film. . . .[29]

It would be irresponsible to dismiss the effects of domestic electronic media coverage of the non-Western world—and with them the displacements that have occurred within print culture—on American attitudes and foreign policy toward that world. I have elsewhere argued the case (which is more true today than when I first made it over ten years ago) that limited public access to the media coupled with an almost perfect correspondence between the ideology ruling the presentation and selection of news (whose agenda is set by certified experts hand in hand with media corporate managers) on the one hand,

and prevailing government policy on the other, maintains a consistent pattern in the U.S. imperial perspective toward the non-Western world. The result has been that U.S. policy has been in the main supported by a mainstream "identitarian" culture that has masked the realities of that policy: support for dictatorial and unpopular regimes, a scale of violence far out of proportion to the violence of native insurgency against American allies, a remarkably steady hostility toward the legitimacy of native nationalism, most of which is compressed into the word *terrorism*. Out of this has come a stubbornly held conviction that American power in the world is the sentinel of freedom, or in President Johnson's words "the guardian at the gate."

The concurrence between such notions and the worldview promulgated by the media is therefore quite close. The history of other cultures is supposed to be nonexistent until it erupts into confrontation with the United States, and hence is covered on the evening news. Most of what counts about foreign societies is reduced first into sixty-second items, then into the question of whether they are pro- or anti-American (freedom, capitalism, democracy). The ultimate choice facing the professional interpreters of, or experts on, "other" peoples, as these experts are framed by the media, is to tell the public whether what is happening is "good" for America or not, and then to recommend a policy for action. Every commentator or expert a potential secretary of state.

The internalization of norms for use within cultural discourse, the rules that must be followed if statements are to be made, the "history" that is judged official as opposed to the history that isn't—all these are some of the ways in which all national states regulate public discussion and private identity. The difference today lies in the truly epochal scale of U.S. global power, and with it the corresponding power of the national consensus created domestically by the electronic media. Conrad saw Kurtz as a European in the African jungle, and Gould as an enlightened Westerner in the South American mountains, as capable both of civilizing and obliterating the natives. The same power, but on a world scale, is held by the United States today.

But my analysis would be incomplete were I not at this point to introduce another important element. In speaking of control and consensus one can use the word *hegemony* advisedly. I do not want at all to suggest that there is a directly imposed regime of conformity in the correspondence I have drawn between contemporary U.S. media discourse and U.S. policy in the subordinate, non-Western world.

What I have been discussing is a system of pressures and constraints by which the whole cultural corpus retains its maddeningly imperial identity and its direction. This is why I think it is perfectly accurate to speak of a mainstream culture as possessing a certain regularity, integrity, or a system of predictable stresses over time.

In relation to mainstream American culture, marginalization by the imperial center means a fate of provinciality. It means the inconsequence associated with what is not major, not central, not powerful— in short, it means association with what are considered euphemistically as alternative modes. And also alternative states, peoples, cultures. There are alternative theaters, presses, newspapers, artists, scholars, and styles. The images of centrality—which are directly connected with what C. Wright Mills called the power elite—supplant the much slower and reflective, the much less immediate and less quick processes of print culture, with its encoding of the attendant and relatively recalcitrant categories of historical class, inherited property, and traditional privilege. Centrality in American culture today is the dominance of the executive presence: the president, the TV commentator, corporate official, celebrity. And, finally, centrality is identity, what *is* powerful, important, and ours. Centrality maintains balance between extremes; it endows ideas with the valances of moderation, rationality, pragmatism; it holds the middle together.

And centrality gives rise to semi-official narratives with the capacity to authorize and embody certain sequences of cause and effect, while at the same time preventing counternarratives from emerging. The commonest and in this instance most effective narrative sequence is America as a force for good in the world, regularly coming up against the obstacle of foreign conspiracies, which are usually perceived as ontologically mischievous and "against" America. Thus American aid to Vietnam and Iran was corrupted either by communists or by terrorist fundamentalists; the result is "our" humiliation and the bitterest sort of disappointment. Conversely, the valiant Afghan *moujahidin* (freedom-fighters) have much in common with Polish Solidarity, Nicaraguan *contras,* Angolan rebels, Salvadoran regulars: "we" support them all. Left to our proper devices "we" would assume their victory, but the meddling efforts of liberals at home and disinformation experts abroad have reduced our ability to help them to the fullest degree.

But to an even greater degree the power of such narratives is to interdict, marginalize, criminalize alternative versions of the same history—in Vietnam, Iran, the Middle East, Africa, Central America,

Eastern Europe. A very simple empirical test of what I mean is what happens when you are given the opportunity to articulate a more complex, less narratively sequential history to the official ones carried by the media, which reinforce what corporate, government, and policy spokespeople already believe. In fact you are compelled to retell "fact" in such a way as to be inventing a language from scratch. The most difficult thing to do, then, is to suggest that the already existing history and presence of foreign societies may not have responded with automatic assent to the imposition of Western political or military power, not because there was anything inherently wrong with that power but because it was felt to be alien. To venture so apparently uncontroversial a truth about how all cultures in fact behave turns out to be nothing less than an act of delinquency, whereupon you feel the enunciative opportunity offered you on the basis of pluralism and fairness is sharply restricted to inconsequential bursts of facts, stamped either as extreme or irrelevant. With no acceptable narrative to rely on, with no sustained permission for you to narrate, you feel yourself crowded out and silenced. No permission to narrate. Anything further you might wish to say or do is likely to become "terrorism."

The bleak picture I have drawn is intended to stress in a heightened way the processes of identity enforcement that are likely to produce rejecting, violent, and despairing responses by groups, nations, and individuals whose place in the scheme is perforce inconsequential. Thus the triumph of identity by one culture or state almost always is implicated directly or indirectly in the denial, or the suppression of equal identity for *other* groups, states, or cultures. Nationalism exacerbates the processes by offering what appears to be ethnosuicide as an alternative to clamorous demands for equality, for sovereignty, for national self-definition. And while it would be a mistake to ascribe all the problems associated with random violence to this maelstrom of escalating identity demands, it would be an even graver mistake to ignore the process altogether. No one in the United States today speaks about limitations on sovereignty, for example, in rhetoric or in political discourse, and few people here assume that there is a real alternative to superpowers running the world. But if untrammeled aspirations based on projections of world power become the norm for political behavior, what checks are there on others who may wish *either* to emulate these gigantic ambitions (the way nineteenth-century novelistic heroes felt that Napoleon was a model to be copied) or to bring down the whole edifice that prevents them from realizing the much smaller ambitions of statehood, cultural independence, self-expression?

As for recent debates on education, my second example, I shall have to be briefer. This audience of readers does not need to be told that postmodernism, post-Marxism, post-structuralism in intellectual discourse have engendered a strongly antagonistic response in many sectors of mainstream culture. Not only has this response involved various defenses of "the canon" of Western humanistic knowledge, it has produced famously discussed screeds on such topics as the closing of the American mind and cultural literacy, all of which have had the effect of clearing the space for a sanctioned rhetoric of national identity, embodied in such documents as the Rockefeller Foundation–commissioned study *The Humanities in American Life,* or, more recently, the more directly politically inspired expostulations of Secretary of Education William Bennett, who speaks not simply as an American cabinet officer, but as self-designated spokesman for the West, a sort of intellectual Head of the Free World.

What do such texts as these "state of the culture" works tell us? Nothing less than that the humanities are important, central, traditional, inspiring. Bennett has gone as far as saying that we can "have" the humanities by "reclaiming" our traditions—the collective pronouns and the proprietary accents are crucially important—through twenty or so major texts. If every American student were required to read Homer, Shakespeare, the Bible, and Jefferson, then we would have achieved a full sense of national purpose. Underlying all such epigonal replications of Matthew Arnold's exhortations to the significance of culture is the social authority of patriotism, the fortifications of identity brought to us by our culture, whereby we can confront the world defiantly and self-confidently. This type of cultural chauvinism is an extremely drastic delimitation of what in other and more interesting contexts we have learned about culture—its productivity, its diverse components, its critical and often contradictory energies, its radically antithetical characteristics, and above all its rich worldliness and complicity both with authority and with liberation. Instead, we are told that cultural or humanistic study is the recuperation of the Judeo-Christian or Western heritage, as free as possible both from Native American culture—which the Judeo-Christian tradition in its early American-Puritan embodiments set about to exterminate—as from the fascinating adventures of that tradition in the peripheral non-Western world.

Yet the cultural disciplines have in fact found a hospitable haven in the academy, a historical truth of extraordinary magnitude. To a very great degree, one of Bennett's most celebrated rhetorical interventions *(To Reclaim a Legacy)* has this accomplishment very much as its target, whereas we would have thought that it has always been a legitimate conception of the modern university's secular mission (as described, for example, by Alvin Gouldner) to be a place where multiplicity and contradiction coexist with established dogma and canonical doctrine. This is now refuted by the rise of a new orthodoxy. Its supposition has been that once having admitted Marxism, structuralism, feminism, and Third World studies into the curriculum (and before that an entire generation of refugee scholars), the American university has sabotaged the basis of its supposed authority: hence, the need for steady, tonic infusions of Homer and Jefferson, especially if these are administered by teachers convinced of our culture's superior mission in the world.

If by now the reader will have felt that I have wandered very far from "terrorism," he/she will be correct, but only because representations of terrorism have been quarantined from the general affirmative and identitarian tendencies in culture at the present time. Yet it would be frivolous for me to suggest that the dreadful violence of terrorist actions can somehow be mitigated by acknowledgment of these tendencies. What I am trying to suggest, however, is that it is a more worthwhile endeavor for us to historicize, analyze, and reflectively consider such tendencies than gregariously and ideologically to go along with the chorus of attacks and patriotic dirges that are raised when the word *terrorism* is pronounced. In other words, there is room for intellectual discussion that partakes neither of the expert discourse of counterterrorism, nor of the partisan affirmations about "our" identity. That kind of intellectual discussion may involve taking positions on specific political conflicts in which terrorism or state-violence is regularly employed, but it would more centrally and interestingly involve enlarging the scope of discussion, and inducing a spirit of criticism, and of negative thought as an antidote to the general yea-saying.

For it must be incumbent upon even those of us who support nationalist struggle in an age of unrestrained nationalist expression to have at our disposal some decent measure of intellectual refusal, negation, and skepticism. It is at precisely that nexus of committed participation and intellectual commitment that we should situate ourselves to ask *how much identity, how much* positive consolidation, *how much* administered approbation we are willing to tolerate in the name of our cause, our culture, our state. What could be more disgraceful an instance of Benda's *trahison des clercs* than the displays of political fervor on the part of intellectuals for "our" side, when so often it has been our side that has been committing the violence in the name of Western virtues, humanism, morality?

Talking about terrorism can therefore become an occasion for something other than solemn, self-righteous pontification about what makes "us" worth protecting and "them" worth attacking. In education, politics, history, and culture there is at the present time a role to be played by secular oppositional intellectuals, call them a class of informed and effective wet blankets, who do not allow themselves the luxury of playing the identity game (leaving that to the legions who do it for a living), but who more compassionately press the interests of the unheard, the unrepresented, the comparatively powerless people of our world, and who do so not in "the jargon of authenticity" but with the accents of personal restraint, historical skepticism, and consciously, politically committed intellect. It is possible, in short, to negate the stale pieties of identitarian politics with other means than violence.

Published in *New Left Review* 171, September/October 1988.

The Orientalist Express:
Thomas Friedman Wraps Up the
Middle East

[1989]

On the face of it, *From Beirut to Jerusalem* is a reporter's journal of a decade in the Middle East spent first as UPI correspondent for a couple of years, then as *New York Times* bureau chief in two major centers.[30] Between 1979 and 1984 Friedman was stationed in Beirut where he covered the civil war, the Israeli invasion of 1982, and the country's tragic dissolution thereafter. He then moved to Jerusalem (traveling rather ostentatiously across the Lebanese–Israeli border with his golf clubs), where he wrote about the Israeli political scene, with particular attention to the *intifadah*. He remained in Israel until mid-1988. He then returned home to become the *Times* man in Washington. For his Middle Eastern coverage Friedman won two Pulitzer prizes, both of them, interestingly enough, about major Palestinian events: the 1982 Sabra and Shatila massacres, and the uprising or *intifadah* that began in late 1987 and continues to the present.

Friedman is no ordinary reporter, however. He is, as he tells us right from the start, a young American Jew who grew up in Minneapolis, was galvanized into Zionist enthusiasm by the 1967 War, studied Arabic and Jewish history first at Brandeis and then at Oxford, and went on to become a major figure in discussions and policy analysis of the Middle East. The complexity and richness of his personal background thus make Friedman's book a compendium of autobiography, journalistic reportage, philosophical reflection laced with a political theory whose main idea is that by virtue of their power and enlightened attitudes Israel and the United States set the standards to which in the end the less gifted and culturally backward Arabs must conform. Yet Friedman is also something of a craftsman. *From Beirut to Jerusalem,* for all its gargantuan length, doesn't often flag or bog down except, it must be said, when Friedman either gets mushy with testimonials about his feelings, or when he offers advice to everyone about how much better they could be doing if they paid attention to him. The result is therefore an interesting book, as much a collection of anecdotes as it is clever writing studded with eye-catching but symptomatic bits of analysis.

What keeps it together as a book is Friedman's own "insider" voice—smart, frequently vulgar and tough, sententious, effortlessly knowledgeable. When Arabs or Jews do things, it is not what they do but how their actions register on Tom's sensibility that matters. Not surprisingly, therefore, it is a strangely ignorant book: Friedman's two main sources of illumination are trusted gurus (e.g., the "philosopher" David Hartman, who—we are not told this—runs a strange religious school in Israel largely on U.S. funds; he doesn't seem to have any "philosophical" works to his credit) or bits of expert and/or folk wisdom, unconnected to specific works or research, asserted rather than argued or proved. I do not disagree with Friedman, for example, in his account of how Hafez al-Assad ruthlessly destroyed Muslim opposition in Hama by massacring thousands of his own citizens; Friedman takes the incident as a case of "Hama Rules" and attributes them to "different political traditions" in the Arab world whose true origin, he pronounces, are such things as a "tribalism" learned in the desert. So astonishing a jump, from modern, predominantly urban Syria to the prehistoric desert, is of course the purest Orientalism, and is of a piece with the moronic and hopelessly false dictum offered later in the book that the Arab political tradition has produced only two types: the merchant and the messiah.

These ludicrous reductions do have sources: In the case of tribalism it is the Israeli "Bedouin expert" Clinton Bailey; in the case of the Arab political tradition "Lebanese Shiite scholar" Fouad Ajami. Friedman deploys these ideas disingenuously, as if there wasn't a fairly active controversy seething in all departments of knowledge about the Middle

East. In fact Friedman belongs very clearly on one side, the side associated with classical anti-Arab and anti-Islamic Orientalism, the world according to Bernard Lewis, Ajami, Bailey, and their ilk. Of course Friedman is perfectly entitled to his views, which are not always unsympathetic, but what is particularly shady is that Friedman palms off his opinions (and those of his sources) as reasonable, uncontested, secure. In fact they are minority views and have been under severe attack for several decades now. They represent a narrow consensus associated not with desirable political change but with the equally political, basically conservative perspective of the *status quo*. People in this camp characterize themselves as pragmatic and realistic, labels that are intended to dismiss the theories of Marxists, non-Western and non-white nationalists, feminists, political economists. The point, of course, is that what Friedman and the Orientalists espouse is a threadbare repertoire of often racist clichés, all of them bearing the marks of colonial knowledge now allied with Naipaulesque disenchantment. People can't change, Friedman says in effect; they are what they are forever. Give Ahmed, or Sambo, a place in the bus and he'll simmer down.

But since this is not a scholarly book, one might say, why shouldn't Friedman traffic in these discredited myths? Because Friedman presents himself as more than a reporter, his book as more than a personal chronicle. No one watching television these days has not seen Friedman, "the expert," on all the right programs—the detached, impartial, authoritative observer who is a sizable cut above the smaller-scale partisans who are so transparently militant and therefore less credible. *From Beirut to Jerusalem* is the marketing strategy by means of which a young reporter consciously elevates himself to the rank of foreign policy sage, there to reap rewards and, alas, to recycle the illusions of American power and visionless realism. In the Middle East, he tells us, America should alternate between being "obstetrician, friend, grocer, and a son-of-a-bitch." Among the prototypes for these largely unattractive roles are Jimmy Carter and Henry Kissinger.

It is not just the comic philistinism of Friedman's ideas that I find so remarkably jejune, or his sassy and unbeguiling manner, or his grating indifference to values and principles by which, perhaps misguidedly, Arabs and Jews have believed themselves to be informed. It is rather the special combination of disarming incoherence and unearned egoism that gives him his cockily alarming plausibility—qualities that may explain the book's quite startling commercial success. It's as if—and I think this is true of his views on both Arabs and

Jews—what scholars, poets, historians, fighters, and statesmen have done is not as important or as central as what Friedman himself thinks. Not only is there scarcely a reference in *From Beirut to Jerusalem* to the latest work on Arab history and society, but Friedman is also quite innocent about the latest in Israeli scholarship that has analyzed the origins of the Palestinian refugee problem, or the birth of Israel, or the internal dislocations within Israeli society.

I do not want to suggest that Friedman is nowhere capable of uncompromising analysis—his remarks on the creepy similarity between Labour and Likud parties are especially trenchant—or that he flinches when it comes to reporting the dreadful, virtually insensate ugliness of recent Israeli policy toward the Palestinians. He is clear about these matters, but he feels somehow that his prized sensibility, saying one thing in one breath and then contradicting it in the next, can carry the whole burden of interpretation and evaluation. And underlying his overestimated sensibility is a patronizing attitude toward all the little people who do not have quite his olympian perspective. Israeli Jews, he tells us in one passage, are closer to the West because their symbol, the star, is close to the cross, "both of which are full of sharp, angled turns. The symbol of the Muslim East is the crescent moon—a wide, soft, ambiguous arc." From such entirely dubious materials he draws conclusions roughly equivalent in explanatory power to theories about a natural sense of rhythm among inferior races that have been discredited at least since World War II. A little later in the book Friedman informs Palestinians that they do not belong to the "biblical super story through which the West looks at the world"—when you come to think of it, not many people have that privilege—and they are "lucky" to have had the Jews as their enemy.

Inside this serenely untroubled cocoon of the purest race prejudice the Friedmanian sensibility ambles from subject to subject. When he arrives finally at the vexed problem of press coverage, he warns us that the media are unfair in their relentless fixation on Israel (this from the journalist-author of a 600-page book on the subject), then he compliments the Israelis on manipulating the media brilliantly, then he blathers on about Israeli troops beating up three-year-olds, and how that vigorous form of outdoor exercise provides them with self-knowledge! Friedman seems to have no inkling that people were and have been killed or beaten when he and his media colleagues were *not* there to report the story, or that such things as imperialism, or demography, or conflicting ideas played a role while he wasn't around to comment on the case. He does not seem quite to have apprehended that other peoples besides Westerners with sharp-angled symbols and superstories might have had a sense of nationhood, or that when a whole society is shattered and its people dispersed and stripped of their lands, it might on its own, without a Biblical superstory or a sharp Western symbol, try to reforge itself and create a new independent society.

One would not fault as seriously *From Beirut to Jerusalem* for its numerous shortcomings were it not that as a collection of anecdotes or as a report on his own apparently omnicompetent sensibility Friedman's writing aspires to an almost regal authority and inclusiveness. There is little self-irony, no twinge of doubt in what he ladles out; mockery and sarcasm are reserved entirely for local Arabs and Jews, not for earnest *Times* reporters. Read his prescriptions at the end of the book and you will quickly realize that Friedman has internalized the norms, if not the powers, of the secretary of state not just of the United States, but of all humanity. Do this, he tells the Israelis; do this, he tells the Palestinians; do this, he tells the Americans—and anyone else who happens to be listening in. His formulas suggest that everyone should try for limits and realism, except, of course, Friedman himself.

His book would have been more interesting had his account of himself included some narrative of how he achieved such awesome powers, or of how being a reporter for the *Times* in the Middle East elevates one to institutional status, or of how the selection of what's fit to print (for example, Friedman's use of the word *indiscriminate* to describe Israel's 1982 bombing of Beirut was removed by then *Times* editor A. L. Rosenthal; Friedman makes no mention of the episode in his book) has a lot to do with what is considered "important" by various powers and interests. I would have also liked to read his opinion of the wall-to-wall coverage of terrorist Shaikh Obeid's kidnapping in which the fact that Israel has been in military occupation of a handsome swathe of South Lebanon is almost totally suppressed by the *Times* and all the other independent U.S. media, along with the fact that although Obeid is an unattractive clerical zealot, he hasn't been concretely accused of any greater or more specific "terrorism" than fighting the Israeli military who have taken over his homeland. Or then again I'd like to have read Friedman's account of how the *Times*'s editorial pages are dominated by the opinions of William Safire and A. M. Rosenthal (whom Friedman credits with having helped his career), opinions about the Muslims and Arabs that could not be printed about any other people on earth.

A treatment of these facts would have been fairer and perhaps less grand than asking Arabs and Jews to bear the brunt of Friedman's ponderous judgments on their infractions and departures from the essences and fates decreed for them by Friedman and his dubious authorities. Yet despite the distorting prism of his official self, Friedman does indeed have an understanding of how people hang on—e.g., the young Palestinian defenders of Beirut in 1982—or of how a self-serving myth of victimization still controls the Israeli self-image. Compassion and affection thus occasionally get through Friedman's remorseless machine, but the really curious thing is how little he seems to be interested in these genuine accomplishments, and how much more determined he is to be an all-knowing White Father composing the ultimate how-to-do-it book for the Middle East.

Published in *The Village Voice,* October 17, 1989.

CHAPTER 35

On Nelson Mandela, and Others

[1990]

Anyone who had access to a television set, a radio, or newspaper during the past several weeks would not have been immune to the powerful effect of Nelson Mandela's dramatic release from a South African jail. Imprisoned twenty-seven years ago for his membership in the African National Congress, Mandela spent the better part of his productive life, first in the fortress of Robben Island—a fearsomely severe and austerely isolated prison off the coast of South Africa—and then as a somewhat better-treated prisoner in a government compound on the mainland. He entered his captivity as a relatively young man in the prime of life, and emerged a clearly old man of seventy-one. A former boxer and powerfully built man more than six feet in height, the Mandela who stepped out of prison was a frail but still dignified black whose first significant gesture as he walked out of prison was to raise a clenched fist in the salute of the still militant ANC.

Watching the events during his first week of freedom, the American viewer was likely to be impressed above all with Mandela's immense dignity; I certainly was. Here was a man who had been under the pressure not only of solitude and punishment, but also of the absolute, unrelenting power of a government determined not to yield one inch in its opposition to an equitable sharing of power for the entire black and colored population. Mandela's post-freedom interviews were dramatically clear about the contest that began the moment he entered prison between him and the government. He said that he knew he had to stand firm no matter what was done to him. In the dehumanizing conditions of a maximum-security prison, the political issues became immediately personal. Thus, he said, he knew he had to resist any attempt made by the guards to treat him contemptuously or cruelly; if asked to kneel or perform some menial duty that was not allowed under the prison regulations (Mandela made a point of knowing the rules better than his guards), he would refuse, despite threats, verbal abuse, or punishment by solitary confinement.

In prison Mandela transformed his captivity not only into a battle of wills, but also into a symbolic struggle between two opposed viewpoints: apartheid, on the one hand, the black majority on the other. Mandela's achievement was to elevate these two interests into opposed *principles*. Gradually, and over an unimaginably long time—twenty-seven years—Mandela's firmness and conviction prevailed in the struggle. On a personal level he was able to convince the government of South Africa that he was not going to give up his principles, regardless of how much power the government brought to bear upon him, and regardless of how much he was made to pay for his position. In the end, as we now know, the government was persuaded not only to release him, but also to agree to negotiations with the ANC. Although no one can say what the main reason for the change was— was it DeKlerk's presence, or the militancy of the ANC, the weakening of South Africa's international position, or the gradual moderation of the Afrikaner position generally?—Mandela's unbending moral principles, as embodied in his unwillingness to modify his position substantively, played a part.

Now that Mandela has been vindicated, it is easy to sympathize with what he did. During his imprisonment, however, I am sure that many people disagreed with his inflexibility, which, even after he left jail, even after an era of political negotiations was dawning, even after the good faith gesture of the government, demanded that he not renounce the need for armed struggle. Twenty-seven years are half an adult lifetime. Many things happened, many things were said both for and against the principles of the ANC, as adhered to by Mandela. Some people must have opined, for instance, that since all of the power was held by the whites, it would be important to placate them, to appeal to them, to conciliate them. This would have entailed showing flexibility on principles: "Let us demonstrate that we are willing to compromise with apartheid so that we can get something in return." Others would have said: "America is very important in the world, and so we should do what Sadat did, appeal to the Americans, and try to get their support as a way of influencing white South Africans to treat us more fairly.'' And then another group would have said that "we, as blacks, should show ourselves to be more attractive, not as terrorists; let us proclaim that we are against violence. Let us make public statements to that effect, and let us also demonstrate our willingness to live in peace with the whites by having public dialogues with them.''

Doubtless many of these things were not only said, but undertaken and acted upon. And I am certain, from what Mandela said after his release, that many of his colleagues in the ANC would have wished him to modify his stance a little in order to reveal to the world that he was a decent, nice family man. When asked by journalists whether he could discuss what inspired him during his years of imprisonment, Mandela's response was always the same: I was inspired by the principles of my party. When he was expected to be a man of vision (in the American press, for example, there was some disappointment when Mandela refused the opportunity to relive the role of Martin Luther King, Jr.), he showed himself to be completely and rigidly bound to his party's codes and principles. There is even a hint now and then, especially in the U.S. media, that maybe Mandela is a bit of a disappointment, that he remains in essence a hard, tough, unbending guerrilla leader, not a saint or a sage like King or Gandhi.

A closer look at other recent leaders of democratic struggles reveals much the same pattern of principled rigidity. Such is equally true of Vaclav Havel and Lech Walesa, who are slightly more acceptable to the West than Mandela because they are European, Christian, and clearly anti-communists. During his recent visit here, Havel was celebrated as a great champion of American-style freedom, but what was not mentioned at all was that one of his first official guests to be invited (then disinvited) to Czechoslovakia was Yasir Arafat. The American media have ignored this fact, doubtless fearing that it might complicate the pure picture of Havel as "one of us." Havel is tougher than that; he can see the importance of the Palestinian struggle, despite its unpopularity in those intellectual and political circles in the United States still dominated either by fear of the Zionist lobby or by the ridiculous and cowardly anxiety that has kept so many people from openly declaring their support for a movement with which they sympathize but are afraid to speak about in public. In any case, the point is that leaders like Walesa and Havel prevailed not by being clever at compromises, or wheeling and dealing, but by sticking to and completely identifying with unchanging principles whose moral content in the end triumphed over their adversaries.

To some people such attitudes appear like fanaticism. And indeed there *is* something fanatical about adhering to principles when your opponents possess overwhelming and apparently unchallengeable power. The plays of Molière are full of characters who, like Cervantes' Don Quixote, are possessed by their ideas and appear to be insane and ridiculous as a result. But there are differences between, for instance, the principles of isolated royalists in republican France today, who are out-of-sync with the times, and people like Mandela and Havel, who support great mass movements. The main difference is that what is silly fanaticism in one case is brave farsightedness in another. The only basis for an extra-parliamentary struggle like that of the blacks in South Africa or the opponents of the Communist regime in Czechoslovakia derives from the irreducible human desire for liberation. Since the constitution of South Africa denied that right to two-thirds of the population, the only resort was to go outside the constitution and state the principle of one person, one vote as morally superior to anything found within present legal and constitutional contexts. Gradually, the principles were shown to occupy the moral high ground, and because enough people, black and white, were persuaded of the virtue of these principles, they gained more adherents, until, as we now know, even the white South African government changed its mind. Believers in the principles of freedom and equality, however, did not.

All these remarks have been occasioned by trying to connect the Mandela story with the current state of the Palestinian and Arab struggle. We are like uninvited guests to an enormous party taking place nearly everywhere else on earth, but not in the Middle East. In Israel the official positions have drifted further to the right. In the days that we regretted the appearance of Begin, we thought we were better off under Labour; then when Shamir came we missed Begin. Now that Shamir is being challenged by Sharon, we find that we prefer Shamir and certainly Rabin. What the Palestinians did in Algiers in November 1988 was a direct result of the *intifadah,* which continues bravely and resourcefully to this very day. At the time we clarified our positions, we stood by our principles of self-determination and self-respect in a decent, morally defensible and politically acceptable way. Since that time, the number of Palestinian dead has mounted; the universities are still closed; the number of houses destroyed, prisoners in jail, villages and camps under curfew has increased tremendously. Israeli troops now shoot Palestinians on sight, not just when they are provoked by stones. A major program of deportation has begun. In November 1989, at a lecture in Tel Aviv, Deputy Foreign Minister Netanyahu said that Israel made a mistake not to deport large numbers of Palestinians when the eyes of the world were focused on what was happening in China. Now we should wait, he said, until there is a massive wave of repression in Albania so that we can deport "our" Palestinians.

In the meantime Shamir announces that at least 100,000 Russian Jews will be coming to Israel every year. Many of them will be settled on the West Bank on land that will have to be taken from Palestinians. No one could have been surprised by this announcement, since it was known for at least thirty years that Jewish and Zionist organizations were putting pressure on both the Soviet and U.S. governments to allow Jewish emigration. The difference came when, in October 1989, the Soviet Union agreed, under U.S. pressure (itself generated by the Zionist lobby and by Israel), to grant Soviet Jews exit visas, principally to emigrate to Israel. For the first time in generations a large mass of new immigrants is destined for the Middle East, with the price for their journey paid for largely by the U.S. taxpayer (who is as unaware as always)—and of course by the Palestinians themselves.

I read in the newspapers last week that the Arab League has been unable to convene an emergency summit to deal with the crisis, which has been called a catastrophe by every Palestinian leader and individual. On the matter of the "peace process," Israel has intransigently maintained its position of not dealing with the PLO, with the result that Egypt, Israel, and the United States are discussing Palestinian representatives with each other, principally and only secondarily with the PLO. For the past several weeks two or three senior representatives of the PLO have been in the United States desperately seeking meetings with the State Department, and failing to secure them; in private, at universities and other public places, these senior PLO people have been saying that they would be willing to discuss modifications of boundaries with Israel, that the 1967 lines are negotiable, that even the principle of a Palestinian state is negotiable.

By now it must be clear that we are experiencing a crisis of leadership and of principles. What had been the principle of Arab liberation and Palestinian independence is slowly slipping from sight. The idea now seems to be that we can bargain our way to our goals. True, the Arab and Palestinian struggle is more complicated and difficult than that of other peoples like the South Africans or Algerians, and true, the odds against us—without a strategic ally, with no economic or cultural infrastructure to withstand the assaults of neo-imperialism—are very great. But how can we expect to rise above the waves of time and fortune if we don't keep our heads clear and fixed on the moral and political principles that guide us in difficult times? How can we persuade ourselves and others of the justice of our cause if we do not keep our principles clear and unchanging? How can we persuade our enemies of our will if we keep changing our minds and keep compromising on nearly everything? *This is both a Palestinian and an Arab concern.*

The answer is clear to me: It is the role of the Arab intellectual today to articulate and defend the principles of liberation and democracy at all costs, and to do so by impressing the leadership of the Arab nation with these realities and values. Otherwise, our future—if we are to have one at all—is extremely grim, and in a sense not worth defending. It seems to me that the lesson of Mandela and others like him for the Arab world is not only something to admire and respect. It is something to emulate, to implement and, yes, to be rigid about. We have been uninvited guests for too long; lingering outside the main march of humanity must not become a habit. Nobody will ask you in; you must march in, believing yourself to be equal to the occasion and suitable for the feast.

Published in *al-Majalla,* March 13, 1990.

CHAPTER 36

Embargoed Literature

[1990]

Eight years before Naguib Mahfouz won the 1988 Nobel Prize for literature, I was asked by a major New York commercial publisher known for his liberal and unprovincial views to suggest a list of Third World novels for translation and inclusion in a new series he was planning. The list I gave him was headed by two or three of Mahfouz's works, none of which was then in circulation in the United States. True, a few novels by the Egyptian master were available in England, but these had never gained entry into the United States and even in Europe were known principally to a few students of Arabic. A few weeks after I submitted my list, I inquired which novels had been chosen, only to be informed that the Mahfouz translations would not be undertaken. When I asked why, I was given an answer that has haunted me ever since. "The problem," I was told, "is that Arabic is a controversial language."

What exactly the man meant is still a little vague to me, but that Arabs and their language were somehow not respectable—consequently dangerous, louche, unapproachable—was perfectly evident to me then and, alas, now. For of all the major world literatures, Arabic remains relatively unknown and unread in the West, for reasons that are quite unique and, I think, remarkable at a time when tastes here for the non-Western are more developed than ever before and, even more compelling, contemporary Arabic literature is at a particularly interesting juncture.

An amusing (but also depressing) sign of the disparity between interest in Arabic literature and interest in all the other literatures outside the Atlantic world is to look at what happened to Mahfouz's work and reputation in English after he won the Nobel Prize in 1988. Doubleday acquired rights to his work and a few months ago began to introduce a handful of his stories and novels, including the first volume of his major work, the *Cairo Trilogy,* in what appeared to be new editions. In fact, with one exception, the translations were exactly the ones already published in England, some quite good, most, however, either indifferent or poor. Clearly the idea was to capitalize on and market his new fame, but to reduce costs by *not* retranslating the works.

Second, and more comically symptomatic, half a dozen profiles of Mahfouz appeared in American magazines such as *Vanity Fair, The New Yorker,* and *The New York Times Magazine.* In effect they were the same article rewritten over and over again. Each talked about his favorite café, his modesty, his position on Israel (in the second sentence of its Nobel Prize story, *The New York Times* had thoughtfully sought the opinion of the Israeli consul in New York), his orderly and extremely uninteresting life. All of the authors, some of them reasonably accomplished essayists, were totally innocent both of the Arabic language and of Arabic literature. All of them regarded Mahfouz as a cross between a cultural oddity and a political symbol. Nothing was said about his formal achievements, for instance, or about his place in modern literature as a whole.

Third is that Mahfouz has more or less dropped out of discussion without having provoked any of even the more venturesome literati into trying to find out what other writers in Arabic might be worth looking into. Where, after all, did Mahfouz come from? It is impossible not to believe that one reason for this odd state of affairs is the long-standing prejudice against the Arabs and Islam that remains in force within Western, but especially American, culture. Here the experts on Islam and the Arabs bear considerable blame. Their doyen, Bernard Lewis, still blathers on in places like *The Wall Street Journal* and *The American Scholar* about the darkness and strangeness of Muslims, Arabs, their culture, religion, etc. . . . . It is still thought to be the correct thing to ask an Israeli or Jewish scholar to comment on things Islamic; the reverse—asking an Arab to comment on Hebrew literature or Jewish culture—is never even contemplated. One of the leading American university centers of Arab and Islamic studies does not have a single native speaker teaching Arabic language or literature.

Critics, book reviewers, and journal editors studiously avoid discussion of Arabic books, even as they attempt prodigious feats of reading and interpretation where, for instance, Czech and Argentinian literatures are concerned.

The unavailability of Arabic literature in translation is no longer an excuse. Small but conscientious publishing houses like Al-Saqi and Quartet in London, Sindbad in Paris, and Three Continents Press in the United States have assembled a diverse cross section of contemporary work from the Arab world that is still overlooked or deliberately ignored by editors and book reviewers. In addition, some larger publishers (Penguin, Random House, a handful of American university presses) have recently put out some truly first-rate literary work that has simply gone unnoticed and unreviewed, as if an iron curtain of indifference and prejudice ruled out any attention to texts that did not reiterate the usual clichés about "Islam," violence, sensuality, and so forth. A seemingly deliberate policy maintains a kind of monolithic reductionism where the Arabs and Islam are concerned; the Orientalism that distances and dehumanizes another culture is upheld, elevating and strengthening at the same time the xenophobic fantasy of a pure "Western" identity.

Some of these reflections have been partially instigated by the truly disgraceful level of reporting on the disastrous Iraqi military intervention in Kuwait. Most of what has passed for journalistic and expert commentary in the U.S. media was simply a repetition of appalling clichés, most of them ignorant, unhistorical, moralistic, self-righteous, and hypocritical. All derive unquestioningly in one way or another from U.S. government policy, which has long considered the Arabs either as terrorists or as mindless stooges to be milked for their money or abundant and inexpensive oil. No one placed the illegal Iraqi move in the context created by Iraq's long war against Iran, the Turkish assault on Cyprus, the Israeli devastation of Lebanon, the American invasion of Panama, etc. . . . Not a single report mentioned that the population of Kuwait was largely—indeed overwhelmingly—non-Kuwaiti, or that the Kuwaiti government had provided Saddam, the so-called Arab champion, with $15 billion in aid to fight Iran, or that with few exceptions governments in the area had little historical legitimacy, deriving their status from colonialism, force, or sheer buying power, and that this situation was long traded on by the major powers, especially the United States. But these and many other lapses are perhaps to be expected in media saturated with their own self-promoting fantasies, their incorrigible vulgarity, and dreadful mendacity portrayed as expertise; what is strange is how little compensating pressure emanates from the culture at large, which seems automatically to prefer the Mahfouz rewrites and the Islamic stereotypes to almost anything else.

The irony is that recent literary material considerably complicates and makes more interesting the current Arab scene. In less than a year three books of unique literary distinction in fine translations have appeared, only to go completely unnoticed. Each in its own way is both a dissenting or oppositional work by a well-known and admired author totally within the Arab and Islamic tradition; none of these works, in other words, expresses the kind of alienation and estrangement from Arab culture that is a staple of attacks by Western Orientalists; each treats the culture as something to be fought over and contested, thereby opposing orthodoxy, unjust authority, uncritical dogma.

The most intellectually stimulating of the three is Adonis's *An Introduction to Arab Poetics,* translated with uncommon intelligence by Catherine Cobham. Adonis is today the most daring and provocative Arab poet; a symbolist and surrealist, he is a combination of Montale, Breton, Yeats, and the early T. S. Eliot. In this compilation of four essays originally given as lectures at the Collège de France, Adonis reinterprets the whole massive Arab tradition, from pre-Islamic poetry, through the Koran, the classical period, and on into the present. Arguing that there has always been a literalist, authoritarian strain in the literature, he presents the thesis that this strain has usually been opposed by poets and thinkers for whom modernity represents renewal rather than conformism, transgression rather than nationalism, creativity rather than fundamentalism.

Far from being an academic statement, *Arab Poetics* is an uncompromising challenge to the *status quo* held in place by official Arab culture. In no uncertain terms Adonis identifies the latter equally with religious and secular authority, clerics and bureaucrats whose retreat either into a reliquary past or the arms of a foreign patron have brought us to the cultural crisis that as Arabs we face today. Adonis's command of the texts is astonishing, as is the simple brilliance of his argument. One would have thought it as important a cultural manifesto as any written today—and this makes the silence that has greeted the work so stupefying.

The two other most recent works are Edwar al-Kharrat's *City of Saffron* and the Lebanese feminist novelist Hanan al-Shaykh's *Woman of*

Sand and Myrrh, both published by Quartet. The first is translated admirably by Frances Liardet, the latter with her customary fluency by Cobham. Kharrat is a Coptic Egyptian writer whose early years in Alexandria form the subject of this semi-autobiographical text, which bears a formal resemblance to Joyce's *Portrait of the Artist as a Young Man.* Readers who have swallowed the journalistic myth that Copts and Muslims hate each other will be informed otherwise by the meditative, yet subversively intimate ruminations about childhood narrated here. One feels not only the *non serviam* of the budding artist, but also a warmly confident exploration of life in a working-class Coptic family, beset with physical dislocation, unhappy sex, political upheaval. Here, too, it is possible to read Kharrat's revelations as very much a part of contemporary Egyptian culture, without ever forgetting that he disputes the official establishment's facile versions of what "realism" and social responsibility are all about. Hanan al-Shaykh's novel is a complex and demanding story of women in the Gulf—oppressed, manipulated, sexually tormented, and confused. Far from simple romance, *Women of Sand and Myrrh* is both breathtakingly frank and technically difficult, taking on such experiences as homosexuality and patriarchy with unexpected power. Would that more Western feminists attended to writers like al-Shaykh, rather than to the overexposed (and overcited) Nawal al-Saadawi.

The point about these three works is that it is less their explicit subject matter than their formal and technical achievements that are so striking, and so accurate an index of how excitingly far Arabic literature has come since Mahfouz was at his peak about twenty-five years ago. The best of today's writers are oppositional figures who have frequently used literary virtuosity as an oblique means to criticize life in the various Arab states, where tyranny and atavism are common features of daily existence. But, one should add, these writers are not alone; their achievement is prepared for and sustained by that of many others. And, to repeat, no one in the Anglo–American literary world has taken any notice whatever of this rich body of writing. Other excellent translations have appeared: Abdel Rahman Munif's monumental *Cities of Salt* (translated by Philip Theroux for Random House), the only serious work of fiction that tries to show the effect on a Gulf country of oil, Americans, and local oligarchy; Gamal al-Ghitani's *Zayni Barakat* (the best of all the translations, done by Farouk Abdel Wahab for Viking Penguin), a superbly elegant Jamesian novel about sixteenth-century Cairo, in effect an allegory of Nasser's rule with its combination of honest reformist zeal and political paranoia and repression; Elias Khoury's *The Little Mountain* (in Maya Tabet's spare translation for the University of Minnesota Press), a postmodernist fable of the Lebanese civil war; Emile Habiby's great *Pessoptimist,* the surreal Palestinian masterpiece (in only a passable version by Trevor le Gassick, published by Three Continents), astonishing in its wit and dark inventiveness.

There are other works, Hussein Haddawy's distinguished new translation for Norton of the *Arabian Nights;* the Sudanese Tayib Salih's *Season of Migration to the North,* translated for Heinemann by the leading Arabic-English translator of our time, Denys Johnson-Davies, and republished in the United States by Michael Kesend; Ghassan Kanafani's *Men in the Sun,* a prescient parable of three Palestinian refugees who are trying to smuggle themselves from Iraq to Kuwait in a tanker-truck and die of asphyxiation and heat at the border post; the collection of poems by Mahmoud Darwish, Samih al-Qassim (today's leading Palestinian poets) and by Adonis, *Victims of a Map,* in a bilingual Penguin edition rendered capably by Abdullah al-Udhari. Salih's novel, for instance, can bear extremely favorable comparison with Naipaul's *A Bend in the River,* although despite the common source in *Heart of Darkness* Salih's work is far less schematic and ideologically embittered, a novel of genuine postcolonial strength and passion.

There are also the enormous compilations by Salma al-Jayyusi, being published over several years by Columbia University Press. It is fortunate that this relatively high number of recently translated Arabic works coincides with their importance and literary reputation in the Arab world. Nevertheless, it is also sadly the case that Arab writers themselves (as well as their publishing houses, ministries of culture, embassies in Western capitals) have done hardly anything to promote their works and the discourse of Arab culture in the West. The absence of an Arab cultural intervention in the world debate is depressing and tragic. I write these lines as the American-led campaign against Iraq's unacceptable invasion of Kuwait increases the likelihood of horrific violence and waste in the near future. Is it too extreme to connect this stark political and military polarization with the cultural abyss that exists on both sides between the Arabs and the West? What impresses one is the will to ignore and reduce the Arabs that still exists in major departments of Western culture, and the unacceptable defeatism among some Arabs, who hold that a resurgent religion and indiscriminate hostility against the West are the only answers. It may seem pathetically utopian to offer the reading and interpretation of contemporary literature as meliorative activities, but what is so attractive about the war we now have going on between Baghdad, the former Abbasid capital, and the entire West?

Published in *The Nation*, September 17, 1990.

CHAPTER 37

The Splendid Tapestry
of Arab Life

[1991]

There is something deeply reassuring and even redemptive about *A History of the Arab Peoples,*[31] which appears just when the United States is attempting in effect to destroy Iraq as a modern Arab nation. Its author, Albert Hourani, is now seventy-five, retired, and living in London after a lifetime of teaching at Oxford. Born in Manchester and educated as an Englishman, he is the son of prosperous Lebanese Protestant parents who came to England early in the century, but never lost contact with the Middle East, its peoples and cultures. Of Hourani it would not be inaccurate to say that he is today's leading historian of the modern Middle East, a scholar whose earlier books on Syria and Lebanon, and on *Arabic Thought in the Liberal Age* (an intellectual history of great insight and craftsmanship) are classics, admired by both scholars and general readers for their scope and their fastidiously refined attention to the fabric of Arab life.[32] In a generously conceived set of essays published over the past several decades, Hourani's sympathy and keen historical sense have also presented to Western and Arab readers a complex structure of innumerable connections: between Arabs and Europeans, Arabs and other Arabs, rulers and ruled, thinkers and their societies.

Now, in what is undoubtedly a masterly summational work, Hourani lays out the whole story of the Arab peoples. There are no other books like it, except—interestingly enough—the similarly grand studies done a generation ago by another Lebanese–Western scholar, Philip Hitti. Hourani has the advantage over Hitti both in the superior contemporary scholarship at his disposal and in greater methodological sophistication. Hourani's guiding ideas, however, are resoundingly classical, drawn from the life and works of Ibn Khaldun, the extraordinary fourteenth-century Arab historian and philosopher. Put simply, Ibn Khaldun's argument in the *Muqaddimah* is that there are variety and unity, stability and fluctuation, shifts in power and permanent realities that organized the Arab world for about a millennium and a half. These were specific to the cohesion of Arab society, whose inner laws Hourani summarizes in a fine passage near the opening:

> A world where a family from southern Arabia could move to Spain, and after six centuries return nearer to its place of origin and still find itself in familiar surroundings, had a unity which transcended divisions of time and space; the Arabic language could open the door to office and influence throughout that world; a body of knowledge, transmitted over the centuries by a known chain of teachers, preserved a moral community even when rulers changed; places of pilgrimage, Mecca and Jerusalem, were unchanging poles of the human world even if power shifted from one city to another; and belief in a God who created and sustained the world could give meaning to the blows of fate.[33]

The story of the Arab peoples therefore begins with late antiquity as an Arab ethos slowly emerges, based upon the developing splendors of a rich language, a generally pastoral life interspersed with trade and travel, the inherited tradition of Rome, Greece, Judaism, and early Christianity. Hourani's naturally synthesizing style next shows how Islam, energized and articulated in seventh-century Arabia by the Prophet Muhammad, flung forth an astonishing new civilization; in a matter of decades it extended all the way to Morocco and Spain. In describing the diverse peoples, dynasties, and styles included in this vast enterprise, Hourani achieves a level of unruffled generalization that is never reductive; conversely, however, he is rarely dramatic or passionate, leaving the reader often wishing for a glimpsed personality, a vignette, a narrative that might somehow deliver the urgency of lived life and compelling advocacy. This lack is especially felt during Hourani's description of Abbasid civilization (749–1258), whose seat in Baghdad brought forth one of the greatest flowerings in the Arab enterprise. Given the present American assault on Baghdad, and the fact that the city was last destroyed by Mongols in 1258, one's sense of outraged grief is only partly attenuated by Hourani's quiet pages.

Hourani is at his best when he considers not the dramatic bursts, but the abiding features and long trends of Arab life and thought as carried forward by the maintainers and sustainers of human community, not principally by its challengers or rebels. Surely there are no finer pages than his on Sufis like Ibn Arabi or metaphysicians like al-Ghazali. No one better than Hourani respects the diversity of Arab societies. The status of Jews and Christians, the role of women, and, above all, the subtle interplay between Islamic doctrine, practice, and social actuality from Andalusia to Syria and Arabia are sifted through with precision and frequently elegance. What emerges from the first half of his history is a surprisingly tolerant, even relaxed Arab *Weltanschauung* dominated, not by frothing zealots, but by courteous and sensitive sages, urbane magistrates, skilled courtiers.

Yet Hourani's is a worldly and, for the most part, a secular history. Ever on the alert for and sensitive to the modulations of fortune, he plots the geography of power with great perspicacity. One feature that characterizes rulers from the eighth-century Umayyads to the Ottomans, for instance, is the physical removal of the sovereign from his principal city to an outlying palace. Another noted by Hourani is the counterpoint between North Africa, on the one hand, and, on the other, the central Islamic lands (Syria, Iraq, Egypt, and Arabia), with their sometimes tense, sometimes cordial relationships with Islamic but non-Arab nations such as Iran, Turkey, and India. And gradually in the second half of his history, Hourani shows how Europe's ascendancy came to overshadow the Arabs' former greatness.

Not that Islam is shown to be the problem: On the contrary. Hourani's pages on the integration of Islamic faith with Arab culture are a masterpiece of cogent and nuanced exposition, largely because here and elsewhere in the book he never mistakes what a text says for reality. Neither does Hourani tolerate the sloppy propaganda that tries to collapse all aspects of Arab life into a so-called Islamic framework. There are always conflicts in interpretation—as between Hanbali, Shafi'i, Maliki, and Hanafi schools—controversies in *ijtihad* (or independent judgment concerning matters of faith), in the role of *ulama',* caliphs, *imams,* and *qadis,* those learned authorities in *shari'ah* law, *sunnah* (orthodoxy) and *shi'ah,* and even on matters of vision. Hourani forever explodes the stupid caricature of Islam as a monolithic and

ageless block, giving us instead an enormously varied tapestry of
religious as well as sociopolitical configurations, changing, recasting,
revising themselves as circumstances around them also change.

Yet while life went on, and the West penetrated more and more
of the Arab universe, the world balance of power shifted more and
more undeniably to the disadvantage of the East and South. The Arabs'
economy seems to have played the central role in the transformation
that Hourani notes, especially in its inability to keep up with the
West's greater entrepreneurial and military skill. This in turn gave rise
to various waves of reform, nationalism, and reaction, from Muhammad Abduh and Jamal al-Din al-Afghani, to Gamal Abdel Nasser and
the struggle over Palestine, and most recently to the appearance of
several brands of Islamic revivalism. What Hourani does with particular effectiveness is, I think, to tell the story in most of its aspects
without alarm or sensationalism. To an Arab or Western reader there
is thus the opportunity to see the almost hopelessly exacerbated circumstances of today in a calmer, more reasonably adumbrated setting,
one in which the excitements and passions of the moment give way
inevitably to an encouraging pattern of mutuality through which Arabs
and Westerners can understand themselves, and each other.

It is difficult to overestimate the signal importance of this book for
this time. Here at last is a genuinely readable, genuinely responsive
history of the Arabs as, I believe, many of them would want to be
known to non-Arabs. Although much in it is perforce either summary
or suggestion, the book is aided by Hourani's bibliography and provides a clear incentive to further reading and exploration. More important, however, is that there isn't a trace in the book of what has been
called Orientalism, that ludicrously inept academic and jargon-ridden
school for which such ideological fictions as "Islamic (or Arab) rage"
or "the Arab mind" are the stock-in-trade. Indeed, Hourani dissolves
most of the Orientalist edifice, with its polemical defenses, its bristling
hostility toward the Arabs and, when they are deployed by modern
Arabs, its grotesque sallies in self-laceration. Not that he is at all either
permissive or triumphalist: very far from it. He completely controls
the best in modern as well as traditional Western scholarship and often
lets the Arabs, their poets, historians, sages, and ordinary people speak
along with, rather than against, that learning. Historical evidence is for
him essentially a *witness,* rather than a symptom, of Arab life.

My main regret is that Hourani's bibliography on Palestine is so
surprisingly stocked with a preponderance of Israeli and Western

sources, some of them admittedly excellent. It is a pity that the quite ample work of Palestinian writers and scholars does not get better exposed or used by him, but with so much else to admire in the book, my complaint is a small one.

Published in the *Los Angeles Times,* February 17, 1991.

CHAPTER 38

The Other Arab Muslims

[1993]

The spring 1993 issue of *Foreign Affairs,* the country's leading quarterly on foreign policy and a bellwether of what policy-makers are thinking about, carried a provocative pair of articles as its feature offering: "Is Islam a Threat? No: Leon T. Hadar. Yes: Judith Miller." Hadar's main point is that the notion of a unified Islamic movement about to engulf "us" with its violence and fanaticism is a "contrived threat." Muslims are neither completely organized, nor totally homogenous. President Clinton would therefore be advised not to lead a crusade against Islam, nor even to try to run the Middle East. Rather he should disengage the United States from interventions or direct pressures on the Islamic countries and allow democracy, peace between the warring factions, and a new prosperity to take over.

For her part Judith Miller is more sweeping in her findings and recommendations. There is an Islamic threat, she insists, whose basis is a fundamental discrepancy between Islam and democracy, modernity, and secularism. Therefore, Muslims should be given tests which, if they fail, will result in strenuous U.S. opposition. A supine fatalism in the face of Islamic militants is a mistake; President Clinton, she says, should fight radical Islam with words, "make a firm commitment to democratic, pluralistic values" for Muslims, and should support regimes like those of Egypt and Jordan. Miller admits that while these regimes have "many, well publicized failings" they are better than any theocratic Islamic regimes that might replace them. She says nothing about already existing struggles for democracy and secularism in the Arab world.

Indeed, whether one believes Hadar or Miller, the overt signs of an extraordinary social and political ferment in the Arab Islamic world—with Iran's simmering Islamic Revolution dangerously adjacent—are there for everyone to see. In Egypt, by far the most significant country in terms of size, volatility, and U.S. interest, the Mubarak government faces an increasingly bold and violently aggressive set of Islamic opponents, with a string of assassinations, indiscriminate bombings, and terrifying threats that proclaim an unremitting defiance; Sudan is in effect controlled by an Islamic party, led by Hassan al-Turabi whose intellectual influence is felt wherever Islamists gather against moderation and secularism; Algeria was about to be overrun by the Islamic Salvation Front, but was protected from this by an unpopular military regime which suffers assassinations and abuse from the proscribed religious party; in the West Bank and Gaza, Hamas and Islamic Jihad have not given up on armed struggle, even though now the PLO has signed an agreement to end its struggle with Israel; Lebanon's Hizballah is supported openly by Iran, and remains the only armed faction in the country, with its resistance against the Israelis and their Lebanese agents, the South Lebanese Army, the party's main arena of violent engagement. Other countries have either made an uneasy peace with the Islamic movements (Jordan, Saudi Arabia) but are mindful of being outflanked by them, or like Tunisia have systematically conducted a protracted war of position against them, using the courts and the military with equal vehemence.

Perhaps with the end of the Cold War, and given our ingrained habits as citizens of a superpower which has divided the world with another (albeit now nonexistent) behemoth, we tend to process all these disturbing bits of information through an us-versus-them filter. There is now also a new attention to what the Harvard former–Vietnam War expert, Samuel Huntington, has called the clash of civilizations: Thus, Islam and the West are seen as irreconcilably at odds. This of course assumes that the West and Islam are watertight categories, and basically ones in which every Westerner and every Muslim is somehow completely at one with his or her respective civilizational category. The fact is that neither Islam nor its alleged opposite is homogenous or all-inclusive. Diversity is a reality that has to be acknowledged.

Now, obviously, to be a citizen of Egypt or of the United States is

not the same thing; but what if at present everyone happens to share
in the difficulty of the question, what does it mean to be an American
(or an Egyptian), and what is the relationship between tradition and
present identity? In the U.S. the tremendously contentious debates
between advocates of multiculturalism and the canon have highlighted
the problem of what in a modern mass society the true components of
a culture are, and how these are best represented. The reason this is
not only an academic question should be plain, since every society
forms an image of itself and of its citizens in order to maintain a
coherent identity, which in a democracy is supposed to be fulfilled or
realized or at least managed by the nation's government. But as more
and more social and ethnic differences appear—as an immigrant culture the United States is particularly liable to the discontent of minority groups who do not feel that Columbus, Jefferson, and Emerson
represent *their* experiences—the dangers of fragmentation or disunity,
in Arthur Schlesinger's phrase, are evident.

In other words, we need to regard society as the locale in which a
continuous contest between adherents of several ideas of the national
identity is taking place. I think this is exactly what is occurring in
Arabic Islamic countries today. The unfortunate thing is that in the
West we tend to think of that contest as already decided in favor of
"Islam" as a war against "us," as if the most significant thing to take
place in Egypt or Saudi Arabia has had to do only with attitudes toward
the West. The contest is deeper, more interesting, and far less determined than that. And as someone who grew up in and still has very
strong ties to the Arab world (even though I live and work in the
United States), I feel much more like a participant in the contest than
a self-indulgent spectator. I am not alone in believing that the prospects
of an Islamic takeover are highly unlikely, and therefore grotesquely
exaggerated in the West, nor am I alone or unrepresentative in my
conviction that for all their vociferousness and enthusiasm the Islamic
parties are not a coherent or viable alternative for the future. My
interest therefore is in personally assessing not so much the grisly
results of Islamic upheaval on the streets of Cairo but rather the
strength of what opposes their efforts. Who and what is *not* interested
in and, in some cases, prepared actively to resist the march toward
Islamic government?

During the summers of 1992 and 1993, I have traveled extensively
in the places I know best—Jordan, Lebanon, the Occupied Territories,
and Egypt—and have been trying to find an answer to these questions

as both an Arab and an American. If there is any point to such investigations, it is to reacquaint oneself with the extraordinary richness and many-layered quality of the terrain: The Arab world today remains turbulent and interestingly unpredictable and, in my opinion, quite resists any neat attempt to compress it into little boxes labeled "Islamic" or "non-Islamic." One of the things that must be factored in is, I believe, that most of these societies, Egypt's certainly, but also Lebanon's and Jordan's, are still largely secular despite the clamorings and debates over Islamic government. The sheer weight of everyday life, with its infinite number of transactions and processes, from the post office, to the public transport system, to currency, buying and selling, electrical power, clothes, medical treatment, diet, construction, television, radio, publishing: all these are worldly (secular, with a small *s*) and are the result not of foreign occupation, imperialism, or Zionism but of willing adaptation, education, and history.

In every Arab country, education, which is now undertaken on a virtually universal scale, is almost completely secular and national. I've lectured in numerous Arab universities over the past several years, and even though you do notice more veils and head-coverings, you also have to take stock of the sheer weight of scientific, social, historical, and aesthetic knowledge imparted to young Muslims, even as in other ways they are also exposed to their religion. If we add to learned or school knowledge all of the myriad components of everyday life that I mentioned earlier, we will have to acknowledge that ongoing life in the Arab world is itself a dense secular information system that deters and inhibits the alternative, otherworldly views provided by theocrats. A recent study of Egyptian television as a national medium by the American anthropologist Lila Abu-Lughod notes that Islam is only marginally represented in the most popular programs, often "as part of a struggle to reappropriate Islamic identity for secular nationalists, a struggle in which the state-controlled mass media . . . are instrumental." Thus, the hero of one popular serial, an intelligence officer, is about to be buried as a disguised spy in Israel; whereupon an Egyptian friend manages to enter where the corpse is lying and reads verses from the Koran over his comrade's body. This sentimentalizes national and religious identities, but it has the potent effect of reaffirming as well as amalgamating them.[34]

What so many of the Islamic parties rhetorically seem to want is somehow to override the secular order, to get on top of it, perhaps change it completely (a fantasy), certainly to regulate it according to their wishes. One must remember, and keep reminding oneself, that this is as possible and feasible a goal as King Canute's wish to roll back the sea. Very little in the enormous literature produced by the Islamic parties for at least two generations suggests any serious way of doing this, except for changing priorities in areas such as civil law, personal behavior, and as the Egyptian writer Nazih Ayoubi puts it in *Political Islam* "the collective enforcement of public morals."[35] Another Arab writer, the Lebanese scholar Asad Abu Khalil, has made the devastating point that if one looks at what has been written by fundamentalists on such matters as economics, industrialization, agriculture, and the like, the most that one finds are vague formulas, such as "we have to reconsider current industrialization policy." Doubtless what Muslim political writers and activists want is the establishment of Islamic states, perhaps resembling Iran's and Sudan's, but one should remember then that political Islam, or the use of Islamic idioms for political ends, is precisely that, and therefore constitutes no more than a party still involved, but by no means victorious, in the cultural and existential contest over identity and secular power.

There is a particularly misleading impression given by Western journalists and academics who write about Islamic fundamentalism that the fanatics and zealots are on one side of some great divide, their victims and opponents (most of whom seem silent) on the other. Phrases like "Muhammad's armies" or the "Islamic threat" suggest an emanation from out of the desert into otherwise faceless societies; it is as if a tribe of aliens suddenly appears over the horizon and invades a placid generic village or town. The reality is very different. All of the major Arab countries with the exception of Lebanon declare in their constitutions that the state religion is Islam. A huge majority of Arabs today are in fact Muslim (the word *Muslim* is less provocative and more habitual for most Arabs, the word *Islamic* has acquired an activist, and even aggressive quality that belies the more ambiguous reality), although of course there are Muslim as well as several Christian Arab minorities too. Islam of course is a religion, but it is also a culture; the Arabic language is the same for Muslims as it is for Christians, both of whom, believers *and* nonbelievers alike, are deeply affected—perhaps the better word is *inflected*—by the Koran, which is also in Arabic.

There are of course distinctly Christian traditions inside the Islamic world. I myself belong to one. But it would be grossly inaccurate to think of them as separate and outside Islam, which includes us all. This, I think, is the most important point of all: Islam is something all Arabs share in, and is an integral part of our identity. I know that I may be speaking only for myself when I say that as an Arab Christian I have never felt myself to be a member of an aggrieved or marginal minority. Being an Arab, even for a non-Muslim, means being a member of what the late Marshall Hodgson called an Islamicate world, or culture. Any attempts at severing the tie are, I believe, doomed to failure.

In Egypt I asked Huda Wasfy, a Coptic woman who is a professor of French at Cairo University, whether she experienced any of the persecution and discrimination she might have expected as a member of the Christian minority. "Not at all," she said. "We are all too much alike, Copts and Muslims, for me to feel like an outsider or a persecuted victim. We speak the same language, we have the same habits, and we even celebrate the same feasts, so as Copts we cannot be considered outsiders in any sense." Ms. Wasfy and I were speaking in the heart of Cairo, not in one of the southern provinces like Asyut, where communal violence has indeed been extremely widespread. Still, in addition to northern cities with sizable Coptic populations like Tanta and Alexandria, Cairo counts for a great deal. If the Muslim insurrectionaries are to win in Egypt, they must win in Cairo. Another Cairo professor—a childhood friend of mine—Huda Guindy, also a Copt and known for her outspoken manner and fearless honesty, confirmed Wasfy's views. But she added that there has been an extra effort on the part of officials and bureaucrats to make Copts feel completely assimilated. This does not mean that Egypt is a paradise for minorities or dissenters. It isn't (which country is?), but most of its people feel that they belong to the same nation, with social and economic problems that derive from within the nation, can be described in the same language, and are therefore common to everyone in it.

If one of the serious misrepresentations of the current crisis is that fundamentalist Islam is depicted as something coming at Arab societies from the outside, another, no less seriously false image is that fundamentalism is a sudden and therefore entirely new eruption from within. For at least a hundred years, the Arab nationalist movement and the Islamic reform movement have been intertwined. No intellectual, political personality, or artist has addressed Arabism without also addressing Islam, and this has been true of Muslims as well as Christians, men and women. There is simply no way of disassociating the two, even though the new debate about *secularism (al-'almanah)*, a relatively unfamiliar word in Arabic, has been gathering momentum

here and there in the Arab world. Western polemicists about Islam—
and this includes some venerable Orientalists—have emphasized the
conjunction in Islam between religion and state *(din wa dawla),* as if the
various Koranic precepts suggesting their correspondence with each
other were somehow absolute. This is a textual fiction, since throughout Islamic history rulers generally acted like rulers everywhere else
and not according to some endlessly consulted text. There is indeed
a curious similarity between recent Western polemics about Islamic
fundamentalism and what the fundamentalists themselves say: Both
argue as if the early Islam the fundamentalists wish to reinstate was in
fact the rather simplistic, not to say Pollyanna-ish confection they have
so violently been fighting for, and they seem to believe that a return
to primitive origins in the late twentieth century is actually possible.

Of course it is not. Polemics in the Arab world today effectively use
Islam as an emotional, attention-getting force to compete with governments and other contestants in the struggle for secular political power.
This is not to say that questions of belief, piety, and interpretation are
not also very much at stake. They are, and I shall come back to them
later. But erudite polemics about law and authority are a small part of
the current political ferment which is so easily discernible to anyone
who looks in from the outside. The best way of grasping this often
quite feverish debate is to identify two or three levels of concern for
Arabs in Muslim societies. First of all at a time when tremendous
political change seems to have occurred everywhere on earth, there has
also been a sudden closeness felt between cultures and peoples that
have usually been both distant and distinct. The worldly culture of
electronic communications, consumerism, transnational commerce
and business that has transformed countries like Egypt and Jordan, for
example, has also sent many people in them back into themselves to
ask, "Who are we, and what does it mean now to be Arab and
Muslim?" In a different way, Europeans are asking themselves the
same question, especially since in France and Britain—to name only
two cases—society now includes large numbers of postcolonial African, Caribbean, and Asian immigrants (many of them Muslim) who
have broken the old homogeneity of Smiths and Duponts.

For many Egyptian and Jordanian men and women, with economic
insecurity a horrifically persistent fact of daily life, there is some
immediate security to be had in dressing demurely, going to prayers,
reciting Koranic verses. Those comforts have always been available,
but now they are part of a more general and ambitious process of

intellectual and political self-questioning. What is modernity for a Muslim? What is our heritage *(turath)*? Who has and ought to have authority? These are major epistemological problems that now occupy a lot of attention among intellectuals and scholars, even though their equivalent among the populace are a much less finicky and more obvious sort of behavior.

Still, there is a paradox to be observed. Commentators and critics who are (of course) usually Muslim, as well as modern and secular, see no difficulty for them in the mere statement of belonging to the Islamic community which is so much a feature of contemporary Egypt. Galal Amin, an economist and social theorist at the American University of Cairo, told me that even though he was a secularist himself he could quite easily identify with women who adopted pious dress or men who seemed to have reespoused Islamic ways. To him, this was a form of self-expression, somewhat playful and carnivalesque, in a dreary time of drabness and even despair. In any case it has to do with regaining a sense of security. With perhaps 58 million out of 60 million people in Egypt waking up each day worried about how they are going to get through the day with enough food for themselves and their children, falling back into simple patterns of Islamic conformity—a scarf over the head, long-sleeved dress, a cap, a beard, frequenting mosques and prayer groups, attachments to a local shaikh—seems easy enough to do if a measure of emotional comfort is achieved. I think it would be foolishly wrong to mistake this for the "fundamentalism" that throws bombs and attempts murders in broad daylight in the name of Islam. That both derive from assertions of an Islamic identity does not mean that they are the same thing at all.

They are related, however, in one very important way, and this is an additional level of concern. I spoke about this at great length with Mohammed Hassanein Heikal, an old friend and the Arab world's leading independent journalist. In his early seventies, Heikal is still an extremely vigorous and fit man; a veritable encyclopedia of information on Egypt and the Arab world (he is really the only journalist who is both pundit and investigative historian), an acute, often quite acerbic critic of both Sadat and Mubarak. He was Gamal Abdul Nasser's closest confidant and, under Nasser, rose to great eminence as cabinet minister and editor of *Al-Ahram,* the Arab world's leading daily. Unlike many prominent figures in Egypt and the Arab world, Heikal has always maintained a critical distance from the Gulf world, its oil, rulers, and favors. He remains an Arab nationalist with a solid presence in Egypt;

he knows what he is talking about, has always been part of the political establishment, and as a solitary intellectual has also become an institution, in his rather baronial but curiously earthy way, opposed to the autocratic methods of Nasser's successors.

Although he is both a secular and modern man, Heikal emphatically rejects the notion that the Islamists are anything more than a vast oppositional and protest movement. Not given to excessively theoretical and exegetic disputes about *ijtihad* (personal interpretation) in readings of the Koran, Heikal's view of Egypt's current turbulence is entirely political. "Those bomb throwers and wild men," he said, "are the result of an almost unimaginably corrupt and mediocre government."

Heikal stated emphatically and persuasively the central secular argument about the rise of Islamic sentiment everywhere in the Arab world. For most citizens the government's indifference and brutality provokes in them a retreat into a relatively inviolate zone of religious observance. A few take the next step—out into the streets. In both instances, says Heikal, "Islam is a natural identity to adopt." As for the Mubarak government, he added, "It has no ideas, no vision, no values." No one I spoke to in Egypt or anywhere else in the Arab world said anything very different about the ruling elites. This, far more than the terrorist threat, is the core of the problem. With literally no exceptions, every Egyptian I know and have discussed these matters with for the past half dozen years says the same disaffected, even disgusted things about the government. Deals on every conceivable commodity are made by middlemen and commission agents, usually with some minister or Mubarak-in-law as a front; public discourse is so devaluated that it is virtually impossible to tell the truth; the country is in effect ruled by a series of autocratic measures licensing the government to stop articles in newspapers, to jail and torture dissidents under emergency laws passed by Sadat but still in force now, and to prevent unions, political organizations, secular human rights groups from assembly or action. Above all, no change is on the horizon.

I happened to turn on the TV one evening in Cairo last July to watch a special parliamentary session convened expressly to hail Mubarak and "convince" him to accept a third six-year term as president. This *mubaya'a,* or convocation of praise, was an astonishing procession of dignified-looking men and women, members of parliament all, heaping the most fulsome and improbable praise on the quite colorless

man—*la vache qui rit;* he is called by some, *Rolex,* i.e., neither advances
nor retards; by others, *moccasin,* you neither have to tie nor untie him;
by still others—who has ruled Egypt for the past twelve years. "O
Mubarak, you bringer of prosperity and tranquillity," roared one
effusive member; "O Mubarak, you intrepid warrior and son of
Egypt," blathered another. So it went more or less uninterruptedly for
the two hours that I watched, all of the speeches reiterating Mubarak's
sterling qualities as a keeper of public order. This was clearly intended
by the government as a show of public democracy, but the total
absence of any other contender, plus the utterly fatuous and empty
praise bestowed on the man who has more or less kept things going
for the Americans, the local rich and the profiteers, gave the convocation a particularly offensive edge—hypocrisy, unreality, servility. "Do
you know," Heikal asked me the next day, "what the state of the
infrastructure is like? Cairo is now a city of almost fifteen million
people, but its grid of basic services is unchanged from the time when
Cairo had a population of four million."

The perception is universally endorsed, even though of course there
have been changes here and there. What matters is that the Egyptian
government, like the Lebanese government, or the Israeli occupation
authorities on the Occupied Territories, appears to be best not at
tending or improving the lot of its people but at its own perpetuation
and profit, regardless of the people it is supposed to be serving. In
Egypt, therefore, this prevalent sense of alienation is best alleviated for
many by Islam, as a communal or oppositional force. Yet whenever I
pressed the issue of such insurrectionary groups as the Gamaat al-
Islamiyya or the shadowy Takfir wal Higra, and especially the redoubtable Shaikh Omar Abdel Rahman, I got all kinds of demurrals. I would
go so far as to say that the stories I heard the most often were first that
Shaikh Omar was an American spy and, second, that the spotty terrorist violence—which the Western press has blown up to the most lurid
proportions and which has simply not totally disrupted everyday life in
Cairo or Alexandria—had made the assailants tremendously unpopular. No one failed to mention that the perpetrators of a recent bomb
attack against a government official riding in his car were apprehended,
beaten up, then handed over to the police—by ordinary Egyptians who
reacted spontaneously to the outrage. I happened to be speaking to a
Cairo journalist by phone on August 19, the day after Interior Minister
Hassan al-Alfi was wounded in a bomb attack just off Tahrir Square.
The striking aspect of the outrage, according to my friend, wasn't the

intended victim but that three Arab passersby were killed. Like the Shubra (a poor section of Cairo) bomb earlier in the summer, these indiscriminate killings may alienate the large majority of Egyptian Muslims for whom presumably an Islamic government is being so energetically pursued.

One speaks here of speculative, impressionistic assessments of course, but it is possible for me to imagine that the average Egyptian man or woman would in the end swing behind these appalling lurches toward something so vague as Islamic government, even though since the methods, to say nothing of the goal, seem in fact to promise little of concrete benefit. In the late eighties there was much attention paid to the sort of parallel economy and services offered to Egyptians by Islamic charities, hospitals, investment companies, and the like. That kind of money, and therefore the services they funded, is no longer available. Now one thing you hear a lot about instead is that well-known movie stars and dancers are publicly declaring their intention to veil themselves *(tahgib)*. Yusef Shahine, Egypt's most distinguished film director, a man now in his late sixties who is apoplectically honest and outspoken, denounced these Tartuffian gestures. "The famous ones are being paid millions to do it; the others do it as a way of perhaps getting money, perhaps of atoning for their past, perhaps because they think it might get them some attention," he said, fulminating against a couple of recent candidates (with whom he has worked over the years) for sanctity. But the focus on arts and artists does suggest the extent to which money for Islamic causes from wealthy funders is now going to symbolic, as opposed to large-scale, social or economic enterprises. (Everyone concedes that their finest moment occurred when the Islamic groups were able to marshal direct aid and support for victims of the Cairo earthquake two years ago.)

Culture and the discourse of everyday life have now become a major battleground between the Muslim acolytes and their secular opponents. I had lunch with Shukry Ayyad, a well-known critic and professor of Arabic literature, and discovered that he was about to complete a long, carefully argued treatise against the fundamentalists. Kamal Abul-Magd, also a professor and Islamic jurist—a man of remarkable fluency and learning—described to me the appallingly slapdash methods of the new shaikhs and religious demagogues who leap to instant denunciations of heresy and apostasy in bloodcurdling language, with scant background in the infinitely complex and pains-taking legal processes that the Islamic tradition spells out explicitly.

The point to be kept in mind, therefore, is that the terrain is Islamic to begin with. How it is charted and how it is fought over are the main issues, and so far as the fundamentalists are concerned the issues are still not settled in their favor. Egyptian culture is too complicated and invested with all sorts of other, more slowly evolving interests that are really quite hybrid (as Egyptian history itself is hybrid) for it to be hijacked by a small band of conspirators, who express a more active disenchantment with the government that has severely limited democratic participation and severely curtails freedom of thought and expression. Besides, even though the extreme fundamentalists do share some areas of belief and tradition with the majority Sunni population, they are in the end felt to be too reductive, ascetic, and unyielding for mainstream Egyptians.

Take the kind of Islamic law flamboyantly administered in Saudi Arabia. That derives first of all from a particular and small branch of Islam, the Wahhabi, and it is now directly connected in the popular mind with the precepts and the monopoly on coercion held by the Saudi royal family. In Egypt, Jordan, Lebanon, such ideas of justice are no match at all for the secular impartiality universally sought for the law in societies where wealth, privilege, or the regime's whimsy has made a travesty of legal procedure. Too many people know about torture, disappearances, and other such abuses of power to wish to endow with even greater autocracy groups perceived as mainly concerned with religious orthodoxy, directly applied, rather than social justice. The fight for an abstract conception of Islamic law is far less popular than a desire for relief from unfair practices right across the board. But many people do see Islam, according to Egyptian political scientist Mamoun Fandy, as "a way of making new rules for society, namely that honesty and hard work rather than family connections should determine social advancement. And in the name of egalitarianism, the young graduates are waging war in Cairo against the old rules."[36]

Sometimes I spend time with Gamal al-Ghitani, probably the best known of the Egyptian writers whose generation immediately follows Naguib Mahfouz's. (He is considered by some as Mahfouz's heir: Both of them come from the same working-class district of Cairo; both have that special combination of historical and political realism with a controlled tendency toward the visionary; both are thoroughly Arab and Egyptian in the best sense and seem only marginally concerned with writing, traditions, and influences outside their immediate orbit.

There is a wonderful book of conversations between the two men that really ought to be translated into English.) Ghitani's best novel is *Al-Zayni Barakat* (I wrote the introduction for the excellent English translation), a complex allegory of Abdel Nasser's Egypt, of which Ghitani himself was a product. The cultural editor of *Al-Akhbar,* Egypt's second largest daily, Ghitani has a very suggestive insight into his society's present volatility, and we have formed the habit of going on rambling walks in Cairo's lesser-known quarters, where we speak meanderingly on the ups and downs of our time; as he points out buildings and mosques to me—he has an astoundingly detailed knowledge of the urban palimpsest that Cairo is—he reflects on the odd unities of Egyptian culture, with its fabulous duration and the persistence of its main themes.

The last couple of times that we spent time together the Islamic resurgence and the methods of its garish fringes kept coming up. ''We are well known for the constant presence in our life as a people commanded by a pharaoh, or sultan, or some grandiose, larger-than-life ruler like Nasser or Sadat,'' he began. ''But things have always changed after the death of a onetime pharoah. Take the Rifai mosque, built in the mid-nineteenth century by Khedive Tawfiq's mother. It was supposed to be a memorial to her power and celebrity, but there was also a very poor man, Ahmad Abu Shibak, in the area who used to come to the mosque for shelter and rest. As he had a saintly reputation it was a matter of only a few years before the mosque became known for his corner in it; people come here to pray and in order to be near him. Although five rulers of Egypt, plus the late shah, are buried there, no one visits their graves, whereas candles are kept lit where Ahmad is buried. Even the mosque is named for the Rifai Sufi order (whose founder is buried in Iraq) to which Ahmad belonged. That's one thing to remember. The other is something that Islamists who have been inspired by desert kingdoms (i.e., the Saudi Wahhabis, whose version of Islam is extremely austere and most unlike Egyptian Islam, which is extremely heterogenous) tend to forget. For us, death and life—tombs and homes, for instance—coexist, nourish each other, are visited with equal familiarity by the people. We are inclusive Muslims; they are exclusivist ones. A person's grave for them is just a hole in the ground, without even a marker next to it. For us it's a recognized part of our daily life.''

On my last visit, he was particularly anxious to take me to the Qaitbay district just at the city's eastern outskirts. A desperately poor area, it nevertheless contains two great mosques, one a jewellike house of worship adjoining the mausoleum of Qaitbay, a Mameluke king; the other a rather more imposing structure, the mosque of Ibn Barquq, also a Mameluke ruler. After showing me a few splendid vistas afforded by Ibn Barquq's skillful architect, Ghitani drew me to a stone slab covered with faint hieroglyphic characters that adorn the floor of the mosque's entryway. Then he quickly took me to the courtyard's central podium, on which a striking birdlike ornament rested. "Both the slab and this ornament draw directly and without any embarrassment on Egypt's pre-Islamic past, which these later Muslim rulers have casually reappropriated for their purposes," Ghitani said. "The mixture is here but isn't much acknowledged by most Muslims today, especially because there's been so much controversy about the so-called purity of Islamic culture stirred up by today's Muslim demagogues." Ghitani's examples were, of course, relatively modest, but they rang true and addressed the larger question of identity—Muslim and Arab—without the anger and resentment that has characterized so many recent debates.

But there was a deeper, perhaps even theological, point being made by Ghitani. One of the major polemical themes constantly elaborated on in the discourse of the new Islamic enthusiasts is the idea of *jahiliyya*. The word derives from the root *j-h-l,* to be ignorant; *jahiliyya* means "the state of ignorance," but in the Islamic context it has a very powerful traditional significance as referring to the condition of the Arabs *before* the Islamic revelation was vouchsafed to the Prophet Muhammad. Historically, therefore, *jahiliyya* refers to a temporal demarcation (like B.C.), although some of the greatest texts of Arabic literature are pre-Islamic, belong to the *jahiliyya* period, and are still studied and memorized as they have been by generations of Arab schoolchildren. Yet in Egypt, *jahiliyya* has now taken on the force of religious condemnation, applied wholesale to contemporary politics, culture, and society. Ghitani was particularly alarmed at efforts made by some of the Muslim preachers (who had once been given a platform by the government when it was prosecuting Leftists and Nasserites) like Shaikh Shaarawi, who were pronouncing sentences of excommunication against the theater, film, dancing, and other arts. The use of blanket charges of *takfir* (or excommunication) he said had roused the cultural community. Yusef Shahine had also mentioned this to me, and while I was in Cairo, the newspapers were reporting the formation of a committee that included Naguib Mahfouz and Egypt's most popular actor, Adel Imam, to fight the fundamentalist assault on virtually the whole of popular culture.

In addition, according to Ghitani, government policy was perceptibly changing, cynically and opportunistically perhaps but enough to encourage opponents of the "extremists" (as everyone now calls them, although the government prefers the wholesome sobriquet "terrorists") to speak up. For television, he said, there has been a noticeable effort to devise programs emphasizing national, perhaps even secular, culture, and for the first time missions of Cairo intellectuals, writers, artists were being sent to Upper Egypt (neglected for decades) where violence has more or less completely taken over. It sounded pretty vague though promising, and I said so to Ghitani. He didn't agree because, having watched the regime's glacierlike slowness for years, he was now encouraged at even the slightest sign of dispatch.

Like all the people I spoke to, he was adamantly opposed to any further concession being made to the religious parties and seemed prepared to go to great lengths to fight them. But what convinced me more was that he kept characterizing the contest as one between those with a sort of forced, sometimes violently applied, and constricting orthodoxy, as formulated by men and women of decidedly mediocre cultural talents, and adherents of a national and Islamic culture that was basically resistant to even the most strenuous pressures of the new, strident orthodoxy. And, indeed, as anyone who knows Egypt's ways—its meandering eclecticism, the joyous untidiness of its public life, the exuberance of its people's wit and perpetual celebration of worldliness, the general ineffectiveness of its police and even its strongmen—there is something profoundly unconvincing about the Muslim fundamentalists. Yes, they offer a devastating rejection of Egypt's dreadful economic and social quandaries but scarcely an alternative or anything resembling an efficient, real worldview.

One cannot disagree with Heikal, who blamed Sadat and Mubarak for robbing the country of its major political assets. "Cairo was once the center of the Arab world," he said with some bitterness. "It is now a large city with all kinds of problems; all the resonances, the dimensions that gave Cairo its status, thanks to Abdel Nasser—Arab, Muslim, Third World, Non-Aligned—have been stripped away. What's left is something very easy for devout Muslims to attack—corruption, mediocre local politicians, extremely opportunistic intellectuals who changed sides en masse as a result of the Gulf War." But he too felt that the extremist Islamic activists had no real chance, although, like the other Egyptians I spoke to, he suggested that the short-run key was probably the army. It is difficult to forget that though the army is often described as the mainstay of anti-Islamic opposition, it was from the army itself that Sadat's assassins came.

According to Mahmoud Amin el Alim, a cultivated and still respected man of the Left, the great triad of army, government, Islamic opposition hinges on the army's internal or perhaps hidden condition. "The three actors are now in an ambiguous and equivocal relationship with each other. Both the government and the Islamics have extensions into the army. On the anniversary of the Revolution [July 23] Mubarak made a great do about spending most of his time at various army camps around Cairo. Yet it is common knowledge that several army officers are Islamic sympathizers, as are many enlisted men. I suppose," he concluded, "it now depends on who has penetrated the army more, the government or the Islamic parties."

Adding to the shifting landscape of domestic power relations is the status of the Muslim Brotherhood, the oldest and most established of all the Islamic groups. They were hounded into silence or prison by Abdel Nasser; they retaliated by trying to assassinate him. Several of their leaders were hanged or tortured to death, but then Sadat revived them as a method for dealing with his other opponents. Their present influence is notable in two ways. First, they represent the original semiclandestine Islamic political party and have created offshoots and branches throughout the *mashriq,* or Eastern Arab world. Theirs is the literature and the ideas, principal among them Sayyid Qutb's *Ma'alim fil Tariq,* 1964 *(Signposts Along the True Way),* which pioneered the use of *jahiliyya* as a term of contemporary description. In the Occupied Territories, Hamas is a local branch of the Brotherhood; Jihad al-Islami, its rival, is a breakaway movement from it whose complaint is that Hamas is not confrontational enough. Second, both in Egypt and Jordan (and to some extent in Palestine) the Brotherhood, in the minds of many, has a symbiotic relationship with the government. In Jordan, for example, they have a considerable number of parliamentary seats and to the more nationalist-minded Islamists are remembered for their use by the king as buffers against Arab nationalism and Abdel Nasser. A similar configuration exists between the Brotherhood and the Egyptian government.

Despite its confusing status the Muslim Brotherhood remains the major Islamic political party, yet it is neither insurrectionary nor extra-parliamentary, and must therefore be counted as part of the mostly discredited official political game in both Egypt and Jordan. Hamas has been given a big play by the Israeli and Western medias, but they too are remembered for having been encouraged as an anti-PLO force by Yitzhak Rabin when he was defense minister in the eighties. So there is a complicated paradox in all this: On the one hand, Islamic groups are opponents to governments in the political arena, although some of the leading contenders are somewhat compromised with the government because of their former alignments. The Egyptian Brotherhood has taken to condemning armed attacks by the smaller and violently inclined extreme parties. On the other hand, these groups are not and probably cannot be mass-based. They have some of the millenarian attributes of, say, the Iranian Shia opponents of the shah, but as Sumnis they have produced neither a charismatic leadership nor a sufficient critical number of proponents who are willing to go the whole way toward taking power. The paradox is therefore that Islamicists are contentious and oppositional, as Heikal continues to argue, but in the moral grayness and intellectual poverty of the landscape, they cannot yet command the hegemony to effect decisive change.

As Ghitani said to me in a formulation that expressed the deeper inner quandary felt by many Arabs: "In the battle between a religious extremism and terrorism seeking to bring down a corrupt and basically repressive government the choice for many of us, lamentable though it may be, is to side with army and regime." Whatever its deplorable shortcomings, the government in place is a lesser evil than Khomeini-style rule (hukm). "Remember," Ghitani added, "that Sunni Islam doesn't provide for clergy with a clearly defined social or political role, and even though clerics like Shaikhs Mohammed Ghazali or Abdel Rahman have influence and some followers they are nowhere near big enough to carry the country forward." Implied in Ghitani's at best qualified support for an unpopular government and a potentially repressive army against the theocrats is the absence of a third alternative. No one said anything about that in Egypt.

Everywhere I went I was most impressed with the size and weight of the mostly silent but sometimes vocal opposition of intellectuals to Islamic fundamentalism as a potential style of government, but equally impressive (and depressing) was the absence of a really alternative political vision and discourse. People who strenuously profess an unwillingness to be ruled by someone like Sudan's Turabi (whose real scope is, I believe, quite overestimated by Western journalists) have become accustomed to living with well-organized Islamists in the

Egyptian professional syndicates (doctors, engineers, etc.), or student groups, or newspapers, magazines, and television. Such cohabitation, particularly since the Islamists overlap with the population in background and tradition, has produced a casual familiarity that has had the strange effect of dulling the sense of shock and urgency that Western outsiders often project onto these societies.

You can see this very plainly in Lebanon, barely recovering from two decades of civil war, invasion, all-out mayhem. I have the feeling that very little of what Lebanon is (or was) has survived in the minds of most Americans except for Beirut, which remains a metaphor for mindless violence, and Hizballah, the "Iranian-backed Shia militia," as it is routinely described in American commentary, which stands for the ultimate in fundamentalist frenzy. Adding to these unattractive qualities is the sad truth that it is still legally impossible for U.S. citizens to visit Lebanon, and in one of those gestures of idiotic denial unworthy of a superpower, American travel agents are not even allowed to sell passage into Lebanon, although of course one can readily do so anywhere in Europe. Such is the pathetic legacy of hostage taking and the destruction of the Marine barracks.

But calm has, in fact, largely returned to Beirut; schools and universities are open and educating eager students; local businesses are once again flourishing; most Arabs now travel there with confidence, as do Europeans; the government of Prime Minister Rafik Hariri is trying to assert itself (with Syria now firmly entrenched as the country's presiding power). Lebanon's confessional politics remain pretty much as they have always been, however, which means that political bosses and sectarian leaders still run things. The big political changes are that adjustments have occurred in the pre–civil war balance: The once all-powerful Maronites are less powerful; the far more numerous Shia Muslims are now relatively more influential.

What about Hizballah's power, I asked Elias Khoury, a brilliant novelist and newspaper editor. "It's true that they are still armed and that they continue to attack the Israelis and their South Lebanese Army stooges in the so-called security zones, but so far as Lebanon is concerned they are to most of us part of the political scene, neither very formidable, nor particularly threatening." As is the case in Egypt, many secular Lebanese have direct access to parties and leaders who are on the opposite side, so one doesn't have the sense of a standing war. On the contrary, Hizballah's leader, Shaikh Fadlallah, is spoken of with respect and some admiration. It is he more than any other local politician who speaks the nationalist discourse, and he seems relatively unencumbered with chiliastic sentiment.

Lebanon's Shias are mostly a disadvantaged community and live unenviably in Beirut's horrendously crowded southern suburbs or in South Lebanon. It was they who bore the brunt of Israel's brand of ethnic cleansing in July 1993—to create hundreds or thousands of refugees, as well as uninhabited towns and villages—and they who for their resistance won the support not only of Hariri's government but also nominally opposed communities like the Maronites. As in Egypt, what was once an international (Third World, Non-aligned, Arabist) platform has become in Lebanon a much more modest polyphony of local voices, all competing for a bit of power. Hariri himself has strong ties to Saudi Arabia and Syria, who themselves play a much smaller game these days. Fabulously wealthy and in the past well intentioned (through his Hariri foundation, he personally financed the studies abroad of thousands of Lebanese students during the worst days of the civil war, a feat unmatched by any individual in the Arab world), he has now become a symbol of cooptation and financial control of anyone who stands in his way.

Lebanon is therefore very far from being any sort of launching pad for worldwide Islamic takeovers—despite the hysterical overreactions of Israeli polemicists like Martin Kramer in the pages of *Commentary*—not just because economic survival in a difficult local environment is the first order of business but also because the Arab world is far too involved in the secular everyday for even the most redoubtable of militant preachers to take it back into the seventh century. Many Arabs do say, "Let them try," but with the proviso that *all* sectors of the population, and not just an unpopular, frequently violent government, be given some credit and support by Western governments, academics, and journalists for opposing such takeovers, in the unlikely event that they should occur.

As with all other fields of social and historical inquiry, "Islam" is not a neutral object of impartial research but enlists the interests of participant and observer alike. Characterizing Islam as *ipso facto* "undemocratic" is not a statement of fact but a sweeping and deeply hostile reaction that simply overrides the efforts of many Muslims—lawyers, women, doctors, intellectuals, even shaikhs—to make their societies democratic and Muslim at the same time. In Pakistan, which for a decade was dominated by the military dictatorship and the fundamentalists, the latter have been completely isolated and the former replaced by parliamentary government. Judaism is not democratic, and its attitudes to women are quite misogynist, yet Israeli Jews are given the benefit of the doubt in their effort to have their society more secular and fair, as should Muslims who want the same social amenities that "we" do.

The role of the present Arab governments is quite problematic, not least because of their alliances, real or imagined, with the United States. In Jordan and Egypt, the American embassy is an imposing, if also monumentally repellent, structure obviously designed to impress locals with the power and authority of the last superpower. Mubarak's regime has in effect completely bought the American discourse on the world, complete with "terrorists," "extremists," and "radicals," all of whom are violent and implacably opposed to the "peace process." Humiliatingly dependent on the United States for money and general support, Mubarak's government, to most Egyptians, has lost its credibility and even its loyalty to its own citizens. An extremely unattractive set of associations has developed therefore: The Americans are seen as abetting Mubarak's regime in its often brutal clamping down on the Muslim activists, and this in turn puts secular or Islamic opponents of the militants in the distasteful position, like Ghitani's, of supporting a government they don't like. Moreover, many Egyptians fall back into implicit support for "Islam" and for some of the militants, if not for their chaotic methods, because Mubarak and the United States are on the same side.

The difficulty of steering a clear path between nationalist and religious identities is even greater in the Occupied Territories, which I visited this summer for the second year in a row. Ibrahim Abu-Lughod, one of my oldest friends, is now Provost of Bir Zeit, the West Bank's leading university. A Muslim himself, he is also an unequivocal secularist and opponent both of Hamas and Jihad al-Islami, the two main Islamic parties. "They are losers and in the end have nothing to offer," he has said for years, and even more insistently now. Yet he acknowledges with some chagrin that they are the only groups publicly willing to mobilize against the Israeli occupation. And as for myself, having for years been involved with the Palestinian struggle for self-determination, I could not disagree with him. In 1992 when I was there, I briefly met a few of the student leaders who represent Hamas: I was impressed by their sense of political commitment but not at all by their ideas. In 1993 I arranged to spend some more hours with them and with their rivals for political sway, Islamic Jihad. I found them

quite moderate when it came to accepting the truths of modern
science, for instance (interestingly the four young men I spoke to were
students with outstanding records: all of them were scientists or
engineers); hopelessly reductive in their views of the West; and irre-
fragably opposed to the existence of Israel. "The Jews have to leave,"
one of them said categorically, "except for the ones who were here
before 1948."

What I did find revealing was the extent to which Hamas and Jihad
oppose each other on crucial points. Indeed, a lot of our time was
taken up with representatives from each side sniping, if not actually
letting loose, against the other. Hamas regards itself as the true Islamic
party, whereas Jihad is more prone to extremism and violence. Jihad
was clear about wanting to kill anyone like Salman Rushdie who was
an apostate (I had informed them that he was not only a good friend
but someone whose writings I fully support); Hamas demurred but
signaled that he would suffer an unpleasant fate just this side of killing.
The punishment wasn't specified. Yet both said that their goals as
militants battling the Israeli authorities were similar: *tawtir wa tath-
wir*—the words in Arabic have a pleasant internal cross-rhyme that
rolls off the tongue liltingly—or in much less attractive English, polarizing and revolutionizing, intensifying and deepening, the sense of
crisis by armed attacks. In turn, such a policy makes it very hard for
the PLO factions who also oppose the occupation but, according to
several informants, have been neutralized by the PLO's conciliatory
and fruitless negotiations. I was there at a particularly low ebb in the
nationalist movement's history; this was two months before the PLO–
Israel agreement was announced and, with no indication that anything
was happening in Washington after twenty months of negotiations,
anti-Hamas Palestinians were very despondent.

The problem, however, seemed then that none of them had anything very much to offer the large majority of people, Muslim and
Christian, who seemed tired and confused. This is why today only
Hamas and Jihad have opposed the new deal but still have no great base
of support, and why Yasir Arafat's dramatic turnabout was cleverly
designed to sweep behind him everyone not for Hamas. The keenest
student of Palestinian Islamic groups, Professor Ziad Abu Amr of Bir
Zeit, has spoken of political schizophrenia to describe the current state
of affairs, yet he has given the Islamists at most 33 percent of popular
sentiment. And he has admitted that the PLO has declined substantially

in the eyes of many, a drop that is not likely to be remedied for some time.

The extraordinary exaggeration of Hamas's power is, I am firmly convinced, part of the same "Islamic threat" furor that has so dominated Western policy and journalistic commentary. On the West Bank and Gaza, they do have the capacity to mobilize people for demonstrations or strikes (mostly useless) and a much smaller number for the occasional attack on Israeli soldiers. But, in the main, their ideas are protests against Israeli occupation, their leaders neither especially visible nor impressive, their writings rehashes of old nationalist tracts, now couched in an "Islamic" idiom. Worst of all, their "threat" has been marketed by policymakers in Israel, the PLO, and the United States, as a way of forcing more concessions on the Palestinians and trying to sell the deal to Israel.

Anyone who wants to get an idea of how an Islamic party can quite easily be coopted and domesticated is advised to look across the West Bank into Jordan. The Muslim Brotherhood there (affiliated with Hamas, whose Jordanian spokesman inhabits and gives statements from the Brotherhood's headquarters) has garnered about thirty seats in the Jordanian lower house in the 1989 election. One of King Hussein's smartest moves was to open out the system enough to let them in; they have since become a sort of dutiful, totally uncharismatic (and finally discredited) opposition, forced to act in effect as part of the establishment. While they do say similar things about the Israeli occupation and Western hegemony that one hears on the West Bank, their voices are freighted with the tired officialese that one hears from most of the sanctioned parties throughout the Arab world. I spent a morning discussing their view of the world and must confess to having been impressed by very little about them: They don't have the same earnest fluency of the young West Bankers I saw a few days earlier; at the same time their command of the facts is so general and derivative as to neutralize all and any attitudes, and their general prospects for action and influence seem confined to remaining in parliament. As compared with a group of high-level businessmen I saw right after them—tough, practical-minded, cynical—you could be certain that Muslim radicalism had in effect been detoured for the duration. The king and his court remain firmly in control.

The real voice of Islamic radicalism in Jordan is that of Laith Shubeilat, an American-educated engineer of remarkable brilliance and attractiveness, on whom both the Brotherhood and the Jordanian establishment heap scorn and abuse. He speaks modestly of a personal conversion in Rome about fifteen years ago; everything about his background—his father was an ambassador—suggests the ease and comfort of the upper-middle-class Jordanian (not Palestinian) population, all of whose members are loyal to the Hashemite dynasty. Shubeilat tells you that *his* Islamic principles are perfectly correspondent with other democratic value systems. He has little affinity for the authoritarianism of the *ulama* (they deal with the shadow of the problem, he said, not the problem itself) and even less time for matters pertaining to whether women should cover their heads or not. He is deeply critical of U.S. policy in the Arab world and has for a long time been an unforgiving critic of the Jordanian government, especially its corruption and lack of real democracy. For his unrelenting attacks on the government's abuses, he was put on trial last year and sentenced to twenty years in jail; the collected documents of the case, plus the well-publicized use of phony witnesses, allegations about hidden arms supplies, and overriding of evidence by the court are almost comic to read through or hear about today. And apparently out of some sense of embarrassment, the king granted him a pardon, although six weeks after I saw him in Amman, Shubeilat (a former member of parliament) retired from politics altogether, protesting both the government and the conventional political parties.

There is no easy way of gauging the extent of Shubeilat's influence or popularity except that, first, he was important enough for the regime to go out of its way to silence, and, second, he was clearly the political focus for anyone in Jordan who was interested in genuine reform and democracy. It is even more significant in my opinion that people like Shubeilat, with their resolute independence of spirit, their uncompromising radicalism, and their utter fearlessness are rarely mentioned in dutiful surveys of "fundamentalism." Why? Because it is quite clear in their case (unlike the Brothers or Hamas or the Egyptian bomb-throwers) that what they speak about is something much more likely to gather large popular support, and is therefore more dangerous and uncontainable. I found an interesting convergence between Shubeilat and a strong, very hard-working woman lawyer, Asma Khidr, a leader of the Jordanian women's movement and one of Jordan's leading human rights activists. In both instances, you notice not only the dedication to clear principles of human equality and real democracy but an almost total absence of theoretical, religious, and sophistic rhetoric. What you get, in effect, is the kind of attention to the concrete world of cases, facts, figures, and conclusions that allows no leap into the Beyond, or any resort to thought-stopping formulas like *"al-Islam huwal hal."* Khidr happens to be a Christian and a Palestinian, Shubeilat a Muslim and a Jordanian, yet the message they both deliver is the same.

The more I read and saw, the less probable was any sign of a coherent Islamic uprising of the kind confected by Western reporters and sages. With the exception of Sudan's Turabi, a brilliant Machiavelli whose decisive disability is that the Sudan is one of the poorest and least influential of any country anywhere, the leaders, their parties, ideas, literature are undistinguished; whatever force they have is parasitic on tired, brutal, and isolated governments that are kept in place partly because the United States gives them so much support. I know of no U.S. policy that supports local human rights movements, or women activists, or independent and critical thinkers. Our allegiance is to the house of Saud, the Kuwaiti Sabahs, Mubarak's Egypt, and so on pretty much down the line. In Cairo and Amman, I heard rumors that U.S. embassy personnel had been meeting with Brotherhood leaders, doubtless because American policymakers had cautioned against being surprised as they had been in Iran. So choked is the official and academic United States with "fundamentalist" projects and books, pamphlets and endless studies of the Islamic threat, that there can be no real dialogue of discovery between Islam and the West. There has simply been too much emphasis on confrontation and incoherent generalization, by which Islam and the West produce caricatures of each other and live off them for far too long. Or there is the "strategic" concept by which Islam is looked at as a contender for power and, therefore, now better courted surreptitiously, just in case one of the militant parties does come to power.

Not being a strategist or a politician, I find all the current alternatives basically insufficient and impoverishing. For by supporting the present governments the United States seems like their accomplice, prolonging their incompetence, repressiveness, survival. By starting to cultivate potentially successful political Muslims (as the United States did during the Afghanistan war, with Shaikh Abdel Rahman and Gulbuddin Hekmatyar as two of the decidedly unattractive prizes), there is the even graver danger not only of giving them unearned stature but of disheartening their secular opponents to whom attention and encouragement needs to be given. But looking at the history of U.S.

relations with the Third World during the past five decades, one can scarcely be optimistic, since only in rare instances have we not opted for local oligarchies and their satellites, like the Muslim fundamentalists, who are unthinkable without the corruption and lack of democracy in so many of the Arab countries whose leaders the United States is close to. So now, in effect, Western powers, journalists, academic opportunists swing from the perspective of the status quo to its most extreme opponents, ignoring the vast middle ground of people who share and are prepared to fight for democratic values that we say we support. Could it be that addressing the large number of secular or, at least, nonextremist Muslim Arabs is not so palatable for us because they would require a dialogue of equals, whereas we want outright servants like latter-day versions of Marcos, Sadat, the shah; outright enemies like Khomeini or Saddam Hussein?

I said at the beginning of this essay that there is a real internal contest in Arab Muslim societies between various interpretations of Islam and that this contest is going on and remains undecided. In the obsession only with rabid fundamentalists (like Omar Abdel Rahman), there has been a quite significant blotting out (avoidance and ignorance perhaps) of the many quite well known Muslim interpreters all across the Arab world who dispute the literalism and dogmatism of the orthodox. Among these figures are men and women like Mohammed Arkoun, Fatima el-Marnissi, Muhammad Abid el Jabiri, Hassan Hanafi, Fuad Zakariya, to mention a few of the better-known names. A new book that offers a rational and modern reading of the Koran by Muhammad Shahrur has recently become a best-seller, surely a sign of how many Muslims thirst for pragmatic interpretations of their faith. In addition, a whole battery of novelists, poets, and dramatists— Adonis, Shahar Khalifa, Hanan al-Shaykh, Abdel Rahman Munif, Kamal Abu Deeb, Mahmoud Darwish, Mahfouz—have either taken outspoken positions against militant political Islam or, by the example of their own work, have opposed its claims. The point about all of them, however, is that they are not marginal or frightened figures cowering in the wings as *ulama* take over center stage, but men and women who have large audiences and speak bravely and openly.

One of the most impressive of these intellectuals has been somewhat in the news lately: the Egyptian academic Nasr Hamid Abu Zeid, a member of the department of Arabic literature at Cairo University. Because of his writings, he told me, a series of university peer committees have ruled against his promotion; more luridly, he has been the target of a risible (but recently failed) lawsuit brought against him by "concerned Muslims," the purpose of which was to force his wife (a Cairo University professor of French, Ibtihal Yunis) to divorce him, since according to Sharia law a Muslim (Ms. Yunis) cannot be married to a heretic (Nasr)! Both the American and English press have portrayed him as a lonely, embattled man, more or less constantly in hiding, acted upon rather than acting. He has also been compared with Farag Foda, the flamboyant Egyptian secularist murdered by extremist assailants in June of 1992.

None of these descriptions is adequate. Intellectually, I found him one of the most exhilarating of all the people I spoke to on my trip, a witty, consciously provocative, and extremely sharp man whose academic specialty and genuine analytical skill place him right up on the front lines against the fundamentalists. A friend told me that Professor Abu Zeid—a man of Falstaffian proportions in his early forties—regularly appears as a panelist at the university where his fearless verbal fireworks and his remarkably alert and good-natured personality are set off handsomely by his bright aquamarine T-shirt. The author of several books, Abu Zeid is best known for his merciless analysis of "Islamic discourse" (the debt to Foucault is evident), in which he refuses the distinction between "moderate" and "extreme" Islamicists—he describes them scornfully as like a sound and its echo—and methodically exposes the ideological bases of everything they say. His summary of the latter is worth quoting for its economy and explicitness:

1. An identification of "thought" with "religion" and an elimination of the distance between "subject" and "object."

2. An explanation of all phenomena by reducing them to a single first principle or a single cause. This explanation includes all scientific as well as social phenomena.

3. A reliance on the tyranny of either "the past" or "tradition," and this by converting secondary traditional texts into primary ones, which are endowed with a sanctity that in many instances is scarcely less than that of the primary texts [e.g., the Koran].

4. An absolute mental certainty and intellectual derisiveness that refuses to brook any disagreement at all, except in negligible details, which in any event have no basis or principle for them.

5.   Avoidance or ignorance of the historical dimension which
manifests itself in weeping over the wonderful past embodied in the
golden age of the Caliph Haroun al-Rashid or the Caliphate of the
Ottoman Empire.[37]

The brunt of Abu Zeid's analysis is directed against the clergy who,
while everyone knows that Sunni Islam is supposed to have no clergy,
nevertheless arrogate to themselves the role of supreme religious
leaders: They require absolute submission to divine precepts which
only they claim to be able to determine and interpret. So far as I know,
none of his work has been translated or cited by Western students of
Islamic fundamentalism. What has given it the force and prominence
it has is not just its salubrious vigor but also that it speaks for many
Muslims who resent the dogmatic mindlessness gradually insinuating
itself everywhere. More interestingly, Abu Zeid's critique also ferrets
out the forced provincial isolationism of the new Muslim extremists
who, as former Leftists in some cases, were greatly influenced by
modern ideas of nationalism and socialism. In rejecting their new
zealotry Abu Zeid reestablishes a sense of intellectual principle appropriate for both secularists and fundamentalists.

Abu Zeid, I think, represents a rising new critical consciousness
within the Arab and Islamic world. His methodology, while to some
extent based on a European model, is nevertheless conducted entirely
within the Arab and Islamic domain; it addresses problems that are of
course local but in a sense universal; and, above all, it exemplifies an
investigative attitude that is both skeptical and affirmative and that has
in fact existed for many centuries in the Muslim tradition. In the
contest over the meaning of Islam, Abu Zeid and many others like him
are key players and by no means easy pushovers for the mediocre
demagogues and tyrants who speak in the name of religion and tradition. I found the reach and panache of his work to be a source of great
encouragement, a sign of energy and vivacity where we have been led
to believe there was none. Such thinkers as he and Shubeilat are a
challenge to the dogmatists who have wanted to shut things down,
capitalize on frustration and despair, lead people toward violence and
negation. Using such figures as these two as models, perhaps we can
interpret the ferment in the Muslim world as not only coming from
fundamentalists and bigots but from democrats, rationalists, and skeptical critics too.

Two concluding observations. One: The Arab world is on the verge of another major change, the onset of an era of peace agreements with Israel. All of these (including the Palestinian) either have been or will be negotiated by leaders all of whom will be seen as doing so from a position of weakness and, in some cases, great unpopularity. Having for years been bombarded with official rhetoric of extreme hostility toward Israel, most Arabs are not prepared for normalization. Egyptians have remained either indifferent or adversarial about Israel, despite the fifteen-year-old peace. So one should expect new unrest, religious *and* secular, in the years to come: This will deepen probably, not alleviate, divisions between rich and poor, ruler and ruled, men and women.

Two: The Arab world is now more obviously inside the American (and Israeli) orbit than ever before. The United States' continuing bombardment of Iraq (in January and June of 1993), its condoning of Israel's late July invasion of Lebanon, the presence of U.S. troops in the Gulf and the Horn, the appearance of a patronizing U.S. attitude toward the Arabs and their rulers—all these exacerbate the gulf dividing the Arabs and the West, the United States especially. There is no dialogue at all; there is vassalage and peremptoriness.

Thus both the era of an impending (and quite imperfect) peace and the continuing pressures of what is in actuality an imperial policy add to the already inflamed situation inside the Arab and Muslim worlds. But it is important to remember that these are secular realities, in which not just "Islam" is involved.

Published in *The New York Times Magazine,* November 26, 1993.

Epilogue

The crisis in Palestinian ranks deepens almost daily. Security talks between Israel and the PLO are advertised as a "breakthrough" one day, stalled and deadlocked the next. Deadlines agreed upon come and go, with no other timetable proposed, while Israel increases the number of its soldiers in the Occupied Territories, as well as the building of settlement residences, the demolition of Palestinian houses, the punitive measures keeping Palestinians from leaving the territories and entering Jerusalem. The Hebron mosque massacre on February 25, 1994, attests to the impunity of Israeli settlers and Palestinian vulnerability.

The September 13, 1993, Declaration of Principles itself, once described as brilliant, has further been revealed as an interpreter's nightmare, a patchwork of old Israeli and American drafts, incomplete procedural suggestions, deliberate ambiguities and obfuscations. In one section, for example, the Israeli army is said to withdraw; in another it is characterized as redeploying. Israel, never compelled to admit it is an occupying power, has been further bolstered in that peculiar denial by the U.S. government. Secretary of State Warren Christopher does not consider it "helpful" to state categorically that the West Bank, Gaza, and Jerusalem are "occupied" territories, thereby perhaps salving whatever conscience may exist in an Administration that continues to provide some $5 billion in annual support while saying little about worsening conditions. Together Israel and its patron seem to be doing all they can—notwithstanding the high-sounding principles of last fall—to make the likelihood of a truly independent Palestine more and more remote. The Cairo agreement on Jericho signed by the PLO and Israel in early February 1994 contains more Palestinian concessions and even more Israeli control.

And the Palestinian response? Yasir Arafat cries betrayal, though he effectively acquiesced to the leverage Israel now exerts by signing the Oslo declaration without establishing any plan for proceeding and without getting much in return but a grudging recognition of the PLO as the representative of the Palestinian people. In Gaza and elsewhere, local leaders resign from the PLO, and its cadres grow more disaffected. No one has anything but complaints about Arafat's leadership: numerous petitions, missions, and articles in the press have kept up a fairly constant pressure on Arafat to reform, change his autocratic ways, open up the decision-making process to talent and proven ability.

None of these petitions, these appeals for reform, have had the slightest effect. Nor will they ever. You cannot change an elephant into a lion by sending it a letter. At this point Palestinians, both in the Occupied Territories and in diaspora, must face up to two central challenges—that of leadership and of serious planning through collective action—or else be resigned to a life of permanent oppression, without land, without a voice in shaping the future, without hope, even without pride, as the leadership stumbles from incoherence to incompetence and worse.

It could not be clearer that the traditional PLO hierarchy, including Fatah and its associated parties, as well as its creatures in the Occupied Territories and elsewhere, should step aside. The leadership has so misunderstood its own people that there is now simmering—and frequently open—revolt more or less everywhere that Palestinians gather and live. No leadership can expect forever to be in sole control of money and political authority and to dole these out according to its whims. Some five hundred schools and eight universities, as well as eleven thousand education workers in the Occupied Territories languish without a budget and no guidance at all (to say nothing of hospitals without medicine). More than most people, Palestinians have been the victims of abuses by every government—Arab and non-Arab—in whose jurisdiction they have lived. Why should they stand for similar practices from leaders who have neither been freely elected nor shown a spirit of self-sacrificing austerity? Why should hard-pressed Palestinians in refugee camps in Lebanon and Gaza accept corruption, Parisian shopping sprees, and continued bumbling among a handful of officials directed from Tunis? How long can Arafat simply assert his prerogative to be in exclusive control of building contracts, foreign aid, lucrative appointments? Are quick profit and a history of servile loyalty the only criteria for service?

Consider, too, the information policies of this leadership. It has yet to tell Palestinians in the Territories, Jordan, and Lebanon the full truth of the present situation. Yes, of course people want an independent state, but—assuming Israel, with the *de facto* collaboration of Arafat and his courtiers, has not already foreclosed that prospect—what sort of state is it to be? Nothing is said. Is there to be resistance to the occupation and settlers or not? No word. Are there to be consultative assemblies or not? No word. What do we tell the world—about where we are in our history, about the killings of our own people, and on and on? No word. What is Palestine's real economic policy (beyond the silly slogan about making Palestine into another "Singapore")? No one seems to know.

Despite the present impasse the PLO will probably finalize its security agreement with Israel on Israeli terms, of course. After that the present PLO leadership can have very little to say and even less to offer. Palestinians should thank the men in Tunis for their past contributions, but they should then take the next logical step and demand that they resign. Their apex was the Declaration of Principles, which, whether one likes it or not, is their legacy to their people. If, on the other hand, the peace process is derailed because of what happened in Hebron on February 25 (and may happen again elsewhere), the PLO leadership is still on the spot.

"And yet," one hears the timorous voices rising, "what is the alternative?" This is a good question were it not so often asked rhetorically. Are Palestinians to be ruled so totally by predetermined fact? As it happens, alternatives only develop by default. The *intifada* is evidence of that: it began because a distant leadership had become bankrupt of ideas and strategies. By chance, the uprising reinvigorated that leadership temporarily. But the lesson of the *intifada* is also the challenge Palestinians face today: that is, that responsibility for what happens next must be a collective one.

Palestinians have to regard the present situation as exposing a much more serious cultural and moral crisis than mere incompetence and corruption among PLO chiefs: as a people, our historical tendency to avoid focusing on a set of national goals and single-mindedly pursuing

them. We have never been able to even undertake a census of our own
people. We rely on Israel for facts about land and water and, to this
day, have rarely produced our own sources of reliable information. Is
there an accurate Palestinian map of the West Bank, Gaza, Jerusalem?

Since the beginning, the struggle over Palestine has been a battle
over territorial sovereignty: "another acre, another goat" was the
motto of the Zionist settlers under Chaim Weizmann. Israel is now in
sole possession of the territory of historical Palestine, although of
course a relatively large population of Palestinians—including the eight
hundred thousand Arab citizens of Israel—is also resident there. The
Zionist idea has always been to coordinate specific concrete steps with
a guiding principle that doesn't change. Thus, the Israelis assert sovereignty *and* they build settlements, they take land and water, build
roads, deploy armed forces. Obviously, they also have the monopoly
on legitimized violence: I do not mean to suggest that there is anything resembling the balance of power between the Israelis and the Palestinians.

Nevertheless, the official political technique pursued by one Arab
government (including the PLO) after another has always been to make
very large general assertions, and then hope that the concrete details
will somehow fall into place later. The PLO accepted the Declaration
of Principles on the grounds that Palestinian autonomy would somehow lead to independence if enough rhetorical statements about an
independent Palestinian state were made. When it came to negotiating
the details (what parts of Jericho and Gaza were in question?), we had
neither the plans nor the actual facts. *They* had the plans, the territory,
the maps, the settlements, the roads: we have the wish for autonomy
and Israeli withdrawal, with few details, and little power to change
anything very much. What is needed is a discipline of detail.

A general idea like "limited autonomy" might lead to independence or it might equally well lead to further domination. In either
case, the main task for Palestinians is to know and understand the
overall map of the territories that the Israelis have been creating, and
then devise concrete tactics of resistance. (In the history of colonial
invasion, maps are always first drawn by the victors, since maps are
always instruments of conquest; once projected, they are then implemented. Geography is therefore the art of war but can also be the art
of resistance if there is a counter-map and a counter-strategy.) The
essence of the Israeli plan for territorial domination, both in theory and

in detail, is (a) effective control over the land within its pre-1967 boundaries; and (b) the prevention of real Palestinian autonomy of the Palestinian inhabitants of the Occupied Territories by maintaining an ever-expanding united Jerusalem as the core of a web extending into the West Bank. Israeli plans for and practices in Jerusalem are therefore central to the future of Palestinians.

Jerusalem has never been the focus of a concentrated Palestinian strategy, nor has there ever been a campaign to systematically resist Israeli control over the city and its surroundings. "Gaza–Jericho" thus seems ever more like a trap or a kind of elaborate distraction, so that Palestinian energies will be absorbed in the administration of the peripheries, while the core is left to the Israelis. As outlined by Jan de Jong, a Dutch geographer who has been studying Israeli policies for Jerusalem for the past eight years, the Israeli idea is to take "the last open spaces that . . . might be claimed by Palestinians . . . to square the circle around the Old City." He describes two rings of settlements that will be the site of Israeli building efforts over the next three years: the first, mainly in annexed Jerusalem; the second, enclosing the first and extending ultimately into most of the central West Bank, from Bir Zeit in the north to Hebron in the south. Within this considerable area (20 percent of the West Bank), Israel will be largely unchallenged, although there and elsewhere in the territories Palestinians will be allowed autonomy "in separated territorial units."

Already the whole of the West Bank and Gaza has been divided into ten or eleven cantons by fifty-seven road barriers. Rabin's government is proceeding with a $600 million road system for the Occupied Territories; it is to be controlled by Israel and will connect the settlements to one another, to Jerusalem, and to Israel, bypassing Arab areas and completing the territories' cantonization. Meanwhile, land confiscation continues at a stunning pace: more than nine thousand acres in the West Bank were forcibly taken and declared Israeli military zones in December 1993 alone. It has even been suggested by Ra'anan Weiz, a former settlement planner for the Labor Party, that Israel build a new capital city for Palestinians near Hizma (in the desert, well beyond the two circles) as a substitute for Jerusalem.

De Jong's main point, however, is that whereas the Israelis are planning, settling, and controlling, the Palestinians have still not even formulated a strategy to resist these moves, whether by initiating collective public building projects or by making metropolitan Jerusalem the center of a *national* development plan. In both instances, since the Israeli vision is to divide the Palestinian population into "islands, cantons, small spheres of containment," de Jong suggests that in response Palestinians "should consider themselves part of a larger unit," of which Jerusalem is not just one district or one main street but a city "from [such disparate East Jerusalem districts as] Al-Azzariah to the Beit-Hanina and Shuafat area, and then to think how we can make a prospect for development there." To discuss that as an alternative, with visible efforts made on its behalf, "will cause people to believe in it," and can then become the basis for collective action.

There has been much talk recently of handing over to "experts'"— Palestinian and non-Palestinian—responsibility for where we go from here in terms of the impending "transfer of authority" to a new Palestinian administration. This notion is seconded by the World Bank, the European Community, and the United States, which emphasize the need for objective and apolitical (i.e., subservient and free-market) strategies. I am unmoved by their arguments ideologically (where development has been dictated from the outside, the net result has been to pauperize the majority and keep those countries even more politically and economically dependent on the developed countries) and practically, since in any case Arafat, designating himself Boss, can exercise arbitrary authority over even the most enlightened experts. Some of Arafat's disaffected (but opportunistic) associates openly favor calling in the "professionals," often proposing themselves as replacements for Arafat.

In this situation experts who sit in Washington or Paris can fix very little: a plan drawn up by the most brilliant and yet faraway intellect cannot be implemented on the ground unless there is a common national will, as well as a national sense of urgency and mobilization. Likewise, freelance Palestinian experts and entrepreneurs cannot be trusted to act for the common good. Throughout the Arab world, Europe, and the United States there are extraordinarily large numbers of gifted and successful Palestinians who have made a mark in medicine, law, banking, planning, architecture, journalism, industry, education, contracting. Most of these people have contributed only a tiny fraction of what they could contribute to the Palestinian national effort. Compared with the Jewish communities in the West, we have done next to nothing, although I am convinced that there is a great potential there. Perhaps the greatest failure of the PLO was not that it signed an ill-considered and stupid Declaration of Principles but that it has failed, both before and after Oslo, to mobilize the vast potential of its own people.

Palestinians today are separated by geography and by Israel's designs in keeping us fragmented and isolated from each other; people in Palestine and those outside it lead different lives, with far too little communication between them. To survive as a nation, it is not enough to repeat slogans or only to insist that Palestinian identity will survive. The first thing is to grasp as concretely and as exactly as possible what the facts really are, not in order to be defeated by them but to invent ways of countering them with our own facts and institutions, and finally of asserting our national presence, democratically and with mass participation.

The Palestine National Council must convene, despite the PLO's opposition. Instead of sitting back and waiting for something to happen, Palestinians can, indeed must, also call assemblies wherever large populations exist (Jordan, Lebanon, North America, England) with enough clout, resources, and potential for contributions that will make a difference. In the territories, divisiveness and factionalism have compounded the situation of helplessness and resentment in which most Palestinians find themselves. Systematic attempts must be made to bridge the distance between the diaspora and those Palestinians. Networks are forming, as are ever-expanding groups of citizens dissatisfied with the PLO's ineptitude. But the key thing is to stop thinking that Arafat and Co. can be reformed, and to begin an open and unafraid discussion about the alternatives, the need to go forward as a nation, and, most important, a strategy to end Israeli occupation.

If Jerusalem is the heart of our predicament with Israel, it is also therefore the heart of the solution. As the Israeli settlement drive continues, Palestinians have to muster the resources and the will to prevent unilateral Israeli control. To do this, Palestinians must start thinking collectively and stop reacting individually. And the main question, of which Jerusalem is the symbol, is how to resist, not how to profit. The Israelis must somehow be convinced that there can be no real peace unless they leave the Palestinian land they now occupy illegally in Jerusalem and their West Bank and Gaza settlements. Yet if they are to be persuaded, it will only be by a people that feels itself to be part of a national effort dedicated to real, not apparent, independence. Those are the facts. There is no such thing as partial independence or limited autonomy. Without political independence there is neither sovereignty nor real freedom, and certainly not equality with an Israeli Jewish state that destroyed Palestine in 1948 and is not anxious to give it another chance in 1993. The challenge is obvious.

E.W.S.
February 28, 1994

Notes

One: Palestine and Palestinians

1. Erik Erikson, *Young Man Luther* (New York: Norton, 1962), p. 14.

2. Jacques Berque, *The Arabs: Their History and Future,* trans. Jean Stewart (New York: Praeger, 1965).

3. Maxime Rodinson, *Israel: A Colonial-Settler State?,* trans. David Thorstad (New York: Monad Press, 1973).

4. Books discussed: Michael Bar-Zohar, *Ben-Gurion: A Biography* (London: Weidenfeld & Nicolson, 1978). Richard Deacon, *The Israeli Secret Service* (New York: Taplinger Publishing, 1978). Martin Gilbert, *Exile and Return: The Emergence of Jewish Statehood* (London: Weidenfeld & Nicolson, 1978). Aviezer Golan, *Operation Susannah* (New York: Harper & Row, 1978). Nahum Goldmann, *The Jewish Paradox* (London: Weidenfeld & Nicolson, 1978). Chaim Herzog, *Who Stands Accused? Israel Answers Its Critics* (London: Weidenfeld & Nicolson, 1978). Sabri Jiryis, *The Arabs in Israel* (New York: Monthly Review Press, 1976). A. W. Kayyali, *Palestine: A Modern History* (London: Croom Helm, 1978). Saul Mishal, *West Bank East Bank: The Palestinians in Jordan, 1949–1967* (New Haven & London: Yale University Press, 1978). Anwar el Sadat, *In Search of Identity* (London: Collins, 1978). Rosemary Sayigh, *The Palestinians: From Peasants to Revolutionaries* (London: Zed Press, 1979). Sammy Smooha, *Israel: Pluralism and Conflict* (London: Routledge & Kegan Paul, 1978). A. I. Tibawi, *Anglo-Arab Relations and the Question of Palestine, 1914–1921* (London: Luzac, 1977). Elia T. Zureik, *The Palestinians in Israel: A Study in Internal Colonialism* (London: Routledge & Kegan Paul, 1979).

5. *Time,* May 15, 1978.

6. See Livia Rokach, *Israel's Sacred Terrorism: A Study Based on Moshe Sharett's Personal Diaries* (Belmont, Mass.: Association of Arab-American University Graduates, 1980), p. 28.

7. Ibid., "He need only be a major."

8. Victor Nee and James Peck, ed., *China's Uninterrupted Revolution: 1840–Present* (New York: Pantheon, 1973), p. 71.

9. See the Executive of the [World] Zionist Organization, *Problems of the Zionist Organization with the Establishment of the State: Summary of the Debate on Ideological and Organizational Problems of the Movement* (Jerusalem: Central Zionist Archives, 1950, vol. 1, p. 2; as cited in Uri Davis and Walter Lehr, "And the Fund Still Lives," *Journal of Palestine Studies* (summer 1978), pp. 5–6.

10. See Ian Lustick, *Arabs in the Jewish State* (Austin, Texas: University of Texas Press, 1980), pp. 173ff; Sabri Jiryis, *The Arabs in Israel*, pp. 83ff.

11. Talal Asad, "Anthropological Textbook and Ideological Problems: An Analysis of Cohen on Arab Villages in Israel," *Economy and Society* 4:3 (August 1975), p. 274.

12. Elia T. Zureik, *The Palestinians in Israel: A Study in Internal Colonialism*, pp. 95–96.

13. Dr. Shlomo Ariel, letter to the editor, *Ha'aretz* (December 1, 1983).

14. Raymond Williams, *Politics and Letters: Interviews with New Left Review* (London: New Left Books, 1979), p. 252.

15. Elisabeth Young-Bruehl, *Hannah Arendt: For Love of the World* (New Haven & London: Yale University Press, 1982), p. 455.

16. Barbara Tuchman, "Israel's Swift Sword," *The Atlantic*, September 1967.

17. Sean MacBride et al., *Israel in Lebanon* (London: Ithaca, 1983), p. 222.

18. See the remarkable denunciation of Avineri by Meron Benvenisti, ex-deputy mayor of Jerusalem, in *Ha'aretz* (July 22, 1982).

19. I have discussed these matters elsewhere: see *The Question of Palestine* (New York: Vintage, 1980) and *London Review of Books* (February 1984), pp. 16–29, focusing, in particular, on Noam Chomsky's book *The Fateful Triangle: Israel, the United States and the Palestinians* (London: Pluto, 1983), although an essentially hostile recent review of the book by Avishai Margalit, an Israeli dove (*New York Review of Books*, July 1984) can easily be added to the corroborating evidence. Margalit's case against Chomsky's is that the latter distorts the horrific evidence on Israel's Palestinian policies which led to the Lebanese invasion; whereas, in Margalit's view, it remains possible to discuss Israel in terms that do not necessarily include the whole atrocious history of what Israel has systematically done to the Palestinians.

20. Martin Peretz, "Washington Diarist on the Record," *The New Republic*, May 7, 1984.

21. Edward W. Said, *After the Last Sky* (London: Faber & Faber, 1986).

22. Mahmoud Darwish, "The Earth Is Closing on Us," trans. Abdullah al-Udhari, in *Victims of a Map* (London: Al Saqi Books, 1984), p. 13.

23. Emile Habibi, *The Secret Life of Saeed, the Ill-Fated Pessoptimist: A Palestinian Who Became a Citizen of Israel* (Columbia, La.: Readers International, 1989).

24. See Martin Bernal, *Black Athena: The Afroasiatic Roots of Classical Civilization* (New Brunswick, N.J.: Rutgers University Press, 1983); and Basil Davidson, "The

Ancient World and Africa: Whose Roots?'' in Basil Davidson, *The Search for Africa: History, Culture, Politics* (New York: Times Books, 1994).

25. Quoted in Christopher Sykes, *Crossroads to Israel, 1917–1948* (1965 reprint; Bloomington, Ind.: Indiana University Press, 1973), p. 5.

26. Edward W. Said, *Culture and Imperialism* (New York: Alfred A. Knopf, 1993).

Two: The Arab World

1. Aaron S. Kleiman, *Foundations of British Policy in the Arab World: The Cairo Conference of 1921* (Baltimore: Johns Hopkins, 1970), p. 244.

2. A curious sideshow of this rivalry has been the polemical literature in the West on postwar radical Arab nationalism. Generally, Abdel Nasser, the Palestinian organizations, and the Baathists are treated as sellouts to, or puppets and stooges of, international communism. This, at least, has been the operative assumption held in official circles. Yet a substantial current of thought, extending from the State Department Arabists to ex-CIA men like Kermit Roosevelt and Miles Copeland (see the latter's *The Game of Nations: The Amorality of Power Politics*, London: Weidenfeld & Nicolson, 1969) and teachers, missionaries, and businessmen, maintains that radical Arab nationalism is substantially the creation of the United States, its foreign service, or its cultural-educational institutions!

3. William B. Quandt, *Palestinian Nationalism: Its Political and Military Dimensions* (Santa Monica: Rand, November 1971), p. iii.

4. Ibid., p. 118. For a different viewpoint, see my article ''Les Palestiniens face aux responsibilité de la défaite,'' *Le Monde diplomatique* (October 1971), in this volume entitled, ''The Palestinians One Year Since Amman,'' pp. 24–29.

5. Ibid., p. 7.

6. Ibid., p. 118. For a RAND study comparing the Vietcong and the Palestinian guerrilla movement, see W. M. Jones, ''Predicting Insurgent and Government Decisions: The Power Block Model'' (Santa Monica: Rand, 1970). Back of Jones and Quandt is *Rebellion and Authority: An Analytic Essay on Insurgent Conflicts* (Chicago: Rand, 1970) by Nathan Leites and Charles Wolf, Jr., two important RAND theoreticians of insurgency who employ a ''systems'' approach. For a series of essays dealing with these issues—both pro and con—see David S. Sullivan and Martin J. Sattler, eds., *Revolutionary War: Western Response* (New York: Columbia University Press, 1971). A peculiarly American approach is found in *Revolutionism* (''a logical political phenomenon in an environment of instability and unknown constants'') by Abdul A. Said and Daniel M. Collier (Boston: Allyn & Bacon, 1971). There is a good useful study, which unaccountably ignores the Middle East, of the methodology, institutions, and mentality of American military foreign policy by Michael T. Klare, *War Without End: American Planning for the Next Vietnams* (New York: Knopf, 1972).

7. Richard J. Barnet, *Roots of War* (New York: Atheneum, 1972), p. 72.

8. Ibid., p. 3.

9. ''The Middle East,'' in *U.S. Foreign Policy: Compilation of Studies,* vol. 2, Senate Foreign Relations Committee (Washington, D.C., 1960). See also the following

House Committee on Foreign Affairs Hearings: *The Near East Conflict* (July 21–23 and 28–30, 1970); *The Indian Ocean: Political and Strategic Future* (July 20, 22, 27–28, 1971); *The Middle East, 1971: The Need to Strengthen the Peace* (July 13–15, 27; August 3; September 30, October 5, 28, 1971); *Soviet Involvement in the Middle East and the Western Response* (October 19–21; November 2–3, 1971); *A Sino-Soviet Perspective in the Middle East* (April 26, 1972). Also, hearings before this committee on the annual Foreign Assistance Act are useful evidence of similar views of the Middle East.

10. In this connection, I have used *American Interests in the Middle East,* a pamphlet issued in Washington by the Middle East Institute (1969). A more sophisticated, but wholly similar, definition of U.S. interests and obligations is found in John C. Campbell and Helen Caruso, *The West and the Middle East* (New York Council on Foreign Relations, 1972).

11. Campbell and Caruso, *The West and the Middle East,* p. 42. Moreover, a domestic shortage of natural gas has made Algeria crucial as a source of supply. See the *New York Times* (June 29, 1972). For an interpretation of the larger picture from the Third World perspective, see Pierre Jalée, *Le Pillage du tiers monde* (Paris: Maspero, 1965); also Harry Magdoff, *The Age of Imperialism* (New York: Monthly Review, 1969); and Jacques Berque, *Déspossession du monde* (Paris: Editions du Seuil, 1964).

12. John C. Campbell, "The United States and the Mediterranean," in *Military Forces and Political Conflicts in the Mediterranean* (Paris: The Atlantic Institute, 1970), p. 15.

13. Eqbal Ahmad in *Africasia* (Paris: September 1970).

14. Campbell, "The United States and the Mediterranean," pp. 21–22. See also Quandt's other RAND paper, *U.S. Policy in the Middle East: Constraints and Choices* (Santa Monica: 1970).

15. A remark by a Soviet negotiator goes as far as saying that up to December of 1969, the United States was arguing that Sharm el-Sheikh was Egyptian territory. Thereafter, the claim was never repeated.

16. That these pressures are being refined is illustrated by an announcement in the *New York Times* of July 9, 1972, that the Synagogue Council of America wished to establish a "think tank," one of whose tasks would be an effort "to illuminate the avenues and processes in the American political system that are available for the advancement of Jewish interests."

17. The phrase is Stanley Hoffman's, from his *Gulliver's Troubles* (New York: McGraw-Hill, 1968).

18. Glen H. Fisher, *Public Diplomacy and the Behavioral Sciences* (Bloomington, Ind.: Indiana University Press, 1972).

19. There are at least half a dozen such RAND studies publicly available, dealing with such subjects as West Bank refugee sociology, Arab radical thought (done by an Arab), inter-Arab politics and the Palestinian resistance, etc.

20. See *Defense Department Sponsored Foreign Affairs Research,* Hearing Before the Committee on Foreign Relations, U.S. Senate, part 1, May 9, 1968, and part 2, May 28, 1968, for a very partial listing of such projects.

21. Ibid., part 1, pp. 17–18 ff.

22. W. G. Weiner, *On Gaming Limited War,* RAND Paper P2123 (1960), p. 4.

23. *Annual Report for 1968,* Institute for Defense Analysis (IDA), p. 18; *Annual Report for 1969,* p. 27.

24. Parts of this have appeared, published by American Elsevier: cf. *Economic Development and Population Growth in the Middle East,* Charles A. Cooper and Sidney S. Alexander, eds. (New York: American Elsevier, 1972).

25. Lincoln P. Bloomfield and Amelia C. Leiss, *The Control of Local Conflict: A Design Study on Arms Control and Limited War in the Development Areas* (MIT: 1967); Robert R. Beattie and Lincoln P. Bloomfield, *Cascon: Computer-Aided System for Handling Information on Local Conflicts* (December 1969); Bloomfield and Leiss, *Controlling Small Wars: A Strategy for the 70s* (New York: Knopf, 1969).

26. This is the title of a study (dated 1966) undertaken by Douglas Aircraft, *Defense Department Sponsored Foreign Affairs Research,* part 2, p. 32.

27. See *Annual Report for 1970,* Institute for Defense Analysis (IDA).

28. Eqbal Ahmad in *Africasia* (Paris: September 1970).

29. In his *Israel and Nuclear Weapons: Present Options and Future Strategies* (London: Chatto & Windus, 1971).

30. This is based on fiscal 1968; see *Defense Department Sponsored Foreign Affairs Research,* part 1, p. 87.

31. "Dealing Arms in the Middle East, part 2," *Middle East Research and Information Project [MERIP] Report* no. 9 (May–June 1972), p. 21. Part I in *MERIP Report* no. 8 (March–April 1972) ought to be consulted also. The source given for the $1.5-billion figure is Secretary Laird's testimony before the Subcommittee on Appropriations, House of Representatives, on Foreign Assistance for 1972.

32. I owe these details to Peter Johnson's paper, "The United States and the Middle East," incorporated in "Nixon's Strategy in the Middle East," *MERIP Report* no. 13 (November 13, 1972), pp. 3–8.

33. On the common program of the three, see the *New York Times,* October 16, 1970, p. 1, and Stewart Alsop, "Why is Israel for Nixon?" *Newsweek,* July 10, 1972, p. 100.

34. Peter Johnson, "The United States and the Middle East," in *MERIP Report* no. 13.

35. William Beecher, "Jordan: On the Razor's Edge," *Army* 22:1 (January 1972), pp. 42–43. On February 14, 1973, in the *New York Times,* C. L. Sulzberger had this to say: "Israel hasn't objected to increasing American support for Hussein. The United States is now committed to a three-year program to modernize the Jordanian Army plus continuing budget support and loans. A few years ago the Israelis would have been deeply worried; now they hint that Washington isn't doing enough to help their least inimical neighbor."

36. For the best, most detailed, and recent study of Israeli economic policy in the Occupied Territories—a study from which some of the details I have cited above are taken—see Sheila Ryan, "Constructing a New Imperialism: Israel and the West Bank," *MERIP Report* no. 9 (May–June 1972).

37. Michael Bruno, "Economic Development Problems of Israel, 1970–80," in *Economic Development and Population Growth in the Middle East,* Cooper and Alexan-

der, eds., p. 117. Alexander teaches at MIT; Cooper is Minister-Counselor for Economic Affairs, U.S. embassy, Saigon; and Bruno teaches at the Hebrew University. Interestingly, Bruno later wrote an impassioned attack on the Israeli government's policy toward the Arabs in the Occupied Territories. He says: "At some point along the way, the future image of the State was forgotten, fundamental values became blurred, and the nation lost the moral and social compass that directed it for so many years. . . . It is a more liberal and enlightened version of Rhodesia or South Africa, but it's not the state in which I would like to educate my children." Quoted from *Davar* (April 7, 1972) in *New Outlook* 15:4 (May 1972), pp. 47–48.

38. For an excellent account of the joint ventures in the Middle East and Africa between Israel and such U.S. arms and electronics manufacturers as Motorola, Chromalloy, Sylvania, and Control Data, see Larry Lockwood, "Israel's Expanding Arms Industry," in *Journal of Palestine Studies* 1:4 (Summer 1972).

39. Noam Chomsky's article, "Indochina: The Next Phase," *Ramparts* 10:11 (May 1972), draws a picture remarkably similar to this.

40. These observations are based on statistics compiled for the years in question from U.S. Department of Commerce, *Highlights of U.S. Export and Import Trade*, monthly, FT 990 (December 1968 and December 1970). I am indebted to Professor Naiem A. Sherbiny for bringing them to my attention.

41. In this connection, it is instructive to see how the United States and France, to name only one erstwhile friend, can orchestrate their interests sufficiently to allow for the special interests of each. A good example of this coordination is found in the proceedings of a Franco-American conference held in 1971 at Beaulieu, and published as numbers 5 and 6 of *Politique étrangère*. The special title is *Intérêts et Politique de la France et des Etas-Unis au Moyen-Orient et en Afrique du Nord* (Paris: 1971).

42. Israel (suggested by many liberals, and even some government officials); the United States (for an example, see Don Peretz, Evan M. Wilson, Richard J. Ward, *A Palestine Entity?* (Washington: Middle East Institute, 1970); and Jordan (King Hussein's plan of March 1972).

43. Eugene V. Rostow, "Vietnam and the Middle East," in his *Law, Power, and the Pursuit of Peace* (Lincoln, Nebr.: University of Nebraska Press, 1968), pp. 82–83.

44. Ibid., p. 76.

45. *Center Report* (June 1972).

46. *New York Times*, February 8, 1973.

47. *Kayhan*, Tehran, December 11, 1972.

48. J. B. Kelly, *Arabia, the Gulf and the West: A Critical View of the Arabs and Their Oil Policy* (London: Weidenfeld & Nicolson, 1980), p. 504.

49. Books discussed: Sean MacBride et al., *Israel in Lebanon: The Report of the International Commission* (London: Ithaca, 1983). Amnon Kapeliouk, *Sabra et Chatila: Enquête sur un massacre* (Paris: Seuil, 1982). John Bulloch, *Final Conflict: The War in the Lebanon* (London: Century, 1983). David Gilmour, *Lebanon: The Fractured Country* (Oxford: M. Robertson, 1983). Jonathan Randal, *The Tragedy of Lebanon: Christian Warlords, Israeli Adventurers and American Bunglers* (London:

Chatto, 1983). Tony Clifton and Catherine Leroy, *God Cried* (London: Quartet, 1983). Salim Nassib and Caroline Tisdal, *Beirut: Frontline Story,* with photographs by Chris Steele-Perkins (London: Pluto, 1983). Noam Chomsky, *The Fateful Triangle: Israel, the United States and the Palestinians* (London: Pluto, 1983).

50. MacBride et al., *Israel in Lebanon,* p. 222.

51. Michael Adams and Christopher Mayhew, *Publish It Not. . . : The Middle East Cover-Up,* (London: Longman, 1975).

52. Yoav, Karni, "Dr. Shekel and Mr. Apartheid," *Yediot Ahronot,* March 13, 1983.

53. In *Critical Inquiry* (autumn 1980).

54. A persuasive study by Mark Heller, an Israeli political scientist at the Centre for Strategic Studies, Tel Aviv University: *A Palestinian State: The Implications for Israel* (Cambridge, Mass., & London: Harvard University Press, 1983), represents an exception. Heller argues that a Palestinian state on the West Bank and Gaza is in Israel's best interest, and is more desirable than either annexation or returning the territories to Jordan.

55. In *Commentary* (September 1982).

56. Richard Poirier, "Watching the Evening News: The Chancellor Incident," *Raritan* 2:2 (fall 1982), p. 8.

57. The background of collaboration between Zionist groups and individuals and various European fascists is studied in Lenni Brenner's *Zionism in the Age of Dictators: A Reappraisal* (London: Croom Helm, 1983).

58. Chomsky, *The Fateful Triangle,* p. 106.

59. Ibid., p. 102.

60. There is one exception to be noted: Lina Mikdadi, *Surviving the Siege of Beirut: A Personal Account* (London: Onyx Press, 1983). This delivers a Lebanese-Palestinian woman's account of life in Beirut during the siege.

61. Kamal Salibi, *The Modern History of Lebanon* (Delmar, N.Y.: Caravan Books, 1977) and *Crossroads to Civil War: Lebanon 1975–1976* (Delmar, N.Y.: Caravan Books, 1976).

62. Elie Salem, *Modernization without Revolution: Lebanon's Experiences* (Bloomington, Ind.: Indiana University Press, 1973).

63. Jacobo Timerman, *The Longest War* (London: Chatto & Windus, 1982).

Three: Politics and Intellectuals

1. See, in particular, Noam Chomsky, "Objectivity and Liberal Scholarship" in *American Power and the New Mandarins: Historical and Political Essays* (New York: Pantheon Books, 1969), pp. 23–158.

2. Noam Chomsky, *For Reasons of State* (New York: Vintage Books, 1973), pp. 302–3.

3. The full title of Chomsky's book is *Peace in the Middle East? Reflections on Justice and Nationhood* (New York: Pantheon Books, 1974). Irene L. Gendzier wrote a foreword for the book.

4. Ibid., p. 164.

5. Edward Grossman, "A Modest Proposal," *Commentary* 59:2 (February 1975), pp. 80–87; Michael Walzer, *New York Times Sunday Book Review,* October 6, 1974, pp. 5–6; Theodore Draper, "War between the States," *New Republic* (October 26, 1974), pp. 21–28.

6. Chomsky, *Peace in the Middle East?,* p. 81.

7. Ibid., p. 38. It is worth indicating that when on page 50, for example, Chomsky speaks of binationalism, he is not referring to the notion of two states, one Arab and one Jewish, on the territory of Palestine. Rather, he refers to a socialist binationalism for Palestine organized around "other than nationalist lines." Presumably this means one or perhaps no state, but it certainly doesn't mean two states.

8. Ibid., p. 25.

9. I. F. Stone, "War for Oil?" *New York Review of Books,* February 6, 1974, pp. 7–10.

10. Richard H. Ullman, "After Rabat: Middle East Risks and American Roles," *Foreign Affairs* 53:2 (January 1975), pp. 284–96.

11. Robert W. Tucker, "Oil: The Issue of American Intervention," *Commentary* 49:1 (January 1975), pp. 21–31; Miles Ignotus, "Seizing Arab Oil," *Harper's Magazine* (March 1975), pp. 45–62.

12. As an example, see *The New Republic* editorial for February 1, 1975, entitled "On Force: Learning the Wrong Lessons," pp. 5–7.

13. Charles D. Creamens, *The Arabs and the World: Nasser's Arab Nationalist Policy* (New York: Praeger, 1963); John S. Badeau, *The American Approach to the Arab World* (New York: Harper & Row, 1968).

14. Creamens, *The Arabs and the World,* p. 325.

15. Chomsky, *Peace and Justice?,* pp. 165 ff.

16. Ibid., p. 150.

17. Mahmoud Hussein, *La Lutte des classes en Egypte, 1945–1970* (Paris: François Maspero, 1971).

18. Chomsky, *Peace in the Middle East?,* pp. 82–84.

19. Musa Khalil, "Al-Hizb al-Shiyu'i al-Filastini (The Palestinian Communist Party), 1919–1948," *Shu'un Filastiniyyah* 39 (November 1974), pp. 111–43.

20. Adnan Abu-Ghazaleh, *Arab Cultural Nationalism in Palestine During the British Mandate* (Beirut: The Institute for Palestine Studies, 1974).

21. Ibrahim Abu-Lughod, "Retreat from the Secular Path? Islamic Dilemmas of Arab Politics," *The Review of Politics* 28:4 (October 1966), p. 475.

22. Janet Abu-Lughod, "The Demographic Transformation of Palestine," in Ibrahim Abu-Lughod, ed., *The Transformation of Palestine: Essays on the Origin and Development of the Arab-Israeli Conflict* (Evanston, Ill.: Northwestern University Press, 1971), p. 139.

23. Israel Shahak, "What Are My Opinions?" *Swasia* 1:48 (December 27, 1974), pp. 1–4.

24. Bernard Lewis, *Semites and Anti-Semites* (London: Weidenfeld & Nicolson, 1986).

25. Walter Laqueur, *The Age of Terrorism* (Boston: Little, Brown & Co., 1987).

26. Ibid.

27. Ibid., p. 11.

28. Giambattista Vico, *The New Science* (Ithaca & London: Cornell University Press, 1970), # 387–88.

29. Theodor Adorno, *Minima Moralia* (London & New York: Verso, 1989), p. 55.

30. Thomas L. Friedman, *From Beirut to Jerusalem* (New York: Farrar, Straus and Giroux, 1989).

31. Albert Hourani, *A History of the Arab Peoples* (Cambridge: Belknap Press of Harvard University Press, 1991).

32. Albert Hourani, *Arabic Thought in the Liberal Age* (Cambridge: Cambridge University Press, 1983).

33. Albert Hourani, *A History of the Arab Peoples*, p. 4.

34. Lila Abu-Lughod, "Finding a Place for Islam: Egyptian Television Serials and the National Interest," *Public Culture* 5:3 (1993) p. 505.

35. Nazih Ayoubi, *Political Islam: Religion and Politics in the Arab World* (London: Routledge, 1991), p. 35.

36. Mamoun Fandy, "The Tensions Behind the Violence in Egypt," *Middle East Policy* 2:1 (1993), p. 31.

37. Nasr Abu Zeid, "Al-Khitab al-Dini al-Mu'asir, al-Yatuh wa Muntalaqatuhu al-Fikriyyah," in *Qadaya Fikriyyah* (October 1989), p. 45.

Permissions
Acknowledgments

The articles in this work were originally published as follows:

· "The Palestinian Experience," Mason, Herbert, *Reflections on the Middle East* (Paris and The Hague: Mouton, 1970). · "The Palestinians One Year Since Amman," *Le Monde Diplomatique*, October 1971. · "Palestinians," *The New York Times*, October 6, 1977. · "The Acre and the Goat," *New Statesman*, May 11, 1979. · "Peace and Palestinian Rights," *Trialogue*, No. 24, Summer/Fall 1980. · "Palestinians in the United States," *The Guardian*, March 23, 1981. · "The Formation of American Public Opinion of the Question of Palestine": Abu-Lughod, Ibrahim, *Palestinian Rights: Affirmation and Denial* (Wilmette, Ill., Medina Press, 1982). · "Palestinians in the Aftermath of Beirut: A Preliminary Stocktaking," *Arab Studies Quarterly*, Vol. 4, No. 4, Fall 1982. · "Solidly Behind Arafat," *The New York Times*, November 15, 1983. · "Who Would Speak for Palestinians?," *The New York Times*, May 24, 1985. · "An Ideology of Difference," *Critical Inquiry*, Vol. 12, No. 1, September 1985. · "On Palestinian Identity: A Conversation with Salman Rushdie," *The New Left Review*, November/December 1986. · "Review of *Wedding in Galilee* and *Friendship's Death*," *The Nation*, Vol. 246, May 28, 1988. · "How to Answer Palestine's Challenge," *Mother Jones*, September 1988. · "Palestine Agenda," *The Nation*, December 12, 1988. · "Palestinians in the Gulf War's Aftermath," *International Herald Tribune*, March 18, 1991. Originally published as "A Plan for Palestinian Self-Determination," *The Washington Post*, March 17, 1991. · "The Prospects for Peace in the Middle East," published as "Peace in the Middle East," in *Open Magazine Pamphlet Series*, November 1991. · "Return to Palestine–Israel," *The Observer*, October 25–November 1, 1992. · "U.S. Policy and the Conflict of Powers in the Middle East," *Journal of Palestine Studies*, Vol. II, No. 3, Spring 1973, p. 336. · "The Arab Right Wing," *Information Paper No. 21*, September 1978. · "A Changing World Order: The Arab Dimension," *Arab Studies Quarterly*, Vol. 3, No. 2, Spring 1981. "The Death of Sadat," *Los Angeles Times*, October 11, 1981. · "Permission to

Narrate," *London Review of Books*, February 16–29, 1984. · " 'Our' Lebanon," *The Nation*, February 1, 1984. · "Sanctum of the Strong," *The Nation*, July 10, 1989. · "Behind Sadam Hussein's Moves," *The Christian Science Monitor*, August 13, 1990. · "A Tragic Convergence," *The New York Times*, January 11, 1991. · "Ignorant Armies Clash by Night," *The Nation*, February 11, 1991. · "The Arab-American War: The Politics of Information," *London Review of Books*, Vol. 13, No. 5, March 7, 1991. · "The Intellectuals and the War," *Middle East Report*, No. 171, July/August 1991. · "Chomsky and the Question of Palestine," *Journal of Palestine Studies*, Vol. IV, No. 3, Spring 1975. · " 'Reticences of an Orientalist'," *The Guardian*, November 21, 1986. · "Identity, Negation and Violence," *New Left Review 171*, September/October 1988. · "The Orientalist Express: Thomas Friedman Wraps Up in the Middle East," *Village Voice*, Vol. 36, No. 42, October 17, 1989. · "On Nelson Mandela, and Others," *al-Majalla*, March 13, 1990. · "Embargoed Literature," *The Nation*, September 17, 1990. · "The Splendid Tapestry of Arab Life," *Los Angeles Times Book Review*, February 17, 1991. · "The Other Arab Muslims," *The New York Times Magazine*, November 21, 1993.

Endpaper maps are based on a map courtesy of Peace Now Settlement Watch Committee.

Index

Abbas, Abul, 280
Abdel Hadi, Mahdi, 191, 192
Abdel-Malek, Anwar, 314
Abdel Nasser, Gamal, xiv, 216, 244,
    399
Abdel Rahman, Omar, 393, 407, 408
Abdel Shafi, Haidar, xxxii, xxxviii,
    195, 196
Abdel Wahab, Farouk, 376
Abu Amr, Ziad, 404
Abu Deeb, Kamal, 408
Abu Ein, Ziad, 68
Abu-Ghazaleh, Adnan, 333
Abu Iyad (Salah Khalaf), xxx, 147–48
Abu Jihad (Khalil al Wazir), xxx, 146
Abu Khalil, Asad, 388
Abul-Magd, Kamal, 394
Abu-Lughod, Ibrahim, xxi, xxviii, xxxi,
    35, 138, 146, 333, 403
Abu-Lughod, Lila, 387
Abu Sharif, Bassam, 274
Abu Shibak, Ahmad, 396
Abu Site, Ahmed Abdul Hamid,
    116–18
Abu Zeid, Nasr Hamid, 408–10
Achille Lauro incident, 113
Acre, Israel, 178, 187
Acre Pedagogical Center, 187

Adams, Michael, 249
Adas, Michael, 162
Adelman, M. A., 222
Adonis, 375, 377, 408
Adorno, Theodor, 353
African National Congress (ANC),
    169–70, 366, 367, 368
Afro-Asian movement, xiv
After the Last Sky (Said), xxv, 107, 120,
    121, 122, 123
  Rushdie's analysis of, 108–12
Aghazarian, Albert, 198
Ahmad, Eqbal, 53, 209, 345–47
Ajami, Fouad, 289, 307, 308, 361
Akili, Ali el, 133
Akleh, Nezih, 133
Algazy, Joseph, 185
Algeria, 145, 161, 385
Alim, Mahmoud Amin el, 399
al-Wafd (Egyptian nationalist party),
    191
Amar, Sonia, 133
Amer, Ibrahim, 14
American-Israel Public Affairs
    Committee (AIPAC), 101, 127,
    251, 273
Amin, Galal, 391
Amman, Jordan, 6–7

Anderson, Benedict, 350
*Anglo-Arab Relations and the Question of
    Palestine* (Tibawi), 35
Anti-Defamation League, 251
anti-Semitism in Arab world, 337–40
Antonious, George, 16
Apple, R. W., 300
Arab Awakening (Antonious), 16
Arab Cultural Nationalism in Palestine
    (Abu-Ghazaleh), 333
Arabia, the Gulf and the West (Kelly),
    234–35
Arabic literature, West's attitude
    toward, 372–78
Arabic Thought in the Liberal Age
    (Hourani), 16, 379
Arab independence, xiii–xiv, 12
Arab League, xvii, xxviii, 370
Arab Mind (Laffin), 339
Arab nationalism:
    Gulf War and, 290–92
    Israel and, 13–14
    Palestinianism and, 12–18
    postwar radical Arab nationalism,
        West's view of, 425n2
    progressivism of, 225–26
    Zionism and, 16–18
"Arab Portrayed" (Said), 11
Arab Predicament (Ajami), 307
Arab Right Wing, 224
    dramatic portrayal of, 226–28
    human rights and, 230
    intellectuals' response to, 230
    oil wealth and, 228–29
    schizophrenic nature, 224–26
    values of, 229–30
Arabs in Israel (Jiryis), 35, 88
Arabs in the Jewish State (Lustick), 88
Arab world:
    anti-Semitism in, 337–40
    Arab dimension in world order,
        enhancement of, 241–42
    Chomsky's perception of, 331–32
    Christian minorities, 388–89
    democratic movements, need for,
        313–15
    education in, 387

Arab world *cont.*
    Europe, relations with, 160–63
    governments, public dissatisfaction
        with, 392–93, 398
    homogeneous Arab state, myth of,
        310
    intellectual establishment, need for,
        292–94, 308–9
    leadership and principles, crisis of,
        369–71
    moderate alternative to Islamic
        fundamentalism, 408–10
    national security state, ideology of,
        232–33
    oil wealth and, 228–29, 233,
        241–42, 292
    secular society in, 387–88
    self-criticism by Arabs, need for, 334
    self-questioning within, 14–16,
        390–91
    terrorism, association with, 342,
        344–45
    United States:
        lack of information about, 214,
            289–90
        relations with, 158, 164
    U.S. cultural war against, 298–99,
        302–3
    West's colonial designs on, 234–35
    West's conflict with, 158–59, 160
    West's distorted image of Arabs,
        235–41
    see also Arab Right Wing; Islamic
        movement
Arafat, Yasir, xvii, xxi, xxv, xxvi, 48,
    141, 176, 191, 312, 368, 404,
    418
    accomplishments of, 78–79
    Camp David peace agreement and,
        xxii
    Israeli-PLO agreements of 1993,
        xxxiv, xxxvi–xxxvii, xli, xlii,
        414
    loss of credibility, xxiii, xxx–xxxi
    media coverage of, xli, 62–63
    peace process of 1990s, xxxi–xxxii
    PLO mutiny against, 78, 79–80

Arafat, Yasir *cont.*
  PNC meeting on *intifadah*, 145, 146,
    147, 148
  as symbol of Palestinian persistence,
    128–29
  terrorism, renunciation of, xx
  "terrorist's" view of, 117
Arendt, Hannah, 18, 95
Arens, Moshe, 257
Arkoun, Mohammed, 408
Armenian holocaust, 253
arms trade, 215
Arnold, Matthew, 357
Asad, Talal, 84, 85
Ashrawi, Hanan, xxix, xxxii, 192
Assad, Hafez al-, 78, 361
Avineri, Shlomo, 97, 98, 99, 263
Avineri, Uri, 98
Awad, Lewis, 14
Ayoubi, Nazih, 388
Ayyad, Shukry, 394

Badeau, John, 330
Baghdad, Iraq, 302
Bailey, Clinton, 361
Baker, James A., III, xxxi, xxxv, 153,
    273–74, 275, 276, 311
Balfour, Arthur, 47, 166
Balfour Declaration of 1917, xiv
Ball, George, 60
Barak, Ehud, xxxv–xxxvi
Baramki, Gaby, 197
Barnet, Richard J., 209
Bar Shelev, Baruch, 250
Bar-Zohar, Michael, 33, 38–39
Battle of Algiers (film), 344
Begin, Menachem, xxvi, xxxvii, 43,
    64, 67, 99, 100, 245, 257, 270
  Israeli invasion of Lebanon, 69, 72
  on religious fanaticism, 36–37
behavioral science approach in foreign
    affairs, 212
Beirut: Frontline Story (Nassib and
    Tisdall), 262
Beirut, Lebanon, 4–5, 30, 401
Beisan, Israel, 182
Beit Shean, Israel, 182

Bellow, Saul, 102, 265
Benda, Julien, 171
Ben-Gurion: A Biography (Bar-Zohar), 33,
    38–39
Ben-Gurion, David, 38–40, 139, 140,
    150, 165, 326
Bennett, William, 357, 358
Benvenisti, Meron, xxvii, xxxix–xl,
    266
Benziman, Uzi, xxxvii
Bercovitch, Sacvan, 57
Berger, John, 108
Bernal, Martin, 163
Berque, Jacques, 15, 16, 306
Berrigan, Daniel, 53, 325, 331
binational socialism, 327, 430n7
Birth of Israel (Flapan), 140
Birzeit University, 197–99
Black Sunday (film), 131
Blaming the Victims (Said), xxv
Brandt, Willy, 231
Bruno, Michael, 217, 427n37
Buber, Martin, 17, 95, 180
Building for Peace (report), 276
Bulloch, John, 259–60
Burton, Sir Richard, 161
Bush, George, xxvii, xxxi, xxxiii, 156,
    158, 173, 190, 282, 293
  Gulf War, 159, 287, 290, 296, 297,
    300, 301
Byrne, Gabriel, 131

Cairo, Egypt, 395–97
Cairo Conference of 1921, 206
Cairo Trilogy (Mahfouz), 373
Campbell, John C., 209
Camp David peace agreement, xvii,
    xxi, 66–67, 140, 232, 244
  Palestinian interests and, xxi–xxii
Camus, Albert, 105
Carioca, Tahia, 227
Carter, Hodding, xxi
Carter, Billy, 241
Carter, Jimmy, 31, 43, 47, 62, 67,
    125, 232
centrality, 355–56
Césaire, Aimé, 294, 318

Chahine, Youssef, 132

Chamorro, Violeta, xl

Chancellor, John, 255–56

Chevalier, Dominique, 260

Chomsky, Noam, xxvi, 53, 94, 113,
    258, 316, 424n19
  Arabs' knowledge of, 324
  on Arab world, 331–32
  on binational socialism, 327, 430n7
  courage of, 333–34
  Jews' attitude toward, 323–24
  liberalism, critique of, 324–25
  orthodoxy, rejection of, 324
  on Palestine, 325–28, 332–33,
      335–36
  on PLO, 328
  on U.S. policy on Middle East,
      328–29, 331
  on Zionist-Palestinian conflict,
      262–68

Christian minorities of Arab world,
    388–89

Christopher, Warren, 237, 413

Churcher, Sharon, 118

Cities of Salt (Munif), 289, 376

City of Saffron (Kharrat), 375–76

Clastres, Pierre, 351

Clayburgh, Jill, 131

Clifton, Tony, 259, 261–62

Clinton, Bill, xxxiv

Cobham, Catherine, 375, 376

Cockburn, Alexander, 113

Cold War, 58, 231

complementary antagonism, 162

"Confessions of a Unionist"
        (Stevenson), 344

Conrad, Joseph, 34, 107, 344, 350,
    354

Copts, 389

Costa-Gavras, Constantin, 131–32,
    251

Covering Islam (Said), 107–8

Creamens, Charles D., 330, 331

cultural chauvinism, 357–59

Dajani, Abir, 131

Damascus, Syria, 6

Daniel, Norman, 161

Darwish, Mahmoud, xxiv, xliii, 108,
    146–47, 377, 408

Davidi, Asher, xxxix

Davidson, Basil, 163

Dayan, Moshe, 36, 45, 139

Deacon, Richard, 37

Death of a Princess (film), 236–39

Debray, Regis, 308

De Gaulle, Charles, 39

Delta Force (film), 131

Dershowitz, Alan, 95, 131, 263

*Development and Economic Situation in
        Judea, Samaria, the Gaza Strip,
        and North Sinai* (Israeli report),
    217

Diaries (Sharett), 45, 261

difference, ideology of, 86–87
  alternatives to, 106
  consequences of, 105–6
  contradictory assertions of, 94–96
  defenders of, 100–105
  "dovish" approach to, 98–99
  military policy and, 97–98
  non-Jews in Israel and, 90–94
  pragmatic and essentialist views,
      99–100
  Zionist orientation, 87–90

Dine, Thomas, 127

Djait, Hisham, 161

Dome of the Rock, 179

Dorat, Tali, 133

Downing, Taylor, 130

Draper, Theodore, 326, 335

Eagleburger, Lawrence, 276

"Earth Is Closing on Us" (Darwish),
    108

Eban, Abba, 172–73, 180, 254

Economist (journal), 222, 237

Eden, Anthony, 297

education:
  in Arab world, 387
  Palestinians' concern for, 187–88,
      191, 197–98

Egypt, xiv, xv, xviii, xxx, 384
  Christian minorities, 389

Egypt *cont.*
European orientation of Egyptian
culture, 163
government, public dissatisfaction
with, 392–93, 398
Islamic movement in, 385, 391–400
Israel, peace agreement with: *see*
Camp David peace agreement
labor disputes, 26
nationalitarianism and, 14
Palestinian autonomy talks (1980),
43–44, 46–47, 67
peace process of 1990s, 153
Soviet Union and, 24
television in, 387
U.S. policy toward, 403
Eichmann in Jerusalem (Arendt), 18, 95
Eliav, Lova, 98
Erikson, Erik, 14–15
European attitudes toward Arabs,
160–63
European Community, 50
Evans, Rowland, 223
*Exile and Return: The Emergence of Jewish
Statehood* (Gilbert), 35
Exodus (film), 130
Explosion of Terrorism (Grosscup), 350
Eytan, Rafael, 36, 105, 138, 249,
257

Fadlallah, Shaikh, 401–2
Fahd, Prince, 45
Falwell, Jerry, 97
Fandy, Mamoun, 395
Fanon, Frantz, 352
Fateful Triangle (Chomsky), 262–68,
424n19
Fawzi, Hussein, 14
Fertile Memory (film), 120, 132
Fisher, Glen H., 212
Flapan, Simha, 98, 140
Foda, Farag, 409
Fonda, Jane, 263
Foreign Affairs (journal), 302, 384
For Reasons of State (Chomsky), 324
Forster, E. M., 89
Foucault, Michel, 352

France, 206, 252, 428n41
Friedman, Thomas, 276, 307, 308,
360–65
Friendship's Death (film), 132, 134–36
From Beirut to Jerusalem (Friedman), 307,
360–65
Fromkin, David, 307
From Time Immemorial (Peters), 102–3,
339
Fulbright, J. William, 212, 214
Future of Culture in Egypt (Hussein),
163

Gamaat al-Islamiyya, 393
Gassick, Trevor le, 377
Gavin, James M., 221
Gaza Strip: *see* Occupied Territories
Gemayel, Amin, 269, 270, 272
Gemayel, Bashir, 261
Gemayel, Pierre, 271
Gendzier, Irene, 328
genocide concept, 253
Ghitani, Gamal al-, 376–77, 395–98,
400, 403
Giacaman, George, 198
Gilbert, Martin, 35
Gilmour, David, 260
Glaspie, April, 299
God Cried (Clifton), 261–62
Goethe, J. W. von, 161
Going All the Way (Randal), 260–61
Golan, Aviezer, 38
Golan Heights, 44, 97
Goldberg, Arthur, 263
Goldmann, Nahum, 39–40
Gouldner, Alvin, 358
Great Britain, 206, 236, 344
Grose, Peter, 96
Grosscup, Beau, 350
Guardian Weekly, 221–22
guerrilla-broadcaster dialogue, 116–18
Guindy, Huda, 389
Gulf War, xxiii, 157–58, 295–96
aftermath of, 301–2
Arab arrangement to avoid military
confrontation, 297
Arab-West conflict and, 159

Gulf War *cont.*
  demonization of Hussein and Iraq, 285, 298
  intellectuals' response, 305–6
  Iraqi invasion of Kuwait, context of, 278–82
  Israeli cities, bombing of, 300
  linkage issue, 282, 288, 296, 304
  media coverage of, 163–64, 285–86, 289, 297, 304–5, 374–75
  nationalism and, 290–92
  Palestinians, impact on, xxx–xxxi, 152–55, 281, 310–11
  as personalized struggle between Bush and Hussein, 296
  public rhetoric on, 290
  Said's comments to Palestinian students about, 198
  sanctions against Iraq, 280
  UN resolutions, 280, 296, 300
  U.S.-Arab relations and, 164
  U.S. imperialism and, 158, 298, 301
  U.S.-Iraqi military confrontation, 283–84, 285, 287–88
  U.S. right of intervention, 297–98
  U.S. war aims, 299
  as war against Iraqi people, 300
Gush Emunim organization, 60, 94, 232

Habash, George, 147, 148
Habiby, Emile, 184, 377
Hadar, Leon T., 384
Hadashot (newspaper), 185
Haddad, Major Saad, 45
Haddawy, Hussein, 377
Haifa, Israel, 178, 186
Haig, Alexander, 248
Hajj (Uris), 102, 103–4
Hama massacre, 361
Hamas organization, xxxiii, xlv, 153, 192, 197, 385, 399, 400, 403, 404–5
hamula (village "clan"), 90–91
Hanafi, Hassan, 408
Hanna K (film), 131–32, 251
Hariri, Rafik, 401, 402

Harkabi, Yeheshofat, 97
Harlow, Barbara, conversation with Said, 304–19
Hartman, David, 361
Havel, Vaclav, 368–69
Hayden, Tom, 263
Heart of Darkness (Conrad), 34
Hebron, West Bank, 188
  mosque massacre (1994), 413
Heikal, Mohammed Hassanein, xxxiv, 293, 391–92, 393, 398–99, 400
Hekmatyar, Gulbuddin, 407
Heller, Mark, 429n54
Hersh, Seymour, 216
Herzog, Chaim, 36–37, 253
History of the Arab Peoples (Hourani), 307, 379–83
Hitler, Adolf, 338
Hitti, Philip, 380
Hizballah organization, 385, 401–2
Hoagland, Jim, 307
Hodgson, Marshall, 389
Hoffer, Eric, 239
Holocaust, 22, 34, 63, 167, 169, 326
Holy Sepulcher, 178–79
Hopkins, Gerard Manley, 19–20
hostage crisis of 1979-81, 58
Hourani, Albert, 16, 161, 260, 292, 307, 379–83
Hourani, Cecil, 13
Hout, Shafiq al-, xxi, xxii, xxiv, xxv, xxvi, xliii
Howe, Irving, 100, 263, 265
Hugo, Victor, 161
human rights:
  Arab Right Wing and, 230
  of Palestinians, 31–32, 46–48, 67–68
  U.S. policy on, 160
Huntington, Samuel, 385
Hussein, Mahmoud, 332
Hussein, Saddam, xxx, 287, 302
  Arab attitude toward, 159, 279, 280
  demonization of, 285, 298
  Gulf War as Bush-Hussein struggle, 296

Hussein, Saddam *cont.*
  Iraqi invasion of Kuwait, 278,
    280–81
  Said's assessment of, 198, 279
Hussein, Taha, 163
Hussein I, king of Jordan, 24, 27, 223,
    405, 406
Husseini, Abdel Kader, 191
Husseini, Faisal, xxix, xxxii, 191–93
Husseini, Fawzi al-, 332

Ibn Barquq mosque (Cairo), 397
Ibn Khaldun, 380
identitarian thought, 353
identity crisis among Arabs, 14–16
identity enforcement, processes of,
    355–57
Idéologie arabe contemporaine (Laroui), 13
Ill-Fated Pessoptimist (Habibi), 109, 119,
    377
Imagined Communities (Anderson), 350
Imam, Adel, 398
Institute for Defense Analysis, 212–13
intellectuals:
  Arab intellectual establishment, need
    for, 292–94, 308–9
  Arab intellectuals' role in West,
    315–16
  Arab Right Wing and, 230
  authority and, 318–19
  criticism of Israel, 171
  Gulf War and, 305–6
  Middle Eastern and Arab concerns,
    disengagement from, 306–8
  "reading list" on Middle East,
    307–8
  responsibilities of, 316–17
  universities' role and, 317–18
  Vietnam War and, 306–7
intifadah, xxvii, xxx, 137, 139, 286,
    311, 312
  casualties of, 166
  Israeli response, 166–67, 274,
    275–76
  message of, 142–44
  as Palestinian self-determination,
    159–60

intifadah cont.
  PNC meeting on, xx, 145–51
  terrorism, comparison with, 349
  as unifying force for Palestinians,
    137–38, 415
Introduction to Arab Poetics (Adonis), 375
Iran, 36, 37, 60, 62, 216, 222, 385
  hostage crisis of 1979–81, 58
  Iraq, war with, 233–34, 288
  "modernization" of, 61
  revolution of 1979, 61
Iraq, xviii, xxx
  cultural achievements, 164, 302
  gassing of Iraqi citizens, 300–301
  Iran, war with, 233–34, 288
  secular society, 157
  see also Gulf War
Ireland, 169, 170, 344
Islam:
  Arab identity and, 388–89
  democracy and, 402–3
  Hourani's analysis of, 381–82
  terrorism, association with, 342
  Western attitude toward, 59–61
Islamic Jihad, xlv, 385, 399, 403–4
Islamic law, 395
Islamic movement:
  cooptation of, 405
  cultural battleground, 394–95,
    397–98
  economic operations, 394
  in Egypt, 385, 391–400
  governments' response, 398
  as historical entity, 389–90
  internal conflicts, 404
  Islamic conformity, attraction of,
    390–91
  in Jordan, 399, 405–7
  in Lebanon, 385, 401–2
  mass appeal, potential for, 406–7
  military forces and, 398–99
  moderate alternative to, 408–10
  in Occupied Territories, 403–5
  as oppositional and protest
    movement, 392–93, 398
  overthrow of secular society, hopes
    for, 387–88

Islamic movement *cont.*
  PLO and, 404
  public's alienation from, 393–94,
    400
  purity of Islamic culture and,
    397–98
  symbolic actions, 394
  as threat to West, 384–85, 386, 405
  U.S. policy on, 407–8
  U.S. relations with Arab
    governments and, 403, 407
Israel, xviii
  Arab nationalism and, 13–14
  Arabs' refusal to acknowledge, 177
  coexistence by Israelis and
    Palestinians, possibility of,
    123–24, 143–44
  criticism of policies, intolerance of,
    100, 170–72, 338–39
  Declaration of Independence, 39
  deportations of Palestinians, 370
  economic power, xxxix
  Egypt, peace agreement with: *see*
    Camp David peace agreement
  enclosure, fixation on, 182
  "existence of Palestinians" issue,
    63–64
  filmic portrayals of, 130–31
  foreign aid, dependence on, 96
  founding of, 65, 70, 85–86, 139
  genocide concept and, 253
  Gulf War and, 300
  intifadah, response to, 166–67, 274,
    275–76
  intelligence services, 38, 261
  Islam's image in Western world and,
    60–61
  Jewish rhythm of life and, 21–22
  as Jewish state, 85–86
  justice and injustice in
    Israeli-Palestinian relations,
    126–27
  kibbutz settlements, 91
  labor disputes, 26
  Law of Return, xliv, 86, 88, 139–40
  Lebanon policy, 45, 261
  Nationality Law, 86

Israel *cont.*
  non-Jews, policy on, 31, 86, 89,
    90–94, 168–69, 186, 250–51
  nuclear capability, 215
  Palestinian autonomy talks (1980),
    43–44, 46–47, 67
  Palestinian elections, proposal for
    (1989), 273–75, 276–77
  Palestinians' national identity,
    attempt to destroy, 71–72
  peace and reconciliation, framework
    for, 48–51
  peace with Arab countries, rejection
    of, 140
  peace with Palestinians, rejection of,
    142, 150, 167
  racism in, 92–93, 339
  religion-based policies, 59–60
  as reparation for Western
    anti-Semitism, 167, 169,
    171–72
  research on Palestinians, 90–91
  "right to exist" issue, 105
  Russian immigrants, 153, 168, 370
  settlements policy, xxxvi, 37, 42,
    60, 140–41, 189–90
  siege mentality, 169
  territorial domination, plan for,
    416–18
  terrorism, policy on, 347–49
  UN's censuring of, 67
  U.S. policy toward, 44–45, 96, 127,
    138, 214–15, 248
  see also difference, ideology of; Israeli
    invasion of Lebanon;
    Israeli-PLO agreements of
    1993; Jerusalem; Occupied
    Territories; peace process of
    1990s; Zionism
Israel: Pluralism and Conflict (Smooha),
  41
Israel and the Palestinians (Davis, Mack
  and Yurval-Davis), 88
Israeli Communist Party (Rakah), 193
Israeli invasion of Lebanon, xvii,
  69–72, 74
  as anti-terrorist action, 348

Israeli invasion of Lebanon *cont.*
  eyewitness accounts of, 258–59
  Israeli brutality, 247–48, 254
  Israeli view of, 254
  journalism on, 259–62
  jurists' report on, 247–48
  media coverage of, 100, 128, 255–56
  Palestinians as targets of, 249
  Sabra and Shatila massacres,
      xvii–xviii, xxiii, 72, 152, 247,
      254, 257
  U.S. response, 248
  Western perception of Israel and,
      84–85
Israel in Lebanon (MacBride
      Commission), 247–48
Israel in the Mind of America (Grose), 96
Israeli-PLO agreements of 1993, xxxiv,
      413–14, 415, 416
  diaspora Palestinians and, xlii,
      xliii–xliv
  economic issues, xxxviii–xli
  governance of Palestinian areas,
      xxxvii–xxxviii
  Israeli settlements and, xxxvi
  Jericho issue, xxxv–xxxvi
  media coverage of, xli
  negotiation of, xlii
  Palestinian response, proposals for,
      xli–xlvii
  as Palestinian surrender,
      xxxiv–xxxvii
  reparations issue, xliv–xlv
  resistance by Palestinians and, xlv
  security arrangements, xxxviii
Israeli Secret Service (Deacon), 37

Jabalya Camp, Gaza, 194, 195
Jabber, Fuad, 215
Jabiri, Muhammad Abid el, 314, 408
Jabotinsky, Vladimir, 39
Jackson, Jesse, xxvii, 248
Jaffa, Israel, 91–92
jahiliyya concept in Islam, 397
James, C. L. R., 294
Jaspers, Karl, 20
Jay, Martin, 353

Jayyusi, Salma al-, 377
Jerbawi, Ali, 193
Jericho, West Bank, xxxv–xxxvi, 178,
      414
Jerusalem, 43, 45, 97, 165, 417, 419
  Said's visit, 177–82
  settler incursions, 188–89
Jew as Pariah (Arendt), 95
Jewish Defense League, 95, 112
Jewish nationalism: *see* Zionism
Jewish Paradox (Goldmann), 40
Jihad al-Islami: *see* Islamic Jihad
Jiryis, Sabri, 35, 88
Jo'beh, Nazmi al-, 192–93
John of Damascus, 161
Johnson, Lyndon B., 59, 354
Johnson-Davies, Denys, 377
Jones, W. M., 25
Jong, Jan de, 417, 418
Jordan, xxx, 146, 177, 222, 384, 385
  Islamic movement in, 399, 405–7
  Palestinianism and, 6–9
  Palestinians, war against (1970), 24,
      27, 29
  refugee camps in, 7–8
  U.S. policy on Middle East and,
      215–17
June 1967 war, xiii
  Palestinians in United States and, 53
  psychological impact of, 11–14
Just and Unjust Wars (Walzer), 95

Kaddafi, Muammar al-, 24
Kahane, Meir, 86, 94, 124
Kanafani, Ghassan, 119, 377
Kapeliouk, Amnon, 254, 259, 347
Karameh, battle of, 9, 20
Karni, Yoav, 253
Kayyali, A. W., 35
Kelly, J. B., 234–35, 239
Kelly, John, 299
Kennan, George, 339
Kennedy, Edward, 68
Kennedy, Robert, 11
Khalaf, Salah: *see* Abu Iyad
Khalidi, Rashid, 177
Khalifa, Shahar, 408

Khalil, Musa, 332
Khalil, Samir al-, 307, 315–16
Kharrat, Edwar al-, 375–76
Khidr, Asma, 406–7
Khleifi, Michel, 120, 132–34
Khodr, George, 180
Khomeini, Ruhollah, 36
Khoury, Elias, 293, 377, 401
Khoury, Makram, 133
Khoury, Ra'if, 14
kibbutz settlements, 91
Kislev, Ran, 91–93
Kissinger, Henry A., xx, xxi, 82, 223
Klieman, Aaron S., 206
Koestler, Arthur, 17
Kramer, Martin, 402
Kramer, Semadar, 250
Krauthammer, Charles, 276
Kreisky, Bruno, 112, 252
Kurds, 157, 300–301
Kuwait, xxxi, 157–58
    Palestinians and, 152, 310–11, 312
    see also Gulf War

Laffin, John, 339
Laird, Melvin, 203
Landes, David, 162
Laqueur, Walter, 343
Laroui, Abdallah, 13, 314
Lautman, Dov, xxxix
Lavon affair, 38
Lawrence, T. E., 12
Lebanese period of Palestinian national
        history, 71–74
Lebanon, 226
    Civil War, xvi, xvii, 30, 269–72
    contradictory character, 5
    crisis of 1969, 5–6
    Gemayel government, 269–72
    Islamic movement in, 385, 401–2
    Israeli policy toward, 45, 261
    journalism on, 259–62
    number of Palestinians in, xliv
    Palestinianism and, 4–6
    Palestinians' ejection from, xvii–xviii
    partition proposal, 271–72
    Right Wing in, 227–28

Lebanon cont.
    U.S. policy toward, 261, 269–72
    see also Israeli invasion of Lebanon
Le Carré, John, 251
Left argument for Palestinianism,
        20–21
Leigh, David, 240
Le Lannou, Maurice, 19
Lenin, V. I., 39
Lerner, Michael, 172
Leroy, Catherine, 261
Lewis, Anthony, 48, 303
Lewis, Bernard, 307, 337–40, 373
Liardet, Frances, 376
Libya, 341
Lilly Foundation, 211
literature of Arab world, West's
        attitude toward, 372–78
Little Drummer Girl (Le Carré), 251
Little Mountain (Khoury), 377
local nationalism, 232
Lustick, Ian, 88
Lutte des classes en Egypte (Hussein), 332

Ma'alim fil Tariq (Qutb), 399
MacBride, Sean, 247
MacBride Commission, 96, 247–48
McGovern, George, 248
McHenry, Donald, 67
Magnes, Judah, 17, 95
Mahfouz, Naguib, 372, 373, 395–96,
        397, 408
Making of Modern Zionism (Avineri), 97
Mandela, Nelson, 170, 366–68
Marei, Mariam, 187
Margalit, Avishai, 424n19
Marnissi, Fatima el-, 408
Massignon, Louis, 161
Mayhew, Christopher, 249
media:
    Arafat and, xli, 62–63
    Gulf War and, 163–64, 285–86,
        289, 297, 304–5, 374–75
    Israeli invasion of Lebanon and, 100,
        128, 255–56
    Israeli-PLO agreements of 1993 and,
        xli

media *cont.*
  Palestinians and, xxvi–xxvii, 62–65
  Saudi Arabia and, 240
  terrorism and, 353–57
Meir, Golda, xvi, 63, 138, 223
Men in the Sun (Kanafani), 119, 377
Miari, Mohammed, 176, 177, 186
Middle East:
  commercialization of international
    relations, 222
  conflict of powers, 204–5
  development disparities, 205
  see also U.S. policy on Middle East
Midnight's Children, 118, 119
Mikhail, Hanna, xiv
Milhem, Mohammed, 47
Miller, Judith, 384–85
Miller, Perry, 57
Mills, C. Wright, 355
Mishal, Saul, 40–41
Mitterrand, François, 252
modernization theory, 58–62
Mohammed, Um, 196
Mohr, Jean, 108, 115, 121, 123
Mondale, Walter, 276
Morris, Benni, 338
Mossad intelligence agency, 261
Mubarak, Hosni, 153, 245, 392–93,
    399, 403
"Muhammad's Sloth" (Hoffer), 239
Munif, Abdel Rahman, 289, 376, 408
Muqaddimah (Ibn Khaldun), 380
Musa, Salama, 14
Musa-Bishouty, Shukry, 184
Muslim Brotherhood, 399–400, 405

Nahda (renaissance of Arabic culture),
    xiii
Najjar, Yusif, 196
Nasser, Gamal Abdel: *see* Abdel Nasser,
    Gamal
Nasser, Kamal, xiv–xv, 196
Nassib, Salim, 259, 262
national security state, ideology of,
    232–33
Nations and States (Seton-Watson), 350
Nazareth, Israel, 183–85

NBC Versus the Jews (film), 128
Netanyahu, Benjamin, 113–14, 343,
    345, 370
New Republic, 104–5
New Science (Vico), 351–52
New York Review of Books, 240
Nicaragua, xl–xli
1949 (Segev), 140
Nixon, Richard M., 209, 221, 223
Non-Aligned movement, xiv
Novak, Robert, 223

Obeid, Shaikh, 364
O'Brien, Conor Cruise, 105
Occupied Territories:
  Islamic movement in, 403–5
  Israeli economic policy on, 217–18
  Israeli expropriation of land, xxvii,
    140–41, 188–90
  laws governing Palestinians, 190–91
  road construction, 190, 417
  Said's visit to Gaza, 194–96
  South Africa, similarity to, 194
  see also Jerusalem
October War of 1973, xvii, 95
oil production, 209, 222
oil wealth, Arab investment of,
    228–29, 233, 241–42, 292
Operation Susannah (Golan), 38
Organization of Petroleum Exporting
    Countries (OPEC), 209
Orientalism, 61, 329, 338, 361, 362,
    374, 382
Orientalism (Said), 107
Origins of Totalitarianism (Arendt), 95
Oslo Declaration of Principles: *see*
    Israeli-PLO agreements of 1993
Other Side of the Medal (Thompson), 127
Oz, Amos, xxxv, 34, 98, 263
Ozick, Cynthia, 112, 125

Pakistan, 402–3
Palestine:
  Chomsky's writings on, 325–28,
    332–33, 335–36
  Jewish-Zionist takeover, 165–66
  Jews' right to settlement in, 266–67

Palestine *cont.*
  religious and cultural significance,
    165
  Said's visit (1992), xxxiii, 175–99
  UN conference on (1983), 252–53
Palestine: A Modern History (Kayyali), 35
Palestine Communist Party (PCP), 332
Palestine Congress of North America, 52
Palestine Liberation Organization
      (PLO), xvi, xvii, xx, 36, 48,
      71, 75, 141
  Chomsky's attitude toward, 328
  information policies, xxvi, 415
  Islamic movement and, 404
  loss of credibility, xxiii, xxx–xxxi,
    414–15
  mutiny against Arafat, 78, 79–80
  negotiations on Palestinian issues
    and, 81–83
  Palestinians in United States and, 53
  peace discussions, informal,
    xxviii–xxix
  peace process of 1990s, xxxi–xxxii
  as quasi-official Arab state
    organization, xviii
  reform, need for, xlv–xlvi, xlvii
  as terrorist organization, 82
  United States:
    dialogue with, xx–xxi, xxiii, 312
    policy toward, xxix–xxx
  U.S. offer of recognition (1978–79),
    xxi–xxii
  see also Israeli-PLO agreements of
    1993
Palestine National Council (PNC),
      xxv–xxvi, xxxii, 141, 167,
      176, 181, 419
  intifadah, meeting on (1988), xx,
    145–51
  peace process of 1990s, 156
Palestine on Film (Downing), 130
Palestine Red Crescent, 52
Palestinian autonomy talks
      (Israel-Egypt-U.S.), 43–44,
      46–47, 67
Palestinian Interim Self-Governing
      Authority (PISGA), 193

Palestinianism, 3–4
  Arab nationalism and, 12–18
  discontinuity of, 8–9
  Jordan and, 6–9
  Lebanon and, 4–6
  obstacles to scrutiny of, 21–22
  Palestinian organizations and, 22–23
  peripherality, isolation, and silence as
      characteristics of Palestinian
      life, 18–20
  political voice, 19
  popular resistance and, 9, 20
  sympathetic views of, 20–21
Palestinian national movement, xiv–xvi
  inclusiveness of, 251–52
  land acquisition policy, 33
  as leadership for Arab world,
    312–13
  Lebanese period in history of, 71–74
  political program, need for, 75–77
  Said's direct involvement,
    xxiv–xxxiv, 145–51
  U.S. policy on Middle East and,
    207–8
  see also Palestine Liberation
      Organization; Palestine National
      Council; Palestinianism
Palestinians:
  art made by, 109
  Camp David peace agreement and,
    xxi–xxii
  census of, proposed, xliii–xliv, 253
  coexistence with Israelis, possibility
    of, 123–24, 143–44
  collective action, need for, 418–19
  deportations of, 370
  diaspora community, xlii, xliii–xliv,
    70, 114
  difficult circumstances of, xviii–xix
  dress of, 118
  education, focus on, 187–88, 191,
    197–98
  elections on West Bank and Gaza,
    Israeli proposal for (1989),
    273–75, 276–77
  "existence of Palestinians" issue,
    xvi–xvii, 10

Palestinians *cont.*
    Arab view, 252–53
    Israeli view, 63–64
    Peters' book on, 102–3
    Said-Rushdie conversation on,
      108–9, 114–19
    Zionism and, 34–35
    "experts" to determine future of,
      418
    expulsion from Palestine (1948),
      139
    extra-dimensionality of, 27, 28
    fall from favor among Arabs
      (1970–71), 26–27
    filmic portrayals of, 120, 130–36
    geographic strategy, need for,
      415–18
    Gulf states, relationship with, 311
    Gulf War and, xxx–xxxi, 152–55,
      281, 310–11
    hamula (village "clan"), 90–91
    human rights issue, 31–32, 46–48,
      67–68
    ideological vacillation, 27–28
    imprisonment of, 193–94
    institutionalized Palestinian history,
      need for, 118–19
    internecine conflict, 192
    Islamic movement and, 403–5
    Israeli invasion of Lebanon and, 249
    Israeli research on, 90–91
    Israeli revisionist view of, 40–42
    Jordan's war against (1970), 24, 27,
      29
    journalism sympathetic to, 259–62
    justice and injustice in
      Israeli-Palestinian relations,
      126–27
    Kuwait and, 152, 310–11, 312
    leadership and principles, crisis of,
      369–71
    leadership change, need for, 414–15
    Lebanon, expulsion from, xvii–xviii
    media's portrayal of, xxvi–xxvii,
      62–65
    name changes imposed by Israelis,
      111

Palestinians *cont.*
    national identity, Israeli attempt to
      destroy, 71–72
    Palestinian citizens of Israel, 168–69,
      176, 186–88
    Palestinians inside Palestine
      ("insiders"), 110–11
    partition of Palestine, proposals for,
      xx, 141–42, 149–50, 167,
      251–52, 266
    peace and reconciliation, framework
      for, 48–51
    peace delegation, 191, 192–93
    political shorthand used by, 193
    public opinion on, xx, xxvii; *see also*
      U.S. public opinion on *below*
    radicalism of 1968–69, 219
    refugees in Jordan, 7–8
    repetition and excess as way of
      existing, 115–18
    self-production by, 36
    statehood declaration (1988), 146–51
    terrorism:
      association with, xxvi–xxvii, 35,
        57–58, 113–14, 116–18, 342
      rejection of, 149–50
    turning inward by, 122–23
    UN protection for, 153
    in United States, 52–55, 112–13
    U.S. policy toward, xxvi–xxviii,
      25–26, 28
    U.S. public opinion on, 56
      foreign policy and, 66–68
      human rights and, 67–68
      ideological background, 57–62
      media's role, 62–65
      Zionism and, 65–66
    women's situation, 120–21
    see also intifadah; Israeli-PLO
      agreements of 1993; Occupied
      Territories; Palestine Liberation
      Organization; Palestine National
      Council; Palestinianism;
      Palestinian national movement;
      peace process of 1990s
Palestinians: From Peasants to
    Revolutionaries (Sayigh), 42

Palestinians in Israel: A Study in Internal Colonialism (Zureik), 41, 88

pan-Arabism, xiv

partition of Palestine, proposals for, xx, 141–42, 149–50, 167, 251–52, 266

Partition project of 1947, 139

Pascal, Blaise, 161

Patterson, Bill, 135

peace and reconciliation, framework for, 48–51

peace discussions, informal, xxviii–xxix

Peace in the Middle East? (Chomsky), 324–36

Peace Now movement, 46

peace process of 1990s, xxxi–xxxii, xxxiii
  Baker's consultations, 153
  inaugural conference, 156
  Israeli domination of, 172–73
  Palestinian peace delegation, 191, 192–93
  Palestinian representation issue, 172
  Said's proposals for, 154–55
  see also Israeli-PLO agreements of 1993

Peace to End All Peace in the Middle East (Fromkin), 307

Peck, James, 58

Peled, Matti, 98

Peres, Shimon, xxxvii, 142

Peretz, Martin, 95, 104–5, 263

pessoptimism, 109, 115

Peters, Joan, 102–3, 126, 339

Peter the Venerable, 161

Phalangists, 254, 261, 269, 270–71, 338

Picot, Georges, 4

Pipes, Daniel, 276, 307

Podhoretz, Norman, 255

Poirier, Richard, 255–56

Poliakov, Leon, 337

Political Islam (Ayoubi), 388

Pontecorvo, Gillo, 344

Popular Front for the Liberation of Palestine, 116, 147

Porath, Yehoshua, 266

Predicting Insurgent and Governmental Decisions (Jones), 25

Preminger, Otto, 130

Project Sierra, 25

Qassam, Izzedin al-, 333

Qassim, Samih al-, 377

Quandt, William, 207, 212

Question of Palestine (Said), xxv, 107, 121

Qutb, Sayyid, 399

Raad, Khalil, 181

Rabbani, Mouin, xlv

Rabin, Yitzhak, xxxiii, xxxvii, 64, 138, 173, 190, 274, 400
  Israeli-PLO agreements of 1993, xxxv, xliv

Ramallah clubs, 52

Randal, Jonathan, 259, 260–61

RAND Corporation, 25, 207, 212, 213

Readings and Writings (Wollen), 134

Reagan, Ronald, xxvii, xxviii, 69, 75, 269, 270, 272, 346

Redgrave, Vanessa, 171

refugee camps, 7–8

Renan, Joseph-Ernest, 161

reparations issue, xliv–xlv

Republic of Fear (Khalil), 307

"Responsibility of Intellectuals" (Chomsky), 316

"Return to Haifa" (Kanafani), 119

Rickover, Hyman, 212

Rifai mosque (Cairo), 396

Right Wing of Arab world: *see* Arab Right Wing

Rodinson, Maxime, 20, 161

Rogers, William, 203

Rosenthal, A. M., 289, 364

Ross, Dennis, 276

Rostow, Walt, 220

Rubenstein, Danny, 266

Rushdie, Salman, 169, 198, 404
  on *After the Last Sky*, 108–12
  conversation with Said, 107–23

Russian immigrants to Israel, 153, 168, 370

Saadawi, Nawal al-, 376

Sabra and Shatila massacres, xvii–xviii, xxiii, 72, 152, 247, 254, 257

Sabra et Chatila: Enquête sur un massacre (Kapeliouk), 254

Sadat, Anwar, xxi, xxxiv, 24, 40, 43, 46–47, 67, 399

  Arab view of, 243–44

  assassination of, 245

  Western view of, 243

Safad, Israel, 183

Safire, William, 289, 364

Said, Edward W.:

  background of, xiii, 11

  conversation with Harlow, 304–19

  conversation with Rushdie, 107–23

  goals of his writings, xvi–xvii, xix, xlviii

  Palestine visit (1992), xxxiii, 175–99

  Palestinian identity, development of, xiii–xvi

  Palestinian national movement, direct involvement in, xxiv–xxxiv, 145–51

  principles advanced by, xix

  South Africa visit, 169–70, 194

  UN conference on Palestine, 252–53

  Vance, meetings with, xxi–xxii

Said, Hilda, 184

Said, Mariam, xxv, 175, 184

Said, Najla, 175, 178, 180, 197

Said, Wadie, 114, 175, 178, 181, 192, 197

St. George's Anglican Cathedral (Jerusalem), 177, 181

Salem, Elie, 260

Salibi, Kamal, 260

Salih, Tayib, 377

Salinas, Franco, 131

Sandouqa, Muhammed, 189

Sartre, Jean-Paul, 13

Saudi Arabia, xviii, 60, 222, 243, 279, 289, 302–3, 385, 395

  Death of a Princess affair, 236–39

  media's portrayal of, 240

Saunders, Harold, xxii, 54

Sayeh, Shaikh Abdel Hamid el, 47

Sayigh, Rosemary, 42, 252

Schelling, Thomas, 213

Schlesinger, Arthur M., Jr., 386

Season of Migration to the North (Salih), 377

Secret Agent (Conrad), 344, 350

Segev, Tom, 140, 338

Semites and Anti-Semites (Lewis), 337–40

Seton-Watson, Hugh, 350

Seven Pillars of Wisdom (Lawrence), 12

Seventh Man (Berger), 108

Shaarawi, Shaikh, 397

Shaath, Nabil, xxix, 147

Shahak, Israel, xxviii, 185, 233, 250, 333

Shahine, Yusef, 394, 397

Shahrur, Muhammad, 408

Shaka'a, Bassam el-, 47

Shamir, Shimon, 97

Shamir, Yitzhak, 138, 142, 172, 173, 274, 275, 338, 370

Sharett, Moshe, 45, 261

Sharon, Ariel, 42, 69, 97, 150, 188, 245, 257

Shaykh, Hanan al-, 375–76, 408

Shehadeh, Raja, 190, 191, 192

Shubeilat, Laith, 405–6, 407

Shultz, George P., xxiii, xxviii, 83, 138

Signs and Meanings in the Cinema (Wollen), 134

Sindbad Misri (Fawzi), 14

Sirhan, Sirhan, 11

Sisulu, Walter, 170

Slovo, Joe, 170

Smooha, Sammy, 41

Society Against the State (Clastres), 351

Sorel, Georges, 352

Sourani, Raji, 194–95, 196

South Africa, xxxviii, 258

  Mandela's release, 366–68

  Occupied Territories, similarity to, 194

  siege mentality, shift away from, 169–70

Soviet Union, xviii–xix, 270, 370

  arms sales, 215

Soviet Union *cont.*
Cold War, 58, 231
Egypt and, 24
U.S. policy on Middle East and, 206, 214, 215
Spain, 216
Spiegel, Steven, 276
Spiro, Gideon, 96, 248
statehood declaration (1988), 146–51
Stein, Fritz, 65
Steinzaltz, Adin, 59–60
Sterling, Claire, 343
Stevenson, Robert Louis, 344
Stone, I. F., 17, 53, 325, 328, 329
Strategy of Conflict (Schelling), 213
Strauss, Robert, 67
Sudan, 26, 385, 407
Sulzberger, C. L., 427*n*35
"Summer of Arab Discontent" (journal article), 302
Swaggart, Jimmy, 97
Swinton, Tilda, 135
Synagogue Council of America, 426*n*16
Syria, xv, xviii, xix, xxx, 6, 45, 226, 228, 270
Hama massacre, 361
PLO mutiny against Arafat, 78, 79

Tabet, Maya, 377
Tabgha (Israel), 182–83
Taha, Sami, 332
Taiwan, 216
Takfir wal Higra, 393
Tambo, Oliver, 170
Teachers, Writers and Celebrities (Debray), 308
technological contest between Europe and Arab world, 162–63
terrorism, 337
Ahmad's analysis of, 345–47
Arab world associated with, 342, 344–45
Arafat's renunciation of, xx
cultural chauvinism and, 357–59
defining terrorism, problems of, 343
exotic aura, 344

terrorism *cont.*
fear of terrorism as justification for mistreatment of Palestinians, 256–57
hysteria about, 341
Islam associated with, 342
isolation of terrorism from history, 342–44
Israeli policy on, 347–49
media practice and, 353–57
new approaches to, 350–59
Palestinians associated with, xxvi–xxvii, 35, 57–58, 113–14, 116–18, 342
Palestinians' rejection of, 149–50
PLO associated with, 82
processes of identity in modern society, connection to, 351–53
retributive response, theory of, 344
terror of, 344
writers on terrorism, agendas of, 347
Terrorism: How the West Can Win (Netanyahu), 345
"Terrorist Couture" (Churcher), 118
Thatcher, Margaret, 297
Theroux, Philip, 376
Third World, U.S. policy on, 58–62
Thomas, Anthony, 236
Thomas, Danny, 53
Thompson, Edward, 127
Thompson, E. P., 127, 231
Tibawi, A. I., 35
Tiberias, Israel, 178, 182
Tillion, Germaine, 162
Timerman, Jacobo, 262
Tisdall, Caroline, 259, 262
To Reclaim a Legacy (Bennett), 358
Trail of the Dinosaur (Koestler), 17
Treglown, Jeremy, 344
Trotsky, Leon, 205
Trudeau, Pierre, 112
Tuchman, Barbara, 95, 102
Tucker, Robert, 329
Tunisia, 385
Turabi, Hassan al-, 385, 400, 407

Udhari, Abdullah al-, 377
United Nations, 47, 50
  conference on Palestine (1983),
    252–53
  Declaration of the Elimination of All
    Forms of Racial Discrimination
    (1963), 87
  Gulf War, 280, 296, 300
  Israel, censuring of, 67
  pro-Palestinian resolutions, 45, 160
  protection for Palestinians, 153
  Security Council Resolutions 242 and
    338, xxii, 82, 141–42, 147,
    149
  Security Council Resolution 681,
    153
United States, xviii
  affirmative action programs, 169
  Arab perception of, xxi, xxix–xxx,
    xxxiii, 214, 289–90
  Arab world, relations with, 158, 164
  centrality in American culture,
    355–56
  Cold War, 58, 231
  common culture, maintenance of, 57
  criticism of Israel, intolerance of,
    249–50, 251
  cultural war against Arabs and Islam,
    298–99, 302–3
  Death of a Princess affair, 237
  Egypt policy, 403
  human rights policy, 160
  imperialist ideology, 158, 283–85,
    298, 301
  Islamic movement, policy on, 407–8
  Israeli invasion of Lebanon and, 248
  Israeli-PLO agreements of 1993,
    xl–xli
  Israel policy, 44–45, 96, 127, 138,
    214–15, 248
  Lebanon policy, 261, 269–72
  Libya, bombing of, 341
  Middle East policy: *see* U.S. policy
    on Middle East
  Palestinian autonomy talks (1980),
    43–44, 46–47, 67

United States *cont.*
  Palestinians, policy toward,
    xxvi–xxviii, 25–26, 28
  Palestinians, public opinion on: *see*
    under Palestinians
  Palestinians in, 52–55, 112–13
  peace process of 1990s, xxxi–xxxii,
    153, 173
  PLO, dialogue with, xx–xxi, xxiii,
    312
  recognition of PLO, Vance's offer
    regarding, xxi–xxii
  South Africa policy, 170
  terrorism policy, 347
  Vietnam War, 25, 59, 213, 306–7,
    324, 325
  Third World policy, 58–62
  Zionism in, 18
  see also Gulf War
U.S. policy on Middle East, 24–25,
    206–7
  arms sales, 215
  authoritarian governments, support
    for, 296
  Chomsky's analysis of, 328–29, 331
  coordination approach, 211, 212–19,
    428n41
  creative participation in processes of
    change, 330–31
  economic concerns, 210–11, 218
  implications of, 220–23
  interests of United States, 209
  isolation approach, 211, 219–20
  linkage principle, 211
  military intervention, 211, 329
  "no real policy" view, 329–30
  Palestine question and, 207–8
  political orientation, 207, 209–10
  pragmatic eclecticism in, 330
  research in support of, 207–9,
    212–13
  selectivity and discrimination in, 211
  status quo, maintenance of, 215–17
  Vietnam experience and, 213
universities, role in society, 317–18,
    358

Uris, Leon, 102, 103–4
Usbat al-Muthaqqafin al-'Arab (League
　　of Educated Arabs), 332

Vance, Cyrus, xxi–xxii
Vico, Giambattista, 351–52
Victims of a Map (Adonis), 377
Vidal, Gore, 113
Vietnam, xl
Vietnam War, 25, 59, 213, 306–7,
　　324, 325

Walesa, Lech, 368–69
Wallerstein, Immanuel, 353
Walters, Barbara, 62–63, 64
Walzer, Michael, 95, 100, 263, 303,
　　326
Wasfy, Huda, 389
Washington Institute for Near East
　　Policy, 276
"Washington Leak that Went Wrong:
　　A CIA Gaffe that Shocked Saudi
　　Arabia" (Leigh), 240
Wazzan, Shafik al-, 269
Wedding in Galilee (film), 132–34,
　　135–36
Weiz, Ra'anan, 417
Weizmann, Chaim, 33, 34, 39–40
West Bank: *see* Occupied Territories
"Western canon" debate, 317–18
White, Hayden, 254–55
Whitehead, Alfred North, 318
*Who Stands Accused? Israel Answers Its
　　Critics* (Herzog), 36–37
Wiesel, Elie, 265
Williams, Raymond, 93
Wollen, Peter, 132, 134–36

women in Palestinian society, 120–21
Woman of Sand and Myrrh (Shaykh),
　　375–76
Wright, Claudia, 68

Yahya al-Wafd (play), 226–27
Yamani, Shaikh, 222
Yariv, Aharon, 44–45
Yemen, 14
Young, Andrew, 63
Young-Bruehl, Elisabeth, 95
Yunis, Ibtihal, 409

Zaghloul, Saad, 191
Zakariya, Fuad, 408
Zayni Barakat (Ghitani), 376–77, 396
Zionism, 111, 251
　　American Zionism, 18
　　Arab nationalism and, 16–18
　　of Ben-Gurion, 38–40
　　colonialist nature, 164–65
　　criticism of Zionism, problems of,
　　　121
　　"existence of Palestinians" issue
　　　and, 34–35
　　extremism of, 17
　　faltering by, 36–42
　　image projected to world, 34
　　Israeli invasion of Lebanon and, 100
　　land acquisition policy, 33
　　racism of, 31
　　U.S. public opinion on Palestinians
　　　and, 65–66
　　see also difference, ideology of
Zuckerman, Mortimer, 128
Zurayk, Constantine, 14
Zureik, Elia T., 41, 88, 90